Threshold Concepts a
Transformational Le

EDUCATIONAL FUTURES
RETHINKING THEORY AND PRACTICE
Volume 42

Series Editors
Michael A. Peters
University of Illinois at Urbana-Champaign, USA

Scope
This series maps the emergent field of educational futures. It will commission books on the futures of education in relation to the question of globalisation and knowledge economy. It seeks authors who can demonstrate their understanding of discourses of the knowledge and learning economies. It aspires to build a consistent approach to educational futures in terms of traditional methods, including scenario planning and foresight, as well as imaginative narratives, and it will examine examples of futures research in education, pedagogical experiments, new utopian thinking, and educational policy futures with a strong accent on actual policies and examples.

Threshold Concepts and Transformational Learning

Edited By

Jan H.F. Meyer
University of Durham, UK

Ray Land
University of Strathclyde, Glasgow, UK

Caroline Baillie
University of Western Australia, Perth, Australia

SENSE PUBLISHERS
ROTTERDAM/BOSTON/TAIPEI

A C.I.P. record for this book is available from the Library of Congress.

ISBN: 978-94-6091-205-4 (paperback)
ISBN: 978-94-6091-206-1 (hardback)
ISBN: 978-94-6091-207-8 (e-book)

Published by: Sense Publishers,
P.O. Box 21858,
3001 AW Rotterdam,
The Netherlands
http://www.sensepublishers.com

Printed on acid-free paper

Cover image: M.C. Escher's "Sky and Water I" © *2009 The M.C. Escher Company-Holland. All rights reserved. www.mcescher.com*

Lintel image page (viii): Pax Intrantibus Salus Exeuntibus: Lintel of threshold (1609), Canongate, Edinburgh, Scotland © *R.Land 2010*

TABLE OF CONTENTS

Pax Intrantibus Salus Exeuntibus. Lintel of threshold (1609),
Canongate, Edinburgh, Scotland

RAY LAND, JAN H.F. MEYER AND CAROLINE BAILLIE

EDITORS' PREFACE

Threshold Concepts and Transformational Learning

INTRODUCTION

At the lower end of the ancient Canongate in Edinburgh there is a worn sandstone lintel over a small seventeenth-century doorway. It bears a Latin engraving on which is inscribed: 'Pax intrantibus, salus exeuntibus'. Peace to those who are entering, and safety to those about to depart. It is a modest reminder that a threshold has always demarcated that which belongs within, the place of familiarity and relative security, from what lies beyond that, the unfamiliar, the unknown, the potentially dangerous. It reminds us too that all journeys begin with leaving that familiar space and crossing over into the riskier space beyond the threshold. So, too, with any significant transformation in learning. As Leslie Schwartzman observes later in this volume, 'Real learning requires stepping into the unknown, which initiates a rupture in knowing'. By definition, she contends, all threshold concepts scholarship 'is concerned (directly or indirectly) with encountering the unknown'.

For readers new to the idea of threshold concepts the approach builds on the notion that there are certain concepts, or certain learning experiences, which resemble passing through a portal, from which a new perspective opens up, allowing things formerly not perceived to come into view. This permits a new and previously inaccessible way of thinking about something. It represents a transformed way of understanding, or interpreting, or viewing something, without which the learner cannot progress, and results in a reformulation of the learners' frame of meaning. The thresholds approach also emphasises the importance of disciplinary contexts. As a consequence of comprehending a threshold concept there may thus be a transformed internal view of subject matter, subject landscape, or even world view. Typical examples might be 'Personhood' in Philosophy; 'The Testable Hypothesis' in Biology; 'Gravity' in Physics; 'Reactive Power' in Electrical Engineering; 'Depreciation' in Accounting; 'Legal Narrative' in Law; 'Geologic Time' in Geology; 'Uncertainty' in Environmental Science; 'Deconstruction' in Literature; 'Limit' in Mathematics or 'Object-oriented Programming' in Computer Science.

In attempting to characterise such conceptual gateways we have suggested in earlier work that they are *transformative* (occasioning a significant shift in the perception of a subject), *integrative* (exposing the previously hidden inter-relatedness of something) and likely to be, in varying degrees, *irreversible* (unlikely to be forgotten, or unlearned only through considerable effort), and frequently *troublesome*, for a variety of reasons. These learning thresholds are often the points at which students experience difficulty. The transformation may be sudden or it may be protracted over a considerable period of time, with the transition to understanding often involving 'troublesome knowledge'. Depending on discipline and context, knowledge might be troublesome because it is ritualised, inert, conceptually difficult, alien or tacit, because it requires adopting an unfamiliar discourse, or perhaps because the learner remains 'defended' and does not wish to change or let go of their customary way of seeing things.

Difficulty in understanding threshold concepts may leave the learner in a state of 'liminality', a suspended state of partial understanding, or 'stuck place', in which understanding approximates to a kind of 'mimicry' or lack of authenticity. Insights gained by learners as they cross thresholds can be exhilarating but might also be unsettling, requiring an uncomfortable shift in identity, or, paradoxically, a sense of loss. A further complication might be the operation of an 'underlying game' which requires the learner to comprehend the often tacit games of enquiry or ways of thinking and practising inherent within specific disciplinary discourses. In this sense we might wish to talk of 'threshold practices' or 'threshold experiences' that are necessary in the learner's development.

This is our third book on the topic of threshold concepts. The first, *Overcoming Barriers to Student Understanding: Threshold Concepts and Troublesome Knowledge* (Meyer and Land, 2006), drew together the early seminal writings and some first disciplinary applications of this approach. It offered, in an exploratory fashion, a tentative conceptual framework and a lens through which to view the pedagogy of higher education anew. After a lively international symposium on this topic in Glasgow, Scotland in the autumn of 2006, a second volume was published. *Threshold Concepts within the Disciplines* (Land, Meyer and Smith, 2008) built and expanded on the first in significant ways. It provided more empirical data concerning the experience of threshold concepts and troublesome knowledge, particularly from the students' perspective. It also extended the range of disciplinary contexts in which thresholds had been studied. This encouraged further work to be undertaken, culminating in a second successful international conference in Kingston Ontario organised by Caroline Baillie in the summer of 2008, from which this third volume has taken shape.

With *Threshold Concepts and Transformational Learning* the empirical evidence for threshold concepts has been substantially increased, drawn from what is now a large number of disciplinary contexts and from the higher education sectors of many countries. The central section of this new volume adds to that evidence base, ranging across subjects that include, amongst others, economics, electrical engineering, education, clinical education, sociology, social justice, modern languages, law, computer science, philosophy, transport and product design, nano-science, mathematics, biology, history and accounting. The authors included here work in colleges and universities in the United Kingdom, the USA, Canada, Sweden, Estonia, Australia, New Zealand, Hong Kong and the South Pacific. The opening section of the volume, moreover, challenges and extends the theoretical boundaries of the thresholds framework in relation to our understanding of transition, liminality and the developmental process of learning, of conceptual structure, of how students experience difficulty, as well as new dimensions of troublesome knowledge and how we might both render conceptual understanding visible and assess it in a more dynamic fashion. The concluding section contains a substantial body of writing which furthers our understanding of the ontological transformations that are necessarily occasioned by significant learning, the learning thresholds, as we might term them, which might not be strictly conceptual, but are more concerned with shifts in identity and subjectivity, with procedural knowledge, or the ways of thinking and practising customary to a given disciplinary or professional community. We see here too, intriguing migratory instances of the application of threshold theory to other sectors of education, to doctoral education, to professional learning and even to the social analysis of an entire nation in transition.

Taking this into consideration we feel emboldened to see the consolidation of the characteristics of threshold concepts, and of learning thresholds more generally, that were proposed in a tentative fashion in the seminal paper by Meyer and Land (2003). If viewed as a journey through preliminal, liminal and postliminal states, the features that characterise threshold concepts can now be represented relationally. In such a view the journey towards the acquisition of a threshold concept is seen to be initiated by an encounter with a form of troublesome knowledge in the preliminal state. The troublesome knowledge inherent within the threshold concept serves here as an *instigative* or provocative feature which unsettles prior understanding rendering it fluid, and provoking a state of liminality. Within the liminal state an integration of new knowledge occurs which requires a reconfiguring of the learner's prior conceptual schema and a letting go or discarding of any earlier conceptual stance. This reconfiguration occasions an ontological and an epistemic shift. The integration/reconfiguration and accompanying ontological/epistemic shift can be seen as *reconstitutive* features of the threshold concept. Together these features bring about the required new understanding. As a consequence of this new understanding the learner crosses a conceptual boundary into a new conceptual space and enters a postliminal state in which both learning and the learner are transformed. This is an irreversible transformation and is marked by a changed use of discourse. These latter effects – the crossing of conceptual boundaries, transformation, irreversibility and changed discourse – can be characterised as *consequential* features of the threshold concept. These dynamics are summarised in Figure 1.

We would not, however, wish to imply that this relational view has an overly rigid sequential nature. It has been emphasised elsewhere (Land et al, 2005) that the acquisition of threshold concepts often involves a degree of recursiveness, and of oscillation, which would need to be layered across this simple diagram. Furthermore, running thoughout this transformational process, in what we might term the 'subliminal' mode, there is often an 'underlying game' in which ways of thinking and practising that are often left tacit come to be recognised, grappled with and gradually understood. This underlying game is a common feature of the processes of entry, meaning making and identity formation typically required for entry to a given community of practice.

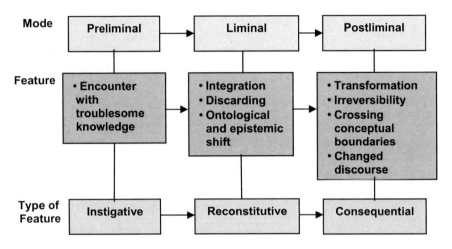

Figure 1. A relational view of the features of threshold concepts.

TRANSFORMATION

It is the nature and process of this transformation or reconfiguring which this volume particularly seeks to address. A number of resonances can be identified between the thresholds approach and work undertaken in the field of transformational learning. The first seminal paper identified correspondences with Mezirow's work (1978, 1990) on 'perspective transformation'.

> Perspective transformation is the process of becoming critically aware of how and why our presuppositions have come to constrain the way we perceive, understand, and feel about our world; of reformulating these assumptions to permit a more inclusive, discriminating, permeable and integrative perspective; and of making decisions or otherwise acting on these new understandings. (Mezirow, 1990, p. 14)

Mezirow saw transformation being triggered by what he termed a 'disorienting dilemma'. In his analysis the meaning schemes that we hold concerning a particular phenomenon or situation are unsettled by the disorienting dilemma or challenging perspective and occasion a series of phases, often involving a phase of withdrawal or disengagement prior to a re-engagement in which the integration of the different perspective is integrated. We recognise a number of correspondences here with the instigative effect of threshold concepts, the liminal phase of thresholds theory and the process of integration it entails.

A recurring critique of Mezirow's work on perspective transformation, however, has concerned its continued emphasis on the rational and analytic nature of the critical reflection that is seen as a primary driver. Boyd and Myers (Boyd, 1989, 1991; Boyd and Myers, 1988) offer an alternative approach, originating in depth psychology, which balances rational reflection with an emphasis on affective processes. They stress, for example that learners must (affectively) be open to the possibility of transformation in the first place and willing to accommodate 'alternative expressions of meaning' (1988, p. 277). Key phases in the process of transformation as they see it are receptivity, recognition and a final stage of 'grieving' in which there is a recognition that an established pattern of meaning is no longer tenable or valid for future practice. This brings about a point or state of *discernment*. The prevailing perception has to be let go of and eventually discarded so that a process of integration might begin. In their framework this is both a psychological as much a social process and ties with our own view that in the liminal phase an ontological shift or change in subjectivity accompanies change in cognitive understanding, often as part of a recognition that such shifts are necessary and appropriate for membership of a given community of practice. In our framework the process is also recognised as troublesome and can incur resistance (see particularly Schwartzman, Chapter 2). The shift is also irreversible, a point noted by O'Sullivan and colleagues:

> Transformative learning involves experiencing a deep, structural shift in the basic premises of thought, feelings, and actions. It is a shift of consciousness that dramatically and irreversibly alters our way of being in the world. (O'Sullivan et al, 2002, p. 11)

METAMORPHOSIS

Kegan (1982) has drawn attention to the ways in which individuals experience such 'shifts of consciousness' through recurring patterns or phases of stability and change during their lives. Julie Timmermans in the opening chapter of this volume points to the elusiveness and inherent difficulty of examining these transitional phases.

> It is these periods of change, these transitions that characterise the learning process, which I find most intriguing. These transitions remain nebulous; however, understanding them is crucial. Cross (1999) notes that 'in developmental theory, the periods of greatest personal growth are thought to lie in the unnamed and poorly-defined periods *between* stages' (p. 262; emphasis in original). We might therefore imagine that the most significant aspect of learning lies not in the *outcomes* of learning, but in the *process* of learning. Understanding this process and how best to facilitate it is thus essential to our work as educators. (Timmermans, Chapter 1)

In her novel *Regeneration*, concerning the trauma and rehabilitation of shell-shocked First World War soldiers, Pat Barker offers a striking, if somewhat unsettling image of transformation. Her character Rivers, a military psychiatrist 'knew only too well how often the early stages of change or cure may mimic deterioration. Cut a chrysalis open, and you will find a rotting caterpillar. What you will never find is that mythical creature, half caterpillar, half butterfly, a fit emblem of the human soul, for those whose cast of mind leads them to seek such emblems. No, the process of transformation consists almost entirely of decay'

(Barker, 1991, p.184). The theme of elusiveness in the process is continued here but also the necessity of discarding the former state. As the American-French writer Anais Nin observed, 'To change skins, evolve into new cycles, I feel one has to learn to discard. If one changes internally, one should not continue to live with the same objects. They reflect one's mind and the psyche of yesterday. I throw away what has no dynamic, living use.' (Nin, 1971, p. 26). But as Rebecca Solnit points out, as yet, 'We have not much language to appreciate this phase of decay, this withdrawal, this era of ending that must precede beginning. Nor of the violence of the metamorphosis, which is often spoken of as though it were as graceful as a flower blooming ... The process of transformation consists mostly of decay and then of this crisis when emergence from what came before must be total and abrupt'. (Solnit, 2006, pp.81–3). The chapters that follow in this volume attempt just that, an articulation of what such transformation – literally a going beyond one's extant form – entails. And, as we will see in the following pages, the transformation will always be determined to some extent by its disciplinary, or interdisciplinary, context. As Crainton emphasises:

> Transformative learning is not independent of content, context, or a discipline. It's not an 'add on' to a course. It is a way of making meaning of knowledge in a discipline in a way that students don't passively accept and believe what they are told or what they read, but rather engage in debate, discussion, and critical questioning of the content. Promoting transformative learning is a part of 'covering' content. (Kelly and Crainton, 2009, p. 1)

Transformative learning, she argues, can be promoted by using 'any strategy, activity, or resource that presents students with an alternative point of view'. These might include 'readings from different perspectives, field experiences, videos, role plays, simulations, and asking challenging questions' all of which have the capacity to effect transformative learning. 'The educator needs to create an environment in which critical reflection and questioning norms is supported and encouraged' (ibid). What would seem to be the enemy of transformative learning, however, is didacticism or any form of coercion. This is persuasively expressed by the American theologian and teacher Walter Brueggemann. The elegance of his argument merits quoting in full:

> We now know (or think we know) that human transformation (the way people change) does not happen through didacticism or through excessive certitude but through the playful entertainment of another scripting of reality that may subvert the old given text and its interpretation and lead to the embrace of an alternative text and its redescription of reality. Very few people make important changes in their description of the world abruptly. Most of us linger in wistfulness, notice dissonance between our experience and the old text, and wonder if there is a dimension to it all that has been missed. Most of us will not quickly embrace an alternative that is given us in a coercive way. Such coercion more likely makes us defend the old and, in general, become defensive. Victor Turner noted that there is an in-between time and place in social transformation and relocation, which he termed

liminality. Liminality is a time when the old configurations of social reality are increasingly seen to be in jeopardy, but new alternatives are not yet in hand. What we need for such liminality is a safe place in which to host such ambiguity, to notice the tension and unresolve without pressure but with freedom to see and test alternative textings of reality. (Brueggemann, 1995, pp. 319–20).

EXTENDING THE THEORY

The opening section of this volume contains six chapters which in different ways move forward our thinking about thresholds. **Julie Timmermans** (Chapter 1) situates the characteristics of threshold concepts within a developmental framework. Informed by Kegan's (1982) interdisciplinary Constructive-Developmental Theory and recognising 'the equal dignity' of both cognition and affect, she examines the process of epistemological transformation triggered by threshold concepts. Seeing each stage within the transformational journey as a kind of new (evolutionary) truce, she draws our attention to the nature of the (alternative) 'commitments', both cognitive and emotional, that may be held by learners. These 'may provide educators with rich insight regarding learners' unwillingness to change' and their reluctance to let go of a sense of integrated selfhood. In asking 'What type of learning leads to development?' she draws attention to the 'complex continuum' of emotional responses likely to be found within the liminal space.

> That some learners 'open up,' while others clearly get 'stuck' … may signal to us as educators that the epistemological transition being instigated by a thres-hold concept lies *beyond* the learner's zone of proximal development (Vygotsky, 1978). That is, it lies too far beyond what the learner may achieve when guided by more skilful others. These variations in response to teaching caution us to be attuned to variations in the ways that learners are making meaning.

In addition to proximal influences this leads her in her conclusion to emphasise the 'multiple layers of context', such as religion and family, that may shape individuals' epistemic beliefs. In a timely note of caution to discipline-based teachers in their attempts to 'teach' threshold concepts she calls for increased attention to the learning *process* and a tolerance of variation in learners' cognitive and affective responses.

From the perspective of phenomenological analysis **Leslie Schwartzman** (Chapter 2) challenges the current theoretical premises of the threshold concepts framework, arguing for a rigorous transdisciplinary theoretical foundation predicated on the scholarship of rupture in knowing (Heidegger, 1927) and the responses, both reflective and defensive, that might ensue (Segal, 1999l). A more productive approach to understanding how students negotiate and traverse liminal spaces, she argues, and to how we might better assist them in this activity, is to be found 'in universal human patterns of encounter and response to the existentially unfamiliar (what appears initially as the unknowable unknown) rather than focusing on variations arising from the sundry disciplinary contexts of learning, or from 'individual inadequacies'. Her analysis leads to a significant contrast in how we might define transformational learning as distinct from deep learning. As a result of deep 'cumulative' learning, she argues:

> one switches dynamically – within the same field of consciousness – among thematic foci, with correspondent restructuring of thematic fields (Booth, 1997, p. 144). The total set of elements in the field remains constant, while boundaries among the thematic foci, the thematic field, and the margin become fluid; and component elements shift between adjacent domains. The mechanism of dynamic switching among extant elements corresponds to *reflection; the operation corresponds to refinement and clarification of one's extant meaning frame.* (Editors' italics).

In contrast, the outcome of transformative learning, she contends, is that:

> the contents of the field of consciousness change. Elements formerly not found in any domain of consciousness, possibly including component parts of elements formerly classified as non-decomposable, now occupy the thematic focus or reside in the thematic field; and some elements formerly found there are now relegated to the margin. The mechanism remains mysterious and corresponds to *reflectiveness; the operation, which results in a different population in the field of consciousness, corresponds to reformulation of one's meaning frame.* (Editors' italics).

In clarifying this nice distinction, she questions whether the proponents of threshold concepts in their teaching are adopting the latter approach, bringing new meaning to bear upon existing experience (which the Meyer and Land framework would seem to condone), or the former approach, which would seem to be attempting the reverse.

The nature of troublesome knowledge is given a further dimension in **Aidan Ricketts'** application of the threshold concepts framework to the teaching of Law (Chapter 3). In relation to transformational learning he points out that 'transformative experiences may enhance a student's critical awareness, but this should not be assumed; in some cases the nature of the transformation may actually reduce the scope for critical thinking'. He coins the term 'loaded knowledge' to refer to the manner in which increased access to and facility with the ways of thinking and practising of a given community of practice (in this case the legal profession) may have a reductive effect more generally in terms of occluding other forms of knowing. The particular instance given here is the way in which students of legal education might find access to certain forms of critical knowing difficult within their curriculum. This is not inevitable but the practice of legal education needs to be carefully designed, he argues, to ensure the inclusion of critical perspectives, including critique of 'the very discipline they have come to study'. In a study of much wider applicability to all disciplines he concludes that it 'appears inevitable that studying law will involve encounters with troublesome and counter intuitive ideas and with loaded knowledge and that one way or another law students are likely to be changed by the experience. The challenge for educators, is to decide whether education should be openly self critical even of its own discipline or simply impose closed intellectual and value systems upon its students.'

If the troublesome transformations occasioned by threshold concepts require a rather different way of looking at the curriculum, then it follows that such transformations will require a more nuanced and generative model of assessment. This would help us identify variation in progress and understanding at the preliminal, liminal, postliminal and subliminal stages of conceptual and epistemological fluency. **Ray Land** and **Jan Meyer** (Chapter 4) argue for a dynamic model of assessment, acting more like a 'flickering movie' of a student's progress along the transformational journey and indicating how structures of a student's understanding might be changing rather than a stationary, one-off 'snapshot'. They argue that the threshold concepts framework points to variation in progressive stages of a student's journey towards, through, and beyond particular conceptual gateways. They ask how we might construct a meaningful assessment process for students for whom, in many instances, what is to be assessed lies outside their prior knowledge and experience, or beyond their ontological horizon. The threshold concept has not fully 'come into view'. This might move us on from traditional assessment regimes in which a student seems to be able to produce the 'right' answer while retaining fundamental misconceptions. They seek an insightful conceptual basis for developing new and creative methods of assessment and alternative ways of rendering learning (and conceptual difficulty) visible. This in turn can inform course (re)design in a generative and sustainable fashion.

Ian Kinchin, Lyndon Cabot and **David Hay** (Chapter 5) demonstrate the kind of approach Land and Meyer advocate, as a means of rendering learning and patterns of understanding 'visible' in professional clinical settings such as dentistry, medicine and nursing. In a piece entitled 'Visualising expertise' they too seek a quality of dynamism – 'a dynamic transformation of knowledge structures, relating competence and comprehension'. They represent the gradual transformation of learners' understanding through concept mapping techniques that render explicit current states of knowing and conceptual linkages that can be represented by 'chains' of practice and 'networks' of understanding. Over a given period of time the structures of meaning-making can be seen to change, with new elements being integrated, others being let go of or discarded, whilst further elements enter understanding but remain unintegrated. In affective terms however, the adoption of expertise-based pedagogy requires a certain confidence and courage on the part of teachers and practitioners both to share their knowledge, and the gaps in their own understanding. This approach often surfaces understandings and misunderstandings which previously might have remained tacit. 'The knowledge structures approach, facilitated by concept mapping tools', the authors contend, 'provides a mechanism to go beyond making learning visible, towards making it tangible (i.e. not only can it been seen, but it can also be manipulated to support development).'

To conclude the opening section on theoretical aspects of threshold concepts **Jerry Mead** and **Simon Gray** (Chapter 6) focus attention on the use of the term *concept* in thresholds parlance in order 'to provide a more secure footing, in the form of a model of conceptual structure on which the term "concept' in "threshold concept" can rest'. They address this issue from a disciplinary perspective, viewing the identification of threshold concepts as something reached consensually over time within the disciplinary community – 'disciplinary constructs that have emerged from the crucible of disciplinary scrutiny as definable abstractions' and with any personal connotations discarded. Hence the role of an educator within a given discipline is to align the structure of students' evolving *personal* conceptions with that of the agreed *disciplinary* conception. They point out that the personal effect of threshold concepts on learners can only be significant 'if the way someone thinks from inside a discipline is different from the way someone outside of the discipline thinks'. But here they take issue with the current threshold concept definition pointing out that 'it leaves threshold concepts isolated from an ontological point of view' without reference, from the student perspective, to other concepts in its disciplinary context. As they put it, 'the idea that a threshold concept "exposes the previously hidden interrelatedness of something" implies that there must be other relevant concepts, i.e., the things that are "interrelated"'.

To address this they set out to provide, within a disciplinary context, a conceptual structure, a 'more secure footing', within which threshold concepts 'can be localized'. They employ Perkins' notion of a *concept episteme* as 'the system of ideas or way of understanding that allows us to establish knowledge of the concept'. They name the kind of conceptual structure they produce a 'disciplinary concept graph' (DCG). This can facilitate student understanding of concepts in a discipline, and, they argue further, the five threshold concept characteristics can be localized within such concept graphs. Using atomic theory as illustration, they seek to identify the concepts that are central to a discipline and which serve as the 'targets of the questions, problems, and judgements' that arise in that discipline. They coin the term *condensation point* to encapsulate 'a unifying and generalizing concept that is definable within an episteme and condenses out of the associated knowledge space a fundamental disciplinary idea or capability'.

CONCEPTUAL TRANSFORMATIONS

The central section of the this volume offers a rich variety of instances of important transformations within the learning of particular disciplines and demonstrates how tutors have tried to understand the kinds of conceptual difficulty faced by their students. In the geosciences **Kim Cheek** (Chapter 7) discusses three possible factors that account for why the notion of 'deep time' proves so troublesome for learners, namely conceptions of conventional time, understanding of large numbers and the student's current state of subject knowledge. She points out the alien and counter-intuitive understanding involved in grasping 'that rocks can behave plastically, continents move, and the mountains we visit will one day be gone'. Much of this difficulty stems from the fact that though deep time is not a qualitatively different construct from a general concept of (conventional) time, it nonetheless requires a logical extrapolation 'to events and processes that are out of the realm of human experience by orders of magnitude'. The processes involved occur at very slow rates and hence are imperceptible to human observers. Such temporal understanding is not within the horizon of the student's experience and neither is the scale of the numbers necessary for such understanding. Issues of scale require an ability to work in different units of measure. The capacity to work in a unit of millions of years, and to differentiate a million year unit from a thousand year unit, 'enables a person to meaningfully conceive of many geologic processes'. However even adults, it seems, will resort to a more logarithmic scale (as opposed to linear mapping) when confronted with such large numbers. A subtle and potentially complex effect arises from the student's prior subject matter knowledge, and their prevailing ways of thinking and practising, i.e. can a student place a particular species in a sequence of events if she doesn't know what it is?

> We may be inferring an understanding (or lack thereof) about deep time when it's really something else directly related to specific geologic knowledge [or even analogical reasoning from some other subject area with which the student is familiar] that's accounting for student responses.

In Chapter 8 **Monica Cowart**, a philosopher, seeks an explanation of 'how to identify, deconstruct, and integrate philosophy-specific threshold concepts so that students can develop disciplinary specific thinking'. What does it mean, she asks, to think like a philosopher? What languages games, rituals, customs and methods come into play? An awareness of threshold concepts, she argues, can guide the decisions professors have to make in terms of prioritising what should be taught in philosophy programmes, how it should be taught and how it might be best assessed. She maintains that philosophy's three sub-disciplines of ethics, epistemology, and metaphysics are the key to recognizing 'core' threshold concepts within the discipline. These core philosophical threshold concepts exist at the *intersection* of the three sub-disciplines because these concepts raise questions within each sub-discipline. This positioning is significant as:

> to truly have an understanding of core philosophical threshold concept x, you must understand the questions threshold concept x raises in metaphysics, ethics, and epistemology. To simply understand the questions the concept raises in only one of these areas will not result in an accurate understanding of the concept.

The location of the concept at the intersection however, adds to its complexity, and hence potential troublesomeness to students. The author examines a specific example of such an intersectional threshold concept in the notion of 'personhood', before moving, in the second part of the chapter, to consider how this concept might be taught and learned. Utilising the specific epistemes (or philosophers' tools) of thought experiments, the Socratic method, and analytic deconstruction, she outlines a pedagogical approach to the teaching and learning of personhood predicated on principles of active learning. This involves the preparation of and participation within a formal team debate, and includes the design of an assignment 'that will enable students to showcase in the public domain knowledge of personhood through the rule-governed use of the discipline-specific epistemes, which enable the exploration of the concept'.

Questions of intersection and the importance of prior learning raised earlier by Kim Cheek, occur again in Chapter 9 where **Rosanne Quinnell** and **Rachel Thompson** consider the points where students are likely to encounter difficulty as they practise academic numeracy in the life sciences and medical statistics. Far from being a transferable skill, numeracy, they suggest, for many students in their field, can become a transferable anxiety. 'A grasp of numeracy is essential to understand the abstraction of the biological phenomenon; failure to appreciate that patterns in biology can be represented in abstracted mathematical forms inhibits students' understanding of scientific practice'. The authors present an experiential learning cycle in science that mirrors their practice of attempting to understand biological phenomena. They map on to this cycle where numeracy and literacy skills intersect, and the points at which they observe that student engagement begins to wane, 'the moments when students experience obstacles to learning'. It emerged that 'most of these points of uncoupling involved numbers and formulae', leading the authors to infer that 'for numerophobic students, this is a key factor affecting student progress through the liminal space in understanding a threshold concept'. Following a process of *unpicking* of numeracy issues based on tutors' and students' experience, the authors identify three main overarching threshold concepts in statistics within their field – the 'sampling distribution' lens, the 'strength of evidence' lens (including hypothesis formation and testing), and the 'applicability of evidence' lens – with the associated basic and threshold concepts that underpin each of these. Two case studies are described in which interventions were made to help students cope with these learning thresholds and overcome anxieties regarding numeracy. In the first the need to explain the concepts using numbers was removed, and with it the concomitant numerophobia, and students were enabled 'to find another route through this difficult learning moment'. In the second study tutorials were constructed around a 'numeracy diagnostic' focused on confidence. The aim of this diagnostic was to pinpoint where numeracy was problematic and where students were uncoupling themselves from the learning process. Interestingly the students who engaged most fully with this challenging task were those least confident in their responses. Both of these approaches have proved fruitful in identifying future paths for skills development and overcoming barriers.

Two further chapters in this section also examine threshold concepts within biological sciences. **Pauline Ross** and her colleagues **Charlotte Taylor, Chris Hughes, Michelle Kofod, Noel Whitaker, Louise Lutze-Mann** and **Vicky Tzioumis** (Chapter 10) explore the nature of student misconceptions in biology. A range of candidates are identified as potentially troublesome content knowledge, including cellular metabolic processes (e.g. photosynthesis and respiration), cellular size and dimensionality (surface area to volume ratio), water movement (diffusion and osmosis) genetics (protein synthesis, cell division, DNA) evolution, homeostasis and equilibrium. In addition to this however the authors identify a number of procedural threshold concepts such as energy, variation, randomness and probability, proportional reasoning, spatial and temporal scales, and thinking at a submicroscopic level. Students lack of such procedural or processual abilities, compounds the inherent difficulty in the subject content knowledge, causing misconceptions. The authors argue that employing thresholds as a heuristic in this fashion permits insights not gained from the existing misconception and constructivist literature, and raises a number of questions for the development of teaching and learning in biology. On the assumption that threshold concepts reflect differences in ways of thinking and practising between acknowledged experts inside the subject and novices on the periphery, they argue that students should be encouraged to acquire facility with the procedural thresholds mentioned above to facilitate their crossing of portals and hence develop a better understanding of hitherto troublesome knowledge. This will enable us to understand 'whether students can subsequently transfer this thinking process to aid their understanding of other similarly difficult content (that is, to see if they have learnt how to cross unfamiliar thresholds)'.

Within biological sciences the capacity to formulate an experimental design and a testable hypothesis within it can be seen as a crucial aspect of how biologists 'think'. **Charlotte Taylor** and **Jan Meyer** (Chapter 11) investigate the processes through which students acquire this capacity for 'apprehending the multivariate complexity of the biological world and hypothesising within it phenomena amenable to experimental verification'. In keeping with threshold theory this apprehension contains an *ontological* dimension and its own *discursive* modes of 'reasoning and explanation'. The authors point out that although higher order abstract dimensions of biological thinking are an indispensable part of this process, and that in discursive terms, 'the mechanics of defining a precisely worded testable hypothesis require an appreciation of the appropriate language and symbolic representations', nonetheless these requirements can to some extent be acquired in a rote manner, with testing procedures for the hypothesis gained through recipe-like formulae. It is the *integration* of ideas, they suggest, which is key, and which:

> demonstrates a transformed understanding, requires a sophisticated articulation of the scale, dynamics, complexity, variability and role of probability in explaining the system under investigation. Dealing with this in the paradigm of scientific thinking encompasses the threshold.

These concerns have led to a consideration of the experience of students in the preliminary space. The students often have limited prior experience of the complexity of biological systems, and encounter scenarios and processes not easily amenable to observation at the molecular or chemical level. Engagement and ownership become the critical factors, with a need for students 'to have the opportunity to take ownership of the process of observation, explanation and hypothesis creation, for successful understanding to occur.' The rich sources of data from students' thinking, as they engage in the process of hypothesising and document their move into the liminal phase, signal the need for significant changes in our approaches to the teaching of biology.

Through a careful analysis of written answers by students in economics examinations **Peter Davies** and **Jean Mangan** (Chapter 12) consider the role of threshold concepts in assessing the progression of students' understanding in economics.

Drawing on both threshold theory and variation theory (Pang and Marton, 2005), they argue that the conception of a phenomenon that is described by a basic concept within a discipline can 'only be attained once a learner is able to use a super-ordinate threshold concept to organise their conceptual structure'. However, for learners to be able to organise their thinking through a threshold concept, they continue, they will also need to use certain associated 'procedural concepts'. As they put it:

> If a discipline threshold can be represented as a 'portal', then procedural concepts provide the means by which the structural form of the portal can be assembled: the guidance that directs the way in which pieces are put together.

Taking an example from economics they argue that without the 'modelling' (or procedural) concept of equilibrium, the set of basic concepts needed to grasp a model of the determination of the level of national income – concepts such as the distinction between injections and withdrawals, savings and investment, stocks and flows, real and nominal values – cannot be made 'to act in concert to produce a coherently structured understanding of an economy as a system'. On the other hand, they suggest, if a student *is* observed to be employing a modelling concept in this way to mobilise one or more basic concepts, then it is probably reasonable to infer that he or she is engaging in the process that can lead them towards incorporating a threshold concept.

The authors' proposition that 'more complex conceptions of a phenomenon rely on the transformation of basic concepts by disciplinary threshold concepts that integrate a learner's conceptual structure' gives rise to significant assessment issues in a massified system of higher education where tutors are faced with large numbers of scripts and seek salient cues to student understanding as a kind of shorthand to facilitate speedier techniques of marking in large first and second year classes. This can prove dysfunctional however. The authors predict that, for example:

> when students are introduced to a concept like 'the circular flow of income' they begin to use the language of a disciplinary conception (such as 'multiplier') well before they have developed the kind of understanding which an expert might infer from use of such terms. This creates an assessment difficulty in the context of 'large-scale' assessment.

The model of the development of a threshold concept provided by the authors here identifies the understanding of procedural concepts, such as equilibrium mentioned earlier, as critical. The evidence gained so far in this enquiry points to this conclusion, though there is a need for further empirical study to confirm these findings.

In a further empirical study drawn from economics **Martin Shanahan, Gigi Foster** and **Jan Meyer** (Chapter 13) build on the earlier observation by Meyer and Land (2006) that individuals proceed at varying rates across conceptual thresholds and exhibit varying states of liminality. These authors also utilise a combination of threshold theory and variation theory to assess the degree of tacit knowledge that students bring to a threshold concept in the preliminary state, for, as with prior content knowledge, students may vary greatly in the amount of prior tacit knowledge they have of particular threshold concepts. The authors then tread new ground in researching whether an association exists between threshold concept understanding and *attrition* from a course of study. The focus of their study is an examination of the association between students' observed grasp of certain threshold concepts in economics at the start of a semester and their likelihood of leaving an introductory microeconomics course in that same semester. An interesting secondary consideration of their study is the hypothesis that an important ontological shift is also required on the part of students – a shift in which one comes to view oneself as a bona-fide student learner – as 'a necessary preliminary stage of thinking that must be attained by students before discipline threshold concepts become relevant'. In terms of attrition they speculate that it is the students who fail to make this shift that are the most likely to leave the course early. Moreover, they suggest that 'the impact of preliminary knowledge of economic threshold concepts is only relevant once this transformation is made'. The findings of the enquiry lead the authors to believe that, though the factors associated with student attrition are many, an important conceptual portal that many students must negotiate as a mark of commitment to their studies is that of 'self-identification as a university student'. An interesting secondary finding is that, once a student has committed to study (roughly completion of the first semester of teaching), then variation in students' grasp of discipline-based threshold concepts may be associated with an individuals' preparedness to sit the exam. Self-identification as a university learner is a clear determinant of student retention in these findings, although, as the authors indicate, 'the distribution of previously acquired threshold concepts does appear to be systematically related to other differences that place students at risk of failing'.

Ference Marton, a leading proponent of variation theory, recently commented that:

The one single thing that would improve the quality of teaching and learning in higher education would be if academics in different disciplines took time to meet together and discuss what they should be teaching in their subject, and how they should be teaching it. This is something that Variation Theory has not done, and I think the Threshold Concepts approach encourages people to do this. In my opinion there is absolute complementarity between Threshold Concepts and Variation Theory. (Marton 2009).

In a significant example of academic specialists engaging in exactly such a conversation, and also reaching conclusions on the possible complementarity between Threshold Concepts and Variation Theory, **Michael Flanagan, Philip Taylor** and **Jan Meyer** (Chapter 14) examine the ways in which 'transmission lines', a threshold concept in electrical engineering may come into view quite differently depending on whether the concept is introduced from a perspective of large-scale systems (power engineering) or small-scale systems (instrumentation and electronics) and whether students are envisaging power transmission along overhead power lines or along coaxial cables. In experimental tests in the former, students struggled with the notion of *reactive power*. As a complex idea of what is in effect 'powerless power', requiring the use of (imaginary) complex number, students found this both counter-intuitive and 'mentally awkward'. With small-scale systems students struggled similarly with the idea of *characteristic impedance*. Students in both engineering contexts were left frustrated, perplexed and confused, and, as we have seen elsewhere in threshold analyses, resorted to 'mimicry' as a coping strategy. For some students, the authors point out, it became clear that 'elaborating the simpler concept of current flow down a wire into a mathematical treatment of the associated electromagnetic field was troublesome and counter-intuitive especially as the concept of the electric or magnetic field itself is troublesome'. Indeed, to exacerbate the problem, the authors comment that 'fields' may operate as threshold concepts in their own right. One source of the conceptual difficulty was that the students found it difficult 'to envisage any associated physical reality in the calculations of the properties of a travelling electromagnetic wave (the signal travelling along the line) using complex arithmetic'. In terms of a 'spiral curriculum' (Bruner, 1960), and an analysis of how earlier preparation in the simplified equations of high school physics might have adversely affected subsequent coping with a more complex university curriculum, the authors conclude that such earlier learning presented three potential barriers to learning. Firstly, the concrete had preceded the abstract; secondly, the detailed had preceded the general; and thirdly, perception was now preceding cognition. The authors' view was that each of these concepts of reactive power and characteristic impedance were in fact acting as portals to usher students into a far more complex liminal space involving understanding of electro-magnetic theory. A number of issues follow from this. One practical problem is that students are not in a position realistically to experiment with large-scale power systems. Though recent computer simulation packages open up interesting and potentially helpful possibilities in this regard there is the danger of students performing calculations in a 'ritualistic' fashion without understanding (Perkins, 1999). Moreover, in relation to possible complementarity between threshold concepts and variation theory the authors observe that:

> If a troublesome concept is flagged by students and/or staff that is, in reality, a portal to a much more complex liminal space there is a risk that a variational approach constructed around this troublesome concept alone may not effectively aide the students in mastering their difficulties.

In terms of the kinds of knowledge that engineering students should encounter during an engineering degree, the study of learning thresholds in relation to electromagnetic theory raises more far-reaching issues of where applied physics might end and electronic engineering begin, and whether engineering graduates are defined by their skills or their particular industry.

In Chapter 15 we encounter another 'disciplinary conversation' taking place. **Lynda Thomas,** with her colleagues **Jonas Boustedt, Anna Eckerdal, Robert McCartney, Jan Erik Moström, Kate Sanders** and **Carol Zander,** report on the findings of a multi-national, multi-institutional project that has now been under way for four years and which is seeking an empirical identification of threshold concepts in the fast-moving and ever-changing domain of computer science. This systematic and detailed enquiry has evolved to date through five phases of enquiry, embarking initially on an extensive review of the computing curriculum literature, and direct interviews with teachers of computing. The characteristics originally identified by Meyer and Land (2003) were employed as the focus of research questions. This shifted in the second phase to interviewing students nearing graduation on their experience of two main threshold concepts of *object-orientation* and *pointers*. As the students' responses tended to emphasise difficulty, a subsequent research question explored the strategies used by students to become 'unstuck'. This opened up a third phase of enquiry, examining the nature of liminality in terms of the student experience of these troublesome concepts. In the fourth, the methodology shifted to the use of conceptual mapping in order to render visible and better gauge the students' understanding of the central ideas of object-orientation, and of what the students themselves regarded as central priorities. The most recent phase, very much in keeping with the theme of this volume, has analysed student biographies to illuminate the transformative aspect of threshold concepts. Here students were asked to identify and describe a computing concept that 'transformed the way they see and experience computing'. The use of 'lure stories' (Schulte and Knoblesdorf, 2007) brought into view a number of other potential thresholds, many of which are related to the key computing science theme of *abstraction*, and which threw light on how the overall concept of abstraction is manifested in students' learning. The authors' point however that

> whether abstraction is a threshold concept; contrary to expectation, it seems unlikely. Rather, it seems likely that there are a number of threshold concepts in computing that could be classified as abstractions of one form or another.

The student biographies, taken from students in three different countries, identified a range of potential candidates for concepts that had transformative potential. These included *modularity, data abstraction, object-orientation, code re-use, design patterns,* and *complexity*. The authors concluded from this wide ranging and large study that changing their data-collection techniques had affected their results. In the light of the link with variation theory discussed earlier they also found considerable individual variability in student experience, and that the students described more specific thresholds than instructors. In a statement which has interesting implications for those researching transformation and learning thresholds in other disciplines the authors found that:

> Whether or not students experience different thresholds, they place greater significance on different transformations. We observed many potential threshold concepts on a single occasion only; we observed some that seemed highly dependent on a particular context. Coming up with an exhaustive 'catalogue' of threshold concepts in a discipline may be impractical. More important, the sequences of partial understandings that students exhibited as they were learning a concept were quite variable: no single path. Rather than seeing a progression of deeper understandings in a concept, we saw different levels of understandings of different parts.

Eun-Jung Park and **Greg Light** (Chapter 16) sought to identify a threshold concept in studies at the atomic and molecular levels in the relatively new field of nanoscience. Their study (after Davies, 2006) adopted both top-down (expert-focused) and bottom-up (student-focused) methods. These methods included 'the construction of concept maps and an interview with the expert (professor), and the construction of pre- and post- course concept maps and the completion of a linked open-ended survey by the students'. Interestingly both methods tended to converge on one particular potential threshold concept, *surface area-to-volume ratio*, as a candidate for nanoscience, at least within this taught programme. Of this threshold concept the expert professor commented:

> Well, *surface-to-volume ratio* is the threshold concept, because you can't get down here (the nano level) without accepting the fact that really tiny particles have large surface-to-volume ratio... So take a gram of something and keep chopping it up until you get down to nano-particles. And what you see is the surface area just goes through the roof. So this is enabling... because, without that, you can't do this. So this would be a threshold concept.

The professor also identified eleven key, or important, concepts within this field. The survey of forty-two student pre- and post-course concept maps revealed thirty-eight further concepts, in addition to the professor's original eleven. The authors employed a phenomenographic approach to analyse the experiential component of these maps to identify variation in the ways students experienced the troublesomeness of the concept. This revealed 'a hierarchical continuum of patterns of understanding, each more complex and inclusive of the preceding patterns' which produced an outcome space comprising the following five patterns of student understanding: 1. Isolated, 2. Unconnected, 3. Detached, 4. Limited, and 5. Integrated. The key aspect of variation characterising the most complex pattern ('Integrated'), and the pattern most closely reflecting the expert's pattern, was the recognition of the central role of *surface area-to-volume ratio* in the integration of the key nano domain concepts. Both expert and student responses reported this as an integrative concept, whilst two thirds of the students selecting this threshold concept also experienced a change of understanding during the course towards a more sophisticated pattern. In consequence the authors conclude that their study presents 'preliminary evidence that a meaningful understanding of *surface area-to-volume ratio* critically contributes to students' ability to integrate other key concepts in the nano-domain'.

Interestingly, however, the concept *surface area-to-volume ratio*, though selected as a threshold, was not regarded as a particularly troublesome or difficult concept to understand. The authors suggest this might be owing to the fact that 'troublesomeness does not necessarily reside directly with the threshold concept but rather in the integration of the domain cluster of concepts within the student's understanding'.

They also report that the representation of student understanding gained from concept maps, though useful, is not a sufficiently rich source of data in itself for analysis and interpretation of student understanding, and their ongoing study will employ subsequent use of interview data.

In the final illustration of conceptual transformation **Marina Orsini-Jones** (Chapter 17) addresses a threshold concept frequently encountered by languages students. This is 'the overarching structure of a sentence', often referred to in linguistics as the *rank scale concept*. The overall concept is formed from acquisition of a range of grammar categories; students must master each of these fundamental grammar 'milestones' before being able to grasp the overall concept. The author proposes that 'encouraging students to actively engage with metacognition relating to the threshold concept identified while they are in the liminal state can also contribute to their "readiness" to cross it'. The data for the study was drawn from a two year action research analysis which highlighted that many languages students experience 'grammar anxiety', despite the aspirations of many of the group to become English as a Foreign Language (EFL) or Modern Languages (ML) teachers, who routinely have to explain grammar to their students.

Active engagement with metacognition relating to grammar anxiety and the *rank scale concept* was fostered through the design of a 'metareflective socio-collaborative assessed task' to help students overcome the troublesome knowledge, though, the author acknowledges, 'it remains a contested notion whether or not engaging in metacognitive grammatical activities can enhance language learning and whether or not a focus on linguistic form can benefit language skills in the target language studied'. The assessed task, *The Group Grammar Project*, is complex and involves students in a range of activities including web site development, group presentation, anonymous self- and peer-assessment, and the writing of an individual reflective report on the project. In both years of the action research it emerged that the most troublesome elements in the overall *rank scale* threshold concept tended to be complex sentences (relationships and identification of verbs); clauses (identifying subject-verb-object); phrases (confusion with clauses); and word classification (adverbs and prepositions). Barriers to learning the threshold concept included unfamiliar terminology that invoked student resistance and conservatism, prior (mis)knowledge of terms, requiring an 'undoing' of pre-conceived definitions of the grammar categories involved, prior knowledge, reliance in group work upon peers who found the grammatical categories 'troublesome' but decided nevertheless to take a lead in the analysis of the sentences, misunderstanding of the concepts and lack of ability to ask lecturers for help; lack of motivation towards grammar and the module, lack of reinforcement or support by other tutors teaching languages, and feelings of grammar fear or inadequacy. Lack of awareness of underlying grammar principles emerged as the main concern for the students interviewed, particularly the native English ones. However a range of strategies were identified as assisting students to overcome the difficulty in understanding the rank scale concept. These included collaborative group work; demonstrating initiative and asking for help; confidence building via grammar analysis; practice via diagnostic tests; inspiration from peers; explaining grammar to peers; tailor-made materials, having fun with grammar, and metacognition. In these ways the *Group Grammar Project* seems to have improved grammar knowledge and confidence for most students.

It would seem that the increase in the amount of work done at the 'meta-reflective' level improved the students' ability for accurate self-assessment in grammar understanding. It could be argued that this in turn had enhanced their 'preparedness' to embrace the ontological shift necessary to cross the threshold. It could be argued that metareflection encouraged students to engage with their state of liminality towards the threshold identified in a positive and constructive way and helped with overcoming the paralysing 'fear of grammar' some had experienced at the beginning of the academic year.

Compared with the ease with which the majority of native French, German, Polish and Italian students, (who had been familiar with formal grammar teaching since primary school) tackled the analysis of the grammar categories, however, many negative attitudes towards grammar arising from the English school system proved difficult to 'undo'. The European students did not perceive the grammar analysis of sentences in the assessed task as a 'terrifying' task like so many of their English counterparts. The author further concluded that the study had confirmed that a learning threshold of such complexity as the *rank scale concept* could not be adequately crossed in one year by many students.

ONTOLOGICAL TRANSFORMATIONS

The concluding section of this volume presents illustrations of the ontological transformations mentioned earlier in this chapter. These 'learning thresholds' might not be strictly conceptual, but seem necessarily occasioned by significant learning and are more concerned with shifts in identity and subjectivity, with procedural knowledge, or the ways of thinking and practising customary to a given disciplinary or professional community. An underlying implication here is that there is always some form of self-relational trajectory to the discipline being learned (Cousin 2009). We are a student and practiser of music in order to become a performing pianist. Being and knowing are inextricably linked. We are what we know, and we become what we learn. As Davies (2006) has pointed out, an act of learning is an act of identity formation.

In Chapter 18 **Jens Kabo** and **Caroline Baillie** examine one such ontological shift required by students of engineering when encountering engineering's relationship with social justice. For much of their engineering education the students envisage their future development and practice as likely to comprise 'problem solving, technical development, efficiency, and profit making'. This 'common sense view', the authors suggest, is likely to be predicated on an 'inherent belief that technical development always equates to progress'. However such a perspective is now open to the challenge that rapidly accelerating technological advances and interventions are implicated in the rise of serious global challenges such as poverty and environmental sustainability (Catalano 2007). The production of biofuels, for example, though encouraged to counter global warming, has occasioned the unintended consequences of increases in food prices and the destruction of rainforests. The critical perspective of 'who benefits and who pays' hence becomes a necessary consideration in the reasoning and judgement of engineers. However, as these authors note, 'the established ways of thinking within a community or a group can serve as barriers toward new knowledge building, i.e. potentially create thresholds.' The 'thought collective' that the engineering students had entered, one of the authors found when teaching a course on social justice, seemed to constitute such a threshold. As students encountered the learning threshold of social justice they seemed to adopt the oscillative behaviour characteristic of liminal states. Students taking the course 'appeared to move into a liminal space, some passing through, some getting stuck and others moving back and forth uncertain of what to do.' For both experienced and novice engineers the required adoption of a socially just perspective to their practice and profession appeared to provoke a 'transformative and troublesome' state of liminality. The authors adapted the phenomenographic framework of Marton and Booth (1997) to assess variation in the response of learners to understanding and integrating the notion of social justice.

> A key thing that varies over the different conceptions is the students' awareness of the complexities surrounding social justice, which goes from simple and superficial to complex and deep. Other shifts are from active to passive and individual to collective.

The outcome space achieved through this approach produced nine conceptions of social justice, ranging from a preliminal state of virtually no understanding, through a (liminal) moral awareness of social justice as duty and responsibility, to a more sophisticated recognition of social justice as a participatory undertaking, and on to a postliminal capacity to employ social justice 'as a lens for deconstruction and critical analysis'. The authors stress however that the nine conceptions are not to be seen as a linear progression 'since they both overlap and can exist simultaneously in how a student views social justice'. The barriers to understanding and progression were found to be often ontological, requiring a letting go of taken for granted collective cultural assumptions that engineering tends to be focused on money, profit making and efficiency rather than social justice. At the level of individual response, the learning threshold required 'sacrifice, risks, doubts and discomfort' and difficulty in moving 'beyond the things they took for granted'. As one student commented:

> [The course] really messed with my head. Sometimes I was scared going to class because I didn't want to think about stuff. [...] it put some guilt on my actions [...] I feel that it might have an impact on my success in a company, for example if I don't do it the next person might.

In her work with colleagues on the Freshman Learning Project at Indiana University **Leah Shopkow** (Chapter 19) has encountered this kind of learning threshold, or as they term it, a conceptual 'bottleneck' or 'impasse' in understanding, across many disciplines. The difficulty may lie in '"basic" concepts, some of which may be threshold concepts, others of which may be clusters of threshold concepts, and some of which constitute disciplinary ways of knowing'.

In a separate but parallel project to the development of thresholds theory, but with a similar chronology, her colleagues have developed an approach to assist colleagues in 'decoding' their disciplines in order to become 'more mindful teachers' and hence more able to assist their students through these learning bottlenecks. She describes the work of Decoding the Disciplines (DtD) as follows:

> DtD approaches the problem of impasses in student learning not from a theoretical perspective (although theory is quite useful in grounding its practices), but from a practical approach that emphasizes both the modelling of expert behaviour for students and the explicit explication of its underlying epistemes; the expert is rendered more self-conscious about these epistemes through a metacognitive dialogue between the expert and interviewers not necessarily within the expert's discipline.

She suggests that the DtD methodology can facilitate the application of the theory of Threshold Concepts in five ways. First of these is that it can help 'identify and order concepts and understandings ...where even the notion of essential concepts can be contested'. This often can apply in the Arts and Humanities, and History is examined here as a particular illustration. The range of learning thresholds identified within this discipline indicates how the conceptual and ontological are inextricably linked, and includes, to take a sample, developing and evaluating historical arguments, recreating historical context, maintaining emotional distance, overcoming affective roadblocks, willingness to wait for an answer, dealing with ambiguity, seeing artefacts from the past as representing choices that change over time, identifying with people in another time/place, understanding historical change, reading critically, writing historically, using appropriate language, and understanding notions of time. Secondly the author argues for the value of DtD in helping to surface tacit knowledge and render it more accessible. The latter she argues is a form of troublesome knowledge 'both drawn upon and expected by the teacher' and which students otherwise merely have to intuit. Her third point relates to the teacher's own academic subjectivity in relation to pedagogy and the greater possibility of engaging discipline-focused academics in considering the difficulties in under-standing faced by their students. 'Because the methodology uses as its launching pad the instructor's own disciplinary modes of thought and teaching concerns', the author contends, it is less likely to be perceived as alien knowledge or foreign knowledge by the instructor'. This is in keeping with the point often made by Glynis Cousin that the thresholds approach invites disciplinary academics 'to deconstruct their subject, rather than their educative practice, thus leaving them within both safe and interesting territory' (Cousin, 2007; see also Flanagan, Taylor and Meyer, and also Weil and McGuigan, in this volume). A further and fourth point made by the author is that because the DtD approach helps clarify both the intended learning outcomes of the teacher and also where barriers to student understanding might lie, the process of course (re)design is made easier, as is also the means of evaluating whether students have achieved the intended learning. This then, in turn, 'provides guidance for interventions'. Her final point raises the important issue of how learning thresholds might be addressed across the span of an entire curriculum lasting for several years. This requires a collaborative engagement at departmental or even institutional level.

> No one faculty member is equally suited or has the kind of continuity of instruction with individuals to help students negotiate them all. If we want students not still to think like novices at the end of their undergraduate programs as they often still do (for a case in History, see Wineburg 2001), many faculty members will have to work collectively to this end. We will have to think about how Threshold Concepts might be sequenced in disciplines, like History, where the content is not sequenced of itself, so as to introduce students to these concepts in a systematic way, to ensure that students keep using the concepts to prevent student knowledge from becoming inert, and to help students learn to coordinate all the concepts that define the epistemes of the disciplines.

Sidney Weil and **Nicholas McGuigan** (Chapter 20) also take up the notion of epistemes, characterised by Perkins (2006, p. 42) as 'a system of ideas or way of understanding that allows us to establish knowledge. ... the importance of students understanding the structure of the disciplines they are studying. ... epistemes are manners of justifying, explaining, solving problems, conducting enquiries, and designing and validating various kinds of products or outcomes.' These authors examine the requisite learning structure for *bank reconciliations*, which is a single, traditionally difficult topic in Introductory Accounting, to determine whether such learning might be characterised as involving threshold concepts or perhaps is better explained through related notions of the episteme or what Lucas and Mladenovic (2006), in an earlier application of threshold theory to Introductory Accounting, have termed *threshold conceptions*.

The authors draw on an empirical study undertaken at the University of the Western Cape in which Accountancy students were questioned in the following manner:

A. If the cash book has a debit balance of 810 Rand, what balance would you expect the bank statement to have?

B. How and why, would you treat each of the following items when preparing a bank reconciliation statement?

(i) Bank charges on the bank statement.

(ii) Cheques made out in the cash book but not yet presented for payment to the bank.

(iii) A cheque from a debtor which has been deposited with the bank, but which is shown as dishonoured on the bank statement.

C. The bank statement shows a debit balance of 410 Rand. There are unpresented deposits of R465 Rand. How will you treat the unpresented deposits in the bank reconciliation statement? What will the cash book balance be?

Such questions give rise to several important aspects of a bank reconciliation process. In A, the authors point out 'students are required to visualize the relationship between a business' cash records and the bank's equivalent for the business. This relationship is a *mirror* image – equal in amount, but opposite in direction – either a debit or a credit'. In B students have to deal with certain unresolved items when preparing a bank reconciliation statement, which exposes the students' understanding of the relationship between a bank statement and a cash book in greater depth, requiring them to be able to manipulate the cause and effect consequences of each situation. C also requires exercise of visualization skills in terms of how the unpresented deposits might affect the respective bank and cash book balances.

The authors conducted a series of protocol analyses of the talk-aloud interviews with the Accountancy students. For this they drew on Feuerstein et al.'s 'deficient cognitive operations' model derived from the psychosocial theory of Mediated Learning Experience (MLE). This postulates that a lack of effective mediation results in deficient cognitive operations, for example, poor visualization of relationships and lack of inferential-hypothetical reasoning. According to Feuerstein et al. (1980, p. 71), such cognitive deficiencies help identify *prerequisites* of thinking, and refer to 'deficiencies in those functions that underlie internalized, operational thought'. Analysis from the talk-aloud interviews revealed, amongst other phenomena, three forms of student difficulty in terms of *lack of inferential-hypothetical reasoning, narrowness of the mental field* and *poor visualisation of relationships.* These deficient cognitive operations overlap and also have an impact on the effective usage of data. In terms of the nature of the learning thresholds that these cognitive operations might constitute, the authors suggest that as they relate more to thinking skills or organizing structures than to concepts, they resemble more Lucas and Mladenovic's (2006) definition of *threshold conceptions*, rather than concepts. Threshold conceptions are defined as 'comprising an *organising structure* or *framework* which provides the explanatory rationale for accounting techniques' (Lucas and Mladenovic, 2006, pp. 153–154). The authors identify similarities in this respect Perkins' notion of the disciplinary episteme mentioned earlier. Interestingly they also point out the likely necessity of an ontological shift in overcoming these deficient cognitive operations:

> Furthermore, the cognitive operations identified in this chapter as being part of an organising structure for studying Introductory Accounting could be argued to represent an ontological shift in how the study of accounting is viewed. A focus on the thought processes underlying a topic area, such as bank reconciliations, rather than on the content itself, may be a spark to ignite a major shift in how student's perceive – and ultimately study – the discipline of accounting.

In their empirical study of design education **Jane Osmond** and **Andrew Turner** (Chapter 21) note the relatively undertheorised nature of this field, observing that 'most research into design has focused on the *process* of design at the expense of the development of the designer'. They applied the threshold concept framework as a lens or 'way in' to research the specific context of Transport and Product Design Courses and to open up a research dialogue with both students and staff on the courses. Initial explorations with staff as to whether 'spatial awareness' might be a threshold concept in Transport and Product Design revealed no common definition and responses ranging from 'all round awareness' to 'design sensitivity'. Student responses, gathered through a combination of qualitative interviews and questionnaires revealed states of 'having no knowledge', 'little knowledge' or 'guessing'. Though the notion of spatial awareness was not pursued further, and seen rather as a 'design capability', the response data had nonetheless provided valuable leads to other candidate thresholds. The notion of 'visual creativity' emerged as a necessary attribute for successful design graduates but integral to this seemed to be an ontological capacity for what the authors term the 'confidence to challenge', and this seemed to operate as a learning threshold. One tutor characterises this as 'the ability to inculcate design conventions and expand upon them using information from a variety of sources and experiences'. It seems a prerequisite to enable designers to tackle what Buchanan (1992) has termed 'wicked problems', that is, those having 'incomplete, contradictory, and changing requirements; and solutions to them are often difficult to recognize as such because of complex interdependencies.' Without this shift in subjectivity, design students, the authors report, 'can remain in a liminal state, constantly "surfacing around" in search of a solution'. Interestingly this threshold seemed to present even more difficulties to those international students used to a more prescribed style of teaching and curriculum:

> I think during the very beginning I really struggled to really know what I should do in my projects - you really spend a lot of time to think about it but the result is not really that good as you expected because you keep surfacing around, you can't really make decisions about doing ... that's one of the most negative feelings because you don't know what to do sometimes - I mean I understand you do projects it is not really satisfying teachers, you learn during the process, but still you want to know what they really want. (First year international student)

The authors draw on the design process literature to gain helpful insights into what the nature of this liminal state might entail, drawing on notions such as Tovey's (1984) 'incubation period' during which 'the two halves of the brain are out of touch or unable to agree', or the idea of 'oscillation' between problem and solution. They cite Archer's view (1979, cited in Cross 1992, p. 5) that:

> The design activity is commutative, the designer's attention oscillating between the emerging requirement ideas and the developing provision ideas, as he illuminates obscurity on both sides and reduces misfit between them.

They also draw on Wallace's (1992, p. 81) representation of this transformational state as 'problem bubbles' involving the solution of countless individual problems, like myriad bubbles within a larger bubble, and in which for the particular design brief to be successfully achieved 'the complete set of problem bubbles associated with the task must be solved; but many, many bubbles not directly related to the task will be entered between starting and finishing the task'.

In order to achieve the confidence to challenge, however, an intervening learning threshold was identified by the authors, namely the need to develop *a tolerance of being in a period of uncertainty.* Significantly, the authors observe, it is only after mastering toleration of this period of uncertainty that the students gain the 'confidence to challenge' and are then ready, or able, to tackle their design briefs which characteristically include the 'wicked problems' discussed earlier. This mastering of the toleration of uncertainty also clearly possesses an ontological dimension and entails a shift in subjectivity. The 'holding environment', or support structures that seemed to enable this shift are identified by the authors as including the 'inculcating skills, capabilities and coping strategies delivered via an apprentice-like immersive method of teaching underpinned by an atelier, or studio-based, environment'. The staff respondents also identified important *transition points*, key moments during the course that moved the students on through the liminal state, and which included 'first year assessments, the use of clay in the second year, exposure to the professional community of practice during the third year, coupled with the ability to work in groups and the development of empathy'.

In an interesting migration of threshold theory to the secondary sector of education **Ming Fai Pang** and **Jan Meyer** (Chapter 22) investigated dimensions of sub- and preliminal variation in secondary school pupils' initial apprehension, via a range of 'proxies', of the threshold concept of 'opportunity cost'. In this case the proxies were short scenarios designed to reveal variation in pupils' under-standing of 'opportunity cost'. The following is an example:

> *Ben woke up at eleven and he planned to study for his exam in the afternoon. At noon, the phone rang. His girlfriend asked him to go to a movie. He decided to spend 4 hours in the afternoon with her. a. What choice did Ben make? Why did Ben have to make choice? What was the cost for Ben to go to see the movie? b. If the movie was boring, would it have increases his cost of going to the movie? Why or why not?*

Forty Secondary 3 pupils of in Hong Kong took part in the study. They were following the 'New Senior Secondary (NSS) Curriculum – Proposed Economics Subject Framework for Secondary 4–6 pupils in Hong Kong', aimed at developing pupils' interest in exploring human behaviour and social issues through a good mastery of fundamental economic themes such as 'economic decisions involving choices among alternatives' and the 'concept of cost in Economics'. The pupils were of both sexes, had not previously taken economics as a school subject and came from schools of different levels of academic attainment and in different physical locations in the city. Interviews were held in Cantonese.

The inquiry drew on Marton and Booth's (1997) 'variation theory' which posits that 'pupils' variation in the understanding of a disciplinary concept or practice, or alternative conceptions of the concept, hinges on those critical features of the concept or practice that pupils are able to *discern and focus on simultaneously'.*

Hence learning is seen as a capacity to discern and focus on the critical aspects of a concept or practice. In this case the threshold concept of opportunity cost became the object of learning whose critical features would need to be discerned and understood. The study also sought to measure variation in the extent to which pupils demonstrated evidence of a subliminal or preliminal state of understanding. The former relates to the learner's awareness and understanding of an underlying game or episteme – a 'way of knowing' – which may be a crucial determinant of progression (epistemological or ontological) within a conceptual domain. The latter concerns how a threshold concept initially 'comes into view' (i.e. is initially perceived or apprehended), and the mindset with which it might be approached or withdrawn from. According to the authors, those experienced in the manners of reasoning and justifying customary to economics are likely, in reaching a rational decision, to take into account both benefits and costs. Significantly 'they focus on both the option chosen as well as the highest-valued option forgone at the same time'. This was not the case with the Secondary 3 pupils however:

> most of the pupils interviewed seem only to have some innate grasp of the allocation of preference or benefit part, and they thus focus only on the option chosen, taking for granted or ignoring the sacrifice or cost involved in choice making. Even though some pupils may have a sense of cost, what they focus on is the monetary cost involved in getting the chosen option, rather than the opportunity cost of getting the chosen option.

At one extreme, pupils failed to understand questioning related to the notions of 'choice' and 'opportunity cost' and could not demonstrate coherent ways of reasoning. At the other extreme a few were:

> conscious of an embedded, consistent way of rationalising the phenomenon, although without the language to formalise it. They have developed an implicit way of using the concept of 'opportunity cost' to make sense of the world through the scenarios and they seemed to be 'thinking like an economist' without being aware of it.

For these few pupils some notion of choice or opportunity cost seemed to have come into view, suggesting the possibility of their already having reached a preliminal stage. Still others frequently *changed their minds* whilst discussing the same scenario, indicating perhaps oscillation between sub- and preliminal modes of variation, or between an economic way of understanding and a lay person's way of understanding. Occasionally students demonstrated an intuitive and quite sophis-ticated, economic way of reasoning.

In seeking to establish a 'transformative pedagogy' the authors propose targeting the *transformation of* pupils' ways of thinking and reasoning. This requires a prior ascertaining of pupils' original, intuitive and normal 'ways of knowing' and an understanding on the part of their teachers of the variation in '*how* pupils initially perceive, apprehend, conceptualise or experience the threshold concept in the absence of any formalised knowledge of the concept itself'. This crucial knowledge will, in turn, the authors argue, 'inform an understanding of where *and why* pupils may find themselves in "stuck places" on their learning trajectory'. It also helps identify the *critical features* of pupils' initial different ways of apprehending phenomena that act as proxies for threshold concepts, and these may involve both cognitive and ontological shifts. This then can open up the possibility, in both secondary and higher education, of genuinely transformative learning designs that can aid learners in their transition from naive or intuitive understandings of economic phenomena to the more sophisticated ways of reasoning and practising normal to the community of practice.

A further interesting migration of threshold theory, in this case from education to social science, and an equally interesting ontological shift, can be found in **Dagmar Kutsar** and **Anita Kärner**'s exploration, from a threshold concepts perspective, of societal transitions in post-communist Estonia (Chapter 23). Their aim is not only to 'broaden the explanatory potential of the threshold concepts perspective of teaching and learning to examine societal transition processes in society' but also 'to develop a cognitive learning exercise from the experiences of students seeking new explanations, visions, and meanings of "the known"'. This involves applying the lens of threshold theory to an entire society at a critical point of political, social and economic transformation in the aftermath of the break-up of the Soviet state, with one political system having collapsed and being exchanged by another. In doing this society is examined as a learning and teaching environment in itself. 'The transitions are meaningful events', the authors observe, 'accompanied by uncertainties, learning the new and changing identities and structures'. During this period of social transformation, society is 'overwhelmed by a liminal space – no longer what it was and not yet what it will be. The liminal space is shared by the actors of transition, the institutions, groups and individuals all filled with a mixture of new and old cognitions, emotions, myths and behavioural patterns'. As was pointed out at the beginning of this section, an act of learning is an act of identity formation, but, as these authors emphasise:

> Learning in rapid societal changes does not have a clear curriculum and all those involved are students. Meeting uncertainties and the 'unknown' leads to new perceptions and ('troublesome') knowledge... Examining rapid societal transitions in a particular country from the threshold concepts perspective, feels like putting the social learning process under a magnifying-glass.

The authors draw on Turner's anthropological notion of liminality, as does threshold theory itself. In their view the entire population of Estonia entered a liminal state at the time of the (peaceful) Singing Revolution. This was the historical moment, in Turnerian terms, of leaving the old and meeting the new, and when the population, the social actors, enter a liminal state of what Turner called a *no-longer-not-yet-status*. The majority of these social actors, in the authors' analysis, emerged into a postliminal state of order at some point in the mid 1990s, with new (and stable) social and economic structures. But this did not apply to all sectors of Estonian society. Continuing the Turnerian analysis, the authors describe the formation of the *Communitas*, with its strong sense of togetherness, group experience and collective goals. This was very much occasioned by large musical gatherings or events such as The Baltic Chain peaceful protest held on the 23 August 1989:

> The *Communitas* of Estonia, Latvia and Lithuania joined together in a human chain, hand–in-hand, from Tallinn, through Riga to Vilnius as a symbol of the shared destiny of the Baltic countries and the expression of the common goals of regaining their independent statehood. Approximately 2,000,000 people joined their hands over the 600 kilometre route to show that the Baltic people had united and shared their visions of the future. During this ritual, a mantra *'Estonia/Latvia/Lithuania belongs to us'* was echoed from person to person the length of the entire human chain.

As in other studies of learning thresholds, the liminal phase was found here to be a troubling experience, not always characterised by positive emotion. The authors speak of 'emotional tensions and fears of loss of cognitive control over the situation, which results in feelings of powerlessness, dissatisfaction and alienation', attributing this to the fact that well-being acknowledges the *possibilities* but also *limitations* for action. A survey of social stress at the time revealed high levels of social distress, 'anxiety, discomfort, different kinds of fears', particularly amongst male, non-Estonian, and older members of society. As this initial period of intense transformation, and transformational learning concluded, the social actors ventured into new and often strange spaces. New social, economic and political structures emerged (popular front, heritage society, green movement, creative unions, the Congress of Estonia) and new actors joined them in these spaces, such as exiles returning from the West and newly released former Soviet dissidents. We see variation entering into the experience of participants here, and also in terms of their role and changed status in the new social space.

> Interestingly, young people who had had a *'missing experience'*, no participatory experience in the Soviet system, were popularly viewed to have more worth in facing the challenges inherent in rebuilding the nation than those, like the nomenklatura, whose experience was deemed an *'invalid experience'*.

What seems to become manifest here is that whilst certain social actors, as social 'learners', successfully negotiate this phase of transformation and emerge into a trans-formed postliminal state, in both senses of that term, others – *The Others*, as the authors characterise them – remain in a liminal mode of oscillation. The non-Estonian (mainly Russian-speaking) population, we are told, 'needed more time for self re-identification and for re-positioning in the transition from being accepted as the dominant ethnic group and the speakers of the former state language (Russian) to being labelled as the ethnic minority with either weak or zero command of the state language (Estonian)'. Meanwhile the formerly powerful Soviet *nomenklatura* could be seen as remaining in a preliminal state, refusing to join the Communitas, seeking to maintain the old identities, and spreading social tension to prevent the new structures form taking hold. In keeping with the threshold theory notion of a holding environment, social myth emerged as a coping strategy for surviving the liminal state, even though the myths later 'disintegrated' in the postliminal state.

Social myths can be interpreted as threshold myths (Atherton et al., 2008), the functional value of which exceeds their value of being true. They are ideological beliefs with strong affective and political elements, which according to Atherton et al., (2008) serve as threshold concepts.

In the concluding chapter of this volume **Margaret Kiley** and **Gina Wisker** (Chapter 24), in a welcome application of threshold theory to postgraduate study, turn the lens of threshold theory to the field of research. In a survey of experienced supervisors in a range of different countries their concern is to identify 'conceptual challenges that candidates encountered when learning to be a researcher, how supervisors recognised that a candidate had successfully met those challenges, and how they might have assisted the candidate in that process'. The purpose of the study was to attempt to identify 'moments of research learning' or 'learning leaps' in the experience of research students, to enable supervisors to develop effective strategies to better assist them in the kinds of conceptual threshold crossing that research undertakings involve.

Their enquiry drew on earlier influential studies such as the Reflections on Learning Inventory (RoLI) (Meyer & Boulton-Lewis, 1997). This was used to inform an action research programme with a large international UK PhD programme to identify when students can be seen, or not, to develop their approaches to, and perceptions of, the learning necessary at doctoral level. This pointed to factors such as identification of research questions, methodology and literature review as well as conceptual levels of enquiry, research design, data management, interpretation of findings and conclusions. The Students' Conceptions of Research inventory (SCoRI) was next consulted. This had aimed to identify what research students and their supervisors envisaged as the nature and purpose of research. Research into the nature of the viva and doctoral examination was then explored to gain insights into the capacity of doctoral candidates 'to present their work conceptually and to theorise and abstract their findings in ways which allowed them to have broader application'.

The convergence of these earlier dimensions of the authors' work – namely student meta-cognition, conceptual level thinking and research students' developing capacity to articulate and theorise their research learning – with the theory of threshold concepts became a catalytic point in their research. These earlier dimensions were seen as 'crucial in the development of postgraduates' doctoral learning journeys through to the crossing of conceptual thresholds and the achievement of their doctorate'. This convergence provided an initial focus to explore the conceptual crossings that students might encounter in the doctoral journey. Six candidate thresholds emerged from research data with staff and students: a) the concept of *argument* or thesis a concept which the research on doctoral examination frequently cites either because of its presence, or lack of it, in the dissertation; b) the concept of *theory* either underpinning research or being an outcome of research; c) *framework* as a means of locating or bounding the research; d) concepts of originality and *knowledge creation*; e) *analysis* (often criticised by examiners as too 'haphazard' or 'undisciplined'); and *research paradigm*, that is 'the epistemological framing of one's approach to research'.

Building on these earlier findings the specific aims of the researchers then became the identification of:

1. How research supervisors recognise the acquisition of the threshold concepts
2. Where and how they recognise evidence they are crossing, and
3. How they 'nudge' candidates in the crossing of this threshold.

By 'nudging' the authors are referring to 'the constructive intervention of the supervisor to aid the student's conceptualised work'. This nudging takes place through 'staged interventions' during the development of the supervisory relationship at various stages of doctoral candidature. The following were recognised as particularly significant:

– The development of research questions.
– The movement from other-directed reading to self-directed and 'owned' reading of the literature leading to the development of a sound literary review.
– Working with data at different conceptual levels, analysing, interpreting and defining findings which make a contribution to understanding as well as factual knowledge.
– Developing an argument or thesis which can be sustained and supported.
– Producing the abstract and the conceptual conclusions.

These interventions were found to be key moments for helping candidates make 'learning leaps' and articulate their understanding at a conceptual level. Supervisors also identified specific elements in their supervision practices which seemed to assist their supervisees in the process of what the authors term 'conceptual threshold crossing'. These specific practices include the following:

– Encouraging engagement with the research question.
– Offering and prompting opportunities for engagement with the literature in relation to themes, issues and then in a dialogue with the candidate's own work.
– Oral prompting of conceptual work in groups, supervisory meetings, and individually.
– Encouraging conceptual and critical work with prompt feedback.
– Pointing out contradictions and tensions.
– Encouraging careful data analysis, developing themes, engaging with theories.
– Encouraging early writing and much editing-sharing and reflection.
– Using the language of 'doctorateness' e.g. conceptual framework, and the ideas, the research and theories of learning e.g. meta-cognition.
– Offering opportunities to articulate ideas and achievements in mock *vivas* and other oral presentations.

The authors contend that evidence of a candidate's behaviour changes is often a proxy indication that the student has crossed a particular conceptual threshold and that this indicates a change in subjectivity, a 'shift, a change, in the learner's appreciation and understanding of her/himself as well as what has been learned'. Though these ontological shifts often incur challenge and a degree of troublesomenes, they generally were found to occasion new insights and access to new levels.

Students are perceived to be changing their ways of working, their contribution to meaning, and also changing in terms of behaviour, particularly their ways of going about their learning. Identity is then an important factor noted by supervisors in terms of the changing ways students engage with, conduct and articulate their research.

CONCLUSION

We hope that the chapters that follow in this book convey something of the vibrancy and engagement that characterised the conference in Ontario where they were first presented and discussed. It is encouraging to see the widespread adoption of the thresholds framework across many disciplines, institutions and countries, and its migration into new sectors and fields. Our thanks are due to the many writers included in this volume, and to the generosity of their colleagues and students in contributing their time, thoughts and feelings in discussion and dialogue about learning thresholds and troublesome knowledge in a common endeavour to gain better insights into student learning and conceptual difficulty. As we go to press with this volume plans are already well under way for a third international conference on thresholds to be held in Sydney in July 2010, jointly hosted by the Universities of Sydney and New South Wales. We look forward with great anticipation to further engagement around this continually intriguing theme, to renewing discussions with old friends and embarking on future explorations with new ones.

REFERENCES

Atherton, J., Hadfield, P., & Meyers, R. (2008). *Threshold Concepts in the Wild*. Expanded version of a paper presented at Threshold Concepts: from Theory to Practice conference, Queen's University, Kingston Ontario 18–20 June 2008. Retrieved 30 January 2009 from http://www.bedspce.org.uk/ Threshold_Concepts_in_the_Wild.pdf

Barker, P. (1991). *Regeneration*. London: Penguin.

Boyd, R. D. (1989). Facilitating Personal Transformations in Small Groups: Part I. *Small Group Behaviour, 20*(4): 459–474.

Boyd, R. D., ed. (1991). *Personal Transformations in Small Groups: A Jungian Perspective*. London: Routledge, 1991.

Boyd, R. D., & Myers, J. G. (1988, October–December). Transformative Education. *International Journal of Lifelong Education 7*(4): 261–284.

Brueggemann, W. (1995). Preaching as Reimagination. *Theology Today*, 52(3): 319–320.

Bruner, J. (1960). *The Process of Education*. Cambridge, MA: Harvard University Press.

Buchanan, R. (1992). Wicked Problems in Design Thinking. In *Design Issues* (Vol. 8, Issue 2). Spring.

Catalano, G. D. (2007). *Engineering, Poverty, and the Earth*. Synthesis lectures on Engineers, Technology and Society #4. San Rafael, California: Morgan & Claypool Publishers.

Collard, S., & Law, M. (1989). The limits of perspective transformation: a critique of Mezirow's theory. *Adult Education Quarterly, 39*(2), 99–107.

Cousin, G. (2007). Exploring threshold concepts for linking teaching and research. Paper presented to the *International Colloquium: International Policies and Practices for Academic Enquiry*, Winchester, April. Available from: http://portal live.solent.ac.uk/university/rtconference/2007/resources/glynis_ cousins.pdf.

Cousin, G. (2009). *Threshold Concepts*. Video webcast, Central Queensland University. Available from: http://onlinemedia.cqu.edu.au/media_request.htm?file=cqu/staff/asdu/interviews/2009_g_cousin&formats=3.

Cross, N. (1992). Research in Design Thinking. In N. Cross, K. Dorst, Roozenbury (Eds.), *Research in design thinking*. Delft University Press.

Cross, P. (1999). What do we know about students' learning and how do we know it? *Innovative Higher Education*, *23*(4), 255–270.

Davies, P. (2006). Threshold concepts: how can we recognize them? In J. H. F. Meyer & R. Land (Eds.), *Overcoming barriers to student understanding: Threshold concepts and troublesome knowledge* (pp. 70–84). New York, NY: Routledge.

Feuerstein, R., Rand, Y., Hoffman, M., & Miller, R. (1980). *Instrumental Enrichment*. University Park Press.

Heidegger, M. (1927). *Being and Time*. Tubingen: Max Niemeyer Verlag.

Kegan, R. (1982). *The evolving self: Problem and process in human development*. Cambridge, MA: Harvard University Press.

Kelly, R., & Crainton, P. (2009, January 19). Transformative Learning: Q&A with Patricia Cranton. *Faculty Focus*. Available at: http://www.facultyfocus.com/articles/instructional-design/transformative-learning-qa-with-patricia-cranton/

Land, R., Cousin, G., Meyer, J. H. F., & Davies, P. (2005). Threshold concepts and troublesome knowledge (3): implications for course design and evaluation. In C. Rust (Ed.), *Improving Student Learning 12 — Diversity and Inclusivity* (pp. 53–64). Oxford, UK: Oxford Brookes University.

Lucas, U., & Mladenovic, R. (2006). Developing New 'World Views': Threshold concepts in introductory accounting. In J. H. F. Meyer & R. Land (Eds.), *Overcoming Barriers to Student Understanding: Threshold Concepts and Troublesome Knowledge* (pp. 148–159). Oxford, UK: Routledge.

Marton, F. (2009). Personal communication to the Steering Committee of the Australian Learning and Teaching Council Project: *A threshold concepts focus to curriculum design: supporting student learning through application of variation theory*. EARLI 2009 Conference, 25 August, Free University, Amsterdam.

Marton, F., & Booth, S. (1997). *Learning and awareness*. Mahwah, NJ: Lawrence Erlbaum Associates.

Meyer, J., & Boulton-Lewis, G. (1997). Variation in students' conceptions of learning: An exploration of cultural and discipline effects. *Research and Development in Higher Education*, *20*, 481–487.

Meyer, J. H. F., & Land, R. (Eds.). (2006). *Overcoming Barriers to Student Understanding: Threshold Concepts and Troublesome Knowledge*. London: Routledge.

Mezirow, J. (1978). Perspective transformation. *Adult Education*, *28*(2), 100–109.

Mezirow, J. (1990). How critical reflection triggers transformative learning. In J. Mezirow & associates (Eds.), *Fostering critical reflection in adulthood*. San Francisco: Jossey-Bass.

Mezirow, J. (1994). Understanding transformation theory. *Adult Education Quarterly*, *44*(4), 222–232.

Mezirow, J. (1995). Transformation Theory of Adult Learning. In M. R. Welton (Ed.), *In Defense of the Lifeworld* (pp. 39–70). New York: SUNY Press.

Nin, A. (1971). *The Diary of Anais Nin 1944–1947*. London: Harcourt.

O'Sullivan, E. V., Morrell, A., & O'Connor, M. A. (2002). *Expanding the boundaries of transformative learning: Essays on theory and praxis*. New York: Palgrave.

Pang, M., & Marton, F. (2005). Learning theory as teaching resource: enhancing students' understanding of economic concepts. *Instructional Science*, *33*(2), 159–191.

Perkins, D. (1999). The many faces of constructivism. *Educational Leadership*, 57, 6–11.

Perkins, D. N. (2006). Constructivism and troublesome knowledge. In J. H. F. Meyer & R. Land (Eds.), *Overcoming barriers to student understanding: threshold concepts and troublesome knowledge*. Oxford, UK: Routledge, 33–47.

Schulte, C., & Knobelsdorf, M. (2007). Attitudes towards computer science-computing experiences as a starting point and barrier to computer science. In *Proceedings of the Third International Workshop on Computing Education Research (ICER '07)*, 27–38. Atlanta, Georgia, USA.

Segal, S. (1999). The Existential Conditions of Explicitness: an Heideggerian perspective. *Studies in Continuing Education, 21*(1) 73–89.

Solnit, R. (2006). *A Field Guide to Getting Lost*. Edinburgh, UK: Canongate.

Torosyan, Roben. (2000). *Encouraging Consciousness Development in the College Classroom through Student-Centred Transformative Teaching and Learning*. Unpublished PhD. New York: Columbia University.

Tovey, M. (1984, October). Designing with both halves of the brain. In *Design Studies* (Vol. 5, Issue 4, pp. 219–228). Elsevier.

Vygotsky, L. S. (1978). *Mind in society: The development of higher psychological processes* (M. Cole Ed.). Cambridge, MA: Harvard University Press.

Wallace, K. (1992). Some Observations on Design Thinking. In N. Cross, K. Dorst, Roozenbury (Eds.), *Research in design thinking*. Delft University Press.

Wineberg, S. (2001). *Historical thinking and other unnatural acts: Charting the future of teaching the past*. Philadelphia: Temple University Press.

Ray Land, Jan Meyer and Caroline Baillie
Glasgow, Durham and Perth WA
October 2009.

DAVID PERKINS

FOREWORD

Entrance...and entrance. Am I repeating myself? Not if you listen really hard. The first 'entrance' has the accent on the initial syllable and the second on the ultimate – EN-trance and en-TRANCE. Such pairs are called heteronyms, same spelling, different pronunciation. Both words trace their ancestry back to the Latin *transire*, to go across, albeit by quite different routes. And both words apply quite well to the notion of threshold concepts, launched through seminal articles by Ray Land, Jan Meyer and their colleagues a few years ago and explored and extended here, as well as in two previous volumes (Land et al 2005, Land, Meyer and Smith 2008, Meyer and Land 2003, 2005, 2006, 2009, Meyer, Land and Davies, 2008).

Meaning 1: EN-trance. When learners acquire a threshold concept, they enter into a new realm of understanding. Quick examples include the concepts of 'limit' in mathematics, 'gravity' in physics, 'depreciation' in accounting, and 'deconstruction' in literature. Innumerable other instances populate the chapters of this volume. Many of these transformative ideas are not concepts in any strict sense but varied ways of thinking and practicing with a threshold-like nature, all of them affording entrance in one sense or another.

Meaning 2: en-TRANCE. This volume and its predecessors give ample evidence that threshold concepts entrance -- they entrance scholars and teachers concerned with the nature and challenges of learning in the disciplines. Discourse around threshold concepts has proven to offer something of a common language, provoke reflection on the structure of disciplinary knowledge, and inspire investigations of learners' typical hangups and ways to help. Indeed, it's been my pleasure to add to this conversation from time to time on the theme of *troublesome knowledge*, the characteristic ways in which learning poses challenges (e.g. tacit knowledge, conceptually difficult knowledge, ritual knowledge) and the value of constructing "theories of difficulty" for the disciplines that chart where the cracks and chasms of learning lie and suggest ways of bridging them.

So why the entrancement? What is it that so many educators have found alluring about threshold concepts? One answer touched on in the upcoming introduction was suggested by Glynis Cousin (2007) a couple of years ago – threshold concepts invite instructors to examine their disciplines rather than looking directly at their teaching practice, both a more comfortable and a more interesting journey for many.

Another related reason seems to be the very fecundity of threshold concepts, the evolutionary proclivity of the idea toward adventurous and fruitful mutation. As an occasional participant in these conversations, I am always struck by how productively imprecise the notion is.

Put the matter this way – Is 'threshold concept' itself an *ideal* threshold concept? For sure, it has brought many scholars to a new view of things. But a truly prototypical threshold concept perfectly fills a critical slot in a mature home discipline, as with the cases mentioned above. Novices may get confused and confounded, but not experts.

In contrast, 'threshold concept' itself seems to have the heart of a nomad. In the chapters to come, it gets stretched, challenged, revised, reconsidered. Back to the evolutionary metaphor, consider today's biological concept of a bird, precisely demarcated by features such as feathers, toothless beak, hard shelled eggs, four chambered heart, etc. All very neat! Now imagine a biologist roaming around in the Jurassic, 150 to 200 million years ago. "Is this a bird?" the biologist asks. – "But it has teeth!" "Is that a bird? -- But those aren't really feathers!" The diversity was startling and the boundaries not yet formed when small theropod dinosaurs fluttered across the threshold of flight into the new world of the air. Moreover, contemporary paleontology suggests that many of the features that today we take as distinctive of birds developed *before* flight...including feathers.

The flock of ideas around threshold concepts seems to me more analogous to the bird-like-creatures of yesteryear than to *Aves* of today, more exploratory and eclectic than categorical and taxonomic. All to the good! -- the richness of this volume testifies to that. So welcome to Jurassic Park! Here we are at the ENtrance. Prepare to be en-TRANCED.

REFERENCES

Cousin, G. (2007). Exploring threshold concepts for linking teaching and research. Paper presented to the *International Colloquium: International Policies and Practices for Academic Enquiry*, Winchester, April. Retrieved on 1 September 2008 from the World Wide Web: http://portal live.solent. ac.uk/university/rtconference/2007/resources/glynis_cousins.pdf.

Land,R.,Cousin, G., Meyer, J.H.F. & Davies, P. (2005). Threshold concepts and troublesome knowledge (3): Implications for course design and evaluation. In C. Rust (Ed.), *Improving Student Learning 12 – Diversity and Inclusivity*. OCSLD, Oxford Brookes University, Oxford, 53-64. See http://www. brookes.ac.uk/services/ocsld/isl/isl2004/abstracts/conceptual_papers/land.html

Land, R. & Meyer, J.H.F. (2009). Threshold concepts and troublesome knowledge (5): Dynamics of assessment. Chapter 4, this volume.

Land, R., Meyer, J.H.F and Smith,J. (Eds) (2008) *Threshold Concepts Within the Disciplines*. Rotterdam: Sense.

Meyer, J.H.F. & Land, R. (2003). Threshold concepts and troublesome knowledge: Linkages to ways of thinking and practising within the disciplines. This seminal paper was published electronically (see http://www.tla.ed.ac.uk/etl/docs/ETLreport4.pdf) and was later republished as a book chapter: Meyer, J.H.F. & Land, R. (2003). Threshold concepts and troublesome knowledge: Linkages to ways of thinking and practising within the disciplines. In C. Rust (Ed.), *Improving Student Learning. Improving Student Learning Theory and Practice – 10 years on*, OCSLD, Oxford, 412-424.

Meyer, J.H.F. & Land, R. (2005). Threshold concepts and troublesome knowledge (2): Epistemological considerations and a conceptual framework for teaching and learning. *Higher Education*, 49 (3) 373-388.

Meyer, J. H. F. & Land, R. (2006). *Overcoming barriers to student understanding: Threshold concepts and troublesome knowledge*. New York, NY: Routledge.

Meyer, J.H.F., Land, R. & Davies, P. (2008). Threshold concepts and troublesome knowledge (4): Issues of variation and variability. In R. Land, J.H.F. Meyer and J. Smith (Eds.). *Threshold concepts within the disciplines*. Rotterdam and Taipei: Sense publishers, 59-74.

David Perkins
Graduate School of Education
Harvard University
USA

PART I:
EXTENDING THE THEORY

JULIE A. TIMMERMANS

1. CHANGING OUR MINDS

The Developmental Potential of Threshold Concepts

INTRODUCTION

In writing this chapter, I have to come to a startling personal revelation: I am a philosopher, if only an amateur one. Perhaps this revelation should not be so startling, for I have always been a lover (*philo*) of wisdom (*sophia*). And I am, after all, in the process of completing a doctor of philosophy degree.

At the heart of a philosopher's approach lies the activity of asking questions. Gaarder (1994) explains, however, that philosophers are generally not captivated by the entire realm of philosophical questions, yet have particular queries with which they are especially concerned. Therefore, philosophers' questions provide valuable insight into their philosophical *projects*.

What, then, is my philosophical project? Broadly, in my work, I am intrigued by questions about learning in higher education. At the beginning of each project, I therefore return to the question 'What is learning?' for I realise that my interpretation lies at the heart of all subsequent thinking. Here, I adopt the perspective that *learning is an active process of meaning-making* (e.g., Anderson and Krathwohl, 2001; Belenky, Clinchy, Golberger, and Tarule, 1986/1997; Kegan, 1982; Perry, 1970). The question that follows, then, is 'How does learning happen?' Indeed, learning is often characterised as a developmental process. In his Constructive-Developmental Theory of Meaning-Making, Robert Kegan (1982) elegantly weaves together the notions of meaning-making and development, and posits that individuals' abilities to construct meaning evolve through regular periods of stability and change throughout their lifespan.

It is these periods of change, these transitions that characterise the learning process, which I find most intriguing. These transitions remain nebulous; however, understanding them is crucial. Cross (1999) notes that 'in developmental theory, the periods of greatest personal growth are thought to lie in the unnamed and poorly-defined periods *between* stages' (p. 262; emphasis in original). We might therefore imagine that the most significant aspect of learning lies not in the *outcomes* of learning, but in the *process* of learning. Understanding this process and how best to facilitate it is thus essential to our work as educators.

How fortunate, then, that we may now turn to the growing body of literature on threshold concepts for, in their identification of threshold concepts, Meyer and Land (2003) appear to have captured the inherently developmental nature of these

J. H. F. Meyer, R. Land and C. Baillie (eds.), Threshold Concepts and
Transformational Learning, 3–19.

trajectories of learning. Indeed, Perkins (2007) notes that threshold concepts are 'especially pivotal to a stage-like advance in understanding a discipline' (p. 36). The focus of my current project is therefore to examine issues central to threshold concepts, such as 'liminality,' and to explore the characteristics used to describe threshold concepts, such as 'troublesome,' 'transformative,' 'irreversible,' 'integrative,' and 'bounded' in light of developmental principles in order to help us better understand the complex nature of the learning process.

In exploring the characteristics of threshold concepts from a developmental perspective, we begin to capture a sense of the work that threshold concepts are doing: they are transforming, integrating, making trouble, but of what? Thus, the question remains as to *what* is changing and allowing us to remark that a threshold has been crossed, that a transformation has occurred, that a learner has moved from one stage, one way of making meaning to the next?

Indeed, what we are witnessing, experiencing, or contributing to is the transformation of the *essence* of a particular position or stage from which meaning of the world is constructed. Kegan (1982) theorises that at the heart of a stage of meaning-making is a way of knowing, an epistemology, which shapes the 'window or a lens through which one looks at the world' (Kegan, with Debold, 2002, p. 3). While we will return to the question of essence later, here, I wish to emphasise that the great value of threshold concepts is that they serve to instigate a process of 'epistemological transitions' (Meyer and Land, 2005, p. 386); that is, transitions not only in *what* learners know, but in *how* they know; transitions that may provide a 'transformed internal view of subject matter, subject landscape, or even world view' (Meyer and Land, 2003, p. 1). This chapter is therefore an attempt to capture and qualify the transitional process instigated by threshold concepts and explore its potential influence on our practice as educators.

UNDERLYING ASSUMPTIONS

Many questions remain to be investigated in our exploration of the developmental nature of threshold concepts, questions such as 'How might a developmental perspective be used to explain variation in learners' responses to threshold concepts?', 'What is the relationship between learning and development?', and 'How might troublesomeness be developmentally productive?'. I would now like to comment briefly on the approach I will take to answering these questions.

One of my fundamental assumptions is that questions are best approached from what I qualify as an *integrationist* approach. As people trained or training to become disciplinary experts, we may so easily become mired in our own contexts that we may fail to consider that the questions about which we feel so passionate are the same questions that intrigue our colleagues in other fields. The question of thresholds and the processes and mechanisms which drive development towards and across thresholds are not only questions of educational psychology (my own field), but also those of the fields in which educational psychology is rooted: philosophy, biology, and psychology. Consequently, in my attempt to situate the characteristics of threshold concepts within a developmental framework, I draw on

Kegan's (1982) interdisciplinary Constructive-Developmental Theory, as well as on work in these other fields, searching for the deeper principles of development that at once underlie, transcend, and thereby unify our specific contextual concerns.

In my exploration, I will also attempt to capture the *simultaneously cognitive and affective* nature of these epistemological transformations. While cognitive processes are often emphasised in accounts of learning, the affective nature of these transitions is often minimised, denigrated, or altogether ignored. Consequently, the appeal of Kegan's Constructive-Developmental Theory (1982) is its acknowledgement of 'the equal dignity' (p. 107) of cognition and affect. It is a theory that recognises that 'we are [evolutionary] activity and we experience it' (pp. 81–82). As we will see later, this conceptualisation has deep implications for the ways in which we view the process of epistemological transformation triggered by threshold concepts.

Thank you for reading. Now let us begin addressing some of our questions.

PRELIMINAL VARIATION, OR, ON BALANCE

A powerful image that Kegan (1982) uses to guide our understanding of the evolution of stages or 'orders' of meaning-making is that of *balance*. Two intriguing questions now emerge: 'How might the notion of balance contribute to our understanding of the learning process?' and 'Might the notion of balance help us account for variation in learners' responses to the process of transformation instigated by threshold concepts?'.

The language of balance permeates our daily lives: we are concerned with maintaining balance in the world's ecosystems, balancing our diets, and finding work-life balance. This concern may be traced to ancient times, where cultural myths reveal that people sought ways to preserve the balance between 'the forces of good and evil' (Gaarder, 1994, p. 25). Hippocrates believed that 'when sickness occurs, it is a sign that Nature has gone off course because of physical or mental imbalance' and that "that the road to health for everyone is through moderation, harmony, and a 'sound mind in a sound body'" (Gaarder, 1994, p. 56). With respect to our cognitive development, Piaget proposes equilibration as a process through which balance is sought by integrating interactions between the organism and the environment (Ferrari, Pinard and Runions, 2001; Piaget, 1950).

What we are balancing, in fact, is *essence*. The question of essence also concerned the earliest Greek philosophers. Gaarder (1994) explains that there existed a shared belief that 'nothing comes from nothing' (p. 41). Parmenides, for example "had refused to accept the idea of change in any form. [...] His intelligence could not accept that 'something' could suddenly transform itself into 'something completely different'" (p. 41). This, then, was the 'problem of change,' the question of 'How could one substance suddenly change into something else?' (Gaarder, 1994, p. 35).

The assumption, therefore, was that "'something' had always existed" (Gaarder, 1994, p. 33). And by examining the notion of essence, we address the question of precisely what is emerging and being organised into qualitatively different (e.g. Kegan, 1982; Lewis, 2000; Schunk, 2000) and more complex forms.

In an edited volume entitled 'Reframing the Conceptual Change Approach in Learning and Instruction,' Baltas (2007) examines the notion of an essential 'something' changing in conceptual change. He states that

> the fact that [...] 'something' remains invariant is faithfully reflected in the pertinent 'Eureka!' experience, for this is an experience that cannot engage but a single thing at both its ends: after having undergone it, we understand exactly what we were incapable of understanding before. (p. 66)

Baltas (2007) suggests that what we were incapable of understanding before were our background 'assumptions' (in quotation marks). These background 'assumptions', which 'were formlessly taken along as a matter of course and to which, accordingly, questions could not be addressed,' once disclosed, become assumptions (without quotation marks), that is, 'proposition[s] that can be doubted and thence conceptually and experimentally examined [...] becom[ing] open to rejection, revision, justification, and so forth' (p. 66).

The notion of balance suggests that there must be more than one component to essence, and that some kind of tension must be resolved between opposites in order to obtain balance. And there is strong evidence in the philosophical, biological, and psychological literatures that supports the existence of opposites in our ideas, physiologies, and psyches. Saussure posits that 'binary opposites' characterise the structure of philosophical discourse; 'Anthropologist Claude Lévi-Strauss maintained that a system of binary codes operates in all cultures as their common logic' (Robinson and Groves, 2004, p. 160). Derrida's deconstructive approach to reading philosophical texts suggests the existence of 'multiple meanings at war with each other in the texts' (Robinson and Groves, 2004, p. 162). Biologists speak of 'evolution and its periods of adaptation – of life organisation – as involving a balance between differentiation and adaptation' (Kegan, 1982, p. 107).

In psychology, Erikson (1959) writes of the various shifts in balances between intimacy and isolation as individuals progress through young adulthood. Jung (1959) posits that our psyches are made up of numerous opposing spheres which we attempt to unite. He powerfully describes a pair of opposites as being 'one of the most fruitful sources of psychic energy' (p. 82). In their theories, Erikson and Jung also succeed in capturing how fundamentally unsettled we feel when our balance is threatened or disturbed. The resulting 'crises' (Erikson, 1959) and 'disequilibrium' (Jung, 1959) may be so powerful that they may lead to a feeling of 'being torn apart' (Magen, Austrian, and Hughes, 2002, p. 187).

Resulting from this process of interaction among opposites is not a static equilibrium, but what philosophers, biologists, and psychologists refer to as a *dynamic equilibrium* (e.g. Homeostatis, 2007; Kegan, 1982; Wood, 1998). This process of interaction among opposites continues throughout the ongoing course of development, and each stage consequently represents a qualitatively different and temporary 'evolutionary truce' (Kegan, 1982).

Kegan describes each truce as the coordination of the two essential elements of epistemology: what we view as 'subject' and what we view as 'object':

What I mean by 'object' are those aspects of our experience that are apparent to us and can be looked at, related to, reflected upon, engaged, controlled, and connected to something else. We can be *objective* about these things, in that we don't see them as 'me.' But other aspects of our experience we are so identified with, embedded in, fused with, that we just experience them as ourselves. This is what we experience *subjectively* – the 'subject' half of the subject-object relationship. (With Debold, 2002, p. 3; emphasis in original)

Each new truce therefore discloses more of that in which we were embedded, thereby enabling us 'to listen to what before [we] could only hear irritably, and [...] to hear irritably what before [we] could hear not at all' (Kegan, 1982, p. 105).

As educators, we must be acutely aware that the construction of meaning, the journey to each new truce, is both a cognitive *and* a deeply emotional venture for learners. Atherton (2008) tellingly writes of the 'cost' of learning, describing 'learning as loss' – the loss of a certain way of thinking about and being in the world. Boyd and Myers (1988) speak of the four phases of 'grief ' learners experience during a transformative learning process. William Perry (1981) also writes compellingly of the emotional upheavals involved in the developmental process:

I have remarked elsewhere (Perry, 1978) on the importance we have come to ascribe to a student's 'allowing for grief ' in the process of growth, especially in the rapid movement from the limitless potentials of youth to the particular realities of adulthood. Each of the upheavals of cognitive growth threatens the balance between vitality and depression, hope and despair. It may be a great joy to discover a new and more complex way of thinking and seeing; but yesterday one thought in simpler ways, and hope and aspiration were embedded in those ways. Now that those ways are left behind, must hope be abandoned too?

It appears that it takes a little time for the guts to catch up with such leaps of the mind. (p. 108)

And, indeed, in the following section, we will explore some of the reasons why it may take our emotions some time 'to catch up with' our minds, and why our minds may be resistant to change in the first place.

Preserving Balance

Inherent in the notion of dynamic equilibrium explored earlier is the idea of *preserving* balance. Indeed, within both human biological and psychological systems, there is a strong tendency to maintain a state of equilibrium, which amounts, in some ways, to *resisting* the ongoing motion of development. Within the biological process of homeostasis, there exist states of dynamic equilibrium in which the system in balance 'resists outside forces to change' (Homeostasis, 2007). As Kegan expresses more colloquially, there is a strong tendency to keep things 'pretty much as they are' (with Debold, 2002, p. 5).

In keeping things as they are, the human (organism) is, in fact, stating, 'I have boundaries that I do not want transgressed.' From a biological perspective, boundaries provide a crucial 'distinction between everything on the inside of a closed boundary and everything in the external world' (Dennett, 1991, p. 174). Dennett (1991) explains that this distinction 'is at the heart of all biological processes' and provides the powerful example of the immune system, 'with its millions of different antibodies arrayed in defense of the body against millions of different alien intruders. This army must solve the fundamental problem of recognition: telling one's self (and one's friends) from everything else' (p. 174).

Human psychological systems are equally adamant in their struggle to prevent change. In his theory of cognitive dissonance, Festinger (1957) explains that individuals attempt to achieve and maintain *consistency*, or *consonance*, between their knowledge, opinions, beliefs, and actions. Piaget's (1950) notion of assimilation captures the attempt to integrate experiences to existing cognitive structures. Perry (1970) notes that these assimilations 'tend to be implicit' (p. 42). That is, we tend to be unaware that they are occurring. Experiences are unconsciously integrated. Consequently, existing cognitive structures remain intact; the current perspective from which we view the world remains acceptable; balance is preserved.

Kegan (with Scharmer, 2000) remarks that these balances are very 'hardy,' (p. 11) particularly during adulthood. It becomes more and more difficult for experiences to undo this balance, to break through a boundary, to 'win through [our] increasingly complex defenses that have better and better ways of deluding us into the belief that we have grasped reality as it actually is' (Kegan, with Debold, 2002, p. 6). These balances are hardy because, 'assimilation is defense, but defense is also integrity' (Kegan, 1982, p. 41). The threat of change is a threat of *dis-integration*: the disintegration of a particular way of knowing that arises from the disclosure of one's assumptions or from disentangling oneself from that in which one was embedded. And if, as we saw earlier, emotion is an integral part of the process of change, there may be great *fear* in losing a self with whom one is familiar (Atherton, 2008; Berger, 2004; Taylor, 1995). In the face of new learning, this fear may reveal itself as a 'numbness,' where the learner may appear to be 'under an anesthetic' and as though 'suspended in time' (Boyd and Myers, 1988, p. 278).

It is not only fear and desire to preserve balance that prevent change, however. At times, people may have 'sincere, even passionate intentions to change'. Kegan explains that a recent medical study

> concluded that doctors can tell heart patients that they will literally die if they do not change their ways, and still only about one in seven will be able to make the changes. These are not people who want to die. They want to live out their lives, fulfill their dreams, watch their grandchildren grow up – and, still, they cannot make the changes they need to in order to survive. (With Carroll, 2007, p. 1)

In fact, Kegan and Lahey (2001) have labelled this tendency to resist change, even when faced the prospect of death, *immunity to change*. Kegan (with Carroll, 2007) describes their work as

> pay[ing] very close – and very respectful – attention to all those behaviors people engage in that work against their change goals [...]. Instead of regarding these behaviors as obstacles in need of elimination, we take them as unrecognized signals of other, usually unspoken, often unacknowledged, goals or motivations. (p. 1)

Kegan refers to these goals and motivations as 'commitments,' and suggests that they may provide educators with rich insight regarding learners' unwillingness to change.

In our exploration of the notions of balance and preservation of balance, we have encountered several ideas that may help us account for why 'mental development is so often steadfastly invariant, so resistant to inspired pedagogy, so limited in transfer' (Bruner, 1997, p. 70). Indeed, learners' fears of giving up a sense of integrated selfhood, as well as commitments, either explicit or implicit, may help explain why learners get 'stuck' (Meyer and Land, 2003) or resist learning, particularly learning of the kind implied by the notion of threshold concepts, that is, learning of an epistemological transformational kind. These ideas suggest that variation in responses to threshold concepts may be linked to learners' readiness for change. That is, there may exist an 'optimal' or 'open period' during which a learner is most likely 'to respond to stimulation' (Kohlberg and Mayer, 1972, p. 490). Consequently, appropriately *timing* the introduction of threshold concepts might be an especially important consideration when designing learner-centred instruction.

TROUBLESOMENESS, OR, ON DISSONANCE

The discussion of variation in learners' responses to threshold concepts leads us to consider the following questions: What is the link between learning and development? Must development precede learning? Are learning and development synonymous? Does learning stimulate development? Vygotsky (1978) reviews these different positions and advances that 'the essential feature of learning is that it creates the zone of proximal development; that is, learning awakens a variety of internal developmental processes' (p. 90).

A logical next question is thus, 'What type of learning leads to development?'. While it is perhaps commonly believed that exposing learners to more and different types of experiences and information, or that 'teaching harder' (Perkins, 2007) will lead to development, the appropriate answer to this question may reveal a more qualitative than quantitative issue. Indeed exposure (even lots of exposure) does not guarantee that an organism will change in any significant way. In order for transformation to occur, learners must first perceive these experiences, knowledge, or phenomena to be 'dissonant' (Festinger, 1957), 'disorienting' (Mezirow, 2000), or what the literature on threshold concepts has come to qualify, 'troublesome' (Meyer and Land, 2003; Perkins, 1999).

Schunk (2000) remarks that 'the dissonance notion is vague' (p. 306). Work by Perkins, however, is doing much to elucidate this concept. His exploration of troublesome knowledge (Perkins, 2006) and theories of difficulty (Perkins, 2007), reveals a variety of reasons that may account for what makes certain sources of knowledge, including threshold concepts, particularly troublesome for learners. And, a deeper understanding of troublesomeness may reveal potentially powerful sources of transformation.

Both the biological and cognitive psychological literature suggest that, to promote development, phenomena must somehow be troublesome enough, inharmonious enough from existing structures, to disturb balance and lead the organism to actively respond (e.g., Festinger, 1957; Homeostasis, 2007). The purpose of this activity is to restore balance and, for humans, constitutes the very *making* of meaning.

Yet, with what actions do we respond to these instigators of change? To address this question, we must consider and acknowledge that, along with the cognitive experience of doubt, may come the emotional experience of self-doubt: the unsettling feeling that arises when one questions one's ways of seeing, of being in, the world.

While 'doubt is an uneasy and dissatisfied state from which we struggle to free ourselves and pass into the state of belief ' (Fisch, 1951, p. 59. In Murphy, 2003, p. 138), there is no guarantee that the state of belief will be a new one. It may, in fact be the already existing state of belief, as the tendency to preserve balance may still be strong at this time. That is, learners may choose to respond to epistemic doubt by 'ignor[ing] their feelings [...] because they feel so strongly about their current beliefs' (Bendixen and Rule, 2004, p. 75). Alternatively, they may experience a range of emotions, from 'a painful pining or yearning for that which has been lost to protest over the present situation' (Boyd and Myers, 1988, p. 278).

It is perhaps Perry (1981) who comments most eloquently on the 'deflections from growth' that might occur when learners become especially adamant in preserving balance even after the infiltration of doubt. He observes that being confronted with information and experiences revealing the inadequacy of their current belief system may not be sufficient to instigate growth in learners, and may, in fact, cause some to react with 'apathy,' 'anxiety,' 'depression,' and even educational 'cynicism' (p. 90). Learners may 'temporize;' that is, they may 'simply wai[t], reconsigning the agency for decision to some event that might turn up' (p. 90). Alternatively, they may 'retreat' to a former position (p. 91). Finally, they might 'escape.' Perry (1981) claims that it is during this period of escape that 'the self is lost through the very effort to hold onto it in the face of inexorable change in the world's appearance' (p. 92).

There are several implications of the above discussion on our interpretation of threshold concepts. First, if we accept that some degree of dissonance is often necessary to stimulate development, then the troublesome or 'nettlesome' (Sibbett and Thomson, 2008) nature of threshold concepts may be the very quality that reveals their developmental potential. Consequently, their power may be that they trigger dissonance not only at the cognitive and affective levels, but also dissonance at the epistemological level, calling upon learners to 'change their minds,' not by supplanting *what* they know, but by transforming *how* they know. Furthermore, that learners respond to discrepancies in different ways, that is, by avoidance, assimilation, or, as we shall see, by accommodation (integration), suggests that there may exist highly individual reasons determining responses to threshold concepts, reasons such as alternative commitments and readiness for change. Finally, given the affective nature of these changes, our task as educators is to acknowledge the difficult journey on which we are asking students to embark. We may thus envision ways of foreshadowing for students the impending sense of loss and help them to live more comfortably with their discomfort.

TRANSFORMATIVENESS, OR, ON OPENING UP OF EPISTEMOLOGICAL, CONCEPTUAL, AND AFFECTIVE SPACES

Kegan (1982) notes that epistemic doubt may indeed lead one to 'the limits of [one's] ways of knowing the world' (p. 59), and, as we have seen, this may cause some learners to temporarily arrest their epistemic development. Yet, is this the response of most learners? Perry (1981) remarks that it is not. The response to epistemic doubt caused by troublesomeness may also take the form of action towards change, action marking the beginning of the transformative process, action which may 'open[…] up a new and previously inaccessible way of thinking about something' (Meyer and Land, 2003, p. 1).

The idea of 'opening up' new ways of thinking is captured in the work of many researchers interested in learning. Baltas (2007) characterises the disclosure of background 'assumptions' in conceptual change as 'widen[ing] up and modify[ing] […] the […] space available to inquiry' (p. 65). In their exploration of professors' developing conceptions of teaching, Entwistle and Walker (2002) characterise professors' sophisticated, learning-centred conceptions of teaching as 'lead[ing] to an expanded awareness – seeing additional goals for teaching and learning which were originally not perceived explicitly at all' (p. 17). Kegan (1994) eloquently notes that

> transforming our epistemologies, liberating ourselves from that in which we were embedded, making what was subject into object so that we can 'have it' rather than 'be had' by it – this is the most powerful way I know to conceptualize the growth of the mind. (p. 34)

We may therefore begin to envision that the transformative process involves not only the expansion of epistemological and conceptual spaces, but also, as Meyer and Land (2005, 2006) explain, the expansion and transformation of identity, of a learner's 'sense of self ' (2006, p. 19). We must also consider that this process of transformation, and hence movement within these liminal spaces, is not unidirectional, yet may 'involve oscillation between stages, often with temporary regression to an earlier status' (Meyer and Land, 2005, p. 376). Boyd and Myers (1988) speak of the 'oscillating movement […] from disorganization to despair' (p. 278) that characterises this phase of grieving in the process of transformational education. Berger (2004) characterises transformational spaces as 'precarious', and Kegan (with Scharmer, 2000) describes entering into a transitional space as feeling much 'like going off a cliff ' (p. 11).

Yet, when standing on the edge of a cliff (or a threshold), might some learners feel terror, while others feel exhilaration? Stated otherwise, 'Does this liminal space feel the same for everyone?' In her thought piece entitled 'Dancing on the Threshold of Meaning: Recognizing and Understanding the Growing Edge,' Berger (2004) suggests that it might not. She recounts the stories of two women, Kathleen and Melody, both facing times of profound transition in their lives. Kathleen is 'excited […] and not knowing about her future leaves her filled with possibility and hope' (p. 341). Melody, on the other hand is both 'frighten[ed]' and 'unhappy' (p. 342) in this space of transformation. Berger's (2004) account of these two women, one who embraces the period of transition, and the other who retreats from it, provides evidence of a 'complex continuum' (p. 343) of emotional responses to the liminal space.

As we saw earlier, underlying this complex variation of individual responses may be issues of alternative commitments and readiness for change. What these issues may signal, in fact, is variation in learners' current ways of making meaning. Perry's seminal study entitled the 'Intellectual and Ethical Development of College Students' (1970) originated in an attempt to account for the variations he had observed in the ways in which college students were responding to the 'the pluralistic intellectual and social environment of the university' (Hofer and Pintrich, 1997, p. 90). What Perry ultimately showed was that different responses to external conditions could be attributed to individual differences in learners' epistemic beliefs. That some learners 'open up,' while others clearly get 'stuck' (Meyer and Land, 2005, p. 380), may signal to us as educators that the epistemological transition being instigated by a threshold concept lies *beyond* the learner's zone of proximal development (Vygotsky, 1978). That is, it lies too far beyond what the learner may achieve when guided by more skilful others. These variations in response to teaching caution us to be attuned to variations in the ways that learners are making meaning.

IRREVERSIBLITY, OR, ON CROSSING THRESHOLDS

Berger (2004) notes that "Bridges (1980) described as the hardest piece of trans-formation the 'neutral zone' when the past seems untenable and the future uniden-tifiable" (p. 343). That the past seems unreachable, suggests that the there is a time in the transformation process when the individual crosses a threshold.

The Oxford dictionary defines that a threshold 'symbolically […] marks the boundary between a household and the outer world, and hence between belonging and not-belonging, and between safety and danger' (Simpson and Roud, 2000) and consequently between the former world and the new world. In biology, a threshold indicates the minimum, yet critical level a stimulus must attain to 'produce excitation of any structure' (Therxold, 2000). Thus interpreted, the inherent troublesomeness of threshold concepts may provide the impulse that 'excites' an individual and leads to the type of action that carries him/her across a threshold towards epistemological transformation.

Might a learner revert to former ways of knowing after crossing a threshold? In characterising threshold concepts as 'irreversible,' Meyer and Land (2003) suggest 'that the change of perspective occasioned by the learning of a threshold concept is unlikely to be forgotten, or will be unlearned only by considerable effort' (p. 4). Baltas (2007) would call the impossibility of "forsaking the 'Eureka!' experience" and returning to previous ways of understanding an 'irreversible achievement' (p. 76). Thus, on a path of development from one way of knowing and meaning-making, one epistemic stage or stance to the next, there seems to exist a point in our journey when we cross a threshold and our old way of knowing is no longer 'tenable'. There is an irreversible shift in the way in which 'essence' is coordinated. There emerges a new space from which to observe and analyse the world.

Accompanying the new, however, is a loss of the old: old 'status,' old 'identity within the community' (Meyer and Land, 2005, p. 376), old ways of knowing, seeing, and being in the world. As we saw earlier, these liminal spaces where one is 'betwixt and between' ways of knowing are understandably deeply emotional, sometimes 'painful' (Boyd and Myers, 1988, p. 277; Love and Guthrie, 1999, p. 72), sometimes exhilarating. They are spaces where 'the individual is naked of self – neither fully in one category or another' (Goethe, 2003. In Meyer and Land, 2005, p. 376). Yet, this state of liminality does not as yet represent the new developmental stage, for, as Kegan (1982) reminds us, 'development is not a matter of differentiation alone, but of differentiation *and* integration' (p. 67; emphasis in original).

THE INTEGRATIVE NATURE OF THRESHOLD CONCEPTS, OR, ON INTEGRATION

The integration after differentiation of which Kegan (1982) speaks is the act of reorganising the essence of one's way of knowing into a new balance. And, as Lewis (2000) notes, self-organisation is a cross-scientific principle which 'explicates the emergence of order in physics, chemistry, biology, ecology, and cosmology' (p. 40). In describing threshold concepts as 'integrative,' and thereby 'expos[ing] the previously hidden interrelatedness of something', Meyer and Land (2003, p. 4) have captured the acts of reorganisation and accommodation (Piaget, 1950) that occur when individuals modify their existing cognitive structures to make sense of the external world. Perry (1970) remarks that these reorganisations are "sometimes [...] sensed as a 'realization.' This is particularly likely in respect to an insight or reconstruction that suddenly reveals 'the' meaning of some incongruity of experience we have been trying for some time to make sense of " (pp. 41–42).

Meyer and Land's notion of integration is not purely cognitive, however, for it refers to the 'indissoluble interrelatedness of the leaner's identity with thinking and language' (2006, p. 21). The integrative nature of threshold concepts is thus also a matter of *integrity* – of the creation of a coherent way of knowing and being in the world. Boyd and Myers (1988) capture the emotion that characterises the final, integrative, phase of the grief work involved in transformational education as 'movement [...] between a hope-filled sense of restabilization and reintegration of identity' (p. 279).

13

We may turn now to the 'newness' of what has emerged through qualitative change. Wood (1998) emphasises that 'the emergence of what is qualitatively new' may be 'understood in terms of the specific essence of that which is in process rather than in terms of general laws applying to simple elements of which it is composed' (p. 2). These qualitative reorganisations, perhaps precipitated by what Meyer and Land (2005) term the '*reconstitutive* effect of threshold concepts' (p. 375; emphasis added), represent the adaptation (e.g. Lewis, 2000) of an individual to his or her environment. And our very survival (biological, academic, or otherwise) depends on our ability to respond to the demands of our surroundings, to our 'life conditions' (Kegan, 1994).

Given the cognitive and emotional complexity involved in reorganising one's epistemic beliefs, Dole and Sinatra (1998) comment rather unsurprisingly that reorganisation is difficult to achieve. As educators and as disciplinary experts, we must consider that we may hold either explicit or implicit expectations regarding the 'appropriate' response or adaptation to the troublesomeness or discrepancy introduced by a threshold concept. Our upcoming discussion of the bounded nature of threshold concepts will urge us to consider, however, that these expectations may arise from the multiple layers of context in which threshold concepts are embedded.

BOUNDEDNESS, OR, ON CONSIDERING CONTEXT

The view of learning expressed in this chapter raises the interesting and ethical question of whether development should be the aim of education (e.g. Fiddler and Marienau, 1995; Kohlberg and Mayer, 1972). This question is important to consider because educational ideologies influence the nature of the outcomes established for and valued in learners (Kohlberg and Mayer, 1972). Moore (2002), commenting on the inherently developmental nature of learning, states that according to Perry and other researchers, 'true education, especially liberal arts education, was fundamentally about this kind of development – namely, the evolution of individuals' thinking structures and meaning making toward greater and more adaptive complexity' (p. 26).

Conceived of in this manner, the purpose of education is much less about fostering growth in *what* learners know than facilitating development of the *ways* in which they know. Such a perspective may partially allay Meyer and Land's (2005) concern about threshold concepts being perceived as prescribing a rigid, unidirectional path toward achievement of particular goals, such as degree achievement or professional accreditation. Focusing on threshold concepts' potential to instigate epistemological transformation enables us to emphasise learning as 'entrance into [...] a community of people who share that way of thinking and practising' (Davies, 2006, p. 71).

While it may seem nobler to discuss the development of ways of knowing and being, rather than the content of knowing, as the aim of education, we must first clarify an important matter. The preceding discussion of essence and end points, of transitions, trajectories, and thresholds in the development of epistemic beliefs reveals an additional underlying philosophical assumption, most notably that there is something orderly and progressive in the way that learners construct meaning in their disciplines and in their lives. Yet, this organismic (or modernist) worldview of development (Goldhaber, 2000) has historically been criticised by those holding contextualist (or post-modernist) views for its failure to integrate a deep consideration for the role played by context in development. In a fascinating illumination of the modernism – post-modernism debate, Chandler (1995) eloquently describes post-modernism's rebellion against modernism's ideas of universal stages and sequences in development. Indeed, some post-modernists claim that development is so entirely context-bound, and individuals' contexts so variable, that any attempt to search for universal patterns and endpoints in development is an attempt to perpetuate hierarchies and oppression. In his analysis of post-modern arguments against modern views of development, Chandler (1995) remarks, however, that

> while a certain incredulity toward the grand political narratives of the past may well be justified, the same suspicions may actually not be appropriate when attention is re-focused on those smaller potato matters having to do with the separate psychological development of individual persons. [...] Many of post-modernism's hallmark questions concerning the essentially political consequences of modernity may actually be irrelevant to the job of deciding whether there is anything like human nature, or universal trajectories in the course of individual psychological development. (p. 8)

Chandler's thoughtful reflections on the post-modern view of development reveal a need for modernists to pay greater heed to the role played by context in development. Meyer and Land's (2003) discussion of threshold concepts as 'bounded' and thereby 'serv[ing] to constitute the demarcation between disciplinary areas' (p. 5) provides an excellent point from which to begin examining the issue of context and its relationship to our developmental perspective of threshold concepts. If, indeed, the learning of threshold concepts is ultimately a matter of epistemological transformation, we might consider the discipline and its inherent epistemology (Meyer and Land, 2005; Perkins, 1997) as only one of the multiple, interacting layers of (epistemic) context in which threshold concepts are embedded.

We might begin by considering, at the macro level, the powerful historical, social, and cultural forces that converge (Goldhaber, 2000) and give rise to the relative prominence of certain disciplines. We may then consider how these forces shape, at the meso level, the epistemic context of the discipline itself; that is, the questions pursued (and funded) and the methodologies judged as appropriate for pursuing them (Perkins, 1997). At the micro level, we may investigate how these forces manifest themselves in the selection by members of the disciplinary community of concepts deemed important, even thresholds, and around which curricula and programmes are designed. Finally, we must consider the ways of knowing and meaning-making of individual learners. Recent research reveals that the development of individuals' epistemic beliefs is shaped by these multiple layers of context (Palmer and Marra, 2008), as well as by more proximal influences, such as religion and family (Gottlieb, 2007). We must therefore be prepared to accept variation in learners' cognitive and affective responses to our attempts to 'teach' threshold concepts.

The value of an approach that acknowledges the existence and influence of the multiple layers of interacting (epistemological) contexts in which threshold concepts are embedded allows us, in Kegan's terms, to make them 'object'. Consequently, rather than being impervious to their influence, we may hold them to light, examine them, and question their influence in shaping our current and future ways of knowing and being.

CONCLUDING THOUGHTS

With increased calls for accountability and the requirements of professional accreditation organisations, we must necessarily be concerned with, and attend to, the outcomes of learning in higher education. Indeed, we must have a clear vision of the direction in which we would like to take students. The questions raised in this chapter caution us, however, against making the acquisition of threshold concepts our sole focus as educators. We are perhaps reminded that increased attention to the learning *process* might help ensure that learners achieve the intended outcomes in a manner that recognises and respects the great cognitive and affective work they must do. Designing such developmentally-appropriate instruction involves having a deep understanding of learners' current ways of making meaning, for what we are facilitating is a process of epistemological transformation so crucial to learners' 'becoming': becoming disciplinary experts, and perhaps, most importantly, becoming more fully themselves.

ACKNOWLEDGEMENTS

This research is partially supported by generous grants from the Social Sciences and Humanities Research Council of Canada (SSHRC) and the Fonds québecois de la recherche sur la société et la culture (FQRSC). I would also like to thank Drs. Cynthia Weston, Alenoush Saroyan, and Krista Muis for their thoughtful responses to my Comprehensive Examination Paper – the document in which the ideas for this chapter originated.

REFERENCES

Anderson, L. W., & Krathwohl, D. (Eds.). (2001). *A taxonomy for learning, teaching, and assessing: A revision of Bloom's taxonomy of educational objectives*. New York: Longman.

Atherton, J. S. (2008). *Doceo: Learning as loss 1* [On-line] UK. Retrieved from http://www.doceo.co.uk/original/learnloss_1.htm

Baltas, A. (2007). Background 'assumptions' and the grammar of conceptual change: Rescuing Kuhn by means of Wittgenstein. In S. Vosniadou, A. Baltas, & X. Vamvakoussi (Eds.), *Reframing the conceptual change approach in learning and instruction* (pp. 63–79). Amsterdam, The Netherlands: Elsevier and the European Association for Research on Learning and Instruction (EARLI).

Belenky, M. F., Clinchy, B. M., Goldberger, N. R., & Tarule, J. M. (1986/1997). *Womens' ways of knowing* (2nd ed.). New York: BasicBooks.

Bendixen, L. D., & Rule, D. C. (2004). An integrative approach to personal epistemology: A guiding model. *Educational Psychologist, 39*(1), 69–80.

Berger, J. G. (2004). Dancing on the threshold of meaning: Recognizing and understanding the growing edge. *Journal of Transformative Education, 2*(4), 336–351.

Boyd, R. D., & Myers, J. G. (1988). Transformative education. *International Journal of Lifelong Education, 7*(4), 261–284.

Bruner, J. (1997). Celebrating divergence: Piaget and Vygotsky. *Human Development, 40*, 63–73.

Carroll, B. B. (2007). Overcoming the immunity to change: Robert Kegan [Electronic Version]. In *Harvard graduate school of education web site: Impact on the world: Stories of impact*. Retrieved June 22, 2007, from http://www.gse.harvard.edu/impact/stories/faculty/kegan.php

Chandler, M. (1995). Is this the end of 'the age of development,' or what? Or: Please wait a minute, Mr. Post-Man. *The Genetic Epistemologist, 23*(1). Retrieved April 2, 2008, from http://www.piaget.org/GE/Winter95/ChandlerW95.html

Cross, P. (1999). What do we know about students' learning and how do we know it? *Innovative Higher Education, 23*(4), 255–270.

Davies, P. (2006). Threshold concepts: How can we recognize them? In J. H. F. Meyer & R. Land (Eds.), *Overcoming barriers to student understanding*. Oxon, UK: Routledge.

Debold, E. (2002, Fall/Winter). Epistemology, fourth order consciousness, and the subject-object relationship or... How the self evolves with Robert Kegan. *What is Enlightenment?: Redefining Spirituality for an Evolving World, 22*. Retrieved June 18, 2007, from http:www.wie.org/i2022/kegan.asp

Dennett, D. (1991). Chapter 7: The evolution of consciousness. In *Consciousness explained* (pp. 171–226). New York: Little, Brown and Company.

Dole, J. A., & Sinatra, G. M. (1998). Reconceptualizing change in the cognitive construction of knowledge. *Educational Psychologist, 33*(2/3), 109–128.

Entwistle, N., & Walker, P. (2002). Strategic alertness and expanded awareness within sophisticated conceptions of teaching. In N. Hativa & P. Goodyear (Eds.), *Teacher thinking, beliefs and knowledge in higher education* (pp. 15–39). Dordrecht, The Netherlands: Kluwer Academic Publishers.

Erikson, E. (1959). *Identity and the life cycle: Selected papers*. New York: International Universities Press.

Ferrari, M., Pinard, A., & Runions, K. (2001). Piaget's framework for a scientific study of consciousness. *Human Development, 44*(4), 195–213.

Festinger, L. (1957). *A theory of cognitive dissonance*. Evanston, IL: Row.

Fiddler, M., & Marienau, C. (1995). Linking learning, teaching, and development. In K. Taylor & C. Marienau (Eds.), *Learning environments for women's adult development: Bridges toward change* (Vol. New Directions for Adult and Continuing Education, 65, pp. 73–82). San Francisco: Jossey-Bass.

Gaarder, J. (1994). *Sophie's world: A novel about the history of philosophy* (P. Moller, Trans.). New York, USA: Farrar, Straus, and Giroux.

Goldhaber, D. E. (2000). *Theories of human development: Integrative perspectives*. Mountain View, CA: Mayfield Publishing Company.

Gottlieb, E. (2007). Learning how to believe: Epistemic development in cultural context. *Journal of the Learning Sciences, 16*(1), 5–35.

Hofer, B. K., & Pintrich, P. R. (1997). The development of epistemological theories: Beliefs about knowledge and knowing and their relation to learning. *Review of Educational Research, 67*(1), 88–140.

Homeostasis. (2007). [Electronic Version]. In *Encyclopædia Britannica*. Retrieved September 26, 2007, from Britannica Online Encyclopædia http://www.britannica.com/EBchecked/topic/270188/homeostasis

Jung, C. G. (1959). *The basic writings of C. G. Jung* (Violet Staub de Laszlo, Ed.). New York: Modern Library.

Kegan, R. (1982). *The evolving self: Problem and process in human development*. Cambridge, MA: Harvard University Press.

Kegan, R. (1994). *In over our heads: The mental demands of modern life*. Cambridge, MA: Harvard University Press.

Kegan, R., & Lahey, L. L. (2001). *How the way we talk can change the way we work: Seven languages for transformation.* San Francisco: Jossey-Bass.

Kohlberg, L., & Mayer, R. (1972). Development as the aim of education. *Harvard Educational Review, 42*(4), 449–496.

Lewis, M. D. (2000). The promise of dynamic systems approaches for an integrated account of human development. *Child Development, 71*(1), 36–43.

Love, P. G., & Guthrie, V. L. (1999). Kegan's orders of consciousness. *New Directions for Student Services, 88*, 65–76.

Magen, R. H., Austrian, S. G., & Hughes, C. S. (2002). Chapter 5: Adulthood. In S. G. Austrian (Ed.), *Developmental theories through the life cycle* (pp. 181–263). New York: Columbia University Press.

Meyer, J. H. F., & Land, R. (2003). Threshold concepts and troublesome knowledge: Linkages to ways of thinking and practising within the disciplines. In C. Rust (Ed.), *Improving student learning: Improving student learning theory and practice – 10 years on.* Oxford, UK: Oxford Centre for Staff and Learning Development.

Meyer, J. H. F., & Land, R. (2005). Threshold concepts and troublesome knowledge (2): Epistemological considerations and a conceptual framework for teaching and learning. *Higher Education, 49*(3), 373–388.

Meyer, J. H. F., & Land, R. (Eds.). (2006). *Overcoming barriers to student understanding.* Oxon, UK: Routledge.

Mezirow, J. (2000). Learning to think like an adult: Core concepts of transformation theory. In J. Mezirow (Ed.), *Learning as transformation: Critical perspectives on a theory in progress.* San Francisco: Jossey-Bass.

Moore, W. S. (2002). Understanding learning in a postmodern world: Reconsidering the Perry Scheme of intellectual and ethical development. In B. Hofer & P. Pintrich (Eds.), *Personal epistemology: The psychology of beliefs about knowledge and knowing* (pp. 17–36). Mahwah, NJ: Lawrence Erlbaum.

Murphy, P. K. (2003). The philosophy in thee: Tracing philosophical influences in educational psychology. *Educational Psychologist, 38*(3), 137–145.

Palmer, B., & Marra, R. M. (2008). Individual domain-specific epistemologies: Implications for educational practice. In M. S. Khine (Ed.), *Knowing, knowledge and beliefs: Epistemological studies across diverse cultures.* The Netherlands: Springer.

Perkins, D. (1997). Epistemic games. *International Journal of Educational Research, 27*(1), 49–61.

Perkins, D. (1999). The many faces of constructivism. *Educational Leadership, 57*(3), 6–11.

Perkins, D. (2006). Constructivism and troublesome knowledge. In J. H. F. Meyer & R. Land (Eds.), *Overcoming barriers to student understanding.* Oxon, UK: Routledge.

Perkins, D. (2007). Theories of difficulty. *British Journal of Educational Psychology Monograph Series II* (4): Student Learning and University Teaching, 31–48.

Perry, W. G. (1970). *Forms of intellectual and ethical development in the college years: A scheme.* New York: Holt, Rinehart and Winston.

Perry, W. G. (1981). Cognitive and ethical growth: The making of meaning. In A. W. Chickering (Ed.), *The modern American college: Responding to the new realities of diverse students and a changing society* (pp. 76–116). San Francisco: Jossey-Bass.

Piaget, J. (1950). *The psychology of intelligence* (M. Piercy & D. E. Berlyne, Trans.). London, UK: Routledge & Paul.

Robinson, D., & Groves, J. (2004). *Introducing philosophy* (Original edition 1998 ed.). Cambridge, UK: Icon Books.

Scharmer, C. O. (2000, March 23). *Grabbing the tiger by the tail: Conversation with Robert Kegan, Harvard Graduate School of Education.* Retrieved July 25, 2007, from http://www.dialogonleadership. org/kegan-1999.html

Schunk, D. H. (2000). *Learning theories: An educational perspective* (3rd ed.). Upper Saddle River, NJ: Prentice Hall.

Sibbett, C., & Thompson, W. (2008, June 18–20). *Nettlesome knowledge and threshold concepts in higher education, organizational and professional cultures.* Paper presented at the 2nd International Conference on Threshold Concepts, Threshold Concepts: From Theory to Practice, Kingston, Ontario, Canada.

Simpson, J., & Roud, S. (2000). 'threshold'. In *Oxford reference online: A dictionary of English folklore.* Oxford University Press. Retrieved August 20, 2007, from http://www.oxfordreference.com/views/ENTRY.html?subview=Main&entry=t71.e1042

Taylor, K. (1995). Speaking her mind: Adult learning and women's adult development. In K. Taylor & C. Marienau (Eds.), *Learning environments for women's adult development: Bridges toward change* (Vol. New Directions for Adult and Continuing Education, 65, pp. 83–92). San Francisco: Jossey-Bass.

Therxold, A. S. (2000, March 5). 'threshold'. In *The online medical dictionary.* Department of Medical Oncology: University of Newcastle upon Tyne. Retrieved September 2, 2008, from http://cancerweb.ncl.ac.uk/cgi-bin/omd?threshold

Vygotsky, L. S. (1978). *Mind in society: The development of higher psychological processes* (Michael Cole Ed.). Cambridge, MA: Harvard University Press.

Wood, A. W. (1998). Dialectical materialism. In E. Craig (Ed.), *Routledge encyclopedia of philosophy.* London, UK. Retrieved September 25, 2007, from http://www.rep.routledge.com/article/N013SECT3

Julie Timmermans
Department of Educational and Counselling Psychology
McGill University

LESLIE SCHWARTZMAN

2. TRANSCENDING DISCIPLINARY BOUNDARIES

A Proposed Theoretical Foundation for Threshold Concepts

ABSTRACT

The constructs of reflective and defensive responses to rupture in knowing are proposed and evaluated as a discipline-independent theoretical foundation for the analytic educational framework of Threshold Concepts (TC). Two premises underlie this work: crucial elements of student experience of difficulty as they encounter existentially unfamiliar, educationally critical content of their respective disciplines occur in common across all disciplinary contexts; and these crucial elements constitute core issues defining the framework of Threshold Concepts. Universally relevant elements require investigation that transcends discipline boundaries in order to be understood well and addressed effectively. From the perspective of phenomenological analysis, student experiences of difficulty under these circum- stances are considered to be founded in reflective and defensive responses to rupture in knowing, and to originate in universal human patterns of encounter and response to the existentially unfamiliar (what appears initially as the unknowable unknown), rather than to result from individual inadequacies or to differ in kind according to the context in which it occurs. A comparison of process and structure in the TC community with that of a classical scientific community of practice and research illuminates the process of generating candidate theoretical foundations in each.

INTRODUCTION

Threshold Concepts (TC) as an analytic educational framework was originated by Meyer and Land during their participation in the *Enhancing Teaching-Learning Environments in Undergraduate Courses* project (Meyer & Land 2005, p. 386). The term *threshold concept (tc)* refers to content of a discipline or profession that poses deep challenges to the learner (and the teaching of which this framework is meant to support). Much of TC work is addressed to considerations of *liminal space or liminality*, which refers to the period between exposure to a threshold concept and its acquisition. *([The term derives] from Latin **limen**, 'boundary or threshold') ... to describe the conceptual transformations that students undergo, or find difficulty and anxiety in undergoing, particularly in relation to ... being 'stuck' ...* (Meyer & Land, 2005, pp. 373–377). Meyer and Land have come to regard an understanding of liminality as the *sine qua non* for the ongoing development of TC (Land, 2008).

J. H. F. Meyer R. Land and C. Baillie (eds.), Threshold Concepts and Transformational Learning, 21–44.

Scholarship in liminality to this point has taken the form variously of description, metaphor, and analogy. Meyer and Land construe approaches to teaching within the TC framework as entirely discipline-specific, and have eschewed those that transcend disciplinary boundaries.

Background

Underlying Premises.   This paper is predicated on two premises: 1) Crucial elements of student experience of difficulty as they encounter existentially unfamiliar, educationally critical content of their respective disciplines occur in common across all disciplinary contexts; and 2) These crucial elements constitute core issues defining TC. I agree with Meyer and Land regarding the importance of *liminality*, but diverge from their dismissal of scholarship transcending disciplinary boundaries. Faculty at TC conferences invariably recognize in each others' descriptions of student behavior – either at formal presentations or in informal conversations, and irrespective of discipline – depictions of their own students' response to encounters with deeply challenging content. Their consistent mutual recognition makes a strong case that the significance and potential of TC as an analytic framework derives from the universality of student experiences of difficulty in encounters with that content in any – and all – of their respective fields. One may conclude that, with respect to the nature of the learner's experience of difficulties in encountering – and the mechanism involved in her / his learning – deeply challenging content, many more elements of commonality than difference hold across disciplinary boundaries.

Certainly the specifics of learning deeply challenging, educationally critical content of a discipline (*tc's*) must be addressed within their respective disciplinary contexts. However, the very notion that liminality will likely be experienced by students in any (and every) field indicates that crucial elements of that experience – which constitute core issues defining TC – are unrelated to disciplinary context. This paper is motivated by an interest in developing TC scholarship of liminality beyond its current forms (description, analogy, and metaphor) to explanation. I argue that doing so requires a theoretical foundation through which these core issues can be investigated and understood independent of disciplinary context.

The argument is based in phenomenological analysis (not psychology or situational dynamics), according to which: student experiences of difficulty under these circumstances are considered to be founded in reflective and defensive responses to rupture in knowing, a universal human pattern of encounter and response to the existentially unfamiliar (what appears initially as the unknowable unknown), rather than to result from individual inadequacies or to differ in kind according to the context in which it occurs. I propose the constructs of reflective and defensive responses to rupture in knowing as a discipline-independent theoretical foundation for TC.

Origins.   The proposal grows out of an exploration of student encounters with the existentially unfamiliar, educationally critical content of computing science (my discipline), where such a framework has proved relevant and illuminating.

Its application in my discipline-specific work was motivated by – and done in preparation to address – the questions of how to engender reflective responses in all students at all times, or, among those students who do respond defensively, how to cultivate transition from defensiveness to reflectiveness (Schwartzman 2007, 2008). Because the conceptual framework organizes exploration around student response to what appears unknowable, rather than discipline content, it transcends disciplinary boundaries.

Organization of the Paper

The paper begins with an introduction to Threshold Concepts (TC) and threshold concepts (tc) and proceeds in sequence: an exposition of motivation and preparation for defining a theoretical foundation (in several parts); a comparison of process and structure in the TC community with that of a classical scientific community of practice and research, which illuminates the process of generating candidate theoretical foundations; a literature-based description of reflective and defensive responses and the rupture in knowing that gives rise to them, as well as the larger context of learning in which all three are situated; an excerpt of student feedback data in my course, from which the work underlying this paper originated; a proposal of the aggregated two response types as a discipline-independent theoretical foundation, both for this investigation specifically, and by extension for TC scholarship more generally; application and evaluation of the candidate theoretical foundation and the associated explanatory theory defined by it; a view toward possible future work.

THRESHOLD CONCEPTS (TC) AND threshold concepts (tc)

The Concept

TC: informally. The frame of Threshold Concepts (TC) is generally understood as an orientation in teaching, for any discipline, that is concerned with how to support students' learning particularly challenging material, aka threshold concepts (tc's).

tc: more formally, definitions. Meyer and Land speak of tc's as conceptual gateways or portals to an otherwise inaccessible – and unknown – conceptual space or way of understanding. *Such conceptual gateways [are characterized as]* ***transformative*** *(occasioning a significant shift in the perception of a subject),* ***irreversible*** *(unlikely to be forgotten, or unlearned only through considerable effort), and* ***integrative*** *(exposing the previously hidden interrelatedness of something).* Transition through the portal to the new space often poses difficulty and is experienced as ***troublesome***. The new space is itself ***bounded*** (bordered by thresholds into further, currently inaccessible conceptual territory) (Meyer & Land, 2005, pp. 373–377).

TC: the entity

The term Threshold Concepts covers a variety of denotations, including an approach to teaching, an existing body of scholarship, and a structure of community.

An approach to teaching. TC is generally understood to mean an orientation toward supporting student learning of deeply challenging material. A concern for student learning, and an emphasis on teaching to support that learning, operate as defining characteristics of this community.

A body of scholarship. Two international TC conferences have been held thus far (2006, University of Strathclyde, Glasgow, Scotland; and 2008, Queen's University, Kingston, Ontario, Canada). Presentations were concentrated in several areas specified by the conference organizers: some analysis, but primarily description of teaching, of liminality, of candidate tc's within a discipline, and of observable student behavior; as well as interpretations of liminality through analogy and metaphor. TC scholarship is initially developing from a variety of sources in a variety of what appear as not-necessarily connected directions; an eclectic mix of description, analogy, and metaphor.

Community structure. The formation, practice, and scholarship of the TC community occur among a membership of individuals who remain committed to their respective disciplines as a primary focus, while also concerned that students learn the deeply challenging material contained therein. This assemblage of individuals is establishing the TC community as an area of common secondary (or occasionally co-primary) focus.

TOWARD DEFINING A THEORETICAL FOUNDATION:
MOTIVATION AND PREPARATION

Content and structure of the TC theoretical foundation is shaped by the role(s) of theory generally in the ongoing development of a field. Content is also shaped by both the requirements the foundation must satisfy and the central question(s) it must address.

The Role(s) of Theory:

From the literature. Padfield notes, in considering the relationship between theory and practice, that *[b]enefits of learning from experience may not materialize without the ability to order [that experience] into understandable patterns and apply theoretical frameworks* (Padfield 1997 p. 91). Most (perhaps all) educators currently drawn to TC are impelled by their experience in teaching discipline-specific content that students find challenging. If some theoretical framework orders such experience – both individually and collectively – into consistent and meaningful patterns, the framework would have value as a communal resource for both teaching and scholarship.

Gurwitsch concisely states the purpose of theory in formal logic; it can be applied here as well: While the practitioner can rely on the nature of a particular conceptual tool as a *'matter of course which goes without saying'*, the theoretician of the discipline has a different task: *to make such tacit presuppositions explicit, to thematize them* [i.e., to place them in their meaningful context], *and to see and attempt to solve their problems* (Gurwitsch 1974 p. 66).

A *theoretical foundation* for any field plays multiple roles. Among those discussed in this paper: 1) It clarifies the nature of a developing field by illuminating an internal coherence among the existing theoretical and applied work, unifying into a body of literature what had appeared as fragments scattered into a variety of not-necessarily connected directions. 2) By defining problems to be addressed and solutions that can be accepted – as Kuhn (1996) describes the role of paradigm – it informs (as organizing principle) future theoretical and application development. 3) It defines an *explanatory theory* for practice within the field (Gurwitsch 1974 p. 81).

An *explanatory theory* defined for TC (whether by the proposed theoretical foundation or otherwise) is required for maturation of the field (Gurwitsch 1974) and education into it. Among its multiple roles: 1) It provides (beyond description, analogy, and metaphor) meaningful explanation(s) of students' experience as they encounter deeply challenging content. 2) It enables faculty to devise more effective teaching strategies for that content by dint of those explanations. 3) It furthers discourse to refine both the designation of what constitutes such content within a discipline and the representation of conceptual elements within TC. 4) It supports a *separation of concerns* (Dijkstra 1972) within TC by, for example, refining and clarifying terminology, and making assumptions explicit.

For this paper. Husserl's view of psychology as a discipline (summarized by Gurwitsch) also applies here: For [it] to be founded and established as an explanatory science, i.e., a theoretical discipline, principles of theoretical explanation are required that can be derived only from a conceptual system (Gurwitsch 1974 p. 81). Such a formulation describes the structure and content of this paper: I propose, as the relevant conceptual system, reflectiveness and defensiveness in response to rupture in knowing; and as principles of theoretical explanation, the setting and implications that are defined as its associated explanatory theory.

Requirements

Transcending disciplinary boundaries. A distinction is noted between the deeply challenging, educationally critical content particular to a discipline, and the universality pertaining to crucial elements of student experiences of difficulty as they encounter such content. Any theoretical result that accounts for universal aspects of student experience by using discipline-specific explanations (the current structure of TC scholarship) cannot be applied across disciplinary contexts. A valid explanatory theory for these crucial elements – and thus its underlying theoretical foundation – must remain unbound by disciplinary context and free of discipline-specific content.

A resource for teaching faculty. Many presenters at the 2008 TC conference spoke about their attempts to reach disengaged, even disaffected, students, and their various successes or difficulties in doing so. A theoretical foundation for TC (and its defined explanatory theory) should serve as a resource for such faculty; suggesting meaningful interpretation(s) of student behaviors and expanding the discourse to explore their causes and origins (Gurwitsch 1974).

Resolving Lacunae: representations of student experience. Lacunae remain in the definitions stated above for threshold concepts. All defining characteristics, except for *troublesome,* describe the aftermath – not the experience – of students' successful acquisition of challenging material. In themselves, these characteristics include no reference to what would facilitate teaching tc content. Like tc's, liminality has been defined by its consequences: anxiety; and by its hoped-for consequences: transformation and ontological shift. To date, TC scholarship regarding liminal space employs a metaphor from anthropology concerning states of being defined by social structure, and transitions among them (Turner 1969, Meyer & Land 2005 p. 375). It depicts implications of journey through that space as transformations or ontological shifts, but does not address the nature of either the space or the journey. In itself, the definition includes no information that facilitates supporting a student on the journey. A theoretical foundation for TC (and its defined explanatory theory) should serve as resources for resolving such lacunae, suggesting useful possibilities to facilitate teaching tc content and support students experiencing difficulty in the face of that content.

Rigorously defined terminology. Existing TC terminology conflates elements with distinct, even divergent meanings, and implicitly expresses assumptions that may not hold; making careful analysis more difficult. For example, "threshold" can be understood to refer to both the experience and the content of an encounter with deeply challenging material. It can also imply that to learn means to be hoisted over an existing (provisionally) stable threshold in a fixed world, so that the *individual acquires ... a new status and identity* (Meyer & Land 2005 p. 376). A theoretical foundation for TC (and its defined explanatory theory) should serve as clarifying resources, enabling greater precision in terminology – and thereby in scholarship.

Questions to be Addressed

A traditional scientific community participates in a *coherent research tradition* (Kuhn 1996 p. 46) delineated by – and communicated through – its extant paradigm. In a traditional scientific field, the paradigm grows out of the central motivating question for the discipline. No such question has yet been defined – or even explicitly sought – in TC scholarship. I propose a central question for TC, and pose it from three perspectives, those of:

1) the practitioner teacher: *How to ensure students' learning of deeply challenging material?*

2) the describer scholar: *How to ensure students' productive journey through liminality?*

3) the theoretician (who makes tacit presuppositions explicit): *What constitutes student learning of deeply challenging material? What happens in an encounter with deeply challenging material? What constitutes liminality?*

The central issue of learning may be pursued in either (or both) of two directions: the **operation** of learning, identifying what it means to have learned; or the **mechanism** of learning, exploring how learning happens. For the former direction, one may use existing and well-established methodologies such as Bloom's taxonomy. Its application, while yielding valuable information, is defined in a discipline-specific way; the results in one area cannot be applied directly to another. Furthermore, it cannot answer the theoretician's multiple questions. Pursuit in the latter – and more challenging – direction is not defined in a discipline-specific way; the results based on one academic or professional area can be applied directly to another. It would also encompass the theoretician's multiple questions.

Teaching faculty drawn to TC are invariably seeking to support student learning. Thus, any useful explanatory theory must address the experience of encounter with deeply challenging content and the process of learning it (productively navigating the ensuing interval of confusion) – or not. The theoretical foundation proposed here (and therefore any explanatory theory defined by it) arises exactly from consideration of the nature of the **encounter** itself, its operation (what occurs), and mechanisms (how it occurs), and their correspondence to possible outcomes.

GENERATING THEORETICAL FOUNDATIONS: COMMUNITY STRUCTURE AND PROCESS

In this section, the structure and process of TC is contrasted with that of a classical scientific community profiled by Thomas Kuhn (1996). It is assumed without discussion that an operative paradigm resembles the explanatory theory defined by an extant theoretical foundation.

A classical scientific community. Thomas Kuhn profiles a classic scientific community of practice and research in *The Structure of Scientific Revolutions* (Kuhn 1996). Kuhn writes about *communities* as the locus of discipline-specific development and discovery. A critical point – so fundamental that it is simply taken for granted and not articulated in the book (likely a *tacit presupposition* on Kuhn's part) – concerns the central and defining role of that particular discipline in community members' professional lives. Conversely, the discipline is completely defined by members' professional practice and scholarship. This process of reciprocal definition is effected through the conceptual construct of (in Kuhn's terminology) a *paradigm*. A paradigm arises from a set of *universally recognized [discipline] achievements [and] for a time provides model problems and solutions to a community of practitioners. ... The defining achievements were sufficiently unprecedented* **to attract an enduring group of adherents away from competing modes of [discipline] activity** ... *[and]* ... *sufficiently open-ended to leave all sorts of problems for the redefined group of practitioners to resolve* ...

The practices of both development and discovery in science *are community-based activities. To discover and analyze them, one must first unravel the changing community structure of the [discipline] over time.* During periods of development, *a paradigm governs, not subject matter but* ... **a group of practitioners.** During periods of discovery, a shifted paradigm is forged by the concentrated collective intention of a group of practitioners. *Any study of paradigm-directed* [i.e., development] *or paradigm-shattering* [i.e., discovery] *research must begin by locating the responsible group or groups.* ... *The pre-paradigm period, in particular, is regularly marked by frequent and deep debates over legitimate methods, problems, and standards of solution, though these serve rather to define schools than to produce agreement* (Kuhn 1996 pp. x, 10, 46, 47, 179, 180) (all emphasis added).

Illuminating TC

Differences and implications.   The formation, practice, and research of a scientific community profiled by Kuhn is impelled by a profession-defining, concentrated, collective intention among its members. They act to formulate and rigorously pursue the most productive questions (from which a theoretical foundation typically evolves) in a content area of shared primary focus. Community cohesion – even perhaps existence – depends on continuing evolution of a workable paradigm. Education into the field does not merit significant attention. In contrast, TC typically occupies a position secondary to their respective disciplinary pursuits in most participating faculty's professional lives. Concern for education and effective teaching defines the TC community. Rather than disputing each other's suggestions (the rigorous debate Kuhn mentions), most of the individuals interested in TC that I have met display receptivity to – even hunger for – any and all ideas about how to support student learning.

Given the combination of secondary focus and readiness to consider proffered solutions, TC is missing the traditional structure and implicit procedures for rigorously producing a paradigm. It lacks the stimulus for normatively generating a set of theoretical foundation candidates, as well as any process for determining the most viable from among the collection of associated explanatory theories. No widely accepted initial paradigm has been established, and the community has engaged in none of the debates that characterize classic pre-paradigm status.

TC: on its own.   Lacking an operative paradigm, TC is valued as an agent of connection and communication by committed teachers who seek others of like mind. TC provides a common vocabulary for discourse and a meeting ground at conferences for a coalescing multi-disciplinary community of teaching practice and descriptive scholarship. Such a community plays a critical role in the ongoing development of faculty who are teaching in their respective disciplines, and even of the disciplines themselves (Lister 2008).

A REFLECTIVENESS / DEFENSIVENESS CONCEPTUAL FRAMEWORK:
THE PROPOSED THEORETICAL FOUNDATION

This section introduces the conceptual framework of reflectiveness and defensive-eeness. A lay person's view of the two is summarized first. A deeper analysis follows, after being set in context.

Reflective vs. Defensive Responses: the Layperson's View

From the layperson's perspective, reflectiveness and defensiveness are understood as radically different from each other. Defensiveness is associated with an incident-specific increase in emotion that overshadows other aspects of an encounter and effectively prevents further discussion of the topic at hand; in shorthand, an ad hoc reaction of: "NO, DON'T". Reflectiveness is associated with diminishment of emotional investment, a kind of long-term stepping back to see better; in shorthand, an attitude of: "Hmmm, I wonder..." Though widely held, these definitions by association do not provide any insight into the origins, operations, or mechanisms of reflectiveness and defensiveness. A deeper analysis follows.

Setting Context: Diverse Sources and Multiple Values

Extending a metaphor from Plack and Greenberg (Plack & Greenberg 2005 p. 3], learning comprises two main aspects, and can be likened to the double helix of DNA. One strand holds the cognitive content specific to a particular domain or discipline; it is acquired by cognitive effort, including memorization. One strand, the focus of this proposal, is composed of context, meaning, and their interplay; it is acquired through reflectiveness, a practice common to all fields of learning. As befits the cross-disciplinary nature of TC, for this paper I draw on literature from a number of disciplines and professions, all directed toward the second strand of learning.

TC practice bespeaks an approach to teaching that is value-laden with respect to reflectiveness, because educators want students to respond reflectively. However, that value-laden orientation may blind one to the possibility of exploring and examining the absence of reflectiveness (a circumstance of many students' experience, and one that must be accounted for by any explanatory theory). Thus, (the search for) a theoretical foundation must take a value-neutral orientation regarding reflectiveness – and defensiveness: rather than being concerned with how one can engender a particular (reflective) response, one explores how students actually do respond to existentially unfamiliar, educationally critical material within a discipline. Following Segal's example (Segal 1999), this sort of exploration in theory produces information epistemologically prior to – and useful for – engendering in practice the desired reflectiveness.

Elements of Explication for Reflectiveness and Defensiveness

This subsection draws primarily on the work of three individuals to explore the roles of meaning and awareness: Jack Mezirow served as an Education Department Chair at Columbia University and reported on both his own research and a wide

29

spectrum of scholarship related to transformation theory (Mezirow 1991). John Dewey (Dewey 1991) played a seminal role in the development of modern education practice and theory. Phenomenologist Aron Gurwitsch, a student of Husserl, suggested that universal patterns of organization characterize fields of consciousness and inform the development of awareness (Gurwitsch 1964).

Meaning. Meaning amounts to a coherent representation of experience, an interpretation that occurs *both prelinguistically and through language ... by processes involving awareness* (Mezirow 1991, p. 4). Meaning arises out of experience, it cannot be arbitrarily imposed. *Saliency of a group of data so that this group emerges and segregates itself from the stream [of experience] is a feature not introduced into the stream, but yielded by the stream itself* (Gurwitsch 1964, p. 31), (James 1890). Dewey believes that the exercise of intelligence requires the existence of meaning; to grasp meaning constitutes the *nerves of our intellectual life.* For Dewey, individual learning may be defined as making meaning; what one can interpret effectively, one understands both differentiated from and in relationship with its surrounding context (Dewey 1991, pp. 116, 117).

Meaning frames. Meaning-making takes place under an orienting frame of reference, a *structure of assumptions within which one's past experience assimilates and transforms new experience, ... a habitual set of expectations.* I use the term *meaning frame* for such structures, which embody the categories and rules that order new experience, shaping how we classify our encounters with the world: what we take in and how we act. They also dictate what we notice and what we ignore by *selectively determin[ing] the scope of our attention ... informed by an horizon of possibility, ... to simplify, organize, and delete what is not salient in sensory input ... and provide the basis for reducing complex inferential tasks to simple judgments.* Thus, they function as both *lions at the gate of awareness and the building blocks of cognition* (Mezirow 1991, pp. 49, 50). Thomas Kuhn (1996) introduced the term *paradigm* to describe the analogous structure(s) within scientific communities of scholarship: a collection of unspoken expectations for, assumptions about, and model of relevant aspects of the world.

Dewey states that *[e]xplicit thinking goes on within the limits of what is implied or understood*, and describes the role of these 'premises', the grounds or foundations, in reasoning: the premises contain the conclusions and the conclusions contain the premises. The importance of coherence as an organizing principle is embodied in that relationship (Dewey 1991, pp. 81, 215). Meaning frames operate below the level of awareness, as an unarticulated, *unconscious* system of ideas. They inhabit the realm of the unseen, taken-for-granted: *The old, the near, the accustomed, is not that **to** which but that **with** which we attend* (Dewey 1991, p. 222).

Meaning frames exist as dynamic entities. In the normal course of our encounters with the world, meaning frames undergo continual refinement; one's *selective and conceptualizing faculties are persistently at work* (Gurwitsch 1964, p. 30). Encounters with the world also occur outside that normal course: Dewey observes that any aspect of the world, no matter how well known, may suddenly present an unexpected and incomprehensible problem (Dewey 1991, p. 120). This section and the next lay groundwork for understanding the (relevant to TC) consequences when meaning frame refinement does not suffice.

Awareness and the organization of consciousness. Meaning frames refer to what one brings within oneself to engage in and interpret an encounter with the world. The work of Aron Gurwitsch enables reference to those aspects of the world that one takes in or one acts upon through the meaning frame. He asserts that every field of consciousness, regardless of content, exhibits a *universal, formal pattern of organization* comprising three domains or dimensions: the *thematic focus* or *theme*, upon which one's mental activity concentrates; the *thematic field*, aspects of the world co-present with the thematic focus and having relevance to it; and the *margin*, aspects of the world co-present with the thematic focus but irrelevant to it (Gurwitsch 1964, p. 56).

Meaning frame operation and field of consciousness organization exist interdependently. Meaning frame dictates what aspects of the world one's awareness encompasses at any given moment, which elements among them have direct significance (corresponding to what occupies the thematic focus); which have significance by association, i.e., *relevance* (corresponding to content of the thematic field (Gurwitsch 1964, p. 341); and which have little or no significance (corresponding to marginalia).

Booth summarizes Gurwitsch's work: The structure of awareness may be thought of as a dynamic relationship between oneself and the object of one's consciousness. One brings the totality of one's experience and awareness to the perception or consideration of some aspect of that object. The object is said to 'present' itself in that awareness; how it does so determines the thematic focus to emerge from it, and the attendant elements of relevance constituting the thematic field. A shift in one's awareness to another aspect of the object brings a corresponding shift in the thematic focus and thematic field. In contemplation of an object, one shifts one's awareness alternately among its different aspects. Each attendant shifting organization of the dimensions of one's consciousness may be enacted by delineation of a different element from the thematic field into thematic focus (Booth 1997, pp. 141,146).

Two critical implications follow from this relationship: The more differentiated one's view of an object (the more aspects one can bring awareness to), the richer the set of elements in the thematic field associated with it and the more varied the set of elements that can serve as a thematic focus during contemplation of the object; thus, the deeper one's understanding. In contrast, a sparsely populated – or empty – thematic field leaves little possibility for deep understanding.

Etiology of Reflectiveness and Defensiveness: A Phenomenological Analysis

Heidegger describes a pattern of encounter with and response to the existentially unfamiliar that he calls the *dynamic of rupture*. Segal's explication of the dynamic (Segal 1999, Heidegger 1927) lays groundwork for a functional definition of rupture and phenomenological analyses of reflectiveness and defensiveness. The dynamic takes the form of a three-step sequence: *rupture, explicitness, response* – either *reflective* or *defensive* (Segal also refers to the response types as alternative *forms of explicitness*). I draw on the literature to examine each step in turn, as well as several underlying concepts on which they're based. The results enable an expanded and refined description of reflectiveness and defensiveness, their origins, differences, and similarities; in preparation for demonstrating their relevance as a foundation to an explanatory theory for TC.

Dynamic of rupture: definition by example. This dynamic can be explained by Segal's example from Dreyfus (Dreyfus 1993) familiar to anyone who is traveling internationally for the first time, perhaps to attend a conference: Each of us 'knows' what particular distance to stand apart from an acquaintance when engaged in conversation. In general, one has no awareness of the specific distance, or even that one is doing it. This 'know-how' resides in the realm of the unseen taken-for-granted. However, when one encounters conference host country natives who use a different conversational distance, one experiences them as standing uncomfortably close or uncomfortably far away, and one suddenly becomes aware that one has an accustomed distance. As will be explained, this discomfort is experienced either productively (reflectively) or unproductively (defensively). Segal's explanation of distinct forms of differentness clarifies the two possibilities. (Note that the traveler's responses in this section actually occur below the level of awareness and language; they are verbalized here for the reader's information.)

Segal, citing Bauman, distinguishes between two kinds of differentness or otherness: the oppositional (in shorthand, *enemy*) and the unknown (in shorthand, *stranger*). The oppositional is defined according to the same rules as oneself, but oppositely. Continuing the example of interpersonal conversational distance, the international traveler may respond: "These unrefined (host country) natives are standing the wrong distance away. I can't possibly carry on a civilized conversation under such conditions."

Their differentness is thus defined in opposition: their 'wrong' vs. one's own 'correct' distance, 'unrefined' vs. 'refined' nature, 'uncivilized' vs. 'civilized' actions. Defining the other in opposition, as *enemy*, confirms one's view of the world; questioning of one's own or the other's behavior has no place. *Enemies* oppose each other but have a common appreciation of the terms on which they meet; *[they] function in the space of the existentially familiar* ...

Alternatively, the unknown is defined by unknown rules, or perhaps not defined at all. The international traveler may respond, "What is happening here?", and eventually, "What does this mean? Do I have an accustomed distance? If so, how did I learn it, what length is it measured at? Do they have an accustomed distance? If so, how do I learn it, what length is it measured at, and how do I figure it out? How long will it take to learn, what will I do in the meantime? ..." Recognizing the other as unknown, as stranger, evinces the inadequacy of one's worldview; questions, but no real answers, abound. *Strangers* have no common understanding of the terms on which they meet; *[they] give rise to the existentially unfamiliar ... [T]here are no ways of reading [such] a situation that can be taken for granted. ... The anxiety of strangeness is experienced not only in the face of the stranger but in the face of strange and unfamiliar situations – in any situation in which we cannot assume our familiar ways of doing things* (Segal 1999 p. 76, Bauman 1990 pp. 143–145).

Enemies and friends, or enemies and oneself, represent two sides of the same coin. Strangers – or strange, unknown situations – represent a different coin altogether.

Note that in this example, conversation with host country natives constitutes the object of the traveler's consciousness, and standing distance between her and them becomes the thematic focus. Elements in the thematic field include observations (of host country natives talking among themselves, out-of-country attendees talking among themselves, and natives and attendees talking with each other); and recollections (of standing distance in conversations at home with close friends or family, or with strangers, and how that distance varied depending on conversational content and the nature of the encounter).

Troublesome knowledge and rupture in knowing. *Anomaly* refers to experience or observation that violates the expectations carried in one's meaning frame. *Troublesome knowledge* denotes an anomaly that cannot be avoided, ignored, or made to conform, leading to a rupture in knowing. Not all anomalies rise to a level of troublesome knowledge; persistence and significance, at a minimum, are required. *Rupture in knowing* (my terminology) arises when *what is known and what must be understood ... conflict.* (Mezirow 1991 p163, Loder 1981). It is created by a conflict or mismatch between one's comprehension of relevant aspects of the world and one's encounters with or observations of those aspects.

It should be noted that anomaly and troublesome knowledge are defined entirely in relation to one's meaning frame, and occur as a violation of expectations carried therein. The frame is required to bring the anomalous nature of a phenomenon to light, but inadequate to resolve the problems raised by its existence (Kuhn 1996 p. 122). In the absence of an extant meaning frame, by definition, neither anomaly nor troublesome knowledge exist. In the example of the traveler, her meaning frame for conversational standing carries the habitual distance to which she'd been socialized; the phenomenon of host country natives' standing distance is defined as an anomaly in relation to it. If the occasional host country native stands at an unaccustomed distance, the traveler can attribute it to that individual's eccentricities. But if virtually every host country native does so, the anomaly becomes troublesome knowledge, an unavoidable phenomenon whose existential strangeness cannot be ignored.

Responses to and consequences from rupture in knowing. According to Mezirow and Dewey, an instance of rupture in knowing forces the inadequacies – and the existence – of one's meaning frame into awareness (*explicitness*, in Segal's explication of Heidegger's dynamic). The sudden unexpected presence of heretofore unseen, taken-for-granted elements in the thematic focus and thematic field(s) of one's consciousness is accompanied by the *shock of estrangement* (Segal 1999) and experienced with much uncertainty and unease. These significant affective components are included in the challenges of explicitness. Segal notes that both cognitive and emotional elements are involved in the responses to rupture and explicitness, because high emotional arousal, either anxiety or excitement, forms an integral part of being attentive. Rupture and explicitness become the requisite, defining pre-condition to subsequent responses, which are restricted to two possibilities: either one avoids those challenges (a defensive response), or one takes on those challenges (a reflective response). Both reflectiveness and defensiveness are freighted with uncertainty and anxiety, and either can follow equally from explicitness.

LEARNING – OR NOT:
CONSEQUENCES OF REFLECTIVENESS AND DEFENSIVENESS

The reflectiveness/defensiveness conceptual framework, which comes to light through effecting the dynamic of rupture, resides within a broader context of learning generally, as illustrated in this section's descriptions of the nature and consequences of reflectiveness and defensiveness.

Defensiveness

The operation of defensiveness (avoiding the challenges of explicitness) shields the responder from having to experience the estrangement and engendered unease and uncertainty. According to Segal's account of the mechanism of defensiveness, it is enacted by *projection* (Segal 1999 p. 86). One disassociates from the uncertainty by recasting the unknown (strange) explicit as the known oppositional (enemy) explicit; one disowns the unease by projecting or displacing all responsibility for difficulty onto that recast source.

As an example, consider the first possible response attributed to the international traveler above. He casts the host country natives as unrefined clods, and (dis)places onto them all responsibility for a lack of productive communication. Details of natives' actual standing distance among themselves and with other visitors, and details of the traveler's and others' habitual behavior in his home country, merit no consideration. In fact, they have no place.

Reflectiveness and Transformative Learning

Reflectiveness (taking on the challenge of uncertainty and its affective components by engaging with the unknown as unknown) serves as the mechanism of trans-formative learning. The operation of transformative learning – the (eventual) reformu-lation of meaning frame after an instance of rupture in knowing – preserves meaning to effect coherence across that discontinuity. With a new meaning frame, one is re-oriented in the world: the same collection of experience, organized along different principles, embodies a radically different set of relationships. In Dewey's terms, *[a clarity illuminates] relations of interdependence between considerations previously unorganized and disconnected ... **binding isolated items into a coherent single whole*** (Dewey 1991 p. 80). Using Gurwitsch's framework, the field of consciousness changes as a result of transformative learning: elements formerly not found in any domain of consciousness, possibly including component parts of elements formerly classified as nondecomposable, now occupy the thematic focus or reside in the thematic field, and some elements formerly found there are now relegated to the margin.

The operation of reflectiveness corresponds to steps 2, 3, and 4 in Barer-Stein's phenomenological analysis of learning as a five-step process of experiencing the unfamiliar: *[1)], being aware ... [characterized by the dominant question,] What is this?; [2)], observing ... How does this compare with what I know?; [3)], acting ... Shall I try it?; [4)], confronting ... Do I know this?, Do I want to?; [(if yes), then] [5)], involving ... How did this come to be?, What are the possibilities, and which makes sense?, What [meaning] is relevant for me?* (Mezirow 1991 p. 84, Barer-Stein 1987). As an example, consider the second possible response attributed to the traveler.

The mechanism of reflectiveness is not well understood; it remains *perhaps ... permanently inscrutable* (Kuhn 1996 p. 90). It might be described briefly (and vaguely) as follows: Once explicitness forces the inadequacies – and the existence – of one's meaning frame into (at least somewhat) conscious awareness, one engages in some combination of conscious and unconscious (Dewey 1991 p. 217) examination of the frame, to determine its inadequacies and correct them. The process is *terminated by ... a relatively sudden ... unstructured event [experienced as] a gestalt switch* (Kuhn 1996 p. 122), corresponding to the newly reformulated meaning frame that is required in order to accommodate the (now formerly) troublesome knowledge. The five-step sequence is thus compressed to: *discontinuity* → *reflectiveness* → *new meaning frame*, or (conforming more to case study course student data): *confusion* → *struggle* → *expanded knowing*.

Revisiting the TC / tc Central Question(s)

In light of the proposed theoretical foundation, TC central question(s) can be reformulated.

1+) from the TC practitioner teacher: *How to ensure students' reflective response to an encounter with the existentially unfamiliar, educationally critical content of the discipline?*

2+) from the TC describer scholar: *How to describe students' (reflective) response to an encounter with the existentially unfamiliar, educationally critical content of the discipline?*

3+) from the TC theoretician, (who is tasked with addressing epistemologically prior considerations (Gurwitsch 1974), which here means understanding how students actually do respond to such encounters and the mechanism(s) of their responses): *What actually occurs in an encounter with the existentially unfamiliar, educationally critical content of the discipline? How does it lead – or not – to learning?*

DATA: PARTICULARS GIVING RISE TO THE UNIVERSAL

Segal has studied the relationship between reflective practice – or its lack – and the interval of confusion that follows an encounter with the existentially unfamiliar. Based on his paper, I assert that a student's exposure to troublesome knowledge in the content domain of a discipline initiates a rupture in knowing, and culminates in reflectiveness or, alternatively, defensiveness.

The current state of education into computing science (my discipline) derives from both immaturity and complexity: no consensus yet exists on a definition for good quality in software, and little beyond complexity is found as a common element among all software. This combination abstracts out much discipline-specific content and placcs in bold relief the issues surrounding student transformative learning – or not. Their exploration can produce results applicable to arbitrary disciplines. Due to space constraints, only a small amount of data is contained here, fuller treatment can be found in (Schwartzman 2007, 2008). In addition, perhaps readers who are drawn to TC will find data closer at hand through their own experience of teaching.

Case Study: A Data Source

The contents of this paper were motivated largely by the experience and outcomes of teaching in my discipline, including an upper-level undergraduate software design and engineering course (which is meant to teach software development fundamentals in a way that transcends software tools and languages, yet engages students in the actual practice of software, not just a theoretical or anecdotal exposition). Data is collected from several sources within that course: all students submit course assignments; some students record and organize thoughts in their group project task log; every student is interviewed at end of term in order to determine the extent of her / his individual learning beyond the group's collective assignment submissions; and students submit anonymous course evaluations at term end. The literature on reflectiveness and defensiveness, especially Segal's article, sheds considerable light on this extensive set of data, through which the course has become a case study for exploration into students' response to deeply challenging content. Data sources are noted.

Representative Data and Analysis

Retrospective indications of reflectiveness: end-of-term interviews. In the case study course, reflectiveness is evidenced retrospectively by students' end-of-semester accounts of transformative learning (the consequence of reflectiveness) in software development. They contrast prior practice (invariably, *It's all about code*) with that now in place, indicating radical – even previously unimaginable – changes and their powerful implications. Consider one student response to the question, 'What will you take away with you from the course?':

(S_r104): Analyzing problems, analyzing software, and ways to go about developing software. I used to code software offhand without going off and thinking about it [first]. This course really helped me to go off and think about it. I'm not afraid

anymore to program, I know that. The real duty behind software development isn't code. Code equals a small percentage. Really: it's sitting down and really thinking it out. ... Now, I don't think about program in terms of lines of code, how many functions. Problems don't seem as big as they used to, they're simplified. [Now,] I'd take a project, break it down to its core elements, and really focus on ... [w]hat is the underlying problem, what underlying job needs to get done? Break down the problem into pieces, each piece has its own duty or task, functionality. Instead of a big, round ball, [it becomes] things more like blocks.

Retrospective indications of defensiveness: anonymous end-of-term course evaluations. In the case study course, retrospective projection onto the teacher and course structure of all responsibility for difficulty in class is interpreted as evidence of defensiveness, for example, this student's comments:

(S_1A1): I think this class was much more difficult than it had to be. ... My main concern was trying to interpret what was being asked, instead of learning the material. A separate point – we spent 2 periods going over the [KWIC index program] – Why? Why the line by line analysis of the ... program? This has little value – except to confuse and bewilder the class.

In-process feedback: indications of anxiety. Almost all feedback data collected at semester's end (representing after-the-fact reportage) satisfies exactly one of the defining conditions delineated in the previous section. However, for most of the group project, qualitative data logged in the midst of students' actual process does not satisfy either definition. It does consistently display a heightened level of affect, indeed anxiety, even among students whose projects later turned out well. Consider student entries from week 1 of the project:

(S_m201): ... It seems to me that we were not getting anywhere very quickly and this undertaking was larger than I previously had thought. What seems like such a straightforward assignment has become very complex ...

(S_m202): ... I'm a very calm and balanced person, and never really get stressed out about anything homework-wise because of the timeline I usually follow when I work. This project is already starting to stress me out because of the seeming lack of progress that we've gotten through so far. It seemed to me to be a fairly straightforward assignment at first, especially given the examples of the circles and the KWIC index, and I had hoped to hammer out a good outline to the [documents] within the first two sessions. We're nowhere near that yet. ... It feels like we're getting nothing done, and right now I don't necessarily know where to work next on my own.

These entries confirm the relevance of Segal's analysis; students are experiencing (effects of) explicitness: the confusion that follows exposure to – but precedes learning (or not) of – existentially unfamiliar material. Distinctions that retrospectively identify reflective and defensive responses do not apply. Analyzing in-process data to distinguish between the two response types poses much more

37

challenge than interpreting feedback given retrospectively, a difference relevant to the TC community concern with understanding and supporting student encounters with challenging material.

These students' group produced an extremely strong project, and their respective individual practices were significantly transformed by completing that project; indicating retrospectively that they responded reflectively. Their journal entries during the project indicate heightened levels of anxiety. Note, therefore, that in-process anxiety does not necessarily equal defensiveness, and reflectiveness neither equals contemplation nor means diminished affect.

THEORETICAL FOUNDATION: EVALUATING THE CANDIDATE

In this section, the proposed candidate theoretical foundation is considered in light of the roles a theoretical foundation should play: illuminating coherence and meaning in the body of existing literature, providing an organizing principle out of which the field can continue to emerge in a coherent way, and defining an explanatory theory for practice.

Illuminating Internal Coherence of Existing TC Literature

Real learning requires stepping into the unknown, which initiates a rupture in knowing. The interval of difficulty that follows exposure to existentially unfamiliar, educationally critical material can be understood as a response to that rupture. It is filled with confusion and uncertainty, even when it is also filled with learning (Brown *et alia* 2001). In the language of Heidegger's *dynamic of rupture*, the interval comprises a form of (response to) explicitness; that is, reflectiveness or defensiveness. By definition, all TC scholarship is concerned (directly or indirectly) with encountering the unknown. In offering meaningful explanation for the interval of confusion and uncertainty that is inescapably engendered by such encounters, a reflectiveness / defensiveness framework illuminates connections and an element of commonality among all TC scholarship.

Informing Future Theoretical and Application Development

Owing to its relevance for all TC scholarship, a reflectiveness/defensiveness conceptual framework (comprising the proposed theoretical foundation) forms infrastructure on which developing TC theory can be anchored. It also enables issues of learning discipline-specific scholarship to be brought more sharply into focus, clarifying relevant questions. The consequences of reflectiveness or defen-siveness, learning – or not, provide an embedding context to contain, shape, and evaluate both developing theory and application.

Defining an Explanatory Theory

The reflectiveness/defensiveness conceptual framework, together with elements of its explication and of its generative phenomenon, form an explanatory theory for student experience, as described in the next section.

A DEFINED EXPLANATORY THEORY: CONSIDERATION OF ROLES

In this section, the explanatory theory defined by the proposed theoretical foundation is considered in light of the roles a TC explanatory theory should play.

Understanding Student Experience: Authenticity / Inauthenticity

In phenomenological terms, Segal is examining elements in the realm of the taken-for-granted unseen, and their transition to a realm of the (seen) explicit, i.e., the development of new phenomenological awareness. Such an orientation relegates discipline content to the sidelines. It thus reduces the complexity – but not the sophistication – of conceptually framing the investigation into student experience. Analysis founded in a reflectiveness/defensiveness conceptual construct becomes a tool for investigating what occurs outside awareness.

One view from psychology holds that defensiveness arises from an individual's inadequacy to manage a situation, and the inadequacy dictates that individual's decisions. Heidegger's phenomenology frames the situation differently: [He] calls defensive responses to rupture *inauthenticity* (Segal 1999 p. 87). Student feedback data from the case study course provides compelling evidence that what I call the *will to authenticity* – an inclination to address the real problem and not be deflected by one's anxiety at doing so – can exert great influence, even in the face of significant difficulty. Consider this student's end-of-term excerpted interview:

(S_m107): [The course appears] very different [to me at the end than at the beginning or middle] ... I'm understanding it better at the end. ... the importance of it is making more sense to me, ... how important it is to have a rational design process. I think if [developers of real software used this approach], the failure rate would not be so high. They'd know exactly where to ... look for [the source of a] problem. I never thought of software that way before. It's fatal: not just with lives (it can be), it also can be fatal economically. ... After realizing it's not just about [code in a particular computer language], I actually went back to the [first design document] – because I didn't understand it; then the [next design document, in order to understand the decomposition of functionality] and what changes might occur, to be prepared for. Second, [I turned to] the [next design document], thinking about procedures (I hadn't thought ... about procedures before realizing it's not just about [code in a particular computer language]), what it does, how to do it. ... I had to keep going back again and again. ... It took awhile for me to get it, I kept talking about [code in a particular computer language] instead of [procedures] with team mates. It was frustrating and difficult. ... [Before I could finish the project], first I had to understand it [my]self. It took 2 weeks; I looked at it each day, and talked with [a team mate] often.

An 'inadequacy/adequacy' frame and an 'inauthenticity/will to authenticity' frame stand in sharp contrast. The former doesn't explain the student's comments, or suggest any way to cultivate similar experience in others. The latter explains the comments perfectly, and indicates possibilities for subsequent teaching through examination of what motivated this student.

39

Strategies for Teaching: The Importance of Experiential Learning

As the mechanism of transformative learning, reflectiveness is required for productively navigating the interval of confusion that follows an encounter with the existentially unfamiliar. Significant difficulties attach to teaching and cultivating authentic reflectiveness (Boud & Walker 1998), which involves becoming aware of one's habitual behavior. Citing Nietzsche, Segal notes that if self-observation is done by rote, it leads to confusion rather than insight. *'Never to observe in order to observe. That gives a false perspective, leads to squinting and something false and exaggerated. ... One must not eye oneself while having an experience; else the eye becomes an evil eye.' ... [A] dogmatic commitment to observation produces a disengaged and decontextualised relationship to one's practice* (Segal 1999 p. 75, Nietzsche 1974). Reflectiveness must come from a student's internal process, as questioning arises out of her dynamic engagement with the content. It cannot be taught in an explicit or linear fashion, experiential learning plays an important role.

Furthering Discourse

Refining the definition of threshold concepts. Currently, no consensus exists on an intellectually rigorous, definitive criteria for identifying tc's. In clarifying how to specify a threshold concept and how to identify the learning that leads to understanding it, a distinction should be drawn between deep cumulative learning and transformative learning. In terms of phenomenological awareness: In the former, the object upon which one's mental activity is concentrated does not change; rather, one moves one's attention with ease among a multiplicity of its aspects (some previously unattended to). In the latter, one's mental activity comes to be concentrated upon a previously unknown and existentially unfamiliar object.

The two can also be distinguished conceptually using Gurwitsch's fields of consciousness: As a result of deep cumulative learning, one switches dynamically – within the same field of consciousness – among thematic foci, with correspondent restructuring of thematic fields (Booth 1997 p. 144). The total set of elements in the field remains constant, while boundaries among the thematic foci, the thematic field, and the margin become fluid; and component elements shift between adjacent domains. The mechanism of dynamic switching among extant elements corresponds to *reflection*; the operation corresponds to refinement and clarification of one's extant meaning frame.

As a result of transformative learning, in contrast, the contents of the field of consciousness change. Elements formerly not found in any domain of consciousness, possibly including component parts of elements formerly classified as non-decomposable, now occupy the thematic focus or reside in the thematic field; and some elements formerly found there are now relegated to the margin. The mechanism remains mysterious and corresponds to *reflectiveness*; the operation, which results in a different population in the field of consciousness, corresponds to reformulation of one's meaning frame.

With this distinction, one can now formulate a question regarding the designation of tc's: Should the term be restricted to content that requires transformative learning (through reflectiveness), or should it also encompass content that depends on deep cumulative learning (through reflection)? Meyer and Land's tc-defining characteristics suggest the former, wherein new meaning arises to be imposed upon (i.e., a reformulated set of expectations, assumptions, and world model are applied to interpret) both old and new experience. However, the papers presented at both conferences suggest the latter, wherein old meaning is imposed upon (i.e., one's extant expectations are applied to interpret) new experience (Mezirow 1991 p. 11). By clarifying the difference, the proposed theoretical foundation brings this question into focus – and into the discourse.

Refining representation of liminality. For Meyer and Land, the ontological shift associated with liminality appears to denote externally defined change (Meyer & Land 2005 p. 376). Following Turner's metaphor (Turner 1969), they focus on *identity transformation* as altered status or place of self within a fixed world. Liminality is understood to be experienced individually, while it is also treated as an entity unto itself: one enters into and exits from a pre-existing – and persisting – liminal space as one's identity and one's place are transformed in the pre-existing – and persisting – world. Students are cast as an exotic other to be placed under anthropological observation. This representation of the encounter and its aftermath rests on *knowing*; it is organized around the principle of presentation of self to the unknown.

I propose instead a phenomenological analysis of a universal human pattern that happens (outside awareness) during encounter with and response to the unknown. Continuity of one's self is preserved; change, if it occurs, appears to occur in the world. Students are immersed in confusion and experience reflectiveness or defensiveness (liminality). This representation of the encounter and its aftermath rests on *meaning*; it is organized around the process of meaning-making, of interpreting the existentially unfamiliar, the principle of presentation of the unknown to oneself.

The phenomenological analysis conforms to student feedback data from the case study course (Schwartzman 2008). It is also supported by an interesting mix of literature; and makes available more nuanced and more wide-ranging interpretation of student experience, and thus greater opportunity for intervention and support of student learning: In Gurwitsch's phenomenological examination of consciousness, he notes that at the moment of solving a problem, one experiences the perceptual field through which one has been confronted with the problem *undergo[ing] reorganization and reconstruction before one's eyes* (Gurwitsch 1964 p. 52). In analyzing scientific discovery, Kuhn writes that *[a]lthough the world does not change with a change of paradigm, the scientist afterward works in a different world* (Kuhn 1996 p. 121).

Separation of Concerns: Definition as Explanation for tc Terms and TC Concepts

In themselves, TC terms of art and tc characteristics enumerated earlier describe but do not explain, and the terminology conflates elements with divergent meanings.

They are redefined here (using a *taxonomy* (Simon 1996) based on the proposed theoretical foundation), to provide both the explanations and the *separation of concerns* (Dijkstra 1972) required for more careful analysis.

TC terms of art:
– *threshold*: a point of rupture in knowing;
– *threshold concept*: existentially unfamiliar (therefore leading to rupture in knowing), educationally critical content of a discipline so fundamental to understanding that it permanently transforms the practitioner's view;
– *liminality*: a period of unresolved explicitness, in the form of reflectiveness or defensiveness; an observer may have difficulty, in process, identifying which response is occurring;
– *troublesome knowledge*: an anomaly that cannot be avoided, ignored, or made to conform, leading to a rupture in knowing.

tc characteristics: If tc learning corresponds to a reformulated meaning frame, it qualifies as
– *transformative*: *by definition;*
– *irreversible*: because meaning frames appear to exist only as dynamic entities in operation at an unconscious level, no structural integrity attaches to a former meaning frame and holds it together for later re-use;
– *integrative*: because a new meaning frame, by definition, illuminates *the relations of interdependence ... binding isolated items into a coherent single whole* (Dewey 1991 p. 80);
– *troublesome*: by definition, one experiences as troubling any encounter with the existentially unfamiliar that cannot be ignored, avoided, or made to conform;
– *bounded new concept space*: as the existentially unfamiliar is never exhausted (Dewey notes that it may arise – always unexpectedly – from any source, at any time, in any place), any concept space is limited in scope.

CONCLUSIONS AND FUTURE WORK

I have proposed here a reflectiveness/defensiveness framework as a candidate (discipline-independent) theoretical foundation for Threshold Concepts. It is intended to illuminate connections in the body of existing TC literature and act as an organizing principle out of which the field can continue to emerge in a coherent way. The explanatory theory defined by it extends beyond description, analogy, and metaphor to provide explanation for TC terms of art and tc-associated characteristics. The two, in combination, also suggest additional possibilities for TC practice and for refining discourse within the developing TC community.

In Husserl's terms, the former constitutes a *conceptual system*, the latter principles of *theoretical explanation*. My exploration and development of the reflectiveness / defensiveness framework continues with the case study course in my discipline. The ultimate usefulness of this framework (in itself) to the developing TC community of practice and scholarship will be determined by whether faculty in a variety of disciplines find it helpful to employ individually: to observe, analyze, and support students' encounters with the existentially unfamiliar, educationally critical content of their respective fields; and collectively: to provide a common vocabulary and establish a common standard for *evidence* (Rowland 2000) of learning – or not – and the exploration of how to support it.

This candidate (if deemed substantive) will be evaluated through community practice and scholarship. The proposal (in itself) is meant to expand the discourse – perhaps others will be encouraged to offer additional candidate theoretical foundations; all this accruing, one hopes, to the benefit of developing Threshold Concepts theory.

ACKNOWLEDGEMENTS

I thank Caroline Baillie for encouraging the role of my work in the developing theoretical foundation for TC; Ray Land for providing his perspective on the current direction of TC scholarship; Lauri Malmi for his repeated suggestions that a reflectiveness/defensiveness framework has relevance to tc's; Keith Miller for his generous assistance; and Raymond Lister, without whom this paper might not have been written.

REFERENCES

Barer-Stein, T. (1987). Learning as a process of experiencing the unfamiliar. *Studies in the Education of Adults, 19*, 87–108.

Bauman, Z. (1990). *Thinking sociologically*. Oxford, UK: Basil Blackwell.

Booth, S. (1997). On phenomenography, learning, and teaching. *Higher Education Research and Development, 16*(2), 135–158.

Boud, D., & Walker, D. (1998, June). Promoting reflection in professional courses: The challenge of context. *Studies in Higher Education, 23*(2), 191–206.

Brown, J., Collins, A., & Duguid, P. (2001, January–February). Situated cognition and the culture of learning. *Educational Researcher, 18*(1), 32–42.

Conolly, J. (2008, June). A term of art introduced by in private communication.

Dijkstra, E. (1972, October). The humble programmer. *Communications of the ACM, 15*(10), 859–866.

Dewey, J. (1991 edition, originally published 1929). *How we think: A restatement of the relation of reflective thinking to the educative process*. Amherst, NY: Prometheus Books.

Dreyfus, H. (1993). *Being-in-the-world: A commentary on Heidegger's being and time, division 1*. MIT Press.

Feldenkrais, M. (1981). *The Elusive Obvious*. Capitola, CA: Meta-Publications.

Gurwitsch, A. (1974). *Phenomenology and the theory of science* (L. Embree, Ed.). Evanston, IL: North-western University Press.

Gurwitsch, A. (1964). *The field of consciousness*. Pittsburgh, PA: Duquesne University Press.

Heidegger, M. (1927). *Being and time*. Tubingen: Max Niemeyer Verlag.

James, W. (1890). *The principles of psychology* (Vol. 1). New York: Henry Holt.

Kuhn, T. S. (1996). *The structure of scientific revolutions* (3rd ed.). University of Chicago Press.

Land, R. (2008, November). Private communication.

Lister, R. (2008). After the Gold Rush: Toward sustainable scholarship in computing. *Proceedings, Tenth Australasian Computing Education Conference* (ACE 2008), Wollongong, NSW, Australia. CRPIT, 78. Simon and Hamilton, M. (Eds.), ACS: 3–18.

Loder, J. (1981). *The transforming moment: Understanding convictional experiences.* San Francisco, CA: Harper & Row.

Meyer, J., & Land, R. (2005). Threshold concepts and troublesome knowledge (2): Epistemological considerations and a conceptual framework for teaching and learning. *Higher Education, 49,* 373–388.

Mezirow, J. (1991). *Transformative dimensions of adult learning.* San Francisco, CA: Jossey-Bass.

Nietzsche, F. (1974 edition). Twilight of the idols. In L. Karl & L. Hamalian (Eds.), *The existential mind: Documents and fiction.* Greenwich, CN: Facett Publications.

Padfield, C. (1997, April). The role of research and reflection in learning from experience: Implications for universities. *Industry and Higher Education, 11*(2), 91–95.

Plack, M., & Greenberg, L. (2005, December). The reflective practitioner: Reaching for excellence in practice. *Pediatrics, 116*(16), 1546–1552.

Rowland, S. (2000). *The enquiring university teacher.* Buckingham, UK: Society for Research into Higher Education (SRHE) and Open University Press.

Schwartzman, L. (2007). Student defensiveness as a threshold to reflective learning in software design. *Informatics in Education, 6*(1), 197–214.

Schwartzman, L. (2008). Student Transformative Learning in Software Engineering and Design: discontinuity (pre)serves meaning, 7th Baltic Sea Conference on Computing Education Research (Koli Calling 2007), Koli National Park, Finland, November 15–18, 2007; *Proceedings Conferences in Research and Practice in Information Technology* (CRPIT) © 2008, v 88, R. Lister and Simon (Eds.)

Segal, S. (1999). The existential conditions of explicitness: An heideggerian perspective. *Studies in Continuing Education, 21*(1), 73–89.

Simon, H. (1996). *The sciences of the artificial* (3rd ed.). Cambridge, MA: MIT Press.

Turner, V. (1969). *The ritual process, structure and Anti-structure.* London: Routledge and Kegan Paul.

Leslie Schwartzman
Chicago
Illinois
USA
sla @ acm.org

AIDAN RICKETTS

3. THRESHOLD CONCEPTS: 'LOADED' KNOWLEDGE OR CRITICAL EDUCATION?

INTRODUCTION

Recent discussion of the idea of threshold concepts in educational literature has highlighted the importance of understanding the transformative nature of disciplinary learning. Transformation occurs when a student finally grasps a key concept within the discipline's view of the world and in the process experiences a change of world view themselves. Transformative experiences may enhance a student's critical awareness, but this should not be assumed; in some cases the nature of the transformation may actually reduce the scope for critical thinking.

Each academic discipline is constructed upon the basis of certain fundamentally important conceptual frameworks that provide the prism through which information is received and reconstructed within that discipline. In accepting and internalising the foundational perspectives of their chosen discipline, students may lose or fail to develop their capacity to critique those perspectives.

This paper explores this particular issue in the context of legal education, and aims to demonstrate that whilst the risk of discipline based indoctrination remains significant, (particularly in law studies) that an educator committed to critical education can nonetheless succeed in encouraging students to critique the very discipline they have come to study. Although the context of this paper is legal education, the discussion is of much wider significance. Most academic disciplines are very strong on encouraging students to critique the external subject matter of the discipline, but many are not so strong in encouraging an internal critique of the disciplinary world view itself.

THRESHOLD CONCEPTS AS TRANSFORMATIONAL EXPERIENCES

The idea that threshold concepts in a discipline can be internalised by students as a result of transformational learning experiences has recently been brought to prominence by the writings of Meyer and Land (2003, 2005 & 2006). The primary concern of Meyer and Land has been to use threshold concept theory as means for exploring ways to design curriculum and other learning experiences in a way which will stimulate students to move through various knowledge thresholds more readily. As such the research has a laudable aim and a practical approach.

The cognitive processes described by Meyer and Land (2003, 2005) cast light on the way in which students' world views can be transformed by education within a discipline. This is neither entirely new nor a cause of concern in itself, unless of

J. H. F. Meyer, R. Land and C. Baillie (eds.), Threshold Concepts and
Transformational Learning, 45–60.

course the transformation is one which narrows rather than expands the students capacity for critical awareness. Meyer and Land (2003, p. 10) actually acknowledge the potential danger of threshold concepts having a 'colonising' effect on student thinking as significant, but have not so far further explored it in their published work on the issue.

Before exploring the potentially troublesome intersection between threshold concepts theory and critical literacy, it is useful to summarise what is meant by threshold concepts. Meyer and Land (2005, p. 1) have used the term 'threshold concepts' to refer to *"concepts that bind a subject together, and that are fundamental to ways of thinking and practising in that discipline"*. The concept casts new light on the internal processes of cognition in students, and seeks to uncover not just cognitive building blocks along a linear trajectory of learning, but particular integrative experiences for students that transform not only their understanding of the subject itself, but potentially a deeper transformation of the student's world view generally.

The exploration of the idea of threshold concepts was sparked initially by inquiry into those particular points at which students commonly become 'stuck' when encountering a new educational discipline or discourse. Earlier descriptions of this process referred to these difficult thresholds as a form of 'troublesome knowledge' that represented particular barriers to a student's further progress in a given subject or discipline (Perkins, 1999, p. 10). It has been observed that a failure to adequately deal with these thresholds leaves a student with little option but to attempt to continue to learn in a fragmented fashion. (Meyer and Land, 2005, pp. 2–3).

To obtain an understanding of what is new about the theory of threshold concepts it is necessary to first distinguish this idea from more familiar educational notions like core concepts, fundamental concepts or conceptual building blocks. These are in fact related to threshold concepts but the key difference lies not so much in the content of the concepts identified, but in the understanding of the cognitive responses required of students to successfully integrate a given concept.

Meyer and Land (2003, p. 4) observe that a *"core concept is a conceptual building block' that progresses understanding of the subject; it has to be understood but does not necessarily lead to a qualitatively different view of the subject matter."*

Conversely, threshold concepts are identified as possessing a transformative character. Until a student successfully 'grasps' or passes through the threshold concept, the ongoing accumulation of knowledge may lack context, meaning or significance and may simply be encountered as a bizarre mass of seemingly unrelated information.

Meyer and Land (2003, pp. 4–5) go on to list five significant features that exemplify their understanding of threshold concepts, paraphrased as follows.

Threshold concepts are:

a) *transformative*, in that once understood the potential effect on student learning is to occasion a shift in the perception of the subject, or part thereof and at times possibly also a shift in personal world view or personal identity;

b) *irreversible*, (probably) in that the new perspective is unlikely to be forgotten, or unlearned, but the previous perspective itself is quite likely to be forgotten.

They point to studies that show the difficulty that expert practitioners have in looking back across thresholds they have long since crossed and attempting to understand (untransformed) student perspectives;

c) *integrative*, in that it exposes the previously hidden interrelatedness of material;

d) *bounded*, (possibly)in the sense that any one threshold concept will have terminal frontiers bordering with thresholds to other ideas or other distinct disciplines; and

e) potentially *troublesome,* in that they represent those very barriers, or 'brick walls' that students reach in learning that can become 'make or break' moments.

Troublesomeness is a key feature of threshold concepts and a key feature of the current discussion as well. Precisely because of their transformative and irreversible effects upon student world views, students can be expected to experience quite a deal of resistance. This resistance may vary in intensity depending upon whether the transformation contradicts deeply held or even cherished belief systems of the student or is merely counter-intuitive in a surprising but not specifically threatening way.

Perkins (1999, pp. 8–10) identifies four forms of troublesome knowledge. The two most significant for our present purposes are his descriptions of 'conceptually difficult knowledge' (counter-intuitive knowledge), and 'foreign knowledge' (knowledge representing perspectives foreign to the student's worldview). Meyer and Land (2003, p. 7) also add a further category—that of 'tacit knowledge'—to refer to complex knowledge that contains paradoxes, seeming inconsistencies or at least subtle distinctions, particularly where these are based upon un-stated assumptions within the discourse.

These forms of troublesome knowledge effectively give rise to the presence of difficult-to-traverse threshold issues within a subject, discipline or discourse. The term, 'threshold issues', as used here describes a step prior to the integration of a threshold concept. The threshold issue represents the resistance of the student to the troublesome knowledge being presented, and the threshold concept represents the eventual resolution of that issue through a conceptual understanding that breaks through the prior resistance. In this sense, successful threshold experiences represent a particularly powerful form of what Gibbs (1992) refers to as 'deep learning'.

An alertness to the presence of potential threshold issues, the need for students to traverse these issues as threshold concepts and a willingness to explore techniques to facilitate this transformative process holds great promise for improving the effectiveness of higher education generally. There is however, a corresponding need to be cautious. The potential ethical dilemmas in designing curriculum to inculcate students to new world views should not be approached lightly.

LOADED KNOWLEDGE

For the purposes of the current discussion, it is useful to identify a further form of troublesome knowledge, which could be described as 'loaded knowledge', which is where the discipline itself attempts to mandate the acceptance of ideological or philosophical assumptions which privilege certain world views over plausible alternatives. As this is new term it requires some explanation.

Loaded knowledge does not refer simply to information or content that contains embedded world views, as it is to be assumed that almost all content contains such elements. It refers only to those particular situations in which the discipline appears to be demanding unquestioned acceptance of a contingent perspective as a precondition to success in the discipline.

Instances of loaded knowledge are not likely to be prominently identified by the discipline itself either. It is in the nature of loaded knowledge that the requirement for unquestioning acceptance is *sub silento*. Indeed if we recall Meyer and Lands description of learning transformations as being irreversible *"in that the new perspective is unlikely to be forgotten, or unlearned, but the previous perspective itself is quite likely to be forgotten"* it is highly likely that teachers within the discipline will be unaware of the presence of loaded knowledge.

What is perceived as loaded knowledge could well differ from person to person because one is only likely to perceive it when it contradicts a strongly held personal perspective. To stay with law as an example, common law legal systems reflect hundreds of years of English history and culture and are structured around deeply embedded world views about individuality, personal volition, property, justice, reasonableness and standards of care, all of which may be loaded knowledge for students, particularly those from different cultural backgrounds.

Finally, there may be good reasons why a particular discipline chooses to adopt the worldview that it has, (biology and evolution for instance) and this critique does not suggest that they should be jettisoned, but rather that every effort should be made to identify such assumptions, and make it explicit that the discipline proceeds from such an assumption. To return to the legal discipline again, the assumption that individuals are independent moral agents is usually presented as an unquestioned ontological truth rather than simply as a deeply held assumption of common law legal systems. The question is not about whether it is essential for a communitarian student for example to understand that the common law perceives humans as ontologically separable individuals, but whether the discipline has become so closed to alternative perspectives that students find no opportunity to critique the world view and feel compelled to internalise the discipline's world view in place of their own prior equally plausible perspectives.

LOADED KNOWLEDGE IN LEGAL EDUCATION: 'THINKING LIKE A LAWYER'

It may be that law more than, for example, physical science is likely to contain more ideologically loaded messages, but this only serves to make it a fruitful place to begin a critique of an issue that has at least some relevance to all disciplines.

Law is famous for its specialised language (jargon) and for the peculiar forms of reasoning (legal reasoning) that are routinely employed. A practice often used by legal educators that aptly illustrates the transformations required of aspiring law students is that of training students to 'think like a lawyer'. This idea is pervasive particularly in first year text and materials, and the quotation below explicitly links this 'transformed thinking' to academic success:

The sooner you learn the intellectual skill of legal analysis, the sooner you will start to 'think like a lawyer'. Thinking like a lawyer is a guarantee of good marks... (Brognan and Spencer, 2004, p. 3)

The very idea of teaching students to think like a lawyer invokes the idea that students need to transform their thought processes and it confirms the existence of a counter intuitive discourse that is central to the disciplines' self image. Specifically 'legal' forms of thinking and analysis become not only essential tools of practice, but key and often exalted aspects of professional identity for the trained (and transformed) legal thinker. Lying beneath the surface rules in the legal discipline are deeply embedded and mostly unconscious assumptions about the ordering of the social, political and economic world.

Harvard University Professor of Law, Duncan Kennedy aptly described the colonising aspect of legal education as follows:

(A) lot of what happens (at law school) is the inculcation through a formal curriculum and the classroom experience of a set of political attitudes toward the economy and society in general...(Kennedy, 1982, p. 42)*...(L)aw school teaching makes the choice of hierarchy and domination, which is implicit in the adoption of the rules of property, contract, and tort look as though it flows from and is required by legal reasoning rather than being a matter of politics and economics...*(Kennedy, 1982, p. 45).

The colonising character of legal knowledge is of special concern when 'thinking like a lawyer' amounts to a demand that a student should jettison personal political, social or even cultural values and internalise a new, but largely uncritical world view. Students could of course be triggered into critical thinking by being confronted by counter-intuitive models of legal reasoning, except for the fact that traditional legal education usually discourages such a response.

There is however no reason why an understanding of the transformative nature of student learning should generate despair in those of us who remain committed to critical education in law or in any other discipline. On the contrary, it provides a powerful opportunity to identify and tackle the colonising tendencies of our disciplines at the deepest cognitive level and intentionally design educational experiences that allow students to identify and critique the very assumptions that are hidden or embedded in the world view of the discipline. At its simplest, what is required is to encourage students to view their discipline from the perspective of an outsider.

A CRITICAL EDUCATORS APPROACH TO LOADED KNOWLEDGE

Educators—at least those who are conscious of and concerned about the potential for discipline-specific indoctrination—have an opportunity to design curriculum to expose the hidden assumptions of the discipline? Ironically, it is these 'critical' educators who are most likely to be viewed by their more conservative colleagues as being engaged in some form of indoctrination. This irony does bear some examination though. We need to be clear about what is meant by designing a critical curriculum. A curriculum that simply aims to indoctrinate students into an alternative belief system that is critical of the status quo is not necessarily any less colonising in its effect upon students. Brookfield (1987) has produced a workable concept of what critical education involves that can be used to examine ways of optimising the intersection of the threshold concepts approach to higher education with an underlying commitment to critical learning.

According to Brookfield (1987, pp. 7–9), the aim of a critical educator should be to provide students with information and experiences that allow students to uncover for themselves the hidden assumptions in the subject matter, this offers students an Archimedean place to stand as they encounter troublesome, counter-intuitive and loaded concepts. A key requirement for an effective strategy to foster critical thinking in adult learners then involves finding ways to provoke others into a new examination of underlying assumptions (Brookfield, 1987, p. 90).

There are actually significant parallels between the processes that Brookfield describes as being essential for critical learning, and the cognitive processes described by Meyer and Land, for example, Brookfield (1987, p. 25), and more recently Mezirow (1997, p. 10) argue that the process of challenging assumptions is usually associated with 'trigger experiences" in which discrepancies between our assumptions and some new information about the world triggers doubt, dis-orientation and ultimately (hopefully) resolution and perspective change. They further argue that teachers can serve as powerful motivators for critical thinking through their enthusiastic presentation of alternative ideas, concepts and interpretative frameworks (Brookfield, 1987, p. 33).

There appear to be at least two distinct sets of assumptions then that need to be challenged to promote truly critical education, one is the prior assumptions of the student, but the other (and most often neglected) is the challenge to the assumptions inherent in the discipline itself. The process of challenging the students own assumptions is a different discussion, what is important here is that—in the process of challenging the students assumptions—the door is left open to also identify and challenge those that are dearest to the discipline.

The educator is in no way absent from this process of challenging assumptions. If we accept that as expert practitioners in the discipline we may have already been indoctrinated by loaded knowledge, then it requires an especially open mind to seriously engage in the process of locating, exposing and critiquing the assume-ptions of our chosen discipline. Such a process is vital for critical education. The educator's own critical reflexivity depends upon such openness and it also produces an atmosphere that invites students to encounter new and potentially confronting critiques as a means of stimulating the students own processes of questioning.

What remains is to attempt to explore how all of this fine sounding theory can actually be put in to practice to successfully teach in a discipline whilst at the same time critiquing its foundational assumptions.

CASE STUDY: DESIGNING A CRITICAL CURRICULUM FOR
FIRST YEAR LAW STUDENTS

This case study relates to some practical experiences in designing critical curricula for first year law students and reveals the possibility of reorienting legal curricula so that the challenging of students' assumptions and challenging and exposing the assumptions of the legal discipline become enmeshed.

This case study tracks the development of two new introductory subjects for first year law students at an Australian University. The two subjects were intentionally designed to stimulate a critical response to some of the most basic assumptions that underlie legal education. What follows is a brief summary of the design and delivery process and analysis of the outcomes based upon feedback from students within the cohort.[1]

Certainly one thing that became apparent from the process is that to be effective, critical education requires the application of strategy and design, based on as much information about the students attributes as is possible to collect.

The strategic approach utilised can be summarised as including the following four steps:

i) Identify the relevant attributes of the learner cohort.
ii) Identify the sites of likely resistance to new concepts.
iii) Provoke fundamental challenge to discipline-specific assumptions.
iv) Design learning experiences to facilitate transformation and promote critical literacy.

IDENTIFYING THE ATTRIBUTES OF THE STUDENT COHORT

The student cohort was a moderately large group of students commencing law study at a regional university in Australia. A baseline survey was designed to gather some basic demographic information about the cohort.

Table 1. (Source: Thiriet, 2005)

First year law student cohort statistics, 2005.	% of Cohort
Under 18 Years of age	35%
18–20	38.8%
Under 25 combined	75.7%
Immediate school leavers	54.4%
First time at University	78.6%
HSC as highest prior education	74.8%

These results revealed a cohort of predominantly young people, with little prior university experience. The development of critical literacy would need to be targeted to this level.

A further set of questions sought answers to socially and politically oriented attitudinal questions.

Table 2. (Source: Thiriet, 2005)

Question 31: Multiple Choice What I think of the relationship between law and justice	
Answers	*Percent Answered*
the law has nothing to do with justice	1.9%
the law has little to do with justice	6.8%
the law attempts to deliver justice	86.4%
the law is nearly always just	1.9%
I don't know	2.9%
Unanswered	<0.0%

Question 32: Multiple Choice I think Australia's system of government is	
Answers	*Percent Answered*
a fair system where all people are treated equally	5.8%
a mostly fair system that tries to compensate for inequality	60.2%
a flawed system where access to justice is not equal at all	23.3%
a system that routinely mistreats underprivileged groups	3.9%
other...specify	1.9%
I don't know	4.9%
Unanswered	<0.0%

Question 35: Multiple Choice If I strongly disagreed with a particular law I would	
Answers	*Percent Answered*
obey it anyway and take no action	8.7%
obey it and work to have it changed	72.7%
disobey it and work to have it changed	2.9%
just disobey it and hope not to get caught	3.9%
openly disobey it	1.0%
openly disobey it and encourage others to openly disobey it	4.9%
I don't know	5.8%
Unanswered	<0.0%

These surveys revealed a significant orientation toward social justice[2], and some concern about the rights of minority groups[3] On the other hand the surveys revealed, a high level of underlying approval of Australia's current legal and political arrangements, (Q31, 32 above), and a strong sense of obedience to law even when disagreed with (Q35 above).

IDENTIFYING THE SITES OF LIKELY RESISTANCE TO NEW CONCEPTS

Attitudinal surveys such as these are invaluable in giving a subject designer some insight beyond personal intuition about the areas where students are likely to experience the kind of resistance, disturbance and confrontation that would be likely to trigger a critical response. A key conclusion of the author based upon the findings (not all of which can be discussed here) was that whilst students were already open to critique the Australian legal and political system from within – as requiring minor reform or modification, to address social injustice, minority disadvantage or the power of big business – they were likely to resist and experience significant discomfort if exposed to a deeper questioning of its underlying foundations. The design conclusions that were drawn from this were that it was vital to take students beyond these comfortable boundaries, to challenge their underlying assumptions and to hopefully provoke critical thinking in relation to the legal and political system.

It was also necessary for this project to challenge not only the students' prior assumptions, but more importantly to challenge some of the deeper assumptions usually embedded in the discipline's world view.

DESIGNING LEARNING EXPERIENCES TO FACILITATE TRANSFORMATION

Brookfield's (1987, p. 26) description of 'trigger events' that stimulate critical reflection and Meyer and Land's (2003, p.1) description of troublesome knowledge that can precipitate student transformation both suggest that learning experiences that deliberately target points of resistance are likely to be the most powerful in provoking a critical response. When applied to the content of the subjects concerned it was predicted that students would be most challenged when provoked to deeply question:

i) existing assumptions about the legitimacy of centralised legal authority; and (to a lesser degree)

ii) the usefulness of law as a tool for social control.

These two ideas could be described as the most likely threshold issues that the students would be challenged to traverse in the process of developing a critical approach to legal phenomena and so were developed as key themes not only of content but more importantly of experiential classroom activities. Fortunately, the attitudinal surveys had suggested that students' prior attitudes could be challenged simultaneously with challenging two important foundational assumptions of the legal discipline.

It is important to understand how radical such a challenge is within traditional legal education. One of the most common criticisms of traditional legal education is the tendency to treat lawful authority and legitimacy as a given (Goldring, 1987, p. 159). The combination of students with little pre-existing inclination to question the fundamental foundations of the legal system with a traditional legal educational approach that puts such questions firmly out of bounds is a classical example of why so much legal education could be described as anti-critical by nature.

Any strategy designed to foster critical literacy in law students would do well to challenge this comfortable orthodoxy before it takes root in students' minds. To this extent the design for the subject in question contained a threshold concept that is usually deliberately absent from positivist legal education—namely the idea that all authority is questionable. Similarly, the idea that law is useful as a tool for social control is almost never seriously questioned in law school.

The first semester subject provided an ideal entry point for a deep questioning of the legitimacy of centralised authority, and of the various 'stories' that have traditionally been employed to legitimate claims of sovereign power and authority such as magic, religion, nobility, social contract and ultimately democracy.

Tutorials were designed to incorporate small group work in which students would be encouraged to reflect on personal experience, express opinions and 'learn by doing' through experiential class activities. Consistent with their focus upon the integration of troublesome knowledge, the tutorials were often designed to be surprising, provocative or confronting, for this reason the actual exercises were often not revealed to students until they arrived in class. Some tutorials required students to collectively draw up power maps, or to engage in role playing exercises specifically designed to encourage integration of the important critical idea (probably a threshold concept) that systems of centralised authority use 'stories' to legitimate power.

The second semester subject maintained the critical focus, but this time upon the theme of the limitations of law as a tool for social regulation. The main strategy for achieving this was to construct the subject around a series of case studies of areas in which legal regulation had been demonstrably problematic (or even unsuccessful). These included drug prohibition, anti terror law, regulation of corporate power and environmental regulation.

It is a fortunate coincidence that the design project related to first year law subjects. These subjects offer great opportunities for deep questioning because there is a strategic advantage to introducing a critical approach from the outset of a student's engagement with the discipline. Confirmation of this was found in the fact that the most strident criticisms of the new approach came from students who had prior experience with law study.

GROUND TRUTHING THE THEORY: OUTCOMES, OBSERVATIONS AND FEEDBACK

It is difficult to measure levels of critical provocation, but the first semester certainly produced some significant displays of discomfort and resistance by students to what was perceived as the radical content of lectures and tutorials. This discomfort fortunately was largely expressed through communication with the presenters which provided an opportunity to reassure students that although a pointedly critical and sceptical approach to current institutions and belief systems was being adopted, that the subject did not require students to adopt any specific alternative belief systems. This is an essential classroom atmospheric if real deeper learning and critical literacy is to be achieved (Brookfield, 1987, p. 72). A student perception that the presenters required students to 'regurgitate' particular opinions would negate the critical value of presenting provocative perspectives.

Somewhat surprisingly (for the author) students with strongly held conservative belief systems (at least those who chose to communicate on the issue) accepted reassurances that the subject did not mandate particular belief systems, but did mandate a preparedness to question dominant explanations for power and authority.

The following extract is from an email sent by a student (for which permission to reproduce has been obtained):

This whole year you have taught me to think and not just to learn facts. You have also challenged me to consider my views and not necessarily whether they are right or wrong but to at least think about the reasoning behind why we (I) have particular views on things...I am not saying that I agree with what you say and generally you can tell that I don't agree, but ultimately you have captured my interest in law by making it thought provoking.

In terms of what has been the greatest catalyst, I would have to say simply having my ideologies challenged has had the greatest influence & the greatest challenge...So for now I will probably continue remembering this year as the year I "learned to think"... It has definitely changed me as a person.

Perhaps surprisingly, whilst some students definitely did find the materials confronting and experienced high levels of resistance at least initially, a greater number responded more positively to new and surprising ideas and experienced the engagement mostly as stimulating rather than as specifically confronting.[4] This indicates that the students were generally a lot more open to deeper questioning than may have at first been assumed. It also confirms Brookfield's (1987) argument that experiences that trigger critical thinking need not always be negative.

STUDENT FEEDBACK SURVEYS

Student feedback surveys[5] were designed to gather feedback from students on their own learning experiences. The second learners experience survey that was conducted towards the end of the second semester was designed to evaluate the effectiveness of the strategy for promoting deep learning, critical literacy and transformational learning.

It is of course very difficult to design surveys to measure whether students have been transformed, have become deep or self reflexive learners or have developed critical literacy. It was all the more difficult to design survey instruments that could adequately address such issues within the compressed time frame within which the subjects were designed, delivered and evaluated for the purposes of this study (less than two years). During that time it was not only the students' understandings of the learning process that was rapidly developing and transforming but also that of the author and all of the teaching staff involved. The process of teaching, learning, evaluation, reflection and re-experimentation was ongoing throughout the study period. Longitudinal study for example was not possible. The surveys provide only a snapshot of the recorded experiences of one group of learners during a single year of delivery. Nonetheless, the surveys in general elicit students own descriptions of their learning experiences and so provide a useful insight into students perceptions of their learning and their own processes of personal transformation.

Table 3. (Source: Ricketts, 2007)

1. Has your experience in studying these subjects changed the way you look at the world?

a) not at all:	3%
b) only to a minor extent:	12%
c) to a significant extent:	51.5%
d) in fundamental ways:	32.8%

2. Has your experience in studying these two subjects changed the way you view particular legal issues?

e) not at all:	4.6%
f) only to a minor extent:	4.7%
g) to a significant extent:	67.2%
h) in fundamental ways:	23.4%

3. Do you find yourself reflecting upon the issues covered in these subjects in your own time outside of class?

a) not at all:	3%
b) rarely	9.3%
c) frequently	68.7%
d) almost constantly	18.8%

TRANSFORMATION

Given the employment of threshold concept theories to promote the development of critical literacy in students in this project, the question of transformation is of key importance. Certainly the students' responses to Q1 of the Semester 2 learners experience questionnaire indicate a very high *sense* of transformation within the student cohort. This result is one of the most powerful confirmations to arise from the data that the subject design strategy was successful in having a transforming effect on students. Put together, the results indicate that 84.2% of students reported that the experience of studying the two subjects significantly or fundamentally changed the way they viewed the world. That 32.8% of students would describe themselves as having fundamentally changed the way they viewed the world is an astonishing outcome, even taking various statistical uncertainties into account.

These conclusions are however further supported by a range of statements offered by students in response to open survey questions (Ricketts, 2007).

I now question things more… everyday I am less of a caterpillar and more of a butterfly!!

I have… developed an approach where I look at both sides of the coin, think outside the square and also take in new and potentially more abstract ideas that I would not have thought about before.

I look deeper into the reason behind the way the world is and why.

The biggest change that I have noticed is a newly found ability to think critically... I look at all the different views on the subject and form my own opinion.

More thoughtful, more compassionate...more sceptical...I look at law in a new way.

DEVELOPMENT OF KEY ATTRIBUTES OF DEEP LEARNING AND CRITICAL THINKING

Transformation on its own is however an ambiguous quality. It has already been noted that transformations can constrain critical thinking just as much as they can promote it. Consequently, an important further question is whether the design strategy was also successful in developing key attributes of critical thinking and deep learning.

Gibbs (1992, chapter 1) observes that as students develop a deeper approach to learning, their descriptions of the learning process move from describing learning as memorising and acquiring facts, towards an understanding of learning as entailing uncovering meaning, and even understanding the world generally in different ways. The learner experience questionnaire provides very useful data because it specifically asks students to describe in their own words what they consider deep learning to be (Q4). The range of common responses showed a marked emphasis upon 'higher order' functions such as critiquing, cross relating and understanding underlying concepts.

Table 4. (Source: Ricketts, 2007)

1. Briefly describe your understanding of 'deep learning'. *The following terms most frequently appeared in students written responses (some students mentioned several of these).*	
Understanding	(42.1%)
Applying/ cross-relating information	(29.6%)
Developing ones own opinions:	(20.3%)
Critiquing analysing:	(15.6%)
Understanding foundational or underlying concepts:	(12.5%)
Reflecting	(3.1%)

2. Do you believe that you have had the opportunity to engage in deep learning in this subject?	
Yes	79.6%
No:	4.6%
Other (includes equivocal and unanswered):	15.8%

These results are consistent with a group of students moving away from a content centred and shallow approach to learning towards what Gibbs describes as a deep approach. Gibbs (1992, chapter 1) identifies "learning as understanding reality' in which the students perception of the world changes as being the most sophisticated level of deep learning. This transformational character of learning is also of course fundamentally important to Meyer and Land's (2003, p. 1) description of learning as passing though 'thresholds'.

Brookfield (1987, pp. 7–9) identifies four key components of critical thinking to include:

i)   Identifying and challenging assumptions
ii) Challenging the importance of context
iii) Imagining and exploring alternatives
iv) The development of reflective scepticism

Whilst the questions were not specifically designed to correspond to Brookfield's schema, student responses to the survey questions still produced a strong indication of the development of these key attributes. In particular, students' responses to Q7 strongly correlate to the kinds descriptions employed by Brookfield. The following responses were extracted and grouped together as representative of significant attributes that broadly correlate to the challenging of assumptions, development of sceptical world view and openness to explore alternatives.

Table 5. (Source: Ricketts, 2007)

7. Briefly describe any new approaches to life, law or learning that you have developed this year.	
The following descriptions were the most commonly used:	
Becoming more questioning:	(20.3%)
Becoming more critical	(14.4%)
Developing new and changed perspective	(12.5%)
Developing own opinions:	(10.9%)
Becoming more sceptical	(9.36%)
Becoming more broad minded	(7.8%)
Looking more deeply into things:	(4.7%)
Thinking about issues outside of class more	(4.7%
Becoming more aware:	(3.1%)
Being more interested in current events	(3.1%)

Whilst the percentages attached to each selected response could be misleading, in that some students nominated several of the key terms, the overall percentage of students who recorded at least one of the responses presented above was 70.3%.

These results give further definition to the changed ways of looking at the world recorded by 84.2% of the cohort in question 1.

CONCLUSION

The data presented above certainly demonstrates that the particular design methodology adopted in this project was highly successful in achieving its stated strategic aims of fostering both a deep approach to learning and the development of critical literacy in first year law students. Such an outcome is of great practical significance as a model for the development of critical education. There are however much deeper lessons to be learnt from these outcomes.

It appears inevitable that studying law will involve encounters with troublesome and counter intuitive ideas and with loaded knowledge and that one way or another law students are likely to be changed by the experience. The challenge for educators, is to decide whether education should be openly self critical even of its own discipline or simply impose closed intellectual and value systems upon its students.

There is much to be gained for students, educators, the disciplines and the professions in producing graduates who are sceptically aware of the assumptions and values upon which their discipline is built. The first necessary step of course is for the educators themselves to become self critical. The process of 'uncovering assumptions' that Brookfield identifies as being fundamental to critical practice requires not only an understanding of the assumptions inherent in the discipline, (as a phenomena external to ourselves) but also of the way that we, as scholars have probably already consciously or unconsciously internalised those assumptions as part of our own education. The challenge for educators is to remain critically reflexive, whilst also ensuring that the threshold experiences that students traverse are presented in a way that expands rather than inhibits the capacity for ongoing critical practice.

It is intended that this study testifies to both, the need for promoting critical thinking in legal and other education as well as providing some practical methodology for achieving this outcome.

NOTES

[1] Ricketts A (2005) Learners Experience Survey 2: Results. (unpublished) Q 15: Over 60% students surveyed listed a concern for social justice as a reason for studying law.

[2] Ricketts A (2005) Learners Experience Survey 2: Results. (unpublished) Q 33: Only 16.5 % felt that the will of the majority should be paramount.

[3] Second survey (not much mention of confronting)

[4] All surveys were conducted on the basis of anonymity, after obtaining the required consents from the participants.

REFERENCES

Brookfield, S. (1987). *Developing critical thinkers: Challenging adults to explore alternative ways of thinking and acting*. San Francisco: Jossey Bass Publishers.

Brognan, M., & Spencer, D. (2004). *Surviving law school*. Melbourne, VIC: Oxford University Press.

Thiriet, D. (2005). *First year experience baseline survey: Results*. Townsville, QLD: James Cook University (unpublished).

Gibbs, G. (1992). *Improving the quality of student learning*. Bristol, UK: Technical and Educational Services Ltd.

Gibbs, G. (1995). *Assessing student centred courses*. Oxford, UK: Oxford Brookes University.

Goldring, J. (1987). The place of legal theory in the law school—A comment. *Bulletin of the Australian Society of Legal Philosophy, 11*(42), 159.

Kennedy, D. (1982). Legal education as training for Hierarchy. In D. Kairys (Ed.), *The politics of law: A progressive critique* (pp. 38–58). New York: Pantheon Books.

Meyer, J., & Land, R. (2003). 'Threshold concepts and troublesome knowledge'. In *Enhancing Teaching and Learning Project University of Edinburgh, Occasional Report 4*. Retrieved September 5, 2006, from http://www.ed.ac.uk/etl/publications.html

Meyer, J., & Land, R. (2005). Threshold concepts and troublesome knowledge (3): Implications for course design and evaluation. In C. Rust (Ed.), *Improving student learning: diversity and inclusivity*. Oxford: Oxford Centre for Staff and Learning Development.

Meyer, J., & Land, R. (2006). *Overcoming barriers to student understanding threshold concepts and troublesome knowledge*. London: Routledge.

Mezirow, J. (1997, Summer). Transformative learning: Theory to practice. *New Directions for Continuing and Adult Education, 74*, 5–12.

Perkins, D. (1999). The many faces of constructivism. *Educational Leadership, 57*(3), 6–12.

Ricketts, A. (2007). *Crossing thresholds in legal education: Transgressing boundaries to promote critical literacy*. Unpublished postgraduate thesis available upon request. Retrieved from ricketts_a @vanuatu.usp.ac.fj

Aidan Ricketts
School of Law
University of the South Pacific
PMB 9072 Port Vila
Vanuatu

RAY LAND AND JAN H.F. MEYER

4. THRESHOLD CONCEPTS AND TROUBLESOME KNOWLEDGE (5):

Dynamics of Assessment

INTRODUCTION

I am a part of all that I have met;
Yet all experience is an arch wherethro'
Gleams that untravell'd world whose margin fades
For ever and for ever when I move.
(Tennyson, *Ulysses*)

This paper considers the implications for assessment of the analytical framework of 'threshold concepts and troublesome knowledge' (Meyer and Land 2006). This framework points to the variation in progressive stages of a student's journey towards, through and beyond particular conceptual gateways. Such journeys involve passage through 'liminal' states of transformed understanding (Meyer and Land 2005). We have seen that knowledge can be troublesome for a variety of reasons. If the troublesome transformations occasioned by threshold concepts are important, and require a rather different way of looking at the curriculum, then it follows that such transformations will require a more nuanced and appropriate form of assessment. This will help us identify variation in progress and under-standing at preliminal, liminal, postliminal and subliminal stages of conceptual and epistemological fluency (Meyer, Land and Davies 2007). The liminal state is the point at which many students 'get stuck' and modes of assessment which can both identify and render visible sources of conceptual difficulty, at the point and time at which they are experienced, would seem to offer helpful forms of support to the learner.

A number of issues concern us. How might we construct a meaningful assessment process for students for whom, in many instances, what is to be assessed lies outside their prior knowledge and experience, or beyond their ontological horizon? How might we get away from traditional assessment regimes in which a student can produce the 'right' answer while retaining fundamental misconceptions? How might a more dynamic approach to assessment, rather than a static 'snapshot' approach, be practically achieved? How might the ontological shift required by threshold concepts be purposefully represented through assessment processes? Can assessment

J. H. F. Meyer, R. Land and C. Baillie (eds.), Threshold Concepts and
Transformational Learning, 61–79.

be optimised by employing threshold concepts as the focus of assessment at programme level? Used as a set of analytical lenses, it will be argued that these new modes of variation present an insightful conceptual basis for developing new and creative methods of assessment and alternative ways of rendering learning (and conceptual difficulty) visible.

THRESHOLD CONCEPTS AND ASSESSMENT

Earlier considerations of the nature of threshold concepts and their implications for course design point to a need:

1) to see how the acquisition by learners of threshold concepts can be usefully assessed, particularly in terms of the *dynamics of liminality*, and
2) how assessment practices can in turn be improved by a threshold concept-based approach.

These questions raise two further substantial issues meriting close consideration. One is how we construct a meaningful assessment process for students for whom, in many instances, what is to be assessed *lies outside their prior knowledge and experience*. These are the situations familiar to many practising teachers when the student 'just can't see it', when the conceptual portal has not yet been discerned or 'come into view', or, if it has, it has more the opaque semblance of a tombstone. In general, because of their transformative property, threshold concepts *by definition* involve a liminal journey in ontological terms, the outcome of which cannot be captured in terms of a simple snapshot. And herein lies the challenge for assessment. The ontological shift required for understanding that threshold concepts often occasion has not yet occurred (Meyer and Land 2005). As the English poet William Blake observed, 'As a man *[sic]* is, so will he see'. We are what we know.

The second important issue concerns how we might get away from traditional assessment regimes in which a student can produce the 'right' answer while retaining fundamental misconceptions. As Marek (1986) puts it, 'They misunderstand, but they'll pass'. The assumption, in the somewhat industrialised models of programme design which economic exigencies currently oblige us to adopt, that in a new module our learners commence, like athletes, from a common start-line, and that all those who achieve a basic pass mark of above, say, forty per cent, arrive collectively in a new conceptual space ready to countenance new conceptual thresholds, is, as we probably all privately acknowledge, untenable. Often learners pass a module and move on, to find themselves negotiating new conceptual complexity and transformation whilst still in a liminal state, or in a state of partial understanding from the previous module's encounter with troublesome knowledge. We know that learners often let go of parts of their prior conceptual stance and manage to meaningfully integrate certain elements of the new knowledge to be understood, but often are not able to accommodate other elements, which remain 'mapped' but not integrated (Kinchin and Hay 2000). And all of this whilst in a state of perhaps discomfiting ontological oscillation.

We have seen that knowledge can be troublesome for a variety of reasons (Perkins 2006). It might be alien, inert, tacit, conceptually difficult, counter-intuitive, characterised by an inaccessible 'underlying game', or equally inaccessible super-complexity. We have argued elsewhere (Meyer and Land 2006, Land, Meyer and Smith 2008) that such troublesomeness and disquietude is purposeful, as it is the provoker of change that cannot initially be assimilated, and hence is the instigator of new learning and new ontological possibility. However, if, as we maintain, the transformations occasioned by threshold concepts are important, and require a rather different way of looking at the curriculum, then it follows that such transformations will require a more nuanced and generative model of assessment to help us purposefully identify variation in progress and understanding between individual learners. So what might this more nuanced model entail?

ACKNOWLEDGING MODES OF VARIATION

The threshold concepts framework has pointed to variation in the spaces occupied in a student's journey towards, through and beyond particular conceptual gateways. States of conceptual transformation can vary at different points on this journey, and it would help both teachers and students to know in what way and at what point. Variation may occur, as we have suggested (Meyer, Land and Davies 2008), within conceptually discrete modes of preliminal, liminal, and postliminal episodes of conceptual and epistemological fluency. There is furthermore possible simultaneous variation within another *subliminal* mode; variation that occurs at the level of tacit knowledge of an 'underlying game' or a 'way of knowing' (episteme). The liminal space is where transformation takes place and needs to occur. It is also the space in which many students 'get stuck' or 'face the tombstone'.

Assessment repertoires, both external *and internal* to the student, which can isolate sources of conceptual difficulty, at the point and time at which it is experienced, would seem to offer helpful forms of support to the learner. This paper argues for a more nuanced model of assessment to help us distinguish between such different modes of variation, and assess student understanding and progress within them. More specifically such an approach helpfully identifies variation in how the portal initially 'comes into view', how it is initially perceived or apprehended, and with what cognitive and ontological mindset it may therefore be approached or withdrawn from. We refer to this mode of variation as *preliminal* variation. Similarly such an approach provides better insight into how the portal, that is the liminal space itself, is entered, occupied, negotiated and made sense of, passed through or not; that is, the dynamics of *liminal* variation.

Within this model we are also able to make informed observation and judgement of variation in the point and state of exit from the liminal state into a new conceptual space, and the epistemological and ontological terrain encountered from that point onwards. This constitutes *postliminal* variation indicating the trajectory of the student's future learning. We know from myriads of assessment data that students do not end up at the same finish line after a course is assessed. There is considerable *post-liminal variation* in students' level of new conceptual understanding and often much residual difficulty, misconception or partial understanding. This has obvious implications not only for the trajectory of the student's future learning, but also for the assumptions by their future teachers of what these students might already be expected to know.

Finally there is variation in the extent of students' awareness and understanding of an underlying game or episteme – a 'way of knowing' – which may be a crucial determinant of progression (epistemological or ontological) within a conceptual domain. Such tacit understanding or epistemic fluency might develop in the absence of any formalised knowledge of the concept itself; it might, for the learner, represent a non-specialist way of thinking as recent investigations by Pang and Meyer (work in progress) with schoolchildren studying Economics concepts clearly illustrate. Variation in such tacit epistemic fluency constitutes a pattern of *subliminal* variation. Perkins describes the episteme or 'the underlying game' as follows:

'...a system of ideas or way of understanding that allows us to establish knowledge...the importance of students understanding the structure of the disciplines they are studying. 'Ways of knowing' is another phrase in the same spirit. As used here, epistemes are manners of justifying, explaining, solving problems, conducting enquiries, and designing and validating various kinds of products or outcomes.' (Perkins 2006, p. 42)

Variation is defined here as the extent or degree to which individuals vary in performance and understanding. Variation is this viewed from the perspective of individual differences. It is assumed that such variation is amenable to observation and estimation in a measurable sense of dispersion (quantitative or qualitative).

We maintain, from analysis of empirical data gathered from UK-funded projects implementing the thresholds framework, that these modal distinctions offer an important set of dimensions of variation for teachers wishing to identify at which points, and in what ways, individual students might experience conceptual difficulty and experience barriers to their understanding. Used as a set of analytical lenses these modes of variation can present an insightful conceptual basis for developing new and creative methods of assessment and alternative ways of rendering learning (and conceptual difficulty) visible. This in turn can inform course (re)design in a generative and sustainable fashion.

RENDERING CONCEPTUAL UNDERSTANDING VISIBLE

We require a means of rendering the student's knowledge visible in some way in these modal spaces. The conceptual mapping research of Kinchin and Hay (2000) at King's College London is valuable in this respect in that it enables us to (a) discover what each student knows (rather than trying to anticipate it); (b) show *what* knowledge a student possesses, and illustrate *how* that knowledge is arranged in the student's mind; (c) move from traditional 'snapshot' testing which often focuses on isolated ideas rather than developmental thought or affective processes, and (d) recognise that some ideas may be resistant to change, but interrelationships with other ideas may be more fluid. These researchers use simple and fast visual concept-mapping techniques which externalise the causal links between students' ideas and thinking. These links serve to clarify which new elements might be appearing within the student's conceptual awareness, and which of these elements are being integrated or not in terms of developing internal cognitive schemata. This form of visual representation also allows us to perceive which aspects of the learner's prior conceptual stance are being 'let go of ', or reconfigured. This requires a technique which they term the *declarative approach*, and which requires students (and their teachers) to represent their current state of knowledge. This needs to be undertaken in a non-threatening fashion (peer groups seem to work extremely well) and leads to interesting dialogues as to why individual students see things in the particular way that they do. As Kinchin and Hay emphasise, drawing on Cohen (1987), there is a need here to monitor progress by revealing thought processes that generally remain private to the learner. So this protocol needs sensitive handling.

SELF EXPLANATION AND THE DYNAMICS OF ASSESSMENT

In similar vein, self explanation theory, after the seminal work by Chi, Bassok, Lewis, Reimann and Glaser (1989), and later work by Chi, deLeeuw, Chiu and Lavancher (1994), recognises that a dialogue with self (an act of 'talk aloud' explanation to self) in the context of problem solving (in Physics and Biology) embodies an externalised learning process that, like the work of Kinchin and Hay, is amenable to analysis and estimation. This process requires an explicit awareness of the dynamics of changed or changing understanding and, in theory at least, 'talk aloud' protocols should be capable of generating explanations of the dynamics involved (the variation) in reaching an understanding (or not) of threshold concepts.

We would argue that consideration of variation through the four modes of variation mentioned earlier, and their subsequent visualisation (or other forms of representation) through methods such as the declarative approach, as well those offered by self explanation theory, can open up an intriguing new research agendas and the development of new tools of estimation and analysis which might do much to alleviate the conceptual difficulty experienced by individual students within specific disciplinary settings. In pursuit of this aim it would be helpful to develop a more nuanced discourse or terminology to discuss the assessment of threshold concepts within courses in terms of following the movie of the personal journey rather than looking at snapshots of it. The next section of this paper attempts to address this issue.

SPEAKING OTHERWISE OF ASSESSMENT: SIGNIFICATION, STIMULUS, AND PROTOCOL (SSP)

The term 'assessment' when brought to bear on threshold concepts tends to refer in a particular way to a community of practice process of *estimation* (forming a measure or mental impression of something) which may include an element of *evaluation* (admitting subjectivity and value judgement, ethical and moral dimensions), as opposed to pretensions of objective measurement in the sense of 'rules' and 'scales'. (That is, crudely put, the purportedly reliable mechanisms by which inferences and judgements are reified and symbols or numbers are assigned to students 'answers' in terms of 'the marking schedule'.) Envisaging how a student might, for example, exhibit an ontological shift at the level of a snapshot 'upper second' (in the parlance of UK degree classification) seems a self-evidently pointless undertaking.

Signification

Signification can be viewed from the perspective of both the teacher and the student. It is for the teacher the process of communicating the impression of what the threshold (portal) is. But how does one communicate such an impression that lies *beyond* the ontological horizon of the student? In terms of modes of liminality, the answer to this question invites a consideration of where the student is positioned, and a recognition that there will be *individual differences* in this positioning.

Hence the notion that, as an act of pedagogy, *all* students will be able to apprehend the impression in the same intended way is therefore unsupportable. A one-size-fits-all statement of intended learning outcomes will simply not work. In the language of variation theory there can be no *discernment* (of the portal) without variation that foregrounds the *critical features* (of the portal). (Note that the term 'variation' in variation theory does not refer to individual differences.) So, as an act of pedagogy, in which mode(s) of liminality can this discernment (in variation) occur?

Stimulus

The stimulus is the mechanism that is employed (by the teacher, or the student in a self regulation of own learning) to evoke and externalise, in a manner amenable to estimation, the state of cognitive and ontological shift.

Protocol

The protocol defines the 'rules of the game' as typically enshrined in the repertoire of well established formative and summative assessment practices. We distinguish between the *response protocol* and the *estimation protocol*. If the stimulus is 'diagnose this patient's illness' in clinical medicine, 'write an essay' in, say, history, or 'set out a proof ' in mathematics, there is in all these examples a specific set of protocols to be followed in the response. This protocol furthermore has to be learned and enshrines disciplinary conventions of reasoning and explanation that have either to be explicitly learned as something new, or are already intuitively known to the student.

An important further point here is that the protocol itself *may also act as a signifier* of a required ontological shift. Consider an example from mathematics. It has been argued that the concept of 'proof' is a threshold concept.

It is common for new students to say that they 'like mathematics' but 'hate proofs'. For many proof technique is a difficult hurdle to overcome and has all of the hallmarks of a *threshold concept*, in the sense of Meyer and Land (2003, 2005). The ability to understand and construct proofs is *transformative*, both in perceiving old ideas and making new and exciting discoveries. It is *irreversible* and often accompanied by a 'road to Damascus' effect, not unlike a religious conversion or drug addiction. The most inspiring mathematical proofs are *integrative* and almost always expose some hidden *counter-intuitive* inter-relations. And of course they are *troublesome*: it can take a long time, even years, for students to learn to appreciate proofs and to develop sufficient technique to write their own proofs with confidence. Wrestling with and finally grasping the concept of proof 'becomes a rite of passage' (Bradbeer 2005), as a student seeks full membership of the mathematical community. (Easdown, 2007, p. 28.)

An issue here is the extent to which an intended *temporal* ontological aspect of the signifier can be apprehended by students otherwise engaged in what might simply be experienced as a ritualistic process of 'ruling out possibilities' in diagnosis, 'writing essays' or 'proving theorems'. How many times does a student have to interrogate historical texts before an ontological horizon appears – the dawning of the realisation of thinking like an historian? This is a crucial point that we need to ponder. What is the role of estimation, of making appropriate inferences, in this crucial process of extended liminality? The protocol may represent a signifier *yet to be apprehended* in terms beyond mimicry. Here it might be the necessity of demonstrating a proof. In other contexts it might be the requirement to offer a critical perspective, justify an ethical stance, or construct a conceptual framework or legal argument.

A CASE STUDY – THE CONCEPT OF INTERFEROMETRY

An articulate illustration of such 'a signifier yet to be apprehended' is provided by Sinclair (2004). In her autoethnographic doctoral study of how students acquire discourse she, formerly trained as a philosopher, kept an analytical journal of her participation in the unfamiliar territory of being a student on a taught programme in Engineering. The particular protocol discussed here, was 'to explain and use the concept of interferometry'.

In many of the cases of difficulties with new concepts and procedures, most of these were eventually overcome, at least to the extent that I could work effectively with them and achieve the associated 'learning outcomes'. There were some expressions, however, that were never understood to the extent that they could be reproduced other than by paraphrasing. One of these was 'interferometry' – a method of measurement using a combination of similar rays of light. (Sinclair, 2004, p. 298)

An extract from her learning journal, included here with the author's permission[1], exhibits the frustration associated with this protocol.

4 March 1999

[the resolution of a vocabulary problem, associated with 'interference' from everyday language]
Still struggling to understand interferometry and in trying to get help from *The Shorter Oxford* have realised that the word 'fringe' has a technical use I need to get to grips with, one of a series of alternate light and dark bands produced by a diffraction-grating. I had understood 'fringe' to refer to the overall pattern, particularly the edge of it…

[questions to do with the procedure itself]
My problem seems to be that there are too many steps to this process – some related to the final condition required for the measurement and some relating to what you need to do to produce light that is in this condition.…
10 minutes later. Still don't understand. Some questions:
What's actually being measured? How?
A – the slip gauge.
By the reflection of the wave of light?
Using known frequency?
Now go back to the original and see whether the maths can be explained in these terms. Why do the rays have to recombine?

[a problem to do with the teacher's instruction]
I was also thrown by the instruction to ignore the final pages of the maths as in fact those contain the explanation or part of it…

[concern with my self-esteem and relationship with other students]
There is also a calculation here about pay-off. I do have to pass this, but I could get away with plagiarism or clever paraphrasing. Other students (A especially) have offered to help. It has become a challenge for various reasons…

[a problem to do with the way information was presented – and this seemed a particularly significant observation at the time and later]
Still struggled with interferometry – spent 90 minutes on it this afternoon with the time just flying by. Sometimes the key information you need is hidden in a whole load of text – e.g. that it is the displacement that is being measured.

Figure 1. Sinclair Journal Extract 34: Attributing causes of barriers (Sinclair, 2004, p. 299)[1]

She identifies, at various times during the struggles of one long day, a range of barriers to her understanding and progress. She attributes these to:
– the complexity of the procedure itself
– the unfamiliar environment (a laboratory)
– interference from everyday vocabulary
– misleading instruction

- attitude – conflict between instrumentalism (and using other students' answers) and desire to 'just see'
- the lack of practical application
- insufficient use in context by the community of practice.

This concurs with Eraut's observation (2008) that conceptual acquisition is often a process of 'overt explanation and tacit acculturation' followed by repeated personal use in a variety of appropriate contexts. Here we see the learner in a troubled liminal state provoked by the concept of interferometry and striving to make sense of the protocol. ('Still don't understand. Some questions: What's actually being measured? How?'). Finally, as a coping mechanism, she acknowledges her own retreat into mimicry. 'In the end', she says, 'I ran out of time and had to paraphrase the answer without really understanding what I was writing' (p. 301). There is a telling ontological dimension to this troublesome concept regarding her 'concern with my self-esteem and relationship with other students' (p. 299). The example also throws revealing light on the discursive aspects of threshold concepts. She links her observation that 'lack of practical application and insufficient use in context might also have contributed to the problem' (p. 300) to Vygotsky's explanation of how a scientific concept develops.

'the development of the corresponding concept is not completed but only beginning at the moment a new word is learned. The new word is not the culmi-nation but the beginning of the development of a concept. The gradual, internal development of the word's meaning leads to the maturation of the word itself.' (Vygotsky, 1934/1987, p. 241)

Sinclair notes that the issue, or absence of, context subsumed all the other causes of difficulty in her understanding. 'More contextual associations' she observes; 'such as additional uses and talk about interferometers could have overcome all the other barriers' (p. 300). Elsewhere in her journal, when encountering difficulty with the engineering concept of 'enthalpy' she observes that:

It was not a dictionary that provided the main step forward in understanding 'enthalpy', but an additional (and practical) application of the notion in an appropriate context. The barrier was removed when further exposure to the word/sign in context rendered its meaning clear...My attempt to pin down a meaning through using a dictionary was not going to take me far in actual engineering discourse, which depends on the interplay of context and the culturally specific practice of engineers using the concept of enthalpy. (Sinclair, 2004, p. 216)

The Sinclair journal is a nice illustration of self-explanation theory mentioned earlier, and of a relatively unstructured protocol of 'talking aloud', or, in this instance, 'writing aloud'. The extracts cited here also powerfully demonstrate the issue running through this piece that what is to be assessed, and even how it might be assessed, is not necessarily 'seen' by the student, even in cases, as here, when a visual demonstration is provided. 'This is a metaphorical use of see,' argues Sinclair, 'meaning to discern and understand all the aspects of a phenomenon simultaneously in order to use that knowledge' (p. 302).

The teaching about interferometry was conducted in a lab with us all crowded round the interferometer. Here was our opportunity to see in the non-metaphorical sense – to observe with our own eyes what happened when certain measurements were being taken. The use of the interferometer was simply a demonstration of how it worked; all we apparently had to do for our assessment (or 'learning outcome') was describe what we 'saw'. While the context was a technical one, it might be expected that we would all 'see' the same thing in the same way – the way that the lecturer wanted us to see it as he talked us through his demonstration. (p. 303)

That however proved to be an erroneous presumption. The phenomenon had not come into view for the learner as it remained, in terms of the threshold concepts analytical framework, beyond her ontological horizon, and in Vygotskian theory, beyond the zone of proximal development. Sinclair compares her own experience with that reported by Säljö and Bergqvist (1997) of secondary school physics students purportedly 'discovering' the properties of light. Again this is not just a question of the students registering self-evident sense data from optical equipment and deriving some form of 'natural' meaning from this, but rather a situation in which the properties being observed required further 'discursive resources' on the part of the students for the properties to be 'seen'. The equipment itself, Sinclair reports, 'is a site of embodied meanings and *was developed for that reason*' (Sinclair, p. 304).

Learning in such contexts implies appropriation of accounts of the world that are neither out there in the objects themselves nor in our brains. Rather, they are cultivated in institutional settings for particular and sometimes highly specialized purposes. (Säljö and Bergqvist, 1997, p. 402)

ISSUES AND CHALLENGES OF THRESHOLD CONCEPTS FOR ASSESSMENT

A primary consideration for us in seeking a productive form assessment to estimate students' understanding of threshold concepts is how to map the signification-stimulus-protocol (SSP) conceptual framework onto the four modes of variation. We would need to consider the 'goodness of fit', and identify issues that need resolving. A second important and related aspect of this approach is the importance of the temporal and dynamic aspects of assessment within this mapping process. In the journey towards the portal, and within the modes of liminality discussed earlier, there is much space for integrating stimuli and protocols in a truly quasi-continuous manner. The use of diarised forms of assessment, portfolios, logs, patchwork texts, sequential conceptual mappings (all viewed here as stimuli) are associated with relatively unstructured protocols that can be further formalised in a manner that resonates with self-explanation theory. One could see blogs, for example, as a kind of travelogue of the learning journey, a form of self directed reflection in the sense of 'write aloud' rather than 'talk aloud' activity (see the Sinclair journal above for an example).

STIMULUS AND PROTOCOL CONSIDERATIONS IN THE PRELIMINAL MODE

How can one form an estimate of whether students are inclined towards disciplinary modes of reasoning and explanation in the subliminal and preliminal mode of variation? Pang and Meyer (work in progress) provide an insight into how variation in these modes can be externalised through stimuli represented by everyday (but not explicitly identified as economic) scenarios in which school pupils can imagine themselves to be situated, and can explain the dynamics of *making choices* (in the face of implicit scarcity that the pupils need to discern). The work described sets out to explore the research question of whether year 10–12 (Secondary 4–6) pupils in Hong Kong with no prior exposure to Economics as a subject, or to economic language, can exhibit within these scenarios an inclination to 'think like an economist' in relation to the (implicitly embedded) threshold concept of *opportunity cost*. This approach has employed proxies – scenarios that act as substitute for (in this case) an economic event, such as the cost consequences of accepting a highly valued invitation to the movies by a girlfriend of boyfriend on an evening when one should be revising for an important examination the next morning. The responses given to explain the cost consequences are not formalised in the syntax of the Economics specialist, but reveal the beginnings of an ontological shift and a capacity to engage with the conceptual language of the discipline in a subliminal or the early stages of a preliminal mode, using a non-formalised discursiveness. This poses an imaginative challenge for teachers in other disciplines to devise similar proxy scenarios which are similarly stripped of formal discursiveness.

What is fascinating about this work is that no single stimulus evokes (or fails to evoke) the exhibited variation in a consistent manner. A *range* of stimuli is required to form an estimate of pupils' inclinations to 'think like an economist' with a consistent (preliminal) response across the range being exhibited in only a minority of students.

A PERSPECTIVE FROM CONSTRUCTIVE ALIGNMENT

It might be helpful here to examine and contrast a fairly well known and popular current practice within other established domains, that of *constructive alignment.* Constructive alignment is a 'sandwich model' of learning and teaching that embraces a philosophy in which learning outcomes are made explicit in congruent intentional and assessment terms, with pedagogical and learning processes aligned in between. It can serve as both a diagnostic and a design model. In the context of reflective practice it can be used as a template to identify discrete aspects of learning and teaching that, in students' perceptions and learning experiences, are not 'aligned' (a classic sign of the 'hidden curriculum'). It is a design template in a very practical sense in requiring the specification of intended learning outcomes that are explicitly reflected in assessment procedures and that are clearly jointly supported by, and articulate with, subject content and pedagogy. In practice, constructive alignment is typically applied to modules, or even entire degree programmes, but it can equally be applied to smaller units of learning and teaching activity, arguably down to the level of discrete concepts including threshold concepts. It has proved successful in engaging academics with an aspect of educational theory that is relatively simple to grasp, has a clear logical appeal, is transferable across disciplinary boundaries, and that is generally actionable; it allows practitioners to think about, reflect on, and actually do something about educational practice. As such, it has been widely embraced by the higher education community of practitioners and professional developers.

Constructive alignment begins by inviting the question of where we think learners are and where we want them to be. In practice, assumptions are made about what students are likely to bring with them to the learning environment in terms of prior knowledge and learning experiences that can be built on and progressed towards the intended outcomes. As a pedagogical strategy in the cognitive domain this theorisation is unproblematic insofar as units of study can be thought of as links in a chain lattice that facilitate vertical and horizontal progression within the broader curriculum. However this notion of progressive linkage brings its own problems. From the perspective of the learner it seems reasonable to assume that, insofar as the first end link is ideally aligned with, and builds on, prior *subject knowledge* and experience, an explicitly stated learning outcome will 'come into view', for students in recognisable terms *in varying degrees*. An expectation of what is required in learning terms and how it will be assessed defines the learning trajectory of students in a very visible sense. In fact reflections of constructive alignment form the basis of many university pro forma templates for the design of new courses, as well as agendas for internal and external cycles of quality assurance.

'THAT UNTRAVELL'D WORLD ...' – A SIGNIFICATION PROBLEM FOR CONSTRUCTIVE ALIGNMENT

But understanding threshold concepts is not just about conceptual transformation bounded by subject matter. It is also about a change in sense of self, a change in subjectivity on the part of the learner. The threshold concepts framework views learning as embracing both a cognitive *and* an ontological shift. It involves a journey into unfamiliar realms. In Tennyson's poem *Ulysses* the eponymous hero reflects on a lifetime of journeying as follows:

> I am a part of all that I have met;
> Yet all experience is an arch wherethro'
> Gleams that untravell'd world whose margin fades
> For ever and for ever when I move.

In general, because of their transformative property threshold concepts, by definition, involve a liminal journey in ontological terms, a 'change in subjectivity' (Pelletier, 2007). As Barnett has pointed out:

'A pedagogy for uncertain times has itself to be uncertain. It is open, it is daring, it is risky, it is, itself, unpredictable... A pedagogy for uncertainty will be ontologically disturbing and enthralling all at once. It will be electric, as one move sparks another and in unpredictable ways...This pedagogy is a form of restrained anarchy; even a disciplined anarchy – with its spaces and its risks.' (Barnett, 2007, p. 137)

As Bayne (2008: 204) has argued, drawing on Kristeva (1991) 'To teach ...is to engage with new ontologies which make students *strangers to themselves*'. And in this question lies the problem for assessment. What do sentences like 'read like a classicist', 'think like a biologist, clinician, lawyer, mathematician, economist, engineer, or an historian' mean to the uninitiated? If, as we saw in the instance of the Sinclair journal earlier, the apprehension of a threshold concept (as an intended learning outcome) lies *outside* the preliminary and subliminal prior knowledge and experience of the student *then so, probably, will an understanding of how it will be assessed, except perhaps in terms of an 'understanding' based on mimicry.* The constructive alignment version of signification lies in the statement of the intended learning outcome. This is fine and well at one level but the model as a whole fails to embrace the complexities associated with threshold concepts. The liminal experience of learning is a much stranger affair, often literally obliging the learner to encounter strangeness, and it is once more difficult to see how this can be communicated to students as part of an intended learning outcome within constructive alignment. Barnett again:

'the student is perforce required to venture into new places, strange places, anxiety-provoking places. This is part of the point of higher education. If there was no anxiety, it is difficult to believe that we could be in the presence of a higher education.' (Barnett, 2007: 147)

This strangeness and uncertainty – further dimensions of troublesome knowledge – are precisely what serve to provoke a liminal state and instigate an ontological shift. These further dimensions should, in our view, be positively embraced as a pedagogical principle.

'Intellectual uncertainty is not necessarily or simply a negative experience, a dead-end sense of not knowing or of indeterminacy. It is just as well an experience of something open, generative, exhilarating (the trembling of what remains undecidable). I wish to suggest that 'intellectual uncertainty' is …a crucial dimension of any teaching worthy of the name.' (Royle, 2003, p. 52, cited in Bayne, 2008: 203).

However a major challenge for the teacher lies in signifying what lies ahead. In an earlier piece (Land, Meyer and Smith, 2008, p. ix) we characterised this experience through the whimsical metaphor of a Desirée potato catching the first glimpse of the fat!

'You are about to enter a state of liminality on the way to becoming a *roast* potato. Aspects of the journey thus far have been troublesome. You have lost your red skin. Your delectable yellow creamy flesh has been exposed. You have been parboiled to get rid of some of your starch. Your outer surface has been roughened. You don't know it, but there is still more trouble ahead. That first glimpse of other potatoes in the hot fat may be the first sign of what things may look like 'on the other side' of the portal. You are not yet a roast potato, and you do not know what it is like to *be* a roast potato. And in the preliminary stages of getting to where you are now you could have entertained other options. Such as keeping your skin on for a start. As a peeled, parboiled potato you still have options. You can, for example, be transformed into mash or something more exotic like *soufflé di patate.* With a bit of creative luck, you might even assume the mantle of *pommes boulangère* or *gratin dauphinoise.* But, once you hit the fat that's pretty much it.'

The most advanced versions of a pedagogy that explicitly addresses the cognitive domain, the affective domain, skills *and* this kind of profound ontological shift is arguably found in the medical profession.

As one medical graduate (anon.) commented, going through medical school is 'like getting your hand caught in a meat grinder. It just keeps grinding and scooping up more of you as it goes. You gradually get bundled into a processed package and pop out as a doctor'. The experience is characterised as a matter of survival. 'If you don't conform you're out'. (Meyer and Land, 2006 p.-)

At another level, and setting the cognitive domain largely aside, the carefully choreographed sequences of human behaviour involving (for the student) a trans-formative rite of passage in beginning to *look* like a doctor (white coat, stethoscope, neat grooming), *talk* like a doctor (what we refer to as the discursive aspect, elaborated use of language, increasing use of medical terminology and language), *act* like a doctor (ward rounds, bedside manner, clinical detachment, elicit a clinical history, perform a physical examination, analyse and present clinical cases), and *think* like a doctor (hypothetico-deductive and probabilistic reasoning, reaching a differential diagnosis). Indeed it is '…the ability to perform a [differential] diagnosis that lies at the very heart of clinical medicine. It is the one critical outcome towards which almost the entire medical curriculum is orchestrated' (Meyer and Cleary 1998, p. 575). Medical education is clearly largely successful in this endeavour and provides a useful ontological perspective for discussion purposes.

PRELIMINAL ONTOLOGICAL SHIFT

We observe that most aspiring doctors enter medical school with some concrete experiences of being treated as patients, as well as an idealised view of what doctors are and do, reinforced by the media, especially television programmes such as *ER* and *House*. The point here is that, even before entering medical school, there is variation in some mental image of what a doctor is and does – the intended and desired outcome. Desire is an important contributory factor in this, as in all identity development. The latter mental image is formed by exposure to multiple examples of signification based on real and vicarious experiences, often additionally explicitly modelled by close family members or relatives working in the various professions allied to medicine. This seems to be a useful exemplar of signification influencing the subliminal and preliminal modes of variation. However the effect of this influence is not simply in terms of signification and goes beyond value judgements about privilege afforded by social and cultural capital. The argument is that, thus influenced, entering medical students have already made a preliminal commitment to becoming a doctor. But, more than this, *they have already made an ontological shift* in viewing themselves as students of clinical medicine. They are thus likely to be advantaged in their engagement with threshold concepts within the discipline. In other words the preliminal ontological shift creates a receptive predisposition *beyond* tacit understanding of the 'underlying game' which prepares the student for threshold concept engagement. This argument raises a question about the degree to which subliminal and preliminal modes of variation also involve ontological shift that are amenable to observation and estimation.

In terms of empirical evidence, in what is believed to be the first study of its kind to address the question, Shanahan, Foster and Meyer (2008) investigated patterns of attrition in a large first-year microeconomics course. The main research question addressed the relationship between prior knowledge of economics threshold concepts and attrition. Unlike the scenario of the medics, what emerged in this context was what was perceived by tutors as a 'lack of commitment' on the part of students who characterised themselves as 'being there to study Economics' but did not see themselves as 'students of Economics'. In this instance the necessary preliminal ontological shift required for the programme was not deemed to have taken place.

THE JEWELS IN THE CURRICULUM: ASSESSING AT PROGRAMME LEVEL

Our considerations to this point have concerned improving the effectiveness and meaningfulness of assessment. A final implication of threshold concepts for assessment however concerns optimising and simplifying assessment for both students and teachers, and the much vaunted need in our higher education institutions to streamline processes. This would involve employing threshold concepts structurally as the foci for learning tasks at programme level, rather than at a more fine-grained and often more burdensome learning outcome level. As Eraut (2008) pointed out in a recent seminar discussion:

'People always think if you go into enough detail about something you'll nail it. But you never can, and you lose sense of the whole context in which that something makes sense. You lose the big picture'.

We have argued elsewhere (Land et al, 2005) that threshold concepts can be used to define potentially powerful transformative points in the student's learning experience. In this sense they may be viewed as the 'jewels in the curriculum' and can lead to a simplified model of assessment at the programme level. They can serve to identify crucial points in the framework of engagement that teachers may wish to construct in order to provide opportunities for students to gain important conceptual understandings and hence gain richer and more complex insights into aspects of the subjects they are studying. And in terms of charting students' learning journeys threshold concepts literally are the waypoints to be navigated. In this respect, we would claim, they are what really matter in a course, and where the key transformations that educators wish to bring about take place. As one of our respondents commented:

'Though I wasn't previously familiar with this terminology, I can see, looking back, that I have always designed the courses that I teach to include threshold concepts. I know where I wish the students to journey to, and I know how I would like them to change. Yes it's often difficult, but otherwise, why would you be interested in teaching the course at all? You could just stick your stuff on the web and they could go and read it.' (Michael, a university lecturer in a research intensive university).

Threshold concepts may also serve a helpful diagnostic purpose in alerting tutors to areas of the curriculum where students are likely to encounter troublesome knowledge and experience conceptual difficulty – the 'stuck places' to which Ellsworth refers (1997 p. 71). But apart from giving a purposeful rationale of why teaching (as opposed to 'facilitation') is necessary and important, above quotation exemplifies a view that teachers know what key conceptual and ontological transformations they wish to see evidence of. There are probably not too many of these transformations in a single programme, but they are what matters in the long run. In the assessment of threshold concepts less is probably more in this regard. Consider for example the experience of two students, later each to become well known writers, on coming to understand the periodic table in their chemistry studies.

'Seeing the table, "getting" it, altered my life. I took to visiting it as often as I could. I copied it into my exercise book and carried it everywhere; I got to know it so well – visually and conceptually – that I could mentally trace its paths in every direction, going up a group, then turning right on a period, stopping going down one, yet always knowing where I was. It was like a garden, the garden of numbers I had loved as a child – but unlike this, it was real, a key to the universe. I spent hours now, enchanted, totally absorbed, wandering, making discoveries, in the enchanted garden of Mendeleev.' (Sacks, 2001, p. 194)

'For the first time I saw a medley of haphazard facts fall into line and order. All the jumbles and recipes and hotchpotch of the inorganic chemistry of my boyhood seemed to fit themselves into the scheme before my eyes – as though one were standing beside a jungle and it suddenly transformed itself into a Dutch garden.' (C P Snow, cited in Sacks, 2001)

But note that, in parallel with the integration of this new conceptual insight, comes an ontological shift in beginning to understand the work and role of the scientist.

'I could scarcely sleep for excitement the night after seeing the periodic table – it seemed to me an incredible achievement to have brought the whole, vast, and seemingly chaotic universe of chemistry to an all-embracing order…And this gave me, for the first time, a sense of the transcendent power of the human mind, and the fact that it might equipped to discover or decipher the deepest secrets of nature, to read the mind of God.' (Sacks, 2001, p. 194)

CONCLUSION

If we were to promote a manifesto for change in our assessment practices, to gain evidence of student understanding of threshold concepts as well as helping to promote that understanding, our desiderata would include the following. We would seek new modes of mapping, representing and forming estimations of students' conceptual formation in all modes of liminality. We would wish to provide a rich feedback environment offered at the point of conceptual difficulty ('stuckness', the liminal state) as well as in the pre-, post-and subliminal states. We would want to develop a more nuanced discourse to clarify variation and experience and achievement through the various stags of the liminal journey. We would hope to bring into being the possibility of an ontological (as well as conceptual) dimension of assessment. We would aim for a more meaningful correspondence of students' coming to terms with troublesome knowledge and transformation to patterns of grading. An 'upper second' in areas of ontological shift does not make sense. We would simplify and optimise assessment by focusing on threshold concepts as the jewels in the curriculum at programme level, where what are assessed are the key transformative dimensions of a learning programme. All of this requires a corresponding emphasis on helping students to become aware of their learning in relation to threshold concepts and in this respect some progress has already been reported by Meyer, Ward and Latreille (2008). There is clear evidence in their study that an opportunity to develop metalearning capacity (after Biggs 1985) can be constituted in the specific context of, in this case, threshold concepts in Economics. 'The concept of metalearning' they argue, 'encapsulates two complementary features of deep level, self regulated, learning capacity; namely an *awareness* of, and *control* over, self as learner in some specified context – a capacity that is also conceptually associated with deep-level learning outcomes' (Meyer, Ward and Latreille, 2008, p. 1).

In these desiderata, we feel, lies the basis for a rich, intriguing, and strategically important research agenda.

'I kept dreaming of the periodic table in the excited half-sleep of that night – I dreamed of it as a flashing, revolving pinwheel or Catherine wheel, and then as a great nebula, going from the first element to the last, and whirling beyond uranium, out to infinity. The next day I could hardly wait for the museum to open, and dashed up to the top floor, where the table was, as soon as the doors were opened.' (Sacks 2001 ibid)

NOTES

[1] We are deeply indebted to Dr Christine Sinclair of Strathclyde University for permission to reproduce extracts from her learning journal. We are also grateful to her for drawing our attention to the links with Vygotsky, Säljö and Bergqvist, and Sacks which we cite elsewhere in this study.

REFERENCES

Barnett, R. (2007). *A will to learn: Being a student in an age of uncertainty*. Buckingham: Society for Research in Higher Education and Open University Press.

Bayne, S. (2008, in press). Uncanny spaces for higher education: Teaching and learning in virtual worlds. *ALT-J: Research in Learning Technology, 1741–1629, 16*(3), 197–205.

Biggs, J. (1985). The role of metalearning in study processes. *British Journal of Educational. Psychology, 55*, 185–212.

Biggs, J. (1999). *Teaching for quality learning at University*. Buckingham: The Society for Research into Higher Education and the Open University Press.

Bradbeer, J. (2005, December). Threshold concepts and troublesome knowledge in the GEES disciplines. *Planet, 15*.

Chi, M. T. H., Bassok, M., Lewis, M. W., Reimann, P., & Glaser, R. (1989). Self explanations: How students study and use examples in learning to solve problems. *Cognitive Science, 13*, 145–182.

Chi, M. T. H., de Leeuw, N., Chiu, M.-H., & LaVancher, C. (1994). Eliciting self-explanations improves understanding. *Cognitive Science*, *18*, 439–477.

Cohen, D. (1987). The use of concept maps to represent unique thought processes: Toward more meaningful learning. *Journal of Curriculum and Supervision*, *2*(3), 285–289.

Easdown, D. (2007, September 27–28). The role of proof in mathematics teaching and *The Plateau Principle*. UniServe Science Symposium proceedings. Science Teaching and Learning Research including Threshold Concepts. The University of Sydney.

Ellsworth, E. (1989, August). Why doesn't this feel empowering? Working through the repressive myths of critical pedagogy. *Harvard Educational Review*, *59*(3), 297–324.

Eraut, M. (2008, June 10). *Research into professional learning: Its implications for the professional development of teachers in Higher Education*. Unpublished seminar paper. HEDG Annual Conference, Madingley Hall, Cambridge UK.

Erdman, D. V. (Ed.). (1988). *The complete poetry and prose of William Blake*. New York: Anchor Books.

Kinchin, I., & Hay, D. (2000, Spring). How a qualitative approach to concept map analysis can be used to aid learning by illustrating patterns of conceptual development. *Educational Research*, *42*(1), 43–57.

Land, R., Cousin, G., Meyer, J. H. F., & Davies, P. (2005). Threshold concepts and troublesome knowledge (3): Implications for course design and evaluation. In C. Rust (Ed.), *Improving student learning 12 — Diversity and inclusivity* (pp. 53–64). Oxford: Oxford Brookes University.

Land, R., Meyer J. H. F., & Smith, J. (Eds.). (2008). *Threshold concepts within the disciplines*. Rotterdam and Taipei: Sense Publishers.

Marek, E. A. (1986). They misunderstand, but they'll pass. *Science Teacher*, *53*(9), 32–35.

Meyer, J. H. F., & Cleary, E. G. (1998). An exploratory student learning model of clinical diagnosis. *Medical Education*, *32*, 574–581.

Meyer, J. H. F., & Land, R. (Eds.). (2006). *Overcoming barriers to student understanding: Threshold concepts and troublesome knowledge*. London and New York: Routledge.

Meyer, J. H. F., & Land, R. (2005). Threshold concepts and troublesome knowledge (2): Epistemological considerations and a conceptual framework for teaching and learning. *Higher Education*, *49*(3), 373–388.

Meyer, J., & Land, R. (2007, August 17). Stop the conveyor belt, I want to get off. *Times Higher Education Supplement*.

Meyer, J. H. F., Land, R., & Davies, P. (2008). Threshold concepts and troublesome knowledge (4). Issues of variation and variability. In R. Land, J. H. F. Meyer, & J. Smith (Eds.), *Threshold concepts within the disciplines* (pp. 59–74). Rotterdam and Taipei: Sense Publishers.

Meyer, J. H. F., Ward, S. C., & Latreille, P. (2008, June 25–27). *Threshold concepts and metalearning capacity*. Paper presented at the 2nd International Conference on Threshold Concepts, Threshold Concepts: from theory to practice, Kingston, Ontario, Canada.

Pang, M. F., & Meyer, J. H. F. (in progress). *Modes of variation in pupils' apprehension of a threshold concept in economics*.

Pelletier, C. (2007). *Learning through design: Meaning and subjectivity in young people's computer game production work*. University of London Institute of Education: Unpublished PhD thesis.

Perkins, D. (2006). Constructivism and troublesome knowledge. In J. H. F. Meyer & R. Land (Eds.), *Overcoming barriers to student understanding: Threshold concepts and troublesome knowledge* (pp. 33–47). Routledge: London and New York.

Ricks, C. (Ed.). (1972). *A collection of poems by Alfred Tennyson*. Garden City, NY: Doubleday & Co.

Royle, N. (2003). *The uncanny*. Manchester: Manchester University Press.

Sacks, O. (2001). *Uncle Tungsten: Memories of a chemical boyhood*. London: Picador (Macmillan).

Säljö, R., & Bergqvist, K. (1997). Seeing the light: Discourse and practice in the Optics Lab. In L. Resnick, R. Säljö, C. Pontecorvo, & B. Burge (Eds.), *Discourse, tools and reasoning*. New York: Springer.

Shanahan, M. P., Foster, G., & Meyer, J. H. F. (2008, June 25–27). *Threshold concepts and attrition in first-year economics*. Paper presented at the 2nd international conference on threshold concepts, Threshold Concepts: from theory to practice, Kingston, Ontario, Canada.

Sinclair, C. (2004). *Students and discourse: An insider perspective*. Unpublished PhD thesis. Faculty of Education and Language Studies, Open University: Milton Keynes, UK.

Vygotsky, L. S. (1934/1987). Thinking and speech. In R. W. Rieber & A. S. Carton (Eds.), *The collected works of L S Vygotsky*. New York and London: Plenum.

Ray Land
University of Strathclyde
Glasgow, UK

Jan H.F. Meyer
University of Durham
Durham, UK

IAN M. KINCHIN, LYNDON B. CABOT AND DAVID B. HAY

5. VISUALIZING EXPERTISE:

Revealing the Nature of a Threshold Concept in the Development of an Authentic Pedagogy for Clinical Education

INTRODUCTION

A reconceptualisation of expertise as a dynamic transformation of knowledge structures, relating competence and comprehension can be represented by chains of practice and networks of understanding revealed by concept mapping. This view of expertise has provided us with a threshold concept for the evolution of university pedagogy, whilst moving away from the problematic binary of student/teacher centredness. Our model also rejects reductionist notions of expertise fostered by an audit culture, preferring an integration of the elements of professional practice. This model facilitates the academic reclamation of pedagogy, placing subject specialists at the centre of pedagogic developments and provides a mechanism to initiate and monitor a more transactional curriculum (*sensu* Cousin, 2008).

The application of concept mapping (Novak, 1998) to the qualitative description of knowledge structures has allowed the visualisation of the process of teaching and learning in novel ways that emphasise the organisation of understanding. The revealed transformation of knowledge structures within the teaching and learning process has lead to a description of clinical expertise that provides functional links between expert knowledge and clinical practice (Kinchin, Cabot and Hay, 2008). The usual reference to these links as 'tacit' or 'intuitive' has previously helped to avoid the issue of how to develop a clinical pedagogy that helps students to develop appropriate links between theory and practice and a trajectory towards expertise. A reconceptualisation of expertise in this way allows a re-appraisal of clinical pedagogy that addresses many of the inadequacies of current teaching programmes and helps us to 'reach the point where expertise can not only be verbalised, but passed on from teacher to pupil' (Rolfe, 1997: 1074).

We are considering the conceptualisation of expertise as a threshold concept by relating our observations to the five characteristics of threshold concepts, as defined by Meyer and Land (2003):

Our view of expertise, as being composed of the dynamic links between chains of practice and underlying networks of understanding, is a *transformative* notion. Once expertise is viewed as both 'dynamic' and 'linking', the traditional transmission view of teaching becomes untenable. The transmission of information only works if the desired outcome is reproduction of a static expert structure. In order to teach

J. H. F. Meyer, R. Land and C. Baillie (eds.), Threshold Concepts and
Transformational Learning, 81–95.
© *2010 Sense Publishers. All rights reserved.*

dynamic expertise, it needs to be modelled in the teaching process. The presentation of information (either clinical or theoretical) only makes sense if it is related to the complementary context in a way that is explicit to the student.

It is probably *irreversible* as, once presented to a teacher, the view of expertise we are proposing appears evident in much of the educational practice that is observable in a clinical school. Our model describes what a few exemplary teachers do intuitively, but what others never seem to identify as important.

Such a view of expertise is certainly *integrative*, and provides a strong link between what is known about the clinical teaching environment and the non-clinical teaching environment. Integrating theory and clinical practice has long been problematic for the student of dentistry, medicine and nursing. Whilst university education is about developing creative, independent thinkers, this has to be reconciled with the need to ensure that a set of professional standards and competencies are met at some threshold level (Manley and Garbett, 2000; Ashley *et al.*, 2006). A dynamic pedagogy of expertise places such a link at its core.

Our view of expertise may, superficially at least, exhibits some degree of *boundedness* within the clinical disciplines - as the distinction between clinical and non-clinical elements is so marked. This may allow some to feel that clinical education is unique. Whilst the distinction between chains of practice and underlying networks of understanding exist in all academic disciplines, the perception of uniqueness among clinical educators may at least serve a purpose in encouraging academics to adopt the proposal in the belief that it represents a bespoke pedagogy for their discipline.

The reconstruction of what counts as pedagogy has been described by Savin-Baden (2006) as one of the most *troublesome* issues to manage. However, academics often fail to recognise teaching as a problematic activity and resort to teaching as telling and learning as receiving (as described by Van Leuven, 1997) as the default setting of university teaching.

PROGRESSION OF TEACHING IN THREE BROAD STEPS

Considering the development of teaching in three broad evolutionary steps is a simplification of reality. However, through simplification, the key characteristics can be highlighted sufficiently to resonate with the experiences of university teachers. The three steps suggest classroom approaches with pros and cons to each:

1. The 'Content-Transmission' Model

This is based around the transmission of information rather than the transmission of understanding. One problem is deciding which content should be transmitted: much of the information that will be given to students in their first years of study will be obsolete before they qualify. Predicting which content will have a longer shelf-life and continue to be of use to the students is a difficult problem. When assessing students' acquisition of content within this model, it is impossible to separate what has been gained from formal and informal sources. In other words, how can you tell how effective the teaching has been, unless students are routinely tested before instruction to determine the level of their prior knowledge? The notion of content transmission implies that there is a fixed 'end-point' of learning (i.e. once the prescribed content has been transmitted). Such a view invites strategic/ rote learning to achieve the end point as quickly and effortlessly as possible, and works against a regime of meaningful/personal learning.

2. The 'Responding-To-Student-Learning-Needs' Model

Responding to the diverse and changing needs of large number of students seems to be setting an impossible goal that represents a 'step too far' for many university teachers (Cousin, 2008: 268). Whilst Simon (1999: 42) is explicit in his criticism of this model in stating that, *'starting from the standpoint of individual differences is to start from the wrong position. To develop effective pedagogy means starting from the opposite standpoint'*. Even if students' learning styles could be reliably determined, it is not clear how teaching should be targeted at matching or complementing these styles. Attempts to classify student learning using learning styles inventories has been shown to reduce the acknowledged range of student learning styles to a small number that in turn, have been used to label students and promote commonality rather than diversity (Ritter, 2007).

3. The 'Expertise-Based' Model

The adoption of an expertise-based pedagogy requires teachers to have the courage to share their knowledge, and the gaps in their knowledge. Patel, Arocha and Kaufman (1999: 89) describe how 'An effective clinical teacher needs to be able to articulate knowledge that would normally be tacit for a practitioner not normally engaged in instruction'. The knowledge structures approach, facilitated by concept mapping tools, provides a mechanism to go beyond making learning visible, towards making it tangible (i.e., not only can it been seen, but it can also be manipulated to support development). The epistemological nature of engaging and inducting students into disciplinary ways of thinking 'invites significant trans-formation of our existing view of pedagogical knowledge and expertise' (O'Brien, 2008: 302). A reconceptualisation of the nature of expertise is offered here.

CONCEPT MAPPING

The principle characteristics of experts in any domain is that they posses an extensive and highly integrated body of knowledge related to their discipline (Patel, Arocha and Kaufman, 1999). This is coupled with the ability to perceive patterns in large amounts of information and to process their responses quickly and efficiently. Uncovering the knowledge bases held by experts to gain insight of the nature of the structures that might be indicative of expert understanding (Bradley, Paul and Seeman, 2006), has led to the use of concept mapping as an exploratory tool (Hoffman and Lintern, 2006).

Concept mapping as developed by Novak (Novak, 1998; Novak and Cañas, 2007; Cañas and Novak, 2008) is a graphical tool used to represent links between ideas. Ideas are written in boxes and linked with arrows carrying explanatory legends. Concept mapping has been used effectively in a variety of contexts as a classroom technique to enhance learning (e.g. Horton *et al.* 1993; Lawless *et al.* 1998; Nesbit and Adesope, 2006). The ability to construct a concept map illustrates two essential properties of understanding, the representation and the organisation of ideas. Halford (1993, p. 7) states that "to understand a concept entails having an internal representation or mental model that reflects the structure of that concept". A concept map is an attempt to make explicit such a mental model so that it can be reviewed with others (Chang, 2007). The construction of concept maps is an excellent way of helping to organise knowledge and so help understanding. Concept maps are increasingly used in higher education to summarise learning, promote critical thinking skills and meaningful learning or as an assessment strategy (e.g. Gravett and Swart, 1997).

Concept mapping may promote the development of thinking skills by providing an explicit point of focus for reflection through the visualisation of the 'learning arena' as portrayed by the map (e.g. McAleese, 1994). The use of concept mapping is often linked to the 'constructivist' view of learning as a concept map makes a good starting point for constructivist teaching. This is a form of student-centred teaching in which understanding is considered to be constructed by the learner rather than absorbed from the teacher as a finished product. Concept maps depict constructed and reconstructed knowledge and teaching that helps this recons-truction process will lead to meaningful learning. The action of mapping is also thought to help the process by revealing to the student connections that had not been recognised previously and by acting as a focus for communication between student and teacher. This is illustrated by Novak & Gowin's (1984) observation that students and teachers often remark that they recognise new relationships and hence new meanings as a result of mapping activities.

An important function of the map is to help make explicit the overall framework of concepts. This is particularly important for complex topics where students may display a fragmentary understanding and are frequently unable to integrate all the components to form a meaningful overview. Identifying these fragments of understanding is vital as these form the foundations for future meaningful learning.

Our application of concept mapping in this context presents some divergence with the philosophy that implicitly underpins much of the literature that has employed' concept mapping in the past. This philosophical tension is particularly evident in the field of science education, in which there exists an epistemological gap between the objectivist philosophy of science and the constructivist philosophy of concept mapping (Kinchin, 2001). Much of the literature on concept mapping is concerned with students' understanding migrating towards an accepted (or expert) view, which is typically hierarchical in nature. However, we have been concerned not with the 'correctness' of response, but with documenting personal change, using concept mapping as an act of rehearsal.

Whilst the 'study-skill' approach to concept mapping has created important benefits for student learning, the potential of concept mapping goes far beyond this. Concept mapping provides a trigger for the development of scholarly, student-engaged pedagogy (Kinchin, Lygo-Baker and Hay, 2008), based on the visualisation of the elements of expertise (Kinchin, Cabot and Hay, 2008). It is this greater potential that we wish to explore here in the practical development and implement-tation of a bespoke approach to teaching that reflects the professional values of the discipline. We encourage the reader to look beyond the implementation of concept mapping merely as a study skill tool to remedy the deficiencies of an outmoded content-delivery-based curriculum, towards an approach to teaching that grants students 'epistemological access' to the discipline (Gamache, 2002; Wingate, 2006; 2007). The use of concept maps to monitor clinical education has revealed the complementary chains and networks that represent competence and understanding.

CHAINS AND NETWORKS

The ability to visualise the clinical reasoning process is considered to represent one of the first steps in the formation of the cognitive skills that are necessary for professional practice by Hill and Talluto (2006). Visualisation of knowledge

Figure 1. The clinician's complex network of understanding may contain uncertainties that are not passed to the patient – who is left with a simplified and 'certain' chain of practice. The student/observer needs to be aware of both structural interpretations and the relationship between them. (After Kinchin, Cabot and Hay, 2008).

structures through concept mapping has enabled us to separate the *chains of practice* that are manifest in teachers' actions from the underlying *networks of understanding* (see figure 1). Chains are indicative of procedural sequences that characterise observable clinical practice and have been described as indicators of 'goal-orientation' (Hay and Kinchin, 2006). This seems entirely appropriate in the clinical setting in that the goal of clinical competence is the effective treatment of patients. If there are no links with an underlying understanding, the chain may be seen as blindly following a recipe.

Networks indicate understanding that is integrated and wholistic. Knowing there are several alternative treatments with varying consequences is not the same as being able to select the most appropriate one within a clinical context. If this was the case, academic study would not need to be backed by clinical training.

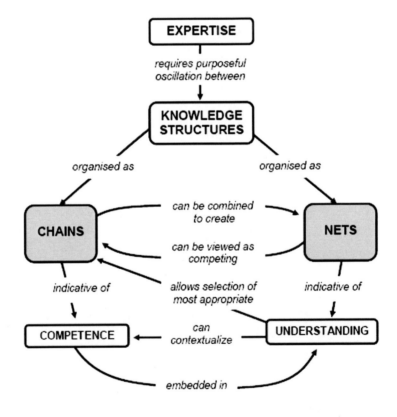

Figure 2. The relationship between chains of practice and networks of understanding. The active engagement in the links between these chains and nets are indicative of expertise. (Modified from Kinchin and Hay, 2007).

APPLICATION TO TEACHING

Patel, Arocha and Kaufman (1999: 89) have explained that 'an effective clinical teacher needs to be able to articulate knowledge that would normally be tacit for a practitioner not engaged in instruction'. It is precisely the articulation of this tacit knowledge that is facilitated by the model and by the concept mapping tool, providing students with the key information they need to develop their own emergent expertise.

The tacit knowledge that needs to be placed in the public arena for teaching is found connecting the chains of practice that are manifest in the clinical teacher's actions and the underlying network of understanding that is usually held privately (Kinchin, Cabot and Hay, 2008). The clinical student needs to gain experience in converting between complementary chains and networks. Such structural transformations can be modelled for the student, once the teacher has recognized them. Engagement in concept mapping activities allows the teacher to recognize the existence of the structures and allows him/her to make them public to the students within the course of teaching. The concept mapping tool also slows down the process (that is usually automated) to facilitate its examination. So, for example, the typical structure of a clinical procedure would be a chain of practice that would be communicated to the student. The student's competence would be assessed through his/her ability to reproduce that chain under varying conditions and with various patients. The student's developing expertise, however, must be assessed through his/her ability to relate the chain of practice to the underlying network of understanding, and explaining how the elements are linked, and how and why the chain of practice should be modified in response to changes of context. This represents a shift in the emphasis of the transactions between teachers and students from fixed end-points to linking activities.

INTUITION AND TACIT KNOWLEDGE

A difficulty in developing a pedagogy of expertise is the central position given to intuition and tacit knowledge in some of the models of expertise used within clinical education (e.g. Benner, 1984; Dreyfus and Dreyfus, 1986). Interpretation of this aspect of Benner's work has been the focus of some debate, exemplified by the divergence of views aired by English (1993) and Darbyshire (1994), illustrating tensions between the 'art' or 'science' of clinical practice (Seymour, Kinn and Sutherland, 2003). If intuition and tacit knowledge cannot be explained or modeled for students, they would not make a good basis for a pedagogy for clinical education. However, we do not see tacit knowledge as a barrier to developing a pedagogy of expertise so long as it is viewed as knowledge that has *not yet* been revealed rather than knowledge that *cannot be* revealed (Eraut, 2000). We see intuition based on tacit knowledge as simply the poorly articulated links between chains of practice and underlying networks of understanding, and agree with Welsh and Lyons (2000) that it would not be possible to use intuition in the clinical context unless it was linked to formal knowledge:

'The use of intuition without reference to a sound knowledge base would reduce it to the sort of thinking which might be expected of an uninformed lay person and has no place in professional practice.'

Yielder, (2004) has shown how some expert knowledge is explicit, and by supporting reflection, theoretical and procedural knowledge can be made more conscious. If colleagues have been unable to verbalise their actions in the past, it may simply be that they have lacked the appropriate tools to uncover what it is that they were doing, and/or the vocabulary or self-awareness to articulate it (Jarvis, 1996). Hoffman and Lintern (2006) argue that there is no indication that tacit knowledge 'lies beyond the reach of science in some unscientific netherworld of intuitions and unobservables', and that appropriate tools (such as concept mapping) can support colleagues in identifying and clearly describing their practice with the aim of improving teaching effectiveness (McLeod *et al.*, 2004). Rolfe (1996) comments that rather than considering intuition as a magical process of knowing, it should be considered as the unconscious workings of the prepared mind. By revealing these workings through the application of concept mapping, the tacit can be made explicit (Hoffman and Lintern, 2006).

RELATING EXPERTISE-BASED PEDAGOGY TO NON-CLINICAL DISCIPLINES.

Within the expertise-based pedagogy for clinical teaching we have discussed the relationship between linear chains of practice and the underlying networks of understanding. The term, 'practice' resonates with the daily activities of clinicians, in 'clinical practice'. At first such terminology might seem confined to the clinical disciplines and so allow non-clinical disciplines to claim that 'it's not the same for us'. We would like to broaden the use of the term 'practice' to include the activities of other disciplines. This is based on the direct observation of teaching across the nine academic Schools within King's College London, relating these to the expertise-based pedagogy described by Kinchin, Cabot and Hay (2008).

Teaching within other disciplines often involves activities that occur as linear sequences (some examples are summarised in Figure 3). These would include the sequential analysis of text that can be observed within humanities teaching. Observations of seminars where text is analysed exhibit the continual relationship of the linear text with a holistic consideration of a much wider historical and social context for the writing (who wrote it for which audience and under what circumstances). For the student to be able to demonstrate a real grasp of the significance of the text, s/he has to be able to oscillate purposefully between text and social background. Whilst McCormick (1994) acknowledges a 'commonsensical' definition of reading as a simple taking of information from the printed page that supplies the whole source of meaning (an objectivist view of reading), she continues to describe a social-cultural view of reading, in which students:

'...*must be given access to discourses that can allow them to explore the ways in which their own reading acts ... are embedded in complex social and historical relations.*' McCormick (1994: 49)

The expertise-based model focuses on the act of making connections between the two.

In Geography, fieldwork is often employed to provide students with opportunities to develop particular skills (e.g. Gold *et al.,* 1991). For example, the first-hand

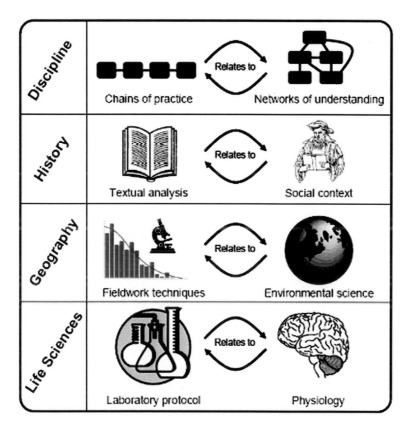

Figure 3. Chains of practice and networks of understanding can be observed to interact within a range of academic disciplines. (After Cabot and Kinchin, 2008).

collection of environmental data may involve the use of procedures and apparatus in a linear manner. The effectiveness of the field course in helping students to think like geographers depends on adequate links to be made between what is learnt in the field with what is developed through classroom and private study (Gold *et al.*, 1991: 29).

In the sciences, the function of laboratory work includes making clear the basic methods of science; adding meaning to abstractions; making information memorable; illustrating connections between topic areas and motivating students to learn. White (1996) has called for theories of how laboratories promote achievement of any of these aims. The application of laboratory protocols is typically arranged as a linear activity, moving towards the collection of data that can be interpreted and related to an understanding of the wider context. Laboratory protocols are typically arranged as a stepped sequence of procedures that may be referred to (in a rather derogatory manner) as a 'recipe to follow', when it is felt that students may be obeying instructions without really understanding the significance of each step. A science student may display competence in following laboratory procedures without necessarily displaying a similar level of understanding.

A WAY FORWARD

Unlike other recent developments in modelling expertise (e.g. Yielder, 2004; Dall'Alba and Sandberg, 2006), the model proposed here addresses a number of the issues that currently inhibit the development of university teaching beyond the cycles of non-learning that have been highlighted by Kinchin, Lygo-Baker and Hay (2008), and challenges the 'safe systems' that dominate university teaching (Canning, 2007):

1. It addresses the theory-practice gap. The content-focused teaching model can result in the separation of that which is learnt in theory from that which is learnt in a practical context (including clinical environments, laboratory practicals and fieldwork exercises). The expertise-based model requires that teaching should actively focus on the links between theory and practice so that, by default, the problem of a gap is overcome.

2. It provides the *epistemological access*, called for by Wingate (2007). The objectivist epistemology that typifies the transmission mode of teaching has given way in the educational literature to a more constructivist epistemology – paralleling the shift from a focus on teaching content to a focus on students' learning. This can cause lecturers difficulties where the epistemology of their discipline is felt to be in conflict with the epistemology of educational development. This is often only considered in broad theoretical terms within the literature that is inaccessible to those teaching within the disciplines as it appears in the specialist literature on academic development, and using jargon that excludes the specialist. In a rare personal account, Taylor (1993) describes in accessible terms how she came to grips with her own internal epistemological conflict by challenging objectivity. Such personal change is seldom acknowledged in public, and the sanitised nature of academic writing never suggests that such conflict may be widespread. However, reflection upon this conflict may be a prerequisite to developing towards a more sophisticated philosophical stance. The paucity of such personal accounts in the literature provides a lack of exemplars against which 'change-ready' teachers may compare themselves.

3. It places the responsibility for learning on the shoulders of the student. This does not mean that the teacher has no part to play. The university teacher has an obligation to be prepared for his/her teaching. Such preparation includes an awareness of the prior knowledge that students typically bring with them and how this will support interaction with the information that is provided through teaching (i.e. pedagogical content knowledge). In addition, the teacher has to be able to manipulate knowledge (from chains to nets and back again) in an explicit manner that is visible to the student. This will model the process that needs to be developed by students as they develop their own emergent expertise.

4. Places teacher development *within* the disciplines, using familiar discourse. The tensions between educational developers and academics teaching within the disciplines can be eased if the complementary roles are made explicit (Kinchin, Cabot and Hay, 2008), and the traditional battles grounds (e.g. student vs. teacher centredness, Cousin, 2008: 261) become obsolete, with the focus now *expertise-centredness*.

The evolution of university pedagogy will only be successful if all involved are committed to the enhancement of student learning, and the discussion of pedagogy is seen as part of the general discourse of higher education rather than the preserve of specialists in teaching and learning (Green and Lee, 1995). A tentative, partial implementation of an expertise-based pedagogy will fail. For success, the model needs to be accompanied by development of an appropriate assessment regime and an explicit acknowledgement of the expectations that are placed on teachers and students. Teachers need to consider the application of the model to their own discipline and be granted time and resources to ensure that cycles of non-learning (*sensu* Kinchin, Lygo-Baker and Hay, 2008) can be avoided.

IMPLICATIONS FOR TEACHING AND ASSESSMENT

Assessment of chains or nets suggests there is a fixed point of reference that would be examined as an 'end-point' of learning. Such a view validates a surface/rote learning approach which can be facilitated by an assessment regime that supports non-learning outcomes (Kinchin, Lygo-Baker and Hay, 2008). Assessment of links is not compatible with rote learning. The appreciation of the links between chains and nets is a dynamic activity that requires a dynamic assessment regime.

If learning is personal (e.g. Gamache, 2002), it seems probable that the thresholds along a particular learning trajectory will also be personal. In this case, the determination of prior knowledge is essential to understand how a particular student may approach a particular threshold – the trajectory of approach being influenced by what is already known. The degree of pre-liminal variation (*sensu* Meyer and Land, 2005) is also an issue for teachers as it will influence the way in which they will approach the concept of 'expertise' in the context of pedagogy. The consequences of teacher variation have been well documented:

'The pedagogical act of teaching remains variably interpreted and enacted within higher education despite decades of praxis. For teaching to become practice directed at both the facilitation of transformative learning, as well as the induction of students into disciplinary ways of thinking and viewing, more is required of the average academic.' O'Brien (2008: 303)

Experts do not agree about established, concrete phenomena (Cabot and Kinchin, 2007), and it is not clear that the less tangible notion of threshold concept is conceptualised in a uniform way, even within a single discipline. The need to develop visual accounts (Hay *et al*, 2008) of the transition through thresholds will help clarify the situation. We need to be clear that not all teaching has to change if the model is adopted. Rather than dictating to academics *how* they should act, part of the reason for visualising the hidden processes of expertise is to make explicit how they already do act. The strength of the pedagogy of expertise therefore lies not in its prescriptive ability, but rather in its descriptive ability. There remains a role for many of the practices that are held dearly within university teaching, so long as they are practiced with understanding. For example, there is a role for the linear presentation of knowledge (exemplified by the traditional lecture), as long as students are given suitable guidance/opportunity to relate the linear sequence to other structures, either through active engagement during the lecture (Jones, 2007) or through active engagement with complementary activities/resources: e.g.

relate lecture → seminar

The seminar should not be a repeat of the lecture with a smaller group, but should offer the students a chance to interrogate the underlying network of understanding that implicitly supported the lecture. The students need to test their restructuring of the information given in the lecture.

relate lecture → lecture notes

Lecture notes should not simply be a record of what was said in the lecture – such as a printout of PowerPoint slides. Notes need to complement the lecture and invite the students to interact with the content and seek to continue their learning after the lecture has finished.

relate lecture → online materials

Materials presented online should also complement the face-to-face materials rather than repeat them.

The competent practitioner needs both technical skill and contextual under-standing, which 'must be combined into a coherent curriculum in which all the mutually reinforcing elements of professional competence form part of a cumulative, interlocking whole which is greater than the sum of the parts' (Lynton, 1990: 21). The expertise-based pedagogy described here provides a transparent mechanism to achieve this.

REFERENCES

Ashley, F. A., Gibson, B., Daly, B., Lygo-Baker, S., & Newton, J. T. (2006). Undergraduate and postgraduate dental students' 'reflection on learning': A qualitative study. *European Journal of Dental Education, 10*, 10–19.

Benner, P. (1984). *From novice to expert: Excellence and power in clinical nursing practice.* Menlo Park: Addison-Wesley.

Bradley, J. H., Paul, R., & Seeman. (2006). Analyzing the structure of expert knowledge. *Information and management, 43*, 77–91.

Cabot, L. B., & Kinchin, I. M. (2007). *Beyond competence: Visualising expertise.* Paper presented at the British Society for the Study of Prosthetic Dentistry (BSSPD) Annual Conference, 3rd – 5th March, Newcastle, UK.

Cabot, L. B., & Kinchin, I. M. (2008, March 3). *Clinical teaching as a template for the development of university pedagogy.* Paper presented at the 2nd Annual 'Excellence in Teaching Conference', King's College London. London, UK.

Cañas, A. J., & Novak, J. D. (2008). *Concept mapping using Cmap tools to enhance meaningful learning*. In A. Okada, S. Buckingham Shum, & T. Sherborne (Eds.), *Knowledge Cartography: Software tools and mapping techniques* (pp. 25–46). London: Springer.

Canning, J. (2007). Pedagogy as a discipline: Emergence, sustainability and professionalisation. *Teaching in Higher Education, 12*(3), 393–403.

Chang, S.-N. (2007). Externalising students' mental models through concept maps. *Journal of Biological Education, 41*, 107–112.

Copperman, E., Beeri, C., & Ben-Zvi, N. (2007). Visual modelling of learning processes. *Innovations in Education and Teaching International, 44*(3), 257–272.

Cousin, G. (2008). *Threshold concepts: Old wine in new bottles or new forms of transactional curriculum inquiry?* In R. Land, J. H. F. Meyer, & J. Smith (Eds.), *Threshold concepts within the disciplines* (pp. 261–272). Rotterdam: Sense Publishers.

Dall'Alba, G., & Sandberg, J. (2006). Unveiling professional development: A critical view of stage models. *Review of Educational Research, 76*(3), 383–412.

Darbyshire, P. (1994). Skilled expert practice: Is it 'all in the mind'? A response to English's critique of Benner's novice to expert model. *Journal of Advanced Nursing, 19*, 755–761.

Dreyfus, H. L., & Dreyfus, S. E. (1986). *Mind over machine: The power of human intuition and expertise in the era of the computer*. New York: The free press.

English, I. (1993). Intuition as a function of the expert nurse: A critique of Benner's novice to expert model. *Journal of Advanced Nursing, 18*, 387–393.

Eraut, M. (2000). Non-formal learning and tacit knowledge in professional work. *British Journal of Educational Psychology, 70*, 113–136.

Gamache, P. (2002). University students as creators of personal knowledge: An alternative epistemological view. *Teaching in Higher Education, 7*, 277–294.

Gold, J., Jenkins, A., Lee, R., Monk, J., Riley, J., Shepherd, I., et al. (1991). *Teaching geography in higher education: A manual of good practice*. Oxford: Blackwell.

Gravett, S. J., & Swart, E. (1997). Concept mapping: A tool for promoting and assessing conceptual change. *South African Journal of Higher Education, 11*, 122–126.

Green, B., & Lee, A. (1995). Theorising postgraduate pedagogy. *Australian Universities' Review, 2*, 40–45.

Halford, G. S. (1993). *Children's understandings: The development of mental models*. Hillsdale, NJ: Lawrence Erlbaum.

Hay, D. B., & Kinchin, I. M. (2007). *Medical students' response to variation in expert knowledge structures: Rote learning?* Paper presented at the Annual Conference of the European Learning Styles Information Network (ELSIN), 12th – 14th June, Trinity College, Dublin, Ireland.

Hay, D. B., Kinchin, I. M., & Lygo-Baker, S. (2008). Making learning visible: The role of concept mapping in higher education. *Studies in Higher Education, 33*(3), 295–311.

Hill, L. H., & Talluto, B. A. (2006). Visualizing the clinical thinking process to prepare students for effective patient counselling. *Journal of Pharmacy Teaching, 12*(2), 69–81.

Hoffman, R. R., & Lintern, G. (2006). *Eliciting and representing the knowledge of experts*. In K. A. Ericsson, N. Charness, P. J. Feltovich, & P. R. Hoffman (Eds.), *The Cambridge handbook of expertise and expert performance* (pp. 203–222). Cambridge, UK: Cambridge University Press.

Horton, P. B., McConney, A. A., Gallo, M., Woods, A. L., Senn, G. J., & Hamelin, D. (1993). An investigation of the effectiveness of concept mapping as an instructional tool. *Science Education, 77*, 95–111.

Jarvis, P. (1996). *Commentary on chapter twelve: A case study of a patient-centred nurse*. In K. W. M. Fulford, S. Ersser, & T. Hope (Eds.), *Essential patient care* (pp. 193–197). London: Blackwell.

Jones, S. (2007). Reflections on the lecture: Outmoded medium or instrument of inspiration? *Journal of Further and Higher Education, 31*, 397–406.

Kinchin, I. M. (2001). If concept mapping is so helpful to learning biology, why aren't we all doing it? *International Journal of Science Education, 23*(12), 1257–1269.

Kinchin, I. M., Cabot, L. B., & Hay, D. B. (2008). Visualising expertise: Towards an authentic pedagogy for higher education. *Teaching in Higher Education, 13*(3), 315–326.

Kinchin, I. M., & Hay, D. B. (2007). The myth of the research-led teacher. *Teachers and Teaching: theory and practice, 13*(1), 43–61.

Kinchin, I. M., Hay, D. B., & Adams, A. (2000). How a qualitative approach to concept map analysis can be used to aid learning by illustrating patterns of conceptual development. *Educational Research, 42*(1), 43–57.

Kinchin, I. M., Lygo-Baker, S., & Hay, D. B. (2008). Universities as centres of non-learning. *Studies in Higher Education, 33*(1), 89–103.

Lawless, C., Smee, P., & O'Shea, T. (1998). Using concept sorting and concept mapping in business and public administration, and in education: An overview. *Educational Research, 40*, 89–103.

Lynton, E. A. (1990). *New concepts of professional expertise: Liberal learning as part of career-oriented education.* Working paper #4. (Massachusetts University, Boston. New England Resource Center for Higher Education). Retrieved from http://www.eric.ed.gov/ERICDocs/data/ericdocs2sql/content_storage_01/0000019b/80/12/fc/7f.pdf

Manley, K., & Garbett, R. (2000). Paying Peter and Paul: Reconciling concepts of expertise with competency for a clinical career structure. *Journal of Clinical Nursing, 9*, 347–359.

McAleese, R. (1994). A theoretical view on concept mapping. *ALT Journal, 2*, 38–48.

McCormick, K. (1994). *The culture of reading and the teaching of English.* Manchester, UK: Manchester University Press.

McLeod, P. J., Meagher, T., Steinert, Y., Schuwirth, L., & McLeod, A. H. (2004). Clinical teachers' tacit knowledge of basic pedagogic principles. *Medical Teacher, 26*, 23–27.

Meyer, J., & Land, R. (2003). *Threshold concepts and troublesome knowledge: Linkages to ways of thinking and practicing within the disciplines.* Enhancing teaching-learning environments in undergraduate courses: Occasional report 4. pp. 1–12. Retrieved from www.ed.ac.uk/etl/docs/ETL report4.pdf

Meyer, J. H. F., & Land, R. (2005). Threshold concepts and troublesome knowledge (2): Epistemological considerations and a conceptual framework for teaching and learning. *Higher Education, 49*, 373–388.

Nesbit, J. C., & Adesope, O. O. (2006). Learning with concept and knowledge maps: A meta-analysis. *Review of Educational Research, 76*(3), 413–448.

Novak, J. D. (1998). *Learning, creating, and using knowledge: Concept maps™ as facilitative tools in schools and corporations.* Mahwah, NJ: Lawrence Erlbaum Associates.

Novak, J. D., & Cañas, A. J. (2007). Theoretical origins of concept maps, how to construct them and uses in education. *Reflecting Education, 3*(1), 29–42.

Novak, J. D., & Gowin, D. B. (1984). *Learning how to learn.* Cambridge, UK: Cambridge University Press.

O'Brien, M. (2008). *Threshold concepts for university teaching and learning.* In R. Land, J. H. F. Meyer, & J. Smith (Eds.), *Threshold concepts within the disciplines* (pp. 289–305). Rotterdam, The Netherlands: Sense Publishers.

Patel, V. L., Arocha, J. F., & Kaufman, D. R. (1999). *Expertise and tacit knowledge in medicine.* In R. J. Sternberg & J. A. Horvath (Eds.), *Tacit knowledge in professional practice: Researcher and practitioner perspectives* (pp. 75–99). Mahwah, NJ: Lawrence Erlbaum.

Ritter, L. (2007). Unfulfilled promises: How inventories, instruments and institutions subvert discourses of diversity and promote commonality. *Teaching in Higher Education, 12*, 569–579.

Rolfe, G. (1996). *Closing the theory practice gap: A new paradigm for nursing.* Oxford, UK: Butterworth.

Rolfe, G. (1997). Science, abduction and the fuzzy nurse: An exploration of expertise. *Journal of Advanced Nursing, 25*, 1070–1075.

Savin-Baden, M. (2006). *Disjunction as a form of troublesome knowledge in problem-based learning.* In J. H. F. Meyer & R. Land (Eds.), *Overcoming barriers to student understanding: threshold concepts and troublesome knowledge* (pp. 160–172). London: Routledge.

Seymour, B., Kinn, S., & Sutherland, N. (2003). Valuing both critical and creative thinking in clinical practice: Narrowing the research-practice gap. *Journal of Advanced Nursing, 42*(3), 288–296.

Simon, B. (1999). *Why no pedagogy in England?* In J. Leach & B. Moon (Eds.), *Learners and pedagogy* (pp. 34–45). London: Paul Chapman Publishing.

Taylor, J. S. (1993). Resolving epistemological pluralism: A personal account of the research process. *Journal of Advanced Nursing, 18*, 1073–1076.

Van Leuven, P. (1997). Using concept maps of effective teaching as a tool in supervision. *Journal of Research and Development in Education, 30*, 261–277.

Welsh, I., & Lyons, C. M. (2000). Evidence-based care and the case for intuition and tacit knowledge in clinical assessment and decision making in mental health nursing practice: An empirical contribution to the debate. *Journal of Psychiatric Mental Health Nursing, 8*, 299–305.

White, R. (1996). The link between the laboratory and learning. *International Journal of Science Education, 18*, 761–774.

Wingate, U. (2006). Doing away with study skills. *Teaching in Higher Education, 11*, 457–469.

Wingate, U. (2007). A framework for transition: Supporting 'learning to learn' in higher education. *Higher Education Quarterly, 61*, 391–405.

Yielder, Y. (2004). An integrated model of professional expertise and its implications for higher education. *International Journal of Lifelong Education, 23*(1), 60–80.

Ian M. Kinchin, Lyndon B. Cabot and David B. Hay.
King's College London, UK.

JERRY MEAD AND SIMON GRAY

6. CONTEXTS FOR THRESHOLD CONCEPTS (I)

A Conceptual Structure for Localizing Candidates

INTRODUCTION

Threshold concepts were first described by Meyer and Land (2003) "as a particular basis for differentiating between core learning outcomes that represent 'seeing things in a new way' and those that do not." As such, threshold concepts are presented as conceptual gateways or portals that lead to previously inaccessible ways of thinking in a discipline. Mastering a threshold concept results in a 'transformed way of understanding, or interpreting, or viewing something without which the learner cannot progress.' This idea has tremendous intuitive appeal and its introduction has sparked interest among many educators, as evidenced by the growing number of papers describing proposed threshold concepts in disciplines ranging from geology to computer science and philosophy to biology.

However, these papers focus on the student's view and their interactions with threshold concepts, paying little attention to the disciplinary side of threshold concepts. Here we seek to fill this gap by defining a mechanism for understanding disciplinary concepts from the discipline's point of view. At the heart of our approach lie two critical observations.

First, threshold concepts are disciplinary constructs that have emerged from the crucible of disciplinary scrutiny as definable abstractions agreed upon, at least implicitly, by members of the discipline. They are also disciplinary abstractions in that, in arriving at an agreed upon definition, the personal views associated with the concept by members of the discipline will have been jettisoned. Of course the same can be said of all *disciplinary concepts*, whether threshold or not: they are concepts (abstractions) which have emerged from the crucible of disciplinary scrutiny to be the focus of curricular attention.

Second, we are struck by the fact that while the word 'concept' appears in the phrase 'threshold concept,' it has received little direct attention in the threshold concept literature.[1] This lack of focus on 'concept' is surprising since it clearly plays a fundamental role and is a notion that continues to receive considerable attention in other disciplines, including philosophy, cognitive science, and education theory.

The goal of this paper, then, is to provide a more secure footing, in the form of a model of conceptual structure on which the term 'concept' in 'threshold concept' can rest. We define a structure, called a disciplinary concept graph, which facilitates understanding concepts in a discipline. We argue that the five threshold concept characteristics can be localized within such concept graphs.

J. H. F. Meyer, R. Land and C. Baillie (eds.), Threshold Concepts and
Transformational Learning, 97–113.
© *2010 Sense Publishers. All rights reserved.*

THE CONCEPTION OF CONCEPT

Our approach depends on a focusing of attention on the notion of *concept*, with the goal of defining a model for the structure of concepts that will facilitate understanding (threshold) concepts within a discipline. This section first presents a somewhat pragmatic discussion of *concept*, followed by a recapitulation and critique of the definition of threshold concept given by Meyer and Land (2003), and finally a discussion of threshold concepts as curricular and pedagogical targets, from both constructivist and structural viewpoints.

Concepts within disciplines. For most concepts we have both private (personal) and public (shared) conceptions (i.e., mental representations). The public is a stripped down version of the private and is usually more or less common to the public conceptions of our friends and colleagues. In addition, while our personal conceptions can change over time, public conceptions tend to be much more stable – changes in public conceptions must somehow be negotiated with others, although perhaps not explicitly.

The same situation prevails when we focus on concepts arising in academic disciplines. A disciplinary concept emerging from disciplinary scrutiny will usually be presented in the form of an agreed upon definition – we see such definitions sprinkled through textbooks and scholarly work in all disciplines. In this way, disciplinary concepts have a stability and formality that outstrips that of other less formal, everyday public conceptions.

But how do students see and interact with these disciplinary concepts? When a student encounters a disciplinary concept, assuming a critical level of interest, they will develop their own conception of it, encrusted with previous experiences and metaphors from everyday life, sometimes leading to misconceptions – this is the essence of the constructivist view. The goal of the disciplinary educator is to work with students to bring the structure of their evolving *personal* conception into alignment with that of the *disciplinary* conception. Notice that this implies two separate conceptual spaces: the formal and more stable shared space of the discipline and the less formal and more volatile personal space of the learner.

Concepts more formally. With respect to the notion of concept, we do not adopt a particular theoretical stance (e.g., classical, prototype, theory-theory, neo-classical), since the definability of disciplinary concepts means they should be stable across these theories. Taking a general view, and working from an excellent review of concepts in Margolis and Laurence (2006), there are two concept characteristics which we adopt.

1. There are *complex concepts* that have a discernible structure, and *primitive concepts* that lack structure.
2. The structure of a complex concept is describable in terms complex concepts (the *components*) and primitive concepts (the *properties*).

Primitive concepts coincide with what we see as properties or attributes – examples being MASS, FORCE, COLOUR, and HAPPINESS. Primitive concepts serve as properties of complex concepts and often have an associated 'measure.' The complex concept CAR, for example, might include the concepts COLOUR and WEIGHT (primitive) and WHEEL and CHASSIS (complex). It is important to recognize that a complex concept can be described with different structures – a CAR can be described in terms of a few large components or in terms of lots of small components.

Note: a complex concept can lack structure (it has no components) and have only properties. For example, the concept SPHERE has no structure, but has many properties (RADIUS, VOLUME, and so on).

Because our focus in the rest of this paper is on disciplinary concepts, we will adopt a couple of simplifying notational conventions. We will use the terms *concept* and *disciplinary concept* to refer to complex concepts, and will explicitly use the modifier *primitive* if we need to reference a primitive concept.

Disciplinary knowledge.   Another issue critical to our discussion of conceptual structure and threshold concepts is the knowledge associated with a disciplinary concept. Actually we are not as interested in the knowledge itself as we are the underlying 'logic' used in establishing that knowledge. In our daily existence we are constantly posing questions, differentiating, seeking justifications, assessing alternative actions. Foucault (1994) introduced the term *episteme* to refer to, as Payne (1997) puts it, an historical period's 'particular *configuration* of knowledge' (emphasis added). Importantly, Payne points out that 'Epistemes both enable and limit the *production* of knowledge...' (emphasis added).[2]

Focusing on disciplinary knowledge, Perkins (2006, p. 41–2) has used *episteme* in a more restricted sense to refer to 'a system of ideas or way of understanding that allows us to establish knowledge' within a discipline. We further focus the use of this term to the context of individual concepts:

A *concept episteme* is the system of ideas or way of understanding that allows us to establish knowledge of the concept.

The concept episteme, then, can be thought of as a set of assumptions about the concept plus ways of reasoning that are appropriate to the discipline and concept. The implication is that an episteme has an associated *knowledge space* that is 'produced' by applying the episteme. This knowledge should be viewed as the conclusions we can make when applying the episteme, either theoretically or in application to some data. Since it is only as a result of applying the episteme that knowledge can be produced, an episteme's knowledge space is necessarily bounded, reflecting Foucault's view of episteme.

As a simple example of a concept episteme, we could discuss the CAR episteme, the system that allows us to establish knowledge of the concept CAR. Significantly, this CAR episteme necessarily implicates the 'epistemes' for its components, the logic of combining these components, as well as areas of economics, mathematics and physics – even culture and personal aesthetics would be drawn in. Using the

CAR example, we could apply the episteme to make predictions about things like fuel economy, wind resistance, crash results at different speeds, etc. One of our goals in this paper is to demonstrate the link between concept episteme and concept structure.

Threshold Concepts – Definition and Critique

Meyer and Land recognized that their simple definition, presented at the beginning of this paper, gave insufficient direction for identifying and prioritizing threshold concepts, so they supplied five characteristics which threshold concepts might satisfy. It is important here to reiterate that the initial definition clearly indicates threshold concepts are transformative. In this light we quote from Meyer and Land (2003):

> Our discussions with practitioners in a range of disciplinary areas have led us to conclude that a threshold concept, across a range of subject contexts, is likely to be:
>
> – Transformative, in that, once understood, its potential effect on student learning and behaviour is to occasion a significant shift in the perception of a subject, or part thereof.
> – Probably irreversible, in that the change of perspective occasioned by acquisition of a threshold concept is unlikely to be forgotten, or will be unlearned only by considerable effort.
> – Integrative, that is, it exposes the previously hidden interrelatedness of something.
> – Possibly often (though not necessarily always) bounded, in that, any conceptual space will have terminal frontiers, bordering with thresholds into new conceptual areas.
> – Potentially (and possibly inherently) troublesome...
> [These are the places where learners are likely to have trouble and become 'stuck' because the concept may be conceptually difficult, counter-intuitive, involve language that is 'alien,' etc.]

These characterizations reflect the constructivist flavour surrounding the threshold concept idea. While the 'integrative' and 'bounded' characteristics may be more structurally based, the other three clearly make reference to the way learners structure their understanding – how they interact with and are affected by threshold concepts. There is an (arguably obvious) implication here – the personal effect on learners can only be significant if the way someone thinks from inside a discipline is different from the way someone outside of the discipline thinks. If, for a learner, the way people think in the discipline is different in very *new* ways, you have the source of alien knowledge, and if it is different in *unexpected* ways, you have a source of counterintuitive knowledge. Both the new and the unexpected can be troublesome. This would seem to be why the notion is so appealing: we have all experienced those aspects of transformation when conquering a concept that was particularly alien or trouble-some, and once the concept is in hand, it is hard to imagine our conceptual landscape without it.

While the constructivist flavour has its appeal and utility, there are questions that emerge with no obvious answers. First, the emphasis on student reaction to threshold concepts hides the importance of how the threshold concept is situated within the discipline. A second problem relates to curriculum and pedagogy: since the definition of threshold concept makes no reference to conceptual surroundings, it will be difficult to understand, much less devise, curricular settings for introducing threshold concepts or pedagogical strategies for guiding students to an under-standing of them.

Moving Forward

The threshold concept definition leaves threshold concepts isolated from an onto-logical point of view, i.e., there is no reference to other concepts in its disciplinary context.[3] The idea that a threshold concept 'exposes the previously hidden interrelatedness of something' implies that there must be other relevant concepts, i.e., the things that are 'interrelated.' Similarly the mention of 'thresholds into new conceptual areas' begs the question: Conceptual areas for what concepts? Our approach in this paper is to bring an alternative and complementary view of the threshold concept idea by focusing attention on the ontological (structural) side, with the goal to provide, within a disciplinary context, a conceptual structure within which threshold concepts can be localized.

A FRAMEWORK FOR CONCEPTUAL STRUCTURE

So what do we do? One problem we have identified is the lack of any description of the conceptual structure surrounding a threshold concept. For now we will focus on understanding the conceptual structure of disciplinary concepts, which we argue provides a framework within which candidate concepts can be localized.

Disciplinary Concept Graph[4]

Remember from our earlier discussion that complex concepts can be described as combinations of other concepts (complex and primitive), while primitive concepts have no structure and are seen as properties or attributes. A concept X, then, is the combination of a set C of complex concepts and a set P of primitive concepts. Since the concepts in C are complex, each can be decomposed in a similar way, giving rise to a hierarchical structure. Assuming X is described as follows

$$C = \{C_1, C_2, ..., C_m\}$$

$$P = \{p_1, p_2, ..., p_n\}, \tag{1}$$

the diagram in Figure 1 illustrates the structure of X. Each complex concept C_i, of course, can be similarly elaborated. There are complex concepts, it should be pointed out, with only properties; that is, that have no complex components. For example, the physics concept ELECTRON has no internal structure, but does have properties, such as *mass* and *charge*. So the set C is empty for ELECTRON.

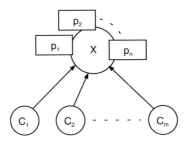

Figure 1. The structure of a disciplinary concept.

We use the phrase X **is the integration of the concepts in** C to mean that the complex structure of X can be defined in terms of the concepts in C *in some meaningful way*. This **meaningful way** describes not only the structure of X (in terms of C), but also the properties of X in terms of the properties of the concepts in C. Since these are disciplinary concepts, we refer to this meaningful way as a discipline's **integration logic** for the concept X.

What we have done in Figure 1 is to illustrate a structure which follows from the notion of integration. We refer to this as a disciplinary concept graph and define it formally as follows.

A **disciplinary concept graph**[5] **(DCG) for concept** X is a diagram consisting of labelled circles (called nodes) and arrows satisfying the following requirements.

- Each node names a complex disciplinary concept and there is a node labelled X.
- If A is a node and C is the set of all nodes with an arrow to A. Then the concept A is the integration of the concepts in C. We refer to the node A as an integrating node and the elements of C as the components of A.
- For each node A there is a path (following arrows) in the diagram leading from A to the node X.
- Each node A has an associated halo of boxes labelled with the names of A's primitive concepts.

The phrase X *is the integration of the set* C also carries the implication that X is the integration of no subset of C – i.e., there are no unnecessary concepts in C. It is also important to recognize that every integrating node in a DCG has an integration logic defining the way the node integrates its components. Because an integrating node A can integrate another integrating node B, the integration logic of A will reference the integration logic of B – i.e., the properties of A are described partly in terms of the properties of B (via B's integration logic). In the next section we illustrate these formal ideas in the context of the concept ATOM from physics.

Illustrating DCGs

Our goal in this section is to present examples that illustrate the use of DCGs in describing disciplinary concepts. We will look at a series of DCGs describing the physics concept ATOM, each exposing a different view of ATOM. What is important here is that the views described either represent a formal or informal way of viewing the concept or, as in the second example, a way that at one time was seen as reasonable, but later shown to be lacking. In each example it is the integration logic that is critical. These examples are not meant to imply any pedagogical strategies or ordering of topics in a course covering atomic structures; rather, they are meant to illustrate the use of DCGs in understanding the disciplinary view of a concept.

A simple model of the atom. Typically a disciplinary concept can be approached in different ways, depending on the pedagogical circumstance. For example, we can talk about the ATOM as a non-decomposable particle that has mass, in which case ATOM is seen as a complex concept comprising no complex components (C is empty) and one property, *mass* ($P = \{mass\}$). We depict this structure in Figure 2(a). The concept ELECTRON is also non-decomposable, but can be described with two properties, *mass* and *charge*, as shown in Figure 2(b) (so, again C is empty, and now $P = \{charge, mass\}$).

(a)   (b)

Figure 2. Representing concept properties.

While ELECTRON is seen by physics as having no complex structure, ATOM is known to have complex structure that can be described in various ways depending on the historical or pedagogical context. For example, another model of ATOM, more complex than that of Figure 2a, has the structure shown in the DCG in Figure 3. Here ATOM is depicted as integrating two complex concepts ELECTRON and NUCLEUS, and the property *mass*. The properties for NUCLEUS reflect that it has *mass* and an electric *charge* (a positive integer value). The properties for ELECTRON are the same, though the charge on an electron has value -1.

As the discussion in the previous section highlights, an integration node in a DCG (e.g., ATOM in Figure 3) also has an integration logic which specifies exactly how the integrating concept is described in terms of its components. In this case the integration logic is very simple.

- An atom is a central nucleus with a surrounding cloud of orbiting electrons and with the electrons behaving as classical particles.
- The number of electrons equals the charge on the nucleus.
- The mass of the atom is equal to the sum of the masses of the orbiting electrons plus the mass of the nucleus.

The ATOM episteme will include the integration logic just described, but will also include classical laws of physics and mathematical reasoning.

There are many other deductions we can make using this episteme. But most of these do not coincide with the behaviour of the physical world. For example, using this integration logic we would expect that over time all electrons will lose their energy and collapse to the middle. However, we know this is not what happens.

There are two characteristics of atoms explained by this simple integration logic. First, since the number of electrons equals the charge on the nucleus, the atom is electrostatically neutral. Second, although this is really quite simple – we know what is meant by the mass of an atom (at least a single atom at rest) – the integration logic tells us this directly. This integration logic is very simple and provides few insights into the behaviour of our physical world. As a very simple example – hydrogen, the atom with a single electron, has a characteristic spectrum and this model gives no insight into its structure.

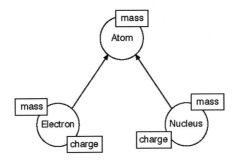

Figure 3. A DCG for the concept ATOM .

The Bohr model of the atom. It is important to recognize that there are other integration logics for the DCG in Figure 3. For example, a more interesting model of ATOM is the Bohr model, described by Niels Bohr in 1913 (see Bohr, 1966). Since the Bohr model has the same DCG as the simple model (above), it must be the integration logic that makes the difference.

The integration logic for this model starts with that for the simple model above, but it puts restrictions on the way electrons behave in their orbits.

- Electron orbits are at a discrete set of distances from the nucleus, with each orbit having a specific energy.
- Electrons lose no energy while in a particular orbit. They gain (lose) a set quantum of energy by jumping from their current orbit to the neighbouring orbit outward (inward).
- Energy for an orbit is a function of the circumference of that orbit.

Again, the ATOM episteme will include the integration logic just described, but will also include classical laws of physics and mathematical reasoning.

So this integration logic is more complex than that for the simple model, with complex relationships between nucleus, electrons, and electron orbits governing the nature of the atom. As in the simple example, we can deduce the electrostatic neutrality of atoms and the mass of an atom based on this integration logic. But the rules Bohr laid down for orbits and electron transitions between neighbouring orbits expose an interesting hidden piece of information: from this integration logic one can deduce the spectrum of hydrogen, which was an important insight at the turn of the 20th century. While this model exposes the structure of the hydrogen spectrum, it provides no insights into the spectra of other atoms – even helium, the atom with just two electrons. In addition, since in the base energy configuration all electrons of an atom will occupy the same orbit, there is no possibility of chemical interactions and thus no molecular structures. So this model exposes something interesting about hydrogen atoms (the spectrum), but no other characteristics we normally associate with atoms (such as chemical interaction).[6]

Particle/Wave model of the atom. The failure of early atomic models to explain how the world we interact with behaves was due to the assumption that sub-atomic 'particles' obey classical laws of physics. The key to progressing past the classically-based models (which expose very little) was the realization that sub-atomic 'particles' have both particle and wave properties. A model based on this assumption, the *particle/wave model*, was described by Schrödinger in 1926 (see Schrödinger, 1966) and also matches the structure of the DCG in Figure 3.

The integration logic for the particle/wave model is too complex to present here, though it does begin with the simple integration logic. In addition, the integration describes the interactions between the electrons and the nucleus in terms of wave equations. Electrons are assumed to be distributed in shells (orbits) around the nucleus, with the distribution determined by certain quantum values based on wave characteristics of each electron.

Based on the integration logic we can understand exactly how electrons distribute into shells for each atom, and in this way understand how chemical bonds and molecular structures come about. In addition, we can understand the spectrum not only for hydrogen, but for all atoms. More generally, based on this integration logic, we can understand why the physical world we are familiar with behaves as it does – the chemical combination of atoms into molecules, the basis for and validity of Newtonian physics, the thermal, optical and magnetic properties and stability of human-scale matter. So with its more complex integration logic, the particle/wave model exposes considerably more hidden properties of the atom than in the simple or Bohr models.

A deeper hierarchy. Before moving beyond the ontological side of the DCG, we will illustrate an important aspect of DCG structure. The three atomic models we discussed were all based on the same DCG – that in Figure 3; we used that DCG to illustrate the notion of integration logic because it has only one integration node. In fact, conceptual structures are often more complex. In the atom, for example, we know that the nucleus is composed of neutrons and protons. We can add this new layer of information and produce the DCG in Figure 4(a). This DCG is not really an extension of that in Figure 3 since the properties of the nodes have changed. These properties were chosen to reflect a particular way of viewing the atom – the atomic weight and number and the isotope being common entries in a periodic table. This diagram requires two integration logics, one for NUCLEUS and the other for ATOM. It should also be clear that the integration logic for ATOM would in some sense incorporate that of NUCLEUS since the properties of NUCLEUS are specified via its integration logic.

The DCG in Figure 4(b) shows a more complete DCG for ATOM – properties have been left off to clarify the DCG's integration structure. It reflects the fact that protons and neutrons have complex structure themselves in terms of sub-atomic particles called up-quarks and down-quarks. Protons contain two up-quarks and one down-quark, while neutrons contain two down-quarks and one up-quark. In this case the integration logic for ATOM will implicate that of NUCLEUS, as before, but also those for PROTON and NEUTRON.

The DCG represents the ontological side of a complex concept, but we are also interested in the epistemic side, which we turn to next.

A Context for Disciplinary Knowledge

It is important to stop here and remember why we are motivated to construct these DCGs. First, we want to address the ontological isolation of threshold concepts by localizing them within a disciplinary conceptual structure. Second, we are

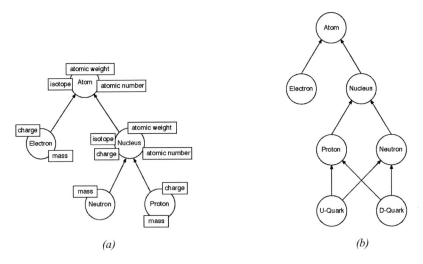

(a)   *(b)*

Figure 4. Two multi-layered DCGs for ATOM.

ultimately interested in disciplinary concepts as they are encountered by students in the course of their education. The fact that we can have *multiple* DCGs for the same concept means that an instructor can order the DCGs for a target concept, introducing the component concepts, their properties, and discipline-defined integration logics in an order that promotes meaningful learning. It is through this process that disciplinary knowledge is both created and comes to be understood by students. Key to this is the role of epistemes within a DCG. The short sections that follow more fully describe this important connection.

Epistemes and integration logics. A node in a DCG represents a concept and consequently an associated episteme which provides a system of ideas that allows us to establish knowledge of the concept. For an integrating node in a DCG, the integration logic describes how, from the discipline's view, the concept, its components, and their various properties are related. Thus, the obvious link between a node in a DCG and its episteme is the integration logic of the node. The episteme of an integrating node in a DCG includes the node's integration logic, which describes the properties of the integrated concepts *in some meaningful way*. In addition, the episteme includes mechanisms for *reasoning* within the discipline. For example, the episteme for ATOM would include (but not be limited to) capabilities for reasoning about mathematics, logic, and objects in motion, both formal (from physics) and intuitive (from everyday life). So, if someone hands us a thing and poses the standard categorization question 'Is this thing an atom?' we will apply the episteme for ATOM in giving our answer.

We also want to remember that an important characteristic of a concept episteme is that it both facilitates and limits the production of knowledge of a concept. The limiting of knowledge production is important as it makes clear the way in which the episteme is seen as bounding a knowledge space.

Condensation points. Our interest in epistemes lies in our desire to localize threshold concepts within some conceptual structure. This localization hinges in part on the nature of the questions, problems, and judgements to which the episteme can be applied. For students these will fall naturally onto a spectrum of difficulty, as described by Perkins (1999). Our interest here is in those concepts that are central to the discipline and are targets of the questions, problems, and judgements.

> We use the term ***condensation point*** to refer to a unifying and generalizing concept that is definable within an episteme and condenses out of the associated knowledge space a fundamental disciplinary idea or capability.

For example, in the particle/wave model questions arise focusing on the diameter of an atom, its mass, or its spectrum. Thus, ATOMIC DIAMETER, ATOMIC MASS, and ATOMIC SPECTRUM could reasonably be termed condensation points of the concept ATOM. Clearly the knowledge space defined by an episteme and condensation points identified within it are of critical interest to educators. It is within the collection of condensation points that we see candidates to be threshold concepts.

LOCALIZING THRESHOLD CONCEPTS IN DCGS

Earlier we discussed the constructivist nature of three of the five threshold concept characteristics and the benefits of localizing all the characteristics in a disciplinary conceptual structure. In this section we discuss the DCG structure as a context for this localization, thus providing a structural model for thinking about threshold concept candidates.

Our claim is that a DCG provides a natural structure for understanding the five threshold concept characteristics. The natural connection between DCGs and threshold concepts will be seen to be the concept episteme, whose associated knowledge space, we argue, is a fertile hunting ground for threshold concept candidates. Table 1 summarizes the localization discussed in the short sections that follow.

Table 1. Threshold concept localization within a DCG

Threshold Concept Characteristic	DCG Component
Integrative, Irreversible	Integrating Node
Bounded	Episteme
Transformative, Troublesome	Condensation Point

Integrative and Irreversible → Integrating Nodes

The notion of concept integration is central to the DCG structure, with all else flowing from it: integration logic, episteme, knowledge space. The 'degree' of integration of component concepts occurring at a node in a DCG can be somewhere along the spectrum from simple to complex, determined by the number and complexity of the interrelationships among the integrated component concepts and their properties, as specified by the integration logic.

In the section illustrating DCGs we discussed three integration logics for atom and the degree to which each exposes properties of atoms that would not have been expected when viewing the integrated concepts on their own. It is the power of the atom episteme in each model that allows us to understand these properties. The interesting thing in the three models is that the first integration logic exposes very little, the second unexpectedly exposes the hydrogen spectrum, while the third exposes the physical world as we know it. These three integration logics illustrate what we mean by the 'degree' of integration.

Our choice of the term 'integration' in the definition of DCG was obviously not coincidental. It is in the integrating nodes of a DCG that we find the 'integrative' characteristic *of threshold concept* clearly represented. The degree to which the integrative property is seen for a particular node is directly related to the degree of integration for that node, as represented in the integration logic.

We also see the integrating nodes in a DCG to be the localization for the 'irreversible' characteristic of threshold concept, arguing that if the integration logic of a node is simple it will be more easily reversed than if the integration logic is useful and complex.

Bounded → Epistemes

It is a fundamental property of an episteme that it both facilitates and limits the production of knowledge about a concept. The knowledge space of an episteme is all statements that can be deduced from the episteme. It is in this limiting way that the episteme acts as a boundary, or, put another way, acts to bound the knowledge space of its concept.

But this rather theoretical take on boundedness doesn't seem to really capture what is experienced by the learner. When the learner takes on a particular concept, many condensation points in the disciplinary knowledge space are encountered. At a particular time some condensation points will have been incorporated into the learner's personal knowledge space, while others remain outside it. To the learner, the portion of the episteme's knowledge space that remains elusive can appear to be a new and separate knowledge space with, perhaps, a threshold concept as the gateway between them. On the disciplinary side there is just one knowledge space, that of the concept's episteme, but viewed from the learner's personal perspective that disciplinary space can appear to have internal boundaries.

The threshold, which for the learner acts as a portal to the new knowledge space, is a condensation point in the discipline's knowledge space. For example, the diagram in Figure 5 illustrates the threshold concept LIMIT within the conceptual space of *real analysis* (known more commonly as calculus). The fact that all statements in the knowledge space are deducible is important on the disciplinary side. It indicates that there are no internal boundaries within the knowledge space, and thus no natural portals. However, as the lightly dashed arrows imply, some deductions are more straightforward than others. In fact, some deductions that follow directly from the episteme may be infeasible even for a practitioner (though theoretically possible). The importance of the LIMIT threshold concept is that,

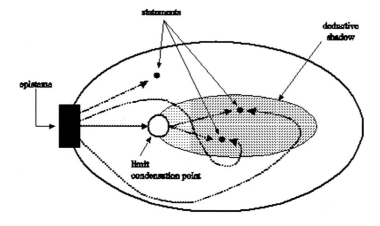

Figure 5. Seeing portals within disciplinary spaces.

once understood, it facilitates deduction of statements within its sphere – the oval extending from LIMIT, which we call the *deductive shadow of* LIMIT. Thus, even on the disciplinary side, we can see a threshold concept acting as a portal to a new bounded knowledge space – the deductive shadow.

Transformative and Troublesome → Condensation Points

A DCG represents a static view of a concept, i.e., it tells us how an instance of the concept is constructed from its components. The episteme, on the other hand, exposes a more dynamic view of the concept: we can ask the question 'How are the electrons distributed around the nucleus?' or 'What is the mass of this atom?' Thus, the episteme captures questions, problems, judgements that focus on fundamental disciplinary ideas or capabilities. When studying a concept, a student is more likely to find troublesome the application of the concept than understanding the concept's structural characteristics. It is for this reason that we see condensation points as likely sources of troublesomeness. An example of such a troublesome condensation point occurs in the wave/particle knowledge space for ATOM: 'Given a particular atom, compute its diameter.' While there may be nothing surprising about the results of such computations, they are still difficult, so the condensation point ATOMIC DIAMETER would seem to be troublesome, though it is not a threshold concept.

We see the transformative characteristic as reflecting a learner's reaction to a conflict between their personal view of the world and the discipline's view, which the learner is trying to acquire. The source of the conflict can vary: it can arise from an inconsistency between the personal and disciplinary views – a theoretical inconsistency; it can arise from a realization that the disciplinary view is inconsistent with the learner's view of himself or herself in the world; or it can arise because the disciplinary view is alien and the learner has no ready conceptions to model the disciplinary view. While conceptual structure could be the cause of a transformative conflict, it is more likely that a condensation point would be the source of conflict.

MOVING FORWARD

The goal of this paper was to provide a more secure footing, in the form of a formally defined conceptual structure, on which the term 'concept' in 'threshold concept' can rest. To this end we have defined the disciplinary concept graph (DCG), which describes both the ontological structure (the graph) and epistemological structure (integration logic, episteme, knowledge space) of a disciplinary concept from the disciplinary point of view. It is important that, in practice, the use of these graphs within a particular curricular context is not meant to specify topic sequences to be covered. Rather, an educator would use a particular DCG to understand the conceptual entanglements (of condensation points within a knowledge space) a student might experience.

We have also related a correspondence between certain structures in disciplinary concept graphs and the five threshold concept characteristics, thus fulfilling the promise of a firmer footing. We have used simple examples drawn from atomic physics and mathematics to illustrate DCG structures and the correspondence to threshold concept characteristics. What is needed now is an example that illustrates how DCGs can be applied in a more realistic teaching and learning context. A start in this direction is presented in Mead and Gray (2009) and in Gray and Mead (in preparation), where specific concepts in Computer Science are discussed in the context of DCGs.

An important consequence of the work presented here is the recognition that there are two parallel and complementary knowledge spaces involved when discussing a disciplinary threshold concept. The learner sees the threshold concept within their personal knowledge space, while the discipline sees it as a condensation point in the knowledge space of a concept's episteme. Though not explored in this paper, there are some obvious questions that arise from this recognition.

- How can the localization of threshold concept characteristics inform the design of pedagogical strategies for confronting threshold concepts?
- How can the localization of threshold concept characteristics help instructors to better understand concepts based on the degree to which the concept reflects each threshold concept characteristic?
- How can the localization of threshold concept characteristics help instructors to formulate approaches to dealing with conceptual bottlenecks, as described in Middendorf and Pace (2004)?
- How can disciplinary concept graphs be used to help organize curricular structures meant to confront threshold concepts?

ACKNOWLEDGMENTS

The authors wish to thank Martin Ligare and David Schepf, of the Bucknell University Department of Physics, for their assistance in vetting the atomic models described in this paper, and Gillian Barker, of the Philosophy Department of the University of Western Ontario, for valuable discussions of concepts in the philosophy of science.

NOTES

[1] In this we are in agreement with Rowbottom (2007), who points out that the original presentation of threshold concepts lacks a discussion of the nature of 'concept,' further opening the door to a wide range of candidates.

[2] Though Foucault's episteme is considerably broader in scope, it seems to capture something similar to Kuhn's paradigm, which describes scientific achievements [read 'knowledge'] that 'attract an enduring group of adherents away from competing modes of scientific activity' and 'are sufficiently open-ended to leave all sorts of problems for the redefined group of practitioners to resolve' (Kuhn, 1996).

[3] When we use the term 'ontological' in this paper, we are referring specifically to the conceptual framework from the discipline's point of view. This is in contrast to the more learner-centred use of the term in Meyer and Land (2005) and Meyer, Land, and Davies (2008).

[4] The disciplinary concept graph structure presented here is a reformulation of the notions *anchor concept* and *anchor concept graph* presented in Mead et al., (2006) and expanded in Mead and Gray (2008).

[5] A *graph* is a mathematical structure which might also be known in other disciplines as a *network* or a *map* (as in concept map (see Novak, 1990)).

[6] This is a nice example of concepts 'emerging from the crucible of disciplinary scrutiny.' In this case, the original model failed that scrutiny, so was revised. The revision was an improvement, but it was also recognized as lacking. This illustrates a *discipline's* epistemological development. Learners also go through phases where they think their understanding explains the world around them, until they encounter something their model can't explain, and they then need to gather enough information to be able to revise (or, in drastic situations, discard) their model.

REFERENCES

Bohr, N. (1966). On the constitution of atoms and molecules. In H. A. Boorse & L. Motz (Eds.), *The world of the atom* (pp. 751–765). Basic Books Inc.

Foucault, M. (1994). *The order of things: An archaeology of human sciences.* Vintage.

Gray, S., & Mead, J. (*in preparation*). Threshold Concepts (in CS): A Promise Unmet? Proceedings of ITICSE'09: The 14th Annual Conference on Innovation and Technology in Computer Science.

Kuhn, T. (1996). *The structure of scientific revolutions.* University Of Chicago Press.

Margolis, E., & Laurence, S. (2006). Concepts and cognitive science. In E. Margolis & S. Laurence (Eds.), *Concepts: Core readings* (chap. 1). MIT Press.

Mead, J., & Gray, S. (2008, June). *Do threshold concepts exist* (in computer science)? (Tech. Rep. No. 08-3). Lewisbug, PA: Department of Computer Science, Bucknell University.

Mead, J., & Gray, S. (2009, January). *Contexts for threshold concepts (II): Applying a conceptual structure in computer science.* (Tech. Rep. No. 09-1). Lewisbug, PA: Department of Computer Science.

Mead, J., Gray, S., Hamer, J., James, R., Sorva, J., Clair, C. S., et al. (2006). A cognitive approach to identifying measurable milestones for programming skill acquisition. In *Iticse-wgr '06 working group reports.* ACM Press.

Meyer, J., & Land, R. (2003, May). Threshold concepts and troublesome knowledge: Linkages to ways of thinking and practicing within the disciplines. *ETL Project: Occasional Report 4.*

Meyer, J., & Land, R. (2005, April). Threshold concepts and troublesome knowledge (2): Epistemological considerations and a conceptual framework for teaching and learning. *Higher Education, 49*(3), 373–388.

Meyer, J., Land, R., & Davies, P. (2008). Threshold concepts and troublesome knowledge (4): issues of variation and variability. In J. Meyer, R. Land, & J. Smith (Eds.), *Threshold concepts within the disciplines* (pp. 59–74). Sense Publishers.

Middendorf, J., & Pace, D. (2004). *Decoding the disciplines.* Jossey-Bass.

Novak, J. D. (1990). Concept mapping: A useful tool for science education. *Journal of Research in Science Teaching, 27*(10), 937–949.

Payne, M. (1997). *Reading knowledge: An introduction to Foucault, Barthes and Althusser.* Blackwell Publishers.

Perkins, D. (1999, November). The many faces of constructivism. *Educational Leadership, 57*(3).

Perkins, D. (2006). Constructivism and troublesome knowledge. In J. Meyer & R. Land (Eds.), *Overcoming barriers to student understanding: Threshold concepts and troublesome knowledge* (pp. 33–47). Routledge.

Rowbottom, D. P. (2007). Demystifying threshold concepts. *Journal of Philosophy of Education*, *41*(2).

Shrodinger, E. (1966). Wave mechanics. In H. A. Boorse & L. Motz (Eds.), *The world of the atom* (pp. 1067–1076). Basic Books Inc.

Jerry Mead
Department of Computer Science
Bucknell University

Simon Gray
Department of Mathematics and Computer Science
College of Wooster

PART II:
CONCEPTUAL TRANSFORMATIONS

KIM A. CHEEK

7. WHY IS GEOLOGIC TIME TROUBLESOME KNOWLEDGE?

What then, is time? I know well enough what it is, provided that no-one asks me;
but if I am asked what it is and try to explain, I am baffled.

(Augustine)

Augustine's sentiment is familiar to many. Time is a fundamental concept that is
a part of our daily existence yet is difficult to define. We have all had the experience
of an hour seeming to pass quickly or perhaps slowly depending upon the activity
in which we were engaged. If it can be difficult to explain or even perceive
conventional time correctly, how much more troublesome is it to conceive of
geologic or deep time? The intent of this paper is to suggest three possible factors
that account for why deep time is such troublesome knowledge.

THRESHOLD CONCEPTS AND TROUBLESOME KNOWLEDGE

Geologic or deep time is a thread that runs through all inquiry in the geosciences. In
any discipline there are some concepts that can be identified as so crucial to that
discipline that if you don't understand them, you will never truly be a practitioner in
the field. In that sense they function as a portal through which one must travel (Meyer
& Land, 2003). We have long recognized that some concepts seem to be particularly
difficult for students to grasp. Many authors have identified deep time as critical to
fuller understanding in geology (Dodick & Orion, 2003a, 2003b; Trend, 1998, 2000,
2001a, 2001b; Hume, 1979; Zen, 2001). Alternative conceptions regarding deep time
often persist after instruction (Libarkin & Anderson, 2005) and become barriers to
understanding certain geologic processes such as mountain building.

Meyer and Land's (2003) notion of threshold concepts provides a metaphor that
is useful when considering how to help students better comprehend deep time. It is
particularly profitable to consider one characteristic of a threshold concept—its
troublesome nature. Thinking about why deep time constitutes troublesome
knowledge can lead to strategies to help students cross the threshold.

WHY MIGHT DEEP TIME BE TROUBLESOME?

Meyer and Land (2003) and Perkins (2006) refer to five types of knowledge that
might be troublesome to students:
- *Ritual knowledge* is routine but often not meaningful. The procedure for finding
  a common denominator for two fractions is an example for many students.

J. H. F. Meyer, R. Land and C. Baillie (eds.), Threshold Concepts and
Transformational Learning, 117–129.
© *2010 Sense Publishers. All rights reserved.*

- *Inert knowledge* can be retrieved for a test but is not connected to other ideas or transferred to real world experiences.
- *Conceptually difficult knowledge* often appears to contradict everyday experiences and notions.
- *Foreign or alien knowledge* arises from a viewpoint that is different from the learner's.
- *Tacit knowledge* might also be termed intuitive knowledge.

Deep time might be considered ritual and/or inert knowledge, particularly if students have memorized an age for the Earth but then proceed to reason about deep time as if that age was irrelevant. More likely deep time can be considered both conceptually difficult and alien. A human lifespan is inconsequential in terms of geologic process such as mountain building or the sculpting of the Grand Canyon. To grasp that rocks can behave plastically, continents move, and the mountains we visit will one day be gone are all conceptually difficult. In order to help students cross the threshold of this troublesome concept of deep time we must determine what requisite knowledge is essential to the development of this idea.

Although they have not all used the term troublesome knowledge, many authors have noted how difficult a concept deep time is for students to grasp (Dodick & Orion, 2003a, 2003b; Libarkin et al, 2005; Trend, 1998, 2000, 2001a, 2001b; Truscott et al, 2006). A review of the literature suggests that students of all ages, and many in-service teachers hold similar alternative conceptions regarding deep time (Orion & Ault, 2007). Several explanatory mechanisms have been suggested for this trouble. Some argue that the scale of deep time makes it qualitatively different from conventional time (Ault, 1982; Dodick & Orion, 2003a, 2003b). While perhaps implicit in their discussion of scale, others have specifically noted that an understanding of large numbers is crucial to understanding deep time (Hume, 1979; Oversby, 1996; Trend, 1998). Trend (2001b) comments on the role of prior knowledge as a mediator in student ability to assimilate new geoscience information. Dodick and Orion (2003b) point out students' subject matter knowledge can be a confounding variable in studies of conceptions of deep time. While not dealing with deep time, Tretter et al. (2006a; 2006b) document the role of experience in students' conceptions of scale involving size and distance.

The authors mentioned above suggest several possible factors that can account for why deep time is such troublesome knowledge. Based upon this body of work, I propose that the concept of deep time can best be represented by a three-legged stool. The three legs are the components that support this understanding: conventional time, large numbers, and the subject matter knowledge of geology. The result, or the seat of the stool, is a concept of deep time. Just as a stool needs all three legs to be sturdy and bear weight, so an understanding of deep time requires all three of these legs to be in place. While a three-legged stool might have legs of equal size, it is also possible for its legs to be of unequal length and yet be stable. At present there is no real evidence to suggest whether the three legs of the "deep time stool" bear equal weight or which, if any, of these factors is more crucial to an understanding of deep time. The nature of the relationship among them is an open question. Nonetheless, the model enables us to explore student understanding

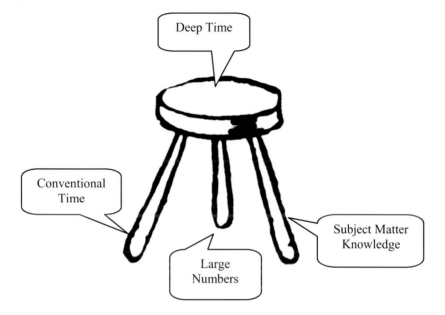

Figure 1. Factors Affecting Conception of Deep Time.

in each area and see how that knowledge is applied to a geologic context. We will examine each of these in turn and discuss why they are essential to a comprehension of deep time.

Hence, in the context of trying to determine why deep time is troublesome knowledge there are these three factors. They are not mutually exclusive and may interact in ways that are not yet clear. A poor understanding of deep time may reflect:

1. Failure to comprehend conventional time or failure to apply notions of conventional time to deep time. While deep time is quantitatively different from conventional time it is not qualitatively different. It requires the same basic concepts but these must be applied to a context that is beyond the realm of human experience. If a student does not comprehend conventional time he or she is unlikely to understand deep time.
2. Poor understanding of large numbers. Deep time differs from conventional time by many orders of magnitude, all of which are outside human ability to directly experience. Spans of time that are very different from one another in terms of human experience are inconsequential in terms of deep time. As one student put it, "A year and 1,000 years are the same in terms of geologic time."
3. Limited subject matter knowledge. Notions about deep time are based on ideas that have nothing to do with time. Absent the requisite subject matter knowledge, time becomes a secondary construct and is not used to reason about events.

A CONVENTIONAL UNDERSTANDING OF TIME

If the model is valid, then we argue that a concept of deep time, while containing confounding variables, is nonetheless a logical extrapolation of a general concept of time to events and processes that are out of the realm of human experience by orders of magnitude. It is not a qualitatively different construct. An individual must take the ideas essential to conceive of time in general and fit them into a new unit of measurement that will encompass vast amounts of time. Clearly this presents unique challenges to a pupil, but it can be argued that the basic principles upon which a concept of time is based are the same principles which underlie a concept of deep time.

What, then, are the necessary components for the acquisition of a general concept of time? Some of the most extensive research into the development of a conception of time in children was conducted by Piaget. His investigations of children's conceptions of time sit within a larger context of research on the development of children's conceptions across a host of domains and are embedded within his overall theoretical framework. As a result of a series of interviews of children aged five to nine Piaget identified two key ideas that he alleges develop in tandem, with the growth of one fostering the growth of the other, namely, succession and duration (Piaget, 1969). While we will deal with them in turn, Piaget repeatedly emphasized that these two ideas develop side by side.

The development of the idea of succession involves the ability to reconstruct the order of events after they have occurred and/or to perceive the correct order of events while they are occurring. While time itself is linear, children who understood succession were able to mentally reconstruct an event and realize that time travelled cannot be deduced solely on the basis of distance travelled if we are considering objects travelling at different velocities (Piaget, 1969, p. 103). This is precisely what students must do when asked to look at static phenomena such as stratigraphic sequences and by employing an operational understanding of reversibility; infer the action that resulted in what one now sees. Principles of stratigraphy such as cross-cutting relationships, original horizontality, fossil succession, and superposition are employed to determine the succession of events that led to a particular formation and require one to work backwards to sequence those events.

The second important idea for a conventional understanding of time is that duration, or amount of time necessary to complete a task, is inversely proportional to velocity. Durations can be judged based upon the starting and ending times of actions. If two actions start and end at the same time their durations are the same even if the rates at which those actions occur is different. Because the rates at which the actions occur are different, the result of the actions will appear different. Conversely, if two events start at the same time and proceed at different rates; their durations cannot be judged simply by comparing the amount of work completed or distance travelled. An example may clarify. Suppose two children begin at the same moment to draw stars on a paper. One draws very quickly while the other draws very slowly. Both stop when they have drawn twenty stars. Although both children have completed the same amount of work, the duration necessary to do so was not the same. Now, suppose those same children again draw stars on paper at the same rates as before but this time for a fixed amount of time. At the end of the time period one child would have drawn more stars than the other. In this case the durations were the same but the amount of work accomplished (number of stars drawn) was different.

This is applicable to geologic reasoning. A student must be able to dissociate size from rate. For example, two layers of sedimentary strata may be the same thickness but have been laid down at very different rates, and, hence, represent different durations. This is important for another reason. In thinking about rates of geologic processes one must not only think about very long units of time, but one must also conceive of processes that happen at very slow rates. The growth rate of the Himalayan Mountains is an example. Currently the Himalayas are growing at a rate of a little more than 1 cm per year. At this rate, they will be ten kilometers taller than they are now in one million years. If someone were to visit the Himalayan Mountains today and then return in 60 years, she would notice no difference in their size. Perception itself will not help a person comprehend a growth rate of 1 cm/year since there will be no observable difference to a person viewing them at a 60-year interval. Rather a student must be able to conceive of very slow velocities. Because the velocity of the event is slow, the amount of time required for the formation of the mountain range (duration) is long. In fact, duration may be a far more difficult concept to apply to a geologic context than succession.

Since deep time doesn't appear in the curriculum until middle school, some have concluded that a conventional understanding of time should be no impediment for students in their understanding of deep time (Ault, 1980). In fact, Piaget concluded that children usually develop an operational understanding of time by age 10. Yet there are indications that this may not always be the case. Dodick and Orion (2003a, 2003b) noted that middle and high school students made the same error as young children who equate size with duration when determining the age of geologic strata. Students in their study alleged that rock layers of equal size represented the same duration and ignored the possibility of different rates of deposition. This could indicate that when confronted with a time scale outside human experience, an individual reverts to a more primitive notion of time that has been previously abandoned when dealing with conventional time. In fairness, to those students, however, there is at least one other possible explanation—that of the role of subject matter knowledge which is discussed more fully below. While student errors could indicate a poor understanding of conventional time, they could also indicate that students simply don't know depositional rates are not constant because depositional environments vary. In the absence of such knowledge, students make what seems to be a reasonable assumption, namely that strata of equal thickness were deposited in the same amount of time.

There are other indications that students older than ten may have difficulty with conventional time. Poduska and Phillips (1986) investigated the ability of 100 college students to perform Piagetian tasks involving distance, time, and speed. The time task was very similar to one used by Piaget with young children and involved water flowing from one container to another. Only 18 of the 100 students in the sample completed this task correctly. It is difficult to evaluate their results since the authors provide limited information about the task, but minimally their work suggests the need for further exploration of whether some older students lack a firm understanding of conventional time.

AN UNDERSTANDING OF LARGE NUMBERS

The second leg of the stool is a solid understanding of large numbers. The role of an understanding of large numbers to a concept of deep time has been noted elsewhere (Hidalgo et al, 2004). Trend (1998) says,

> Not surprisingly for 10- and 11-year-old children, their conception of large numbers becomes a dominant influence on their answers (p. 980).

Oversby (1996), in describing the results of a cross-age study of earth science conceptions of 9–11-year-olds, 14–16-year-olds, preservice non-science student teachers and preservice science student teachers, remarks,

> A minority held the accepted scientific view that the Earth is older than 10^9 years but the results could be partly explained by assuming that the respondents had a poor understanding of large numbers and an inability to distinguish between millions and billions (p. 95)

There are several aspects to this leg that could be problematic for students. The first is an understanding of our decimal number system (i.e., a system based on "ten"), and that adjacent places in a multi-digit number are related multiplicatively by a power of 10. A poor understanding of that relationship can make estimating relative distances of numbers difficult (Siegler & Opfer, 2003). Second, students need to possess proportional reasoning skills to be able to move among powers of ten efficiently (Jones et al., 2007).

It might be suggested that difficulty comprehending large numbers would only be a problem for elementary school age children, but that does not appear to be the case. Children's early notions of how numbers map onto a number line appear to be intuitively logarithmic (Siegler & Opfer, 2003). While a change from logarithmic to linear mapping seems to occur in mid-elementary school, even adults resort to a more logarithmic scale when confronted with large numbers (Dehaene et al, 2008). Confrey (1991) describes a series of interviews with a female college student who was asked to place events from the Big Bang to the Renaissance on a timeline. Her initial attempts at the task were logarithmic as she moved left on the timeline with a space representing ten times as long an interval as the space to its right. In other words, the amount of space she allotted between 1.5×10^8 and 1.5×10^9 was identical to the amount of space between 1.5×10^9 and 1.5×10^{10}. This young woman did not understand that the distance between 1.5×10^9 and 1.5×10^{10} should be ten times as great as the distance between 1.5×10^8 and 1.5×10^9. She gave no indication that she realized she was changing the size of the interval with each successive space (p. 125).

Related to these ideas are issues of scale and the ability to work in different units of measure. Tretter et al (2006, 2006a) adapted Trend's methodology (1998, 2000, 2001a, 2001b) to conceptions of size and distance. They found increasing accuracy in students' concepts of large and small scale phenomena with age (and perhaps more importantly, educational experience). Experts (science doctoral students) in their study relied on measurement units to categorize sizes of objects. They often thought of an object that represented a particular size (1,000 to 1 million meters) and then used that object as a reference point. The ability to conceive of long units of time is important in two ways where deep time is concerned. The first deals with absolute ages of events. The second is in terms of processes that occur at very slow rates. As a result, those processes are imperceptible to human observers. Having the capacity to work in a unit of millions of years enables a person to meaningfully conceive of many geologic processes. It further enables an individual to differentiate that million year unit from a thousand year unit. Of course, this is dependent upon the understanding of large numbers and their proportional relationship discussed above.

There is some indication that a facility with standard numerical units could account for more accurate estimations of size and may be operative for conceptions of time as well. Jones et al (2008) compared concepts of size of experienced and novice science teachers. While experienced teachers were more accurate at the extremes of scale than novices, it was only true when using standard metric units. When using non-standard units, such as body length, both groups were equally inaccurate. This may indicate the experienced teachers genuinely had more accurate conceptions of size than novices. However, it could also be interpreted as a more precise numerical understanding of the metric system, powers of ten, and a greater ability to reason efficiently about the numbers involved.

SUBJECT MATTER KNOWLEDGE

The role of subject matter knowledge permeates all and may be the most difficult to tease out as a separate factor. Minimally a cognizance of its role provides a caution in data interpretation. It is exceedingly difficult to control for the effect of subject matter knowledge when investigating student conceptions of deep time.

Tretter et al mentioned earlier, noted that direct experience was a crucial factor in the ability to correctly perceive relative and absolute sizes and distances. While experts who worked with small scale phenomena were adept at dealing with sizes or distances at that scale, they had difficulty with large scale distances and sizes. The reverse was true for experts used to dealing with large scale phenomena (Tretter et al., 2006a; Tretter et al., 2006b).

> When students have had prior experiences with objects and distances, their relative and absolute understandings are more accurate than when they have had limited experiences such as those for large and small scale.... Understanding of relative scale comes with age and/or direct experience with objects of different sizes (Jones et al., 2007, p. 199).

These results are consistent with Ault's (1982) observation for a similar phenomenon with time. In fact Ault indicates children in his study were unable to apply reasoning from a hypothetical compost activity to a geologic setting primarily because the geologic phenomena were unfamiliar to them. In the absence of the requisite geologic knowledge children used other factors to determine age such as color or "crumbliness" of the rocks. Dodick and Orion (2003b) fault many studies that have looked at student conceptions about deep time. In their words those studies, "largely reflect the subjects' knowledge of particular events rather than the underlying cognitive basis for their understanding of geological time itself (p. 709).

How can a student place bryozoans in a sequence of events if she doesn't know what they are? She may somehow place them correctly. However, her correct placement would not be due to an understanding of deep time but rather to some other reasoning process, e.g., *"I've never seen one before so it must be old. It doesn't look like anything we have today."* How could a student sequence strata if he knows nothing of principles of stratigraphy? If he has never heard of original horizontality then a failure to order layers correctly would say nothing regarding his conception of time. We may be inferring an understanding (or lack thereof) about deep time when it's really something else directly related to specific geologic knowledge [or even analogical reasoning from some other subject area with which the student is familiar] that's accounting for student responses.

Two examples will illustrate the point. Preliminary interviews were conducted prior to this current research that included a card sequencing task modeled after Trend (1998, 2000, 2001a, 2001b). One of the cards in the set was the Big Bang. Several students indicated they had never heard of the Big Bang. Their subsequent inability to place it correctly in a sequence of events cannot be taken as evidence of confusion regarding deep time. Rather, it indicates nothing more than a guess about the placement of an event of which they had no knowledge. The second example comes from a study investigating the effect of the film "Powers of Ten" on student conceptions of scale. Students who viewed the film improved on their ability to sort objects according to size in a post-test *if* the objects were in the movie. They showed no improvement for objects that were not in the movie (Jones et al., 2007).

HOW CAN WE INVESTIGATE *WHAT* IS TROUBLESOME ABOUT DEEP TIME?

A qualitative investigation designed to explore the role of these three explanatory factors for student difficulty with deep time is currently underway. The sample consists of eighth graders, eleventh graders, and university students from schools in southeastern Pennsylvania. The eighth and eleventh graders attend the same public charter school. The twelve university students are drawn from two institutions. One is a comprehensive state university. The other is a small, religiously-affiliated liberal arts college. At the time of the interview all university participants were enrolled in either an introductory geology or earth science course that fulfills a general education requirement and contains students from a wide variety of majors across the university. Tasks were designed to explore each of the three factors discussed above. After each question participants were asked to explain their reasoning or how they got their answer.

PRELIMINARY RESULTS

Data analysis is at the beginning stages so it is not yet possible to speak collectively about the data or to make justifiable inferences. Examples of responses that are indicative of the range of responses for selected items exploring each of the three factors are reported here. They will be confined to university participants since data analysis of responses for the eighth and eleventh graders has not commenced.

Conventional Time

Certain tasks involving duration are more troublesome for students than others. A series of computer animations was used to explore understanding of conventional time. In each animation students watched six colored layers fill up one after the other. In animation 1, each layer was the same size but the time necessary for adjacent layers to fill (duration) was different. In animation 2, the size of the layers varied but each took the same amount of time to fill. Participants had difficulty distinguishing the amount of time required for two different colored layers to fill if the sizes of the layers were different, but they took the same amount of time to fill (animation 2). In this case the duration is the same (because layers fill at different rates) but the end product (size of the layers) is different. Students found it easier to distinguish duration when two layers were the same size but filled at different rates (animation 1). When asked how they determined which layer filled more slowly than another, some students said they counted in their heads. However, counting was not necessarily indicative of a correct answer. Others said one layer *seemed* to move faster than another. Explanations of incorrect responses for the animation in which layers of varying sizes took the same amount of time to fill tended to focus on the thickness of the layers, i.e. *Brown is taller so it takes longer.* When later asked to compare two sedimentary layers of different thicknesses and to comment on which one probably took longer to form, three of the twelve students said the thicker layer took longer to form because it's thicker, indicating that they may be applying faulty reasoning about conventional time to a geologic context.

Large Numbers

While numeric timelines presented no difficulty for some students, they were problematic for others. Two examples illustrate those difficulties. In one item students were asked to place these numbers on a timeline: 1,000 years, 100,000 years, 1 million years, and 100 million years. A 22-year-old female drew the timeline

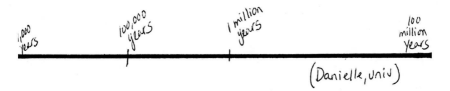

Figure 2. Timeline for a Female Undergraduate.

in Figure 2. Her explanation of her placement of points for the timeline appears below the timeline. Interviewer's comments are in regular font and indicated with an (I); student responses are in italics and indicated with an (S).

I: Tell me how you decided where to put the numbers.
S: *Ok, 1,000 years is the beginning and 100 million years at the end. 100,000 years I estimated the amount of spaces from the 1,000 years. Then the 1 million years closer to the 100,000 years because it only takes…what was I thinking? Originally because I was thinking this took 10 more, 10,000 more years so it would be closer to the 100,000.*
I: But now you aren't sure?
S: *Now I don't know if that's right. I'm not sure. I don't know… The numbers in between 100,000 and 1 million are very blurry. I don't know what the amount of difference is so I can't really say if that is my guess.*

Both the timeline and this student's explanation indicate confusion about the proportional relationships among large numbers as well as more basic confusion regarding the numbers themselves. Her timeline was fairly typical of those who had trouble with the task in that she spread the numbers out fairly evenly with a slightly larger space between 1 and 100 million years than the others, exaggerating the differences between smaller intervals of time while underestimating the differences between larger intervals.

She was not the only student to express confusion about the size of the numbers as a male student's comments illustrate,

I'm just thinking of how big these numbers are compared to each other. I'm not quite sure 'cause we don't deal with numbers this big normally in our average day. So I really don't know how long one million years is compared to a thousand. I really don't know how long a thousand years is. It's kind of hard to put that in the reference when I don't know how long a thousand years is much less a hundred million years. It's kind of hard to put that on the timeline. I'll do my best but I don't know so I'm just gonna keep going.

Subject Matter Knowledge

Participants' subject matter knowledge appeared to play a critical role in their responses. Several students indicated the Moon orbits the Earth in one day. Some identified a lack of knowledge as the reason for being unsure of their responses. The following is from a 20-year-old male's description of the items he was unsure about on a questionnaire asking participants to estimate the amount of time necessary for certain events to occur.

The Appalachian Mountains to form (He chose hundreds of years); *I know it probably wasn't just; I don't know, it could be years. It's definitely not days. I don't think mountains go up in days. It was just in years to hundreds of years.*

Later when explaining his reasoning for why he thinks it takes hours for light to travel from the Sun to the Earth,

The Sun was probably the trickiest one just because I'm not sure. I forget what the speed of light is, and I forget what the distance between Earth and the Sun is.

The effect of subject matter knowledge was apparent on two items dealing with succession. The university students in this sample were able to sequence events accurately *if* specific subject matter knowledge was not required. Prior to watching an animation showing fossil succession of three stratigraphic columns, students suggested a variety of reasons to justify why one layer of strata containing an index fossil probably preceded another. Even though some students answered correctly their answers were based on faulty reasoning such as which fossil picture was larger, which one looked older, or which fossil they had never heard of before, thereby making it older. After watching the animation, students had no difficulty placing the strata in the proper order. Conversely, some students had problems with a card sequencing task in which each card named an event from the past. In their explanations for their sequencing, several made reference to a lack of familiarity with some of the events on the cards.

Preliminary analysis of the interviews appears to suggest that each of these three factors may affect student understanding of deep time. A more complete analysis and synthesis of the data is required to make any further comments and to draw any substantial conclusions.

WHAT DOES THIS SUGGEST FOR AN INVESTIGATION OF DEEP TIME AS A THRESHOLD CONCEPT?

Several ideas emerge:

1. A conception of deep time seems to rest upon several factors, namely a conventional understanding of time, an understanding of large numbers, and subject matter knowledge in the geosciences.
2. Although data is limited, early indications are that some university students lack solid understanding of one or more of these critical factors that could enable them to comprehend deep time. There are indications that it is also true for younger students.
3. Fuller exploration of how these three factors are related to a conception of deep time is needed. The nature of the relationship among them is an open question. As additional research is able to articulate that relationship, efforts to help students better cross the threshold of deep time should improve.

The model of the stool of deep time with its three legs enables us to explore more fully why deep time is troublesome knowledge. The goal, of course, is to design instructional practices that will help students move from current alternative conceptions to scientifically correct ones. Thinking about why deep time is troublesome knowledge may suggest particular avenues for instructional practice to improve student understanding and may also explain why practices commonly suggested have not been highly successful. Simply providing students with a scale model of deep time will not be terribly useful if that student lacks either an understanding of conventional time or large numbers. We would do well to recognize that, "Troublesome knowledge of various kinds invites constructivist responses to fit—not one standard constructivist fit," (Perkins, 2006, p. 45). As we are better able to articulate specifically what makes deep time troublesome knowledge, we will be better equipped to design instruction that will specifically address its troublesome nature and allow students to cross the threshold into understanding.

REFERENCES

Augustine. *Confessions, Book XI* (p. para. 17).

Ault, C. (1982). Time in geological explanations as perceived by elementary-school students. *Journal of Geological Education, 30*, 304–309.

Ault, C., Jr. (1980, May). *Children's concepts about time no barrier to understanding the geologic past.* Unpublished doctoral dissertation, Cornell University.

Confrey, J. (1991). Learning to listen: A student's understanding of powers of ten. In E. von Glaserfeld (Ed.), *Radical constructivism in Mathematics education* (pp. 111–138). Netherlands: Kluwer Academic Publishers.

Dehaene, S., Izard, V., Spelke, E., & Pica, P. (2008). Log or linear? Distinct intuitions of the number scale in western and Amazonian indigene cultures. *Science, 320*, 1217–1220.

Dodick, J., & Orion, N. (2003a). Cognitive factors affecting student understanding of geologic time. *Journal of Research in Science Teaching, 40*(4), 415–442.

Dodick, J., & Orion, N. (2003b). Measuring student understanding of geological time. *Science Education, 87*, 708–731.

Hidalgo, A., Otero, J., & de Henares, A. (2004). An analysis of the understanding of geological time by students at secondary and post-secondary level. *International Journal of Science Education, 26*(7), 845–857.

Hume, J. (1979). An understanding of geologic time. *Journal of Geological Education, 26*, 141–143.

Jones, M. G., Taylor, A., Minogue, J., Broadwell, B., Wiebe, E., & Carter, G. (2007). Understanding scale: Powers of ten. *Journal of Science Education and Technology, 16*(2), 191–202.

Jones, M. G., Tretter, T., Taylor, A., & Oppewal, T. (2008). Experienced and novice teachers' concepts of spatial scale. *International Journal of Science Education, 30*(3), 409–429.

Libarkin, J., & Anderson, S. (2005). Assessment of learning in entry-level geoscience courses: Results from the Geoscience Concept Inventory. *Journal of Geoscience Education, 53*, 394–401.

Libarkin, J., Anderson, S., Science, J. D., Beilfuss, M., & Boone, W. (2005). Qualitative analysis of college students' ideas about the Earth: Interviews and open-ended questionnaires. *Journal of Geoscience Education, 53*(1), 17–26.

Meyer, J., & Land, R. (2003). *Threshold concepts and troublesome knowledge: Linkages to ways of thinking and practising within the disciplines*, Enhancing Teaching-Learning Environments in Undergraduate Courses. (p. 12). Occasional Report 4, Edinburgh: School of Education, University of Edinburgh.

Orion, N., & Ault, C. (2007). Learning earth sciences. In *Handbook of research on science education* (pp. 653–687). Mahwah, NJ: Lawrence Erlbaum Associates.

Oversby, J. (1996). Knowledge of earth science and the potential for its development. *School Science Review, 78*(283), 91–97.

Perkins, D. (2006). Constructivism and troublesome knowledge. In *Overcoming barriers to student understanding: Threshold concepts and troublesome knowledge* (pp. 33–47). London: Routledge.

Piaget, J. (1969). *The child's conception of time* (A. J. Pomerans, Trans.). New York: Ballantine Books. (Original work published 1927).

Poduska, E., & Phillips, D. (1986). The performance of college students on Piaget-type tasks dealing with distance, time, and speed. *Journal of Research in Science Teaching, 23*(9), 841–848.

Siegler, R., & Opfer, J. (2003). The development of numerical estimation: Evidence for multiple representations of numerical quantity. *Psychological Science, 14*(3), 237–243.

Trend, R. (1998). An investigation into understanding of geological time among 10- and 11-year-old children. *International Journal of Science Education, 20*(8), 973–988.

Trend, R. (2000). Conceptions of geological time among primary teacher trainees, with reference to their engagement with geoscience, history, and science. *22*(5), 539–555.

Trend, R. (2001a). An investigation into the understanding of geological time among 17-year-old students, with implications for the subject matter knowledge of future teachers. *International Research in Geographical and Environmental Education, 10*(3), 298–321.

Trend, R. (2001b). Deep time framework: A preliminary study of U.K. primary teachers' conceptions of geological time and perceptions of geoscience. *Journal of Research in Science Teaching, 38*(2), 191–221.

Tretter, T., Jones, M. G., Andre, T., Negishi, A., & Minogue, J. (2006). Conceptual boundaries and distances: Students' and experts' concepts of the scale of scientific phenomena. *Journal of Research in Science Teaching, 43*(3), 282–319.

Tretter, T., Jones, M. G., & Minogue, J. (2006). Accuracy of scale conceptions in science: Mental maneuverings across many orders of spatial magnitude. *Journal of Research in Science Teaching, 43*(10), 1061–1085.

Truscott, J., Boyle, A., Burkill, S., Libarkin, J., & Lonsdale, J. (2006). The concept of time: Can it be fully realised and taught? *Planet Special Issue, 17*, 21–23.

Zen, E. (2001). What is deep time and why should anyone care? *Journal of Geoscience Education, 49*(1), 5–9.

Kim A. Cheek
Department of elementary and early childhood education
Valley Forge Christian College

MONICA R. COWART

8. A PRELIMINARY FRAMEWORK FOR ISOLATING AND TEACHING THRESHOLD CONCEPTS IN PHILOSOPHY

INTRODUCTION

Threshold concepts are defined by Meyer and Land (2003) as concepts that are transformative, irreversible, integrative, bounded and potentially troublesome. Once students are able to understand these concepts, they experience a transformative shift in their understanding of a particular discipline that can be viewed as "passing through a portal, or conceptual gateway, thus opening up a new and previously inaccessible way of thinking about something." Moreover, as students become more advanced in their understanding of a field of study, they begin to see the ways in which different threshold concepts relate to and inform one another to create a holistic, interwoven epistemological system. However, a necessary condition for this advanced conceptual shift is the passing through the initial portal. In this case, the threshold concepts can be viewed as jointly representing the key that opens the door to the discipline. Once one travels inside the structure, other rooms and levels may remain locked until more advanced disciplinary-specific concepts are grasped and interwoven into the emerging epistemological structure. Yet, an awareness of this process raises an important question. How can experts within a given field help students grasp and utilize threshold concepts so that these students can begin their intellectual journey?

While a growing body of research is directed at uncovering the threshold concepts in certain disciplines, such as economics, there are a number of disciplines that have not benefited from this same level of analysis. This paper will focus upon uncovering the threshold concepts in an area of study that has received little attention: philosophy. I maintain that what is missing from the literature is an explanation of how to deconstruct philosophy-specific threshold concepts in such a way that students can identify, grasp and integrate their meanings, resulting in a conceptual scheme that reflects disciplinary conventions. I maintain that this preliminary analysis will augment both the discipline of philosophy and the emerging literature on threshold concepts.

This paper is divided into two parts. In Part I, I will outline a preliminary framework for isolating threshold concepts within philosophy, including isolating what I term core philosophic threshold concepts. In addition, I will discuss a few of the common problems that students encounter when trying to master these threshold concepts, regardless of whether they are taking an introductory course or

J. H. F. Meyer, R. Land and C. Baillie (eds.), Threshold Concepts and
Transformational Learning, 131–145.
© *2010 Sense Publishers. All rights reserved.*

a senior seminar. Finally, I will demonstrate how the core philosophical threshold concept I identify adheres to Meyer and Land's (2005) criteria. In Part II, I will discuss classroom techniques and projects that I have developed, which are specifically designed to help students develop and integrate threshold concepts in an Introduction to Philosophy course. Therefore, the goal of this portion of the paper is to trace an identified philosophical threshold concept (e.g., personhood) through the stages of assignment formation, evaluation, and student assessment. The progression will include a discussion of what success would look like for student learners, how the assignment construction utilizes scaffolding techniques to facilitate comprehension of the threshold concept, and the role of student assessment in determining success. The final section of the paper will consider the strengths and weaknesses of this pedagogical approach. Specifically, I will focus upon how the use of analytically-focused experiential learning techniques helped students understand the connections between the threshold concept of personhood and the discipline-specific epistemes used to analyze it.

PART I

BOOTH'S PRELIMINARY ANALYSIS OF PHILOSOPHY AS A DISCIPLINE

Before examining potential threshold concepts within philosophy, it is important to consider why introductory students might find the discipline to be so difficult. Although little has been published about the specific content and nature of threshold concepts within philosophy, Jennifer Booth (2006) offers a preliminary analysis in which she argues that the discipline is "rife" with threshold concepts, which are the key to unlocking student understanding (173). Yet, this raises the question: why are so many introductory philosophy students struggling in the first place? Booth maintains that there are two central reasons why novice students state that philosophic subject matter is difficult to grasp. First, since many students take their initial philosophy course in college, students are often surprised when they are asked to consider questions and ponder ideas that require a completely new, and arguably foreign, skill set (Booth, 173). Second, Booth notes that "in order to evaluate the material, the student must re-evaluate or distort parts of their common-sense understanding about the world" (174). Booth concludes by stating that novice philosophy students will encounter "troublesome knowledge" given the "the origin-nality and conflict-inducing nature of the material" found within the discipline (174). Put another way, philosophical threshold concepts tend to be counterintuitive in nature since they require students to question long held assumptions concerning the world, and it is for this reason that they are classified as troublesome (176).

With a clearer understanding of why introductory philosophy students struggle to grasp these concepts, let's turn to Booth's pedagogical suggestions for improving student mastery. Booth states that when teaching it is just as important to keep in mind what not to do in the classroom. Consequently, Booth isolates two peda-gogical techniques that she claims will prevent students from grasping a threshold concept: "dogmatically forcing new material on students at a fast pace, or with little or no explanation of the reasons behind the motivation for the material" or "trying to slow down the pace of learning by offering an easier or simplified version" of the concept (177). In addition, Booth notes that professors must become more aware of student affect and its impact upon learning, especially in a discipline such as philosophy, which often utilizes the Socratic method. Since the Socratic method involves the questioning and testing of student assumptions within a public space, students can feel intimidated, embarrassed, and anxious when asked to engage in the process in front of their peers. Booth suggests that instructors adopt a modified Socratic approach that utilizes a less confrontational and less aggressive stance (180). Therefore, Booth concludes by noting that professors can minimize the degree of negative emotions students experience while attempting to acquire threshold concepts, if professors consciously choose or modify techniques based upon an awareness of their impact upon student "affectivity" (180).

WHAT IS MISSING FROM BOOTH'S ANALYSIS

I maintain that Booth's analysis correctly articulates 1) why introductory students might find philosophy to be difficult as a discipline, given that it forces them to question their long-held assumptions about the world, including assumptions of an extremely personal nature, and 2) why professors need to closely monitor how student affect can impact learning, especially when traditionally confrontational techniques, such as the Socratic method, are utilized.

While I grant that Booth provides a helpful first account of the importance of isolating threshold concepts within philosophy, more needs to be said about the exact nature of these concepts and how they can be isolated. Moreover, since Booth claims that philosophy is "rife" with such concepts, I argue that we must consider which threshold concepts are most central to the discipline and thus most appropriate for an introductory course. In other words, since professors must make strategic decisions about what readings to include in the syllabus, what teaching techniques to employ (e.g., lecture, group presentation, etc.) and what assessment tools to test the effectiveness of the overall learning experience, I contend that an awareness of threshold concepts can guide these decisions (e.g., what readings are chosen).

I maintain that what is missing from the current literature is an explanation of how to identify, deconstruct, and integrate philosophy-specific threshold concepts so that students can develop disciplinary specific thinking (e.g., what does it mean to think like a philosopher?, what languages games, rituals, customs and methods would come into play?, etc.). Since developing a comprehensive theoretical framework for isolating philosophical threshold concepts is beyond the scope of this paper, I will offer only a preliminary sketch of this theoretical framework here. However, this sketch will serve as a first attempt to explain why certain threshold concepts might be considered more central to the discipline than others. In the next section I will describe what sets these "core" threshold concepts apart from others. Moreover, I will explain why designing a course that highlights core threshold concepts presents a greater opportunity for students to grasp disciplinary-specific thinking (i.e., thinking like a philosopher).

PRELIMINARY FRAMEWORK FOR ISOLATING THRESHOLD
CONCEPTS IN PHILOSOPHY

Philosophy as a discipline is composed of multiple sub-disciplines, including the philosophy of science, philosophy of art (aesthetics), and philosophy of religion. Although the various categories seem to proliferate on a yearly basis, there are three central sub-disciplines that all others can be, arguably, categorized within: ethics, epistemology, and metaphysics. A section of the course devoted to ethics will include readings on morality; a section on epistemology will examine the study of knowledge; a section on metaphysics will ask questions concerning existence. Given the centrality of these three sub-disciplines within philosophy, it is not surprising that many introductory courses divide the semester into coverage of these three areas of philosophy. However, having an awareness of the sub-disciplines does not necessarily translate into an awareness of the threshold concepts, but I maintain that these sub-disciplines are the key to recognizing "core" threshold concepts within philosophy. In other words, I maintain that a special type of foundational threshold concept exists within the discipline of philosophy: core philosophical threshold concepts. I define core philosophical threshold concepts as threshold concepts that reside at the intersection of metaphysics, epistemology and ethics. In other words, core philosophical threshold concepts exist at the intersection of the three sub-disciplines because these concepts raise questions within each sub-discipline. Consequently, to truly have an understanding of core philosophical threshold concept x, you must understand the questions threshold concept x raises in metaphysics, ethics, and epistemology. To simply understand the questions the concept raises in only one of these areas will not result in an accurate under-standing of the concept. Yet, if the concept resides at the intersection of these sub-disciplines, then the complexity of the core concept can account for it being "troublesome" to students. Let's consider an example, involving personhood, in order to further illustrate the above theoretical points.

PERSONHOOD AS A CORE PHILOSOPHICAL THRESHOLD CONCEPT:
APPLYING THE FRAMEWORK

If personhood truly is a *core* philosophical threshold concept, then it must satisfy two criteria. First, it must meet all of the requirements set forth by Meyer and Land (2003) to qualify as a threshold concept (i.e., transformative, irreversible, integrative, bounded and potentially troublesome). Second, a core philosophic concept also must demonstrate that it raises questions in metaphysics, epistemology and ethics. Moreover, I hypothesize that core philosophic threshold concepts will be easier to identify as threshold concepts since they will most likely present as even more transformative, more irreversible, more integrative, more bounded and more potentially troublesome than traditional philosophic threshold concepts. To consider this point, let's deconstruct personhood in order to see how this process of classifying core philosophic threshold concepts would work.

Step 1: Meeting the Requirements of a Threshold Concept

Personhood As Transformative: Meyer and Land (2005) characterize trans-formative as "occasioning a significant shift in the perception of the subject" (373). Studying personhood through a philosophical lens commonly provides a shift in awareness. Students often report being surprised at how so many philosophical debates can "turn" depending upon how this concept is defined. The study of the concept often results in a shift in identity as students begin to grasp how the way in which personhood is defined can impact their beliefs concerning abortion, artificial intelligence, the death penalty, etc.

Personhood As Integrative: Meyer and Land (2005) define integrative as "exposing the previously hidden interrelatedness of something" (373). Personhood is integrative as a threshold concept because students think they understand what it is at the start of the class, but then after more study begin to recognize the concept as much more complex and harder to define than originally thought.

Personhood As Irreversible: Meyer and Land (2005) define irreversible as "unlikely to be forgotten or unlearned through considerable effort" (373). The various interrelated connections that students uncover about personhood make them realize that they did not have an adequate understanding of the concept prior to the class. Consequently, the irreversible change is that they exit the class knowing not what it is, but what it is not.

Personhood As Potentially Troublesome: Students find it particularly troublesome that they thought they had such a clear understanding of personhood at the start of the semester, only to discover that the concept is more difficult to define than they imagined. When the naïve concept that was seemingly firm is shattered into a thousand unanswered questions, the students take one step closer to under-standing philosophy as a discipline. Moreover, they struggle with recognizing that part of what makes the concept a *philosophical* threshold concept is that there is not a fact of the matter (even though there often is a fact of the matter in other disciplines); in philosophy, there are only competing theories that must be evaluated in terms of the strengths and weaknesses of their arguments. When describing the nature of philosophy, Russell states "as soon as definite knowledge concerning any subject becomes possible, this subject ceases to be called philosophy and becomes a separate science" (23). Russell's point is that philosophy can lead to advances in fields, but as soon as the question at hand is answered definitively, then it can no longer exist within the realm of philosophy. In addition, I maintain that philosophical threshold concepts that reside at the intersection of the three sub-disciplines are particularly difficult for students to grasp because in order to master the concept, they must understand its ethical, metaphysical and epistemological implications.

Personhood As Bounded: The above point made by Russell also highlights how philosophical concepts can be bounded. In terms of personhood, we do not have one theory that has emerged as "the truth" concerning this concept; the concept is widely debated today. However, if one day personhood is found to have one conclusive definition, then it will no longer remain in the realm of philosophy. Yet, the very nature of personhood as a concept makes the "discovery" of an airtight definition unlikely.

Step 2: Meeting the Requirements of a Core Threshold Concept

Personhood must exist conceptually at the intersection of ethics, epistemology and metaphysics to be considered a core philosophical threshold concept. To exist at the intersection of these sub-disciplines would mean that personhood plays a crucial role in key questions that are asked by these various sub-disciplines within philosophy. To consider whether or not this is true, we will examine each sub-discipline to see whether personhood is a factor in analyzing central questions, while keeping in mind that what is merely sketched here is not designed to be an exhaustive analysis. If the philosophic threshold concept in question can be found to raise key issues in each sub-discipline, then this will suffice for further classification as a core philosophic threshold concept. In other words, other areas of connection might exist within a particular sub-discipline than those identified here, but since only one is needed to establish the existence of connections within that sub-discipline, the analysis will conclude (however prematurely) once one connection is found in each sub-discipline. If a connection cannot be found within one of the three sub-disciplines, then the concept will not qualify as a core philosophic threshold concept. However, it can still count as a traditional threshold concept provided that Land and Meyer's criteria are met. Let's turn to the sub-disciplines within philosophy to examine how one would determine if personhood is a core philosophical threshold concept.

Personhood and Ethics (Morality/Values): A number of theorists argue that the abortion debate turns on the issue of personhood. Specifically, if the fetus can be shown to be a person, then the fetus should be granted the full rights of a person, and the pregnancy would be immoral to terminate. However, Thompson famously argued that there are circumstances in which it would be moral to terminate a pregnancy, even if the fetus is granted personhood status. In short, it is impossible to adequately study the issue of whether abortion is ethical without also considering the concept of personhood. Thus, personhood meets the criterion of being an important concept for deciding key issues within ethics.

Personhood and Metaphysics (Existence): The concept of personhood also resurfaces when we turn to metaphysics or the study of existence. One question that emerges is what "stuff " might a person be made of? For instance, must you have a body and a soul to be a person? Is it possible that a person can be made out of any "material" as long as the functional connections are in the right order? Given this, would it be possible for an advanced robot to be classified as a person? If so then, why did the robot qualify for personhood and if not, then what was the robot missing that prevented this classification? These metaphysical questions help to highlight the uncertainties around what it means to exist as a person. Thus, personhood meets the criterion of being important to central issues within metaphysics. Moreover, these issues concerning existence tie back to the ethical issues raised. For instance, if organism x meets the criteria for personhood, then what are the implications concerning how organism x should be treated? This point demonstrates the further inter-related nature of the concept.

Personhood and Epistemology (Knowledge): The ways in which the concept of personhood surfaces in epistemology relates to the previous examples. For instance, once the ethical question concerning abortion, which involves a meta-physical element, is asked (i.e., is it moral to terminate a fetus, if the fetus is a person?), then the epistemological question emerges (i.e., how can we *know* with any certainty that the fetus is a person?). Similarly, in metaphysics, the question of whether the robot should be granted personhood is followed by the consideration of the different methods that might enable one to address this concern. In both cases, the epistemological questions soon follow once the central questions in ethics and metaphysics have been asked. This shows a further way in which these concepts are integrated and inter-related. Thus, personhood meets the criterion of raising important questions in epistemology. Moreover, the emerging episte-mological questions directly develop from the earlier metaphysical and ethical concerns.

The above example of personhood demonstrates that there are certain concepts within philosophy that raise equally central ethical, metaphysical, and episte-mological concerns. These core concepts can be particularly difficult for novice students to grasp because their mastery requires that students understand the ways in which the three sub-disciplines within philosophy inform the concept. Even though these core philosophic threshold concepts can be more difficult to teach, I argue that they are worth the extra trouble because once a student grasps one, the student has a better idea of how the sub-fields within philosophy relate to one another.

In summary, I have argued that the degree to which a philosophic concept is fundamental to understanding the discipline typically will map onto the degree in which the concept raises metaphysical, epistemological, and ethical issues. If the concept resides at the center of the discipline and is a core philosophic concept, then it will meet Meyer and Land's criteria for a threshold concept as well as raise central metaphysical, epistemological, and ethical questions. The above analysis demonstrates that personhood meets Meyer and Land's criteria for a threshold concept as well as satisfies the outlined requirements for classi-fication as a core threshold concept. Now that this core threshold concept has been isolated and the process for isolation has been briefly outlined, we will turn our attention to how the concept of personhood can be introduced in an Introduction to Philosophy course. In particular, once a threshold concept has been identified, what do you do in terms of course planning to help students grasp the concept? Answering this practical pedagogical question will be the focus of Part II of this paper.

PART II

IN THE CLASSROOM: PERSONHOOD AS A PEDAGOGICAL CASE STUDY

Part II focuses upon the very practical matter of course design that takes place once a threshold concept has been identified. In short, the identification of the concept is merely the first step in the pedagogical process since other questions immediately arise. For instance, how can professors design assignments that will enable students to grasp the threshold concept in a way that gives the students insights into the field (i.e., practitioners within the field use the concept)? Put another way, can we design assignments to help students uncover the discipline-specific conventions that govern the use of a threshold concept? If so, then how can we accomplish this in a systematic manner so that additional threshold concepts can be mastered within the discipline?

I argue that within the field of philosophy it is possible to teach introductory students to engage with a philosophic threshold concept in such a way that the students demonstrate a basic understanding of how language games operate within the field. However, in my personal experience, creating a pedagogical space in which these connections can occur requires a willingness on the part of the professor to calibrate and re-calibrate his/her interventions in direct response to student need. While this task can be tiring since no two classes are the same, the positive student learning outcomes that can result can make the process worthwhile, especially if one teaches at a university that provides institutional support. Therefore, the goal of this portion of the paper is to trace an identified philosophical threshold concept (e.g., personhood) through the stages of assignment formation, evaluation, and assessment. The progression will include a discussion of what success would look like for student learners, how the assignment construction utilizes scaffolding techniques to facilitate comprehension of the threshold concept, and the role of student assessment in determining success. The final section of the paper will consider the strengths and weaknesses of this pedagogical approach.

RECOGNIZING SUCCESS: THINKING LIKE A PHILOSOPHER

Before assignment construction can begin, we must consider the aim of the assignment or what we hope the assignment will achieve. On a simplistic level, one might argue that the assignment is successful, if the threshold concept in question is grasped. However, what will it look like, from the perspective of the instructor, for a student to grasp the threshold concept? Or to highlight the epistemological concern, how will we *know* that the student has grasped the threshold concept?

Since we cannot get into the student's head to experience first hand his/her subjective experience, we are forced to depend upon more outward manifestations of concept acquisition. In short, we must depend upon the discipline-specific language games and practices that convey that the student understands the concept. For instance, Davies (2006) argues that disciplinary ways of thinking about a subject "necessarily entail particular ways of *practicing*" (70). Moreover, Davies clarifies this relationship between the theoretical concept and the manner in which it is practiced within the public domain when he states that "teaching should encourage a subject-specific pedagogy that aims to expose the 'ground rules' or...'epistemes', so that these become a focus for dialogue between teachers and learners" (71).

Perkins(2006) makes a related point when he states that:

"The disciplines are more than bundles of concepts. They have their own characteristic epistemes...An episteme can be defined as a system of ideas that allows us to establish knowledge... 'ways of knowing' is another phrase in the same spirit. As used here epistemes are manners of justifying, explaining, solving problems, conducting enquiries, and designing and validating various kinds of products or outcomes" (42).

Applying Davies' and Perkins' analysis to philosophic threshold concepts, the next step would be to determine which epistemes are commonly employed in philosophy to enable the emergence of the threshold concepts. However, identifying all of the epistemes within the discipline of philosophy is well beyond the scope of this paper, so I will limit this discussion to identifying two previously unidentified philosophic epistemes that directly impact the acquisition of person-hood: thought experiments and the analytic deconstruction of terms (e.g., necessary and sufficient conditions for x, rules governing a language game, etc). Since Booth (2006) already identified the Socratic method as an episteme within philosophy, I am arguing that the identification and use of these additional epistemes will shed more light on what it means to 'think like a philosopher'. In part, thinking like a philosopher occurs when one utilizes thought experiments, the Socratic method, and analytic deconstruction to understand a concept. Put another way, these three tools can be found in every philosopher's tool kit and they enable the philosopher to build and test assumptions concerning the world. Therefore, one of the goals of the assignment will be to enable students to demonstrate that they grasp the meaning of the philosophic concept of personhood by correctly using it in a variety of language games, which employ the above-mentioned epistemes. In this case, the language games enable students to examine and explore the implications of the concept through the use of the epistemes.

To clarify this relationship between epistemes and threshold concepts , let's turn to an example from the abortion debate to see how the threshold concept of personhood is explored via a common philosophical episteme: the thought experiment. Thomson (1971) constructs a number of famous thought experiments to consider the implications of personhood on the abortion debate. In particular, she questions whether there are circumstances in which abortion would be permissible, if it was granted that the fetus is a person. In these scenarios, each thought experiment provides the hypothetical framework in which the reader can test common assumptions about personhood. Yet, to grasp Thomson's arguments, students must "play the game" by realizing that hypothetical thought experiments often include extremely unlikely to nearly impossible scenarios in order to highlight one's intuitions about the assumption in question. Consequently, if a student rejects a thought experiment on the grounds that seed people do not exist or on the grounds that you wouldn't really wake up to find a famous violinist hooked to your kidneys, then it is clear that the student does not understand how the thought experiment works as an episteme. In other words, they simply do not understand the rules necessary to play this philosophical game.

Given the above-mentioned relationship between epistemes and threshold concepts, I maintain that the next step is to design an assignment that will enable students to showcase in the public domain knowledge of personhood through the rule-governed use of the discipline-specific epistemes, which enable the exploration of the concept. Given this, in the next section I outline a team debate assignment that provides such opportunities.

ASSIGNMENT CONSTRUCTION: UTILIZING ACTIVE LEARNING TO GRASP PERSONHOOD

The personhood debate assignment occurs over seven classes, two of which involve the actual formal debates. Here is a class-by-class breakdown of the content covered on each day:

Day 1: (Pick Teams & Debate Format). Students are given two debate resolutions to examine for homework before day 1. When they arrive in class, they are asked to sign-up to be on either the negative or the affirmative team for one of the resolutions. Consequently, the twenty-four students in the course quickly divide themselves into four 6 person teams. During this first day, students are given an argument workshop in which they are shown how to formulate arguments to support or refute a resolution. Since the debate readings have not been assigned, students are taught the structure for the first formal speeches through a hypothetical resolution that does not involve any philosophical concepts (e.g., resolved: vanilla ice cream is better than chocolate ice cream). This non-philosophical example is discussed and as a class we outline the structure of the formal speech for the mock topic. These speeches consist of three main parts: defining key terms from the resolution, reformulating the meaning of the resolution to convey your definitions of the terms, and creating at least three well-developed arguments to argue for your team's position (either affirming or negating the resolution). Finally, students use class time on the first day to look up definitions for their resolutions. We have a discussion in class about the role of key words within a resolution, and how opposing teams will want to find definitions that support their interpretation of the resolution. With the basic structure of the first formal speeches explained, students are instructed to read the first two of the three journal articles on the abortion debate for homework. Students are given the following schedule that outlines the times for each speech:

1st Formal Affirmative Speech (5 minutes)
Questions from Negative Team (3 minutes)
1st Formal Negative Speech (5 minutes)
Questions from Affirmative team (3 minutes)
3 minutes of preparation time for both teams
2nd Affirmative Rebuttal Speech (5 minutes)

Questions from Negative Team (3 minute)
3 minute of preparation time
2nd Negative Rebuttal Speech (5 minutes)
Questions from Affirmative team (3 minute)

The two resolutions to be debated are as follows:
Resolved: Abortions are morally permissible, even if the fetus is granted personhood.
Resolved: Marquis' "future-like-ours" standard should be used to determine if an abortion is moral.

Day 2: (Argument Workshop on Formal Speeches; Lecture on Articles). The second day of the assignment begins with a detailed lecture on both articles. The instructor asks questions during the lecture to highlight potential debate strategies for both teams. Students sit with the rest of their teams and are given class time to discuss strategies for their first formal speech. Typically, it is during this class that students remark that they did not realize that the abortion debate "turns" on the notion of personhood.

Teams sub-divide into those individuals who will write the first formal speech (which is typed in advance and read) and those team members who will write the rebuttal briefs. A brief explanation is given on how to write a rebuttal brief. In particular, students must guess as to which arguments the opposing team will use against them and then write counterarguments to address these concerns. If students do not have a prepared brief to address an argument, then they must provide a counterargument on the spot or lose the point. Students often state that they feel overwhelmed and unsure at this point in the assignment. Rough drafts of the formal speeches must be sent to the instructor over the weekend for feedback.

Day 3: (Lecture on Final Article & Rebuttal Brief Workshop). Day three focuses upon formulating counterarguments to use in rebuttal briefs. In addition, special attention is devoted to supporting or refuting arguments that depend upon thought experiments. A portion of day 3 involves lecturing on the final article. Whereas the first two articles are clearly for and against the topic, the third article can be used in a number of strategic ways by both sides, depending upon interpretation. Teams that will debate first meet individually with the instructor to discuss the feedback on their rough drafts. Specific team strategies are discussed at this time.

Day 4: (Team Meeting Continued). Professor meets with teams that will debate first. Feedback is given on proposed strategies and questions are answered concerning the rough drafts. Optional drafts of rebuttal briefs can be sent to the professor for feedback. Some students request private meetings at this time to make sure that their arguments are appropriate.

Day 5: (Final Preparations). Final questions are answered concerning the debate. In addition, students are given pre-drawn "flow charts" so that they can track the arguments stated during the debate. The individuals who are not debating are expected to write down all of the arguments stated in the debate and to pay special attention to the arguments that are not answered.

Day 6 & Day 7: (Debate Days). At the end of the debate, the teams that debated write a two minute "immediate reflection" on the experience while the audience members write a detailed paragraph explaining who they think won the debate. The summary comments , flow charts and immediate responses are collected at the end of class. The debate results and summary comments are emailed to all of the students later that day. On day 7, the two groups switch sides so that both resolutions are debated over the two days. Each team turns in a final copy of their first formal speech and all of their debate briefs. Each team must turn in an assessment of their personal experience as well as an assessment of the overall team dynamic on the day after their team debates.

The debate assignment is designed to be highly scaffolded while still leaving room for student creativity. For instance, students must use the same three articles, regardless of which resolution they choose; the only outside sources permitted are dictionaries to define words from the resolutions. Since the three journal articles are considered to be classics within the field that demonstrate the opposing views on abortion, students are provided with a bounded pedagogical space that forces them to carefully consider nuanced interpretations of each article. Moreover, each of the articles chosen includes thought experiments, clear arguments and an analytic discussion of personhood. Consequently, the articles enable students to examine personhood by way of epistemes that are central to philosophy (e.g., thought experiments, argument and counterargument construction, and analytic deconstruction of terms).

Finally, the debate assignment gives students the opportunity to "do philosophy" by actively engaging with arguments concerning personhood in real time. In addition, audience members see their classmates succeed and stumble, while they track the arguments on their flow charts. Therefore, the assignment is designed to facilitate the learning of a core threshold concept and corresponding epistemes in a manner that challenges the student, but without being confrontational. In fact, even the Socratic method is (potentially) employed during the structured cross-examination period of the debate, but this time all participants are students; thus removing the hierarchical confrontative element that Booth (2006) stated might adversely impact affect. In short, the assignment provides a space in which students can use the formal debate format to explore the epistemes that help shape the core threshold concept of personhood. While some will learn to play the game better than others, the assignment is structured so that introductory students might feel the rush of thinking like a philosopher…if only for the day.

ROLE OF STUDENT ASSESSMENT IN DETERMINING SUCCESS

A common complaint of group assignments is that team members do not always put forth the same amount of effort and that this is "unfair" if a group grade is assigned. In response to this concern, students are informed that they will write an assessment of each team member, including themselves at the end of the debate assignment. The assessment instructions are as follows:

A typed response from every member of the team explaining *exactly* what you did to help your team prepare for the debate and your assessment of how other team members contributed. You will give each team member (including yourself) a grade (0–100%) based upon his/her contributions. This is due the day after the debate. In addition, you will describe your team dynamic, including a discussion of what went well and what aspects would require improvement if you had to debate again with your group. What were the strengths and weaknesses of this assignment? What, if anything, did you learn? Finally, what is one piece of advice that you wish you had been given concerning the successful completion of this assignment.

Since students know from day one that they will be evaluated by their teammates, I have found that there have been fewer reports of teammates being accused of not doing their share of the work. Moreover, answering the questions provides students with an opportunity to process and evaluate what they learned. Here are a few representative responses from students who have completed this assignment:

> I have never worked so hard in my life. I didn't know anyone in my group, but we all pulled together and met a lot outside of class (even Mike). At first I had no idea what I was doing. The rough draft deadline forced us to meet and then we started to panic because we didn't know what we were doing. We turned something in but it was pretty bad and your comments scared us even more, but at least we could hand in more than one draft. I hate public speaking too, but it all came together in the end.

> I didn't know anyone in my group, but we were all hanging out together by the end of the assignment. It was a real bonding experience because we had to work really hard….there were some really late nights. Some people in our group had a better understanding of the articles and some people were less scared by the public speaking. We all helped each other out and started making philosophy jokes by the end. I learned a lot and now I have some new friends.

> I won't say I loved the debates but I do know the articles inside and out. I even had a dream about having a violinist hooked up to me. Too much philosophy.

> I thought I would hate this assignment. I couldn't believe we were going to do another debate on abortion (I got burned out in high school when people would just yell at each other). This time it was different because everything was sooo structured. I actually got into it and was surprised that I understood the articles really well by the end (but had no clue at first and neither did my group). Can we have another debate instead of a final exam?

These excerpts from the informal assessments are representative of the themes that students reported concerning their learning experiences. To date, this assignment has been utilized with over ten sections of introductory students. The section size varied from 20 to 24 students. When asked to evaluate the debate experience, over 95% of these students reported at least one positive outcome including: increased understanding of course content (i.e., personhood), increased understanding of philosophical methods, and increased understanding of argument isolation and formation. In addition, only three negative outcomes were mentioned. The assignment was said to 1) require too much work for an introductory class, 2) force students to engage in public speaking, which was viewed as "unfair to introverts" and 3) make students meet outside of class, which was reported as difficult for students engaging in outside activities (e.g., sports, part-time jobs, clubs, etc). Interestingly, even the majority of students who reported a negative experience noted that they left the course with a more nuanced understanding of personhood. However, they argued that as non-majors the time consuming nature of the assignment was not worth their increased understanding of personhood and/or philosophy as a discipline. Finally, 2% of the students noted that they still felt "completely lost" at the end of the assignment. While it is unfortunate that these students did not see any shift in understanding at the end of the assignment, 98% of the students noted an increase in understanding (even if a small percent felt that it was not worth the time and effort).

In conclusion, the various student self-assessments as well as their written debate speeches indicated the majority introductory philosophy students were able to grasp the complexities associated with the threshold concept of personhood. While this might be viewed as a success, some might argue at what cost? In the next section we will examine a few of the advantages and disadvantages to utilizing the debate format to teach a threshold concept in philosophy.

STRENGTHS AND CHALLENGES OF USING DEBATE FORMAT TO FACILITATE TC ACQUISITION

The strengths of using this highly scaffolded debate format are that it provides an opportunity for integration, transformation, and the chance to practice "thinking like a philosopher." In addition, it offers the chance to gain a deeper understanding of discipline-specific epistemes by making explicit a number of the language games that shape philosophy as a discipline.

The challenges involved are also important to note. First, professors will find that setting up the assignment, especially for the first time, can be extremely time-consuming. This is especially a concern if the instructor has a heavy teaching load and/or works at an institution that does not grant release time for pedagogical pursuits. In addition, professors must be prepared to problem-solve often, given the variable nature of group activities and debate formats.

Therefore, the current assignment achieves its goal of exposing students to a number of different epistemes while helping them understand a core threshold concept in philosophy: personhood. While the assignment is admittedly time consuming it can be further refined to attempt to diminish the amount of energy it requires. Yet, importantly, it is a first step and it provides a case study of how a threshold concept can be traced from its initial isolation to assignment construction to student reflection on outcomes.

REFERENCES

Booth, J. (2006). On the mastery of philosophical concepts: Socratic discourse and the unexpected 'affect'. In J. H. F. Meyer & R. Land (Eds.), *Overcoming barriers to student understanding: Threshold concepts and troublesome knowledge* (pp. 173–181). London and New York: Routledge.

Davies, P. (2006). Threshold concepts: How can we recognize them? In J. H. F. Meyer & R. Land (Eds.), *Overcoming barriers to student understanding: Threshold concepts and troublesome knowledge* (pp. 70–84). London and New York: Routledge.

Meyer, J. H. F., & Land, R. (2003). Threshold concepts and troublesome knowledge: Linkages to the ways of thinking and practicing within the disciplines. In C. Rust (Ed.), *Improving student learning: Improving student learning theory and Practice-ten years on*. Oxford, UK: OCSLD.

Meyer, J. H. F., & Land, R. (2005). Threshold concepts and troublesome knowledge (2): Epistemological considerations and a conceptual framework for teaching and learning. *Higher Education, 49*, 373–388.

Perkins, D. (2006). Constructivism and troublesome knowledge. In J. H. F. Meyer & R. Land (Eds.), *Overcoming barriers to student understanding: Threshold concepts and troublesome knowledge* (pp. 33–47). London and New York: Routledge.

Thomson, J. J. (1996). A defense of abortion. In R. Munson (Ed.), *Intervention and Reflection: Basic Issues in Medical Ethics* (pp. 69–80). Belmont: Wadsworth.

Russell, B. (2003). The value of philosophy. In D. Abel (Ed.), *Fifty readings in philosophy: An introduction to philosophy* (pp. 21–27). New York: McGraw-Hill.

Monica Cowart
Philosophy Department
Merrimack College

ROSANNE QUINNELL AND RACHEL THOMPSON

9. CONCEPTUAL INTERSECTIONS

Re-Viewing Academic Numeracy in the Tertiary Education Sector as a Threshold Concept

INTRODUCTION

Tertiary educators expect that students have developed sound numeracy skills from their previous studies in mathematics and that they are able to transfer and apply these skills to their studies in other discipline contexts, such as the life sciences. In reality, each year a proportion of our students fail to meet this expectation. The "maths problem" persists despite resources being directed to improve levels of academic numeracy. It is important to note that there is a requirement to complete mathematics prior to and/or as part of their degrees in life sciences and in medicine. However, the simple mathematical operations of multiplication and division addition and subtraction remain problematic for a significant subset of students. There is likely to be a raft of factors that underpin this maths problem and here we are considering only a few. This maths problem prevents students from embracing the quantitative dimension of the life sciences. The relevance of undertaking a quantitative approach to gain a better understanding of a biological phenomenon is lost on some students particularly if the calculations involved are perceived to be impenetrable. So, rather than witnessing numeracy as a "transferable skill", we see students transferring their maths anxiety i.e. "a transferable anxiety"; commonly expressed as "*I can't do maths*". Instead of our students seeing the relevance of numeracy to their studies in the life sciences, subjects such as mathematics and statistics are perceived as unconnected to their discipline, and therefore "*maths is boring*". Student comments: "*I can't do maths*", and "*maths is boring*" exemplify rigid standpoints, standpoints that we need to challenge if we are to aid students to enter their liminal space. Both of these standpoints speak to our students' prior conceptions of a subject which has been highlighted as important (Biggs, 1989).

Our focus is at the point where students stumble as they practice academic numeracy in the life sciences and medical statistics. We are concentrating on the moments when students withdraw from learning at the point of entering their liminal space, as described by Meyer and Land (2003, 2005) and further examined by Savin-Baden (2008). An obvious indicator of when students have disengaged in a class is when they fail to make eye contact. For instance, this occurs when one begins to shift from describing a biological phenomenon in words to presenting a mathematical abstraction of that same phenomenon (e.g. an equation, or data

J. H. F. Meyer, R. Land and C. Baillie (eds.), Threshold Concepts and
Transformational Learning, 147–163.

points tabulated or graphed). A grasp of numeracy is essential to understand the abstraction of the biological phenomenon; failure to appreciate that patterns in biology can be represented in abstracted mathematical forms inhibits students' understanding of scientific practice.

REEXAMINING OUR PRACTICES AS SCIENTISTS AND IN TEACHING SCIENCE

As scientists we examine the patterns in our discipline; we observe phenomena and assert hypotheses about phenomena. In our attempts to explain the world, we test our hypotheses by conducting experiments using the hypothetico-deductive method almost exclusively. Experiments need to be undertaken in accordance with this method, requiring a sound understanding of the parameters being measured, and of when and how to measure and record the important data. The conduct of the experiment needs to be coupled to an understanding of the aims of the study and its limits and feasibility. Scientists are expected to be confident with their practice.

So how does this description of scientific method relate to student learning in science? Many undergraduate practical classes provide opportunities for students to observe like a scientist, and then to record the observed data. It is, however, rare that the raw data will be the final data, particularly numeric data. Data sets may need to be clustered, units of measure may need to be converted, and control data need to be accounted for. Formulae may need to be applied to determine statistical significance. Also, when presenting the results, the patterns within the data need to be displayed clearly. Students often attend practical classes unaware of these underlying procedures. Rather, they arrive under the impression that they will be presented with a dull data-handling or statistics practical that they perceive to have no relevance in their future career. Asking students to learn how to observe and explain like a scientist is one of the "underlying games" in life science teaching practice; being more explicit about what we expect students to do, resonates with Taylor and Meyer's work on how biologists work i.e. the testable hypothesis as a threshold concept (2008).

We present an experiential learning cycle in science that mirrors our practice of attempting to understand biological phenomena (Figure 1) (Quinnell and Thompson, 2008; LeBard and Quinnell 2008). We have mapped on this cycle where numeracy and literacy skills are required. Process A is focused on calculations and involves making observations, recording raw data, processing this data into evidence which is represented mathematically. Process B is where the experimental evidence is placed in the disciplinary context and involves describing and explaining the patterns evident in the data. We have indicated some of the points where students appear to uncouple themselves from this process: As part of the experimental process (Process A) students are expected to: (1) understand the relevance of participating in the process, and to participate by, (2) make scientific observations of a scientific phenomenon, (3) record the required data, (4) process the raw data and, (5) translate these data into evidence by clustering the data to generate figure, table or equation that make the patterns in observations evident. Process B is translating the data summary into a scientific explanation and involves: (6) describing the

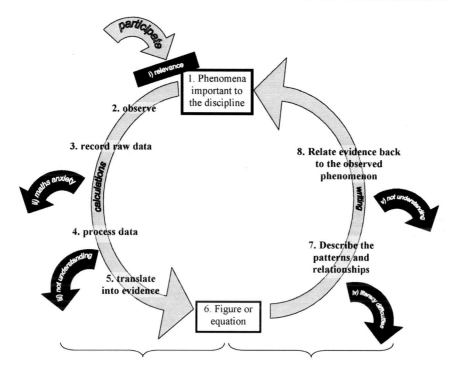

Figure 1. Generalised process in undergraduate science practical classes.

| *A. Experimental process: translating* | *B. Interpreting process: translating* |
| *observations into data summary* | *evidence into an explanation* |

patterns in the data and the relationship between data sets and (7) making critical statements about how well these data support, or refute, the premise (or hypotheses) upon which the observations were made. We have indicated some of the points (thick black arrows) where we observe student engagement wane: i) failing to see relevance at the outset, ii) experiencing maths anxiety, iii) not understanding the computational processes, iv) not being able to describe the patterns in the data in words, and v) not being able to relate the results to the original aim. This diagram can be mapped onto the experimental component of the scientific method; we are dealing with science learning that is common to both students and practitioners of science.

In Figure 1, the black arrows indicate the moments when students experience obstacles to learning. These obstacles are not identified as being exclusively around threshold concepts but appear to be at points where concepts are linked and where numbers play a major part. We have begun to map these obstacles onto this generalized model of scientific method; the movement from observing scientific phenomena to the process of representing those phenomena in abstracted form (Figure 1 Process A). In medicine, the same uncoupling of student learning is seen when the students are required to translate these abstracted forms back into a concrete explanation of the phenomena (Figure 1 Process B). This is apparent in the interpretation of epidemiological figures or the results of clinical studies, for example. The obstacles shown in the Figure 1 are not exclusively caused by numeracy issues but we argue that they all are modulated by numeracy skills. The importance of this seems small initially as students in our classes are those who have achieved a high grade in at least level 3 Mathematics at the Australian final year (year 12) school examinations (the HSC). This is an above average level of attainment, yet a significant number of the students still have a problem with manipulating and interpreting numbers that can precipitate discomfort and even anxiety within the classroom (Ben-Shlomo, Fallon, Sterne and Brookes, 2004; Tariq, 2007). The term "numerophobia" was coined for this phenomenon by Ben-Shlomo et al, (2004). This is a fear of using numbers that tends to occur more with interpreting formulae, working out equations and basic mathematical manipulation (Klinger, 2004; Quinnell and Wong, 2007; Moss, Greenall, Rockcliffe, et al., 2007). Numerophobia initiates a strong emotional response that can overwhelm the student so that their work is compromised. In lectures, a wider effect of this can be seen when students react en masse by a communal sigh or exclamation followed by disengagement when a PowerPoint slide accompanying description of formulae or equation is displayed. Students in some disciplines may be able to get by with limited mathematic involvement, but medicine and life sciences have a surprising amount of formulae, equations and mathematical explanation that are essential to the students' progress. For example, patterns of populations are expressed in statistical parameters and the patterns of physiology are expressed in the parameters of physics.

So where does that leave us with student numeracy? What is it that we want students to make sense of, and be critical of, when they are "doing calculations" in these disciplines? How does student confidence affect competency? Can strategies to improve student numeracy be created by re-viewing and deconstructing the problem and therefore discover the threshold concepts buried within academic numeracy obstacles? We sought answers to these questions and present our findings in the following case studies, one in medical statistics and one in biology. Two solutions are presented: the first proposes teaching numeric concepts without the numbers; the second proposes addressing student confidence as a mechanism to reduce transference of students' maths anxiety across to science.

PRESENTING NUMERIC CONCEPTS WITHOUT THE NUMBERS

Unpicking Statistical Concepts

Teaching medical students statistics relevant to their future practice is hampered in two ways. Firstly, because it is a "Cinderella" subject; statistics is far less glamorous or medical than the disciplines and topics of anatomy and physiology and so on (Altman and Bland, 1991; Sinclair, 1997). Secondly, it is perceived to involve mathematics and numbers and hence is often viewed by students as difficult, complicated, unpleasant or just plain boring. Consequently at UNSW in 2005, we strove to make a medical statistics course (embedded within an evidence-based medicine element in the new undergraduate medical curriculum) as relevant as possible to clinical practice. Following a poor result in the first formative examination of this course in 2005, several points of student disengagement were identified in the mainly online mode of learning environment. We re-viewed the content and teaching methods with the aim of finding a more engaging and successful way to approach teaching these topics. Threshold concepts as proposed by Meyer and Land (2003) seemed to fit some of these obstacle points perfectly. As Meyer and Land state in their original paper on this topic, a threshold concept:

> ...represents a transformed way of understanding, or interpreting, or viewing something without which the learner cannot progress (ibid, p. 1).

In statistics there are few publications that discuss threshold concepts, but, over ten years ago, Kennedy (in a paper on learning and economics) noted that students of statistics could carry out appropriate statistical exercises adequately but fail to understand the "big picture" (Kennedy, 1998). He proposed an elegant reason for this:

> What they are missing is the statistical lens through which to view the world, allowing this world to make sense. The concept of sampling distribution is this statistical lens. My own experience discovering this lens was a revelation, akin to the experience I had when I put on my first pair of eyeglasses – suddenly everything was sharp and clear (ibid, p. 142).

The sampling distribution is the distribution of all the possible sample means for a variable taken from one population or set of values. Arguably, it is fundamental in understanding how statistics work as it is the basis of inferential statistics. In describing his own experience, Kennedy suggests that understanding the sampling distribution provides a statistical "lens" through which the rest of statistics becomes clearer. We assert that this meets a key characteristic of a threshold concept according to Meyer and Land (2003, 2005): that is, that it is transformative. Once students understand the sampling distribution, they approach statistics in a different way; less that this is a mathematical process, and thinking more as a statistician would. This is similar to the way in which Shanahan and Meyer (2005) suggest that students studying economics learn "to think like an economist". This transformation is usually irreversible and enables the student to understand other troublesome concepts that are based upon this essential premise.

On examining sampling distribution in more depth one sees that the concept is not only transformative and likely to be irreversible but that it contains troublesome knowledge and language, and also is integrative. Detecting troublesome knowledge and language in statistics is not difficult. Those of us who are non-statisticians will still remember how impenetrable the language was on first learning statistics (our peers calling it "gobbledegook") and even more worrying were the mystifying concepts that seemed to tie one's brains in knots, over and over again. For instance, central tendency (the measurement of average and dispersion) is a common stumbling block, but is essential if one is to understand the concept of sampling distribution. It may be troublesome as there are several measures of central tendency, useful with different distributions. Also, one has to understand distributions, symmetry, skewness (which can be rather tricky and counter-intuitive) and dispersion (which involves the derivation of several more confusing formulae and itself requires a tacit understanding of measurement and spread). Additionally, statistical language itself can be difficult and often heavily mathematical. Even in encountering the seemingly easier concept of central tendency, a student will come across: "sum of squares", "degrees of freedom", "variance" and "deviations from the mean". Furthermore, the concept of sampling distribution integrates several basic statistical concepts (along with their derivations and formulae) such as: population, generalizability, sampling, randomisation, distributions, central tendency, estimation, sampling error, and standard deviation.

So, in statistics, the example of sampling distribution is relatively easy to identify as a threshold concept; Kennedy's wonderful visual metaphor identifies this is an essential key to "thinking like a statistician". One could argue that the whole of inferential statistics hangs on this premise, so that a failure to understand this would be a hindrance to comprehending this area of statistics. On the other hand, a deep understanding of the sampling distribution leads a student to survey the whole aspect of statistical practice in a different light. The whole curriculum can be viewed through the "statistical lens" as described by Kennedy (1998). This lens then allows a plethora of other concepts and new practical applications to become apparent and be approached by the student with a better degree of understanding.

To identify other threshold concepts in our teaching of statistics to medical students at UNSW, we followed Eckerdal, McCartney, Moström, Ratcliffe, Sanders et al's (2006) proposal of approaching this by first listing all the core concepts taught in the content. This is their "breadth-first" approach that proposes that among these listed concepts will be some threshold concepts. Simultaneously, the evaluations and feedback received from students were examined in order to identify where they felt that they were stumbling. This information was then analysed with the characteristics of threshold concepts in mind (Meyer and Land, 2003, 2005). To identify whether there is troublesome knowledge and language in the concepts, they were *unpicked*; stripped back to their fundamental elements. Added to this were the experiences of the teachers in their own learning of these concepts and experiences of teaching these concepts. In looking at our own learning we were able to identify the points where we struggled, faltered and failed (Bonner, Harwood and Lotter, 2004).

Two other overarching threshold concepts were identified in this manner (see Figure 2): the "Strength of evidence lens" (centred around hypothesis testing and statistical significance) and the "Applicability lens" (centred around the applicability of evidence). This third threshold concept was identified with assistance from Mayer (2004) who has deftly unpicked this area, clarifying the application of evidence in a clinical situation for the practitioner. These overarching threshold concepts are not intended to be placed in any order, for instance, most statisticians

Threshold Concept a) Kennedy's (1998) - "Sampling distribution lens"
- Sampling and sampling distribution
- Sampling error
- Randomisation
- Central tendency
- Central limit theorem and Normal distribution
- Other continuous and discrete distributions, including t and chi squared
- Regression to the mean

Tacit knowledge required/allied concepts: types of data; frequency distributions; study designs; placebo effect

Threshold Concept b) Statistical significance –"Strength of evidence lens"
Hypothesis formation and testing:
- Null and alternative hypothesis
- Effect size
- Statistical testing
- P values and significance
- Confidence intervals
- Type 1 error
- Power and Type 2 error
- Research design and validity
- Strength of evidence criteria

Tacit knowledge required / allied concepts: understanding how statistical distributions convert into statistical significance tables; and Probability (and Bayesian theory)

Threshold Concept c) Applicability of evidence – "Applicabilty lens"
In medicine / health this is clinical significance = peculiar to medical / health statistics and can be thought of as "applicability" (Mayer, 2004):
- Best evidence
- Clinical evidence
- Patient values
- Clinical situation

Figure 2. The three main overarching threshold concepts in statistics with the associated basic and threshold concepts that underpin them.

and epidemiologists would discuss hypothesis formation before sampling. All three of these lenses overlap so that some concepts are found within more than one "lens" and unsurprisingly, these lenses integrate other theories, for instance: Bayesian theory and probability (both likely candidates for threshold concepts as well).

We acknowledge that the interaction of these concepts is highly complex as they integrate many basic and threshold concepts. The learning of basic concepts is recognised as "basic conceptual changes" as described by Davies and Mangan (2007, 2009). They are not transformative concepts in themselves but contribute to the "discipline conceptual change" of the threshold concept (ibid). Clearly, a student might understand all of these basic concepts separately but still may not be able to grasp the full threshold concept. Practical application of these concepts helps the student to understand them more fully, especially if applied with what Davies and

Mangan (ibid) dub "procedural concepts". These concepts "provide the means by which the structural form of the [threshold concept] portal can be assembled (Davies and Mangan, 2009). They allow the "discipline conceptual change" (threshold concept) to be understood by organising the concepts in a modelling process. This interaction between concepts feeds back until the students' understanding "deepens" to the transformative point (ibid). Examining statistics with this theory has assisted in unravelling the links between the concepts. Furthermore, we concur with Davies and Mangan (ibid) that the identification of procedural concepts will assist in the development of better teaching and assessment methods.

Unpicking Numeracy Issues

We propose then that these threshold concepts are built up of the basic concepts listed below them. Some of these might be threshold concepts in their own right and are themselves informed by several other concepts of an even more basic level. In unpicking all of these concepts, it becomes obvious that they contain some basic numerical processes (e.g. summation, equations and ratios) and also a great deal of basic probability theory. Subsequently, numeracy skills are extremely useful in navigating the mathematical and probability language used in explaining and deriving the formulas for these concepts. A student who has poor numeracy skills or numerophobia could fail to learn many basic concepts in statistics and then would be more likely to flounder in understanding the threshold concepts. On the other hand, students who like numbers and understand probability are likely to have a much easier ride through the liminal process as described later in this chapter.

A mapping exercise is being undertaken to reveal the networking of all of these concepts and to see how they map onto the overall learning cycle in Figure 1. This process is already revealing that there is a close interlinking of the basic and threshold concepts. It shows that there is a possible natural progression in terms of teaching from one threshold concept to the next. This is not surprising in terms of the manner in which inferential statistics originated but is surprising when one analyses the established methods used to teach it. Standard text books (for medical statistics) do not seem to agree on a particular order of learning these concepts, although most have chapters devoted to the threshold concepts identified above in Figure 2. However, they are not explicitly identified as threshold concepts, nor are the links between these concepts identified or emphasized in a consistent way. Interestingly (though uncorroborated), from our own experience, the better statistics courses that we have encountered were those where teaching was focused on these specific areas and progression between them was mapped and described. We would argue that by identifying these threshold concepts we have found another way to observe and analyze how students learn statistics and hence can target our teaching.

With these threshold concepts identified, the next step to unpicking the difficult learning areas was to identify the numeracy issues underlying and making up the threshold concepts and to examine this in terms of student learning and our teaching approaches. Bulmer, O'Brien and Price (2007) have carried out a detailed online evaluation of 555 biology students being taught basic statistics. One of their aims was to begin to identify the content areas that students considered most "difficult to learn". They found that a frequent issue raised was to do with numeracy: "Maths/Formulas" and choice of "Tests". In examining the basic content taught to our medical students, numeracy was also identified as being of key importance in all of the statistical threshold concepts and student feedback commonly mentioned maths or numbers as being a problem (Thompson, 2008). Bulmer et al. (ibid) further suggest that the derivation and application of concepts is more important to student learning than actual mathematical skills. Students are able to do the maths but cannot apply this to the content or in the application of the content. Davies and Mangan's (2009) procedural concepts may be of vital importance here in explaining how these learning processes occur or are hindered.

Traditionally statistics, even when taught in non-mathematical disciplines, is taught through the formulae and equations that represent the statistical concepts. It is standard practice to derive or present the formulae as part of the explanation of an important theory, concept or statistical test. However, for the numerophobic, this can present an insurmountable challenge due to the anxiety that this provokes. This anxiety may result in a misunderstanding or complete failure to understand. Further study on our part and Bulmer, et al (2007) has shown that the students fail to apply the statistical techniques correctly, which is a failure of application:

> So while the students do not find the underlying mathematics knowledge to be challenging or particularly "threshold" in nature, the conceptually difficult bridge to traverse appears to be in the selection and application of statistical techniques within relevant contexts (ibid, p. 13).

Do students who are just beginning to understand a threshold concept, entering into that *liminal space* of learning and preparing to cross a *learning bridge* (Savin-Baden, 2008), falter and fail to cross the final threshold due to inability to understand the formulaic explanation or the numerical calculation that is inherent in the explanation? Does the discomfort experienced and the fear of numbers and equations cause confusion and disengagement that forces an affected student to back out of the liminal space (Savin-Baden, 2008)? If so, this leaves the student with only a partial understanding of the concepts involved and interrupts the transformative process that will lead the student into a higher level of under-standing or practice as described early on in threshold concept research by Meyer and Land (2003). This failure to engage fully with the concept may also leave them with a lack of confidence in learning this particular content and may even initiate a full blown aversion.

To overcome this problem in a mainly online teaching environment (which has its own limitations when it comes to engagement and knowledge transfer) we chose to target the mathematic formulae by presenting them in a less mathematical way than previously and with an emphasis on functionality, theory and application. The main aim in teaching evidence-based medicine and basic statistics at this early stage of the undergraduate medical program at UNSW is to develop the students' ability to interpret results and apply this clinically; the learning skills targeted by the course are the interpretation of results which includes mastering and under- standing of statistical tests, statistical significance and clinical significance. This process is depicted in the second half of the cycle shown in Figure 1. What can be seen from this figure is that there are places where numeracy holds the key to understanding and so this is where an effort was made to analyse the concepts further in order to develop parallel but non-numerical explanations. To support those students who could not approach statistical formulae, visual and narrative explanations were expanded and developed. For example, the difficult threshold concept of the central limit theorem (in the Sampling distribution concepts, Fig. 2) is usually explained in terms of formulae and complex graphs, however, we also taught this using a narrative example of sampling in order to describe it and a picture to visually impress this further (Figure 3).

Furthermore, lectures are now targeted at explaining the threshold concepts and the underlying basic concepts underlying them using both maths and non-math based approaches. More face to face tutorials are provided in the course: an increase from three to ten practical classes (over the first two years of the medical program) with tutors on hand to advise as students attempt the exercises in the online tutorials and whole class discussion of key points. This change has been appreciated by the students; there has been a good response from both informal and formal feedback (Thompson, 2008). By offering several "variations" of the same

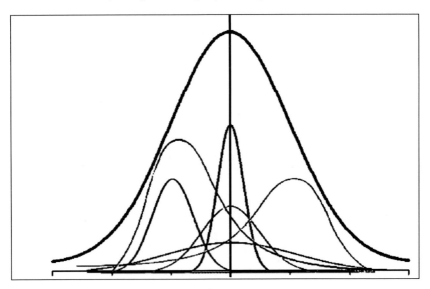

Figure 3. Example from an online statistics tutorial. This is the final figure of a series depicting the distribution of the means of samples (central narrowest distribution) used to explain the central limit theorem. A definition and questions with detailed explanations sit adjacent the figure series.

content to a student in terms of perceptive modalities (narrative, visual and mathematical), the improved tutorials, practical classes and lectures are providing a richness of perspectives or different views, of numeric concept (Dienes, 1959 cited Meyer, Land and Davies, 2008) and in doing this the student is better prepared to traverse and reach the bridge of liminality and eventually cross the threshold for this concept (Savin-Baden, 2008).

Evaluation of these improvements to the online tutorials is continuing and will be described elsewhere. However, preliminary evaluation has shown that the students are completing the online tutorials in higher proportions and are showing an improved understanding of the key assessable elements around the threshold concepts of Strength of evidence and Applicability (Figure 2). There were students who still found these examination questions difficult but more passed these than previously and overall the students appeared to have a better grasp of the threshold concepts: less than 15% of the students failed the short answer questions after the changes (2007–8), compared to over 30% in 2005, the mean average mark increasing by 7%. On the other hand, the qualitative tutorial feedback revealed that there were a few students who would like more mathematical explanations: one student suggested "More maths-background behind each of the explanations!" (Thompson, 2008). These could be dubbed the "numerophilic" students; those who find that mathematics and formulae are the best way for them to understand these trouble-some concepts. In contrast, the numerophobic students appear to prefer the narrative, visual or written styles of learning and maybe the best way for these students to cope with the formulae and these troublesome concepts is to understand it fully this way first. One student felt most distanced in a module "when numbers are brought in" whilst another found that an "illustration on odd ratio is clear" (Thompson, 2008). Concurrently, Freeman, Collier, Staniforth and Smith (2008) have carried out similar improvements to their medical statistics course at the University of Sheffield, UK. Although not focussing on threshold concepts as such, they concentrated on teaching basic statistical concepts with less emphasis on requirement for inherent numeracy skills and using "materials... created that presented the same information in a number of ways, maximizing the opportunities for students with different learning styles and approaches" (ibid, Methods section, para. 3). Their evaluation of this particular improvement showed a statistically significant increase in understanding of definitions of basic concepts but, interestingly, not for the question: do you "Feel comfortable with the basics of medical statistics"? (ibid).

In summary, our first case study shows that students are struggling with the numeracy within troublesome concept areas. In bypassing the numerical explanation initially we have helped them to enter the liminal space with less anxiety and more readily achieve understanding of the basic and threshold concepts in statistics. The overarching threshold concepts of Sampling distribution, Strength of evidence and Applicability of evidence (Figure 2) were identified and ways of explaining them without an emphasis on numbers were developed and implemented. These concepts were then more easily grasped by students and in so doing they were more able to process the information presented to them in epidemiological studies and in clinical trials (Figure 1, Process B – evidence interpretation). The barriers to understanding and interpretation were lifted by reducing the exposure to this numerophobic problem. By removing the need to explain the concepts using numbers, the anxious environment that these numbers and formulae had caused in the liminal space cleared and the numerophobic students were able to find another route through this difficult learning moment. These students describe how they are then more readily able to approach the numerical explanations and understand them more fully.

HOW ARE CONFIDENCE AND ABILITY LINKED WITH RESPECT TO ACADEMIC NUMERACY?

The link between student confidence and their numeric abilities when studying science is beginning to be explored. Current findings highlight that there is a lot that we do not understand about the role of student confidence in applying their numeric skill when learning about science. Klinger (2004) has identified that a proportion of students who are not engaging in numeric tasks within the context of science are maths anxious and that these students are at risk of failing or withdrawing from university. Because engaging constructively with available course resources (whether these are online or resources offered more traditionally) is required for success in a course, the issue then becomes how to assist those students who are not engaging with these resources because of their anxiety and to explicitly address student confidence.

Having spent many months designing a series of online modules to assist students with the calculations involved in their plant physiology practical work, the lack of engagement with the numeric content of biology persisted after these online modules were implemented. Although most students used the numeracy modules and found them useful for consolidating their understanding, there was still a percentage of students whose difficulties with calculations persisted (Quinnell, May and Lloyd, 2004). The inference here is that the online "how to" guides seemed to not solve the maths problem for all students; not all students were able to engage meaningfully with these and did not use the modules to improve their numeric proficiency (Tariq, 2007; Quinnell, 2006).

Furthermore, most online learning systems seem to lack the capacity to interrogate students about their confidence at the point of undertaking data analysis. In a face-to-face tutorial, which the online modules were designed to replace, it is possible to *read* the student, and student body language is powerful feedback for tutors. To linger at those moments when the students *break eye contact* (the "*look away*" moments, which we see as being an indication that a "threshold" has been reached) and to modify tutorials and lectures in response to this, is a powerful teaching strategy, that to our knowledge, has not been replicated in the online learning environment.

As a result of these findings our teaching strategy was modified. Face-to-face tutorials were re-introduced and constructed around a numeracy diagnostic focused on confidence. The aim of this diagnostic was to pinpoint where numeracy was problematic and where students were uncoupling themselves from the learning process (Quinnell and Wong, 2007). This diagnostic was designed and implemented in a second year undergraduate plant physiology course. The vast majority of students have completed both first year mathematics and first year chemistry as prerequisites for entry into plant physiology. The diagnostic task was implemented at the start of the semester and allowed each student to determine their confidence: (a) with articulating their understanding physical parameters used in physiology, (b) with understanding the units of measure of these parameters; and, (c) in their ability to calculate and convert between units of measure. For many students this was the first time their discomfort and their lack of confidence with calculation was acknowledged in a practical class task. Enabling students to address their discomfort and engage in their own skills development has proved to be a useful approach, particularly for students lacking confidence (Quinnell and Wong, 2007). In this study those students who had the highest engagement with the task were those with the least confidence in their responses. This diagnostic has proved to be valuable to academic staff and initiated a dialogue about course expectations that included a discussion on skills development.

The literature shows that even students of mathematics have anxiety when studying maths (e.g. Meece, Wigfield and Eccles, 1990; Phan and Walker, 2000); these studies provided an important starting point to understand maths anxiety in a discipline other than mathematics (Klinger, 2004; Tariq, 2007). One of the main tasks that we expect students to carry out is to recognise data sets or clusters of data that logic dictates relate to each other (Figure 1, Steps 2–5). But how are students expected to focus on the biological principles in practical class when confronted with the relatively complex measures such as one used for the rate of photosynthesis: mol $O_2.s^{-1}.mg^{-1}$ chlorophyll? In this example, students are required to measure the change in concentration of oxygen dissolved in the buffer solution containing photosynthetic plant tissue or algae using an oxygen electrode; the units of measure recorded by oxygen electrode are mM O_2. min^{-1}. Using the volume of the assay buffer, the amount (in mmol) of oxygen liberated by the photosynthetic tissue can be calculated to give mmol. O_2. min^{-1} that, using the conversion factor 60 s. min^{-1}, can be expressed as mmol. O_2. s^{-1}. The final units of measure to describe the rate of photosynthetic activity are mmol O_2. s^{-1}. mg chl^{-1}; so the amount of chlorophyll in the system needs to be measured and incorporated into the calculations. The chlorophyll in the photosynthetic tissue is extracted into solution and the absorbance readings at the λ_{max} for Chl a and Chl b of this solution are measured using a spectrophotometer. The amount of total chlorophyll (expressed in mg) is calculated from i) the Chl a and Chl b absorbance readings ii) the corresponding extinction coefficients of each pigment and, iii) the volume of the chlorophyll extract. In the final step of the calculation the data derived from the oxygen electrode (mmol O_2. s^{-1}) is divided by the data derived from the spectro-photometer (mg Chl) to generate mmol O_2. s^{-1}. mg chl^{-1}. By the end of the experimental process, each student will generate a table that displays the results of the test with the controls so that comparison can be made and interferences drawn. Documenting the number and detail of the calculations involved in this single practical exercise shows that what we are asking our students to do is not trivial. There are many points were students can incur difficulties; students can lose

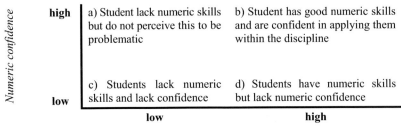

		low	high
high		a) Student lack numeric skills but do not perceive this to be problematic	b) Student has good numeric skills and are confident in applying them within the discipline
low		c) Students lack numeric skills and lack confidence	d) Students have numeric skills but lack numeric confidence

Numeric skills within the discipline

Figure 4. Linking students' numeric skill competence with their confidence with these when operating within Life Sciences. Motivating students to shift from low to high with respect to confidence and/or skills requires require our teaching practices to be re-thought.

their way when undertaking a multistep process (Trott, 2007) and that applying calculations in life sciences is considered, by some students, to be more difficult than just executing those calculations (Koenig, 2007; Tariq, 2008). Further to this, generating the table of data may be end of the experimental process but it marks the beginning of data interpretation process (Figure 1); the work does not end with the calculations. It is no wonder then that "data analysis" in life sciences has been proposed to be a learning threshold (Taylor, 2006).

The learning strategy that a student needs to adopt to develop their numeracy skills will depend on several factors, two of which are whether they i) lack confidence or ii) the ability to map their numeracy skills into the discipline. Strategies can be designed to engage and challenge the maths anxious biology student (Quinnell and Wong, 2007) and mark a departure from focusing directly on how to 'do' calculations. When a student makes an educationally positive transitions by developing i) their confidence or ii) their numeric skills and/or their confidence (Figure 4), it directly challenges the standpoints of "*I can't do maths*" and "*maths is boring*", which we believe makes the hitherto rigid boundaries around these standpoints dissolve a little and the student's chances of entering their liminal space greater.

CONCLUSION

The academic numeracy skills of tertiary students are being explored more fully and have resulted in the creation of networks and resource hubs that focus on learning maths, for example: the Maths, Stats & OR Network at http://www. mathstore.ac.uk/ in the UK; and the Australian Network in Learning Support in Mathematics and Statistics at http://silmaril.math.sci.qut.edu.au/carrick/sites.html. It has become clearer that numerophobia needs to be accepted as an important factor in student learning difficulties at the tertiary level. Our research has added to this work by examining the processes and concepts wherein numeracy skills are important in our students' learning. In outlining our two case studies we have shown advantages of targeting teaching improvements at those key moments where students stumble over numeracy. In the first case study we unpicked the medical statistics topics to identify the key threshold concepts and the concepts that underpin them. Once the overarching threshold concepts were identified, we found it easier to isolate where students uncoupled from the learning process. We discovered that most of these points of uncoupling involved numbers and formulae, and infer that, for numerophobic students, this is a key factor affecting student progress through the liminal space in understanding a threshold concept. Subsequently, successful changes were made to teaching modes and content to enable the numerophobic students to approach both basic and threshold concepts without encountering explanations filled with confusing numbers or formulae. In contrast, the second case study shows a different approach to numerophobia; by challenging students in a diagnostic, students' confidence in their numeracy skills can be improved so that they approach their learning with less anxiety. Both of these methods have proved useful to us and we continue our investigations into how confidence in numeracy affects students learning in practical classes in other life sciences (including genetics and physics). Our future research will focus on threshold concepts and numeracy issues in medical statistics, extending this into the life sciences, as these conceptual intersections appear essential to teaching students how to practise as a statistician or a scientist.

NOTES

The model presented in Figure one resulted from collaboration between the authors and Dr Rebecca LeBard, in the School of Biotechnology and Biomolecular Sciences at the University of New South Wales, Australia. We acknowledge A/Prof Mike Bennett (UNSW) and A/Prof Deborah Black (UNSW & USyd) for their assistance in the development and revision of the medical statistics content in the undergraduate medical program at UNSW.

REFERENCES

Altman, D. G., & Bland, J. M. (1991). Improving doctors' understanding of statistics. *Journal of the Royal Statistical Society, Series A (Statistics in Society)*, *154*(2), 223–267.
Australian Network in Learning Support in Mathematics and Statistics. Retrieved February 16, 2009, from http://silmaril.math.sci.qut.edu.au/carrick/sites.html
Ben-Shlomo, Y., Fallon, U., Sterne, J., & Brookes, S. (2004). Do medical students with A-level mathematics have a better understanding of the principles behind evidence-based medicine? *Medical Teacher, 26*, 731–733.
Biggs, J. B. (1989). Approaches to the enhancement of tertiary teaching. *Higher Education Research & Development, 8*, 7–25.
Bonner, J., Harwood, W., & Lotter, C. (2004, December). One bottleneck at a time. *The Science Teacher*, 26–29.
Bulmer, M., O' Brien, M., & Price, S. (2007). Troublesome concepts in statistics: a student perspective on what they are and how to learn. In I. Johnston & M. Peat (Eds.), *UniServe Science National UniServe Conference – Symposium Proceedings Science Teaching and Learning Research including Threshold concepts*. Uniserve science, University of Sydney, (9–15), 28–29 September. Retrieved February 13, 2008, from http://science.uniserve.edu.au/pubs/procs/2007/06.pdf

Davies, P., & Mangan, J. (2007). Threshold concepts and the integration of understanding in economics. *Studies in Higher Education, 32*(6), 711–726.

Davies, P., & Mangan, J. (2009). *Assessing progression in students' economic understanding: The role of threshold concepts*. In R. Land, J. H. F. Meyer, & C. Baillie (Eds.), *Threshold concepts and transformational learning*. Rotterdam, The Netherlands: Sense Publishers.

Eckerdal, A., McCartney, R., Moström, J. E., Ratcliffe, M., Sanders, K., & Zander, C. (2006, June 26–28). Putting threshold concepts into context in computer science education. In *Proceedings of ITiCSE 2006*. Bologne, Italy. Retrieved February 16, 2009, from http://portal.acm.org/citation.cfm?id= 1140154&dl=GUIDE&coll=GUIDE&CFID=22125449&CFTOKEN=62763002

Freeman, J., Collier, S., Staniforth, D., & Smith, K. (2008). Innovations in curriculum design: A multidisciplinary approach to teaching statistics to undergraduate medical students. *BMC Medical Education, 8*(28). Retrieved February 13, 2009, from http://www.biomedcentral.com/1472-6920/ 8/28

Kennedy, P. E. (1998, May). *Teaching undergraduate econometrics: A suggestion for fundamental change*. Papers and Proceedings of the Hundred and Tenth Annual Meeting of the American Economic Association. *The American Economic Review, 88*, 487–492.

Klinger, C. M. (2004). Study skills and the math-anxious: Reflecting on effective academic support in challenging times. In K. Dellar-Evans & P. Zeegers (Eds.), *Language and academic skills in higher education* (Vol. 6, pp. 161–171). Adelaide: Flinders University Press.

Koenig, J. (2007). Essential maths for medics and vets. In D. Green (Ed.), *Conference Proceedings. Continuing excellence in the teaching and learning of mathematics, statistics and operational research* (pp. 93–96). Retrieved December 2007, from http://www.mathstore.ac.uk/

LeBard, R., & Quinnell, R. (2008). *Using assessment audits to understand students' learning obstacles*. In Proceedings of the UniServe Science Symposium on Visualisation for concept development. Sydney: UniServe Science. Retrieved February 14, 2009, from http://science.uniserve.edu.au/pubs/ procs/2008/182.pdf

Mathstore | maths, stats & OR network. Retrieved February 16, 2009, from http://www.mathstore.ac.uk/

Mayer, D. (2004). *Essential evidence-based medicine*. Cambridge, UK: Cambridge University Press.

Meece, J., Wigfield, A., & Eccles, J. (1990). Predictors of maths anxiety and its influence on young adolescents' course enrolment and performance in mathematics. *Journal of Educational Psychology, 82*, 60–70.

Meyer, J., & Land, R. (2003). Threshold concepts and troublesome knowledge (1): Linkages to ways of thinking and practising within the disciplines. In C. Rust (Ed.), *Improving student learning – Ten years on*. Oxford: OCSLD.

Meyer, J., & Land, R. (2005). Threshold concepts and troublesome knowledge (2): Epistemiological considerations and a conceptual framework for teaching and learning. *Higher Education, 49*, 373–388.

Meyer, J. H. F., Land, R., & Davies P. (2008). Threshold concepts and troublesome knowledge (4): Issues of variation and variability. In R. Land, J. H. F Meyer, & J. Smith (Eds.), *Threshold concepts within the disciplines* (pp. 59–74). Rotterdam, The Netherlands: Sense Publishers.

Moss, K., Greenall, C., Rockcliffe, A., Crowley, M., & Mealing, A. (2007). Threshold concepts, misconceptions and common issues. In P. Chin, K. Clark, S. Doyle, P. Goodhew, T. Madden, S. Meskin, et al. (Eds.), *Proceedings of the science learning and teaching conference* (pp. 190–196). Liverpool: The Higher Education Academic Subject Centres for Bioscience, Materials and Physical Sciences. Retrieved February 14, 2008, from http://www.bioscience.heacademy.ac.uk/ftp/events/ sltc07papers/o31moss.pdf

Phan, H., & Walker, R. (2000). The predicting and mediational role of mathematics self-efficacy: A path analysis. *The Australian Association for Research in Education conference*. Melbourne 1999. Retrieved December 2006, from http://www.aare.edu.au/00pap/pha00224.htm

Quinnell, R. (2006, November 2). *When instructions are not enough: Strategies to engage students in numeracy and written skills development*. College of Science and Technology Teaching and Learning Showcase. The University of Sydney. Retrieved September 2008, from http://science. uniserve.edu.au/courses/showcase/

Quinnell, R., & Thompson, R. (2008, June 18–20). *Re-viewing academic numeracy in the tertiary education sector as a threshold concept*. Threshold Concepts Conference, Kingston Ontario.

Quinnell, R., & Wong, E. (2007). Using intervention strategies to engage tertiary biology students in their development of numeric skills. In *Proceedings of UniServe Science Symposium Science Teaching and Learning Research, including Threshold concepts*. September 27 & 28, 2007, Sydney (pp. 70–74). Retrieved February 15, 2009, from http://science.uniserve.edu.au/pubs/procs/2007/16.pdf

Quinnell, R., May, E., & Lloyd, H. (2004). *A comparison of student usage of traditional verses ICT learning resources in the Life Sciences*. Proceedings of the UniServe Science Symposium on the Scholarly Inquiry in Flexible Science Teaching and Learning Symposium. Sydney, NSW: UniServe Science (pp. 80–84). Retrieved February 15, 2009, from http://science.uniserve.edu.au/pubs/procs/wshop9/schws005.pdf

Savin-Baden, M. (2008). Liquid learning and troublesome space: Journeys from the threshold? In R. Land, J. H. F. Meyer, & J. Smith (Eds.), *Threshold concepts within the disciplines*. Rotterdam, The Netherlands: Sense Publishers.

Shanahan, M. P., & Meyer, J. H. F. (2005). The troublesome nature of a threshold concept in Economics. In J. H. F. Mayer (Ed.), *Overcoming barriers to student understanding* (Ch. 7). Abingdon, UK and New York, USA: Routledge.

Sinclair, S. (1997). *Making doctors: An institutional apprenticeship*. Oxford, UK: Berg.

Tariq, V. (2007). Can't do maths, won't do maths – don't want help. In D. Green (Ed.), Conference Proceedings. *Continuing excellence in the teaching and learning of mathematics, statistics and operational research* (pp. 124–127). Retrieved September 2008, from http://www.mathstore.ac.uk/

Taylor, C. E., & Meyer, J. H. F. (2008, June 18–20). *The testable hypothesis as a threshold concept for biology students*. Threshold Concepts Conference, Kingston Ontario.

Taylor, C. E. (2008). Threshold concepts, troublesome knowledge and ways of thinking and practicing – can we tell the difference in biology? In R. Land, J. H. F. Meyer, & J. Smith (Eds.), *Threshold concepts within the disciplines*. London: Routledge.

Thompson, R. (2008). *Sexing up stats: Dealing with numeracy issues and threshold concepts in an online medical statistics course*. Australasian and New Zealand Association for Medical Education. Retrieved September 2008, from Retrieved from http://www.anzame.unsw.edu.au/conf_past.htm

Trott, C. (2007). Mathematics and neurodiversity. In D. Green (Ed.), *Conference Proceedings. Continuing excellence in the teaching and learning of mathematics, statistics and operational research* (pp. 161–166). Retrieved December 2007, from http://www.mathstore.ac.uk/

Dr Rosanne Quinnell
Faculty of Science
University of Sydney and University of New South Wales

Dr Rachel Thompson
Faculty of Medicine
University of New South Wales

PAULINE M ROSS, CHARLOTTE E. TAYLOR, CHRIS HUGHES,
MICHELLE KOFOD, NOEL WHITAKER, LOUISE LUTZE-MANN,
AND VICKY TZIOUMIS

10. THRESHOLD CONCEPTS:

Challenging the Way We Think, Teach and Learn In Biology

INTRODUCTION

Students generally come to tertiary institutions with misconceptions of some of the key content and concepts in the disciplines they are studying. Their misconceptions commonly relate to conceptually difficult or troublesome content knowledge and can be: incomplete and contradictory; stable and highly resistant to change; and remain intact despite repeated instruction at successively higher levels perhaps reinforced by teachers and textbooks. Troublesome or difficult content knowledge in Biology includes cellular metabolic processes (for example, photosynthesis and respiration), cellular size and dimensionality (surface area to volume ratio), water movement (diffusion and osmosis) genetics (protein synthesis, cell division, DNA) evolution, homeostasis and equilibrium. We suggest that the threshold concepts of Meyer and Land, (2005) in biology are the ability to work with concepts and processes; energy, variation, randomness and probability, proportional reasoning, spatial and temporal scales, thinking at a submicroscopic level, and that these abilities, or lack thereof, underlie the difficult content or troublesome knowledge causing misconceptions. Threshold concepts thus provide a powerful heuristic to interrogate the cause of troublesome content knowledge in biology and to aid in the development of teaching interventions, to surface the tacit knowledge within the biology discipline.

MISCONCEPTIONS AND DIFFICULT OR TROUBLESOME CONTENT

The seminal work of Driver and Easley (1978) over thirty years ago and the subsequent research (Driver, 1983; Driver, 1985; Driver, Guesne and Tiberghien, 1985; Osborne and Freyberg, 1985; Driver and Bell, 1986; Driver, Squires, Rushworth and Wood-Robinson, 1994) highlighted that children possess numerous ideas that are inconsistent with scientific knowledge even after teaching. These erroneous ideas have been called misconceptions, alternative concepts, alternative frameworks, naïve explanations, preconceptions and pre-scientific concepts, being found in textbooks and are also held by teachers and students at school, college and university level (Yip, 1998). Much of the early misconception literature focused on

*J. H. F. Meyer, R. Land and C. Baillie (eds.), Threshold Concepts and
Transformational Learning, 165–177.*

identifying misconceptions in younger students of primary and high school age and determining their understanding of basic concepts of living, plants and animals (e.g. Stavy, Eisen and Yaakobi, 1987; Stavy and Wax, 1989; Eisen and Stavy, 1992, 1993; Wandersee, 1983; Wandersee, Mintzes and Novak, 1994). More recently the renewed interest in the alternative conceptions or misconceptions of biological concepts has occurred because even the best quality, high achieving biology students at elite institutions (taught by universally admired academics), continue to fail to understand the conceptual foundation in key content areas of biology after passing through multiple conventional biology courses (Wandersee et al., 1994). This renewed emphasis in diagnosing misconceptions has lead to the development of summative assessment tests such as the Biology Concept Inventory (Klymkowski & Garvin-Doxas 2008).

Some authors have suggested that it may be useful to distinguish between the misconceptions generated prior to informal instruction and those that occur during or because of formal instruction (Yip, 1998). Misconceptions of the first type which occur prior to formal instruction, arise through children's life experiences and indiscriminate use of everyday language being characterised as basic biological errors e.g. living, animal, plant, gas exchange. Yip (1998) suggested that because these misconceptions are established early in the cognitive structures of children, they are highly stable, resistant to change, show in students as often incomplete and contradictory understandings, are personal in nature and can impact on the receipt of formal instructional approaches, despite repeated instruction at successively higher levels. A wide range of previous studies have identified misconceptions in biology (Driver, 1983; Driver Guesne and Tiberghien, 1985; Driver and Bell, 1986; Osborne and Freyberg, 1985; Seymour and Longdon, 1991; Gabel, 1994; Songer and Mintzes, 1994; Wandersee et al., 1994; Mann and Treagust, 1998; Alparsian, Tekkaya and Geban, 2003) and although misconceptions in biology are personal in nature, not all such misconceptions arise because of personal experience. Children and students have substantially less personal experience in daily life of abstract biological content, such as the dynamic electron transport chain (at the core of cellular metabolic processes including photosynthesis and respiration) and the kinetic gas theory (underlying osmosis). Without a formal school setting students have little opportunity to develop misconceptions about biological content including such areas as the submicroscopic world of photosynthesis. The abstract, counter-intuitive, conceptual difficulty of some biological content and the ritualisation of knowledge may aid the development of misconceptions (Perkins, 2006). It can be difficult within a cohort of students to determine who has misconceptions, but identification can occur when students try and apply conceptual knowledge outside the classroom (Perkins 2006). Regardless of how and where misconceptions arise, they have a real influence on *what and how students learn*. The challenge for teachers is to change student misconceptions into deep understandings of more scientifically accepted conceptions (Posner, Strike, Hewson and Gertzog, 1982; Duit and Treagust, 1998; Gabel, 1994; Tytler, 2007) and this is where the identification of threshold concepts assists.

THRESHOLD CONCEPTS AND THEIR IDENTIFICATION

Meyer and Land (2003, 2005) recently proposed the notion of threshold concepts, and described such concepts as akin to passing through a portal or conceptual gateway to a previously inaccessible and initially perhaps troublesome way of thinking about something. These conceptual gateways or thresholds are characterised as being transformative (occasioning a significant shift in the perception of a subject), irreversible (unlikely to be forgotten or unlearned) and integrative (exposing the previously hidden interrelatedness of something) (Meyer and Land, 2005). This transformed internal view is typified by a cognitive and ontological shift (Meyer, personal communication), often accompanied by an extension of the student's use of language (Meyer and Land, 2005). Although threshold concepts are conceptually difficult or troublesome, being 'particularly tough conceptual nuts' (Perkins, 1999), they are not necessarily troublesome by definition (Perkins, 2006) but they can be content which has become ritualised by students and teachers. It is this tacit, ritualised nature which makes threshold concepts difficult to identify within the discipline. Difficulty in understanding threshold concepts may leave a student in a state of liminality where they get 'stuck' (Perkins 1999; Meyer and Land, 2006). Such liminal or 'stuck' places prevent the learner from undergoing a transformation which may be integrative and irreversible extending their understanding of formal and symbolic language while at the same time paradoxically characterising the change (Meyer and Land 2005).

In the Sciences, students often encounter conceptually difficult or troublesome knowledge (Perkins, 2006). While the literature is rife with examples of misconceptions and mistaken expectations based in physics and chemistry (Meyer and Land, 2006), there are relatively fewer comments about conceptually difficult or troublesome knowledge in biology. This is because it is perhaps easier in the discipline of biology for students to achieve 'success' through learning ritual responses to definitional questions which have become instituted and resistant to change, while still maintaining significant misconceptions about key biological concepts. For the notion of threshold concepts to make a significant contribution to the learning of biology, however, teachers must first be able to identify them. This is not an easy task, even with such a powerful heuristic (Perkins, 2006). Other authors such as Davies and Mangan (2007), have used evidence from interviews with experienced staff and novice students within the discipline, to develop a framework to identify and distinguish threshold concepts as types of conceptual change, namely 'discipline' and 'procedural' from 'basic'.

It would appear that there is consensus within the biology discipline that certain content and concept areas are difficult. Ask experienced biology academics and beginning students to identify which biological concepts are most difficult to teach and learn and they will state cellular metabolic processes (including photosynthesis, respiration and enzymes), cellular size and dimensionality (surface area to volume ratio), water movement (diffusion and osmosis) genetics (protein synthesis, cell division, DNA) evolution, and homeostasis and equilibrium (e.g. Gabel, 1994; Wandersee *et al.,* 1994; Brown, 1995; Canal, 1999, Griffard, 2001, Taylor, 2006; Ross and Tronson, 2004; 2007; Köse, 2008; Taylor, 2008), the processes of hypothesis and null hypothesis testing (Taylor and Meyer this volume) and more broad scale issues of thinking and practising within the discipline such as scale (spatial and temporal) and again surface area to volume ratio, probability, uncertainty, dynamics and change. Although these content and concept areas prove difficult for teachers and learners, they are not necessarily threshold concepts. For example, protein synthesis is frequently identified as a difficult troublesome content area in biology, perhaps because students need to operate simultaneously at several hierarchical, subcellular and submicroscopic scales, but that does not automatically make it a threshold concept. It has been suggested that to identify threshold concepts, which may be currently tacit (Davies, 2006), we need to lift our eyes above the particular (Perkins, 2006) to determine which concepts operate in a deep integrating way in the discipline, while simultaneously being taken for granted, rarely being made explicit (Davies, 2006).

Using the definitions and exemplification of the three types of conceptual change; 'basic', 'discipline' and 'procedural' described by Davies and Mangan (2007), we propose that the threshold concepts in biology which are transformative, irreversible and integrative across the discipline are not the troublesome difficult content of cellular metabolic processes, genetics, evolution, protein synthesis, ecology, enzymes or osmosis alone, but the underlying cognitive commonalities of energy, transformation, variation, probability, proportion, predictive reasoning (hypothesis testing), randomness, linkage of the subcellular with the macroscopic, temporal and spatial scales and equilibrium (Table 1). Further we divide the basic conceptual change category of Davies and Mangan (2007) into pre-basic and basic, neither of these being threshold concepts (Table 1).

The pre-basic type of conceptual change develops prior to formal instruction, through childrens' life experiences and indiscriminate use of everyday language. Our pre-basic type of conceptual change differs from the basic conceptual change of Davies and Mangan (2007) because the concepts are formed through an integration of personal experience, but arise independently of ideas within the formal discipline. For example, very small children have an understanding of animal, but will not often even start to equate a human as an animal until a formal presentation of the definition of animal. Even then the idea that a human is an animal can be simultaneously rejected for religious, social and ethical reasons.

Similarly, very small children have little idea that a seed contains a living embryo of a plant, until this concept is introduced, generally in a formal setting. Once again this conception can change over time (Osborne and Freyberg, 1985). The basic type of conceptual change occurs (Davies and Mangan, 2007) once these personal experiences have been integrated with ideas from the discipline. This constitutes the basic stage, which is often the focus of lower school curriculum, and it is here that students start to acquire the language of biology (Table 1).

Discipline conceptual changes (Davies and Mangan, 2007) in biology are those concepts where there is an integration of the theoretical view within the discipline including a transformation. For example, students might have a basic concept of chlorophyll (and a pre-basic knowledge that plants are green), but can only integrate and transform this content within the theoretical perspective of photolysis and energy conversion occurring in the leaf. Similarly a basic conceptual change of membranes is required to integrate and transform the processes whereby carbon is converted from a gas (carbon dioxide) to a solid compound (sugar/starch). Although these are integrative and transformative experiences, the acquisition of the discipline type of conceptual change, does not require irreversibility. Irreversibility occurs at the next step where a web of threshold concepts occurs. Such irreversibility characterises threshold concepts. We argue that the pre-basic level occurs prior to formal schooling while the 'basic' and 'discipline' areas become the focus of formal schooling and it is here where many misconceptions in biology occur (Yip, 1998). There is generally an expectation that students entering university have the background knowledge and understanding of pre-basic, basic and discipline content, although university lecturing staff may also anticipate that many students are operating at levels beyond these columns in Table 1.

The irreversible and threshold-crossing step occurs when there is integration of discipline concepts and the emergence of a commonality or web of conceptual change. In biology, the threshold concepts equivalent to the procedural conceptual changes of Davies and Mangan (2007) are energy, transformations, variation, probability and randomness, proportional reasoning (surface area to volume ratio), predictive reasoning (hypothesis and null hypothesis testing), thinking at the subcellular level and integrating these observations with the macroscopic, temporal and spatial scales and equilibrium (Table 1). If we take several of these troublesome or difficult content knowledge areas (column 1 of Table 1) we find they have a series of threshold concepts in common (described in column 6 of Table 1). For example, the concept of variability is key to several content areas including ecology, evolution and genetics, while an understanding of energy transformations and dynamism are some of the threshold concepts or 'big ideas' critical in cellular metabolic processes including enzyme action and ecology.

Similarly, the development of the visuo-spatial concept of proportionality, space and perspective and the ability to mentally rotate and relate two dimensional figures into their three dimensional structures is crucial in the conceptual understanding of enzyme action and many biochemical processes. The dynamic nature of biological systems and the energetics which drive biochemical processes also apply broadly across abstract biological content areas such as biochemical processes, homeostasis and equilibrium. The concepts of variability and probability underlie understanding in genetics, evolution and a number of cross disciplinary areas (e.g. quantum mechanics), as does the process of empirically combining factors in a scientific investigation (hypothesis creation) or genetic recombination (Good, 1977). Scale, visuo-spatial dynamics, thinking at the submicroscopic level, variability and probability are acquired developmentally (Inhelder and Piaget, 1955 in Good, 1977), apply broadly and combine synergistically.

The acquisition of language and understanding of language, in context, is critical within the discipline of biology. The linguistic demands of biology, being particularly challenging at the basic and discipline stage (Table 1) often create barriers. For many students, the language developed to describe specific biological conditions becomes confused with the students' natural language form (Meyer and

Land, 2003; 2005). For example, there is an everyday meaning to 'animal', non-human, 'live', 'living fire' or a 'live wire' and respiration, 'that's breathing isn't it?', while the scientific construct is specific and relates to the presence of cells, cellular membranes or cellular metabolism (Osborne and Freyberg, 1985). Also, many students, not having completed Latin at school, tend to concentrate on acquiring the language of biology, rather than meaning, thus facing a cognitive overload. Further, especially in genetics and molecular biology there are often shifts from biological text to symbolic, abbreviations and acronyms (Taylor, 2006), exacerbating and increasing the intensity of the language barrier, and preventing a holistic viewpoint needed to acquire threshold concepts. Paradoxically, however, language, complexity, dynamism and dimensionality are common threshold concepts in biology. For example, thinking in three dimensions is required in ecology, evolution, genetics, cellular metabolic processes and almost all other subject areas. In contrast, often the teaching of biology offers the learner a plethora of two-dimensional representations due to the inherent restrictions and visual imagery of microscopic investigations and the abstraction of the molecular world in textbooks.

Like language, the extension of the students' use or thinking about scale, dimensionality, variability, dynamics and energetics leads to a transformed internal view, rather like the passage from a novice to an expert, of biology beliefs about the nature of knowledge (Perry, 1968; Schommer, 1988; 1993; McCune and Hounsell 2005). The threshold or procedural concepts we have identified form 'epistemes' or ways of understanding, and systems of ideas, but often receive little direct attention in the teaching of biology. They are concepts which are unifying themes across biological systems, are less frequently explicitly taught and which many students (even at graduate level) never get the hang of or do so only slowly (Perkins, 2006) if they can read between the tacit lines (Davies, 2006). Yet these threshold epistemes shape one's sense of the entire biological discipline (Perkins, 2006), by forming the tacit knowledge within the discipline of biology. We need to emphasise that while academics and teachers identify the content knowledge (on the left hand side of Table 1) as troublesome or problematic, the threshold concepts (on the right hand side of Table 1), which underlie the problematic difficult content knowledge, *receive the least attention* in teaching.

Table 1. The relationship between content knowledge which may be conceptually difficult and troublesome, and pre-basic, basic, discipline and threshold concepts, and threshold epistemes

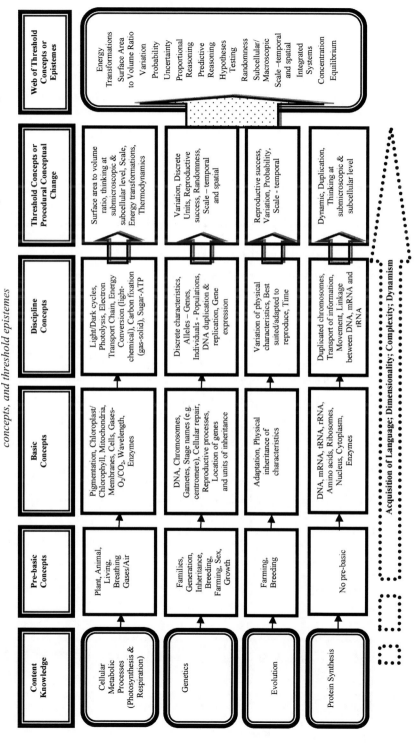

Content Knowledge	Pre-basic Concepts	Basic Concepts	Discipline Concepts	Threshold Concepts or Procedural Conceptual Change	Web of Threshold Concepts or Epistemes
Cellular Metabolic Processes (Photosynthesis & Respiration)	Plant, Animal, Living, Breathing Gases/Air	Pigmentation, Chloroplast/ Chlorophyll, Mitochondria, Membranes, Cells, Gases-O_2/CO_2, Wavelength, Enzymes	Light/Dark cycles, Photolysis, Electron Transport Chain, Energy Conversion (light-chemical), Carbon fixation (gas-solid), Sugar-ATP	Surface area to volume ratio, thinking at submicroscopic & subcellular level, Scale, Energy transformations, Thermodynamics	Energy Transformations, Surface Area to Volume Ratio, Variation, Probability, Uncertainty, Proportional Reasoning, Predictive Reasoning, Hypotheses Testing, Randomness, Subcellular/ Macroscopic, Scale –temporal and spatial, Integrated Systems, Concentration, Equilibrium
Genetics	Families, Generation, Inheritance, Breeding, Farming, Sex, Growth	DNA, Chromosomes, Gametes, Stage names (e.g. centromere), Cellular repair, Reproductive processes, Location of genes and units of inheritance	Discrete characteristics, Alleles – Genes, Individuals - Populations, DNA duplication & replication, Gene expression	Variation, Discrete Units, Reproductive success, Randomness, Scale – temporal and spatial	
Evolution	Farming, Breeding	Adaptation, Physical inheritance of characteristics	Variation of physical characteristics, Best suited/adapted to reproduce, Time	Reproductive success, Variation, Probability, Scale - temporal	
Protein Synthesis	No pre-basic	DNA, mRNA, tRNA, rRNA, Amino acids, Ribosomes, Nucleus, Cytoplasm, Enzymes	Duplicated chromosomes, Transport of information, Movement, Linkage between DNA, mRNA and tRNA	Dynamic, Duplication, Thinking at submicroscopic & subcellular level	

Acquisition of Language; Dimensionality; Complexity; Dynamism

Table 1(Continued). The relationship between content knowledge which may be conceptually difficult and troublesome, and pre-basic, basic, discipline and threshold concepts, and threshold epistemes

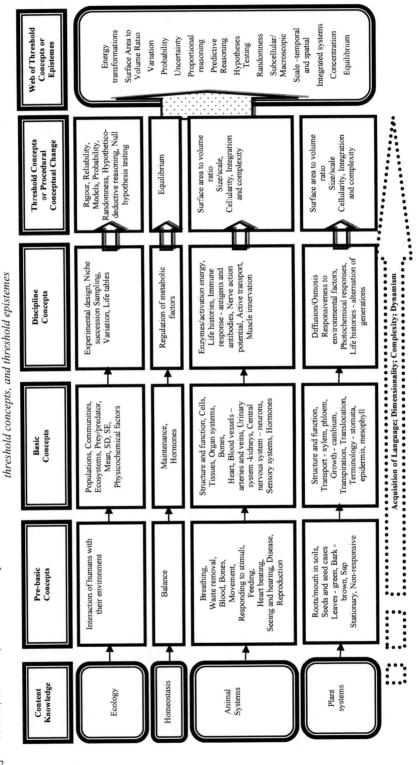

THRESHOLD CONCEPTS AND EVIDENCE

There is some evidence within the science education literature to support the identification and classification of threshold concepts described above. A number of researchers have identified students' lack of experience in 'thinking at the cellular level' (Songer and Mintzes, 1994), particle theory (Meyer, 2007) and scale (spatial and temporal) as causing conceptual difficulties(Russell, Netherwood and Robinson, 2004; Canal, 1999; Ross and Tronson, 2004; Ross, Tronson and Ritchie, 2005; Ebert-May, Batzli and Heejun, 2003; Tretter and Jones 2003; Modell, Michael and Wenderoth, 2005; Taylor, 2006). In two recent studies (Taylor, 2006; 2008), thinking at the submicroscopic or subcellular level and scale were frequently identified by junior and experienced academics as threshold concepts. For example:

> What is the scale at which you define something …there are so many different scales, you have to keep redefining all the time …with this context in mind (Taylor, 2008 p. 188).
> Biochemistry works so well because you have all these little compartments doing different things which link together and help things work at different levels (Taylor, 2006 p. 94).
> You've got to be able to think about water moving in cells and what's going on across membranes and then see the intercellular level, and that feeds into action potential and then muscles come in and how you move your elbow. Then the whole thing comes together at a level where you can actually see something happen (Taylor, 2006 p. 93).
> You cannot see things which are subcellular in most cases, but students expect to be able to see the structure of DNA under the microscope (Taylor, 2006 p. 94)

The model proposed in this paper refines Taylor's (2006, 2008) perspective of process and abstract concepts, often encompassed in the same threshold concept. We argue that many difficult and troublesome biological concepts are a web of threshold concepts. For example the same threshold processes (energetics, dynamics, dimensionality, submicroscopic, language and scale) in cellular metabolism are essential in the development of an understanding of the troublesome knowledge of photosynthesis. Similarly the threshold concepts of variability, dynamics, language and scale are essential in an understanding of evolution and a combination of the thresholds of dynamics, thinking at the submicroscopic level, dimensionality, probability, language and scale are necessary to prevent the content of genetics becoming troublesome. Further, the threshold concepts of variability and probability are inherent in experimental design and analysis (Taylor, 2008). These threshold concepts are found throughout the sciences including chemistry and physics and some cross disciplines into economics – in this way they are not bounded (Meyer and Land, 2003; 2005). The mechanism for determining a threshold in biology thus centres on its transformative, irreversible and integrative nature (Meyer and Land, 2003; 2005), ways of thinking and practising (McCune and Hounsell, 2005) and is parallel with the movement from the novice to expert.

The novice often has a view of the discipline as isolated pieces of content to be memorised as handed down by authority, but this changes as the novice progresses throughout the undergraduate degree to an understanding of the underlying coherence and structure of the discipline (Schommer, 1988; 1993).

IMPLICATION FOR IDENTIFICATION OF THRESHOLD CONCEPTS IN BIOLOGY

Certainly the heuristic of threshold concepts allows insights not offered by the misconception and constructivist literature, raising a number of questions for the development of teaching in biology. For example, where should we be spending our energies as teachers of biology? If we continue to spend our entire time with the basic and discipline concepts, how will our students be able to develop the tools or facility with threshold concepts required to develop a solid understanding of troublesome content? Perhaps using the threshold heuristic we can devise ways to help the students develop the crossing or portals and thereby develop a better understanding of hitherto troublesome knowledge. What is clear from the literature, is how difficult it has been to change students' misconceptions into more scientific conceptions (Duit and Treagust, 1998; Gabel, 1994) perhaps because of the assumption that learning is rational (Posner *et al.*, 1982) and the notion that misconceptions are stable, dependent on the context and individual orientation (Tytler and Peterson, 2004). They may not be. Tytler (2007) suggests a focus on the development of a mental representation of concepts and an integration of different representational models of learning and a socio-cultural approach for shared meaning with high quality conceptual discussion to create conceptual change. It may be that the surfacing of the tacit threshold game within disciplines, through analytic discussion, deliberative practice and alignment of the threshold with instructional approaches could make a big difference to the teaching and learning within disciplines. We do know that experts can transfer across contexts (Hesketh and Ivancic, 2002) and perhaps we can assist students explicitly to cross these thresholds across contexts and thus make troublesome content less troublesome.

FUTURE DIRECTIONS

Future work is needed to: test the hypothesis that the threshold concepts outlined in this paper underlie difficult Biological concepts; develop intervention strategies to improve student mastery of these processes with the aim of improving their understanding in one or more related concept areas, (that is, to help the students cross a conceptual threshold); and finally to test whether students can subsequently transfer this thinking process to aid their understanding of other similarly difficult content (that is, to see if they have learnt how to cross unfamiliar thresholds). Since threshold concepts are meant to reflect the difference in ways of thinking and practising between those who are inside the subject and acknowledged as experts in the field (academics), and novices (students), we propose that future empirical studies should focus on these underlying threshold processes with a view to characterising and evaluating effective teaching intervention strategies.

ACKNOWLEDGEMENTS

This project is being undertaken collaboratively by academics from three Universities in Australia: the University of Sydney; the University of New South Wales; and the University of Western Sydney, funded through the Australian Learning and Teaching Council (ALTC).

REFERENCES

Alparsian, C., Tekkaya, C., & Geban, O. (2003). Using the conceptual change instruction to improve learning. *Journal of Biological Education, 37*(3), 133–137.

Brown, C. R. (1995). *The effective teaching of Biology.* London: Longman.

Canal, P. (1999). Photosynthesis and 'inverse respiration' in plants: An inevitable misconception? *International Journal of Science Education, 21*(4), 363–371.

Davies, P. (2006). Threshold concepts: How can we recognise them? In J. H. F. Meyer & R. Land (Eds.), *Overcoming barriers to student understanding: Threshold concepts and troublesome knowledge* (pp. 70–85). Abingdon: Routledge.

Davies, P., & Mangan, J. (2007). Threshold concepts and the integration of understanding in economics. *Studies in Higher Education, 32*(6), 711–726.

Driver, R. (1983). *The pupil as scientist?* Milton Keynes, UK: Open University Press.

Driver, R. (1985). Beyond appearances: The conservation of matter under physical and chemical transformations. In R. Driver, E. Guesne, & A. Tiberghien (Eds.), *Children's ideas in science* (pp. 145–169). Milton Keynes, UK: Open University Press.

Driver, R., & Easley, J. (1978). Pupils and paradigms: A review of literature related to concept development in adolescent science students. *Studies in Science Education, 5*, 61–84.

Driver, R., & Bell, B. (1986). Students' thinking and the learning of science: A constructivist view. *The School Science Review, 67*(240), 443–456.

Driver, R., Guesne, E., & Tiberghien, A. (1985). *Children's ideas in science.* Milton Keynes, UK: Open University Press.

Driver, R., Squires, A., Rushworth, P., & Wood-Robinson, V. (1994). *Making sense of secondary science: Research into children's ideas.* New York: Routledge.

Duit, R., & Treagust, D. F. (1998). Learning in science: From behaviourism towards constructivism and beyond. In B. J. Fraser & K. G. Tobin (Eds.), *International handbook of science education* (pp. 3–25). Dordrecht, The Netherlands: Kluwer.

Ebert-May, D., Batzli, J., & Heejun, L. (2003). Disciplinary research strategies for assessment of learning. *BioScience, 53*(12), 1221–1228.

Eisen, Y., & Stavy, R. (1992). Material cycles in nature: A new approach to teaching photosynthesis in junior high school. *The American biology Teacher, 54*(6), 339–342.

Eisen, Y., & Stavy, R. (1993). How to make learning of photosynthesis more relevant. *International Journal of Science Education, 15*(2), 117–125.

Flavell, J. H. (1963). The developmental psychology of Jean Piaget. *Journal of Research Science Teachers Association, 2*(3), 267.

Gabel, G. L. (1994). *Handbook of research on science teaching and learning: A project of the national science teachers association.* New York: Macmillan Publishing Company.

Good, R. G. (1977). *How children learn Science: Conceptual development and implications for teaching.* New York: Macmillan Publishing.

Griffard, P. B. (2001). The two-tier instrument on photosynthesis: What does it diagnose? *International Journal of Science Education, 23*(10), 1039–1052.

Hesketh, B., & Ivancic, K. (2002). Enhancing performance through training. In S. Sonnentag (Ed.), *Psychological management of individual performance.* New York: Wiley.

Köse, S. (2008). Diagnosing student misconceptions: Using drawings as a research method. *World Applied Sciences Journal, 3*(2), 283–293.

Klymkowski, M. W., & Garvin-Doxas, K. (2008). Recognizing student misconceptions through Ed's tools and the Biology concept inventory. *Plos Biology, 6*(1), 14–15. Retrieved from www.plosbiology.org

Mann, M., & Treagust, D. F. (1998). A pencil and paper instrument to diagnose students' conceptions of breathing, gas exchange and respiration. *Australian Science Teachers Journal, 44*(2), 55–59.

McCune, V., & Hounsell, D. (2005). The development of students' ways of thinking and practising in three final-year biology courses. *Higher Education, 49*, 255–289.

Meyer, H. (2007). Is it molecules? Again? A review of students' learning about particle theory. *Chemical Education Journal.* Retrieved from http://www.juen.ac.jp/scien/cssj/cejrnlE.html

Meyer, J., & Land, R. (2003). *Threshold concepts and troublesome knowledge: Linkages to ways of thinking and practising within the disciplines.* Enhancing Teaching-Learning Environments in Undergraduate Courses. Occasional Report 4.

Meyer, J., & Land, R. (2005). Threshold concepts and troublesome knowledge (2): Epistemological considerations and a conceptual framework for teaching and learning. *Higher Education, 49*, 373–388.

Meyer, J., & Land, R. (2006). Threshold concepts and troublesome knowledge: An introduction. In J. H. F. Meyer & R. Land (Eds.), *Overcoming barriers to student understanding: Threshold concepts and troublesome knowledge* (pp. 3–19). Abingdon: Routledge.

Modell, H., Michael, J., & Wenderoth, M. P. (2005). Helping the learner to learn: The role of uncovering misconceptions. *The American Biology Teacher, 67*(1), 20–26.

Osborne, R., & Freyberg, P. (1985). *Learning in science: The implications of children's science.* New Zealand: Heinemann Publishers.

Perkins, D. (1999). The many faces of constructivism. *Educational Leadership, 57*(3), 6–11.

Perkins, D. (2006). Constructivism and troublesome knowledge. In J. H. F. Meyer & R. Land (Eds.), *Overcoming barriers to student understanding: Threshold concepts and troublesome knowledge* (pp. 33–48). Abingdon: Routledge.

Perry, W. G., Jr. (1968). *Patterns of development in thought and values of students in a liberal art college: A validation of a scheme.*

Posner, G. J., Strike, K. A., Hewson, P. W., & Gertzog, W. A. (1982). Accommodation of a scientific conception: Toward a theory of conceptual change. *Science Education, 66*, 211–227.

Ross, P. M., & Tronson, D. (2004). Towards conceptual understanding: Bringing research findings into the lecture theatre in tertiary science teaching. In *Proceedings of scholarly inquiry into science teaching and learning symposium* (pp. 52–57). Sydney, NSW: UniServe Science.

Ross, P. M., & Tronson, D. (2007). Intervening to create conceptual change. *UniServe Science Teaching and Learning Research Proceedings*, 89–94.

Ross, P. M., Tronson, D., & Ritchie, R. J. (2005). Modelling photosynthesis to increase conceptual understanding. *Journal of Biological Education, 40*(2), 84–88.

Russell, A. W., Netherwood, G. M. A., & Robinson, S. A. (2004). Photosynthesis *in silico*. Overcoming the challenges of photosynthesis education using a multimedia CD-ROM. *Bioscience Education e-journal, 3*.

Seymour, J., & Longdon, B. (1991). Respiration – that's breathing isn't it? *Journal of Biological Education, 25*(3), 177–183.

Schommer, Z. M. (1988). Effects of beliefs about the nature of knowledge on comprehension. *Journal of Educational Psychology, 82*(3), 498–504.

Schommer, Z. M. (1993). Comparison of beliefs about the nature of knowledge and learning among postsecondary students. *Research in Higher Education, 34*(3), 355–370.

Songer, C. J., & Mintzes, J. J. (1994). Understanding cellular respiration: An analysis of conceptual changes in college biology. *Journal of Research in Science Teaching, 31*(6), 621–637.

Stavy, R., Eisen, Y., & Yaakobi, D. (1987). How students aged 13–15 understand photosynthesis. *International Journal of Science Education, 9*(1), 105–115.

Stavy, R., & Wax, N. (1989). Children's conceptions of plants as living things. *Human Development, 32*, 88–94.

Taylor, C. (2006). Threshold concepts in biology: Do they fit the definition? In J. H. F. Meyer & R. Land (Eds.), *Overcoming Barriers to Student Understanding: Threshold concepts and troublesome knowledge* (pp. 87–99). Abingdon: Routledge.

Taylor, C. E. (2008). Threshold concepts, troublesome knowledge and ways of thinking and practising – can we tell the difference in Biology? In R. Land, J. H. F. Meyer, & J. Smith (Eds.), *Threshold concepts in the disciplines* (pp. 185–197). Rotterdam, The Netherlands: Sense Publishers.

Tretter, T. R., & Jones, G. M. (2003). A sense of scale: Studying how scale affects systems and organisms. *The Science Teacher, 70*, 22–25.

Tytler, R. (2007). Re-imagining science education: Engaging students in science for Australia's future. *Australian Educational Review, No. 51*. Australian Council for Education Research, ACER press.

Tytler, R., & Peterson, S. (2004). Young children learning about evaporation: A longitudinal perspective. *Canadian Journal of Science, Mathematics and Technology Education, 4*(1), 111–126.

Wandersee, J. H. (1983). Students' misconceptions about photosynthesis: A cross-age study. In H. Helm & J. D. Novak (Eds.), *Proceedings of the international seminar on misconceptions in science and mathematics* (pp. 441–463). Ithaca, NY: Cornell University.

Wandersee, J. H., Mintzes, J. J., & Novak, J. D. (1994). Research on alternative conceptions in science. In G. L. Gabel (Ed.), *Handbook of research on science teaching and learning: A project of the national science teachers association*. New York: Macmillan Publishing Company.

Yip, D. Y. (1998). Identification of misconceptions in novice biology teachers and remedial strategies for improving biology learning. *International Journal of Science Education, 20*(4), 461–477.

[1]*Pauline Ross*
College of Health and Science
University of Western Sydney, Australia
Locked Bag 1797, Penrith South DC, 1797
Penrith South DC 1797, Sydney, Australia
Corresponding author pm.ross@uws.edu.au

[2]*Charlotte Taylor and Vicky Tzioumis*
School of Biological Sciences
University of Sydney
Sydney 2006, Australia

[3]*Chris Hughes*
School of Public Health and Community Medicine
University of New South Wales
Sydney, 2052, Australia

[3]*Louise Lutze-Mann and Noel Whitaker*
School of Biotechnology and Biomolecular Sciences
University of New South Wales
Sydney, 2052, Australia

[3]*Michelle Kofod*
Australian School of Business
University of New South Wales
Sydney, 2052, Australia

CHARLOTTE E. TAYLOR AND JAN H.F. MEYER

11. THE TESTABLE HYPOTHESIS AS A THRESHOLD CONCEPT FOR BIOLOGY STUDENTS

INTRODUCTION

The key characteristics of biology as a discipline encompass the study of complex processes in living systems (Taylor 2006, 2008). In this context the epistemological status of the testable hypothesis in biology is fundamental, since new knowledge is confirmed through experimental results. Inherent in this role of *hypothesis testing* is the broader consideration of the conceptualisation of experimental design and the role that variation in this design may play in terms of verifying and extending previous findings. The concept of hypothesis testing thus provides a framework for experimentation and investigation, and provides a necessary context for developing an understanding of biological systems which are characteristically dynamic and exhibit temporal and spatial variability.

The capacity to formulate an experimental design and a testable hypothesis within it also represents an aspect of how biologists 'think' (Entwistle and McCune 2001; McCune and Hounsell 2005, Entwistle 2005). This characteristic has been further elucidated by Becher and Trowler (2001) in terms of a capacity to look at the world and focus 'in and out' through the various layers of complexity in living systems, working between the 'big picture' and the 'minutiae'. There is therefore an *ontological* shift associated with the capacity to think in this way; a shift in terms of 'sense of being' in apprehending the multivariate complexity of the biological world, and hypothesising within it phenomena amenable to experimental verification. This shift carries with it its own specialised forms of 'thinking and practising' and modes of 'reasoning and explanation'. The associated vocabulary represents another postulated aspect of threshold concepts; that of *discursiveness* (Meyer and Land, 2005). This chapter will discuss hypothesis creation and testing in the context of *threshold concepts* as defined by Meyer and Land (2003) and analyse the role played by troublesomeness, integration, irreversibility, and bound-edness. In particular we will focus on how the 'portal' of the threshold in hypothesis testing 'comes into view' and is subsequently negotiated. Within this transfer we distinguish a transition in the development of understanding from the preliminal through the *liminal* stages and beyond (Meyer and Land, 2006).

A study of the threshold status of hypotheses requires discussion of the nature of hypotheses in scientific thinking and practice. Their use in understanding biological systems is based on the premise that they confer rigour and precision on the process of investigating, and allow a degree of reliability to be assumed when

J. H. F. Meyer, R. Land and C. Baillie (eds.), Threshold Concepts and Transformational Learning, 179–192.

interpreting information (Conner and Simberloff, 1986; Underwood 1986, 1997). Practising biologists argue that an investigational framework built around models and hypotheses allows

... clear definitions to define the world that you're working in so that you can understand the limitations of the world

Biology lecturer 1

Testing hypotheses also requires information to be collected and interpreted in such a manner that unequivocal evidence for conclusions can be provided and explained. The limits to such statements are also inherently understood by biologists as part of the process of analysing information, as described by a teacher who discussed the thinking of senior biology students:

the threshold is coming to terms with ... one thing you've got to overcome, when you're giving expert evidence and you've got to give a definitive answer, even though the full response is not black and white ... we work with shades of grey

Biology lecturer 1

... but afterwards, they realise there's more than criticising methods, spatial and temporal replications ... there are more important issues, and that's just background noise that they've got to deal with

Biology lecturer 1

Meanwhile, there continues to be vigorous debate amongst biologists as to appropriate methodologies for using hypothesis testing approaches in research (Fidler *mult al*, 2005; Anderson, Burnham and Thompson, 2000), which discusses the validity of the null hypothesis and problems of a lack of rigour in reporting outcomes e.g. misinterpreting significance of results and interpretations. The field of hypothesis testing thus remains a focal point for biologists reflecting on their practice.

Examining the threshold status of hypotheses and their testing requires an understanding of the context in which students and teachers approach the topic. We provide an overview of the teaching of hypotheses across the curriculum and include discussion of areas of dispute in thinking about the cognitive development of children's scientific understanding and the problems arising from an inappropriate introduction to the topic. A detailed study of written responses, to questions on hypotheses, has allowed us to deconstruct the troublesome nature of this topic for undergraduate students and to determine where possible conceptual thresholds might lie. We discuss our findings in relation to the ways in which biologists think and practise in a complex and dynamic field, and reflect on the changes which may be made to the teaching of hypothesis testing.

THE CONTEXT IN WHICH HYPOTHESES ARE TAUGHT

The concepts of prediction, measuring, and interpreting, associated with understanding the dynamic living world, are fundamental to developing childrens' views of biological systems. As such, they are key to the science and biology syllabus at primary and secondary school, and as part of the induction into undergraduate biology degree programs (Lawson *mult al* 2000a). Within the introduction to science in the primary school syllabus in Australia, hypotheses and the underlying scientific method are not discussed explicitly but their use forms part of reasoned discussions of explanations for observations of natural phenomena. It is often assumed that such discussions with children will be characterised by naïve articulations of scientific thinking, and that more complex conceptions will be developed over time (Vass, Schiller and Nappi, 2000). However, anecdotal observations of children's investigations of obvious ecological interactions such as feeding behaviour, and abundance and distribution of organisms, can provide interesting insights into the challenges being confronted, and the following statements display sophistication in scientific thinking which could readily translate into a hypothetico-deductive train of reasoning.

For example, faced with the challenge: *'What problems are there in counting living things?',* as part of an observing and counting exercise in the playground (Taylor, pers obs), primary school children reflected on the following problems, all of which are routinely faced by professional field biologists:

you can't cownt (sic) all the ants in the playground

you might keep count (sic) the same one more than once if they keep running around

what if all the ants are here and none over there?

Such questioning demonstrates an acknowledgment of aspects of rigour, reliability, and precision, in measuring and interpreting information, which are fundamental to biological investigations.

Understanding the act and its links to statistics, in sort of understanding variability, and how you know if you use the results you get in one situation they may not necessarily apply in another situation because there's inherent variability in biological ecological systems and I think that's a threshold. One that many do get but it does take a little while for them to appreciate.

Biology lecturer 1

As part of this thinking biologists use models, predictions and hypothesis testing to take into account such aspects of variability and dynamics in natural ecosystems, and rely on the results of statistical tests and discussions of probabilities to explain the limitations of the outcomes.

Following the pattern of thinking displayed above, it is clear that young children may also be engaged in providing explanations of cause and effect relationships relating to organisms, their environment and behavioural activities. A progression into more formalised discussions of investigations and experimentation in high school biology generally introduces children to the concept of the hypothesis and prediction, and the high school syllabus will require demonstrations of competence in generating and testing a hypothesis (White, 2004). Examples of tools to teach the rationale and practice of hypothesis testing have been devised for incorporation into high school classrooms and field studies e.g. National Health Museum Accessing Excellence: Hypothesis writing (1994) and the University of Tasmania (2005). Much discussion on teaching in schools has focused on the potential to lose sight of the *thinking* inherent in the creation of a hypothesis to explain puzzling phenomena, depending on the approaches used by teachers and activities with which children engage. (Lawson *mult al*, 2008). MacPherson (2001) has argued that poor teaching frequently leads to considerable difficulty in understanding and using hypotheses, and confusion about the role of hypotheses and predictions in scientific investigations. The whole premise of the hypothetico- deductive method can be lost at this point, with misconceptions becoming entrenched in children's thinking. It is clear that problems in understanding this concept may be exhibited at all stages of cognitive development, as evinced in White's (2004) review of studies in hypothesis understanding.

In this chapter we present quantitative and qualitative data from responses of undergraduate biology students, focusing particularly on those beginning their degree, and compare their experiences of creating hypotheses with those of third year students. Data were collected from activities in a laboratory course for first year biology students, where the concept of hypothesis creation and testing was integrated into investigations in the laboratory program (Figure 1).

Activities included formal lectures, practical hands-on lab investigations, group discussions, and formal examinations. Student written responses were subjected to thematic analysis to determine categories of understanding of creating and testing hypotheses. The first question (Appendix 1) was presented during a laboratory class, and described a preliminary scenario for students to discuss in groups. As a result of the discussion they were asked to formulate a hypothesis and describe an appropriate testing procedure. These responses were reviewed by tutors and any misconceptions apparent in the answers were discussed, in a subsequent class, before the next phase of the investigation proceeded. Students then engaged with hands-on data collection, in this case counting invertebrates in samples of leaf litter, using materials from field sites described in the scenario, to test their hypothesis. A class discussion of the resulting data allowed students to decide whether to accept or reject their hypothesis and to interpret outcomes in terms of limitations to their investigation and variability in the materials sampled. At the end of the course an examination question about hypotheses required students to answer a similar question to that posed at the beginning of the course. This was designed to provide more detailed observations from a field situation, and to postulate a model explaining the observations. Students were required to write a testable hypothesis and describe a protocol for testing this hypothesis. The scenario was more structured than that in the earlier hypothesis question, which had been designed to encourage broad discussion about possible explanations.

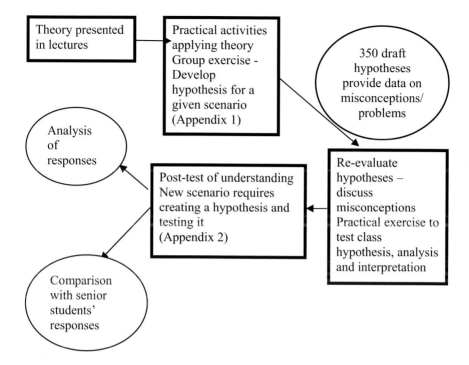

Figure 1. A flowchart for introducing, practising and reflecting on creating and testing hypotheses in a first year biology course.

DECONSTRUCTING THE TROUBLESOME COMPONENTS OF HYPOTHESES

The current investigation uses data from students in an undergraduate biology program to answer the following questions:
– Where might the troublesomeness lie in hypothesis creation and testing?
– Does it encompass the underlying notion of testability?
– Does it also involve the capacity to foreground a 'slice' or 'view' of something against a background of multivariate complexity?

In addition there is usually a requirement that a testable hypothesis should also be amenable to falsification; to what extent does this prove troublesome? Once you can formulate a testable hypothesis, is the process of conceptualising an experimental design something separate that comes before, after, or during formulation itself? We argue that the *'what' are we going to test* is conceptually separate from the *'how' are we going to test it,* but that the 'what' only becomes testable when we can answer the 'how' question. This premise has been previously raised in the context of teaching hypothesis testing in the curriculum, and also in terms of the *modus operandi* of scientists conducting research investigations and reporting the outcomes. (Lawson, *mult al*, 2008; White, 2004).

An examination of the initial qualitative responses identifies points at which students demonstrate a state of *preliminality*, in which they struggle to develop the ability to see the relationship between an experimental sample and the background complexity of a biological system. It also highlights differences in the way that students may conceptualise the creation of a hypothesis as they progress in their studies and begin to emerge from the preliminal state.

Data from the preliminary question (Table 1) indicated that many responses had no recognisable hypothesis, simply having instead a description of variables in the scenario. It is clear that while students understood the need to formulate a precise statement about the observations they could not see what is relevant to such an explanation. Frequently, where a hypothesis was stated, answers focused on too many variables which inevitably lead to problems in describing a testing protocol for the hypothesis. A majority of students only worked with one variable, effectively demonstrating no understanding of an explanation of the observations and a prediction of outcomes. This confusion created further problems in that proposed hypotheses were frequently phrased imprecisely such that an appropriate test was impossible. In the testing process, problems were compounded when students demonstrated a lack of understanding of their explanations such that there were no variables to measure when testing. Other students reverted to the experimental paradigm used in their school studies as an appropriate mode of answering the question. There were thus numerous examples of students trapped in a vicious circle of liminality. The concepts we postulate as integral to the 'entrapping' process, namely the 'how' and the 'what', are shown to indeed be problematic. The subsequent stages of the biology course provided students with further opportunities to reflect on their ideas and misconceptions and to create new, and testable,

Table 1. Categories of response by first year biology students to a question requiring hypothesis creation and testing

Categories of responses	% responses
Categories about creation of a hypothesis	
Appropriate hypotheses which were testable	22%
Hypotheses linking too many variables and not testable	18%
Hypotheses not related to the scenario or variables	12%
Descriptions of the variables or the scenario	48%

Categories about testing a hypothesis	
Collected data on applicable variables	15%
Collected data on only one variable	41%
Carried out an experiment	15%
Collected no applicable data	29%

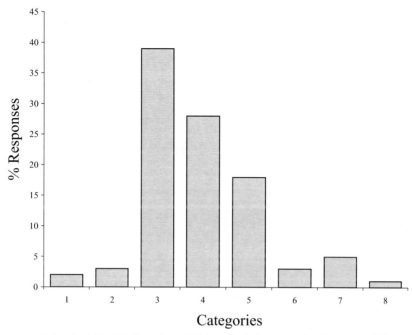

Categories 1, 2 and 6: Created a testable hypothesis, but some using incorrect variables
Category 3, 4: Descriptive hypothesis showing links between the variables
Category 5,7, 8 : Descriptive and vague

*Figure 2. Categories of hypothesis created by first year undergraduate biology students
in a post-test examination.*

hypotheses. Analyses of their responses to a post- test at the end of the course
indicated that problems persisted with the 'how' and the 'what' (Figure 2). Only a few
students could create a testable hypothesis, using appropriate variables, and based
on the model described:

*There will be more lizards present in forest patches with more fallen tree
trunks present.*

The majority continued to create hypotheses which were descriptive but did show
links between appropriate variables. However, since the question described the
appropriate variables more explicitly this would be expected.

*Forest patches with more fallen trees trunks will attract more lizard
populations.*

*To evaluate if the presence of fallen tree trunks relate to the number of
lizards in forest patches.*

Lizard numbers are determined by numbers of fallen trees.

A key problem in some responses indicated that students were only planning to measure one variable during their testing.

Choose samples from 2 area types, one with lots of fallen tree trunks and one with few. Count the number of lizards found in the areas. Record results and compare.

Many still struggled with what they would measure or count in their testing, and some responses pointed to an experiment which manipulated the variables.

Put equal amounts of lizards in environments with 10 fallen tree trunks, 20 fallen tree trunks up to 100 fallen tree trunks. After 3 months counting the number of lizards in each tree trunk, analyse whether the number of lizards increase with the number of tree trunks or not.

A minority of responses were clearly inappropriate in a hypothesis testing framework, and did not answer the question.

There are more lizards located where there are less tree trunks.

Lizard populations thrive when there is plentiful access to decaying organic matter, provided by fallen tree trunks.

Lizards dwell in fallen tree trunks.

Lizards prefer to live in areas with lots of fallen tree trunks.

Answers describing a testing procedure again suffered from being associated with hypotheses which were not clearly defined or testable (Figure 3).

Select several different environments which have different pattern of fallen tree trunks. Within each environment select a fixed size of area to recording down the amount of fallen tree trunks available and population size of lizards. The population size of lizards can be determined by its area size. Grouping the data into table and finding the relationship.

Find several forest patches to test in. For each one, determine whether they are similar enough to produce accurate results (i.e. eliminate or determine any other variables present). In areas with similar abundance of food source, temperature, etc count the number of fallen trees and number of lizards present.

Collect samples of lizards and tree trunks. In an experimental tank, which is filled with soil, the tree trunk is placed at a corner of the tank. Place the lizards in the tank and observe the movement of the lizard, whether it is towards the tree trunk.

In contrast senior students specialising in studying field ecology responded to the same post-test question with much more sophisticated answers (Figure 4). They demonstrated an understanding of the fundamental concept of hypothesis creation, and devised detailed protocols for testing which not only satisfied the requirements

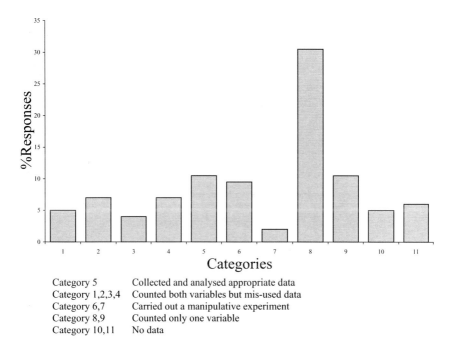

Category 5   Collected and analysed appropriate data
Category 1,2,3,4   Counted both variables but mis-used data
Category 6,7   Carried out a manipulative experiment
Category 8,9   Counted only one variable
Category 10,11   No data

Figure 3. Categories of hypothesis testing procedure described by first year
biology students in a post-test examination.

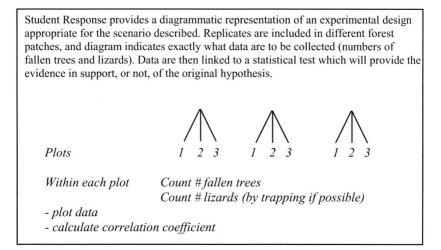

Student Response provides a diagrammatic representation of an experimental design appropriate for the scenario described. Replicates are included in different forest patches, and diagram indicates exactly what data are to be collected (numbers of fallen trees and lizards). Data are then linked to a statistical test which will provide the evidence in support, or not, of the original hypothesis.

Plots

Within each plot   *Count # fallen trees*
                       Count # lizards (by trapping if possible)
- plot data
- calculate correlation coefficient

Figure 4. A response to the post- test question formulated by a senior biology student.

of the hypothesis, but also took into account issues associated with replication, sampling design error, statistical analysis of the data, variability in the system and controlling for confounding factors. These students had experience a range of learning opportunities involving hypothesis creation and testing following their experiences in first year courses but were all actively engaged, at the time of answering the post-test question, in curriculum activities based in discussion and thinking about hypotheses. Students developed answers which demonstrated the development of an experimental design and a mind model of this process. Their design incorporated a hypothesis which was clearly testable, and in most cases they indicated an appropriate test for the design. It seemed likely that the students could visualise the scenario and make appropriate predications and workable experimental methods; this would be consistent with the assumption that their prior experience in field situations was being applied to this new problem.

CHARACTERISING THE THRESHOLD

The troublesomeness of the concept is clearly related to a number of factors, including the formal approach to creating and testing a hypothesis, and the links to conceptualising testability. Initial visualisation of the context allows the investigator to distinguish the appropriate variables for testing and then to frame an explanation and hypothesis relating to the relationship between the variables. Many students know they have to count or measure something, but the question is 'what'? This question is inextricably tied to the statement of link or causality, without which data cannot be collected. Students are engaging with the 'how' at the prediction level (Lawson *mult al* 2000b; MacPherson, 2001) but not seeing the underlying hypothesis which provides the structure. It therefore appears essential that the link between 'how' and 'what' must be understood at an early stage in developing hypotheses. The measuring of variables is further tied to strict requirements of a statistical test and the concept of falsification. This formality is another aspect of the concept which involves tacit knowledge of the context in which we validate results and interpret data, and another area which students did not link to their observations, explanation and interpretation. *Senior students* had this structured thinking in place, possibly as a result of working in the field, collecting data, and using statistical tests in various experiments. They could place these experiences into the bigger picture of the ecological context and its inherent complexity, dynamics and variability. They had thus passed through the portal associated with an under-standing of this concept, and had engaged with the challenges of the liminal space at some time between first year and their senior studies. Hypothesis testing thus demonstrates the web of interrelated biological and philosophical concepts which have to be rationalised and integrated to make sense of biological practice

How does this inform our understanding of the threshold concept, and explain the presence of the transformation, integration and liminal stages in hypothesis testing. We argue (Ross *mult al* 2008), that higher order abstract dimensions of biological thinking play a critical role in developing students' thinking in this area. The mechanics of defining a precisely worded testable hypothesis require an appreciation of the appropriate language and symbolic representations, but this process can be 'learnt' in a rote manner, as demonstrated by many of the student responses. Similarly a generally acceptable testing procedure for the hypothesis may be described, which allows students to rely on a recipe-like formula. However the *integration* of ideas, which demonstrates a transformed understanding, requires a sophisticated articulation of the scale, dynamics, complexity, variability and role of probability in explaining the system under investigation. Dealing with this in the paradigm of scientific thinking encompasses the threshold.

USING THRESHOLDS TO INFORM TEACHING

In rising to the challenge of helping students to understanding hypotheses, teachers need to engage with the experiences of working in the preliminal space. This will require a shift in thinking to appreciate the ways in which students struggle with approaching the portal and entering 'unknown' territory. As such, Martin and Leuckenhausen (2005) studied the extent to which teachers change their perceptions of their subject and its context when confronted by evidence of misconceptions about the topic in their students. Interpretation of the data described in this study necessarily requires reflection on the process and outcomes of our teaching. Such reflection provides a rich vein of information about student thinking and liminality which can direct changes in our teaching approaches. As discussed by Timmerman, Strickland and Carstensen (2008), students need to have the opportunity to take ownership of the process of observation, explanation and hypothesis creation, for successful understanding to occur. An obvious example of this is shown with senior students who had been exposed to a variety of such experiences during their intervening years of study. It will obviously be of great relevance to investigate further the learning processes occurring during this time, and to characterise the degree to which students recognise their ownership of knowledge and under-standing. Such ownership activities are also essential, at an early stage, to allow us to take into account the fact that many students have minimal prior experience of the complexity of biological systems. Lawson *mult al* (2000b) describes problems for students in visualising scenarios in investigations which deal with organisms or processes which cannot be seen, in particular at the molecular or chemical level. While this would not appear to be a limitation for the activities described in this study, it may have been a contributing factor for some students. In future classes, where large class sizes may preclude visits to field sites, it could be useful to provide pictures or video of the habitat, plants and animals described in the scenario. The problem of identifying the relevant and related variables, in an explanation of a phenomenon, may be further alleviated by extending the preliminary discussion activity such that students document their progress to making a decision about variables to be included in their hypothesis. Thus the 'what' of the hypothesis can be elucidated and informs the development of the 'how'. In addition a fundamental change in teachers' approach to the topic would allow us to articulate more explicitly the way in which we conceptualise the higher order abstractions when engaging with biological challenges (Lawson 2003).

This investigation of threshold concepts in biology, with its analysis of portals and liminalities reveals further issues associated with starting to think as a biologist. An extension of the study is proposed to characterise the learning journey undertaken by undergraduate students as they approach, experience and emerge from the liminal state.

REFERENCES

Anderson, D. R., Burnham, K. P., & Thompson, W. L. (2000). Null hypothesis testing: Problems, prevalence and an alternative. *Journal of Wildlife Management, 64*(4), 912–923.

Becher, T., & Trowler, P. R. (2001). *Academic tribes and territories: Intellectual enquiry and the culture of disciplines*. Open University Press.

Connor, E. D., & Simberloff, D. (1986). Competition, scientific method and null models in ecology. *American Scientist, 74*, 155–162.

Entwistle, N. (2005). Learning outcomes and ways of thinking across contrasting disciplines and settings in higher education. *Curriculum Journal, 16*(1), 67–82.

Entwistle, N. J., & McCune, V. (2001). Conceptions, styles and approaches within higher education: Analytic abstractions and everyday experience. In R. Sternberg & L.-F. Zhang (Eds.), *Perspectives on cognitive, learning, and thinking styles* (pp. 103–136). (Erlbaum).

Fidler, F., Burgman, M. A., Cumming, G., Buttrose, R., & Thomason, N. (2005). Impact of criticism of null-hypothesis significance testing on statistical reporting practices on Conservation Biology. *Conservation Biology, 20*(5), 1539–1544.

Lawson, A. E. (2003). The nature and development of hypothetico-predictive argumentation with implications for science teaching. *International Journal of Science Education, 25*(11), 1387–1408.

Lawson, A. E., Alkhoury, S., Benford, R., Clark, B. R., & Falconer, K. A. (2000a). What kinds of scientific concept exist? Concept construction and intellectual development in college biology. *Journal of Research in Science Teaching, 37*(9), 996–1018.

Lawson, A. E., Drake, N., Johnson, J., Kwon, Y. J., & Scarpone, C. (2000b). How good are students at testing alternative explanations of unseen entities? *The American Biology Teacher, 62*(4), 249–255.

Lawson, A. E., Oehrtman, M., & Jensen, J. (2008). Connecting science and mathematics: The nature of scientific and statistical hypothesis testing. *International Journal of Science and Mathematics Education, 6*(2), 405–416.

Martin, E., & Leuckenhausen, G. (2005). How university teaching changes teachers: Affective as well as cognitive challenges. *Higher Education, 49*, 389–412.

McCune, V., & Hounsell, D. (2005). The development of students' ways of thinking and practising in three final-year biology courses. *Higher Education, 49*, 255–289.

MacPherson, G. R. (2001). Teaching and learning the scientific method. *The American Biology Teacher, 63*(4), 242–245.

Meyer, J. H. F., & Land, R. (2003). Threshold concepts and troublesome knowledge: Linkages to ways of thinking and practising within the disciplines. In C. Rust (Ed.), *Improving student learning. Improving student learning theory and practice — 10 years on* (pp. 412–424). Oxford: OCSLD.

Meyer, J. H. F., & Land, R. (2005). Threshold concepts and troublesome knowledge (2): Epistemological considerations and a conceptual framework for teaching and learning. *Higher Education, 49*(3), 373–388.

Meyer, J. H. F., & Land, R. (2006). *Overcoming barriers to student understanding - Threshold concepts and troublesome knowledge*. London: Routledge.

National Health Museum. (1994). *Access excellence – Writing hypotheses: A student lesson*. Retrieved August 2008, from http://www.accessexcellence.org/L C/TL/filson/writhypo.php

Ross, P. M., Taylor, C. E., Hughes, C., Kofod, M., Whitaker, N., & Lutze-Mann, L. (2008, July). Using thresholds concepts to generate a new understanding of teaching and learning biology. *Proceedings of the 2nd Threshold Concepts Conference*. Queens University, Kingston, Canada.

Taylor, C. E. (2006). Threshold concepts in Biology: Do they fit the definition? In J. H. F. Meyer & R. Land (Eds.), *Overcoming barriers to student understanding: Threshold concepts and troublesome knowledge*. London: Routledge.

Taylor, C. E. (2008). Threshold concepts, troublesome knowledge and ways of thinking and practising. In R. Land, J. H. F. Meyer, & J. Smith (Eds.), *Threshold concepts within the disciplines* (pp. 185–197). Rotterdam, The Netherlands: Sense Publishers.

Timmerman, B. E., Strickland, D. C., & Carstensen, S. M. (2008). Curriculum reform and inquiry teaching in biology: Where are our efforts most fruitfully invested? In *Integrative and comparative Biology*. Advanced Access Publishing.

Underwood, A. J. (1986). The analysis of competition by field experiments. In J. Kikkawa & D. J. Anderson (Eds.), *Community Ecology: Pattern and process* (pp. 240–268). Melbourne, VIC: Blackwell.

Underwood, A. J. (1997). *Experiments in ecology*. Cambridge, UK: Cambridge University Press.

University of Tasmania. (2005). *Scientific experimentation and writing hypotheses*. Retrieved August 2008, from http://www.utas.edu.au/sciencelinks/exdesign/HF2C.HTM/

Vass, E., Schiller, D., & Nappi, A. J. (2000). The effects of instructional intervention on improving proportional and correlative reasoning skills among undergraduate education majors. *Journal of Research in Science Teaching, 37*(9), 981–995.

White, B. (2004). Reasoning maps: A generally applicable method for characterising hypothesis-testing behaviour. *International Journal of Science Education, 14*, 1715–1731.

APPENDIX 1

Field observations have been made in a number of Eucalypt woodland areas in the Sydney region and the following point noted. There appear to be more slaters in woodland areas 1 and 2 as compared with areas 3 and 4.

- Discuss these observations in your group and write down possible models to explain this difference.
- Then write down one hypothesis, derived from one of the models, which you could test.
- To test this hypothesis, what information and materials would you need to collect from the areas?

Additional Information - Slaters

These are small arthropods in a group called the isopods. They are related to shrimps and also to other crustaceans. The live in spaces in leaf litter and feed on dead plant material. The body is flattened dorso-ventrally and the animal can roll up to protect the undersurface if necessary. Slaters require a moist habitat and cannot live in very dry areas.

APPENDIX 2

Preliminary observations of a number of forest patches indicate that lizards are much more numerous in some forest patches than in others. Previous studies have shown that their presence is highly dependent on the presence of fallen tree trunks.

A model has therefore been proposed that the observed differences in numbers of lizards are explained by differences in the number of fallen tree trunks present.

- Write a testable hypothesis based on this model.
- Briefly describe how you would go about testing this hypothesis.

Charlotte E. Taylor
University of Sydney
Australia

Jan H.F. Meyer
University of Durham
United Kingdom

PETER DAVIES AND JEAN MANGAN

12. ASSESSING PROGRESSION IN STUDENTS' ECONOMIC UNDERSTANDING:

The Role of Threshold Concepts

PROGRESSION IN STUDENT UNDERSTANDING IN HIGHER EDUCATION

The intellectual journey of students in higher education has typically been described in general terms. Several strands have been suggested: (i) epistemological beliefs; (ii) integration of knowledge; (iii) approach to learning and (iv) interest in, and emotional commitment to, the pursuit of particular kinds of knowledge. For example, Perry (1970) charts a development in students' epistemological beliefs in a four stage model from dualism to commitment within relativism. Schommer (1990) provides an instrument by which such changes might be measured, whilst Trautwein and Ludtke (2007) find that students' achievements in the final years of secondary schooling are positively associated with development in epistemological beliefs in the manner suggested by Perry and Schommer. An important way in which epistemological beliefs are expressed is through the exercise of 'critical reasoning.' There is a widespread belief that students' progress in Higher Education should be demonstrated in an increasing ability to engage in critical reasoning (Giancarlo and Facione, 2001). Christopoulos et al. (1987) found that as students progressed from secondary to higher education they experienced a greater demand on them to integrate domain knowledge, whilst Vermetten et al. (1999) found that an increasing proportion of students report using a 'meaning-directed' approach to learning as they progressed beyond their first year of study in HE. These three strands are combined with the fourth strand (students' interest in, and commitment to, a particular knowledge domain) in a model proposed by Alexander et al. (1995) who suggest three stages in students' progression: from naivety through competence to expertise.

However, assessments of students' progress that contribute towards their degree classifications are routinely conducted with no reference to any of these strands. Academics construct assessments and mark students' work on the basis of their tacit professional knowledge of what students should be expected to do at each stage in their learning. One interpretation of this disjunction is that academics are ignoring a body of evidence that is directly pertinent to their work and that they should revise their practice. An alternative interpretation is that the nature of progression varies from domain to domain in ways that are inadequately captured by schemas that abstract from the peculiarities of particular subjects for study.

J. H. F. Meyer, R. Land and C. Baillie (eds.), Threshold Concepts and Transformational Learning, 193–206.

Phenomenography, and more recently variation theory, have provided an alternative approach to the identification of stages in progression in understanding. Researchers in this tradition have tried to reveal different ways of understanding particular phenomena. These different ways of understanding or experiencing a phenomenon can then be placed in a hierarchy of quality that defines progression (Pang and Marton, 2005). Between the generalist approach and the highly specific approach of variation it is pertinent to ask if there are characteristics of progression in understanding that are typical of one domain, but not of others.

Threshold concepts have been proposed as a way of characterising progression at domain level. It has been suggested (Meyer and Land, 2003 and 2005) that within each domain there are certain ideas that present themselves to students as portals that can open up a new way of thinking within a particular domain. Meyer and Land (2003) suggest that threshold concepts integrate, transform, set boundaries to domain and probably are irreversible and troublesome for the learner. The integrative and transformative characteristics echo two of the strands in the generalist approach to students' progression. However, the form taken by integration and transformation are now determined *within* the domain. That is, increasing complexity of understanding is *not* characterised simply by more connections between conceptions. Within the current thinking in any domain some connections are held to be valid whilst others are not. Moreover, super-ordinate conceptions or threshold concepts require a transformation of more basic concepts, so that these become aligned with an emerging structure of understanding that characterises a way of thinking within a domain (Davies and Mangan, 2008).

Table 1. Definition and exemplification of three types of conceptual change

Type of conceptual change	Type of transformation and integration	Examples in economics
1. Basic	Newly met concepts some of which transform understanding of everyday experience through integration of personal experience with ideas from discipline.	Distinctions between income/wealth (stocks/flows); nominal/real values; investment/saving; withdrawals/ injections.
2. Discipline Threshold Concepts	Understanding of other subject discipline ideas (including other threshold concepts) integrated and transformed through acquisition of theoretical perspective.	Partial equilibrium, welfare economics, marginality, opportunity cost, cumulative causation.
3. Procedural Concepts	Ability to construct discipline specific narratives and arguments transformed through acquisition of ways of practising.	Comparative statics (equilibrium, ceteris paribus), time (short-term, long-term, expectations), elasticity.

An approach to distinguishing between 'basic' and 'threshold' concepts is suggested by Davies and Mangan (2007) on the basis of evidence gathered from students and lecturers in economics. It is reproduced here as Table 1. Basic concepts (Table 1, Row 1) provide ways of categorising phenomena in ways that are necessary for the understanding of threshold concepts. As such they create a particular and infrequently observed problem for learners. Whilst they are necessary steps along the way towards a more integrated and complex form of understanding, the form in which they are initially understood is likely to be only a shadow of their full significance. That is, the full significance of a basic concept is only grasped once a transforming threshold concept has been subsequently incorporated into a learner's thinking. Another way of expressing this point is that the conception of a phenonmenon that is described by a basic concept within a discipline is only attained once a learner is able to use a super-ordinate threshold concept to organise their conceptual structure. But for learners to be able to organise their thinking through a threshold concept they will also need to use any associated procedural concepts. If a discipline threshold can be represented as a 'portal', then procedural concepts provide the means by which the structural form of the portal can be assembled: the guidance that directs the way in which pieces are put together. Figure 1 indicates the linkages between these sets of concepts. Student progression from basic to threshold discipline concepts cannot take place directly (along the grey line) without an understanding of the procedural concepts. Understanding of procedural and threshold discipline concepts are also expected to feedback to and deepen understanding of basic concepts. Before acquiring the framework provided by the procedural and threshold discipline concepts, there is often only shallow understanding of basic concepts, often from rote learning.

This, then, carries some implications for assessment. First, the literature on conceptual change has long established that a phenomenon can be understood in qualitatively different ways. That is, to speak of acquisition of a basic concept in terms of 'understanding' or 'not understanding' misrepresents the situation. Students may have an understanding of a phenomenon and they may use the language of a discipline to express their understanding, without having the kind of understanding associated with expert knowledge in a discipline. Therefore, it is

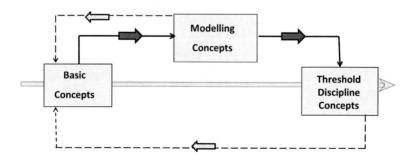

Figure 1. Learning and Integration between Concepts.

desirable that assessment should distinguish between limited and more complex ways of understanding a phenomenon. The more complex understanding will be that way of understanding that is aligned with a threshold concept. Second, we might therefore interpret a more complex understanding of a basic concept as an indication that a learner is, at least, becoming aware of a threshold concept. Third, a learner's journey towards incorporating a discipline threshold concept in their thinking requires that they learn to use procedural concepts to generate structures of thought from. For example, an important stage in introductory economics is learning to combine a number of basic concepts (such as the distinction between injections and withdrawals, savings and investment, stocks and flows, real and nominal values) in a model of the determination of the level of national income. Use is made of a simple model of the whole economy in which relationships between different components are regulated by the way the whole model tends towards an equilibrium position. Without this modelling (or procedural) concept of equilibrium the set of basic concepts that are pertinent to the model are not made to act in concert to produce a coherently structured understanding of an economy as a system. Therefore we may also infer that when a student uses a modelling concept in conjunction with one or more basic concepts they are engaging in the process that can lead them towards incorporating a threshold concept (in this case of 'cumulative causation' – 'the multiplier') in their thinking.

In this chapter we focus on the understanding of non-economics students in the context of a first year undergraduate module on introductory economics, although the process described above equally applies to students specialising in economics[1]. Understanding the learning of non-economics students is important to the discipline, as a considerable proportion of students who are take economics at this level are not taking economics degrees. At this stage in students' learning we are interested in the way in which students have understood basic concepts and the ways in which they try to combine modelling (procedural) and basic concepts in order to make sense of economic problems, which they need to do in order develop an understanding of threshold concepts. Whilst written examinations are fairly crude methods of exploring the structure of students' understanding they are the standard method used in assessing undergraduates' understanding and that is the rationale for focusing on formal examinations in this study. They are also a readily available source that can be widely used for such analysis.

In the following section we consider the extent to which the examination questions used in this study provided adequate opportunities for students to provide evidence of their thinking and describe the method of analysis. Section 3 presents the results. In Section 4 we discuss some implications and in Section 5 conclude.

METHOD

The Students

We use end of year examination scripts sampled from 133 students who sat the examination of an introductory economics module taken by first-year business studies students. The sample came from those who gained on overall pass on the paper.

Since these answers included failures on the particular questions of interest, this did not restrict the range of our categorisation and we were concerned to get variation that showed higher levels of understanding. One of the major objectives of the module is to help students to understand how businesses are affected by the macroeconomic environment and this was considered in terms of the analysing the determination of the level of national income by the 'circular flow of income' framework. Few had studied economics in their school curriculum, although many of the students had studied business in their final years at secondary school. However, teaching on the external environment of business on these courses takes variation in aggregate demand (usually referred to as 'the business cycle') as a given. Our sample of thirty four scripts was taken from students who chose to answer a selection of questions that required analysis of the determination of national income as a major part of a reasonable answer.

Question Design

Since assessment serves a number of purposes the question design was guided by several criteria that generated some tensions. First, the question design aimed to serve summative purposes. That is, the assessment formed part of students' examinations at the end of their first year of undergraduate study. As such it was required to contribute to the decision about whether students should be permitted to proceed to their second year of study. This criterion encourages the design of questions that give borderline students a good chance of demonstrating their 'just passing' level of understanding. That is, it encourages the design of questions that give students considerable support (such as through directing them towards a concept/ model they should use in their answer). Second, the question design aimed to uncover students' understanding rather than their rote knowledge and this criterion stood in almost direct opposition to the first in that, in order to do this, the question should present something unfamiliar to the students which they have to use their understanding to unravel (Eisner, 1993). Unfamiliar in this case does not mean 'odd', it simply means that students should not be able to reproduce more or less verbatim a rehearsed answer. Third, the design aimed to create opportunities for students to demonstrate a range of levels of understanding through their answers.

The first section of the paper gave more weight to the first and third criteria. Students were presented with a list of economic terms and asked to explain and give an example of the use of two of the microeconomic terms and two of the macroeconomic terms (from the list of five). They should have spent approximately 12 minutes on each of these questions. The investigation here concentrates on students' explanations of two of the macroeconomic terms 'discretionary fiscal policy' and 'withdrawals'. This assessment task served criterion one by guiding students towards a term that had featured in teaching and, as such, failed to satisfy criterion two. However, it did give students opportunity to demonstrate a range of ways of understanding the term. In giving an example of the use of 'discretionary fiscal policy' or 'withdrawals' students were expected to demonstrate the way they understood the 'circular flow of income': how the economy can be portrayed as a system of flows of goods and payments that tended towards equilibrium. When compared with in-depth interviews, students' answers under examination conditions might be expected to provide an inferior basis for identifying the range of ways of understanding a phenomenon and the way in which any particular student understands a phenomenon. Nevertheless, written examinations are the standard means of assessment in undergraduate examinations and it is pertinent to ask what qualitative differences are evident under these conditions. To date, there has been no published phenomenographic study of qualitative differences in understanding of 'flows of income' in an economy.

In the second section of the paper students were asked to choose one from three questions on macroeconomics. Our investigation focuses on two, which are presented in Table 2.

Table 2. Questions from a first year economics examination for non-specialists

1.	The following is a short extract from the minutes of the Monetary Policy Committee (MPC) meeting of the 8th and 9th November 2006.
	'… Most measures of investment intentions had strengthened…….. Most surveys of export orders had also picked up. That was probably in large part due to the euro-area recovery, which appeared to have been sustained during the second half of 2006.'
	Explain the effect of these changes on the economy (you may want to use an appropriate diagram). The MPC recommended raising interest rates given these changes in the economy. What would be the expected effect of this increase?
2.	What factors affect consumer expenditure? What would be the influence on the whole economy of a fall in consumer confidence?

These questions were designed so that students would have to identify the concepts they should use to answer the question. There was no direction to the model that should be used or indeed that a model should be used[2] (though a diagram is asked for in question 1). As such, these questions were more focused on criteria two and three. These questions were, therefore more open than the questions in the first section and they invited students to show their understanding of a wider set of connections. Nonetheless, answers to these questions in the second section were expected to draw upon students' understanding of 'the circular flow of income' and this provided a basis for comparison between answers to the questions in the two sections and it was on this aspect of their answers that our analysis concentrated.

Method of Analysis

Students' answers to the examination questions were analysed to identify qualitative differences between the ways of understanding the phenomena. This post-examination qualitative analysis involved an initial careful examination of a sub-sample of answers to note the characteristics of each. The analysis was undertaken by two researchers who initially studied the examination scripts independently and then compared their classifications. The notes on these answers were then compared to produce an initial list of characteristics of answers to each question. The wording of these characteristics was closely related to the way that answers had been expressed by students. A second level of analysis then took place to classify these characteristics into qualitatively distinct categories that might generalise beyond the specific requirements of an individual question. Examples of the application of this process, which gave four categories, are detailed in the following section.

We also obtained responses to the same questions from a small number of economics lecturers and master's students for comparison of the understanding revealed. These were analysed by the two researchers and two additional categories were recognised. One of these was included as the highest classification in the ensuing analysis as lecturers teaching the model considered it had been covered in the curriculum and had hoped, indeed expected, to find it in some of the better undergraduate responses. The second additional category of response in the answers of this group was criticism of the 'circular flow' model as a basis for answering these questions and the hence more appropriate use of advanced models. This are not included as a categorisation as our first year students had not covered such models in their course, thus they could not be expected to reveal such conceptions (and indeed did not). Although some of the undergraduate students did include aspects that could be classed as 'criticism', these were ideas were that were likely to simply be learnt as isolated objects rather than indicating more advanced understanding.

The full sample of thirty-four scripts was then analysed and the answers to the chosen questions given one of the five categorisations. A check between the two researchers found that their classification of the student answers was consistent at this stage.

RESULTS

Qualitative Differences between Students' Answers

We begin illustrating the two stages in the qualitative analysis by explanations of 'withdrawals' offered by two students. One student explained 'withdrawals' in the following terms:

This is when income is withdrawn from the economy it can be by either savings or taxation etc. For example the government may want to withdraw money from the economy so they may put up taxes, this leaves consumers with less disposable incomes. (Student 33)

The first stage of analysis noted:
– correct identification of types of 'withdrawal' (savings, tax)
– increase in tax leads to less disposable income

A second student wrote:

If on the circular flow of income withdrawals outweigh injections then the economy shrinks and aggregate demand falls. If we then look at the multiplier effect we can see if this downward spiral continues as demand for GDP products would decrease, causing job losses and unemployment levels to rise. (Student 29)

The first stage of analysis noted:
- balance of 'withdrawals' and 'injections' leads to change in economy, directional change appropriate
- 'multiplier effect' referred to appropriately but only as linear sequence.

The second level of analysis compared the responses of all the students on the basis of the established categories. The response of Student 1 was categorised as showing understanding of 'directionality' ('so they put up taxes, this leaves consumers with less disposable income'), but no more. Student 2 directly refers to the balance of 'injections' and 'withdrawals' as determining the direction of overall change in the economy. They also show some appreciation of 'knock-on' effects through a 'multiplier' process, but there is no indication whether the student appreciates this process as leading to a new equilibrium. The idea that changes in an economy can be understood in terms of movements between two equilibrium positions is identified in Table 1 as a key procedural concept. Although Student 2's answer improves upon the answer offered by Student 1 it does not demonstrate an understanding of an economic system in terms of equilibrating forces and so was categorised as showing the 'beginnings of understanding of the process', but not as understanding a 'limit to the process'.

In analysing the problem-focused questions from the second section we concentrated on the aspects of the question that directly linked to the use of the economic model of flows of goods and payments in the economy. This aspect was important in the answering of both questions, but was not the only aspect that could be deemed relevant. Considering these aspects we found similar qualitative differences in students' explanations of these problem-focused questions in the second section to the 'withdrawals' and 'discretionary fiscal policy' questions in the first section of the examination. For instance, in the 'discretionary fiscal policy' question better responses referred to an effect of an increase in government spending (G) or taxation (T) on the 'circular flow' but insofar as 'multiplier' effects were referred to there was no reference to a decline in the 'knock-on' effect and exemplification was restricted to highly localised examples. Similarly to the example on 'withdrawals' from the second student, 'multiplier' effects were not explained as an attribute of an economic system and we categorised such answers under the same heading. In particular, these answers gave no indication that an economy was understood as a system that tended towards an equilibrium position and that effects of changes in any particular variable should be understood in terms of disturbing an equilibrium position and prompting a shift towards a new equilibrium. More complex answers did begin to recognise some systemic effects, distinguishing between discretionary and automatic effects, by contrasting a rise in tax revenue that was a result of increasing national income and an increase that resulted from a rise in the rate of tax, but did not consider the relationship between these and the adjustment to a new equilibrium.

The Distribution of Conceptions across Questions

Tables 3 and 4 present the classifications derived for each question. The overview categories are the same for each question; the features illustrate ways these link to the particular question.

We now turn to evidence of the distribution of the different conceptions across questions as given in Table 5. Since the examination paper gave a choice of questions to answer in each section, the number of answers per student varies. We found that our students were lacking in understanding of the procedures in economics and in particular their lack of understanding of the role of equilibrium in modelling was preventing them from having a deeper understanding. This was our highest conception, which was not initially found in our student sub-sample that determined the categorisation, but in our economics lecturer/master's student sample. Indeed, it was found to be absent from the whole student sample – categorisation e is zero for all the questions[3]. That is no student fully understood the threshold concept of 'cumulative causation' ('the multiplier') although some were beginning to indicate an emerging sense of the system that may indicate that they were not far from such a position.

Table 3. Categories of response to questions requiring students to explain 'withdrawals' and 'discretionary fiscal policy'

	Overview	Features of response to a question requiring students to explain 'withdrawals'	Features of response to a question requiring students to explain 'discretionary fiscal policy'
a	No clear understanding	Incorrectly identifies the components of withdrawals.	Misunderstanding of what is meant by fiscal policy.
b	Identification of elements of system	Correctly identifies the components of withdrawals and other elements of the 'circular flow'.	Correctly defines fiscal policy.
c	Understands directionality	Recognises that increases in withdrawals reduce in national income.	Rise in G or fall in T will increase the 'circular flow', expand economy etc.
d	Beginnings of understanding of process of cumulative causation.	Recognises that there are 'knock-on' effects, but not as a limited process.	Refers to discretionary/ automatic distinction or 'multiplier' (but treats this as a sequence of 'knock-on' effects without any sense of interactions in a system).
e	Understanding of limit to process.	Considers how 'knock-on' effects reduce and the economy tends towards equilibrium.	Shows an understanding of 'the multiplier' and how this is limited process; differentiates between automatic/ discretionary policy and considers how these interact.

Table 4. Categories of response to longer questions requiring students to respond to problems focused questions

	Overview	Features of response to question about increase in rate of interest	Features of response to question about consumer confidence
a	No clear understanding	Does not identify how the changes relate to the components of the 'circular flow'.	Does not correctly associate changes in consumer confidence with components of the 'circular flow' and changes in national income.
b	Identification of elements of system	Correctly relates the changes to the components of the 'circular flow' and their role (as injections/ withdrawals) in the system.	Associates changes in consumer confidence to consumption/saving in the 'circular flow', but no clear direction of relationship to changes in national income made.
c	Understands directionality	Understands that increased investment/ export orders leads to a rise in national income and an increase in interest rates leads to a fall.	Suggests a fall consumer confidence will lead to a fall in consumption and increase saving and will reduce aggregate demand.
d	Beginnings of understanding of process of cumulative causation	Recognises that there are 'knock-on' effects of the changes and these relate to the business cycle, but not as a limited process.	Suggests a fall has 'knock-on' effects on lower aggregate demand, but not as a limited process/there is a two-way process between consumption and income/ the effect is contingent on any countervailing changes in G or T.
e	Understanding of limit to process.	Considers how the 'knock-on' effects reduce and the economy tends towards equilibrium.	Explains the 'multiplier' effects of the changes and how the economy tends to equilibrium.

Table 5. Numbers of students replying by category of response

Category of response	Section 1		Section 2	
	Withdrawals	Fiscal Policy	Monetary Policy	Consumer Confidence
a	2	2	1	2
b	10	4	0	0
c	11	11	4	10
d	3	5	4	5
e	0	0	0	0

It might be expected that students who gave indications of more sophisticated answers in one question should be more likely to show more sophisticated understanding in another, given the overlap of many of the procedures and many of the concepts required needed to answer these questions. Although there was some connection, this was far from complete. For example, while three of the students achieved the same category on all of these questions they answered, one student was given *a* on his/her short question answer but *c* on the longer, while yet another student achieved a different category (*b*, *d* and *c*) on each of the three questions he/she attempted. However, Meyer et al. (2008) argue that the liminal journey through the portal provided by a threshold concept may be oscillatory between states and what we observe in terms of these latter students may be a manifestation of this.

DISCUSSION

We turn at this point to the differences in the ways that students express their understanding of *'discretionary* fiscal policy'. Many of the students correctly referred to this in terms of explicit choices made by a government in attempting to set levels of government spending and taxation so as to manage the level of income in the economy. However, only a small number of students showed any recognition that levels of government spending or taxation may change as a result of changes in the level of income in the economy. That is, they did not distinguish between automatic and discretionary changes in the levels of government spending and taxation. The question is how should we characterise this difference in ways of understanding?

The key problem for students here appears to be the relationship between circularity and equilibrium. Take for example from one student's answer, which was amongst the better responses to the question:

> In a recession the government can cut taxes to try and reflate the economy. This happens as consumers have more disposable income and more money to spend. Or it can inject money into the economy by extra government expenditure. For example, if they build a new school they will have to hire a firm to build it. This firm will employ workers who will earn a wage and would be able to spend their disposable income on goods and services, benefiting other firms and reflating the economy as a whole. (Student 32)

This student provides an account that suggests a 'circular flow of income': government spend money, firms hire new employees, increasing disposable income, 'reflating the economy as a whole'. This is an 'integrated' answer but there is a more desirable form of integration that could be shown. That is, as it stands, this student's explanation suggests that an infinite increase in income will be initiated. There is no hint here that the economy will converge on a new equilibrium. Like other students, this student had shown in an answer on withdrawals that they understood that there were withdrawals from an economy, but they did not bring this understanding to bear on their discussion of 'discretionary fiscal policy'.

203

They did not proceed as far as the subsequent effect of a change of income on 'withdrawals', leading to a convergence towards a new equilibrium. That is, they had not developed a way of integrating their understanding in a way that, from the point of view of the discipline, would be more desirable. Therefore, to simply label a response as 'integrated' is not sufficient to capture critical differences between ways of understanding from the point of view of the discipline.

There is a further difficulty that suggests that the teaching strategy proposed by variation theory may be insufficient in this particular case. Variation theory (Pang and Marton, 2003 and 2005) argues that students can be taught to understand a phenomenon in a particular way if they are presented with simultaneous variation in those features that are critical to that way of understanding. In this case a critical feature is the relationship between government taxation and income. The problem here is that understanding this relationship in terms of the 'circular flow' requires appreciation of two simultaneous relationships: an increase in T (exogenous) leading to a fall in Y and a decrease in Y leading to a decrease in T (endogenous). Data showing simultaneous changes in T and Y cannot differentiate easily between these two relationships.

CONCLUSION

Threshold concepts create challenges for received approaches to assess the progress of undergraduates. However, the implications of our analysis are less far reaching than those suggested by Meyer and Land (2008). The focus of our investigation was on variation of students' understanding of a phenomenon ('the circular flow of income') that is a standard part of an introductory course in economics. Our interest in students' understanding of this phenomenon is derived from the proposition that more complex conceptions of a phenomenon rely on the transformation of 'basic concepts' by disciplinary threshold concepts that integrate a learner's conceptual structure. We would predict, from this proposition that when students are introduced to a concept like 'the circular flow of income' they begin to use the language of a disciplinary conception (such as 'multiplier') well before they have developed the kind of understanding which an expert might infer from use of such terms. This creates an assessment difficulty in the context of 'large-scale' assessment where lecturers are aiming to use salient cues in students' scripts to facilitate rapid marking of large numbers of scripts in Year 1 and Year 2 examinations.

None of the students in our sample revealed the understanding of 'circular flow of income' that was expressed by lecturers and which is described in standard introductory textbooks. In particular, they did not express an idea of the 'circular flow of income' as a self-equilibrating process. Many of the students expressed the idea of a linear process, some referring to a single step in the process and others suggesting 'knock-on' effects. Those students who suggested circular and/or contingent processes appeared to have made a significant step towards lecturers' target understanding as such ideas make it more likely that the question of equilibrium would be subsequently considered.

The model of the development of a 'threshold concept' that we have suggested identifies understanding of procedural concepts – such as equilibrium – as critical. Whilst the data we have presented are consistent with this proposal there is a need for more directly confirming evidence. Our analysis suggests that teaching of this topic should give much greater emphasis to the contrast between the notion of a self-equilibrating system and a set of 'knock-on' effects. Further research is required to examine the efficacy of such a change.

Outside of economics, other disciplines may find our method useful in facilitating learning. The data in this study were the answers by students in examinations, a resource which is available to academics in abundance. Our work suggests analysis of student assessments may be a fruitful source for the categorisation of responses and identification of possible critical concepts to emphasise in teaching and learning.

NOTES

[1] Work on this project was carried out under the Embedding Threshold Concepts in First-Year Undergraduate Economics Project which was based at Staffordshire University, UK. The project was funded by the Higher Education Funding Council for England and the Department for Employment and Learning (DEL) under the Fund for the Development of Teaching and Learning and it involves a partnership with Coventry, Durham and West of England Universities. We are grateful to our evaluators Noel Entwistle and Steve Hodkinson and the members of the project team, Dave Allen, John Ashworth, Ray Land, Jan Meyer, John Sloman and Peri Yavash for their support in developing the ideas presented in this chapter. We would also like to express our thanks for the continued support of the Economics Network of the Higher Education Academy.

[2] Recordings during the Embedding Threshold Concepts project of students working in groups suggest that students do not immediately recognise the need to use a model when analysing an applied problem.

[3] A lack of students at the highest conception level was also found in the study by Pang and Marton (2005), where they had one student in this category.

REFERENCES

Alexander, P. A., Jetton, T. L., & Kulikowich, J. M. (1995). Interrelationship of knowledge, interest, and recall: Assessing a model of domain learning. *Journal of Educational Psychology*, *87*(4), 559–575.

Christopoulos, J. P., Rohwer, W. D., & Thomas, J. W. (1987). Grade level differences in students' study activities as a function of course characteristics. *Contemporary Educational Psychology*, *12*(4), 303–323.

Davies, P., & Mangan, J. (2007). Threshold concepts and the integration of understanding in economics. *Studies in Higher Education*, *32*(6), 711–726.

Davies, P., & Mangan, J. (2008). Embedding threshold concepts: From theory to pedagogical principles to learning activities. In J. H. F. Meyer & R. Land (Eds.), *Threshold concepts within the disciplines*. Rotterdam, The Netherlands: Sense.

Eisner, E. W. (1993). Reshaping assessment in education: Some criteria in search of practice. *Journal of Curriculum Studies*, *25*(3), 219–233.

Giancarlo, C. A., & Facione, P. A. (2001). A look across four years at the disposition toward critical thinking amongst undergraduate students. *The Journal of General Education*, *50*(1), 29–55.

Meyer, J. H. F., & Land, R. (2003). Threshold concepts and troublesome knowledge: Linkages to ways of thinking and practising within the disciplines. In C. Rust (Ed.), *Improving student learning. Improving student learning theory and practice — 10 years on*. Oxford: OCSLD.

Meyer, J. H. F., & Land, R. (2005). Threshold concepts and troublesome knowledge (2) Epistemological considerations and a conceptual framework for teaching and learning. *Higher Education, 49*(3), 373–388.

Meyer, J. H. F., Land, R., & Davies, P. (2008). Threshold concepts and troublesome knowledge (4): Issues of variation and variability. In R. Land, J. H. F Meyer, & J. Smith (Eds.), *Threshold concepts within the disciplines*. Rotterdam, The Netherlands: Sense Publishers.

Meyer, J. H. F., & Land, R. (2009). Threshold concepts and troublesome knowledge (5): Dynamics of assessment. In R. Land, J. H. F. Meyer, & C. Baillie (Eds.), *Threshold concepts and transformational learning*. Rotterdam, The Netherlands: Sense Publishers.

Pang, M., & Marton, F. (2003). Beyond "Lesson study": Comparing two ways of facilitating the grasp of some economic concepts. *Instructional Science, 31*(3), 175–194.

Pang, M., & Marton, F. (2005). Learning theory as teaching resource: Enhancing students' understanding of economic concepts. *Instructional Science, 33*(2), 159–191.

Perry, W. (1970). *Forms of intellectual and ethical development in the college years: A scheme.* New York: Holt, Rinehart, and Winston.

Schommer, M. (1990). Effects of beliefs about the nature of knowledge on comprehension. *Journal of Educational Psychology, 82*(3), 498–504.

Trautwein, U., & Ludtke, O. (2007). Epistemological beliefs, school achievement, and college major: A large-scale longitudinal study on the impact of certainty beliefs. *Contemporary Educational Psychology, 32*(3), 348–366.

Vermetten, Y. J., Vermunt, J. D., & Lodewijks, H. G. (1999). A longitudinal perspective on learning strategies in higher education: Different view-points towards development. *British Journal of Educational Psychology, 69*(2), 221–242.

Peter Davies and Jean Mangan
Institute for Education Policy Research
Staffordshire University

MARTIN P. SHANAHAN, GIGI FOSTER AND JAN. H.F. MEYER

13. THRESHOLD CONCEPTS AND ATTRITION IN FIRST-YEAR ECONOMICS

INTRODUCTION

Threshold concepts have been characterised as transformative, irreversible, integrative, troublesome, and bounded (Meyer and Land, 2006). They have been and are likely to be identified in a range of discipline areas (Land, Meyer, Smith, 2008). Importantly, they appear to represent a major source of variation between individual learners within discipline-specific boundaries.

Identifying and defining threshold discipline-specific concepts, however, is not straightforward. Within economics for example, there has been debate as to the form and nature of these concepts. They are not necessarily equivalent to the 'key concepts' frequently listed in text-book chapters, nor do they appear to be discrete and separate entities (Davies, 2006; Davies and Mangan 2005, 2007). Indeed they may be more accurately viewed as a 'web' of concepts that underlie the shift in thinking that is associated with learning (Davies and Mangan 2007). In earlier work within the economics discipline, Davies and Mangan (2006) proposed three categories of threshold concepts: those they labelled 'personal' (economically-orientated perspectives on everyday life); 'procedural' (ways of practicing and articulating economics) and 'discipline-based' (related to use of the concept within the discipline). A similar categorisation is adopted in the analysis presented in this paper, although we also explore the association of individual threshold concepts with outcomes.

To the extent that threshold concepts in particular disciplines are difficult to master, they also represent potential barriers to student learning. Variation in the rate at which students master threshold concepts has begun to be explored in the discussion on liminality (Meyer and Land, 2006). The concept of liminality has been used to describe the process whereby an individual student becomes conscious they are beginning to think, for example, like an economist. The idea of liminality therefore, attempts to capture the process whereby the individual learner is transformed from learner to practitioner or from student of a discipline to a member of the discipline (albeit still a novice). This requires a transformative shift in ontological belief – that one shifts from 'learning about' economics, to 'thinking like' an economist, to 'acting like' an economist, to 'being' an economist. Extending this idea further, Meyer and Land suggest that individuals proceed at varying rates across conceptual thresholds and exhibit varying states of liminality. Of particular interest to this paper, the state they label as 'pre-liminal' refers to the 'tacit' knowledge students bring to a threshold concept. As with prior content knowledge, students

J. H. F. Meyer, R. Land and C. Baillie (eds.), Threshold Concepts and
Transformational Learning, 207–226.

may vary greatly in the amount of prior tacit knowledge they have of particular threshold concepts. Some evidence of this has previously been reported in Shanahan, Foster and Meyer (2008). In that study, the tacit knowledge of some selected threshold concepts in economics were more highly correlated to examination performance at the end of one semester than some measured dimensions of learning.

While the association of threshold concept understanding with student success in university courses has been explored in prior research, virtually no research examines whether an association exists between threshold concept understanding and attrition from a course of study. If threshold concepts are troublesome, or represent a barrier as much as a threshold, then some students must fail to make the transition across the threshold. We would thus anticipate that students who do not exhibit an understanding of certain threshold concepts may be more likely to drop out of courses than students who appear to have acquired such concepts before commencing a course. The focus of this study is to examine the correlation between students' observed grasp of certain threshold concepts in economics at the start of a semester and their likelihood of leaving an introductory microeconomics course in that same semester.

We also posit a further speculation linking threshold concepts with attrition. We suggest that based on evidence drawn from students' surveys, a necessary preliminary stage of thinking that must be attained by students before discipline threshold concepts become relevant is the ontological shift required to view oneself as a student learner.[1] We speculate that students who fail to make this transformation are the most likely to leave the course early, and that the impact of pre-liminal knowledge of economic threshold concepts is only relevant once this transformation is made. We suggest therefore that the correlation between prior acquisition of discipline threshold concepts and attrition is likely to be of secondary importance. Although consistent with the data we have, this conjecture remains relatively unexplored.

In addition to extending existing empirical research on the causes and consequences of threshold conceptual understanding, our results may also inform the debate about potential avenues of intervention universities could follow to understand and control student attrition.

This remainder of this paper is in five sections. Section 2 describes the theoretical, methodological and institutional context for the present study. Section 3 provides details about the data and Section 4 reviews some existing results regarding attrition for a larger group of students of which we then examine a subset in detail. Section 5 reports our results focusing on this subset, and Section 6 discusses some interpretations, notes some caveats on the research, and concludes with some possible policy implications.

THEORETICAL BACKGROUND AND METHODOLOGICAL CONTEXT

Attrition is widely regarded in the tertiary sector as a costly and regrettable phenomenon. Previous studies have identified a range of student characteristics associated with attrition.[2] These include whether English is a second language; university entrance score; the number of hours a student works outside university; socioeconomic background; schooling experience; and initial university experience, to name a few. Unfortunately, the results of existing studies are not consistent across institutional context. Further, while most studies have examined the external, quantifiable characteristics of students, few have asked the students themselves their reasons for leaving, and thus have, by and large, failed to isolate additional factors such as health and personal issues, motivation, financial and work related issues, institutional (administrative) factors or issues with the teaching and learning of academic material.[3] While the reasons underlying a student's decision to leave a course or program of study may be related to the difficulties they have in mastering threshold concepts, no previous research has examined students' individual level of discipline-specific prior acquisition of threshold concepts.

After commenting on student withdrawals from microeconomics at the University of South Australia, we suggest that a major explanatory factor is individual commitment to the course. Using administrative data, we then ask whether a student's expectations of success in the course are correlated with withdrawal from the course, and to what extent students' acquisition of threshold concepts, as revealed through their multiple choice responses from week 3, correlated with the likelihood of leaving the course.

To detect variation in students' individual level of discipline-specific prior acquisition of threshold concepts, this study uses students' responses to multiple choice questions completed in the first two weeks of the semester, and submitted by week three. Previous work has demonstrated that multiple choice questions can be used to detect variation in students' grasp of threshold concepts (Shanahan, Foster and Meyer 2006). Such questions can reveal variation in students' levels of understanding of these concepts: some students display an absence of even the most fundamental threshold conceptual understanding while others possess a deep, wide-ranging understanding of economic concepts even before they begin the course (Shanahan, Foster and Meyer 2008).

We initially employed simple regression-based methodologies to explore the data. We regressed measures of attrition from the course on measures of threshold conceptual understanding and an array of student-specific control variables, using ordinary least squares. These analyses revealed comparatively little.[4] Robustness checks using binary logistic models yielded no qualitative shift in our results. The results suggest that apart from 'external' measures of difference (such as the number of hours a student is committed to work outside the university) there are only small differences in the distribution of previously acquired discipline-specific threshold concepts between those who leave the course, and those who remain.[5] When we examined selected sub-sets of 'at risk' students, however, we detected large differences in the distribution of prior threshold concepts that appears consistent with our exploratory hypothesis.

EMPIRICAL SETTING

Institutional Context

A public university, the University of South Australia is primarily located in Adelaide, South Australia.[6] The university services approximately 33,000 students and employs approximately 1,000 academic staff. A key mission of the institution is to provide tertiary-level studies that are accessible and equitable to a diverse student body.

The Division of Business comprises approximately one-third of the university. Within the Division, all undergraduate students study a first-year-level core of business-related courses before continuing on to more specialised areas. The core courses include introductory subjects in microeconomics, accounting, marketing, statistics, management, law, information systems, and communications. Depending on their program, full-time students study up to four courses in each semester.[7]

One of the courses taught to full-time students in their first year is micro-economics.[8] In the first semester as many as 800 students may be enrolled in the course, of whom 150 may study exclusively via on-line materials ("external" students), and the remainder attend face-to-face classes as well as utilising web-based materials ("internal" students). The course is a standard first year microeconomics course whose principal text is an Australian adaptation, by colleagues in the department, of the introductory American textbook by McConnell.[9]

Data Collection and Measures

Our data on attrition rates are drawn from study period 2, 2007 (February – July) as part of a broader study of attrition.[10] On each Tuesday of classes (weeks 1 to 13), the enrolment list was downloaded from the university information system, and each student's enrolment status in microeconomics was recorded. Three sample surveys were administered during the semester in which enrolled students were asked their views about different aspects of the course and about the university.[11] This weekly tracking provides the data on attrition, while responses to the first survey provide additional background information on students, including the extent to which they reveal a commitment to being a student. Questions included whether the student had attended orientation programs; whether they had resolved problems related to determining their program and courses and course expectations, and if they still had basic problems such as knowing where their program director or classes were located. Finally, they were asked to respond on a Likert-type scale (ranging from 'a lot' to 'none') to their expectations of courses in regard to intellectual stimulation, fun, personal attention, and difficulty with balancing competing demands. These questions were designed to provide insights into student expectations and commitment to university life.

The study also uses a second set of data collected from microeconomics students studying in the same period. An important component of the microeconomics course aims to raise students' meta-learning capacity.[12] Two components of the assessment, in weeks 2–3 and 12–13 of the course, require students to complete an online discipline-specific 'learning inventory', and to respond to a series of 40 multiple-choice questions that test their understanding of economic concepts – including threshold concepts. Students also write a short essay about their learning profile. In this study, we use students' responses to the first iteration of the learning inventory and multiple choice questions, completed in weeks 2 to 3 of the course, to gauge students' grasp of an array of threshold concepts prior to, or very early into, the course.[13]

Within the 40 multiple-choice questions, each contributed toward revealing one of 27 basic conceptual elements that the authors considered potentially relevant to learning economics. These 27 elements were then categorised into Davies and Mangan's three categories.[14]

To summarise this categorization rationale briefly, Davies and Mangan (2007) have proposed that transformative learning can be described by the acquisition of a web of threshold concepts organized into three groups. The first category is personal conceptual change, where the novice learner's "naïve or 'common-sense' understanding" is replaced by the more powerful discipline mode of thinking. Associated with this is the use of more specialist language. This category represents the transformation of everyday experiences via the integration of personal experience with ideas from the discipline. The second category is discipline-based conceptual change, which "integrates and reworks" the disciplinary ideas already learned. This category represents a transformation that occurs via the acquisition of the discipline's theoretical perspective. Third procedural conceptual change is defined as a change associated with "ways of practicing the subject"; the discipline-specific procedures required to construct arguments, and so on. There is a necessary and mutual interdependence between the personal, discipline and procedural threshold concepts, all of which must be acquired in order for the student to gain full mastery of the discipline.

In the present study, our initial attention was on the student-level association between these categories of threshold concept acquisition and persistence in or attrition from the course. Our expectation was that students whose grasp of any of these three threshold concept categories was well-developed on entry to university will find the academic material and their own interaction with it to be less troublesome. They have already partially integrated and been transformed by some of the concepts, and are thus less likely to leave the course because of the degree of difficulty caused by mastering threshold concepts. To investigate this basic hypothesis more deeply, we examined the association between students leaving the course and the 27 threshold concepts that are grouped to form the three categories proposed by Davies and Mangan. These groupings are detailed in Table 1.

As part of the microeconomic students' self-assessment of their personal approach to learning, and in the process of completing the learning inventory and multiple choice questions, students were also asked to complete other 'background' questions. These included questions on their expectations about the course (e.g., How well do you anticipate you will do in this subject?); their expectations about the course and its academic requirements (I don't expect I will be stretched too much in this course...); whether university study takes a 'top priority' in their life; whether they are the first member of their family to attend university and so on. Other questions included whether they had studied economics before, and whether English was their first language. We also asked students to identify how committed they were to activities outside of their study. Students were asked to indicate the number of hours per week they were in paid employment or other non-leisure activities (such as running a household).

*Table 1. Categorisation of multiple-choice questions following Davies' and
Mangan's (2007) taxonomy*

Category	Davis & Mangan's categories	Concepts covered in MC questions	MC questions
Personal			
	Price/cost; Income/wealth	Price and cost	2, 32
	(stocks/flows)	Stock and flow	24,
	nominal/real	Real v nominal	11, 30, 31
	investment/saving	interest	9
		incentives	12, 15
		Living standards	40
		profits	10, 14
		Economics definition	37
		TOTAL number in this section	13/40
Discipline	Partial equilibrium	Partial equilibrium	25
	General equilibrium	Inter-related markets	16
	Welfare economics	Public good	23
	Opportunity cost	Opportunity cost	4, 8, 35
		Fallacy of composition	27, 29, 33
		Scientific model	26
		Zero sum game	3, 6
		Gains from trade	13
		Comparative advantage	36
		Marginality	18, 38
		Economic system	1
		Prod'n possibility Frontier	
		Trade-offs	5
		Markets	21
		Market Failure	
		TOTAL number in this section	19/40
Procedural	Comparative statics	Supply and demand	17, 19, 39
	Equilibrium		
	Ceteris paribus		
	Time short/long term		
	Expectations		
	Elasticity	Elasticity	7
		Competition	20
		Cost-benefit	22
		Externalities	28
		Sunk costs	34
		Behaviour of firms (includes cost decisions)	
		TOTAL number in this section	8/40

As the discussion below reveals, responses to these questions were used in part, to assist in the identification of students who were realistically committed to their studies, and those who were not. The issue of self-identified commitment emerged as the dominant factor associated with students who left the course early in the semester.

SOME FACTORS LINKED TO ATTRITION

Before proceeding to the issues associated with threshold concepts we briefly examine some of the issues associated with student attrition in microeconomics.[15] In all first year business courses, a large amount of student attrition, as measured using weekly class-list downloads, takes place in the first seven weeks of the semester. In our study, between 10 and 15 percent of students leave business courses by week seven; in microeconomics the figure is 12.4 percent. Significant levels of attrition also occur after lectures have ended, but before the exam is held. For example, the proportion of students who are recorded as not sitting the exam in first-year business courses ranges from 22 to 35 percent. In microeconomics the figure is 28.7 percent.

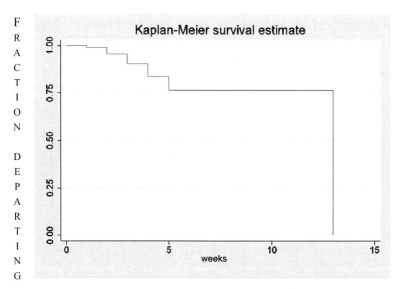

Figure 1. Departure pattern of all students who left microeconomics, by week.

Note: total n = 178
:A census of the enrolled students was collected each Tuesday. Students who left the course departed sometime between census dates and were recorded as leaving as from the beginning of each week.
:The figure shows the departure pattern of all students *who leave the course*. Approximately 25% leave by week five and the remainder leave after lectures end (week 13) and before examination (week 16).

Among microeconomics students who leave, the pattern of attrition across the teaching semester is shown in Figure 1 using a survival curve, which documents the departure pattern of all students who left the course in any given week. The figure reveals that among students who left, approximately a quarter had departed by week five after which point little attrition occurs until after lectures end. Between week 13 and the final exam, the remaining three quarters of those leaving the course, depart. These are caught in our records as students who did not sit the exam, despite being officially enrolled for all weeks of the semester. As a general observation, it would appear that students who leave the course can be divided into two groups: those who leave early (before week 5 in the case of microeconomics), and those who stay in the course officially but are observed to drop out in the period between the end of teaching and the examination. We hypothesise that these two student groups, of 'early' and 'late' leavers, may differ fundamentally, not just in their attachment to the course, but in their personal view of themselves as student learners.

We know that all students who leave have lower expectations across a range of issues at the start of their course experience. Students who leave during the semester initially expect their course experience to involve less intellectual stimulation, fun, individual freedom, and attention and commitment from university personnel than students who complete the course. There is some evidence that students who leave also may expect more trouble balancing university demands with other demands, though they actually predict lower academic workload than eventual stayers. Students who left the course were statistically less likely to have attended orientation events than students who sat the final examination. They were also statistically more likely than completing students to have experienced something that made them doubt the decision to accept the university's offer of admission. Finally, when they enrolled in their program, students who would leave were also statistically significantly less certain than stayers that they wanted to work in the area of their program after leaving university.

Of those students who responded to the questions regarding hours of outside commitments such as paid work and other non-leisure activities, course leavers reported statistically significantly higher levels of non-study commitments – in the range of three hours more per week on average (17.5 hours compared to 14.4 hours for non-leavers). The pattern of withdrawal from the microeconomics course by those who left the course can be further categorised by students' level of outside commitments. This pattern is shown in Figure 2.

There, the 'work-hours' variable is defined as 0 if the student reported no hours of outside commitments; 1 if 4 or fewer hours per week; 2 if 4.1–8 hours per week (i.e., around a day a week); 3 if 8.1–21 hours (i.e., up to 3 days a week); 4 if 21.1–30 hours per week; and 5 if over 30 (and usually 38 hours per week - in effect a full time job) or more (for example, a full-time job plus family responsibilities). Categorising students who leave the course on the basis of their outside commitments reveals the somewhat surprising result that it is not those with the greatest hours of outside commitments (groups 4 and 5, and less strongly 3) who

F
R
A
C
T
I
O
N

D
E
P
A
R
T
I
N
G

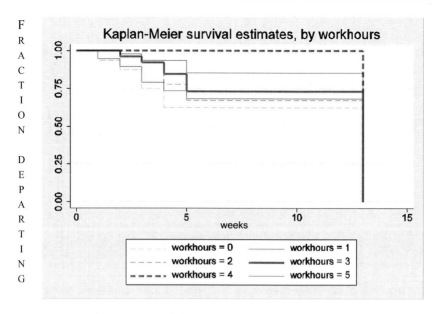

Figure 2. Departure pattern of all students who left microeconomics, categorised by declared hours of 'outside work' and 'family commitments'

Note: total n = 178
0 = Corresponds with no hours committed to activities outside university
1 = Corresponds to ≤ 4 hrs/week of outside commitments
2 = 4.1–8 hours/week (around one day a week)
3 = 8.1–21 hours (i.e., up to 3 days a week)
4 = 21.1–30 hours / week
5 > 30 hours/week (in effect a full time job) or more (for example, a full-time job plus family responsibilities).
:The figure shows the departure pattern of all students who leave the course. Students with higher levels of outside commitments (Categories 3, 4 or 5) tend to remain longer in the course before departing than those with lower outside commitments.

tend to leave early. Students with high outside commitments, if they leave, tend not do so until shortly before the exam. By contrast, a higher proportion of students with lower levels of outside commitments leave early.

These patterns suggest that of the students who are recorded as leaving a course, many may have not really 'entered' the course, other than on paper. The statistically significant differences between eventual stayers and leavers in expectations, orientation function attendance, certainty about the area of study, and simultaneous employment and other non-leisure commitments suggest that many students who are recorded as leaving a course – even as judged through simply not sitting the final examination – may well have not committed to it in the first place.[16] That departing students with high levels of outside commitments tend to 'hang-on' rather than leave early, compared to students with lesser outside commitments, suggests that something other than outside commitments is important here. We speculate that it is students' self-identification as student learners. It appears that in relative terms, students who already work long hours make a stronger commitment to university learning than those with lesser outside commitments- at least among those who eventually leave the course.

Students who left microeconomics after week two or three, and who submitted the first piece of assessment, are caught in the data reported below. It was this sub-group of microeconomic students that we initially hypothesised may hold different levels of previously acquired threshold concepts.

RESULTS

Descriptive Analyses

Table 2 presents descriptive information on the sample of all students in micro-economics, not just those who left the course.[17] Data were obtained from the initial learning inventory and multiple-choice question array on 529 students, of whom

Table 2. Descriptive statistics of all microeconomic students

Variable	Mean	Std. Dev.
Left in first 7 weeks	0.10	.
Did not sit final exam	0.34	.
Personal Threshold Concept	0.51	0.16
Discipline Threshold Concept	0.62	0.15
Procedural Threshold Concept	0.61	0.19
Test of Economic Literacy Score	22.79	4.55
Female	0.52	.
Took economics elsewhere	0.42	.
English is not first language	0.25	.
Expect to be stretched in the course	0.76	.
Feel ready for the course	0.86	.
Family member has gone to university	0.63	.
Study takes top priority	0.54	.
Academic work is not top priority	0.64	.
Prefer to work alone on academic work	0.63	.
Work < 5 hours per week	0.13	.
Work 5–8 hours per week	0.33	.
Work 9–21 hours per week	0.14	.
Work 22–30 hours per week	0.06	.
Work full time or more outside university	0.15	.
Performance expectations: Excellent	0.47	.
Very good	0.46	.
Average	0.03	.
Bare Pass	0.00	.

Note: N = 529; TEL Score (Test of Economic Literacy) is out of 40. The TEL is based on the work by Walstad (1987) and is used with permission.

216

52 percent were female; 25 percent reported that English was not their first language; and 42 percent reported having taken economics elsewhere. Students' expectations of academic success in the course were generally good, yet their external commitments were substantial: 35 percent reported non-leisure activities of 9 hours per week or more, and only 19 percent did not report other non-leisure activities at all. Just over a third (34 percent) of the sample ended up leaving the course, and 10 percent of students left in the first seven weeks.

Table 2 also presents students' average initial scores on each of three aggregates relating to their original mastery of economic threshold concepts. On the initial test of economic literacy-based multiple-choice question array, students averaged a total score of 22.79 out of a possible 40. On the three threshold concept taxonomies discussed above – personal, discipline-specific, and procedural threshold concepts – students averaged scores of 0.51, 0.62, and 0.61, respectively, out of a possible 1, with a substantial degree of variation across students in each case. Students' mastery of economic concepts therefore appears to be midrange and given the size of the standard deviation, quite variable.

Regression Results and Discussion

As a first exploratory look at the data, we examined the association between failure to sit the final exam (leaving the course), students' initial threshold concept scores and the array of background variables available to us on the initial learning inventory and multiple-choice test. In these first regressions, we used the three-part aggregation of threshold concepts into personal, discipline-specific, and procedural concepts. We ran the model with several different subsets of students. Very little was statistically significant in these regressions, including our measures of prior acquisition of the three 'formal' types of threshold concepts. What were highly significant, however, were students' concurrent employment commitments. For the overall sample and even more so for native English speakers, having outside work commitments drastically cut the chance of course completion. Working 22 or more hours a week was estimated to increase the chance of eventually not sitting the final exam by 45 to 55 percentage points, and the impact of working was significant across the spectrum of hours from five per week upwards (and, for non-ESL students, even working 4 or fewer hours per week was significantly negatively associated with course completion).

When we examined the same issues, but made departure in the first seven weeks the dependent variable, (i.e. 'early leavers') employment commitments did not appear to matter, but nor did personal, discipline-specific, or procedural threshold concepts. What did matter was whether students had taken economics elsewhere; those who had, tended to be 10 to 13 percentage points less likely to leave in the first seven weeks. Students who replied 'yes' to the statement on the learning inventory that 'people who know me would tell you that my university study takes top priority in my life' were estimated to be about six percentage points less likely to leave in the first seven weeks. It was also of note that we could not explain as much of the variation in students' leaving early as we could of the variation in students' leaving at any stage during the semester: the R-squareds for these models were less than 0.05, compared to over 0.10 previously. This may suggest the triumph of hope over good judgment in students' decision making, whereby those with very little objective chance of completing the course nonetheless persevere against the odds (and perhaps irresponsibly, at least from a financial standpoint) beyond the midpoint of the semester.

To examine the possible impact of threshold concepts by themselves, we grouped students into three categories: those who left the course 'early' (first 7 weeks); those who left later (did not sit the exam) and those who did not leave. We then examined the distribution of scores for each of the threshold clusters (personal, discipline and procedural). Figures 3, 4 and 5 reveal these distributions. As can be seen from these figures, there is relatively little difference in the distribution of threshold concept scores between these three groups.

We next disaggregated the threshold concept measures to see whether any specific concepts were associated with either measures of attrition. There was still a strong relationship between hours of paid employment and likelihood of leaving the course at some point during the semester. We also saw a statistically significant relationship between attrition and several specific threshold concept measures. These included one question that was linked to student's understanding of living standards; three linked to opportunity cost and one on student's understanding of economic systems as a whole. That opportunity cost appeared in this regression as statistically significant was consistent with earlier findings (Shanahan and Meyer, 2006; Shanahan, Foster and Meyer, 2008), that the concept was threshold concept within the discipline.

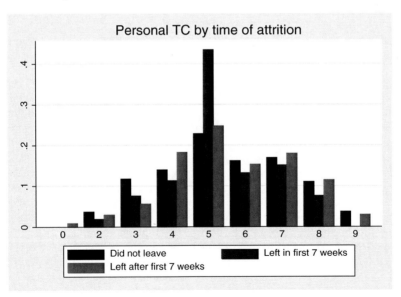

Figure 3. The distribution of personal threshold concept scores by time of attrition.

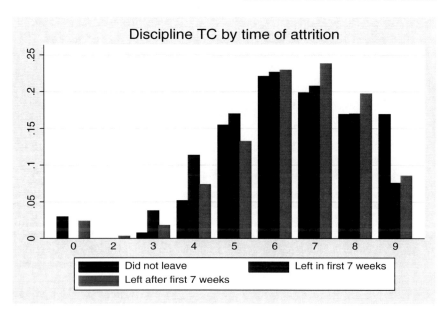

Figure 4. The distribution of discipline threshold concept scores by time of attrition.

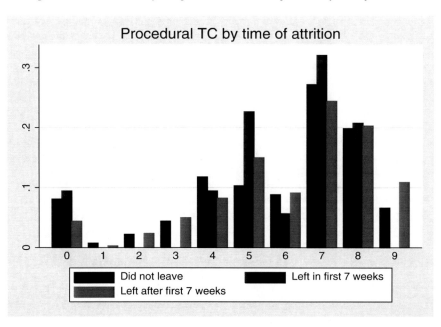

Figure 5. The distribution of procedural threshold concept scores by time of attrition.

Other regressions, also not reported here, looked at the student group as a whole and reaffirmed that having taken economics previously and having stated that university is a top priority were both negatively associated with attrition in the first seven weeks. There was also a negative relationship between female gender and the likelihood of attrition: women were less likely than men to leave the course in the first seven weeks, once we controlled for individual rather than grouped threshold concepts. However, only one individual threshold concept was further associated statistically with attrition in the first seven weeks of the course; the concept of the necessity of trade-offs when choosing between outcomes – a concept that itself underlies opportunity cost.

The fact that we found different predictors for attrition overall, and for attrition in the first seven weeks, lends credence to the notion that there is a different process underlying each of these outcomes. Indeed, apart from the tantalising statistical 'hints' that some threshold concepts may be involved, our strongest conclusion was the overall importance of how 'connected' students were with the university. Students who rated university as a 'number one priority were less likely to leave, while having large time commitments outside the university were statistically influential in students' decision to leave the course.

Given these interim results, we partitioned the data differently. We grouped students into students 'at risk' of leaving and those who were not 'at risk'. Students who were 'not at risk' of leaving the course were identified as students who worked 21 hours a week or less outside the university and who agreed with either 'I feel ready for this course'; 'study takes top priority' or disagreed with 'academic work, while important, is not the most important thing in my life'. The rationale for using these criteria was to identify students whose responses indicated they were prepared to give a reasonably high priority to university studies. Students who were 'at risk' were by definition, all other students. We then examined the distribution of previously acquired threshold concepts.

Interestingly, an inspection of these distributions suggested that a small group of 'at risk' students exhibited the classic 'progression' through threshold concepts as originally outlined by Davies and Mangan (2005; 2007). None of the 'at risk' students revealed particularly low scores on our admittedly crude measures of personal threshold concepts in economics. A higher proportion of students at risk of leaving, however, appeared in the low scores on discipline threshold concepts and a slightly higher proportion again appears in the low scores of procedural concepts. While there was slight evidence in the patterns to suggest that prior acquisition of these clusters of concepts may in some cases prove a tipping point for students persistence in the course; the evidence was weak.

Finally, we took advantage of previous research on student learning (Meyer and Shanahan, 2001). In that study a series of factors that would increase a student's risk of failing first-year microeconomics was identified, based on measures detectable in the first weeks of semester. Factors that increased the risk of failing included: having English as a second language; if the student had not studied economics previously (at school); whether the student held 'economic misconceptions'; and whether the individuals' approach to learning put them at risk.

This last element included high scores on learning scales that revealed the student was motivated by a duty to others rather than herself; if she saw knowledge being made of discrete 'units' to be 'collected'; if she had a preference for memorising before understanding; and whether the student tended to focus on details in preference to gaining an overview of material.

Figures 6, 7 and 8 report the distribution of previously acquired threshold concepts of two student groups. The first are students who are 'at risk' because they were 'above average' in holding economic misconceptions, above average in holding approaches to learning that put them at risk of failing (labelled 'problematic learning' in the graphs) and who had not previously studied economics before. The second group consists of all students who did not fall into the first category.[18]

Unlike the previous comparisons, the distributions of previously acquired threshold concepts are strikingly different. The distribution and mean of the scores on previously acquired personal threshold concepts among 'at risk' students is clearly to the left of students not so 'at risk'. The difference in distributions between the two groups is slightly less marked for discipline specific thresholds but strongly marked again for procedural threshold concepts. The results suggest that earlier work focussing on student learning, and prior discipline knowledge in particular, and English language skills to a lesser extent, is consistent with measureable variation in prior threshold concept acquisition. This itself suggests potentially important avenues for future research – to measure the congruence between learning dimensions and threshold concept acquisition.

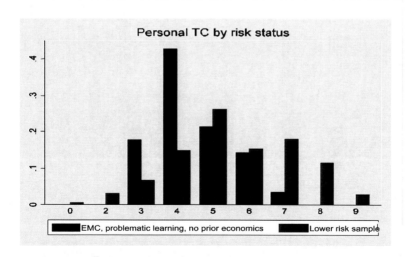

Figure 6. The distribution of personal threshold concept scores; students grouped into 'at risk' and 'lower-risk' subgroups.

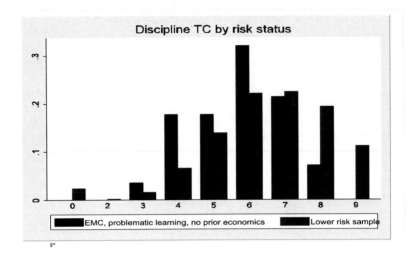

Figure 7. The distribution of discipline threshold concept scores; students grouped into 'at risk' and 'lower-risk' subgroups.

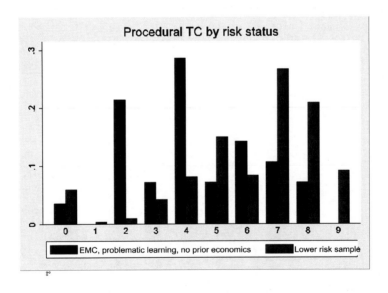

Figure 8. The distribution of procedural threshold concept scores; students grouped into 'at risk' and 'lower-risk' subgroups.

Note for figures, 6, 7 and 8: At risk students are those who were 'above average' in their recorded economic misconceptions; above average in scales estimating poor learning processes and had not previously studied economics.

222

The results may also have important policy implications. Universities who are concerned with student attrition may already provide advice regarding the optimum number of hours of external commitment students can successfully manage. More telling, however, may be advice about the level of personal commitment to becoming a student learner that is required. Further, the results here suggest that relatively simple methods to detect students at risk of failing (i.e. asking students to reflect on their approach to learning; determining whether they have prior knowledge of the subject; whether English is their second language) may allow universities to detect students whose prior acquisition of threshold concepts is also lower than those of others. This may mean universities will be able to intervene to assist students whose learning approaches, prior knowledge and previously acquired concepts place them at risk. Better understanding the interplay of these factors and their relative importance for student success is an important area for future research.

CONCLUSIONS

The factors associated with student attrition are many. An important conceptual portal that many students must negotiate, however, before they begin their university studies is that of self-identification as a university student. We conjecture that many students who leave a course, particularly those who leave in the first seven weeks, may have failed to identify themselves as university student learners, and thus have failed to commit to their studies with the same level of intensity as others who have enrolled.

Once a student has committed to study (in this paper this is associated with completing the first 13 weeks of teaching), variation in students' grasp of discipline-based threshold concepts may be associated with an individuals' preparedness to sit the exam. While the work here suggests relatively little difference in the distribution of previously acquired threshold concepts between students who have large 'outside commitments' and those who report that university study is a high priority, there is still a group of students whose acquisition of threshold concepts varies greatly from others. Students identified as 'at risk' in previous studies; those with high scores on poor learning processes or who have high levels of economic misconceptions or who have not studied economics previously and for whom English is a second language also demonstrate a markedly different distribution of previously acquired threshold concepts relative to other 'not at risk students'. [19]

We conclude that in the case of factors associated with attrition, variation in students' prior acquisition of threshold concepts is likely to be of 'second order' importance to variation in students' prior belief in themselves as university student learners. We conjecture that self-identification as a university learner will be fundamental to all students in all university disciplines before issues of discipline-specific threshold concepts. Nonetheless, the distribution of previously acquired threshold concepts does appear to be systematically related to other differences that place students at risk of failing.

These conclusions from this exploratory study are based on quite crude measurement instruments; much more work needs to be done to refine these. In particular, efforts to detect and measure variation in discipline-specific threshold concepts are in their infancy. Similarly, efforts to examine the association between threshold concepts and learning processes have not been explored to any extent. Our work suggests that efforts to detect whether students have crossed various portals of self identification as learners will also repay future research.

ACKNOWLEDGMENTS

The authors would like to thank Ken Adams, Matt Giro, and George Bredon for their assistance in this project.

NOTES

[1] As a further consideration, it may be argued that what is also required is an ontological shift to viewing oneself as a student learner of economics, rather than just as a university student learner. This issue cannot be explored properly in this chapter, as the students under review were majoring in a number of discipline areas, including accounting, marketing, management and commercial law. It is an area for future research.

[2] There is an extensive literature on attrition. For a summary of recent Australian studies see McMillan (2005) and Marks (2007). For older but insightful reviews on attrition by 'nontraditional' students see Bean and Metzner (1985), and more generally Evans (1999).

[3] For a recent Australian study that considers variations in attrition by discipline area, see Danaher et al (2008). One that considers in part, variation in student motivation is Dancer and Fiebig (2004).

[4] We interpret the estimates from our linear probability models as marginal probabilities of leaving the course in response to changes in each independent variable, conditional on all other variables in the regression remaining unchanged.

[5] Such a finding also begs the question whether differences would have been detected if different threshold concepts (such as those related to learning more generally) had been examined.

[6] While the majority of students are located in Adelaide, the university also has campuses in Whyalla (250 km north of Adelaide) and Mt Gambier (400 km south-east of Adelaide. It also has students in Hong-Kong, Singapore and Malaysia. All students in this study were located in Adelaide.

[7] Part-time students may take as few as one course. Students may also elect to take 'non-core' courses in their first semester, generally from other divisions (e.g. maths or computing). Thus not all full-time students will take four core courses in their first semester.

[8] Although this course is taken by most students in their first semester (February to July), they may also undertake the course in semester two (August to November), depending on their individual timetable.

[9] The course introduces a number of basic economic concepts and models such as opportunity cost; supply and demand; equilibrium; elasticity; markets; perfect competition; the theory of the firm; imperfect competition, including monopoly, oligopoly, monopolistic competition; regulation; externalities; and the economic role of government. Actual delivery of the course to internal students consists of two hours of lectures and a weekly 1.5 hour tutorial. Given the overall class numbers, group work is used in tutorials, with the total number of students per tutorial around 25. There are several pieces of assessment including individualised learning exercises at the beginning and end of the course, an individual written assignment and in-tutorial questionnaires together with a final, closed-book examination.

[10] The report is available on request from the authors.

[11] The survey of students was taken during the weekly lecture.

[12] See Meyer and Shanahan (2003) and Shanahan and Meyer (2001) for further details.

[13] While multiple-choice questions may be considered to produce only 'crude' indicators of an individual's grasp of a threshold concept, they have several practical and theoretical advantages that make them eminently suitable for this task. See Buckles and Siegfried (2006) and Shanahan, Foster and Meyer (2006) for a discussion.

[14] The individual questions were a combination of purpose-written questions (some based on ideas from the Embedding Threshold Concepts project at the Institute for Education Policy Research at Staffordshire University), and questions taken from the United States-based Test of Economic Literacy. The spread of conceptual elements covered in these questions, their mapping into the three categories suggested by Davies and Mangan and examples of the questions are provided in Shanahan, Foster and Meyer (2006). See also Table 1.

[15] The observations in this section are taken from a University of South Australia report on attrition. It is available on request from the authors.

[16] Students who left one or more courses were followed-up and asked why they left. Eighty-two responses were obtained. The top two reasons for attrition, both of which attracted an average rating above 3 on the 1 to 5 scale of importance, were associated with problems managing the work required at university.

[17] These data were collected separately within the microeconomics course as part of students' assessment. As all microeconomic students were included, the number of observations is higher than for the attrition survey.

[18] Two distributions were also compared that grouped students as those for whom English is a second language verses all others; and students for whom English is a second language and who held economic misconceptions compared to all others.

[19] As demonstrated in Meyer and Shanahan (2001), whether a student holds economic misconceptions is only weakly correlated to whether they have or have not received prior formal training in economics (i.e. at school).

REFERENCES

Bean, J. P., & Metzner, B. S. (1985). A conceptual model of non traditional undergraduate student attrition. *Review of Educational Research, 55*(4), 485–540.

Buckles, S., & Siegfried, J. J. (2006, Winter). Using multiple-choice questions to evaluate in-depth learning of economics. *The Journal of Economic Education, 31*(1), 48–57.

Dancer, D. M., & Fiebig, D. G. (2004). *Modelling students at risk*. Department of Econometrics working paper, University of Sydney, NSW, Australia.

Davies, P. (2006). Threshold concepts: How can we recognise them? In J. H. F. Meyer & R. Land (Eds.), *Overcoming barriers to student understanding. Threshold concepts and troublesome knowledge* (pp. 70–84). London: Routledge.

Davies, P., & Mangan, J. (2005). *Recognising threshold concepts: An exploration of different approaches*. Paper presented at the European Association in Learning and Instruction Conference (EARLI) August 23–27th, Nicosia, Cyprus.

Davies, P., & Mangan, J. (2007). Threshold concepts and the integration of understanding in economics. *Studies in Higher Education, 32*(6), 711–726.

Evans, M. (1999). *School-leavers' transition to tertiary study: A literature review*. Department of Econometrics and Business Statistics, Monash University Working Paper. Victoria, Australia.

Marks, G. N. (2007). *Completing University: Characteristics and outcomes of completing and Non-completing students longitudinal studies of Australian youth*. Report 51, Australian Council for Educational Research, Victoria, Australia.

McMillan, J. (2005). *Course change and attrition from Higher Education, Longitudinal Studies of Australian Youth*. Report 39, Australian Council for Educational Research, Victoria, Australia.

Meyer, J. H. F., & Land, R. (Eds.). (2006). *Overcoming barriers to student understanding: Threshold concepts and troublesome knowledge*. London: Routledge.

Meyer, J. H. F., & Shanahan, M. P. (2001). A triangulated approach to the modeling of learning outcomes in first year economics. *Higher Education Research & Development, 20*(2), 127–145.

Meyer, J. H. F., & Shanahan, M. P. (2004). Developing metalearning capacity in students — Actionable theory and practical lessons learned in first-year economics. *Innovations in Education and Teaching International* (Special issue), *41*(4), 443–458.

Shanahan, M. P., & Meyer, J. H. F. (2006). The troublesome nature of a threshold concept in economics. In J. H. F. Meyer & R. Land (Eds.), *Overcoming barriers to student understanding: Threshold concepts and troublesome knowledge* (pp. 100–114). London: Routledge.

Shanahan, M. P., Foster, G., & Meyer, J. H. F. (2006). Operationalising a threshold concept in economics: A pilot study using multiple choice questions on opportunity cost. *The International Review of Economic Education, 5*(2), 29–57.

Shanahan, M. P., Foster, G., & Meyer, J. H. F. (2008). Associations among prior acquisition of threshold concepts, learning dimensions, and examination performance in first-year economics. In R. Land, J. H. F. Meyer, & J. Smith (Eds.), *Threshold concepts within the disciplines*. Rotterdam, The Netherlands and Taipei, Taiwan: Sense Publishers.

Walstad, W. B. (1987). Measurement instruments. In W. E. Becker & W. B. Walstad (Eds.), *Econometric modelling in economic education research* (pp. 73–98). Boston: Kluwer Nijhoff.

Martin P. Shanahan
Centre for Regulation and Market Analysis
University of South Australia

Gigi Foster
Centre for Regulation and Market Analysis
University of South Australia

Jan. H.F. Meyer
University of Durham
University of South Australia

MICHAEL T. FLANAGAN, PHILIP TAYLOR AND JAN H. F. MEYER

14. COMPOUNDED THRESHOLDS IN ELECTRICAL ENGINEERING

INTRODUCTION

In the five years since Meyer and Land (2003) introduced the idea of a Threshold Concept it has been embraced by many disciplines, not only for its value in exploring difficulties in student learning but also in aiding the development of rational curricula in areas of rapidly expanding knowledge where there is a strong tendency to overload the curriculum (Cousin, 2006). Though both these aspects are highly relevant to electrical engineering there are, to date, few threshold concept studies reported for electrical engineering. This might have been anticipated as, as Entwistle and his colleagues (2005: 9) have noted, the pace of pedagogic change in the engineering disciplines, especially electrical engineering, has traditionally been slow. However, change does appear to be in the air. Two aspects of the threshold concept give rise to an expectation of an eventual more ready acceptance among the traditionally conservative, subject-centred engineering community than it usually gives to new pedagogic approaches. The above mentioned overcrowded curriculum is particularly marked in electronic and electrical engineering where there is general agreement that 'discarding what is no longer important, to make room for new material is much easier said than done' (Penfield, 2002). Cousin (2006) has suggested that a sensible curriculum development might proceed from an identification of threshold concepts thus 'enabling teachers to make refined decisions about what is fundamental to a grasp of the subject they are teaching'. Such an implementation would only ensue if individual staff were prepared to examine their own teaching practice in an unaccustomed manner. Thus more significantly she has observed that, in discussing threshold concepts, academics are asked 'to deconstruct their subject, rather than their educative practice, thus leaving them within both safe and interesting territory' (Cousin, 2007). This observation certainly resonates with one of the authors of this paper, an engineering lecturer, who found this aspect so highly attractive that it facilitated his move from engineering to pedagogic research. Atherton (2008) has already commented on the unusually high number of engineers who attended the conference leading to the publication of this book and there is an increasing flow of studies on the role of the threshold concept in the sister discipline of computer science, including studies of its teaching within electrical engineering (Mead & Gray, 2009, Flanagan & Smith, 2008, Boustedt et mult. al. 2007, Flanagan, 2009).

J. H. F. Meyer, R. Land and C. Baillie (eds.), Threshold Concepts and Transformational Learning, 227–239.

However, starting in 'safe and interesting territory' holds no promise of remaining there especially when considering potential transformations integral to the threshold concept. The outcome of a threshold concept study may not only be perturbing in a suggested radical curriculum redesign but may also, in a semi-vocational subject as interdisciplinary as electrical engineering, become enmeshed in the ever-present problems of identifying what 'electrical engineering' is and what an 'engineering student' is; embodied, if in somewhat simplified manner, in such questions as

> Where does applied physics end and electronic engineering begin?
> Are engineering graduates defined by their skills or their industry?

> Penfield (2002).

In this chapter we examine, with these issues in mind, the way in which a threshold concept in electrical engineering may come into view in a very different manner depending on whether it is introduced from the perspective of large-scale systems (power engineering) or small-scale ones (instrumentation and electronics). In a joint study between UCL (University College London) and Durham University we compare the difficulties students meet in coming to terms with *transmission lines*, one group on a telecommunication and instrumentation oriented course, the other on a power engineering course. The work is in progress but the initial study suggests the likelihood of a common *liminal space* linking two superficially disparate portals.

The Teaching of Transmission Lines

The term 'transmission line' covers a wide range of structures for transmitting either power or information from one place to another. To a power engineer a transmission line is likely to evoke a picture of overhead power lines – large diameter conductors, typically 50 to 65 mm, supported by tall lattice steel towers (pylons), designed to facilitate bulk *power* transfer over long distances at high voltages (kV) and relatively low frequencies (50 Hz). To an electronic engineer it is likely to evoke something rather more modest in size - possibly the coaxial cable running from the back of your television set to the aerial socket on your room wall – a much smaller structure transmitting *information* but at a much higher frequency (kHz to GHz) and a much lower voltage. In a joint study between UCL and Durham University two troublesome concepts, identified by both staff and students alike, arose in the teaching of transmission lines; *characteristic impedance* in coaxial cables and *reactive power* in power lines. A grasp of the latter is critical in understanding how efficient transfer of power from generators to load centres, e.g. a sub-station, is achieved. However, reactive power confounds the students' everyday concept of power – the rate of doing work. The transmission line carries real **and** reactive power. Both are important, but only real power can actually be drawn from the line and perform work – reactive power is 'trapped' in the line and cannot perform work. Controlling *reactive power* is critical in achieving efficient transfer of the real power even though it itself is both conceptually and mathematically imaginary; i.e. it is in effect a powerless power. A grasp of characteristic impedance is critical in understanding how the efficient transfer of information is achieved, e.g. in avoiding reflection along the line giving rise to a ghost image on your television or ringing in an audio system. Characteristic impedance confounds students' everyday concept of 'impedance' which they see as a more general form of resistance. The resistance of the conductor forming the cable doubles if its length is doubled; however characteristic impedance of the cable is independent of the cable's length. It is likely that it is the counter-intuitive nature of these two concepts that puts them high on students' list of problematic concepts. The difficulties encountered in attempting to grasp these two concepts may not initially appear to be closely related as they are counter-intuitive in different ways. The identification of the two counter-intuitive concepts arose from standard course evaluation procedures, i.e. course questionnaires, tutorial discussions and laboratory class observations. However the convergence of these two concepts in the way they are calculated suggested that they may be two portals to a common *postliminal* space whose recognition may be critical in teaching transmission lines. Consequently a deeper study probing the students' difficulties in these two areas has been initiated.

Studies at UCL and at Durham University

At UCL this deeper study centres on a transmission line laboratory experiment and on a revised approach to tutorial discussions. The experiment is one in which the students observe the reflection of electrical signals injected into a series of simple transmission lines of different configuration[1]. The experiment was originally designed as a classical variational approach, following Dienes (1967) but here applied to the teaching of transmission lines, with the aim of clarifying the role of characteristic impedance and the origin of reflections. This experiment was known to be failing and appeared to encourage mimicry rather than understanding, this trait becoming clearer when the relevant analytical instrument, a time domain reflectometer, was replaced by a new one in which some of the experiment's necessary calculations were performed within the new instrument's microprocessor. The deeper study involved a rewriting of the laboratory script to include questions aimed at revealing the stages at which the failing students met problems. The interrogatory role of the demonstrator was extended and the demonstrator-to-student-pair ratio greatly increased for this experiment. In an additional exercise the concept of reactive power was introduced to the students in a first year tutorial in which the five students present had not previously met the concept and who had had no lectures on transmission lines either in a communications or power engineering context. The concept was introduced by presenting them with a circuit slightly in advance of those that they were familiar with but one in which the concept of reactive power would arise when they tried to calculate the power dissipated, which is what they were asked to do. Their perplexity and discussions on how they might resolve an apparently nonsensical result were recorded. At Durham University the deeper study centres on an interactive power systems analysis (IPSA) software package. This package allows final year students to construct a section of a power network and to study how real and reactive power flows within the network. The students are asked to carry out a number of experiments over a wide range of power flow conditions. The flexibility of this package allows the lecturer to tailor the examples in order to examine more readily the source of the perplexity and frustration of the students in grasping the role of reactive power in the efficient transmission of real power.

Liminal Space

In calculating the value of either of these two parameters, characteristic impedance or reactive power, two very different physical structures, a coaxial cable and a high voltage power line, are first reduced to an identical abstract representation, an 'equivalent circuit diagram' (Figure 1).

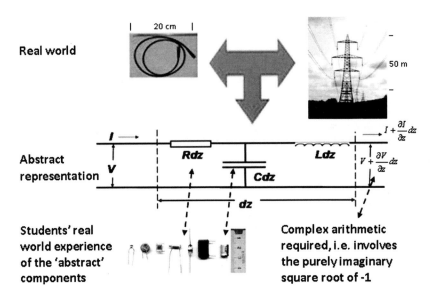

Figure 1. Representations of transmission lines.

This abstraction contains representations of several electrical components, i.e. resistors, capacitors, inductors, with which the students are familiar but in a very different form. Though the use of equivalent circuits as abstractions of complex systems is common in engineering this one is strange enough that, in a discipline in which the text books are not noted for their pedagogic asides, one text book does make an exception –

> There are also systems, such as power and telecommunication transmission lines, where it is not immediately obvious where the capacitance, inductance or resistance reside, ... they are not built using components obtained from

stores, where each component comes with a declaration of its function.... All three are mixed together and the practice of separating (lumping) each component is called into question.

Christos Christopoulos (1990)
Introduction to Applied Electromagnetism

The equivalent circuit diagram is an abstraction that facilitates the calculation of such properties of the transmission line as characteristic impedance and reactive power. Such calculations are performed in complex arithmetic involving the purely imaginary square root of minus one, a troublesome concept already discussed as a threshold concept (Meyer and Land, 2003). A large proportion of the calculations carried out by electronic and electrical engineers are much simplified by working with complex numbers – despite their intrinsic troublesome character they are a valuable 'engineering mathematical shorthand' –

the shortest and best way between two truths of the real domain often passes through the imaginary one.

French mathematician, Jacques Hadamard (1945)

This complex representation is, along with equivalent circuits, the second example of common engineering practice that may well be considered, when viewed from the students' perspective, as a form of tacit knowledge. Though both the formal procedures for drawing an equivalent circuit and for describing an 'electromagnetic field' in complex terms are undoubtedly examples of explicit knowledge and not of tacit knowledge, the reasons leading to their ubiquitous use throughout electrical engineering are less easily articulated and often are done so inadequately. Complex analysis is especially appropriate in this case as a signal travelling down a transmission line is best analysed as an *electromagnetic field*, i.e. as fluctuating electric and magnetic fields, entities that are routinely represented as complex numbers. For some students it became clear that elaborating the simpler concept of current flow down a wire into a mathematical treatment of the associated electromagnetic field was troublesome and counter-intuitive especially as the concept of the electric or magnetic field itself is troublesome. Fields may even be threshold concepts in their own right as will be considered below in the discussion of preliminal variations.

Thus we have a morass of mildly and deeply troublesome concepts; analysis of signals travelling in both time and space (some students find this juxtaposition counter-intuitive but even when they do not its mathematical representation can, to quote one student, be 'mentally awkward'), counter-intuitive abstractions with oscillation between the abstract and the concrete (Smith, 2006), calculations in complex arithmetic, electromagnetic field theory and counter-intuitive entities such as characteristic impedance or reactive power. Such a compounding suggests that we may be looking at a common liminal space in which the two counter-intuitive aspects first encountered in student questionnaires and interviews are simply different portals to understanding. The exploratory deeper study is confirming this view.

For example, the revised UCL strip line laboratory experiment identifies students failing to envisage any associated physical reality in the calculations of the properties of a travelling electromagnetic wave (the signal travelling along the line) using complex arithmetic. They resort to mimicry which may enable them to obtain the immediate intermediary value within a transmission line calculation but which will not carry them on to the next stage. This coping mechanism may well lead a student to identify as troublesome a set of issues that are peripheral to the threshold concept under consideration.

Within the Durham University IPSA package a reactive power compensator is included in the simulated network which automatically provides all of the reactive power required to facilitate significant levels of real power flow. The students examine the network over a range of power transmission conditions. The amount of reactive power required varies in relation to the amount of real power required. The presence of the compensator means that this variable reactive power requirement can easily be overlooked and a simplistic view of power transfer maintained. The students are asked to comment on the network's ability to transfer real power. The students often comment on how strong the network is and how it can transmit what seems like limitless power. The students are then asked to disconnect the reactive power compensation device. They then repeat the tests and are shocked and confused to see that the power systems ability to transfer real power has deteriorated drastically. They often think the software package has malfunctioned. They become frustrated and confused.

At this point the issue of reactive power is highlighted and the source of their frustration can be probed with the underpinning complex representation of the properties of the equivalent circuit now coming to the foreground. The responses of the UCL 'naive' first year tutorial students presented with a problem that led to them having to face a strange entity – reactive power – is instructive in the light of this discussion. They first decided that they had made a mistake in calculating the power in this 'novel' circuit. Eventually they satisfied themselves that they had not made a mistake (they had calculated it correctly). They spent even more time querying their understanding of the concept of 'power' which was correct for real power. Some frustration was now beginning to surface but nonetheless they systematically identified two areas leading to their frustration and, without resolving the issues, began to query both their own appreciation of why we use complex arithmetic in such calculations and their own understanding of what an electrical current is even in apparently simple circuits.

This exploratory study also suggests both a transformative aspect and an integrative aspect consistent with such a liminal space. In mastering the concept of reactive power or characteristic impedance students can not only handle the derivative concepts, e.g. power matching and impedance matching, but more distantly related concepts, e.g. resonance in tuned circuits, in a quite professional manner. The integrative aspect is reflected in that grasping either counter-intuitive aspect appeared to illuminate the other. Such integration in their learning matches well the common but not obvious aspect of the two apparently very different transmission lines, e.g. the characteristic impedance of a transmission line and of a device or system to which either power or information is to be transferred must be equal to ensure either efficient power transfer or reflection free information transfer.

Several students, in failing to come to terms with transmission lines at this level, demonstrated a mode of learning that is characteristic of a student mired within a liminal space, i.e. in a 'stuck place' – an extensive use of mimicry and ritual learning with a confusion of different aspects of the transmission line. Ritual learning at this level can be nicely illustrated by one student's problem in writing a computer program that modelled a simple aspect of a transmission line which involved complex arithmetic. The student had successfully completed the exercises, in his mathematics module, in manipulating complex numbers but then was perplexed when he found he had to use a special programming convention to represent a complex number, incorporating both its real and imaginary parts, and could not understand why he could not use the programming language's conventional representation of a real number.

Preliminal Variation

Meyer and Land (2005) have suggested that preliminal variation is a means of distin-guishing between variation in students' 'tacit' understanding (or lack thereof) of a threshold concept and of understanding why some students approach and manage threshold concepts while others cannot. When students enter university to study engineering their 'tacit' knowledge, acquired within their school physics course, is clearly relevant. We suggest that one such example, highly relevant to an understanding of transmission line theory, but also relevant across the electrical engineering discipline, is students' concept of a 'field' in physics; in this case the electric and the magnetic field. We would like, at this point, to give the reader a short, simple and clear definition of what a field means in physics. That we cannot is one measure of its troublesome nature. It is a concept, first introduced by Faraday, to picture and to explain the way in which objects separated in space exert a force on one another. The objects may be electrical charges (electric field), magnets (magnetic fields) or simply masses (gravitational fields). The word field itself is being used in a manner that does not readily relate to its everyday usage and engineering students may well meet two more, but different specialized meanings, of the word in their accompanying mathematics and computer science modules.

That electric and magnetic fields, or more generally *electromagnetic theory* encompassing and linking both, are problematic is indicated by the almost universal aversion to electromagnetic theory shown by engineering students, the continuing discussions of the place of electromagnetic theory in the engineering curriculum and the confusion shown by some students about devices whose basic operation cannot be fully appreciated without a grasp of the electric field. It should not be surprising that a concept that was very much a threshold concept for its originators should still be one for present day students – consider the 19th century obsession of physicists with the non-existent, invisible, all-pervasive, mass-less, solid-like support for electromagnetic waves, the 'ether'. Meyer and Land (2003) have already discussed the gravitational field as a threshold concept and much of that discussion could easily be transferred to electric or magnetic fields. Capacitors and inductors are electrical devices that store energy within their internal electric fields. Both may take quite diverse physical forms, many of which differ considerably from those first encountered in typical school physics courses, e.g. two parallel metal plates separated by an insulator. Some students immediately recognize a capacitor in a 'strange dress' but many do not. A typical example is the above discussed contrast of a transmission line and a single physical capacitor component where both the scale and structure are different, the latter corresponding to the school physics capacitor. Similarly some students do not readily identify the capacitor at the heart of a field effect transistor where the scale is more comparable but where the physical materials are very different. The importance of the teaching of these devices in the context of an electric field has been given weight by a correlation noted by one of the present authors. Those of his students who had difficulties in recognising 'unconventional capacitors' correlated well with those who continued, incorrectly, to use the 'school physics' simplified equation describing an electric field, applicable only to the uniform fields[2] typical of many school examples, long after their relevant university courses had abandoned this simplification. Electric fields are rarely uniform in engineering.

Drawing on the work of Bruner (1960) and Reigeluth and Stein (1983) we can postulate that, in some schools, the teaching of this branch of physics has failed to construct an appropriate base supporting a spiral curriculum that will facilitate the fruitful revisiting of the concepts of field and field dependent devices in the first year of a university course, i.e.

- The concrete has preceded the abstract; a circuit element presented without a fully appreciated accompanying concept of charge storage in the context of the associated electric field relationships and its consequences for current flow.
- The detailed has preceded the general; two planar metal plates and a planar insulator instead of the field relationships governing charge on a conductor or semiconductor.
- Perception is now preceding cognition; students can manipulate capacitance only in the simplest of circuit equations. They cannot extend the concept to, or recognise the concept in, a more complex situation, e.g. field effect transistors or transmission lines.

Such failures present significant difficulties for the university lecturer even if the relevant concepts are not themselves troublesome and these difficulties are likely to be even more unfortunate if they bear upon a threshold concept such as the one proposed here, i.e. an electric field.

Computer Assisted Teaching and Transmission Line Teaching

It is especially important that good pedagogic practice is followed in the above two examples of transmission lines. The teaching of both large scale power delivery systems and large scale telecommunication networks, because of their size and/or the high voltages involved, preclude students experimenting with and experiencing full scale real systems. The advent of a range of computer simulation packages in both areas offers the potential of a significant contribution to the alleviation of this problem. Such packages do, however, carry the very real risk that, though offering a taste of real systems and *enabling the student to avoid excessive manual arithmetic,* they may become *a means of avoiding understanding* (Shepstone, 2002). The propensity of students to adopt such an approach has been much discussed, e.g. ritualistic knowledge (Perkins, 1999) and the well-worked and oft-quoted deep versus shallow learning paradigm. Unfortunately many of these simulation packages were designed for research groups and their shoe-horning into courses as teaching aides may well compound an inappropriate pedagogic approach.

However, a well designed computer assisted approach may well facilitate the students' passage across a liminal space. The IPSA power system analysis software package has been quite successful in taking the students on the Durham University course through an engaging journey into a world where reactive power is a crucial element in power transfer systems.

Implications for Curriculum Development

The implications for curriculum development of this exploratory study present themselves at two levels – local considerations of the best way to teach trans-mission lines irrespective of the wider curriculum, and more global considerations of where the teaching of transmission lines should sit in our overcrowded curricula.

A local implication may be best illustrated by returning to Dienes' variability principle and the UCL strip line experiment. If a troublesome concept is flagged by students and/or staff that is, in reality, a portal to a much more complex liminal space there is a risk that a variational approach constructed around this troublesome concept alone may not effectively aide the students in mastering their difficulties. Dienes exemplified his variational approach with the teaching of the parallelogram. He suggests focusing on the properties of each geometric shape, e.g. square, rhomboid, and on transitioning from one shape to the other. In a comp-ounded threshold concept failure to identify the true nature of the liminal space may lead to the construction of variations that, extending the Dienes example, are NOT equivalent to varying the angles and the lengths of the sides of the parallelogram but simply the colour of the pen with which the parallelogram is drawn. The failure of the original strip line experiment, which superficially appears to be an excellent example of the variational approach but centred on characteristic impedance alone, would seem to support this analysis. The analysis of the threshold concept within electrical engineering presented here is less advanced than comparative analyses in e.g. economics. It is nevertheless appropriate to speculate that we may, in this example of a compounded threshold, discern a hierarchy of basic, discipline and procedural conceptual changes with which Davies and Mangan (2007) characterize the learning, by economics students, of the selection, amendment and testing of economic models.

Globally we may return to the questions Penfield (2002) addressed in his presentation to the US Accreditation Board for Engineering and Technology:
– What is an engineering degree?
– Where does applied physics end and electronic engineering begin?
– Are graduates defined by their skills or their industry?

Applied science is similar to engineering science and though a science department may, and usually does, have a different ethos to that of an engineering department the second question cannot be easily answered. Many engineering lecturers tend to assume that the correct alignment of the underpinning basic sciences with the appropriate engineering topics will ensure that this question is reduced to a tautology. Discussions on whether mathematics should be taught by the mathematics department or taught in-house by engineers, whether computer science should be taught by the computer science department or in-house, loom large in such development. However recognition of a greater complexity in answering these questions, and an appreciation of the care with which such a fragmented and interdisciplinary subject must be presented, has been emphasised by Entwistle et al. (2005: 11)

> Of course, students cannot be expected to see the long-term benefit of skills they are required to develop, so an important part of an engineering degree programme or a course unit involves explaining the relevance of the various parts, and how they contribute towards the vocational goal towards which most of the students will be looking. And simply telling students about the broad aims is not sufficient.

The third question is no more easily answered and the increasingly *multiple, unpredictable career paths* that students take can easily be underrated in such discussions. In 2006 only 31% of UK electronic and electrical engineering graduates entered careers that could be unequivocally described as engineering professional and this figure only rises to 52% if IT professional is included (Graduate Prospects, 2008). There is not even agreement amongst lecturers as to whether this is a good or a bad situation, though, anecdotally, we feel that most think it to be unfortunate.

The transmission line example presented here will probably please those who feel strongly that electrical and electronic engineering should be underpinned by a strong base in physics more so than those who advocate a rigorous systems approach. On the other hand a single example of a threshold concept alone will not carry that much weight in the often passionate discussions on what an electrical engineering degree should be. However the implications of this example do suggest that a continuation of this study and similar ones may help to define more clearly some of the issues at the heart of these discussions.

For example, the depth to which electromagnetic theory should be taught and the year in which it should be introduced are often debated but in a way that conflates the latter two Penfield questions. Both the year of introduction and the depth to which it is taught vary dramatically between departments in the UK. This variation often depends on whether the department favours a *discipline-based* [3] or *sector-based* [4] approach to curriculum design. Consequently it is only too easy for discussions on facilitating effective learning, and those on deciding whether a sector-based or discipline-based approach is appropriate, to become unnecessarily and confusingly intertwined. The analysis presented in this chapter touches significantly on electromagnetic theory and a clearer understanding of the nature of our students' difficulties, both in this and further examples, would greatly improve these debates, especially if it helped place problems of mastering difficulty, disciplinary direction and departmental ethos in a more sensible relationship.

Though, as yet, there are few studies on the possible role of the threshold concept in electrical engineering a consensus nonetheless does appear to be emerging on the nature of a common liminal space as can be seen in comparing the liminal space described in this chapter with the troublesome knowledge identified by the extensive studies of Bernhard's group (Bernhard & Carstensen, 2007; Carstensen & Bernhard, 2007). They have identified a complex concept in examining the teaching of the application of the Laplace transform[5] to the related area of circuit analysis. Their complex concept is complex both arithmetically, i.e. involves complex numbers, and in the more conventional sense of involving a complicated set of relationships. They discuss the development of an effective variational strategy. If this consensus is borne out by further studies the threshold concept will indeed play an important role in these debates.

ACKNOWLEDGEMENTS

This work is an extension of the preliminary studies first presented at the 6th Annual American Society for Engineering Education Global Symposium on Engineering Education, Istanbul, 1–4 October 2007 (Flanagan) and the 15th Improving Student Learning Symposium, Ireland, 3–5 September 2007 (Flanagan and Meyer). Mick Flanagan also thanks Jan Smith (CAPLE, University of Strathclyde) for the in-depth discussions on Jerome Bruner's spiral curriculum.

NOTES

[1] Technically the laboratory experiment transmission lines were strip lines formed by depositing strips of metal on a layer of an insulator itself layered on a metal plate. The various strips differed in their shape – rectangular, wedge shaped, decreasing or increasing gradually in width, increasing or decreasing in width sharply at a point within the line, branched lines – and in the load, i.e. in the impedance terminating the line.

[2] A uniform electric field is one that does not vary from place to place. e.g. is constant between the plates of a parallel plate capacitor.

[3] We have borrowed the term *discipline-based education* from Penfield (2002), i.e. *graduates can work in many industrial sectors — they have greater career flexibility — they can adapt to changes more easily*, but with a typical UK electrical engineering slant of a curriculum stressing the underlying principles often addressing the necessary physics in some depth.

[4] We have also borrowed the term *sector-based education* from Penfield (2002), i.e. *graduates plug right in to a company — they start a career faster*, but with a UK electrical engineering slant of a typically system oriented curriculum.

[5] The Laplace transform is a powerful mathematical tool that allows the transformation of many difficult mathematical problems into a more readily soluble form.

REFERENCES

Atherton, J. (2008). *On threshold concepts*. Retrieved September 8, 2008, from the World Wide Web http://www.doceo.co.uk/reflection/2008/06/on-threshold-concepts.

Bruner, J. (1960). *The process of education*. Cambridge, MA: Harvard University Press.

Bernhard, J., & Carstensen, A.-K. (2007, August 21–25). *Modelling and learning a complex concept – an exploration in light of some examples from electric circuit theory*. Paper presented at *ESERA2007*, Malmö. Retrieved February 12, 2009, from the World Wide Web http://staffwww. itn.liu.se/~jonbe/fou/didaktik/papers/ESERA2007_Bernhard.pdf

Boustedt, J., Eckerdal, A., McCartney, R., Moström, J. E., Ratcliff, M., Sanders, K., et al. (2007). Threshold concepts in computer science: Do they exist and are they useful? *ACM SIGCSE Bulletin, 39*, 504–508.

Carstensen, A.-K., & Bernhard, J. (2007). Threshold concepts and keys to the portal of understanding: Some examples from electrical engineering. In R. Land, J. H. F. Meyer, & J. Smith (Eds.), *Threshold concepts within the disciplines* (pp. 143–154). Rotterdam, The Netherlands: Sense Publishers.

Christopoulos, C. (1990). *Introduction to applied electromagnetism*. Chichester and New York: John Wiley and Sons.

Cousin, G. (2006, December). An introduction to threshold concepts. *Planet*, No. 17. Retrieved September 1, 2008, from the World Wide Web: http://www.gees.ac.uk/planet/p17/gc.pdf

Cousin, G. (2007). *Exploring threshold concepts for linking teaching and research*. Paper presented to the International Colloquium: International Policies and Practices for Academic Enquiry, Winchester, April. Retrieved September 1, 2008, from the World Wide Web http://portal live.solent.ac.uk/university/ rtconference/2007/resources/glynis_cousins.pdf

Davies, P., & Mangan, J. (2007). Threshold concepts and the integration of understanding in economics. *Studies in Higher Education, 32*(6), 711–726.

Dienes, Z. P. (1967). *Building up mathematics* (Rev. ed.). Education Ltd. London: Hutchinson Education Ltd.

Entwistle, N., Nisbet, J., & Bromage, A. (2005, December). Electronic Engineering. *ETL Project, Subject Overview Report*. Retrieved February 7, 2009, from the World Wide Web http://www.etl.tla. ed.ac.uk//docs/EngineeringSR.pdf

Flanagan, M. T. (2009). *Threshold concepts and undergraduate teaching: A short introduction and reference list*. Retrieved February 7, 2009, from the World Wide Web: http://www.ee.ucl.ac.uk/~ mflanaga/thresholds.html

Flanagan, M. T., & Smith, J. (2008). From playing to understanding: The transformative potential of discourse versus syntax in learning to program. In R. Land, J. H. F. Meyer, & J. Smith (Eds.), *Threshold concepts within the disciplines* (pp. 91–104). Rotterdam, The Netherlands: Sense Publishers.

Graduate Prospects. (2008). *Electrical and electronic engineering - 2006 graduates*. Retrieved September 1, 2008, from the World Wide Web: http://www.prospects.ac.uk/cms/ShowPage/Home_page/What_ do_graduates_do__2008/charts_and_tables_pages/p!eaLjjjF?subject_id=11

Hadamard, J. (1945). *An essay on the psychology of invention in the Mathematical field*. Princeton, NJ: Princeton University Press.

Mead, J., & Gray, S. (2009). Contexts for threshold concepts I: A conceptual structure for localizing candidates. In J. H. F. Meyer, R. Land, & C. Baillie (Eds.), *Threshold concepts and transformational learning* (pp. 97–113). Rotterdam, The Netherlands: Sense Publishers. [this book!]

Meyer, J. H. F., & Land, R. (2003). Threshold concepts and troublesome knowledge: Linkages to ways of thinking and practising. In C. Rust (Ed.), *Improving student learning – ten years on*. Oxford, UK: OCSLD.

Meyer, J. H. F., & Land, R. (2005). Threshold concepts and troublesome knowledge (2): Epistemological considerations and a conceptual framework for teaching and learning. *Higher Education, 49*, 373–388.

Penfield, P., Jr. (2002, March 16). What is a discipline? *Presentation to the US Accreditation Board for Engineering and Technology (ABET) Board of Directors*. Baltimore, MD. Retrieved September 1, 2008, from the World Wide Web http://www-mtl.mit.edu/~penfield/pubs/abet-02.html

Perkins, D. (1999). The many faces of constructivism. *Educational Leadership, 57*, 6–11.

Reigeluth, C., & Stein, F. (1983). The elaboration theory of instruction. In C. Reigeluth (Ed.), *Instructional design theories and models*. Hillsdale, NJ: Erlbaum Associates.

Shepstone, N. M. (2002). Teaching power systems using computer simulations. *International Journal of Electrical Engineering Education, 40*, 72–78.

Smith, J. (2006, June 8–9). Lost in translation: Staff and students negotiating liminal spaces. *SEDA Spring Conference 2006: Advancing Evidence-Informed Practice in HE Learning, Teaching and Educational Development*.

Michael T. Flanagan
Department of Electronic and Electrical Engineering
UCL (University College London)
Torrington Place
London
WC1E 7JE
United Kingdom

Philip Taylor
School of Engineering
Durham University
South Road
Durham
DH1 3LE
United Kingdom

Jan H. F. Meyer
Centre for Learning, Teaching and Research in Higher Education
School of Education
Durham University
Leazes Road
Durham DH1 1TA
United Kingdom

LYNDA THOMAS, JONAS BOUSTEDT,
ANNA ECKERDAL, ROBERT MCCARTNEY, JAN ERIK MOSTRÖM,
KATE SANDERS AND CAROL ZANDER

15. THRESHOLD CONCEPTS IN COMPUTER SCIENCE:

An Ongoing Empirical Investigation

INTRODUCTION

Computer science is a complex, technical, and rapidly changing field. One of the challenges that this offers to educators is how to structure courses when much of the content is continually changing. A possible solution to this problem is through the use of threshold concepts (Meyer and Land, 2003; 2005), which could be used to organise and focus the educational process. For this to be successful requires that we identify and characterise the threshold concepts that computing students learn, and how they fit in with the other concepts that are part of a computing degree program.

This chapter describes an ongoing multi-national, multi-institutional project aimed at empirically identifying threshold concepts in Computer Science, and describing students' experiences of learning these concepts. The project has collected and analyzed data from students and educators in Europe and North America. In doing so it has identified some threshold concepts in computing, and characterised aspects of the learning experience associated with these concepts. These results are based on a number of different data collection and analysis approaches that focus on different aspects of threshold concepts.

In the next section, we present a temporal overview of the work in terms of our evolving research questions. In subsequent sections we describe individual aspects of the work: the research questions, the techniques used to gather and analyze data, and the results. We then provide some general observations of the study and its methods, followed by a discussion of some relevant related work. Finally, we present our conclusions to date and the future directions of this research effort.

OVERVIEW OF OUR RESEARCH

We have been empirically investigating threshold concepts in Computer Science since 2005. As the work has progressed, our research questions and data collection methods have evolved based on previous results and observations. An overview of our efforts to date is given in Table 1.

J. H. F. Meyer, R. Land and C. Baillie (eds.), Threshold Concepts and
Transformational Learning, 241–257.

Table 1. Research foci, questions, and data analysed

Phase	Focus	Main Research Questions	Data Collection
1	Threshold concepts in general	– What are the threshold concepts in computing according to instructors? – What threshold concepts in computing are suggested by the literature?	Informal interviews (instructors), Literature review
2	Threshold concepts in general; Troublesome	– What are the threshold concepts in computing according to students? – What strategies do students use to get unstuck?	Semi-structured interviews (students)
3	Liminality	– Is the 'liminal space' a useful metaphor in aiding our understanding of the conceptual transformation students undergo in learning computing?	Semi-structured interviews (students)
4	Integration	– How do students who have recently learned about object-oriented programming express the relationships among those concepts? – What do those students see as the most important concepts in object-oriented programming?	Concept maps drawn by beginning programming students
5	Transformation	– What concepts and experiences transform the way students view computing? – How is abstraction manifested in students' transformative experiences?	Student biographies

The first phase of the research looked for threshold concepts in computer science as seen by instructors; indirectly through review of the computing curriculum literature, and directly by interviewing and surveying computing instructors. Both the literature review and the interviews were organised around characteristics of threshold concepts as defined in Meyer and Land (2003): transformational, irreversible, integrative, and troublesome. The results suggested some changes in approach: more formal data collection, and a greater emphasis on student rather than instructor experience.

In the second phase, we revisited the "What are the threshold concepts?" question by interviewing students nearing graduation from computing programs. These interviews allowed us to identify two threshold concepts, object-orientation and pointers. While we looked at the same characteristics as in phase 1, the student focus was generally on troublesome, and on the experience of being stuck and getting beyond that. The second research question – What strategies do students use to become unstuck? – followed from this particular focus in the interviews.

In the third phase, we looked more closely at the notion of liminality. As suggested by Meyer and Land (2005), difficulty in attaining concepts may leave students in a suspended state of partial understanding. By re-analyzing the student interview data on object-orientation and pointers with respect to liminality, we verified that many of these liminal space characteristics are experienced by students learning threshold concepts.

In the fourth phase, we changed our data-collection techniques, using concept maps to explore the integrative characteristics of a threshold concept, object-orientation. These data also provided a way to evaluate students' understanding of the central ideas of object-orientation – and what they themselves see as central.

In the fifth phase, we used student biographies to shed more light on the transformative aspect of threshold concepts. By focusing on transformation, we have identified a number of other potential thresholds that were not discussed in the semi-structured interviews in phase 2. Many of the concepts thus identified are related to abstraction, a central theme in computing, and provide insights into how the overall concept of abstraction is manifested in students' learning.

The research evolved: what we learned in each phase led to more questions and different data collection and analysis. In the following sections, we examine these phases in more detail.

PHASE 1: PRELIMINARY INVESTIGATION

The first part of this study addressed a simple research question:

– What are the threshold concepts in computing (if any)?

This question was approached in two ways: by interviewing (or surveying) computing educators and asking them for threshold concepts based on their experience, and by looking for likely candidates in the computing education literature.

Preliminary Investigation: Data collection

We started Phase 1 with unstructured interviews and questionnaires to educators at two international conferences on computer science education. In the interviews we gave the five criteria for threshold concepts to 36 instructors, and asked them if they could name any such concepts. The interviews were performed by two researchers: one asking questions, the other taking notes. The notes were transcribed for analysis. The questionnaires (5 responses) were similar: they gave the threshold concept characteristics and asked the respondent to identify concepts that meet these characteristics.

Preliminary Investigation: Results

In 36 interviews, the instructors suggested 33 possible threshold concepts. While some concepts came up multiple times (for example abstraction, object-orientation, and recursion), there was no universal consensus on topics. Most participants found the idea of threshold concepts interesting.

Although this work suggested a number of areas for further study, the data were not directly usable. First, the interview data were notes, not transcriptions, so a lot of detail and rationale was lost. Second, the instructors tended to focus on topics that they saw as difficult for students to learn, and said little about the other threshold concept characteristics. The surveys collected from instructors were consistent with this focus. More details about this phase of the work are given in Zander et al, 2008.

The literature survey suggested two threshold concepts, object-orientation and abstraction, as well as positioning threshold concepts within a number of other educational traditions in computer science; see Eckerdal et al. (2006) for details.

PHASE 2 THRESHOLD / TROUBLESOME CONCEPTS

In the second phase of the study, we investigated threshold concepts from the students' perspective using interviews. The research question investigated was
  – What are the threshold concepts in computing?

As these interviews discussed concepts where students were originally "stuck" before learning, there was a good deal of discussion about "getting unstuck". This led to an additional research question:
  – What strategies do students use to get unstuck?

Threshold / Troublesome Concepts: Data Collection

We completed 16 semi-structured interviews (Kvale, 1996) with students at 7 institutions in a total of 3 countries, ranging from 20 minutes to over an hour long. In these interviews, we began by asking the students to talk about a concept they had been stuck on before learning (troublesome), then continued discussing whether the transformative, integrative, and irreversible criteria were also met for that concept. These interviews were recorded and transcribed, and translated to English if necessary.

Threshold/Troublesome Concepts: Results

The analysis of these interviews provided evidence that threshold concepts exist in computer science. Specifically, by demonstrating the transformative, integrative, irreversible and troublesome characteristics, they suggested that object-oriented programming and pointers were threshold concepts (Boustedt et al., 2007, Zander et al., 2008). The analysis of the second question led to a rich categorization of strategies that students used successfully (McCartney et al., 2007) to get unstuck.

PHASE 3: LIMINALITY

Through the semi-structured interviews we also investigated the metaphor of "liminal space". Was it useful in aiding our understanding of the conceptual transformation students undergo in learning computing? Meyer and Land (2005) list the following defining characteristics of people in the liminal space: they are being transformed, acquiring new knowledge and acquiring a new status and identity within the community. The process of being in this liminal space takes time; may involve oscillation between old and new states; involves emotions, of anticipation, but also of difficulty and anxiety; and may involve mimicry of the new state.

We looked for evidence of the different features of a liminal space given in this definition. It follows from the definition of a threshold concept that by learning it, the student is being transformed and acquiring new knowledge. Because threshold concepts are core concepts within a discipline, students learning them can also be said to be acquiring a new identity - that of an insider, someone who understands the central ideas of a field. We focused, therefore, on the remaining aspects of the definition of a liminal space, looking for answers to the following questions in our interviews:

- Does the process of learning threshold concepts take time?
- Do the students appear to oscillate between the old and new states (i.e., not understanding and understanding)?
- What emotional reactions do students express?
- Does the process of learning threshold concepts involve mimicry?

The data also led us to formulate some questions that are not explicitly addressed by Meyer and Land, but notwithstanding seem to be important for a rich description of the learning of the threshold concepts studied.

- What kinds of partial understandings do students possess within the liminal space?
- Do students know that they have crossed a threshold, and if so, how?

Liminality: Results

In the structured interviews conducted with graduating students, the students described the features that define liminal space according to Meyer and Land.

Time: Many students mentioned a prolonged time in the liminal space. Across the board, the time to gain understanding was lengthy. In addition to having spent time learning the concepts, they also demonstrated understanding that the prolonged process was necessary for learning.

> Subject 13: I think there was definitely a point where I definitely got the understanding, whether I was still confident in doing it, that probably took a lot of time.

Oscillation: Students also discussed oscillation in their learning. They describe the nature of going back and forth between knowing and not knowing, thinking that they know it, but realizing they're not quite there:

> Subject 4: It was clear to me, it just seemed like while I was in the thick of it I would forget. I spent a lot of time lost in the - it was that forest for the trees. I don't know. Lost in the jungle.

Emotion: Meyer and Land refer to the liminal space as "problematic, troubling, and frequently involv[ing] the humbling of the participant." (Meyer and Land, 2005) They also warn that students may experience "difficulty and anxiety" in relation to learning threshold concepts. We examined our student quotes from this perspective, to see if we could find evidence of emotionally laden terms. Students frequently mentioned that they found that learning threshold concepts was frustrating:

> Subject 3: Felt? I think I felt frustrated. My thoughts were that I didn't understand why we needed pointers when references worked perfectly well beforehand.

Others referred to feelings of depression:

> Subject 13: During ... well if I found it difficult then I would probably mope slightly for a while and then got down to it.

There was evidence of students feeling humbled:

> Subject 2: Another thing that was very frustrating. I'm usually quick to understand things.

Mimicry: During the interviews some of the students mentioned that in beginning to learn a subject they "imitated" someone or some existing code. Subject 9 discusses starting object-oriented programming:

> Subject 9: And then ... when ... to learn something from an example, for example, it had to be exactly almost the same example as the thing you are trying to solve. You are trying to find exactly the information how to solve this problem in the textbook always search in the textbook.

Partial Understanding: Some of the more interesting findings in this phase of the research related to students' partial understandings of concepts. We saw a number of common themes emerge. Students identify a number of different sorts of understanding including abstraction of the concept, concrete implementation of the concept, and the ability to go back and forth between the two. The observed understandings could be placed into these general categories:
– An abstract (or theoretical) understanding of a concept;
– A concrete understanding—the ability to write a computer program illustrating the concept—without having the abstract understanding;
– The ability to go from an understanding of the abstract concept to software design or concrete implementation;
– An understanding of the rationale for learning and using the concept; and
– An understanding of how to apply the concept to new problems—problems beyond those given as homework or lab exercises.

As Subject 2 says:

> Subject 2: You understand how a theory works but how do you take that theory and how it works and apply it to a practical sense? I think that is one of the hardest leaps to make.

For more details on this part of the work, see (Eckerdal et al., 2007).

PHASE 4: INTEGRATION AND OBJECT-ORIENTATION

Students' interviews had led us to identify "object-oriented programming" as a potential threshold concept. But this term covers a wide range of sub-concepts, and raises questions of granularity. In this phase of the research we examined novice students' understandings of the main object-oriented concepts by asking them to draw concept maps. Specifically we were looking at three questions:
– What do students who have recently learned about object-oriented programming see as the most important OO concepts?
– How do they express the relationships among those concepts?
– Do student concept maps show the integrative nature of object-orientation?

Integration and Object-orientation: Data Collection

Concept maps are based on the theory "that people think with concepts and that concept maps serve to externalise these concepts and improve their thinking." (Novak and Gowin, 1984, p. 2]) They have been used to help students learn, to

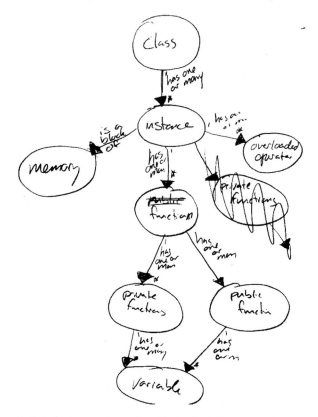

Figure 1. A student concept map for object-oriented programming concepts.

gain a static picture of what they know, and to measure changes in student understanding (Ferguson, 2003; Nash et al, 2006; Steyvers and Tenenbaum, 2005). The concept maps were used in order to focus on what concepts within the larger category of object-oriented programming students might be finding the most challenging.

Each participant was given the following task:

Put the concept map here that starts with the two concepts "class" and "instance" with labelled arrows and other concepts that creates a partial map of object-oriented programming, as you have learned it so far.

Included with the task was a sample concept map that included the concepts "kitchen", "dinner", and a number of meal-related concepts.

Data were collected during the 2006–2007 academic year at six institutions in three countries. We collected maps from 107 participants. The participants included 71 novices, 12 intermediate students, 15 graduating students, and 9 instructors. We have so far focused our analysis on the 71 novice maps.

Integration and Object-orientation: Results

Our analysis produced quantitative results having to do with graph topologies and frequencies of nodes, edges, and node-edge-node combinations. Structural features such as these may provide insights to the overall knowledge organization. Additionally, we examined qualitative details – whether concepts were implicitly present in a map, how groups of various related concepts are linked, and so forth.

Table 2 shows the frequencies of concepts given in (Armstrong, 2006), a list of nine concepts that most commonly occur in the object-oriented programming literature; all of these concepts had been covered in class before the students did the maps. As *Class* and *Instance* were specified in the assignment they would be expected to be in all maps; *Method* was also present in nearly all of the maps. Few students included concepts like *Encapsulation, Polymorphism, Abstraction,* or *Message Passing.*

Table 2. Number and percent of concept maps showing concepts from (Armstrong, 2006), explicitly in node or edge name, or implicit in map structure

Concept found	Explicit (no. maps)	Implicit (no. maps)	Percentage
Class	71	-	100%
Instance	67	0	94%
Method	63	4	94%
Object	34	0	48%
Inheritance	23	13	51%
Encapsulation	2	16	25%
Polymorphism	1	0	7%
Abstraction	1	-	2%
Message Passing	0	0	0%

The relationships between concepts were expressed by the labelled edges. Overall, 36% of the edges were unlabeled, indicating a poor understanding of these relationships. Additionally, the labels used suggest that many students do not fully understand the meaning of essential concepts like class, object, and instance.

In previous phases, we identified object-orientated programming as a threshold concept, and students expressed how it integrated other concepts. In these maps we looked for links to a broader context as evidence of this integration, specifically interaction between the program and other software or hardware, interaction between the program and potential users, or connection between the program and the real world. We observed such "integration" in about 35% of the maps, which were generally focussed quite narrowly on programming.

More details regarding this phase are reported in (Sanders et al. 2008).

PHASE 5: TRANSFORMATION AND ABSTRACTION

In this phase, we focused on the transformative aspect of threshold concepts, because that is arguably the most important criterion, and it had been given little attention by the students in our semi-structured interviews. The research question was:
– What do students describe as their transformative computing experiences?

As we analysed the data, we found that many of the topics discussed by the students were related to various kinds of abstraction. Abstraction is frequently used by instructors when discussing core concepts in computing, and it was proposed as a threshold concept by instructors in phase 1. This led us to address these questions as well:
– How is abstraction manifested in students' transformative experiences?
– Is abstraction a threshold concept in computing?

Transformation and Abstraction: Data Collection

Data were collected as "transformation biographies" from computing students – the data are written documents submitted by the students that describe their experiences in some context. Schulte and Knoblesdorf (2007) explain how using biographical research explores how individuals interpret their experiences in retrospect, adding their attitudes and opinions.

The students were asked to identify and describe a computing concept that transformed the way they see and experience computing. Like Schulte and Knoblesdorf, we used "lure stories" as a way to focus the structure of the student biographies: included in the instructions were two sample transformation biographies – one about modularity, another about abstraction. (The questions and sample biographies are given in Moström et al, 2008.) These data were collected from 86 students from 5 institutions in 3 different countries. The student biographies, where necessary, were translated into English by the researcher. Nearly all of these were collected as a regular assignment associated with a course taken by computing majors in the second half of their computing degree programs. The majority of the biographies (75 of 86) were collected at two institutions in different countries.

Transformation and Abstraction: Results

The biographies mentioned many different topics as having led to a transformation. The overall analysis of the first (and most general) research question has not been completed. We have some partial results, however, based on those biographies that dealt with concepts that relate to abstraction – the topic of the other two research questions.

Preliminary analysis of the 86 biographies identified 47 that involved concepts related to abstraction. Abstraction was manifest in several ways, including modularity, data abstraction, object-orientation, code reuse, design patterns, and complexity.

Modularity: Twelve of the biographies referred in one way or another to code modularization. They typically referred to the students' old practice of writing long linear code, usually in one single file, and contrast this with code arranged into modules.

Subject 18: The new realisation for me was that a programming problem could be broken up into classes all containing relevant code to that class.

The biographies make it clear that the ability to abstract code into larger chunks, whether modules or classes, is an important part of learning to program. Without this ability, programming is a daunting task.

Data Abstraction involves the aggregation of related data items into logical structures, with access allowed through defined operations. It allows the programmer to use the structure without knowing the details of its implementation. Judging from the biographies it seems that when they were novices some students assumed that they were required to manage each piece of information separately.

Subject 28: Object reuse and grouping relevant and coherent pieces of data or variables together was now really helping my understanding of many things in computing.

Object-orientation is an approach to designing and implementing programs that includes encapsulation of data and function into objects. The functionality of each object is defined by its class, and classes are hierarchically related using inheritance.

In many of the biographies, students mentioned object-orientation but then discussed a concept that is not exclusive to that paradigm, such as modularity, data abstraction, or functional decomposition. In other biographies, however, when the students discussed object-orientation, the transformative aspects discussed were essential components of object-orientation: ten students discussed inheritance and polymorphism, and one discussed encapsulation.

Code Reuse: Twenty-one of the biographies mentioned code reuse, the ability to extract parts of earlier programs and use them as components in new programs. Frequently, this was in a simple list that described the advantages of object-orientation and/or modularity, and in these instances it was not always clear whether the students were simply echoing standard wisdom. Some students, however, discussed reuse further and displayed a clear understanding. For example, for Subject 27, reuse was tied to reusing parts of his or her own code:

Subject 27: Writing code in methods allowed me to reuse methods in other programs...

While other students discussed reusing code written by other people. Subject 32, for instance, shows a deeper level of understanding in a biography entitled "Libraries":

Subject 32: I found I was able to achieve a lot more with the software I was writing allowing me to focus on higher level concepts.

Design Patterns are ways to specify solutions to common design problems in a discipline, including a specification of the problem and the context in which the solution can be applied. Originally used in architecture (Alexander et al. 1977), these were popularised in computer science by (Gamma et al. 1995). Ten students expressed experiences related to software modelling; six used the term "pattern" explicitly. Two specific design patterns were discussed: Factory and Model-View-Control. High cohesion and low coupling were mentioned as separate principles. Some students focused on the principle of programming to an interface and how the use of models, such as UML diagrams, helped them to understand complicated large-scale systems. The evidence suggests that the essence of design patterns is often deep, subtle and not very easy to understand at first. Some students had to make these abstractions meaningful by using the patterns in concrete programs, before they could understand them. For example, Subject 22 thought design patterns were pointless and useless when first confronted with them, but after using them changed his or her attitude:

Subject 22: When design patterns were introduced I didn't really see the point in them, they seemed very abstract and not very useful. ... After trying to use them I discovered that they were useful and they provided your code with more structure and help keep your code loosely coupled rather than everything being tightly linked together.

Complexity: Asymptotic time complexity abstracts away the details from algorithms, placing them in groups based on how fast they would run on an idealised computer. Three of the biographies discussed time complexity or "big-Oh" analysis in their biographies. When they did, they referred to it as one aspect of programming they now take into consideration. Part of the changed perspective here is realizing that algorithmic changes can have a larger effect than increasing the speed of the underlying hardware.

Finally, with regard to the third research question, whether abstraction is a threshold concept; contrary to expectation, it seems unlikely. Rather, it seems likely that there are a number of threshold concepts in computing that could be classified as abstractions of one form or another. These specific concepts (the ones above, for instance) were described as transformative, and it is likely that they also exhibit the other threshold concept characteristics.

Results from this investigation are reported in greater detail in (Moström et al., 2008).

DISCUSSION

In looking at this project as a whole, we can make some general observations:

Using different data-collection techniques affected our results.
- The informal interviews worked well as a way to collect hypotheses, sort of like brainstorming. Since they were done in an informal setting, and not recorded and transcribed, they were not particularly useful beyond that.
- The semi-structured interviews provided rich, detailed data. The order of questions, however, introduces a particular focus, which could be positive or negative. They are relatively hard to collect and analyze, requiring a lot of effort from the interviewer, the subjects, and the researchers doing the analysis.
- The concept maps also provided rich data, good for seeing how people relate various concepts. We found it difficult to get a global view, however. We saw less integration than expected, but that may have been an artefact of the way we asked the question – unlike interviews, there were no follow-up questions.
- The biographies with lure stories were n effective way to collect a large amount of data, focussed as desired, with a reasonable structure to analyze. The ability to collect more data means there is more to analyze, however, and the lack of follow-up questions (as with the concept maps) means that answers may be relatively shallow and ambiguous. The lure stories have the potential to bias the results.

Using a combination of approaches has allowed us to vary our focus and triangulate across data sources, across groups of students, and across modes of analysis.

There is a lot of individual variability in student experience. Whether or not students experience different thresholds, they place greater significance on different transformations. We observed many potential threshold concepts on a single occasion only; we observed some that seemed highly dependent on a particular context. Coming up with an exhaustive "catalogue" of threshold concepts in a discipline may be impractical. More important, the sequences of partial understandings that students exhibited as they were learning a concept were quite variable: no single path. Rather than seeing a progression of deeper understandings in a concept, we saw different levels of understandings of different parts.

Students seem to describe more specific thresholds than instructors: Faculty interviews in Phase 1 suggested abstraction (in general) as a threshold concept, but students describe particular examples of abstraction. It may be that instructors naturally try to view the bigger picture, abstracting away from the real thresholds. This is likely a problem in any discipline that has concepts, or themes, that apply throughout the discipline.

Rich data may afford opportunities for other useful questions. We started out with straightforward research questions, and collected data to answer them. What we found, however, was that the data suggested other questions and analyses as well. Looking at stuck places led to a categorization of how students get unstuck, and an examination of liminal spaces. Looking at concept maps (for integration) led to a richer understanding of student understanding of object-oriented programming.

RELATED WORK

There are a number of papers about threshold concepts in computing that relate to this study. Flanagan and Smith (2008) divide programming thresholds into two kinds: (1) localised threshold concepts, e.g. Java interfaces, and (2) the programming language itself as a threshold. Their focus is on "operationally challenged students" for whom the programming language itself is troublesome. These students are generally motivated, highly qualified and successful in other subjects. The authors apply theory and terminology from linguistics and identify "markedness" of logically related oppositional attribute pairs in Java, e.g., true/false, public/private. Asymmetric pairs may cause problems for the students, especially if one of the key words is only implied in the language, such as in the pair static/non-static. Another problem is that these students read code as if it were natural language, and as they do not understand it, they desperately need notes or templates to be able to mimic it. The authors point out debugging as another problem for such students. Long error listings filled with unfamiliar words such as exception, symbol and thread make them overwhelmingly hard to read. They conclude that the language itself needs to be addressed much more, e.g. by using language games inspired by Wittgenstein.

These results are consistent with Bonar and Soloway (1989), who attributed many student problems to mismatches between natural language and programming language, as well as our observations (Eckerdal et al., 2007) that students often had problems with the syntax of the unfamiliar programming language but not with the underlying computing concepts.

Shinners-Kennedy (2008) claims that everyday notions conceal important threshold concepts within computing, and that searching for "the big" significant concepts that really transform the computing students risks missing some of the simple and obvious ones. For instance, the notions "empty list" and "end of list" are the most troublesome parts for students when they are solving list-related problems, not the algorithms they have to formulate. *State* is another example of a concealed everyday life concept that can be very troublesome when learning CS, because in everyday life: "… we are not conscious of the fact that our next action is determined by the current state or that our actions that change the state are the critical ones." However, in programming the understanding of the concept "state" is central.

He advocates a state-based way to introduce several other related concepts, such as parameter passing and iteration. His arguments are based on his experience with students rather than empirical study. Parameter passing is one of the concepts that our student interviews identified as a particularly troublesome concept, but we have not seen "state" mentioned, possibly because it is a more abstract version of other concepts that are more natural to the students.

Mead et al. (2006) extend the notion of threshold concepts into *anchor concepts*, roughly speaking either a threshold concept or a fundamental concept in a discipline, which are arranged into *anchor graphs*, with edges from concepts to other concepts that integrate them. They suggest that part of the cognitive load in learning a threshold concept is learning the concepts that it integrates; the anchor graphs, therefore, can provide a partial ordering of concepts that minimises the student's cognitive load. This work draws upon and applies the theories of threshold concepts, fundamental ideas, and cognitive load.

While Mead et al.'s work considers other threshold concept work in computing and elsewhere, it provides no empirical evaluation. The authors' use of the term "integrates" seems to be equivalent to "has prerequisites of ", which is good justification for the cognitive load arguments, but does not exactly correspond to the meaning of integration in threshold concepts. A key question is whether these relationships between concepts hold for all students – which would make these anchor graphs very useful in planning instruction – a strong claim that would need to be empirically evaluated.

Rowbottom (2007) argues that threshold concepts cannot be investigated empirically. His major arguments are:

1. The definition is too vague, since Meyer and Land (2003) list five criteria, but indicate that none of these is essential
2. Thresholds may not be universal (i.e. the same for all students) and
3. It is impossible to know what concepts students understand.

Although Rowbottom's work concerns threshold concepts in general rather than computing, it addresses the feasibility of empirical studies such as this one. While we would agree that a hard-to-operationalise definition, variation among students, and difficulty of assessment makes empirical investigation more difficult, our experience suggests that such investigations can produce useful results.

CONCLUSIONS AND FUTURE WORK

In our study of threshold concepts in computer science, we have identified a number of threshold concepts, and characterised parts of the student experience in learning these concepts. This work is primarily empirical and qualitative, collecting and analyzing rich student data: interviews, concept maps, and biographies. The researchers and students being in Sweden, the UK, and the USA provides evidence that these results should be applicable over a fairly broad geographical scope.

Figure 2 summarizes the research to date, and the potential threshold concepts that have been identified. Examining this from the perspective of the data collected, the instructor interviews correspond to Phase 1 (Preliminary Investigation), and although they suggested some potential threshold concepts, the data are not of sufficient quality to analyze. The student interviews were used in Phase 2 (Threshold/Troublesome Concepts), and allowed us to identify Pointers and Object-orientation as threshold concepts. In Phase 3 (Liminality), those interviews were re-analyzed to characterise students' experience of liminal spaces. The concept maps were used in Phase 4 (Integration and Object-orientation) to look closer at Object-orientation and what concepts it might integrate. Finally, the student biographies were used in Phase 5 (Transformation and Abstraction) to focus on transformative experiences; that work has identified six concepts so far.

Methodologically, the research has been triangulated by studying three groups of participants – novice students, graduating students, and to some extent educators – as well as using several data gathering techniques. As these are rich data, the analysis has involved primarily qualitative techniques. The richness of the data has also allowed us to examine learning questions outside of threshold concepts.

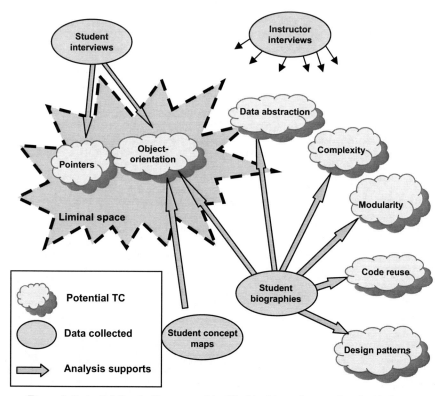

Figure 2. Potential threshold concepts identified in this study, associated with the corresponding data and analysis.

REFERENCES

Alexander, C., Ishikawa, S., & Silverstein, M. (1977). *A pattern language: Towns, buildings, construction.* Oxford University Press.

Armstrong, D. J. (2006). The quarks of object-oriented development. *Communications of the ACM, 49*(2), 123–128.

Bonar, J., & Soloway, E. (1985). Preprogramming knowledge: A major source of misconceptions in novice programmers. *Human-Computer Interaction, 1*(2), 133–161.

Boustedt, J., Eckerdal, A., McCartney, R., Moström, J. E., Ratcliffe, M., Sanders, K., et al. (2007). Threshold concepts in computer science: Do they exist and are they useful? In *Proceedings of the 38th SIGCSE Technical Symposium on Computer Science Education (SIGCSE '07)* (pp. 504–508). Covington, Kentucky, USA.

Eckerdal, A., McCartney, R., Moström, J. E., Ratcliffe, M., Sanders, K., & Zander, C. (2006). Putting threshold concepts into context in computer science education. In *Proceedings of the 11th Annual SIGCSE Conference on Innovation and Technology in Computer Science Education (ITiCSE)* (pp. 103–107). Bologna, Italy.

Eckerdal, A., McCartney, R., Moström, J. E., Sanders, K., Thomas, L., & Zander, C. (2007). From Limen to Lumen: Computing students in liminal spaces. In *Proceedings of the Third International Workshop on Computing Education Research (ICER '07)* (pp. 123–132). Atlanta, Georgia, USA.

Ferguson, E. (2003). Object-oriented concept mapping using UML class diagrams. *Computing in Small Colleges, 18*(4), 344–354.

Flanagan, M. T., & Smith, J. (2008). From playing to understanding: The transformative potential of discourse versus syntax in learning to program. In R. Land, J. H. F. Meyer, & J. Smith (Eds.), *Threshold concepts within the disciplines* (pp. 91–103). Rotterdam, The Netherlands: Sense Publishers.

Gamma, E., Helm, R., Johnson, R., & Vlissides, J. (1995). *Design patterns.* Boston: Addison-Wesley Professional.

Kvale, S. (1996). *InterViews: An introduction to qualitative research interviewing.* Thousand Oaks, CA: Sage.

Lister, R., Berglund, A., Clear, T., Bergin, J., Garvin-Doxas, K., Hanks, B., et al. (2006). Research perspectives on the objects-early debate. In *Working Group Reports on ITiCSE on innovation and Technology in Computer Science Education (ITiCSE-WGR '06)* (pp. 146–165). Bologna, Italy.

McCartney, R., Eckerdal, A., Moström, J. E., Sanders, K., & Zander, C. (2007). Successful students' strategies for getting unstuck. In *Proceedings of the 12th Annual SIGCSE Conference on innovation and Technology in Computer Science Education (ITiCSE '07)* (pp. 156–160). Dundee, Scotland.

Mead, J., Gray, S., Hamer, J., James, R., Sorva, J., Clair, C. S., et al. (2006). A cognitive approach to identifying measurable milestones for programming skill acquisition. *SIGCSE Bulletin, 38*(4), 182–194.

Meyer, J., & Land, R. (2003). Threshold concepts and troublesome knowledge: Linkages to ways of thinking and practising within the disciplines. *ETL Project Occasional Report 4.* Retrieved June 29, 2007, http://www.ed.ac.uk/etl/docs/ETLreport4.pdf

Meyer, J., & Land, R. (2005). Threshold concepts and troublesome knowledge (2): Epistemological considerations and a conceptual framework for teaching and learning. *Higher Education, 49*, 373–388.

Moström, J. E., Boustedt, J., Eckerdal, A., McCartney, R., Sanders, K., Thomas, L., et al. (2008). Concrete examples of abstraction as manifested in students' transformative experiences. In *Proceeding of the 2008 international workshop on Computing education research (ICER'08)* (pp. 125–136). Sydney, Australia.

Nash, J., Bravaco, R., & Simonson, S. (2006). Assessing knowledge change in computer science. *Computer Science Education, 16*(1), 37–51.

Novak, J., & Gowin, D. (1984). *Learning how to learn.* Cambridge, UK: Cambridge University Press.

Rowbottom, D. P. (2007). Demystifying threshold concepts. *J. Philosophy Educ., 41*(2), 263–270.

Sanders, K., Boustedt, J., Eckerdal, A., McCartney, R., Moström, J. E., Thomas, L., et al. (2008). Student understanding of object-oriented programming as expressed in concept maps. In *Proceedings of the 39th SIGCSE Technical Symposium on Computer Science Education (SIGCSE '08)* (pp. 332–336). Portland, OR, USA.

Schulte, C., & Knobelsdorf, M. (2007). Attitudes towards computer science-computing experiences as a starting point and barrier to computer science. In *Proceedings of the Third International Workshop on Computing Education Research (ICER '07)* (pp. 27–38). Atlanta, Georgia, USA.

Shinners-Kennedy, D. (2008). The everydayness of threshold concepts: State as an example from computer science. In R. Land, J. H. F. Meyer, & J. Smith (Eds.), *Threshold concepts within the disciplines* (pp. 119–128). Rotterdam, The Netherlands: Sense Publishers.

Steyvers, M., & Tenenbaum, J. (2005). Graph theoretic analyses of semantic networks: Small worlds in semantic networks. *Cognitive Science, 29,* 41–78.

Zander, C., Boustedt, J., Eckerdal, A., McCartney, R., Moström, J. E., Ratcliffe, M., et al. (2008). Threshold concepts in computer science: A Multi-national empirical investigation. In R. Land, J. H. F. Meyer, & J. Smith (Eds.), *Threshold concepts within the disciplines* (pp. 105–118). Rotterdam, The Netherlands: Sense Publishers.

Lynda Thomas
Department of Computer Science
Aberystwyth University
ltt@aber.ac.uk

Jonas Boustedt
Department of Mathematics, Natural, and Computer Science
University of Gävle
bjt@hig.se

Anna Eckerdal
Department of Information Technology
Uppsala University
Anna.Eckerdal@it.uu.se

Robert McCartney
Department of Computer Science and Engineering
University of Connecticut
robert@cse.uconn.edu

Jan Erik Moström
Department of Computing Science
Umeå University
jem@cs.umu.se

Kate Sanders
Department of Mathematics and Computer Science
Rhode Island College
ksanders@ric.edu

Carol Zander
Computing and Software Systems
University of Washington, Bothell
zander@u.washington.edu

EUN-JUNG PARK AND GREG LIGHT

16. IDENTIFYING A POTENTIAL THRESHOLD CONCEPT IN NANOSCIENCE AND TECHNOLOGY:

Engaging Theory in the Service of Practice

INTRODUCTION

Since Feynman (1959) invited us to the room at the bottom, studies at the atomic and molecular levels have accelerated and generated enormous achievements in the field of science. In recent years, startling developments in science and technology at the nano level have attracted particular interest, from scientists and engineers as well as the general public, and initiated a new field in science: nanoscience and technology (Mehta, 2002; Roco, 2003; Roco & Bainbridge, 2005; Venema, 2006). Excitement about the technological potential of this new field has also drawn attention to the need for and importance of corresponding educational developments in the field to prepare the future workforce (Fonash, 2001; Laurillard, 2002, 2005). However, compared to the recent attention and development given to the science and technology, there have been very few studies exploring the educational implications of the field. Recent research by the National Center for Learning and Teaching in nanoscale science and engineering has identified a core set of key concepts or "big ideas" central to the development of students understanding of nanoscience and technology (Stevens, Sutherland, Schank, & Krajcik, 2007; Wansom, Mason, Hersam, Drane, Light, Cormia, Stevens, & Bodner, 2008). These big ideas include such concepts as size and scale, the particulate nature of matter, surface area to volume ratio, dominant forces as well as others. Additional research has begun to explore student understanding of these different concepts within a range of educational levels (Park & Light 2008; Light, Swarat, Park, Drane, Tevaarwerk, & Mason, 2007; Tretter, Jones, Andre, Negishi, Minogue, 2006).

This paper presents research examining whether or not one of these key concepts might be a *threshold concept* within the field of nanoscience and technology. *Threshold concepts* are regarded as central to the organization of a particular knowledge domain or field, but also critical to the understanding of that domain or field. A *threshold concept* is defined by Meyer and Land (2003, 2006) as a conceptual gateway representing 'a transformed way of understanding, or interpreting, or viewing something without which the learner cannot progress.' It is characterized as being transformative, integrative, probably irreversible, potentially troublesome, and often a boundary maker. As such, it is believed that identifying

J. H. F. Meyer, R. Land and C. Baillie (eds.), Threshold Concepts and Transformational Learning, 259–279.

potential *threshold concepts* in nanoscience will help focus research on student learning of nano concepts, and on subsequent developments in the teaching and assessment of nano concepts.

Methodologically, the identification of threshold concepts is a problematic exercise. The two indispensable characteristics of a threshold concept – that it is integrative of the domain and that it is transformative for the student – suggest two distinct units or components of analysis: a conceptual component and an experiential component. The former focuses on the nature of the concept in the domain and the latter on the nature of the student's experience of the concept. While methods for ascertaining these features are not necessarily mutually exclusive, they need to be carefully calibrated. Davies (2006) notes that concept identification by experts could draw upon expertise to identify problems for student understanding in what might be referred to as a 'top-down' approach. In contrast, a 'bottom up' approach identifying concepts which lead to a transformative the variation experience would focus on research with students, themselves. In addition, such studies can map out the experiential component by further identifying in the ways in which students experience the concept and the key dimensions of variation which might constitute the troublesomeness of the concept - such as the aspects of variation revealed in phenomenographic studies (Marton & Booth, 1997). While this study takes both 'top down' and 'bottom up' approaches, it primarily focuses on the less frequently taken 'bottom up' approach to identify *threshold concepts*.

THEORETICAL FRAMEWORKS

Threshold Concept

In order to understand the "transformed way of understanding," which Meyer and Land (2003, 2006) argue are "conceptual gateways" to understanding a particular domain, they explore the ontological status of threshold concepts as a *liminal space*, following the use of the term in ethnographic studies by van Gennep (1960) and Turner (1969). The term *liminality* has a Latin origin *limen* meaning boundary or threshold and has been characterized by Turner as a transition phase in van Gennep's threefold structure of rites of passage rituals: a pre-liminal phase (separation), a liminal phase (transition), and a post-liminal phase (reincorporation). The troublesomeness of knowledge associated with this transition means knowledge is conceptually difficult, meaningless, inert, alien or implicit (Perkins, 1999 & 2006). Meyer and Land cite examples of threshold concepts in different disciplines; *opportunity cost* in economics, *central limit theorem* in statistics, *limit* in mathematics, and *entropy* in physics. The *threshold concepts* identified in a specific discipline also suggest useful approaches for instruction and curriculum development. Curriculum design and instruction should carefully consider how to provide the necessary scaffolding to help students overcome key conceptual barriers to understanding a threshold concept, as the latter can be a critical building block to progress in a particular subject.

Davies (2003) makes a distinction between applying fundamental or key concepts and phenomenographic approaches in the context of identifying threshold concepts. According to Davies, fundamental concepts are identified 'through professional reflection on the nature of the subject as a conceptual entity' (2003, p. 7). On the other hand, phenomenographic approaches (see below) based on variation in ways of understanding can identify student conceptions inductively through analysing their responses based on their own experience. Davies (2003, 2006) explains that threshold concepts can be identified by extending the two approaches in the context of subject communities. In addition, identification of threshold concepts requires inquiry about the characteristics. Davies suggests, for example, comparing responses of multiple experts, those of experts and students, and those of students in different situations as a way of identifying threshold concepts. Davies pointed out the importance of threshold concepts as 'a diagnostic tool of student understanding and development' and as 'a link between deep or surface approaches to learning and the outcomes of learning. (2003, p. 13)'.

Variation Theory and Phenomenography

Phenomenography is "the empirical study of the limited number of qualitatively different ways in which we experience, conceptualize, understand, perceive, [or] apprehend various phenomena" (Marton, 1994, p. 4424). The findings of a phenol-menographic study are usually presented in terms of the qualitatively different categories of experience of the phenomenon, and their logical relationships, sometimes referred to as the "outcome space" (Marton & Booth, 1997). The logical relationship between the categories of experience is usually hierarchical in nature, with some being more comprehensive and inclusive of others. Generally, each succeeding level of category includes an understanding of those that came before and an awareness of the difference between them. A study by Renstrom, Andersson, & Marton (1990), for example, introduced variation in students' conceptions of the nature of matter. The study categorized 20 students' interview responses into six qualitatively different categories of conceptions, hierarchically structured in terms of inclusiveness. These six categories comprise the 'outcome space' of the students' intended object of learning (i.e. their understanding of the nature of matter). These categories are also differentiated with respect to critical aspects of variation in the students' awareness of the intended object of learning. In addition, through an analysis of course textbooks, using these critical aspects of variation, the study provides possible reasons for student learning difficulties.

By identifying the ways in which the experience of a phenomenon or a particular concept varies from other less comprehensive ways, phenomenography, moreover, provides a way of studying the learning of that phenomenon. Indeed, a "theory of variation" (Pang, 2003) emerges which explains how learning can result through the experience of recognizing differences or variations that a student has not been able to discern previously. This, in addition, raises substantive implications for teaching and curriculum design, primarily that giving students opportunities to recognize the variation between their current experiences or understanding of a concept and one which is more comprehensive will facilitate their learning (Akerlind, 2005; Neuman, 1997; Renstrom, Andersson, & Marton, 1990). Drawing upon aspects of variation which distinguish different conceptions, activities have been developed and used to enhance student learning in mathematics and physics (the color of light & Newton's third law) and findings from the studies suggest pedagogical benefits of using variation in learning (Ling, Chik, & Pang, 2006; Marton & Pang, 2006; Runesson, 2005).

Meaningful Learning and Concept Maps

In order to highlight effective teaching and learning, Ausubel used a term "meaningful learning" that became the foundation of his assimilation theory. In the 1960s, by realizing the limitation in discovery learning, Ausubel (1963) differentiated his theory of "meaningful learning" from rote and discovery learning. More recently, Entwistle (1997) and others (Beattie, Collins, & Mcinnes, 1997), have described a similar distinction between deep and surface approaches to learning. Meaningful learning occurs when new knowledge is meaningfully linked to prior knowledge (prepositions) through assimilation of subordination (he used the word "subsumption"), superordination, and coordination "in a non-arbitrary and substantive way" (Ausubel, 1963, p. 24–26). In rote learning, new concepts are presented to the learner's conceptual framework in an "arbitrary and verbatim way" (Ausubel, 1963, p. 22) producing a weak and unstable cognitive structure. Through meaningful learning, on the other hand, the learner can make a real change in her/his individual experience of the world (i.e. "a conceptual change") which could be real, meaningful learning (Ausubel, 1963). By applying Ausubel's assimilation theory of meaningful learning to sketch students' conceptual understanding, Joseph D. Novak and his research team at Cornell University in the 1970s developed concept maps to evaluate student learning. Since then, concept maps have been used for over 25 years in research and classroom practice to assess student understanding and knowledge structure. A concept map is a knowledge represent-tation tool showing concepts and explicit links forming a hierarchical branching, and dendrite structure. A map is composed of concepts and connecting lines (indicating the relationship between concepts). The core element of a concept map is a "proposition" that is composed of two or more concept labels connected by a linking relationship that forms a semantic unit (Novak, 1988). Concept mapping is a technique with which one can clarify and describe one's idea about some topic in a graphical form (Novak & Gowin, 1984). Basic knowledge can be connected through a rich set of relations among important concepts within a discipline. In addition, concept maps can be made by learners, teachers, or resear-chers. Because a concept map is an effective means of representing, visualizing, and communicating knowledge, it has been used as a valuable tool for instruction and assessment. The utility of concept maps has been discussed in many studies in learning science (Al-Kunifed & Wandersee, 1990). In order to identify potential threshold concepts in nanoscience, the current study investigates concept maps in detail.

METHODS

As noted above, this study employed both 'top down', expert-focused and "bottom up", student-focused methods for identifying a threshold concept in nanoscience. These methods included the construction of concept maps and an interview with the expert (professor), and the construction of pre and post course concept maps and the completion of a linked open-ended survey by the students.

Participants, Research Site and Course Context

Data for this study were collected from the instructor (expert) of an advanced level course for engineering majors at an American Midwestern research university and 21 second-year college students who enrolled in the course. The course was designed as an introduction to thermodynamics in materials science and included a week-long unit on nanoscience, specifically nanomaterial thermodynamics, toward the middle of the course. In addition to this unit, a group project relating to the nanoscience unit comprised 30% of the course grade. Students were required to develop a computer–assisted learning tool to help high school students and/or non-science college students learn how thermodynamic properties, especially melting point, change with particle size as size approaches the nanometer range. At the end of the course, each group presented their instructional materials (in the form of a guide for teachers) and it was assessed by both the instructor and the other students.

Data Collection and Analysis

(1) Expert (Instructor)

Drawing on the learning goals for the nanoscience unit of the course (table 1 below), the course instructor (expert) was asked to make a list of the key nano related concepts addressed in the course and to create a concept map depicting the relationship between those concepts. He was also informed that the list of concepts he constructed (but not the concept map) would be given to the students prior to the construction of their student concept maps. The expert was also interviewed following the construction of his concept map to elaborate on the concepts and conceptual links on his map. In addition to the elaboration of his map, the expert was asked to classify the concepts within three different categories: important concepts, difficult concepts, and threshold concepts (see table 2 below). He was given a short definition for a *threshold concept*: a concept that can be conceptual gateways that lead to a previously inaccessible and initially troublesome way of thinking (Meyer & Land 2003). Other information about the course (learning goals, structure of the course, prerequisites, assessment, etc.) and the teacher's teaching experience in general were also obtained. Table 1 shows the learning goals of the nanoscience unit.

Table 1. Learning goals for the one-week unit on "Nanomaterials Thermodynamics"

Students completing this unit on "Nanomaterials Thermodynamics" should be able to:

1. Describe and quantify changes in surface area-to-volume ratio as particle size is reduced into the nanoscale regime.
2. Articulate and predict how free energy changes with surface energy/surface tension and with surface area.
3. Name and describe key materials kinetic phenomena driven by surface free energy differences/gradients.
4. Predict how melting temperature changes with particle size for nanosized crystallites.
5. Predict how solute solubility changes with particle size in the nano-regime.
6. Determine quantitatively an approximate upper size range for surface-dominated thermodynamic behaviour.

(2) Students

Twenty-one of the 25 students enrolled in the course volunteered to participate in the study. These students were asked to construct two concept maps describing and explaining the relationships between the 11 concepts provided from the expert's list. In the construction of their concept maps, they were informed that they could drop concepts from this list and/or add other concepts they felt were important. They completed their concept maps before the beginning of nanoscience unit and, again, after the course ended. In addition, after the students constructed their second concept map, they were asked to complete a survey comprised of six questions which asked them to select one or more concepts or links from their maps and group them in the same three categories in which the expert was asked to classify them: difficult concepts, important concepts, and threshold concepts (see below table 2).

Table 2. Student survey questions

Category	Questions
Difficult Concept	a. Could you list which concept or relationship between concepts was the most difficult for you to understand?
	b. Why do you think the concept or relationship between concepts is difficult?
Important Concept	a. Could you list which concept or relationship is the most important for you to understand Nanoscience/technology?
	b. Why do you think the concept is the most important?
Threshold Concept	a. Could you list which concept can be a *threshold concept* (a concept that can be conceptual gateways that lead to a previously inaccessible and initially troublesome way of thinking) for learning Nanoscience/technology in this course?
	b. Why do you think the concept is a threshold concept for learning Nanoscience/technology in this course?

The pre- vs. post nanoscience unit concept-maps and the student vs. expert maps were explored in detail. A first level quantitative analysis focused on differences in the numerical nature of the concept maps. For the analysis of the concept maps, the researcher and two other experts in science with Ph.D's in engineering developed a coding scheme. The expert's concept-map and two randomly selected student concept-maps were used for the preliminary analysis and code development. In some cases, students did not include explicit semantic links describing the relationship between the concepts in their maps. In those cases, the link was interpreted conservatively as simply meaning "is related to." To ensure inter-rater reliability, 8 sets of student pre-and post concept maps were selected and individually coded by the researcher and two science and engineering experts. The analysis was conducted with respect to four areas: (1) concepts (number of concepts, change in the pre/post-list of concepts), (2) links (number of links, change in the pre/post-link between concepts), (3) format of concept maps, and (4) conceptual levels (number of levels). The results were compared among the three raters. The inter-rater reliability between the three raters was 85.94 % across these four areas. For those student maps where agreement was not achieved among the three raters, further discussion was processed and agreement among all three was reached. The rest of the student concept maps were coded by the researcher. A second level of qualitative analysis was conducted drawing on the results obtained in the first analysis. One researcher analyzed the conceptual links of the 42 pre and post concept maps to identify differences in the overall conceptual patterns of the maps. The analysis revealed five conceptual patterns differing in the way they linked four general concept areas: NA (nanoscale/nanoscience); SV (surface, volume, surface-to volume-ratio); SE (Surface energy and forces) and PR (size dependent properties). These preliminary patterns were then subjected to further analysis by two researchers. This analysis added a fifth conceptual area NE (nanoscale entities), and focused on the contrast in student understanding as expressed by the variation in the overall conceptual meanings of the links.

FINDINGS

(1) Expert (Instructor)

In the interview and in his concept map, the course instructor identified 11 concepts as being the key concepts in the nanoscience unit of the course. They were provided to the students for the construction of their concept maps. Table 3 shows the 11 concepts.

Table 3. Key concepts for the nanoscience unit in a materials science course

– Atoms	– Surface forces
– Molecules	– Surface energies
– Nanoscale	– Thermodynamic behaviour
– Nanoscience	
– Volume	– Melting point
– Surface	– Solubility

The expert identified *surface area-to-volume ratio* as a potential threshold concept that offered students in his class a conceptual gateway for accessing critical ways of thinking and integrating the other key concepts of the unit and for developing advanced knowledge and understanding of nanoscience. It is worth noting that this concept was not specifically included in the above list of concepts for students, but rather its components surface area and volume were given. It was agreed by the researchers and the expert that the students were able and needed to show the link between surface area and volume in their concept maps. The following excerpt gives the expert's reasons for selecting *surface area-to-volume ratio* as a threshold concept.

> **Expert:** Well, *surface-to-volume ratio* is the threshold concept, because you can't get down here (the nano level) without accepting the fact that really tiny particles have large surface-to-volume ratio. ... So take a gram of something and keep chopping it up until you get down to nano-particles. And what you see is the surface area just goes through the roof. So this is enabling.... because, without that, you can't do this. So this would be a threshold concept.

With respect to important and difficult concepts, the expert reported *surface energy* to be an important and difficult concept with some potential to be a threshold concept. *Surface tension* and *surface forces* were also considered to be both important and difficult concepts but they were not felt to constitute threshold concepts. There was no overlap between threshold and difficult concepts.

(2) Students

Concept Maps – Concepts. SelectedIn addition to the 11 concepts provided by the expert, 38 additional concepts were identified as key concepts for nanoscience on at least one of the 42 student pre- and post-concept maps. Table 4 list the additional concepts used in student maps. As can be seen in the list, students added a diverse range of concepts including concepts related to the size and scale continuum, to properties, to tools and to application.

Table 4. Additional concepts used in student concept maps

− Science, materials science, engineering on the nanoscale
− Bulk, non-nanoscale, particle size, 10^{-9}m, macroscale, 0.1–100nm, Size of atoms/molecules, microscale, unit of measurement
− reaction rate
− free energy, phase diagrams, matter phase
− solution
− kinetic behavior, physical behavior, electronic behavior, mechanical behaviour
− macroscopic properties, atomic properties, properties of how particles change as they approach the nanoscale, properties of materials, bulk properties, nanoscale properties
− physical tension

Table 4. (Continued)

– % of atoms on surface, atoms/molecules on surface, atoms/molecules in bulk volume – Surface science, surface tension – Tools (SEM, AFM, TEM, ESEM) – Bonding – Surface area to volume ratio, area – Light absorption – Application

Survey Response - Concepts Categorized. Table 5 (below) shows the distribution of the students' concept selection within the three categories of concept: Difficult concept (DC), Important concept (IC), and Threshold Concept (TC) with a comparison to the expert's selection (see asterisks).

Table 5. Category and number of student responses to three different concepts
(DC: difficult concept, IC: important concept, TC: threshold concept)

	Category of Student Responses	Expert			Student		
		DC	IC	TC	DC	IC	TC
1	Nanoscale/size				3	4	4
2	Surface				2	0	2
3	Surface Area to Volume Ratio			*	0	8	9
4	Surface energy or Surface forces	*	*		9	5	3
5	Thermodynamic property change (Solubility or Melting point)				5	4	3
6	Atoms/Molecules				1	0	0
7	Conductivity				1	0	0

As can be seen in the table 5, student responses were distributed across 7 concepts with the majority of the student's matching the expert's selection on two of the three types of concepts. Nine (43%) students agreed with expert's selection of *surface energy* or *surface force* as a difficult concept and a further 5 students (24%) chose *property change* as a difficult concept. *Surface area-to-volume ratio* was chosen as the most important concept by eight (38%) students, in contrast to the expert's choice, *surface energy/forces* which were selected by only five (24%) students as the most important concept. Interestingly, while no students felt that *surface area-to-volume ratio* was a difficult concept, nine (43%) students mirrored the expert's selection and chose it as a threshold concept, a concept they felt provided a conceptual gateway for understanding the other concepts. In addition, four students (19%) selected *size* as a threshold concept.

Overall, student concept selections ranged over at least four different types of concepts in each of the three categories. The pattern of selection for the different categories, however, revealed some interesting results. Student selection of the most important concept, for example, was very similar to that of their selection for threshold concept, indicating that they may not have fully understood the difference. However, a further analysis of the student surveys found that 71% of the students chose different concepts for IC and TC. Across the three categories, the students' choices agreed with the expert's choice only 36% (23/63) of the time. More interesting, perhaps is the choice distribution against the conceptual patterns. Difficult and threshold concepts appear to differ substantially with, for example, the most cited difficult concepts, *surface energy/forces*, cited only 3 times as a threshold concept. And as noted above, the most cited threshold concept, *surface area-to-volume ratio* not being cited at all as a difficult concept.

Concept Maps - Patterns of Understanding.   The analysis of the concepts and conceptual links characterizing the 42 student concept maps resulted in five quailtatively distinct patterns of conceptual expression which, we suggest, reflect critical variations in student understanding of key concepts of nanoscience. These five patterns constitute a preliminary outcome space with respect to student understanding. These patterns are, moreover, constituted by the relationships between five categories of concepts:

− NA - nanoscience, nanoscale/size,
− NE – nanoscale particles (atoms, molecules),
− SV – surface, volume, surface area to volume ratio,
− SE - surface energy, surface force, surface tension,
− PR – size dependent properties (size dependent thermodynamic properties, solubility, and melting point).

The five patterns of student understanding are described below in table 6. They are illustrated by a concrete example of a student concept map[1]. These student concepts maps, originally hand drawn, have been faithfully re-constructed in this paper for reading convenience. No change in the nature or number of concepts, links, propositions, and/or shapes have been made.

Table 6. Five student patterns of understanding from concept map analysis

Student Patterns of Understanding (As Expressed by Concept Maps)	
Types	*Description*
1. Isolated	Nanoscience is primarily understood in terms of the nanoscale particles. Nanoscience is essentially an isolated concept. No links are constructed to nanoscale properties and mediating or explanatory concepts such as surface, volume, surface energy/forces.
2. Unconnected	Nanoscience is understood as relating nanoscale particles and nanosize properties, but there is no meaningful connection to the key mediating concepts: surface, volume, surface energy/forces are often missing.

Table 6. (Continued)

3. Detached	Nanoscale particles and properties are related and they are mediated by relationships to surface and volume, but these mediating concepts are not integrated and describe an apparently detached or divided understanding of nanoscience and the nano domain.
4. Limited	Nanoscale particles and nano properties are related and they are mediated by relationships to surface, surface energy/forces in an integrated understanding but the explanatory mechanism is limited to surface area alone; reference to volume missing.
5. Integrated	Nanoscale particles and nano-properties are related; and they are mediated by relationships to surface, volume, surface energy/forces in a fully integrated understanding which explains the central role of surface area-to-volume ratio with reference to surface energies and forces.

Pattern 1 (Isolated):   Concept maps in this pattern express an understanding of nanoscience and nano-phenomena which is primarily focused on nano-entities – atoms and molecules. Nanoscience is essentially isolated from the other types of concept which are regarded as basically related to macroscale phenomena. Figure 1 shows an example of student maps in this category. There are no links at all between nanoscience, size dependent properties and surface forces/energy. Surface forces/energy is linked to surface area only. The student does not appear to understand the importance of *surface area-to-volume ratio* to explain nanoscale phenomena and properties: indeed nanoscience is understood simply in terms of nanoscale entities such as atoms and molecules.

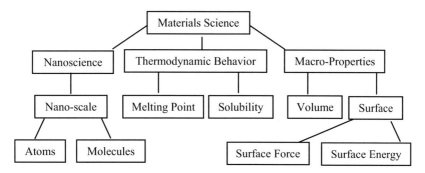

Figure 1. Student pattern of type 1 understanding.

Pattern 2 (Unconnected):   Student concept maps in this category show that nano-science is understood by more than its entities and is linked to particular phenomena and properties (such as thermodynamic behavior, melting point, solubility). There is, however, no meaningful explanation given for the links and relationships described in terms of the key relationship with surface area or surface area to volume ratio. As can be seen in Figure 2, while nanoscience properties are described in terms of nanoscale entities there is no meaningful link provided for the relationship between the thermodynamic properties and nanoscience. In particular there is no reference to the key change in surface area to volume ratio to explain the surface dominant behavior at the nano level.

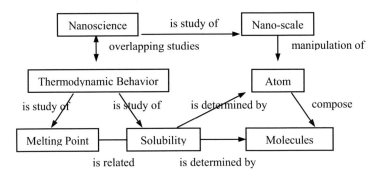

Figure 2. Student pattern of type 2 understanding.

Pattern 3 (Detached): In this pattern there is an expression of understanding that recognizes the relationship of nanoscience to both the nanoscale entities and the nanoscale properties of matter with a reference to the concepts of surface area and volume which provide an explanation for those nanoscale properties. The concept map (Figure 3), however, indicates that students in this category do not fully understand the importance of *surface area-to-volume ratio* for explaining size dependent properties at nanoscale. Although nanoscience can be described by the two, there is no meaningful link between surface side of the map and the volume/thermodynamic behaviour side of the map that explains the critical aspect of size dependent properties at nanoscale. The two are detached. Indeed the map shows them as representing two different types of nanoscience.

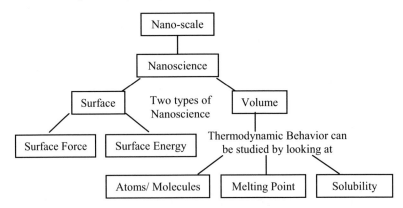

Figure 3. Student pattern of type 3 understanding.

Pattern 4 (Limited): This pattern expresses an understanding of property change at the nanoscale in an integrated but limited way. The concepts are linked in a manner which suggests that the properties of nanoscale phenomena are determined by surface behaviour of nanoscale entities characterized by surface energy/forces linked to properties. The concept map (Figure 4), however, does not appear to recognize the key concept of *surface area-to-volume ratio* which accounts for the unique, size dependent characteristics of nano-materials. Properties are described in surface terms only. The concept map shown in Figure 4 depicts the integration of the five key concept groups but the group of mediating concepts is limited to surface area and its relationship to surface energy/forces, The concept of volume is left out, presumably as unnecessary.

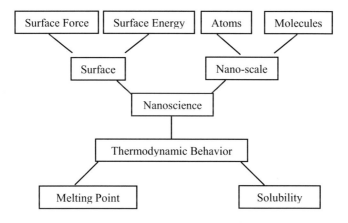

Figure 4. Student pattern of type 4 understanding.

Pattern 5 (Integrated): Concept maps exhibiting pattern 5 type understandings have integrated the key concepts and conceptual groups in a meaningful pattern which explains size dependent properties at the nano level. The relationship between nanoscale particles and nano-properties is mediated and explained by meaningful links with surface, volume, surface energy/forces which explains the central role of *surface area-to-volume ratio*. This pattern varies from pattern 4 primarily in its recognition of the importance of *surface area-to-volume ratio* (which was not provided as a direct concept but its components were given). Integrated understandings are depicted by two kinds of concept map pattern (Figures 5a and 5b) reflecting different student expressions of this ratio. In pattern 5a, the concept map links surface and volume as distinct concepts, indicating that their interrelationship is important to the determination of the unique properties of nano phenomena. Pattern 5b differs in that these concept maps specify *surface area-to-volume ratio* directly and usually place it in the central location.

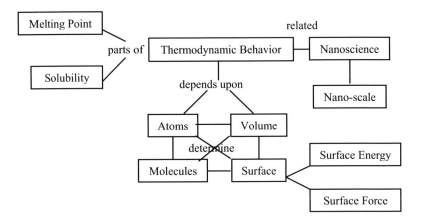

Figure 5. Student pattern of type 5a understanding.

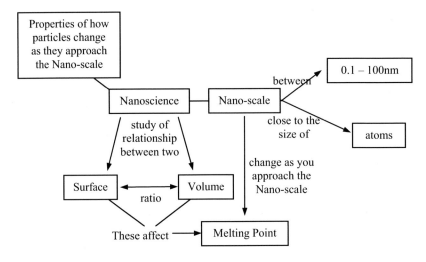

Figure 6. Student pattern of type 5b understanding.

Pre- and post- concept maps: change in patterns of understanding. An additional analysis was conducted on the 42 pre and post concept maps to determine whether there was meaningful change in the distribution of patterns of understanding prior to the nano-unit and project and after the students had completed them. The results of the analysis (Table 7) indicate that where only one third (7) of the students' concept maps displayed an integrated pattern (type 5) of understanding prior to the unit, two thirds (14) of the concept maps depicted an integrated map upon completion. In addition, it appears that where 6 (29%) of the pre maps were in the lower two patterns, only one (4%) was in those two groups upon completion.

Table 7. Change in student concept maps

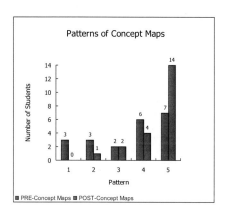

Instruction and project work in nanoscale concepts appear to have resulted in a change in many students understanding of the unique qualities of nanoscale properties. More importantly, this change appears to be primarily focused on understanding the relationship and mechanisms of size dependent property change at nanoscale by integrating *surface area-to-volume ratio* into their thinking. The increased complexity of student concept maps integrating thermodynamic properties at the nanoscale appears to be due to their recognition and understanding of the key concept of *surface area-to-volume ratio*.

Selection of threshold concept by pattern of understanding. To verify that *surface area-to-volume ratio* was indeed the critical concept in the development of the most complex pattern 5 understanding, an analysis of the concepts the students selected as threshold concepts, with respect to the different patterns of understanding their post concept maps expressed, was undertaken. The results are given in figure 7 below.

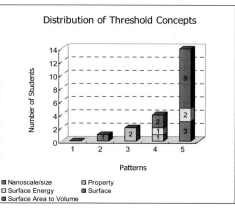

Figure 7. Distribution of threshold concept selection by pattern of understanding.

The post concept maps of all 9 students who chose *surface area-to-volume ratio* as a threshold concept were identified as exhibiting type 5 patterns of understanding. The other five students in the pattern-5 group chose a range of other concepts including size and surface energy/forces. No students with post concept maps in the other four patterns chose *surface-to-volume ratio* as a threshold concept. In an attempt to look at the transition experiences of those students with type 5 patterns, a further analysis was conducted looking at the pre concept maps for those students who had final concept maps exhibiting type 5 patterns of understanding. The results for this analysis are given Figure 8 below. The number in the boxes shows the number of students expressing the particular pattern shown.

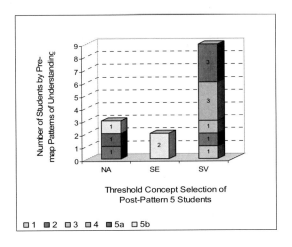

Figure 8. Post nanoscience pattern 5 threshold concept selection by all pre patterns.

It is worth pointing out that of the 5 students who did not select *surface area-to-volume ratio* as a threshold concept, 4 students had type 5 patterns of understanding prior to the beginning of the nanoscience unit. However, of the 9 students who selected *surface area-to-volume ratio* as a threshold concept, only three exhibited a type 5 pattern in their pre nanoscience unit concept map. Those three students, moreover, all exhibited type 5a patterns. Six students changed their pattern of understanding from a less complex or sophisticated pattern to a more complex pattern of understanding.

DISCUSSION

In its goal of identifying a potential threshold concept within the nano-domain, this study employed two different methodological approaches: a top-down approach based on the reflective experience of an expert and a bottom-up approach examining student experiences of a cluster of related concepts which describes size-dependent properties at the nano level. Both methods converged on *surface area-to-volume ratio* as a potential threshold concept of nanoscience at least within the context of the particular engineering course in which the study was situated. The expert described it as a threshold concept "because you can't get down here (the nano level) without accepting the fact that really tiny particles have large *surface area-to-volume ratio*." The identification process drew upon the instructor's expertise as a scientist in the field, as a student who learned these concepts, and most significantly as a teacher with over two decades of experience teaching these concepts, developing learning outcomes, constructing curricula and reflecting on student difficulties in understanding these concepts. It requires the expert's thoughtful reflection on his experience and on students' experience of nano-phenomenon.

While taking a similar approach to the identification of a threshold concept with students – i.e. surveying them against a definition after they had completed the nano unit and project in the course – the study of student experience also examined the different patterns of student understanding with respect to the key nano-phenomena of the curriculum. The assumption, here, is that if *surface area-to-volume ratio* was, indeed, a potential threshold concept, a study of student understanding should show indications of its integrative and transformative (Meyer & Land, 2006) impact on student understanding as those understandings became more complex and sophisticated. In this regard, the study employed a phenomenographic approach using the construction and analysis of student concept maps to derive an outcome space describing the different types of understanding and the aspects of variation differentiating them.

Analysis of the student concept maps revealed a hierarchical continuum of patterns of understanding, each more complex and inclusive of the preceding patterns. The key aspect of variation which characterized the most complex pattern, and the pattern most closely reflecting the expert's pattern, was the recognition of the central role of *surface area-to-volume ratio* in the integration of the key nano domain concepts. In this respect, the study found not only that the expert reported *surface area-to-volume ratio* to be an integrative concept, but that an examination of student understandings revealed that it appears to behave in that way in the defined domain. This was further supported in an analysis of the student selections of threshold concept against their post patterns of understanding. Nine of the 14 (64%) students, expressing type 5 patterns of understanding, selected *surface area-to-volume ratio* as a threshold concept. No student expressing other patterns selected this concept as a threshold concept.

If the study findings support the critical integrative aspect of a threshold concept (Meyer & Land, 2006), the second key aspect of a threshold concept, transformative experience, is more problematic. While the continuum of patterns of experience represented by the outcome space, describe a transformative arc of liminality, the concept maps by themselves may be limited in their scope for revealing individual expressions of student transformation. Combined with interviews, for example, they could be a powerful instrument for revealing transformative experience. The analysis of the change in student patterns over the nano portion of the curriculum, however, does suggest that *surface area-to-volume ratio* may have contributed to a transformative experience within this domain cluster of concepts. Two thirds (6) of the students selecting *surface area-to-volume ratio* as a threshold concept, experienced a change of understanding from a less sophisticated pattern of understanding prior to the course. (Furthermore, the three students with pre type 5a patterns of understanding, who chose *surface area-to-volume ratio* as a threshold concept, all had experienced a change to 5b patterns post the nanoscience unit.) Indeed, it was those students who did not undergo a change or transformation of pattern of understanding – 4 of 5 (80%) including all three who had 5b patterns of understanding – who did not select *surface area-to-volume ratio* as a threshold concept. The suggestion here is that recognition or awareness of a concept's role in the transformation of an understanding of a domain is an essential ingredient of the selection of a concept as a threshold concept. For the expert, this recognition came as a result of reflection on many years experience teaching the concepts (Davies, 2003 & 2006). For the students, however, it appears that the experience of a recent transformation of understanding may have played that role.

One preliminary finding was that *surface area-to-volume ratio* was not regarded as a particularly troublesome or difficult concept. Indeed, if anything, it appears to be regarded as rather easy concept to understand. This may be due to the different ways in which this ratio is understood. As a simple ratio, it is a relatively straightforward mathematical concept which students in engineering would be expected to have little trouble with. There is evidence (Park et al. 2008), however, that within the nano-domain, this concept is understood in increasingly complex ways, a full understanding of which engages a cluster of troublesome concepts. The argument here is that troublesomeness does not necessarily reside directly with the threshold concept but rather in the integration of the domain cluster of concepts within the student's understanding.

CONCLUSIONS

Meyer and Land (2003) characterized *threshold concepts* as having two essential and three associated characteristics. Such concepts were transformative, integrative, probably irreversible, potentially troublesome, and often boundary makers. This study provides evidence arguing that *surface area-to-volume ratio* may be such a threshold concept within the nanoscience and technology domain. This study presents preliminary evidence that a meaningful understanding of *surface area-to-volume ratio* critically contributes to students' ability to integrate other key concepts in the nano-domain. In addition, it appears to be a central concept in transforming students' understanding of that domain. Finally, while not regarded as troublesome prima facia, there is evidence that the concept is critical to the understanding a cluster of concepts regarded as troublesome or difficult. The paper does not comment on the "irreversibility" nature of the concept, nor does it address the "boundary making" aspect of the concept, except to note with respect to the latter that by definition the study is examining student understanding of the differences between phenomena crossing the boundary between the macro level and the nano level. In this respect, the concept, *surface area-to-volume ratio* may assist students to make a critical conceptual leap across the visible/non-visible (macro-submacro) border.

From the nanoscience perspective, the identification of *surface area-to-volume ratio* as a potential threshold concept supports earlier research (Wansom et al., 2008) identifying it as one of the "big ideas" in nanoscience at the higher education level. From the broader educational perspective, the identification of threshold concepts within a key area of the nano-domain provides educational practitioners and policy makers useful information in the recent goal to prepare students for careers in the developing nanoscience industry. More specifically identifying such concepts will help teachers focus their instruction, curriculum and assessment materials and activities on concepts that have important learning implications for a wider range of related concepts.

Finally, the limitations of the study need to be noted. As mentioned above, the identification of threshold concepts are by definition problematic. In particular, they require methods by which student understanding of concepts can be described and mapped. The construction of understandings by concept maps alone, while useful, is qualitatively limited in terms of their provision of data for analysis and interpretation.

The data obtained from concept maps such as those presented above constrain analysis to interpretation at a relatively broad level. While they can provide useful information for detecting variation in patterns of conceptual expression, they would be aided by fuller commentary by the students explicating their meaning. They do not, moreover, lend themselves very easily to ascertaining the transformative element of threshold concept. As such, additional studies which included interviews were conducted with a selection of students and are now being analyzed. A second critical limitation of this study was the relative lack of variation in the student sample selected. Students in the study all came from one class. They were all engineering majors who had been highly selected for their ability in science and math. This may account for the predominance of student patterns of understanding in the two higher categories. In response to this, the researchers have developed plans for enhancing their study methods and extending them across additional populations of student studying nanoscience and technology.

ACKNOWLEGEMENTS

This work was supported by the National Center for Learning & Teaching in Nanoscale Science and Engineering (NCLT) under the National Science Foundation Grant No. 0426328. We also thank Dr. Thomas Mason for his support of our inquires.

NOTES

[1] While maps 1 and 4 (as shown) are not technically complete concept maps (see above), they are helpful illustrations of their respective patterns.

REFERENCES

Akerlind, G. (2005). Learning about phenomenography: Interviewing, data analysis, and the qualitative research paradigm. In J. Bowden & P. Green (Eds.), *Doing developmental phenomenography*. Melbourne, VIC: RMIT University Press.

Al-Kunifed, A., & Wandersee, J. H. (1990). One hundred references related to concept mapping. *Journal of Research in Science Teaching, 27*(10), 1069–1075.

Ausubel, D. (1963). *The psychology of meaningful verbal learning*. New York: Grune & Stratton.

Beattie, V., Collins, B., & Mcinnes, B. (1997). Deep and surface learning: A simple or simplistic dichotomy? *Accounting Education, 6*(1), 1–12.

Davies, P. (2003, August 26–30). Threshold concepts: How can we recognize them? In *The Proceedings of the European Association for Research on Learning and Instruction Conference*. Padova, Italy.

Davies, P. (2006). Threshold concepts: How can we recognize them? In J. H. F. Meyer & R. Land (Eds.), *Overcoming barriers to student understanding: Threshold concepts and troublesome knowledge* (pp. 70–84). New York: Routledge.

Entwistle, N. (1997). Contrasting perspectives on learning. In F. Marton, D. Hounsell, & N. Entwistle (Eds.), *The experience of learning*. Edinburgh, UK: Scottish Academic Press.

Feynman, R. P. (1959). *Plenty of room at the bottom*. Presentation to American Physical Society. Viewed September 8th 2008. Retrieved from http://www.its.caltech.edu/~feynman/plenty.html

Fonash, S. J. (2001). Education and training of the nanotechnology workforce. *Journal of Nanoparticle Research, 3*(1), 79–82.

Laurillard, D. (2002). *Rethinking university teaching: A conversational framework for the effective use of learning technologies*. London: Routledge.

Laurillard, D. (2005). Rethinking university teaching. *Physical Science Educational Reviews, 6*(1), 59–62.

Light, G., Swarat, S., Park, E.-J., Drane, D., Tevaarwerk, E., & Mason, T. (2007, June 23–24). Understanding undergraduate students' conceptions of a core nanoscience concept: Size and scale. In *the Proceedings of the International Conference on Research in Engineering Education*, Honolulu, Hawaii.

Ling, L. M., Chik, P., & Pang, M. F. (2006). Patterns of variation in teaching the color of light to primary 3 students. *Instructional Science, 34*, 1–19.

Marton, F. (1994). Phenomenography. In T. Husen & T. N. Postlethwaite (Eds.), *The international encyclopedia of education* (2nd ed., Vol. 8, pp. 4424–4429). Oxford, UK: Pergamon.

Marton, F., & Booth, S. (1997). *Learning and awareness*. Mahwah, NJ: Lawrence Erlbaum.

Marton, F., & Pang, M. F. (2006). On some necessary conditions of learning. *The Journal of the Learning Sciences, 15*(2), 193–220.

Mehta, M. D. (2002). *Nanoscience and nanotechnology: Assessing the nature of innovation in these fields*. Bulletin of Science, Technology, & Society, *22*(4), 269–273.

Meyer, J. H. F., & Land, R. (2003). Threshold concepts and troublesome knowledge: Linkages to ways of thinking and practicing within the disciplines. In C. Rust (Ed.), *Improving student learning. Improving student learning theory and practice-ten years on* (pp. 412–424). Oxford, UK: OCSLD.

Meyer, J. H. F., & Land, R. (2006). *Overcoming barriers to student understanding: Threshold concepts and troublesome knowledge*. New York: Routledge.

Neuman, D. (1997). Phenomenography: Exploring the roots of numeracy. *Journal for Research in Mathematics Education*, Monograph, *9*, 63–177.

Novak, J. D., & Gowin, D. B. (1984). *Learning how to learn*. New York and Cambridge, UK: Cambridge University Press.

Novak, J. D. (1988). Learning science and the science of learning. *Studies in Science Education, 15*, 77–101.

Pang, M. F. (2003). Two faces of variation – On continuity in the phenomenographic movement. *Scandinavian Journal of Educational Research, 47*(2), 145–156.

Park, E.-J., & Light, G. (2008). Identifying atomic structure as a threshold concept: Student mental models and troublesomeness. *International Journal of Science Education*.

Park, E.-J., Light, G., & Mason, T. (2008, June 24–28). *Identifying threshold concepts in learning nano-science by using concept maps and students' responses to an open-ended interview.* Poster presented at the International Conference in Learning Science, Utrecht, Netherlands.

Perkins, D. (1999). The many faces of constructivism. *Educational Leadership, 57*(3), 6–11.

Perkins, D. (2006). Constructivism and troublesome knowledge. In J. H. F. Meyer & R. Land (Eds.), *Overcoming barriers to student understanding: Threshold concepts and troublesome knowledge* (pp. 33–47). New York: Routledge.

Roco, M. C. (2003). Converging science and technology at the nanoscale: Opportunities for education and training. *Nature Biotechnology, 21,* 1247–1249.

Roco, M. C., & Bainbridge, W. S. (2005). Societal implications of nanoscience and nanotechnology: Maximizing human benefit. *Journal of Nanoparticle Research, 7,* 1–13.

Renstrom, L., Andersson, B., & Marton, F. (1990). Students' conceptions of matter. *Journal of Educational Psychology, 82*(3), 555–569.

Runesson, U. (2005). Beyond discourse and interaction. Variation: A critical aspect for teaching and learning mathematics. *Cambridge Journal of Education, 35*(1), 69–87.

Stevens, S. Y., Sutherland, L., Schank, P., & Krajcik, J. (draft, 2007). *The big ideas of nanoscience.* Retrieved June 2, 2007, from http://hi-ce.org/PDFs/Big_Ideas_of_Nanoscience-20feb07.pdf

Tretter, T. R., Jones, M. G., Andre, T., Negishi, A., & Minogue, J. (2006). Conceptual boundaries and distances: Students' and experts' concepts of the scale of scientific phenomena. *Journal of Research in Science Teaching, 43*(3), 282–319.

Turner, V. W. (1969). *The ritual process: Structure and anti-structure.* Chicago: Aldine Publishing Co.

van Gennep, A. (1960). *The rites of passage.* (1909). Reprint, London: Routledge & Kegan Paul.

Venema, L. (2006). Nanoscience: Small talk. *Nature, 442*(31), 994–995.

Wansom, S., Mason, T., Hersam, M., Drane, D., Light, G., Cormia, R., et al. (2008). A rubric for post-secondary degree programs in nanoscience and nanotechnology. *International Journal of Engineering Education.*

Eun-Jung Park and Greg Light
Searle Center for Teaching Excellence
Northwestern University

MARINA ORSINI-JONES

17. TROUBLESOME GRAMMAR KNOWLEDGE AND ACTION-RESEARCH-LED ASSESSMENT DESIGN:

Learning from Liminality

FOREWORD

Sempre caro mi fu quest'ermo colle,
E questa siepe, che da tanta parte
Dell'ultimo orizzonte il guardo esclude.
Ma sedendo e mirando, interminati
Spazi di là da quella, e sovrumani
Silenzi, e profondissima quiete
Io nel pensier mi fingo; ove per poco
Il cor non si spaura. E come il vento
Odo stormir tra queste piante, io quello
Infinito silenzio a questa voce
Vo comparando: e mi sovvien l'eterno,
E le morte stagioni, e la presente
E viva, e il suon di lei. Cosí tra questa
Immensità s'annega il pensier mio:
E il naufragar m'è dolce in questo mare[1].

(Giacomo Leopardi, L'infinito)

The above poem was written by Giacomo Leopardi, one of the greatest Italian poets, between 1818 and 1821. It is uncanny how this poem can be seen as a metaphor illustrating the epistemological and ontological discussion surrounding the acquisition of troublesome knowledge that is taking place within the relatively new field of threshold concepts (e.g. Meyer, Land & Davies, 2008; Land, Meyer & Smith, 2008). In the poem, Leopardi writes how he holds dear the hedge ('la siepe') that is both real - there was a large hedge around his house that obscured the view to the open landscape of the Appennine's 'Sibillini' mountain range beyond it, and of the plain lying at its feet - and metaphorical - the hedge was literally the boundary, the threshold, of his paternal home's land, of his 'safety area'. At the same time, Leopardi is drawn to what lies beyond the hedge, the seemingly 'never-ending spaces beyond it': *'interminati spazi di là da quella'*, even if this 'unboundedness' fills him with fear: *'ove per poco il cor non si spaura'* ('wherefore my heart almost loses itself in fear'). The dialectic between the threshold (the hedge – *'la siepe'*) and the 'never-ending' horizon

J. H. F. Meyer, R. Land and C. Baillie (eds.), Threshold Concepts and
Transformational Learning, 281–299.

beyond it, reflects the oscillation between the relative safety of the 'known' and the risky territory that is the unknown. Leopardi, a great erudite, who was translating Greek tragedies into Italian by the age of 12, finds it delightful, albeit scary, to imagine 'drowning' in the infinite space beyond the threshold and embrace the unknown. This contrasts with the approach to troublesome knowledge of many present-day undergraduate first year students in the UK, who tend to hover around what they perceive to be the 'safe' side of the hedge and come from a secondary school system that often encourages them to strictly adhere to set rules in order to pass examinations set with rigid criteria that do not allow for creative risk-taking and independent thinking.

Crossing thresholds is part of the ontological journey necessary to become independent thinkers at university level. It is a risky journey (Barnett 2007), but an exciting one too that could open new, challenging, but possibly pleasant horizons: '*e il naufragar m'è dolce in questo mare*' ('and to shipwreck is sweet for me in this sea').

It is the indefinite nature of what lies behind the threshold that scares students, particularly in their first year of undergraduate studies. The curricular actions carried out in a variety of disciplines following the identification of threshold concepts (e.g. Gray & Yavash, 2007; Davies & Mangan, 2007; Osmond & Turner, 2008) to help students cope with and understand troublesome knowledge, aim at turning the fear of the indefinite into a love for the endless epistemological horizons that can be viewed once a conceptual threshold is crossed. Meyer, Land and Smith illustrate the transformation brought about by the crossing of the threshold concept with the original choice of the journey of a raw Desirée potato becoming a roast one (2008, p. ix), understanding threshold concepts is not confined to the conceptual transformation bounded by subject matter, it also about a 'change in sense of self, a change in subjectivity on the part of the learner'.

The liminal state is pivotal to the change process. The anthropologist Victor Turner's definition of the liminal state as the ambiguous 'betwixt and between' space (1967) is quite fitting. As argued in Meyer, Land and Smith (2008, pp. x–xi), the liminal state is a pre-cursor of the ontological shift. Students who become 'stuck' on the 'pre-liminal' position (which has been previously compared to Dante's Hell in the *Divine Comedy*, Orsini-Jones, 2008, p. 213) lack the flexibility necessary to oscillate in the liminal state. Not all students in the latter state will cross the threshold, and might regress to the 'stuck' position, but those who can live with the uncertainty of troublesome knowledge are those who will not feel too threatened by the uncertain change-process area of the *limen*.

There is some evidence that tailor-made assessment tasks based upon threshold concepts that have been identified in some disciplines have helped students with understanding troublesome knowledge (Davies & Mangan, 2007; Orsini-Jones & Sinclair, 2008; Gray & Yavash, 2007). It is proposed here that encouraging students to actively engage with metacognition relating to the threshold concept identified while they are in the liminal state can also contribute to their 'readiness' to cross it.

INTRODUCTION

This study summarises the findings of two academic years of action-research cycles of curricular intervention (2006–2007 and 2007–2008) aimed at helping undergraduate languages students with troublesome grammar knowledge. It is based upon the outcomes of a research project carried out by staff in Languages at Coventry University and evaluated in collaboration with an educational researcher from the University of Strathclyde, entitled *Grammar: Researching Activities for Student Progress* (GRASP)[2].

The work develops from earlier research projects (Orsini-Jones & Jones, 2007; Orsini-Jones, 2008; Orsini-Jones & Sinclair, 2008) highlighting a 'threshold concept' encountered by languages students: the overarching structure of a sentence also known in linguistics as the '*rank scale concept*' (e.g. Coulthard, 1985, p. 121; Halliday, 1985; Crystal, 2006, p. 251, see Table 1). This overall concept is formed by the grammar categories illustrated in the table below, which means that students needs to master each of the fundamental grammar 'milestones' listed in the table before being able to grasp the overall concept.

The study has taken an action-research approach to curriculum change (as illustrated in McNiff, 1988 and in McKernan, 1992). Successive cohorts of students in their first year of studies at Coventry University have provided active input and feedback on the actions taken. In the academic years 2006–2007 and 2007–2008, the intervention took place within the module entitled *Methods and Approaches* that supports learning on both generic and subject specific skills for students majoring in languages.

The data collected for this study highlighted that many students reading languages experienced 'grammar anxiety'. It was worrying that many of them were also planning to become English as a Foreign Language (EFL) or Modern Languages (ML) teachers and would therefore have to explain grammar to their students. Moreover, as stressed in previous literature (Orsini-Jones, 2008, p. 215), there is a requirement from the Quality Assurance Agency for Higher Education in England and Wales (QAA, 2002, p. 9) that students reading languages and

Table 1. The hierarchical structure of a sentence - rank scale concept - (Crystal, 2006, p. 251) - 'Glossary' provided in Appendix 2

sentences	morphemes
which are analysed into	which are used to build
clauses	words
which are analysed into	which are used to build
phrases	phrases
which are analysed into	which are used to build
words	clauses
which are analysed into	which are used to build
morphemes	sentences

linguistics should develop the ability to carry out formal grammar analysis of thelanguages studied. It was therefore crucial to try and put measures in place that could help students with overcoming troublesome grammar knowledge and design both targeted curricular activities and a grammar analysis assessed task that, in Perkins' words (2006, pp. 42–43) would equip students with the 'conceptual arsenal' of linguistic analysis and would make them fluent in the 'foreign' epistemic game of linguistics.

The grammar sessions designed for module *Academic Methods and Approaches* aimed therefore to raise students' awareness of the threshold concept identified and of its individual troublesome components (individual grammar categories in Table 1). Feedback and data from the previous action-research cycles indicated that a socio-collaborative assessed task in particular had helped students with understanding the concept: the *Group Grammar Project*, a web-based grammar microteaching unit used by students to demonstrate their understanding of grammar categories to each other. The assessed task was re-designed and re-focused to help students further with crossing the threshold concept identified.

MODULE ACADEMIC METHODS AND APPROACHES

Module *Academic Methods and Approaches* is a 20 credit mandatory module, one out of six for the first year of study on a BA Honours in French or Spanish for both Single Honours and Joint Programmes. It started in academic year 2006–07 and was based upon module *Academic and Professional Skills for Language Learning* – that had ran between 2001–2005 (details in Orsini-Jones, 2004 and in Orsini-Jones & Jones, 2007).

The aims of *Academic Methods and Approaches* are to prepare students for academic study at degree level, to illustrate the nature and processes of research in humanities and to encourage students to engage with the tasks set in an academic and professional way using appropriate e-learning tools. The assessment tasks for the module are designed to provide practical experience of applying academic and professional skills in actual case studies relevant to their study programme, engage in personal development planning and in team work. Students are given the opportunity to reflect upon and record their personal development both via the e-portfolio *PebblePAD and* in discussion forums within the Virtual Learning Environment used (*Blackboard Vista*).

The intended learning outcomes are that, on completion of this module, languages students should be able to:

1. Search for, review and correctly reference literature relating to their languages degree using the Harvard style.
2. Interpret data from a variety of sources, evaluate it and indicate how it can be used for specific academic tasks relating to their course.
3. Illustrate their knowledge and understanding of texts, concepts and theories relating to their course.

4. Demonstrate the ability to work as part of a team, design a website on grammar categories - English and other language(s) studied - and present it to their peers.
5. Reflect on the experience of the group grammar project in an individual reflective report.

(Module Information Directory Coventry University 2007)

The module outcomes are assessed as follows:

– Coursework 1 – 20%, *Information retrieval and academic writing online in-class test* assesses outcomes 1, 2 and 3.

– Coursework 2 – 50% - *Group grammar project and presentation* assesses outcomes 1, 2, 3 and 4.

– Coursework 3 – 30% *Individual reflective report on the group grammar project* assesses outcomes 1, 3, 4 and 5.

This study focuses in particular on coursework tasks two and three which were designed to engage students with the threshold concept identified, stimulate a debate on troublesome grammar knowledge and encouraged them to reflect upon their grammar learning journey. This work also builds on one of the findings from the previous cycles of the action research process, i.e. that metacognition appears to help undergraduate first year students with 'coping' with troublesome knowledge (Orsini-Jones & Sinclair 2008).

GRAMMAR LEARNING AND METACOGNITION

Students engaging with language learning at Higher Education level are usually expected to reach a level of proficiency in both written and oral skills comparable to that of **educated** native speakers.

Relationships between reflection and learning are complex and multifaceted (Moon, 2004, p. 85). There is however evidence that reflection on what is being learnt and on the processes involved in learning can enhance learning and foster understanding (e.g.: Bransford, Brown & Cocking, 2000).

The role of metacognition features as a (contested) topic in the field of formal grammar learning. It is generally acknowledged that there is a difference between 'tacit' grammar knowledge and 'active' application of that knowledge (this relates to Chomsky, 1968, further details in Mitchell & Myles, 2004). There is an ongoing debate relating to whether or not engaging in metacognitive grammatical activities can enhance language learning and whether or not a focus on linguistic form can benefit language skills in the target language studied (Klapper, 2006, pp. 396–405).

The benefits of stimulating the language learner's proficiency via metacognition at university level have been highlighted by many linguists (e.g. Hurd, 2000; Hauck, 2005; Orsini-Jones, 2004; Klapper, 2006). For the above reasons, for the duration of the *Group Grammar Project*, students were encouraged to engage in reflective practice upon the activities carried out. Specific assessment tasks, both formative and summative, were designed for this purpose.

DESIGNING A 'METAREFLECTIVE' SOCIO-COLLABORATIVE ASSESSED TASK TO OVERCOME TROUBLESOME KNOWLEDGE: THE GROUP GRAMMAR PROJECT

The Group Grammar Project is a rather complex task (Table 2), attempting to develop subject-specific skills while consolidating the generic ones covered in the first term in module *Academic Methods and Approaches* and encouraging students to become reflective learners. The task involved an analysis of the structure of sentences, clauses, phrases and words in terms of the item immediately below each one on the rank scale and a taxonomy of clauses, phrases, words and morphemes (Table 1). Diagnostic activities were carried out before the students started on the group task, such as formative multiple choice tests on grammar terminology that were administered to students to identify grammar issues before they started creating the web-pages for the *Group Grammar Project.*

Working in groups, students had to create a website containing linked web pages. In each page they had to analyse a sentence. At least one of the sentences had to be in one of the target languages studied, and the other(s) in English. In academic year 2006–2007 students chose their own sentences (which had to be approved by the module leader), while in 2007–2008 they had to choose from a list given to them (in view of the results obtained in 2006–2008, more on this point below), and each group had to create the relevant analysis and website. The latter had to be created with the *Webfolio* tool in *PebblePAD* and shared with the rest of the group and tutors via the module's *Gateway.* Each *Webfolio* had to be presented to the rest of the class by the group which had created it.

The choice to ask students to use the *Webfolio* tool of the e-portfolio *PebblePAD* to create the grammar web-pages was deliberate as the software is designed to encourage students to engage in reflective practice when writing an entry – or 'asset' - as it is called in *PebblePAD. PebblePAD* also makes it relatively easy to create active hypertextual nodes, so that students could add active links to grammar explanations of the grammar categories analysed in their *Group Grammar Project.* Moreover, *PebblePAD* maximises the socio-collaborative and constructivist aspects of the task, as assets can be created and shared both individually and via a shared *gateway* that operates like a 'content-rich' forum, where students can peer-review each other's work (Orsini-Jones *et al.*, 2007).

Table 2. The Group Grammar Project 2006–2008

1. Analyse sentences in English and French (and or Spanish) according to the Hallidayan '*rank scale*' (Halliday, 1985; Crystal, 2006 – see Table 1) in group;
2. Create a website in a collaborative way, sharing online files using the *Webfolio* tool in the e-portfolio *PebblePAD* to illustrate the group's grammar findings/ analysis;
3. Each group to reflect on the collaborative process and present the website with the analysis of the findings and reflections to tutor and peers;
4. Each student to write a reflective individual report on the group grammar presentation and webfolio creation.

After the presentation had taken place, students had to engage in anonymous self- and peer-assessment and then write an individual reflective report on the project.

RESEARCH METHODOLOGY

The results reported in this study are part of a larger, iterative work for which the overarching methodology is action-research – Table 3 (Orsini-Jones and Jones 2007, pp. 96–97; Orsini-Jones & Sinclair, 2008, p. 77).

Both qualitative and quantitative data (mixed method approach) were used, with a stronger stress on qualitative data ('QUAL-quant' model, Dörnyei, 2007, pp. 170–175).

Informed consent to participate in the research was sought from each participant and the staff involved adhered to the guidelines issued by the British Educational Research Association (BERA). Information sheets and consent forms (adapted from Mackey & Gass, 2005) were used with both Languages and English Degree Students.

The sample of interviewees for the semi-structured interviews was a self-selected group from the whole population on module *Academic Methods and Approaches*. Out of 29 students in 2006–07, 10 volunteered for the semi-structured interviews (7 female and 3 male) and 14 (10 female and 4 male) out of 40 in 2007–08. Although most students were 18–19 years of age, the age range was 18–45.

The data were subsequently anonymised, transcribed by the research assistant, transferred to the software package for qualitative data analysis *Atlas-Ti* (Muhr, 1997) and coded independently by the module leader (who was also the principal investigator for the research project) and the research assistant. The codes were then compared and subsequently discussed with the co-researcher from the University of Strathclyde. The research assistant took hand-written minutes of each grammar session and recorded the students' reactions to the activities.

Table 3. Stages in an action-research project

1. A problematic issue is identified (**reconnaissance** stage);
2. Change is **planned** collaboratively (staff and students) to address the issue;
3. The change process is **implemented – 'acted out'**;
4. All agents involved in the change process **reflect** upon its outcomes, both while it is happening and at the end of the first phase of implementation;
5. Actions are taken to **re-plan** the changes and the second phase of the action-research cycle starts (McNiff, 1988; McKernan, 1992; Kemmis & McTaggart, 1990 and 2005; Kember, 2000).

All three researchers participated in the design of the following questions:

1. When did you feel most 'stuck' during the grammar project?
2. Were there any times when you suddenly realised something important? If so, what had helped you?

3. Do you feel any differently about grammar now than you did at the start of the grammar project?

4. Were you surprised at grammar issues you knew about and other people didn't?

5. How do you feel about the way grammar was taught to you at school?

6. What remains the main issue for you now about grammar?

7. What do you wish you had known before you started the grammar project?

8. What 'grammar tips' would you give to a first year undergraduate student?

9. How would you describe your 'grammar journey' on this module?

The questions were administered to the students on 1 March 2007 (2006–2007 cohort) and on 17 April 2008 (2007–2008 cohort).

The quantitative data mainly consisted of an analysis of the results obtained by the students in their two attempts at the formative grammar tests on grammar categories/terminology and the marks they obtained for the *Group Grammar Project* (both presentation and individual report components).

The diagnostic online grammar tests designed by the research team were released to students in the second week of term two, at the beginning or the grammar part of the programme for the module. They were then hidden from 'View' in the VLE and released again at the end of the term to be re-taken after the completion of the *Group Grammar Project*. The VLE's assessment tool automatic processing of the diagnostic tests provided statistical data on the students' performance in each test.

The participating students' individual reports were also inputted into *Atlas-Ti*, coded with reference to problematic issues relating to grammar and 'triangulated' with the previously collected data and discussed with colleagues in Spanish, French and English in December 2007 and June 2008.

DATA RESULTS AND DISCUSSION OF THE FINDINGS

In both years it was confirmed that the concepts listed below were the most troublesome components of the overall *rank scale* threshold concept identified:
– Complex sentences (relationships and identification of verbs);
– Clauses (identifying subject-verb-object);
– Phrases (confusion with clauses);
– Word classification (adverbs and prepositions).

Also, the following points were confirmed as those that impacted negatively upon the crossing of the identified threshold concept and/or one or more of its components:

1. 'New to me' terminology (students opposed to change, refusing new type of analysis, refusing its semantics);
2. Prior (mis)knowledge of terms such as 'phrase' or 'clause' – lecturers had to 'undo' pre-conceived definitions of the grammar categories involved;
3. 'Prior knowledge' – background and previous grammar learning experience;

4. Reliance in group work upon peers who found the grammatical categories 'troublesome' but decided nevertheless to take a lead in the analysis of the sentences;
5. Misunderstanding of the concepts and lack of ability to ask lecturers for help;
6. Lack of motivation towards the module and/or grammar ('grammar boring');
7. Lack of reinforcement/support by other tutors teaching languages;
8. Grammar fear (feeling inadequate/not up to the task set).

Lack of awareness of underlying grammar principles emerged as a main concern for the students interviewed, particularly the native English ones (Semi-Structured Group interviews March 2007):

Extract 1 (where 'I' is interviewer and 'P' participant)

P: ...I can't really recall a lot of grammar being done at secondary school or primary school at all really. As I said only really from doing languages have I picked up the grammar side of things but I can't recall any time of actually doing grammar at school.

I: yeah. Do you think it should be taught in the schools?

P: I think it should really. I think there's been a lot of times when I've been sitting in whether it's a French or a Spanish class and you can see everyone sitting there racking their brains to try and understand what the teacher's saying and it's not necessarily the fact that the teacher's confusing matters, it's just the fact that we don't know the English to then learn the French.

On a positive note, it would appear that the following strategies/actions helped with understanding grammar:

– Collaborative group work;
– Initiative (strategic approach and asking for help);
– Confidence building via grammar analysis;
– Practice via diagnostic tests;
– Inspiration from peers;
– Explaining grammar to peers;
– Tailor-made materials (students commented positively on the chapter on sentences by Sinclair, 2007, pp. 55–74);
– 'Working out' grammar for yourself as part of the Grammar Task;
– 'Fun' with grammar;
– Metacognition.

The extract below illustrate that enjoying grammar analysis and adopting a process-based approach to its 'deconstruction' both appear to be key to understanding (Semi-Structured Interviews, March 2007):

Extract 2

P4: I like the analysis because it's also a bit of logic, like, not mathematics but it is kind of...there is a structure behind it obviously so I did enjoy analysing it and going into a deeper structure or deeper...I don't know.

I: and you've done this before have you? That kind of analysis?

P4: not really.

I: not really. But you quite enjoyed doing it? So nobody's really done it much before. Is that right? This is the first time you've had to do it.

P3: I did it a bit for English A-Level. Like you had to look at the different aspects of grammar but like never applying it to like a French text or anything, which is a bit different. .. it's like finding out for yourself, you learn a lot more.

As a consequence to findings in 2006–2007, it was decided to action the following changes for academic year 2007–2008:

1. Ask students for their definition of grammar both before *and* after the project to better explore the 'affective' and motivational dimensions relating to grammar learning (Krashen, 1981; Dörnyei, 2001).
2. Re-write the marking scheme for the collaborative component of the project to highlight the importance of grammar analysis.
3. Create a new marking scheme for the individual report.
4. Create new marking criteria for both components of the project (presentation and report).
5. Allocate a limited number of sentences chosen by the tutors.
6. Collaborate with Spanish and French tutors to reinforce grammar analysis and understanding.
7. Highlight common features in grammar amongst the languages studied (both native and target) as opposed to stressing the differences.
8. Provide examples of reflective discourse (Moon, 2004).
9. Make attendance compulsory for grammar sessions (change module descriptor).
10. Make students carry out the grammar analysis on paper before they start creating the website.

The above actions 1, 2, 5, 9, 7 and 10 appeared to work: students' grammar confidence was boosted in 2007–2008, the task appeared to have been understood better and the overall 'learning experience' during contact hours was enhanced by the fact that most students had attended regularly.

A further interesting finding emerged: although the stress during the grammar sessions had been on the identification of common underlying grammar principles amongst the three languages under study (English, French and Spanish), the comparison between textbooks highlighted the fact that there are some major differences in the grammar explanations in the textbooks used on the degree courses that could create confusion amongst students. It was in fact noticed that some English grammar manuals (like Thomson & Martinet, 1986, pp. 352, 338 and 337 and Swain, 1980, p. 480) distinguish between 'possessive adjectives' and 'possessive pronouns' and so do the French and Spanish textbooks (e.g. Kattan-Ibarra & Hawkins, p. 138), but some English grammar textbooks and course books for English linguistics and TEFL don't (e.g. Quirk & Greenbaum, 1973, p. 105; Kuiper &

Scott Allan, 1996, which is the main mandatory textbook for students on Spanish/ French and TEFL), where both 'possessive pronouns' and 'possessive adjectives' are classified as 'possessive pronouns'.

The module leader therefore realised that the students who had taken English language/linguistics 'A' level (secondary school qualification in the UK after 4–5 years of studies) and were quite confident in their grammar analysis classified the 'sa' in 'sa vie' as a pronoun because this was the grammar definition they had been taught in English for 'his' in 'his life' either at school or by colleagues in English. Following consultation with members of staff in both languages and linguistics, it appeared that all languages staff (the *Academic Methods and Approaches* tutor included) felt very strongly that students should use the 'possessive adjective' definition and be taught how a 'possessive adjective' differs from a 'possessive pronoun', while the tutors in linguistics felt that the classification 'pronouns' should now be used for both. Needless to say that this 'epistemic ambiguity' caused some confusion amongst students, and made the understanding of some of the individual grammar categories within the threshold concept more troublesome. This critical incident highlighted that languages and linguistics tutors need to engage in a discussion on grammar terminology in order to implement a consistent approach to its teaching and make it less troublesome for students.

COMMON ISSUES ARISING IN BOTH 2006–2007 AND 2007–2008

Despite the difficulties encountered, the most positive result of the two cycles of actions carried out as part of the curricular intervention appeared to have made the understanding of some components of the threshold concept - morphemes and word classification - easier – even if some issues still remained with word classi-fication, mainly relating to the understanding of pronouns and adverbs. It was confirmed however that the understanding of clauses and phrases is still eluding many students who often failed to see the links between identifying the subject, verb and object in a simple sentence and identifying a clause.

In both years it was also observed that the weaker students did not read the carefully selected and structured literature on grammar provided by the lecturers both in class and online, but chose to find their own grammar material online. This resulted either in confusion and further 'grammar fear' or in false security inspired by non-academic web-sites providing incorrect information.

It emerged that students reading Teaching English as a Foreign Language (TEFL) and a Language (e.g. Spanish and TEFL; French and TEFL) had an advantage over students on other degree combinations (e.g. Spanish and International Relations; French and Business). This was because the TEFL degree course is underpinned by grammar analysis of English in the first year and these students were therefore able to reinforce the grammar knowledge learned in *Methods and Approaches* in their other modules.

There was one particular student in the TEFL and Spanish group, mature and bilingual in Spanish and English, who scored '0' in each of the diagnostic tests he took at the beginning of the term in January 2008 and '80/100' at the end of term in

March 2008. In his case the crossing of the grammar threshold had been particularly visible as he moved from grammar fear – he had never studied grammar formally before - to grammar confidence in eight weeks. When interviewed, he explained that his 'eureka' grammar moment had happened during a lecture given by one lecturer in the English department who was explaining one of the fundamental components of the *rank scale* threshold concept – the phrase - on the mandatory English module *The Nature of Language*, at a time in which the student was carrying out the *Group Grammar Project* and struggling to 'see' the overarching structure of the sentences he was analysing. He decided to ask specifically for further clarifications on the concept of 'phrase' from the English lecturer after struggling with the deconstruction of his Spanish sentence. The English linguistics lecturer then explained that one way to check if a phrase is a phrase is to try and rearrange the phrases identified in a sentence to create a new sentence. If the new sentence still makes sense, the phrases have been identified correctly. This 'revelation' set the student on a path of grammar discovery and, as he put it to the interviewers (March 2008), in the end he could 'see' the grammar in a sentence - like the Matrix in the homonymous film: 'I could not see anything before. Now I look at a sentence and I can see grammar, it's there, it's like the Matrix' (Semi-structured interviews March 2008).

This above student's 'grammar journey' would appear to illustrate how for some students one of the abstract components of the *rank scale* threshold concept (the phrase) can be crossed via the support of concerted curricular actions, targeted assessment (both formative and summative), collaborative group work and metare-flection. The abstract teaching on his linguistics module reinforced by his practice on the *Group Grammar Project* enabled him to 'see' the connection between theory and practice, to make the link that opened a new world of understanding to him and cross the threshold.

In view of the difficulties encountered by English-educated students in tackling the *rank scale* threshold concept and its individual troublesome components in a sentence both in English and in the target language(s) studied, it could be argued that more work on basic grammar concepts could be carried in schools before pupils reach the secondary level sector. Some of the interviewees pointed out that their grammar fear had been triggered by the fact that grammar was first mentioned to them in year 7. The ease with which most of the native French, German, Polish and Italian students in the two years tackled the analysis of the grammar categories in the sentences allocated for the *Group Grammar Project* would appear to be linked with having engaged with a considerable amount of formal grammar instruction from primary school level. This does not mean that their analysis was always correct, but they did not perceive the grammar analysis of sentences in the *Group Grammar Project* as a 'terrifying' task like so many of their English peers. Languages lecturers who have not been educated in England are not always fully aware of this 'grammar gap' and sometimes assume a basic level of 'meta-grammatical' knowledge on the part of their students. This would appear to add a 'cultural' dimension to the understanding (or not) of the threshold concept identified.

The research findings also corroborated the proposition that embedding metacognitive work into the teaching and learning of grammar via the *Group Grammar Project* had enhanced the students' ability to deal with troublesome grammar knowledge. In academic years 2006–2007 and 2007–2008 students had become better at self-diagnosing their grammar strengths and weaknesses in comparison with previous academic years. This was demonstrated by the fact that while in 2003–2005 there had been a wide discrepancy between the students' estimated mark for the grammar analysis and the real one, in 2006–2007 and 2007–2008 the students' predictions were quite accurate. It could be argued that this is a result of having offered students more opportunities for metareflection with the support of dedicated e-tools. During the interviews, in 2007–2008 in particular, most students stated that they now knew what to do to improve their grammar understanding. As previously highlighted, it could be argued that this is a positive step towards the crossing of the threshold concept. These findings would appear to indicate that encouraging students to 'metareflect' upon the threshold concept identified can trigger a 'self-assessment ontological shift' that will help them at least at the level of the 'estimation' and 'evaluation' (Meyer, Land & Davies, 2008, pp. 70–71) of their position *vis a vis* the threshold concept and give them the confidence to at least assess their understanding of the 'protocol', 'the rules of the game'. So, although students might still be pre-liminal with reference to the concept itself, the confidence acquired via self-assessment will have prepared the ground for the ontological shift that can lead to the 'eureka' moment of grasping the concept.

CONCLUSION

The assessed task designed to help students with overcoming grammar fear, the *Group Grammar Project,* appears to have boosted grammar knowledge and confidence for most students, but many negative attitudes towards grammar 'nurtured' within the English school system are difficult to 'undo'.

However, in the cases in which the students started to understand how to analyse a sentence, the impact of the action-research-led curricular intervention illustrated here proved to be very beneficial and wide-ranging, also improving grammar performance and understanding in related modules, as reported by both the students and other colleagues in languages.

As already stressed, another emerging outcome will require further investigation. Although some students did not appear to improve their understanding of some of the threshold concept's components, they were better at self-assessing their understanding (or lack of) for each of them. So, while in previous years there had been a discrepancy between students' perception of progress and actual results (Orsini-Jones and Jones 2007: 100), in 2006–08 the students appeared to have a very accurate perception of their own grammar analysis proficiency. It would seem that the increase in the amount of work done at the 'metareflective' level improved the students' ability for accurate self-assessment in grammar understanding. It could be argued that this in turn had enhanced their 'preparedness' to embrace the ontological shift necessary to cross the threshold. It could be argued that meta-reflection encouraged students to engage with their state of liminality towards the threshold identified in a positive and constructive way and helped with overcoming the paralysing 'fear of grammar' some had experienced at the beginning of the academic year.

The findings also confirm that the overarching structure of a sentence (*rank scale*) is a threshold concept for linguists and is (as from Meyer & Land, 2003 and 2005):

- Troublesome;
- Transformative;
- Integrative;
- Bounded.

However, as highlighted previously (Orsini-Jones, 2008, p. 224), its *irreversibility* is still under discussion, as during this action-research cycle, like in the 2003–2005 one, some students appeared to be able to grasp it for one language, but to be unable to transfer it across the other languages studied.

The analysis of the data from this study also confirms that the threshold concept identified is complex and cannot be crossed in one academic year by many students. Further explorations of long-term curricular interventions are needed to help students on languages further with grasping this concept.

APPENDIX 1

Translation of the poem 'L'infinito' – Infinity - by Giacomo Leopardi. The translation (slightly edited here) was found at http://www.tcm.phy.cam.ac.uk/~mdt26/poems/leopardi2.html

Always dear to me was this lonely hill,
And this hedge, which precludes the view of such a great a part
Of the farthest horizon.
But as I sit and watch
I figure in my mind the endless spaces beyond it, and the superhuman
silences, and the deepest quiet wherefore my heart
almost loses itself in fear. And as I hear the wind
rustle through these plants, I compare
that infinite silence to this voice:
and I recall to mind eternity,
And the dead seasons, and the current one
alive, and what it sounds like. So in this
Immensity my thoughts drown:
And it is sweet for me to shipwreck in this sea.

APPENDIX 2

Glossary for the *Group Grammar Project*

Morphemes

A morpheme can be defined as the smallest meaningful unit of language: a morpheme can only be further divided into sounds which do not carry any meaning.

Morphemes can be defined as:

– **free** – morphemes which can stand alone, e.g. "*strawberry*" consists of 2 free morphemes ("*straw*" and "*berry*")
– or **bound** – morphemes which cannot stand alone, e.g. "*unfortunately*" consists of 1 free morpheme ("*fortune*") and 3 bound morphemes
– ("*-un-*", "*-ate-*" and "*-ly*").

Bound morphemes can be further divided into:

– **inflection** – morphemes which add extra information to the basic word, e.g. "-s" in "runs" or "-ed" in "started".
– **derivation** – morphemes which change one word into another word of a different class, e.g. "*-ly*" in "*luckily*" or "*-ion*" in "*demonstration*".
A word consists of one or more morphemes.

Words

Words can be seen as the basic building blocks of language, and can be recognised in the written language by the space before and after each word.

There are 8 basic classes of word (also known as "parts of speech"):

- **verb** – sometimes defined as "doing" or "action" words, they can also indicate states or conditions. They are the central unit of a sentence, and can best be recognised grammatically, as they show tense as well as person and number.
- **noun** – sometimes described as "naming" or "object" words, they can also indicate abstract qualities. They accompany verbs and can again best be described grammatically: they show number and sometimes case, but not tense or person.
- **adjective** – usually accompany a noun, and qualify or modify the noun in some way. Sometimes defined as "describing" words.
- **adverb** – very hard to define as they are essentially the residual category: if a word doesn't fit any of the other definitions, it must be an adverb. They qualify or modify verbs, adjectives, other adverbs or whole sentences.
- **pronoun** – words such as *"he"*, *"she"*, *"which"*, *"them"*. They stand in for and replace a noun.
- **preposition** – words such as *"for"*, *"with"*, *"in"*, *"under"*. They are placed before nouns or noun phrases to form preposition phrases.
- **article** – essentially three words in English: *"the"*, *"a"*, *"an"*. In some languages they combine with some prepositions to form a single word.
- **conjunction** – words which join together two elements within a sentence, most commonly two nouns or noun phrases or two clauses. Words such as *"and "*, *"because"*, *"until"*, *"while"*.

Many words may function as 2 or more different parts of speech, depending on the context.

A phrase consists of one or more words.

Phrases

A phrase is a group of words which taken together form a meaningful unit. The function they perform in a clause or sentence can also be performed by a single word.

There are 5 basic types, each named after their main or "head" word:

- **noun phrases**
- **verb phrases**
- **adjective phrases**
- **adverb phrases** and
- **preposition phrases**

Pronouns are considered to be noun phrases, and articles never occur as head word of a phrase.

A clause consists of one or more phrases.

Clauses

A clause is a meaningful group of words which includes a verb, and is sometimes defined as a sentence within a sentence. Three basic types can be distinguished:

- **Main clause** - all sentences have at least one "main" clause, possibly more. If there is more than one main clause they are normally joined together by "*and*" or "*but*".
- **Subordinate clause** - a "subordinate" clause is one whose meaning depends on that of the main clause for a full interpretation, and they can be joined to the main clause by a variety of different conjunctions.
- **Reduced clause** - a "reduced " clause in one which does not have a complete verb phrase.

A clause can be divided into

- **subject**
- **verb**
- **object (direct or indirect)** and
- **adjunct**

It may have several adjuncts, but not more than one of the other elements. **All** clauses have a verb, and in some languages (such as English and French) **must** have a subject. They do not always have a direct and/or indirect object or any adjuncts. The subject determines the person and number of the verb.
A sentence consists of one or more clauses.

Sentences

Sentences are the largest units of language which have a grammatical structure. They normally start with a capital letter and end with a full stop (or question or exclamation mark).
Sentences can be:

- simple
- compound
- complex

Refer to Sinclair (2007) for further details on what simple, compound and complex sentences consist of.

NOTES

[1]   Translation in Appendix 1.
[2]   The project was allocated £4,000 pedagogical research funding by the Higher Education Academy Subject Centre for Languages, Linguistics and Area Studies (UK). Please note that some of the findings illustrated here have been previously published (as conference proceedings in Orsini-Jones & Sinclair, 2008).

REFERENCES

Barnett, R. (2007). *A will to learn: Being a student in an age of uncertainty*. Buckingham: SRHE and Open University Press.

Bransford, J. D., Brown, A. L., & Cocking, R. R. (2000). *How people learn: Brain, mind, experience and school*. Washington, DC: National Academy Press.

British Educational Research Association (BERA). (2008). Retrieved April 30, 2008, from http://www. bera.ac.uk/welcome/index.php

Chomsky, N. (1968). *Language and mind*. New York: Harcourt, Brace and World.

Coulthard, M. (1985). *An introduction to discourse analysis*. Harlow: Longman.

Crystal, D. (2006). *How language works*. London: Penguin.

Davies, P., & Mangan, J. (2007). Threshold concepts and the integration of understanding in economics. *Studies in Higher Education, 32*(6), 711–726.

Dörnyei, Z. (2007). *Research methods in applied linguistics*. Oxford, UK: OUP.

Gray, K., & Yavash, P. (2007). *An evaluation of the challenges MBA students encounter in acquiring and applying threshold concepts in Economics*. Project Report for the HEA Economics Network Pedagogic Funded homonymous project, available online at: Retrieved February 15, 2009, from http://www.economicsnetwork.ac.uk/projects/mini/gray_mba.htm

Halliday, M. (1985). *An introduction to functional grammar*. London: Edward Arnold.

Hauck, M. (2005). Metacognitive knowledge, metacognitive strategies, and CALL. In J. Egbert & G. Petrie (Eds.), *Call: Research perspectives* (pp. 65–86). Mahwah, NJ: Lawrence Erlbaum.

Hurd, S. (2000). Helping learners to help themselves: The role of metacognitive skills and strategies in independent language learning. In M. Fay & D. Ferney (Eds.), *Current trends in modern languages provision for non-specialist linguists* (pp. 36–52). London: CILT.

Kattan-Ibarra, J., & Hawkins, A. (2003). *Spanish Grammar in context: Analysis & practice*. London: Arnold.

Kember, D. (2000). *Action learning and action research: Improving the quality of teaching and learning*. London: Kogan Page.

Kemmis, S., & McTaggart, R. (Eds.). (1990). *The action research reader*. Victoria: Deakin University.

Kemmis, S., & McTaggart, R. (2005). Participatory action research: Communicative action and the public sphere. In N. K. Denzin & Y. S. Lincoln (Eds.), *The sage handbook of qualitative research* (pp. 559–603). London: SAGE.

Klapper, J. (2006). *Understanding and developing good practice: Language teaching in higher education*. London: CILT.

Krashen, S. D. (1981). *Second language acquisition and second language learning*. Oxford, UK: Pergamon.

Kuiper, K., & Scott Allan, W. (2004). *An introduction to English language: Word, sound and sentence* (2nd ed.). Basingstoke, UK: Palgrave McMillan.

Land, R., Meyer, J. H. F., & Smith, J. (Eds.). *Threshold concepts within the disciplines* (59–74). Rotterdam, The Netherlands: Sense.

Leopardi, G. *L'infinito* (1818–1821). Retrieved from http://www.tcm.phy.cam.ac.uk/~mdt26/poems/ leopardi1.html (Italian) Retrieved February 15, 2009, from http://www.tcm.phy.cam.ac.uk/~mdt26/ poems/leopardi2.html (English)

Mackey, A., & Gass, S. M. (2005). *Second language research: Methods and design*. London: Routledge.

McKernan, J. (1992). *Curriculum action research*. London: Kogan Page.

McNiff, J. (1988). *Action research: Principles and practices*. London: Routledge.

Meyer, J. H. F., & Land, R. (2003). Threshold concepts and troublesome knowledge (1). Linkages to ways of thinking and practising within the disciplines. In C. Rust (Ed.), *Improving student learning – Ten years on* (pp. 412–424). Proceedings of the 2002 10th International Symposium, The Oxford Centre for Staff and Learning Development. Oxford, UK: OCSLD.

Meyer, J. H. F., & Land, R. (2005). Threshold concepts and troublesome knowledge (2): Epistemological considerations and a conceptual framework for teaching and learning. *Higher Education, 49*, 373–388.

Meyer, J. H. F., & Land, R. (2006). *Overcoming barriers to student understanding: Threshold concepts and troublesome knowledge*. London: Routledge/Falmer.

Meyer, J. H. F., Land, R., & Davies, P. (2008). Threshold concepts and troublesome knowledge (4): Issues of variation and variability. In R. Land, J. H. F. Meyer, & J. Smith (Eds.), *Threshold concepts within the disciplines* (pp. 59–74). Rotterdam, The Netherlands: Sense.

Meyer, J. H. F., & Land, R. (2010). Threshold concepts and troublesome knowledge (5): Dynamics of assessment. In press in this volume.

Mitchell, R., & Myles, F. (2004). *Second language learning theories* (2nd ed.). London: Hodder Arnold.

Module Information Directory (MID). (2008). *Coventry University*. Retrieved February 15, 2009, from http://mid.coventry.ac.uk

Moon, J. (2004). *A handbook of reflective and experiental learning: Theory and practice*. London: Routledge/Falmer.

Muhr, T. (1997). *ATLAS.Ti: The knowledge workbench*. Berlin: Scientific Software Development.

Orsini-Jones, M. (2004). Supporting a course in new literacies and skills for linguists with a Virtual Learning Environment: Results from a staff/student collaborative action-research project at Coventry University. *ReCALL, 16*(1), 189–209.

Orsini-Jones, M., & Jones, D. E. (2007). Supporting collaborative grammar learning via a Virtual Learning Environment (VLE): A case study from Coventry University. *Arts and Humanities in Higher Education: An International Journal of Theory, Research and Practice, 6*(1), 90–106.

Orsini-Jones, M., Adley, D., Lamari, C., Maund, N., & Paruk, K. (2007). Integrating PDP (Personal Development Planning) and *PebblePAD* into the curriculum – Students' perspectives. In F. Deepwell (Ed.), *Proceedings of the ELATE (Enhancing Learning and Teaching Environments) Conference 2007. Internationalisation* (pp. 31–35). Coventry, UK: Coventry University.

Orsini-Jones, M., & Sinclair, C. (2008). Helping students to GRASP the rules of grammar. In C. Rust (Ed.), *Improving student learning – For what?* (pp. 72–86). Proceeding of the 2007 15th International Symposium – The Oxford Centre for Staff and Learning Development. Oxford, UK: OCSLD.

Orsini-Jones, M. (2008). Troublesome language knowledge: Identifying threshold concepts in grammar learning. In R. Land, J. H. F. Meyer, & J. Smith (Eds.), *Threshold concepts within the disciplines* (pp. 213–226). Rotterdam, The Netherlands: Sense.

Osmond, J., & Turner, A. (2008). Measuring the creative baseline in transport design education. In C. Rust (Ed.), *Improving student learning – For what?* (pp. 87–101). Proceeding of the 2007 15th International Symposium – The Oxford Centre for Staff and Learning Development. Oxford, UK: OCSLD.

PebblePAD. Retrieved February 15, 2009, from http://www.pebblelearning.co.uk/

Perkins, D. (2006). Constructivism and troublesome knowledge. In J. H. E Meyer & R. Land (Eds.), *Overcoming barriers to student understanding: Threshold concepts and troublesome knowledge* (pp. 33–47). London: RoutledgeFalmer.

Quality Assurance Agency (QAA) for Higher Education. (2002). *Languages and related studies, subject benchmark statement*. Gloucester: QAA.

Quirk, R., & Greenbaum, S. (1973). *A University grammar of English*. London: Longman.

Sinclair, C. (2007). *Grammar: A friendly approach*. Milton Keynes: OU/McGraw-Hill.

Thomson, A. J., & Martinet, A. V. (1986, 1992 print). *A practical English grammar* (4th ed.). Oxford, UK: OUP.

Turner, V. (1967). Betwixt and between: The liminal period in Rites de Passage. In V. Turner (Ed.), *The forest of symbols* (pp. 93–111). Ithaca, NY: Cornell University Press.

Marina Orsini-Jones
Department of English and Languages
Coventry University (UK)

PART III:
ONTOLOGICAL TRANSFORMATIONS

JENS KABO AND CAROLINE BAILLIE

18. ENGINEERING AND SOCIAL JUSTICE

Negotiating the Spectrum of Liminality

INTRODUCTION

Throughout their education, engineering students develop an understanding that engineering is mostly about problem solving, technical development, efficiency, and profit making. Thus the idea of engineering focussed on social justice challenges the view many engineering students have of their future profession. This study explores these challenges as a potential threshold for students. However, rather than only being a threshold for students entering engineering we suggest that social justice serves as a threshold for the whole discipline and that this in turn implicates the development of current ways of thinking and practising of engineering. This discussion brings to the forefront the question of expertise and who may judge what are these ways of thinking.

What is Engineering?

The view of engineering often found in engineering text books represents what we are calling the 'common sense' view of the profession both among educators and practitioners. A classical definition by Thomas Tredgold on behalf of the Institution of Civil Engineers in 1828, states that: '[engineering is] the art of directing the great sources of power in nature for the use and convenience of man [sic]'(Johnston, Gostelow, & King, 2000, p. 26). 180 years later the essence of this definition can be found in the American Accreditation Board of Engineering and Technology's (ABET) view of engineering, but emphasis on economics has been added (Voland, 2004). These views of engineering place the profession at the service of humanity, but signal that nature is there for humans to use as they see fit. Andrews *mult al.* (2006) view engineers as people who use their knowledge and skills to create, operate, manage, or maintain products and processes in a rational and economic way. This marks a shift away from an ideological emphasis to a more practical one, i.e. engineers build things. More recently, some people within the profession have started to focus more on the social dimension of engineering. According to Johnston *et al.* (2000, p. 26) engineering is '[a] total societal enterprise, with significant influences on all aspects of human life and a major role to play in moving the world towards particular goals.' However, Vesilind (2006, p. 283) suggests that engineers have never been very good at this, since '[t]he engineer is

J. H. F. Meyer, R. Land and C. Baillie (eds.), Threshold Concepts and
Transformational Learning, 303–315.

sophisticated in creating technology, but unsophisticated in understanding its application. As a result engineers have historically been employed as hired guns, doing the bidding of both political rulers and wealthy corporations.' Overall, the current, or 'common sense' understanding of engineering among students, practitioners and even professors is that engineering is mostly associated with efficiency and profit making, and there is usually an inherent belief that technical development always equates to progress.

Engineering in a Social Context

Critics of the common sense view such as Catalano (2007) believe that technology and rapidly accelerating technical advances have played key roles in the creation of two of our largest challenges – those of poverty and environmental sustainability. A present and ongoing issue that highlights the nature of the complexities engineers face today is the international debate about biofuel (e.g. Vidal, 2008). Biofuels have been seen as a part of the solution of countering global warming since their net carbon dioxide imprint on the environment is zero. An increasing demand for biofuel in the world has lead to farmers switching from food production to fuel production. A decrease in food production will contribute to an increase in food prices, which has the greatest impact on the poor of the world. In addition, production of crops for biofuel has lead to the destruction of rainforests in some parts of the world because forest areas are cleared for fuel production.

To deal successfully with increasingly complex and interdisciplinary challenges, Catalano and Baillie (2006) believe that it is important that engineers broaden their horizons and become more aware of the impact of their actions. Ursula Franklin (1999), who is a key thinker in the area of technology and society, offers advice on how to ensure a socially just engineering practice by proposing that engineers always ask about their projects, 'who benefits and who pays?' An important skill to enable us to properly ask the questions and to appropriately define our problem is critical thinking, the ability to see beyond what we consider to be 'common sense'. It is important for engineering students to question the very essence of what they assume engineering to be.

Thought Collectives

According to Baillie and Rose (2004, p. 20): 'it is important to realise that for something to be known, it must fit within the relevant community's paradigm or thought collective.' The term 'thought collective' originates with Fleck (1979, p. 39) who says:

> If we define 'thought collective' as a community of persons mutually exchanging ideas or maintaining intellectual interaction, we will find by implication that it also provides the special 'carrier' for the historical development of any field of thought, as well as for the given stock of knowledge and level of culture. This we have designated thought style.

Fleck then goes on and discuss consequences of these thought styles (1979, p. 99):

It constrains the individual by determining 'what can be thought in no other way.' Whole eras will then be ruled by this thought constraint. Heretics who do not share this collective mode and are rated as criminals by the collective will be burned at the stake until a different mode creates a different thought style and different valuation.

And when two different thought styles collide (1979, p. 109):

The alien way of thought seems like mysticism. The questions it rejects will often be regarded as the most important ones, its problems as often unimportant or meaningless trivialities.

Wenger (1998, p. 175) discusses, on a related note, potential consequences of belonging to a community of practice:

The understanding inherent in a shared practice is not necessarily one that gives members broad access to the histories or relations with other practices that shape their own practice. Through engagement, competence can become so transparent, logically ingrained, and socially efficacious that it becomes insular: nothing else, no other viewpoint, can even register, let alone create a disturbance or a discontinuity that would spur the history of practice onward. In this way, a community of practice can become an obstacle to learning by entrapping us in its very power to sustain our identity.

So what both Fleck and Wenger are saying is that the established ways of thinking within a community or a group can serve as barriers toward new knowledge building, i.e. potentially create thresholds. As an example of this, Baillie and Johnson (2008), by studying the attitudes of first year engineering students in a professional skills class, found that the students experienced 'professionalism' as a threshold. The view of engineering presented in the class clashed with some students' perceptions which were more aligned with applying science to solve problems in a classroom than the communication and collaboration required in real world engineering. These students could be said to form a thought collective based on their high school experience and this worked as a barrier when presented with a new view of engineering. After some time in an engineering program, students will most likely become part of a new thought collective represented by engineering education. We might imagine then that seeing through the lens of social justice might prove to be a barrier for engineering students who are in this thought collective. This was observed in practice when one of the authors of this paper, Baillie, together with Richard Day, Sociologist, in 2006 developed a class entitled 'Engineering and Social Justice: Critical Theories of Technological Practice'. Students taking the course appeared to move into a liminal space, some passing through, some getting stuck and others moving back and forth uncertain of what to do. It was hypothesised, therefore, that for engineers, both practising and students, adopting a socially just perspective to their practice and profession can be seen as a threshold that needs to be crossed and that this transition might prove both transformative and troublesome. The current study aimed to explore this liminal space in order to help students navigate through in future years.

THE THRESHOLD CONCEPT FRAMEWORK

The threshold concept framework represents a relatively recent and growing area in educational research as discussed in the rest of this book and at the conference at which the paper that forms the basis of this chapter was presented. The idea is that there exist certain concepts within a discipline that have transformative qualities concerning ways of thinking and seeing that are crucial to a learner's progress in the discipline. However, the process of grasping these concepts might prove trouble-some for some learners, leaving them stuck and unable to move forward (possibly for some time).

The term 'concept' does not necessarily have to be interpreted in the narrow sense of a scientific concept. For example, social justice is not a concept in the same sense as gravity or complex numbers are concepts in engineering. Social justice represents a way of seeing the world. However, the metaphor of the threshold is still useful for describing engineering students' attempts to approach social justice. Meyer and Land (2003) raise the notion that there might exist ways of thinking or seeing that will have the same transformative effect as their proposed concepts.

Part of grasping a threshold concept seems to involve the learner moving closer to how people think within a discipline. In other words threshold concepts are likely to be key points in a gradual shift from a novice mindset to an expert mindset in relation to a subject or discipline. This leads to the notion of 'thinking like an engineer' or 'thinking like an economist' etc. However, we maintain that social justice (as related to engineering) cannot be seen in this light since it both originates outside the discipline and challenges the status quo of the disciplinary community.

Meyer and Land (2006, p. 25) relate the new ways of seeing that Einstein introduced into his community of practice:

> Einstein, in this instance, was not traversing a threshold concept already in existence, *he was creating the threshold*, and perhaps to a certain extent creating his own liminality. It is feasible that this form of liminality may be quite common to the process of conducting fundamental research, which creates new thresholds rather than extending or elaborating the domains (boundedness) of existing ones. Indeed it might be argued all creative movements in forward research share a similar quality of liminality as that which appears within the Einstein story.

In addition to being conceptually difficult, general relativity represents a very different way of conceptualising space and time than the Newtonian way most physics students are used to. From this example it can be speculated that the introduction of new ways of seeing in to a disciplinary community can create new thresholds. Einstein was still working within the discipline of physics, but came up with a new way of seeing.

Flanagan (2007) speculates that new thresholds can arise in cross-disciplinary contexts and observes that computer science and non-computer science students, e.g. electrical engineers, negotiate liminal spaces or cross thresholds related to learning to program in different ways. He suggests that a possible factor behind this is that non-computer science students do not 'benefit from being in an environment that facilities their embracing of the ethos of the computer science community and from the reinforcement of a wider computing curriculum' (Flanagan, 2007, p. 2). However, non- computer science students who successfully cross the thresholds 'move rapidly into a mode of discussing their work in a manner [similar to that of computer science] and can be observed volubly attempting to take a partner over the threshold' (Flanagan, 2007, p. 4).

Due to their transformative qualities the process of internalising a threshold concept can be seen as a transition from one state of knowing. This transition can be quick or drawn out over a considerable period of time depending on how troublesome a learner finds the concept in question. Meyer and Land (2006) use the terms liminality or liminal space to describe this transition. The idea of a liminal space is useful to illustrate the variation in how different students progress towards adopting social justice as a perspective to engineering problem solving. The liminal space will be expanded through the idea of *pre-liminal*, *liminal* and *post-liminal* variation (Meyer, Land and Davies, 2008), that is variation in the ways in which students see the concept come into focus, pass through the threshold and come out the other side. An illustration of this can be seen in Figure 1.

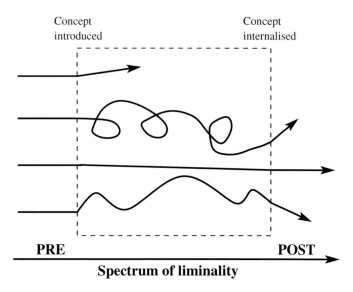

Figure 1. A visual representation of the variation present among students navigating a liminal space connected to a threshold. Based upon the work of Meyer et al. (2008).

RESEARCH PROJECT BACKGROUND AND APPROACH

The focus of this study was a course entitled 'Engineering and Social Justice: Critical theories of technological practices' which was an elective course at Queen's University in Canada. The course was cross-disciplinary both in content and student composition (engineering and social science). Its aim was to help students see the wider context of, and develop critical perspectives toward, technology in general and engineering practices in particular. Social justice was the guiding ideal of the course and the ways in which it can be applied in the engineering context were explored. The classes were carried out in a seminar manner with discussions usually centred on the assigned weekly readings. These readings covered key concepts, the dominant engineering paradigm, critical perspectives and alternative paradigms. Based on these readings the students had to write two critical response essays, which encouraged them to deal with the ideas presented on a more personal level. In addition, the students were required to carry out community based group projects in which they were to critically examine an element of engineering practice.

This study is situated in an adapted phenomenographic (Marton and Booth, 1997) framework – a non-dualist position, focussed on collective experiences of phenomena, and pooling of data. The 'outcome space' differs from traditional phenomenographic studies by focusing on liminal variation of the paths through the threshold. This facilitates the study and description of the range of experiences of a group of engineering students approaching social justice as a lens for looking at engineering practice. Data were collected at two stages (first and second half) of the course through semi-structured interviews with a total of 13 students from both engineering and social science. 11 of the students were interviewed during the first round and 10 were interviewed during the second round. Interviews were transcribed verbatim. The transcripts were read with the following in mind: What were the students' conceptions of social justice? What helped their learning? What hindered their learning? When relevant quotes were found these were highlighted and collated to form a pool of meaning. Initially, the quotes from each interview round were analysed separately, but were later pooled. The iterative process then continued until the themes could be formalised.

RESULTS AND DISCUSSION

Variation along the Spectrum of Liminality

When the students were asked to describe what social justice meant to them, different conceptions of how they conceptualized social justice emerged – nine in total. These conceptions can be seen as different points on a spectrum of liminality – going from a pre-liminal state to bordering on a post-liminal state. A key thing that varies over the different conceptions is the students' awareness of the complexities surrounding social justice, which goes from simple and superficial to complex and deep. Other shifts are from active to passive and individual to collective. The nine conceptions are illustrated by the quotes given below and a visual summary can be found in Figure 2.

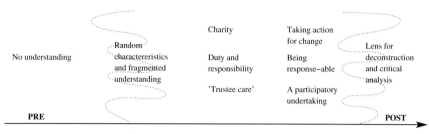

Spectrum of liminality

Figure 2. A visual representation of the nine conceptions of how students conceptualise social justice scattered over a spectrum of liminality. Conceptions situated further to the right in the figure represent a more complex understanding.

Pre-liminal state before social justice comes into view – no understanding. Some students showed at times during the interviews no or little understanding for various critical aspects of social justice. This indicates that at least some parts of the threshold had not come into view for them yet. The following quote shows this:

> S11: [In response to worker recovered factories in Argentina] I'm really glad I don't live in Argentina and I really think anybody in their right mind would want to live in a society where even if you weren't per se seeing the profits, you would want to live in a society where someone was. [...] I don't think you can just get rid of it [hierarchical workplaces], like they did in Argentina, I would be surprised if anyone is happy with the situation in Argentina.

This student seems to miss that the main reasons behind why workers in Argentina took over enterprises that had closed down during the country's economical meltdown around the turn of the century were desperation and pure survival and not because they thought it was a better system. The 'common sense' of profit making is very strong.

Social justice as random characteristics and fragmented understanding. Here the students spoke about social justice in general terms focusing on random and isolated characteristics which indicated a fragmented understanding.

> S2: Yeah, for sure like I always thought of social justice as like going and like feeding people like foreign aid and stuff like that, my idea of social justice now has changed in the sense that like it's broader than just foreign aid, like you can do a lot of things like with our pro bono project, it's not like we're going to a third world country and helping them with their cars and what not, we're like helping people who need to be helped and you can you know, you can have social justice in your everyday life whether you live in a first world country or a third world country.

309

Social justice as charity. Here students had a stronger focus on one thing they considered to be social justice namely charity or a one-way transfer of something, the act of giving. The critical aspect here is that there is a giver and a receiver.

> S5: It is the same kind of idea for engineering, if we don't help them rebuild their infrastructure, who is gonna rebuild it? Who is gonna educate them? Show them that there is a better way?

> S9: If we did this [the interview] in week one, you'd ask me: what's social justice? I'd probably say charity. Like giving money and just, I don't know, helping out the poor person, walking by throw them two bucks, that's social justice.

Social justice as duty and responsibility. Here the focus is less on a specific act and more on the moral underpinnings of social justice, which take the form of having a duty or responsibility.

> S5: It all comes down to doing what is right. Do you think it's right? Like, if you saw, you know, someone weak being bullied by someone in the street, would you do something about it? Well, you should. Morally you should do something about it. It is having the moral courage to act.

> S13: Every human being has a responsibility to work toward social justice. [...] When I think of social justice I think of not having any negative impact on anything by anybody's actions, and that's obviously impossible.

Social justice as telling people what to do or 'trustee care'. This conception of social justice is somewhat similar to charity but the focus is less on giving and more on a limited form of collaboration between giver and receiver. The giver provides the receiver with 'know how' but maintains a position of power.

> S5: Instead of us going in and building it for them [...] it's like a mentorship program, apprenticeship as well. We take people from [local university] and teach them how to do it. [...] So we don't do it, we get them to do it and we pay a local elder to pay workers to do it. We show them how to do it. [...] trying to educate them not just doing it for them. [...] We have interaction with the local population. Obviously we want to build trust. Without trust nothing happens.

Social justice as taking action for change. The critical aspect of this conception of social justice is that students have realised that only having a responsibility or providing help or 'know how' is not enough and that more direct personal action is needed for truly promoting social justice.

> S12: First of all when you know something, when you have the knowledge you can start thinking about what choices you want to make. So you take a choice, you decide to get involved and once you make a choice even then you still have to take action. It doesn't matter, I could make the choice to go help someone, but until I actually do it I haven't really done much, right?

S8: At the same time I do think that you have to feel passionate about it and I sort of realize the things that I do feel passionate about, it's not enough to just talk to them, talk about them to my friends, that I should actually be seeking out people who might feel the same way and who are, you know, wanting to put together different initiatives to do something about it.

For this student the taking action part is also critical but the action itself involves collaborating with people to actually change how things work.

Social justice as being response-able. Being response-able means being aware of the consequences of different actions and trying to respond accordingly, i.e. to be able to respond. The critical point here is the combination of awareness and corresponding appropriate action, even if the necessary action is not clear.

S7: I feel that what I understand of social justice is what I'm doing is at the expense of others as opposed to this is what I do to help others, this is how social justice works to help people, so I guess my concept is this is what I need to stop doing, this is what I need to stop other people from doing and this is like, this is the system I need to understand and understand how to change and I understand less about what to do as an alternative you know like how to, I just know that what is happening is unjust.

The following student focused on a specific issue to point out the link between awareness and appropriate action.

S3: I don't think that you can geographically just look at one thing and see if it benefits, like have that as your scope, because there can be a lot that happens because of that outside of there. Like right now garbage is shipped to other countries and thing like that. If you just looked at Canada, you'd be like: oh yeah we are doing pretty good for waste in Canada, but maybe that's because we are shipping it to other places. So I think it is completely global scale, especially in this day and age with technology that we have.

Social justice as a participatory undertaking. The critical aspects of this conception are that change comes through collaboration and that power relationships between participants need to be levelled.

S8: You realize that social justice can't come from one and it has to, it's a dynamic process where you have to communicate with people. [...] collaborating with different people and their ideas to synthesize all these ideas and to make sure that you know whatever practice you're doing everyone benefits.

S10: It would be sort of taking into account like a variety of perspectives and how different sorts of social, cultural, political influence [...] affect those different perspectives [...] I guess it's taking into consideration like the broader social influence that impact a variety of people as opposed to speaking of it as a top down theory. [I: So more bottom up?] Yeah.

Social justice as a lens for deconstruction and critical analysis. The critical aspect of this conception is the insight that awareness about, for example, social injustices can only be gained by critical analysis and deconstruction of what one takes for granted. While some of the earlier dimensions highlighted the role of awareness this dimension highlights how awareness can be achieved and also how appropriate actions can be devised.

> S9: You should try and see what actually caused this to happen, cause if it burst once it can burst again and the same thing with social justice and charity is that if you just kind of perform charity acts, yeah you might have helped one person in one situation, but who's to say the underlying factor won't cause the exact same thing to somebody else. So social justice, social change is trying to figure out well what's the fundamental problem or what's the root cause of […] what you're seeing.

> S8: I think that it's really important that different people from different faculties sort of break down the boundaries between them and come and together and learn a lot about other things that you normally would have certain assumptions on.

In summary, different conceptions of how the students conceptualised social justice go from simple toward more complex understanding and the variation along the spectrum of liminality helps to illustrate how the students pass through the threshold. The conceptions cannot be seen as a linear progression since they both overlap and can exist simultaneously in how a student views social justice.

Student Perceptions of Barriers to their Understanding of Social Justice

The students mentioned several things, both at a collective and an individual level, that they experienced as blocks or barriers when trying to approach social justice as a lens for their practice.

Collective barriers – 'Common sense' views in Engineering. Some students felt that their previous experiences of the engineering culture and engineering education strongly emphasised money, profit making and efficiency as well as being conformist and traditional. The students felt that all of these served as obstacles for shifting engineering more toward social justice as well as providing personal challenges.

> S7: [In class] everyone kept bringing up efficiency. […] and I just thought why is efficiency so important and my personal kind of conclusion was that it's because we have to make a profit and be, you know everyone is taking commerce classes or business classes that are talking about the economy. […] So I feel like that concept being so prevalent is why the environmental crisis seems inevitable to me is that, unless we stop growing, I mean we just can't continue to grow and this idea of growth just doesn't seem to get questioned. […] I mean I know people who are very environmentally conscious

and they do their best and they're really pro uh, they're very positively favoured towards environmental causes, but the idea of not growing still seems just so hard to imagine to them and I think those two things conflict.

S9: Especially in engineering where you're always told these are the courses you need to take if you want to be a professional engineer, here's your core curriculum and this is the way you're thinking. It's almost like a little cookies cutter, you just go along and you make little engineers and then you throw them out into the real world. But yeah, once you're the little gingerbread cookie cutter guy out there you have to realize there are so many different viewpoints.

S9: After the [traditional Canadian engineering] ceremony I brought the feminism aspect to kinda say well why is it so male dominated and some people, yeah, some people flat out said well that's the way it's always been.

Individual barriers – personal challenges and risks. Some students perceived that at a personal level approaching social justice could potentially involve sacrifice, risks, doubts and discomfort. In addition they felt it was difficult to move beyond the things they took for granted.

S13: [The course] really messed with my head. Sometimes I was scared going to class because I didn't want to think about stuff. [...] it put some guilt on my actions [...] I feel that it might have an impact on my success in a company, for example if I don't do it the next person might.

S5: I can see that this kind of engineering [pro bono] is not going to happen without government sanction. You know liabilities, [...] you cannot do anything without being sued nowadays. So the fact that doctors can do pro bono work and are covered by the government, lawyers can do pro bono work and are covered by the government, it should be extended to goodwill for any sort of profession, but engineers should actually be covered...

S10: I've really noticed that it's really hard to break down some of those taken for granted assumptions that people have and that, like, often you really, like, revert back into your old thinking patterns even though you're challenging those kinds of things.

As can be seen above most of the barriers (even on the individual level) students experience when approaching social justice can be tied to the culture of the engineering profession and consequently these barriers most likely arise from the current ways of thinking and practising dominating engineering and will thus be present among many practising engineers and engineering educators.

IMPLICATIONS FOR TEACHING THE COURSE 'ENGINEERING AND SOCIAL JUSTICE: CRITICAL THEORIES OF TECHNOLOGICAL PRACTICES'

The results of this study indicate that social justice can be experienced as a threshold by engineering students. Approaching it can be both transformative and troublesome. Courses such as the one studied can help students get a deeper understanding of the complexities of social justice but there will be a large variation in the ways students cope with the task of seeing engineering from a socially just perspective. Developing the students' ability to think critically is the aim of the course but it is clear that not all students are achieving this goal. One of the purposes of this study was to explore the dimensions of variation in the way students conceptualise the phenomenon of social justice with regard to engineering, in order that the results might throw some light on ways of approaching the teaching in future years. Helping students to experience the ways of understanding of fellow students, by experiencing each of the conceptions discussed above, will allow them to focus on the critical aspects encountered whilst attempting to move through the liminal space. Students could, for example, critique the role of 'trustee' or 'dutiful engineer', understand what the difference might be between being charitable and being socially just, being aware and taking action or what it means to involve clients in a participatory way.

Alongside focussing on the critical aspects found along the dimension of variation, students could be made aware of the typical barriers that they might face, so that when they reach a place of confusion and uncertainty, they know they are not alone. Students might be encouraged to share these perspectives with classmates in an informal class session.

SUMMARY

The threshold concept framework has proven useful for exploring how engineering students approach the notion of social justice in their current and future profession and practice. Drawing on Fleck (1979) and Wenger's (1998) ideas that *thought collectives* and *communities of practice* can provide resistance toward new ways of thinking or seeing we conducted a study of students endeavouring to pass through a new threshold for engineering, that of 'seeing through the lens of social justice'. We propose that social justice not only is a threshold for engineering students, but for the whole disciplinary community of engineering.

To help facilitate the transition for engineering students to approach social justice as a lens to their practice, we recommend that engineering educators centre the discussion of social justice around the critical aspects, contained within the conceptions students adopt, as they move along a spectrum of liminality. These dimensions can then be contrasted and compared to enhance understanding of social justice and help students successfully navigate the liminal space. Furthermore, students might also be encouraged to share with one another some of the barriers which prevent their movement through liminal space.

ACKNOWLEDGEMENTS

Thanks to SSHRC for the financial support of this study, to the students of the Engineering and Social Justice class, to Richard Day, Martin French the course professor during 2008, and to John El-Khazen, who helped with part of the data analysis.

REFERENCES

Andrews, G. C., Aplevich, J. D., Fraser, R. A., Macgregor, C., & Ratz, H. C. (2006). *Introduction to professional engineering in Canada* (2nd ed.). Toronto: Pearson Education Canada.
Baillie, C., & Johnson, A. (2008). A threshold model for attitudes in first year engineering students. In R. Land, J. H. F. Meyer, & J. Smith (Eds.), *Threshold concepts within the disciplines* (pp. 143–154). Rotterdam: The Netherlands: Sense Publishers.
Baillie, C., & Rose, C. (2004). Travelling facts. In C. Baillie, E. Dunn, & Y. Zheng (Eds.), *Travelling facts: The social construction, distribution, and accumulation of knowledge* (pp. 17–26). Frankfurt: Campus Verlag.
Catalano, G. D. (2007). *Engineering, poverty, and the earth*. Synthesis lectures on Engineers, Technology and Society #4. San Rafael, California: Morgan & Claypool Publishers.
Catalano, G. D., & Baillie, C. (2006, June 18–21). *Engineering, social justice and peace: A revolution of the heart*. Paper presented at ASEE Annual Conference & Exposition, Chicago, Illinois.
Flanagan, M. T. (2007). *The threshold concept in electrical engineering*. Paper presented at 6th ASEE Global Colloquium on Engineering Education, Istanbul.
Fleck, L. (1979). *Genesis and development of a scientific fact*. Chicago: University of Chicago Press.
Franklin, U. (1999). *The real world of technology*. Toronto: Anansi Press.
Johnston, S. F., Gostelow, J. P., & King, W. J. (2000). *Engineering and society*. Toronto: Prentice-Hall.
Marton, F., & Booth, S. (1997). *Learning and awareness*. Mahwah: Lawrence Erlbaum Associates.
Meyer, J. H. F., & Land, R. (2003). Threshold concepts and troublesome knowledge: Linkages to ways of thinking and practicing within the disciplines. In *ETL Project Occasional Report 4*. Retrieved January 28, 2009, from http://www.etl.tla.ed.ac.uk/docs/ETLreport4.pdf
Meyer, J. H. F., & Land, R. (2006). Threshold concepts and troublesome knowledge: Issues of liminality. In J. H. F. Meyer & R. Land (Eds.), *Overcoming barriers to student understanding: Threshold concepts and troublesome knowledge* (pp. 19–32). London: Routledge.
Meyer, J. H. F., Land, R., & Davies, P. (2008). Threshold concepts and troublesome knowledge (4): Issues of variation and variability. In R. Land, J. H. F. Meyer, & J. Smith (Eds.), *Threshold concepts within the disciplines* (pp. 59–74). Rotterdam, The Netherlands: Sense Publishers.
Vesilind, P. A. (2006, October). Peace engineering. *Journal of Professional Issues in Engineering Education and Practice*, 283–287.
Vidal, J. (2008). Crop switch worsens global food price crisis. In *The Guardian*. Retrieved January 28, 2009, from http://www.guardian.co.uk/environment/2008/apr/05/food.biofuels/print
Voland, G. (2004). *Engineering by design* (2nd ed.). Upper Saddle River, NJ: Pearson Education, Inc.
Wenger, E. (1998). *Communities of practice: Learning, meaning, and identity*. Cambridge, UK: Cambridge University Press.

Jens Kabo
Faculty of Applied Science
Queens University
Kingston
Canada

Caroline Baillie
Faculty of Engineering
University of Western Australia
Perth WA

LEAH SHOPKOW

19. WHAT DECODING THE DISCIPLINES CAN OFFER
THRESHOLD CONCEPTS[1]

The punctuated equilibrium of student learning so richly explored by the ground-breaking explorations of Meyer and Land in the theoretical field of Threshold Concepts is something that all instructors have encountered in their own classrooms. (Meyer & Land 2005a and 2006b) Students stall out, making little progress, only to leap forward in unpredictable ways. Decoding the Disciplines (DtD), a method-ology developed at Indiana University (see Middendorf & Pace 2004), and Threshold Concepts have in common a philosophy that sees ways of knowing as disciplinary and both posit the goal of education as transforming students (Meyer & Land 2005a; Díaz et al. 2008), although they have evolved different vocabularies to describe the phenomena. However, DtD approaches the problem of impasses in student learning not from a theoretical perspective (although theory is quite useful in grounding its practices), but from a practical approach that emphasizes both the modeling of expert behaviour for students and the explicit explication of its underlying epistemes; the expert is rendered more self-conscious about these epistemes through a metacognitive dialogue between the expert and interviewers not necessarily within the expert's discipline. It is thus a methodology that may help to bridge the gap between the theory of Threshold Concepts and classroom practice, cutting down on and informing experimentation in the classroom.

I argue in this paper that the methodology can facilitate the application of the theory of Threshold Concepts in five ways. First, the methodology can help identify and order concepts and understandings, some of which may be threshold concepts, in disciplines (particularly the Arts and Humanities) where even the notion of essential concepts can be contested. Second, this methodology can help reveal the tacit knowledge, one form of troublesome knowledge (Perkins 2005), both drawn upon and expected by the teacher. When the knowledge that supports the architecture of the disciplines is tacit, students have to intuit its existence, but when this knowledge is rendered visible and made explicit it can be made less "troublesome" for students. My third point is that because the methodology uses as its launching pad the instructor's own disciplinary modes of thought and teaching concerns, it is less likely to be perceived as alien knowledge or foreign knowledge by the instructor (Perkins 2005, 1999). It thus provides an incentive for the instructor to investigate his or her own teaching and has, in our experience, left instructors more open to the vast body of research on student learning available to inform practice. Fourth, because the methodology clarifies the learning that the teacher is intending to help the students achieve, it is easier to design lessons to

J. H. F. Meyer, R. Land and C. Baillie (eds.), Threshold Concepts and
Transformational Learning, 317–331.
© *2010 Sense Publishers. All rights reserved.*

teach it and metrics for assessing whether students have learned it, and so provides guidance for interventions. The fifth point is that when the methodology is applied to instructors within a discipline, it provides the shared vocabulary of goals and techniques that can encourage the institutional change needed to guide students through a process that may take a number of semesters–extended or repeated periods of liminality–while also providing the basis for fruitful conversation and collaboration among faculty in different disciplines. These are large claims, but I will substantiate them by drawing on evidence from two groups using the methodology at Indiana University, the Freshman Learning Project (FLP) run by Joan Middendorf and David Pace, and the History Learning Project (HLP) run by Arlene Díaz, Joan Middendorf, David Pace and Leah Shopkow.

THE METHODOLOGY

Most of our inquiries begin with an assignment with which a significant number of students who are doing the work have had difficulty. These difficulties may arise from the failure of students to master what might be termed a single threshold

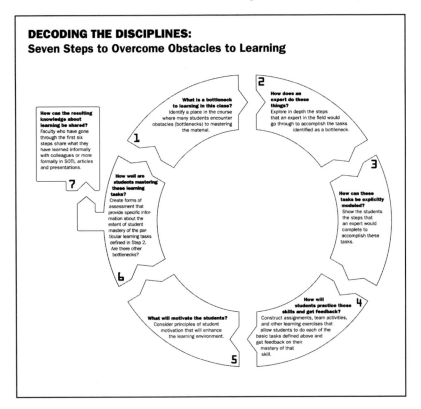

Figure 1. The Decoding the Disciplines process.

318

concept, but which might also be a cluster of such concepts, or even a fundamental disciplinary way of knowing. It makes a difference, of course, which of these is the case, because the difficulties students have may not reside only in their failure to have navigated the component concepts, but also in their difficulty in building the schemas to integrate those concepts. To begin with, however, it is sufficient to identify the task the students are having difficulty with and to clarify what a successful performance would look like. (For this and subsequent steps, see Figure 1.)

Step two of the process calls for the teacher to identify the steps the expert would go through to accomplish the task the students have not done well at. This is a difficult process for experts to do, because much of their knowledge operates so tacitly, they are not aware of possessing knowledge inaccessible to their students. This interview with a faculty member specializing in European history shows how difficult it can be for faculty to see all the things they do without consciously thinking about them or to see how to bridge the gap between the intellectual resources available to them as expert practitioners and students as learners.

(Beginning of interview)

Subject: One conceptual problem I find is just a general tendency, that they [students] have difficulty appreciating that historical actors didn't know what was going to be happening in the future...

Interviewer 1: What does an historian do ...an historian looking at the 1920s or 30s...that the students aren't doing? Can we nail down what it is that we do that they don't do?

(Around 5 minutes)

Subject: The sheer the number of similar sources that one has read.

Interviewer 1: Okay.

Subject: I think it is hard to read one source and fully get an appreciation for it.

(Around 8 minutes)

Interviewer 2: If I had that problem as a student I would have that a problem whether I read one document or 200 documents. I would still be wondering why these people don't know what is going to happen in the future.

Subject: I actually think it does make a difference if you read one document or you read 200 documents.

Interviewer 2: You do?

Subject: That actually is the point. If you read one document, that is just hard to believe...I think the students are thinking, "How could somebody not know that this was happening? How could somebody be so stupid or be so blind," or however they want to put it?

(At around 47 minutes)

Interviewer 1: One of the standard student ways resolving differences in an electoral history is to determine who was right, which is completely destroying the whole thing you are trying to do here in a certain way.

Subject: Yeah. But again the more opinions you get the more difficult. If you have one person says X, one person says Z. It is easy to come up with Y...But if you have one person says A the other B C D E. I mean then it is much more difficult to come up with one resolution...Multiple sources makes it more difficult to be simplistic about the period itself.

Although the second interviewer, not an historian by training, continually questioned the historian's assumption that reading simply more primary source documents would get students through this particular threshold, it is quite possible that if students did read hundreds of documents, as the expert has, they would arrive at a more complicated view of the past. Graduate students, by imitating expert behaviours (like wide reading) do seem to advance in just this way (Cole 2000), and those who have more domain knowledge and better organized domain knowledge can build more effective schemas. (Meier, Reinhard, Carter & Brooks, 2008) However, in the context of an undergraduate class there is never the time to have students read so extensively. Students may read three documents or five, but then it is time to move to another topic. Thus this particular route to expertise is blocked for the student. But even knowing that allows the instructor to consider possible interventions.

The third step of the process to model what experts do. In the above case, for example, the historian might show how historians go back and forth between a small number of documents, a practice well documented by Sam Wineberg (2001, 77) or lead students through a think-aloud (see Calder 2002). In the process, the instructor explicitly lays out the rules for a particular epistemic game within the discipline (Collins & Ferguson 1993). There has been extensive research on what these "moves" look like in History (see Wineberg 2001; Stearns, Seixas & Wineburg 1999), research that can be deployed by the instructor once he or she is clear about what particular student difficulty seems most pressing to solve. The students are then given an opportunity to practice the skill and receive feedback on their practice (step 4). The modeling and practice we advocate fits well into the paradigm Meier has called "elaborated worked example modeling," which her research has shown assists novices in schema building (Meier, Reinhard, Carter & Brooks 2008). An essential element of this sort of modeling is simultaneous explanation of the reasons for certain procedures and approaches. Practice also takes more than one form, so that students working on understanding the concept of "audience" might practice by researching the characteristics of a particular audience and also by rendering that audience's ideas in a drawing. While these two steps are going on, the expert is also trying to motivate the students, often by explaining why the students are doing it and what concepts the teacher is trying to help them learn and by pointing out the applications of student mastery (step 5) (also consistent with "elaborated worked example modeling). The instructor also designs a means of measuring whether students have successfully negotiated the threshold or mastered the understanding (step 6), whether they are still struggling with the concept or concepts involved, or whether they have fallen back into old ways of doing things. These four steps, modeling, practicing, motivating, and assessing may well overlap; they are most effective when done iteratively. It is worth noting in passing that what this methodology calls upon faculty to do is the kind of metacognitive reflection that we enjoin students to do and for the same reasons: that "going meta," reflecting on one's own learning, promotes "proactive learning" (Perkins 2008), and in this case, the instructors themselves are learners.

REVEALING THRESHOLD CONCEPTS AND MODES OF THOUGHT IN THE ARTS AND HUMANITIES

Arts and Humanities courses pose a distinctive challenge to student learning, because there is often no prerequisite content knowledge. A history student may well take an advanced course in which he or she has little prior domain knowledge. In addition, there are dazzling arrays of potential contents and techniques, and practitioners themselves don't use all of them or use them equally well. An historian cited by Meyer and Land, for example, suggests that

If pressed, most historians would be able to define what they would think of as threshold concepts for history...but because History tends to be rather anti-theory, or at least sceptical of theories like postmodernism and deconstruction etc, we might not have the jargon that other disciplines have to describe it. (23)

I would argue that the issue is not so much history's allergy to theory (theory being a boundary issue for the discipline) so much as the way historical knowledge is structured. Historical knowledge is not linear, but rather is organized in networks (Mink 1970), and history's mode of explanation is narrative (White 1971, Carr 2008). Explanations are pluralistic, something also true of the social sciences (Van Bouwel & Weber 2008); this can make these disciplines seem particularly elusive forms of knowledge. What theory or approaches could be absolutely essential for the expert to master in this context? For every candidate, one could point to scores of successful practitioners who would disagree. What contents are essential? Practitioners again would disagree. In history, enthusiastic amateurs may well know more in a given field than an historian specializing in a different field (Wineburg 2001). There are practices which practitioners share, for instance, the "sourcing heuristic" in history (Wineburg 2001, 76), but there is considerable variation in the kinds of sources historians deploy, the way they approach those sources, and, when they act as instructors, the understandings and skills they consider most important. If history students occupy states of liminality, it may well be because they are cognitively overloaded by the content on the one hand, and because they are confused by conflicting messages arising from the different and frequently tacit schemas employed by their instructors and have not yet developed schemas of their own.

The DtD interviewing process, however, can untangle some of that complexity or at least make that complexity evident to instructors. Consider the following essay question assigned by a faculty member in Gender Studies:

Today, many people in the United States use the word "feminism" as if it describes a single worldview or political program that has remained more or less unchanged over time. As we've seen this semester, the term "feminism" is actually something of a generalization that encompasses a broad range of historically contingent and sometimes conflicting worldviews and political programs. What are some of the specific forms that feminism has taken over the past two centuries? How have feminist agendas changed in response to specific historical events, like the passage of the 19th Amendment? Which people or texts have played important roles in catalyzing the emergence of new forms of feminist consciousness at particular moments? You need not answer all of these questions, but you should consider them as you generate a coherent response that maps some of the different feminisms that have come into being during the period covered in this course and situates the examples you choose to present relative to broader historical changes in US and society and culture.

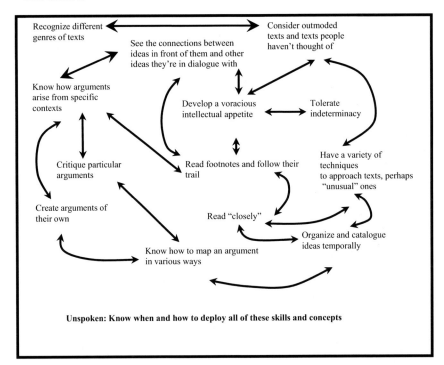

Figure 2. Mapping the understandings a student would need to write a successful essay.

The faculty member who provided this essay topic was questioned by some ten people about what a student would have to do to write a successful essay on this subject (this was a training session for interviewers for which the faculty member had kindly volunteered). At various points in the interview, the faculty member identified at least thirteen explicit "threads" or "threshold concepts" or clusters of concepts, some of them relating to processes, some of the relating to content, some of them relating to feelings. Interestingly, none of them related to the "classic" steps of writing an essay (such as organizing evidence or creating an outline). (See Figure 2).

Each of these threads could be inquired into more deeply, as some of them involve more than one threshold concept; indeed, our normal practice is to focus on one thread and break it down into its component parts, rather than, as in this training exercise, to uncover as many as possible. One can also see that the threads tend to overlap somewhat, but not entirely, and are certainly connected to each other (connections are indicated with arrows). Some are practical (read the footnotes!), some involve ideas (critique arguments), some involve intellectual techniques (deploy lots of them!), and some are affective (tolerate indeterminacy). In other words, to answer an essay question even at an elementary college level requires the coordination of a complex performance, and while the faculty member assuredly did not expect students to do all those things or to do them all well, to write an effective essay a student would have to do at least some of those things passably well.

As the result of the interviews of the History Learning Project, we have come up with a list of student impediments to learning in three broad classes: disciplinary, evidentiary, and affective (Diaz et al. 2008). It is very clear, however, that the impediments are interconnected and difficult to work on in isolation, even given the issues raised by Entwistle (2008) about the importance of integration and by Perkins about integration and also situating knowledge proactively (2008). Change on the largest scale would therefore be beyond ability of the solo practitioner, although it would be possible to work successfully on one impediment and this would probably lead the student to develop more robust disciplinary schemas. I will turn to the implications of this situation at the end of the paper.

REVEALING TACIT KNOWLEDGE

The process of being interviewed and repeatedly questioned about what one does as an expert has often pushed the historians we have interviewed to recognize their own tacit knowledge and tacit assumptions, to see that what is simple and self-evident for them is nothing of the kind for students.

Subject: I think it is pretty simplistic …

Interviewer 1: All these interviews are that way in a sense...but it is only simplistic to the expert.

Subject: Right. I mean you are asking what we do intuitively and it is very difficult to determine what we are doing intuitively.

Interviewer 1: That is right; it is like breathing air. You just do that.

Subject: Right.

Interviewer 1: But students don't do that.

Subject: No.

Interviewer 1: So that is the gap. That is what the whole research is really about. How do you bridge that gap? Well the first thing is you have to actually recognize that it is there and in asking very simple questions to really complex matters.

Subject: You are asking us to do exactly what we are trying to get the students to do... That is very useful.

In some cases, however, faculty have responded in a way that suggests they have navigated a major threshold in teaching themselves.

Subject: Yeah. Yeah. Yeah. Now this is very good. It actually means that...when you are spelling out the course objectives, they can be much more meaningful...

Interviewer 1: Right. So it is a very nuanced environment you are working in with students.

Subject: Yes. I mean it is so very historiographically dense...[that] if I was just reading out the titles of the books on the issues, I wouldn't have enough time to lecture.

Interviewer 2: But it seems that then one of the issues here is that they don't have a map. Of how to understand these different parts of the puzzle, or the complexity you want them to understand, and they have this understanding that this should be a straight-forward type of story and they don't have a map to navigate themselves through this sea of information. It is evident to us, but it might not be evident to them.

Subject: Yeah. (Long pause.) Has anybody else been this shocked?

Interviewer 1: Yes. We work really hard at doing this. We explained at the beginning. When you start to look shocked, then we know we are really on to something. The more panicked you look, the happier we are, but it's not vindictive; it's meaningful!

Subject: So glad this is not on video! (Laughter from subject and interviewers)

After the interview, this historian rewrote the syllabus for the course, creating a "Course owner's manual" for the students based on his new understanding of his own tacit knowledge. In so doing, this instructor also rejected the hermetic tendencies of academia, the sometimes deliberate mystification of the academic learning process. (Hilsdon & Bitzer 2007, Graff 2004) Until the practitioner is clear about the schemas he or she employs, it is difficult to help students to construct them; the failure to create an effective schema undoubtedly explains why some students remain so long in liminal states.

DRAWING CHANGE FROM FACULTY MEMBERS' OWN CONCERNS

In the case of the Gender Studies essay, we identified fourteen interview "threads" pointing to concepts and practices students would have to master to write a successful essay. Which of these threads gets followed would be up to the practitioner, based on what most bothers him or her about the students' lack of understanding. If a faculty member were deeply concerned about having students examine a rich variety of primary texts, a thread like "reading the footnotes" might be summarily dealt with by simply instructing the students to read them. But a faculty member interested in getting students to understand that academic knowledge is a conversation might create a more structured lesson in which the connection between the footnotes and the contested points of the domain is explicitly modeled, with the students then doing an elaborated worked model.

Even where faculty are interested in the same learning problem, there is often considerable room for choice, based on the materials the faculty use in their classrooms. For instance, many of the historians the HLP interviewed were interested in helping students to understand primary sources, but the kinds of sources they used and the kinds of problems associated with those sources varied considerably. A modern European historian wanted her students to understand that maps have ideological content, that they are artefactual; an historian of American Latino history wanted students to understand how to use memoirs as historical sources and to make connections between those memoirs and larger currents of history; an American historian wanted students to be more analytical about images, to notice the fingernail polish on the nail of Rosie the Riveter and to speculate on why it was there; an African historian wanted students to understand how praise tales might be used as historical sources. Ultimately students would need to construct schemas sufficiently robust to accommodate all of these sorts of sources, but each historian chose the source because it was particularly problematic or revealing in his or her class.

That the decision is the practitioner's is important because otherwise, faculty members may respond just as students do to the imposition of someone else's ideas: they may treat it as alien knowledge, some horrible and foreign imposition. Katharine Burn found just that among trainee history teachers, who although presented with constructivist approaches to history learning and teaching tended to fall back on their "folk pedagogies." (Burn 2007; Bruner 1999). Burn's hypothesis was that "their professional identities as experienced practitioners was under threat and they were no longer willing to expose their own practice to detailed scrutiny." (457) But if the practitioner himself or herself identifies the learning issues and subjects those issues to his or her own scrutiny, it instead reinforces the instructor's sense of him or herself as an experienced, and indeed, highly competent practitioner. In the middle of one interview, the historian ran to get materials to take notes:

Interviewer 2: As you mention, [there is a] rich historiography that exists on the Holocaust, and... if they [students] do understand history as this dialog between different people of the past or whether they understand history as a series of names and dates.

Subject: Right.

Interviewer 1: [Students may think] "maybe we get the facts from you and then you want us to write an essay," whereas you may want something else; you may want to share what all the voices are on all this...

Subject: Yes. Yes. Let me just get my notes because I need to know some things you have mentioned....Yeah. Yeah. That is very good. You already made me realize that there are things I need to say that I'm not saying.

There is a secondary issue as well. When History faculty are simply presented with educational research, they are being asked to absorb alien knowledge, the product of a social science discipline, one which they may feel has poor understanding of history. They may feel (as so many students do) that they have no criteria upon which to evaluate the contents of this alien literature or that this literature is not "for them" but for secondary school teachers (much of the literature on history learning has been done in the context of pre-collegiate education). But when they approach this literature from the perspective of their own teaching concerns, they have a means to sift through it based on its pertinence to the problem that concerns them and they are also already thinking about how they might deploy the knowledge contained in it.

GREATER CLARITY IN DESIGNING INTERVENTIONS AND METRICS

Identifying exactly the problem that students face makes it easier for the instructor to find the literature on student learning with respect to that issue, incorporate it in instruction, and even to become involved in research in the scholarship of teaching and learning. (Middendorf & Pace 2007) For instance, our study identified a cluster of concepts and understandings relating to the analysis and deployment of primary sources that students find it difficult to master. One of these is the ability to take an historical perspective, that is, to see historical actors as acting out of a particular historical context. There is a literature on this subject to be accessed (see Davis, Yeager & Foster 2001); Hartmann and Hasselhorn (2008) have devised a metric for measuring student ability in this regard; and Tally and Goldenberg have designed inquiry tools (2005). Once it is clear to the instructor that his or her students need to learn to take historical perspective and the ways that historical perspective taking differs from what is commonly meant by the term empathy (VanSledright 1999), not only is it clearer what goal the students need to achieve, but also the ways in which they can be derailed en route or stuck in a state of liminality are clearer as well.

Even without this history-specific literature, however, it is easier to devise a lesson for a clearly defined problem. To give one example, a fellow of the History Learning Project and the Freshman Learning Project, Eric Sandweiss, began with the concern that his students were taking poor notes in class. When he considered what good notes were, he concluded that they organized information in hierarchies, generally comprising interpretations (judgments about the meaning of historical events), themes (recurrent topics), and evidence (examples used to support interpretations). This led to some changes in the contents of instruction, in that he became more mindful of the organization of his lectures, but he also devised a way to model the existence of these three categories for students, by assigning portions of the class to each category of material and having them each call out an utterance made famous by a television character. Finally, he assessed their mastery by using "word dumps," that is, providing a list of terms that students had to sort to render them coherent and meaningful, a variation on the Categorizing Grid described by Angelo and Cross (1993). This kind of assessment is both formative and summative, because it represents practice and assessment, and it required a great deal of practice with much feedback on the part of the instructor. But because the problem and goals were clear, Sandweiss was able to draw a way of assessing mastery came from the general pedagogical literature.

A BASIS FOR COLLABORATION

While individual teachers can become more mindful teachers by means of the methodology, perhaps its greatest usefulness is in its collaborative applications, particularly since most of the changes in understanding we want to see in students take place over the course of years, not the weeks of the semester. As the table of 'bottlenecks' (some of which may be "basic" concepts, some of which may be threshold concepts, others of which may be clusters of threshold concepts, and some of which constitute disciplinary ways of knowing–see Entwistle 2008, Davies & Mangan 2007) compiled by the History Learning Project show (Table 1), a student who has successfully come to the end of his or her program will have had to negotiate many concepts, threshold or otherwise, across a span of years. No one faculty member is equally suited or has the kind of continuity of instruction with individuals to help students negotiate them all. If we want students not still to think like novices at the end of their undergraduate programs as they often still do (for a case in History, see Wineburg 2001), many faculty members will have to work collectively to this end. We will have to think about how Threshold Concepts might be sequenced in disciplines, like History, where the content is not sequenced of itself, so as to introduce students to these concepts in a systematic way, to ensure that students keep using the concepts to prevent student knowledge from becoming inert, and to help students learn to coordinate all the concepts that define the epistemes of the disciplines.

By talking about the disciplines in this way, I do not mean to reify the disciplines, which are cultural constructions or communities of practice. To render visible what the practices are, the History Learning Project engaged in series of interviews of history faculty (seventeen faculty members in the summer of 2006, with more interviews carried out in the summer of 2008), to identify all the concepts their students find difficult and how experts navigate these difficulties. In that way we have begun to creation what Jauss (1984) has referred to as the 'horizon of expectations' in literature or what in Bordellian terms would be a *habitus*; the space within in most historians would be mostly comfortable; the centre of the intellectual galaxy if not each individual star; what most of us would agree that students have to learn.

We then compiled these points of difficulty into a table. These tend to fall into three rough groups: one set relates to the nature of History as a discipline and the practices necessary to participate in it; a second set relates to evidentiary practices and primary sources in history; and the third relates to affective understandings and abilities. (See Table 1) However, each of the three groups can be broken down into a number of concrete difficulties students have, and there is some interconnection between the groups, as was true in the Gender Studies case above.

Table 1. Frequency of Bottlenecks in Interviews with 17 Faculty Members from the History Department

Bottlenecks[2]	Frequency	Total	Percentage
Nature of the Historical Discipline		38	27.7
Understanding History as discipline	19		
Developing and evaluating historical arguments	6		
Recreating historical context	13		
Affective Issues		35	25.5
Maintaining emotional distance	1		
Overcoming affective roadblocks	21		
Willingness to wait for an answer	4		
Dealing with ambiguity	9		
Primary Sources		26	18.9
Interpreting primary sources	13		
Seeing artefacts from the past as representing choices that change over time	11		
Employing effective research methods	2		
Analysis		19	13.8
Going back and forth between evidence and analysis	3		
Identifying with people in another time/place	15		
Understanding historical change	1		
Reading		14	10.2
Learning how to use the textbook	4		
Reading critically	4		
Distinguishing main/secondary points	5		
Knowing how to skim books	1		
Writing		3	2.2
Writing historically	3		
Other		2	1.5
Using appropriate language	1		
Understanding notions of time	1		
Total	137	137	100.0

At a departmental workshop, attended by fifty-eight people, faculty and graduate students, the Project presented a working document in which the things we wanted students to know how to do when they completed their degrees were broken down into stages to be handled at each course level, so that our curriculum would be developmentally coherent (with attention to Perry and Bloom). This represents a step away from a common tendency of teachers when confronted with teaching challenges, to concentrate on the content of the instruction (Burn 2007) and to see the difficulties of learning as being inherent in the difficulty of the material. The faculty revised this plan at the workshop. The faculty were then surveyed by the Undergraduate Affairs Committee about their teaching practices in each of the courses they had taught for the past seven years (all but two faculty members in a department of around fifty people complied), with questions about the kinds of readings they assigned, about which of the areas of difficulty they provided *explicit* instruction, about the kinds of written assignments they made. This data is being used to restructure the department's curriculum in ways in which we hope to report on in future years. The cooperation of members of the department is particularly extraordinary in an institution which, like most high-intensity research institutions, puts more emphasis on research than on teaching and learning and in a context unlike the British or Australian HE environment, where there is, as yet, no government-mandated attention to learning outcomes.

The History Learning Project, however, is just one example of collaboration using DtD. The larger project out of which the HLP grew, the Freshman Learning Project (FLP), where DtD was developed, has brought together scholars both within and across disciplines to share their inquiries into student learning. (Middendorf & Pace, 2002; 2004) Scholars within disciplines have published collaborative work in English, in history, in biology, in business and in astronomy, while Whitney Schlegel and David Pace have offered an example of collaboration between physiology and history (Schlegel & Pace, 2004). Participants in the FLP from disciplines as diverse as sociology and astronomy (to say nothing of art education, studio art, anthropology and the university library), have formed the Visual Methods in Teaching and Learning Project to explore how visual learning might be applied in their various disciplines.

Without collaboration of this kind, even if we can successfully identify all the ways students get stuck in their studies, we are unlikely to be able to apply what we know about individual areas of getting stuck as effectively. Sometimes the impediments to our students learning one threshold concept arise from their difficulties with another, perhaps one they have never encountered. We can see the appearance of liminality in their work, but only the large picture can reveal its source. We need collaboration within disciplines because we have a shared charge in educating our students and we need collaboration across disciplines not only because there are common problems we might confront or because the way in which we confront student difficulties might have a greater impact than in our disciplines alone, but also because it can clarify for us what thresholds our discipline might be constructing for our students as we consider other thresholds shaped by other disciplines within the shared architecture of higher education.

NOTES

[1] I would like to thank the other members of the Freshman Learning Project, Arlene Díaz, Joan Middendorf (especially for her feedback on an earlier draft), and David Pace, and the faculty members who gave their explicit consent for me to use their interviews in this article. I learn

something significant from Eric Sandweiss every time he opens his mouth. Without the leadership of Jennifer Meta Robinson, who has been the soul and heart of SoTL at Indiana, I would not be doing this work. I also wish to thank Colin Johnson, Mark Roseman, and Jeff Veidlinger. The History Learning Project has been supported by the Dean of the Faculties at Indiana University through a SoTL Leadership Grant, and has enjoyed great encouragement from Jeanne Sept, the Dean of the Faculties, and Ray Smith of Academic Affairs. George Rehrey has been a friend of the project in every way possible. I would also like to acknowledge the Teagle and Spencer Foundations who are supporting the next phase of our research., along with Academic Affairs, the College of Arts and Sciences, and the History Department at Indiana University.

[2] This table was created by Arlene Díaz for the History Learning Project. These categories are provisional.

REFERENCES

Angelo, T. A., & Cross, K. P. (1993). *Classroom assessment techniques: A handbook for college teachers* (2nd ed.). San Francisco: Jossey-Bass.

Bruner, J. (1999). Folk pedagogies. In J. Leach & B. Moon (Eds.), *Learners & pedagogy*. London: Paul Chapman and Open University.

Burn, K. (2007). Professional knowledge and identity in a contested discipline: Challenges for student teachers and teacher-educators. *Oxford Review of Education, 33*(4), 445–467.

Calder, L. (2002). Looking for learning in the history survey. *American Historical Association Perspectives, 40*, 43–45.

Carr, D. (2008). Narrative explanation and its malcontents. *History and Theory, 47*, 19–30.

Cole, C. (2000). Inducing expertise in history doctoral students via information retrieval design. *The Library Quarterly, 70*, 86–109.

Collins, A., & Ferguson, W. (1993). Epistemic forms and epistemic games: Structures and strategies to guide inquiry. *Educational Psychologist, 28*(1), 25–42.

Davies, P., & Mangan, J. (2007). Threshold concepts and the integration of understanding in economics. *Studies in Higher Education, 32*, 711–726.

Davis, O. L., Yeager, E. A., & Foster, S. J. (2001). *Historical empathy and perspective taking in the social studies*. Lanham, MD: Rowman & Littlefield.

Díaz, A., Middendorf, J., Pace, D., & Shopkow, L. (2008). The history learning project: A department 'decodes' its students. *Journal of American History, 94*, 1211–1224.

Entwistle, N. (2008). Threshold concepts and transformative ways of thinking within research into higher education in Land, Meyer & Smith, 21–35.

Graff, G. (2004). *Clueless in academe: How schooling obscures the life of the mind*. New Haven, CT: Yale University Press.

Hartmann, U., & Hasselhorn, M. (2008). Historical perspective taking: A standardized measure for an aspect of students ' historical thinking. *Learning and Individual Differences, 18*, 264–270.

Hilsdon, J., & Bitzer, E. M. (2007). To become an asker of questions: A functional-narrative model to assist students in preparing post-graduate research proposals. *South African Journal of Higher Education, 21*(8), 1191–1203.

Jauss, H. R. (1982). *Toward an aesthetic of reception* (T. Bahti, Trans.). Minneapolis: University of Minnesota.

Land, R., Meyer, J. H. F., & Smith, J. (2008). *Threshold concepts within the disciplines*. Rotterdam, The Netherlands: Sense Publishers.

McCullagh, C. B. (1978). Colligation and classification in history. *History and Theory, 17*(3), 267–284.

Meier, D. K., Reinhard, K. J., Carter, D. O., & Brooks, D. W. (2008). Simulations with elaborated worked example modeling: Beneficial effects on schema acquisition. *Journal of Science Education and Technology, 17*, 262–273.

Meyer, J. H. F., & Land, R. (2005a). Threshold concepts and troublesome knowledge (2): Epistemological considerations and a conceptual framework for teaching and learning. *Higher Education, 49*, 373–388.

Meyer, J. H. F., & Land, R. (Eds.). (2005b). *Overcoming barriers to student understanding: Threshold concepts and troublesome knowledge*. London: Routledge.

Middendorf, J., & Pace, D. (2002). Overcoming cultural obstacles to new ways of teaching: The Lilly Freshman Learning Project at Indiana University. *To Improve the Academy: Resources for Faculty, Instructional, and Organizational Development, 20*, 208–224.

Middendorf, J., & Pace, D. (Eds.). (2004). Decoding the disciplines: Helping students learn disciplinary ways of thinking. *New Directions for Teaching and Learning, 98*. San Francisco: Jossey Bass.

Middendorf, J., & Pace, D. (2007). Easing entry into the scholarship of teaching and learning through focused assessments: The "Decoding the Disciplines" approach. *To Improve the Academy, 26*, 63–67.

Mink, L. (1970). History and fiction as modes of comprehension. *New Literary History, 1*, 541–558.

Perkins, D. (1999). The many faces of constructivism. *Educational Leadership, 57*(3), 6–11.

Perkins, D. (2005). Constructivism and troublesome and knowledge, in Meyer & Land, (pp. 33–47).

Perkins, D. (2008). Beyond understanding, in Land, Meyer & Smith, (pp. 3–19).

Schlegel, W., & Pace, D. (2004). Using collaborative learning teams to decode disciplines: Physiology and history in Middendorf & Pace, (pp. 75–83).

Stearns, P. N., Seixas, P., & Wineburg, S. (2000). *Knowing, teaching, and learning history: National and international perspectives*. New York: New York University.

Tally, B., & Goldenberg, L. B. (2005). Fostering historical thinking with digitized primary sources. *Journal of Research on Technology in Education, 38*(1), 1–21.

Van Bouwel, J., & Weber, E. (2008). A pragmatist defense of non-relativistic explanatory pluralism in history and social science. *History and Theory, 47*, 168–182.

VanSledright, B. (2001). From empathic regard to self-understanding: Im/Positionality, empathy, and historical contextualization in Davis, Yeager, & Foster.

White, H.. The value of narrativity in the representation of reality. *Critical Inquiry, 7*(1), 5–27.

Wineberg, S. (2001). *Historical thinking and other unnatural acts: Charting the future of teaching the past*. Philadelphia: Temple University Press.

Leah Shopkow
History Department
Indiana University
Bloomington

SIDNEY WEIL AND NICHOLAS MCGUIGAN

20. IDENTIFYING THRESHOLD CONCEPTS IN THE BANK RECONCILIATION SECTION OF AN INTRODUCTORY ACCOUNTING COURSE:

Creating an Ontological Shift for Students

INTRODUCTION

The study of Introductory Accounting has traditionally proved challenging to students (Weil, 1989; Lucas and Mladenovic, 2006). Much research (*inter alia* Sharma, 1997; Lucas, 2000; Mladenovic, 2000) has considered the many possible causes for this. An emerging theory of learning, which has recently enjoyed considerable attention in the education literature (Meyer and Land, 2006a, 2006b) and increasing exposure in the accounting education literature (Lucas and Mladenovic (2006; 2007), is called threshold concepts. Developed by Meyer and Land (2006a), they describe this emerging theoretical framework as:

> akin to a portal, opening up a new and previously inaccessible way of thinking about something. It represents a transformed way of understanding, or interpreting, or viewing something without which the learner cannot progress. As a consequence of comprehending a threshold concept there may this be a transformed internal view of subject matter, subject landscape, or even world view (p. 3).

Lucas and Mladenovic (2007) ask whether threshold concepts will develop 'its own distinctive theoretical framework' (p.245). To do so, they state that the theoretical development of threshold concepts should draw on other fields of research, such as cognitive psychology. This chapter addresses this need, drawing on a study in accounting education by Weil (1989) which utilised a 'deficient cognitive operations' paradigm known as Mediated Learning Experience (Feuerstein, Rand, Hoffman, and Miller, 1980). The chapter reassesses the findings of the Weil (1989) study in terms of the criteria enumerated by Meyer and Land (2006a) for the classification of accounting-specific content as a threshold concept or conception (Lucas and Mladenovic, 2006) – in effect, performing a threshold concepts analysis of a challenging area in the introductory accounting curriculum.

BACKGROUND AND LITERATURE REVIEW

This section initially describes the Weil (1989) study and briefly reviews the relevant literature. Threshold concepts' theory is then explained and discussed and

J. H. F. Meyer, R. Land and C. Baillie (eds.), Threshold Concepts and Transformational Learning, 333–345.

its relevance to the study considered. The section concludes by explaining the motivation for the study.

The Weil (1989) study was conducted at the University of the Western Cape, a university serving predominantly the Coloured[1] community. These students traditionally had very low success rates, which compared unfavourably with results at White universities (Financial Mail, 1981). At that time, pass-rates in Introductory Accounting of the order of 25% to 30% had resulted in fewer than twenty black chartered accountants in South Africa (Mehl and Weil, 1988).

The objective of the Weil (1989) study was to identify requisite thinking skills for success in the study of accounting. Using a cognitive operations approach to the teaching of thinking (Nickerson, Perkins and Smith, 1985), the study used Feuerstein et al.'s (1980) theory of Mediated Learning Experience to examine 'novice' problem solving. Using verbal protocol analysis (Konold and Well, 1981; Mehl, 1984; and Ericsson and Simon, 1985), Weil (1989) analysed the ways in which 'novices' (Introductory Accounting students) solve accounting problems. The thirty students' talk-aloud interviews were analysed using the deficient cognitive operations' paradigm of Feuerstein et al. (1980). Weil (1989) then used the protocol analyses to formulate a cognitive problem-solving profile for the group of subjects.

The interview subjects were presented with three questions, covering prepaid expenses, bank reconciliations and inventory, during a 45 minute talk aloud interview (Chi, Bassok, Lewis, Reimann and Glaser, 1989; Chi, de Leeuw, Chiu and LaVancher, 1994), which was recorded. Due to the limited duration of the interviews, most interviews covered only two of the three questions. To ensure that all of the questions received approximately equal coverage, they were rotated during the different interviews.

The interviews were transcribed and combined with the subjects' written data to produce student protocols (Ericsson and Simon, 1985; Chi et al., 1994). The subsequent protocol analyses enabled certain deficient cognitive operations of students (Feuerstein et al., 1980), as well as problems with definitions and concepts, to be identified.

Feuerstein et al.'s deficient cognitive operations derive from a psychosocial theory called Mediated Learning Experience (MLE), which postulates that a lack of effective mediation results in deficient cognitive operations, for example, poor visualization of relationships and lack of inferential-hypothetical reasoning. According to Feuerstein et al. (1980), these '....deficient functions relate to and help identify the *prerequisites* of thinking. In this sense, they refer to deficiencies in those functions that underlie internalized, operational thought' (1980, p. 71). Feuerstein et al. (1980) do not claim that their list of deficient functions is either definitive or exhaustive and they acknowledge that overlaps exist between the functions, as well as the fact that the three phases of the mental act can not be viewed in isolation from each other. Their model provides a useful paradigm for the identification of deficient cognitive operations which students may bring to the study of a discipline at university level and permits the formulation of a cognitive profile of these students.

The 'problems with definitions and concepts' were an additional category of student difficulties that emerged during the protocol analyses. Unlike cognitive difficulties, which manifested themselves as difficulties in how students think, this category reflected a lack of a fundamental understanding of a basic concept, for example, a bank cheque, or a bank debit order – what it meant and how it functioned. During the analyses, it became evident that a lack of understanding of these basic concepts provided a barrier – often severe – to students manipulating these concepts in more advanced scenarios.

This chapter reports on the findings for the bank reconciliation question, which was as follows:

A. If the cash book has a debit balance of R810^2, what balance would you expect the bank statement to have?

B. How and why, would you treat each of the following items when preparing a bank reconciliation statement?

    (i)   Bank charges on the bank statement.

    (ii)   Cheques made out in the cash book but not yet presented for payment to the bank.

    (iii)   A cheque from a debtor which has been deposited with the bank, but which is shown as dishonoured on the bank statement.

C. The bank statement shows a debit balance of R410. There are unpresented deposits of R465. How will you treat the unpresented deposits in the bank reconciliation statement? What will the cash book balance be?

The question covers several important aspects of a bank reconciliation process. In Part (A), the student is required to be able to visualize the relationship between a business' cash records and the bank's equivalent for the business. This relationship is a *mirror* image – equal in amount, but opposite in direction – either a debit or a credit. Part (B) tests the ability of the student to deal with certain unresolved items when preparing a bank reconciliation statement. By using three specific, common situations, Part (B) examines the student's understanding of the relationship between a bank statement and a cash book in greater depth. In addition to understanding what each of the concepts means, a student will need to under-stand – and be able to manipulate – the cause and effect consequences of each situation. As for Part (A), the student will need to demonstrate strong visualization skills to complete each of the three scenarios successfully. Part (C) requires the student to prepare a simple bank reconciliation statement which includes unpresented deposits. As for Parts (A) and (B), Part (C) requires the exercise of visualization skills – how do the unpresented deposits affect the respective bank and cash book balances? – as well as the ability to demonstrate an understanding of cause and effect. Table 1 summarises the findings of the protocol analyses for each section of the question.

By identifying Introductory Accounting students' problems with definitions and concepts and cognitive difficulties, as illustrated in Table 1, the Weil (1989) study provides an overview of the types of difficulties that these students encounter in their studies. The findings provide a broad range of difficulties, but do not indicate

Table 1. Protocol analysis findings for bank reconciliation question

Part of question	Problems with definitions and concepts	Cognitive difficulties
A	Inadequate knowledge of definitions and concepts	Resistance to logical analysis of concepts
B(i)	Inadequate knowledge of definitions and concepts	Blurred and sweeping perception Lack of verbal skills Lack of inferential-hypothetical thinking
B(ii)	Inadequate knowledge of definitions and concepts	Blurred and sweeping perception Lack of inferential-hypothetical thinking Narrowness of the mental field Resistance to logical analysis of concepts
B(iii)		Blurred and sweeping perception Lack of verbal skills Lack of inferential-hypothetical thinking Narrowness of the mental field
C	Inadequate knowledge of definitions and concepts	Impulsivity Lack of precision and accuracy Poor visualization of relationships Lack of inferential-hypothetical reasoning

either the extent or the severity of each difficulty, or its likely impact on learning. If learning in accounting is to be made more accessible to students, it is desirable that curriculum design identify those specific areas of the course that need either more emphasis, or a different pedagogical approach. In other words, an analysis of a course, or a section of a course, is required that identifies fundamental barriers to student mastery of a topic, by way either of a core concept, a principle or way of thinking.

Such an analysis requires a suitable paradigm for analysis. One such emerging theoretical framework, developed by Meyer and Land (2003), documents a new perspective on students' conceptual understanding through the introduction of 'threshold concepts'; a contention that certain concepts in a discipline often present students with barriers to learning. Such 'threshold concepts' are described by Perkins (2006) as 'pivotal but challenging concepts in disciplinary understanding. They act like gateways. Once through the gate, learners come to a new level of understanding central to the discipline' (p. 43). This distinguishes threshold concepts from core concepts found within a course, as threshold concepts represent more than simply a building block towards student understanding; they are 'akin to a portal, opening up a new and previously inaccessible way of thinking about something. It represents a transformed way of understanding, or interpreting, or viewing something without which the learner cannot progress' (Meyer and Land, 2006a, p. 3).

Meyer and Land (2006a) propose five main criteria for qualification as a threshold concept; the concept should be transformative, irreversible, integrative, bounded and troublesome. They suggest that a threshold concept is transformative in nature, representing a significant shift in the perception of a subject. Secondly, it is probably irreversible, meaning that students who encounter and successfully pass through a threshold concept possess a differing world view to that held previously and it cannot be unlearned. Thirdly, a threshold concept is integrative, displaying a previously hidden interrelatedness of something to a student. Fourthly, it may represent a boundary in a student's learning between the academic discipline in which the student operates and that of another. Finally, it is proposed that threshold concepts may be troublesome to the student, that is, counter-intuitive, alien or incoherent (Perkins, 2006). He develops the concept of troublesome knowledge further by identifying five categories of such knowledge, namely, ritual, inert, conceptually difficult, foreign or alien and tacit.

Lucas and Mladenovic (2007, p. 239) argue that such an emerging theoretical framework encourages educators to 'view current concerns within the curriculum in a different, and productive, way'. Embracing a threshold concept framework allows the educator to review a specific discipline by focusing on the nature of key concepts, the curriculum and how this is related in educational practice (Lucas and Mladenovic, 2007). Cousin (2007) provides further support for threshold concept theory, by highlighting its ability to encourage educators to review and discuss their specific discipline, as opposed to their educative practice, allowing them to remain within their area of expertise.

This theoretical framework is clearly aligned with a highly student-centred approach to research in which the nature of the student's understanding and approach to learning is emphasised. Davies (2003, p. 13) states that a threshold concept 'offers a theoretical construct that enables the results of phenomenographic studies to be reinterpreted from the perspective of the social construction of disciplines'.

This chapter revisits the findings of the Weil (1989) paper, with a view to considering their appropriateness in terms of the threshold concept literature. The chapter aims to contribute to the emerging literature on threshold concepts by reconsidering the deficient cognitive operations (Feuerstein et al., 1980) and problems with definitions and concepts (Weil, 1989) in terms of Meyer and Land's (2003) theory of threshold concepts. In doing so, it addresses the question posed by Lucas and Mladenovic (2007), namely, whether or not threshold concepts will develop into its own distinctive theoretical framework.

FINDINGS AND DISCUSSION

In conducting a threshold concept analysis of the findings of the Weil (1989) study, this section initially considers 'problems with definitions and concepts', followed by Feuerstein et al.'s (1980) cognitive difficulties.

Problems with Definitions and Concepts – or Threshold Concepts?

As illustrated in Table 1, 'Problems with definitions and concepts' were encountered in each part of the question, except Part B(iii). These were manifest as *Inadequate knowledge of definitions and concepts*, referring to the numerous bank reconciliation-related concepts that are essential to a student's mastery of the topic, for example, unpresented cheques and deposits, dishonoured cheques, bank fees and debit orders.

An example is found in interview 12 (Weil, 1989), when the student attempts Part B(ii) of question 2. The student explains the meaning of unpresented cheques to be, ' ....old in the previous period and they're still not paid in this period....' (p. B53, Weil, 1989). While this may be true of some unpresented cheques, it is not exhaustive, as unpresented cheques may also originate in the current period. The student's knowledge of the concept 'unpresented cheques' is incomplete. Understanding the nature of an unpresented cheque is essential for the successful completion of a bank reconciliation statement, as unpresented cheques from both the present and from prior periods need to be identified and included in the statement.

A second example, found in interview 12 (Weil, 1989), relates to the treatment of bank charges. The student says that the business will make out a cheque to pay for these charges. This is clearly incorrect and will represent double payment, as the bank has already debited its account (statement) with the amount for bank charges.

A further example of difficulty with concepts is found in the analysis of interview 14 (Weil, 1989, B61), when discussing how unpresented deposits should be treated in the bank reconciliation statement. The student describes unpresented deposits as 'the deposits are not yet received, therefore it is not yet in our cash book' (p. B61). This statement is incorrect; unpresented deposits are already in the cash book, but have not yet been entered on the bank statement. Such flawed understanding could lead to a student entering unpresented deposits in the cash book, rather than as a reconciling item in the bank reconciliation statement.

Unpresented cheques, deposits and bank charges – and their treatment – could be argued to be 'core concepts', which are described by Meyer and Land (2006a) as representing 'conceptual 'building block[s]' that progress[es] understanding of the subject' (p. 6), in this case, bank reconciliation statements. Does an understanding of these concepts, however, lead to a 'qualitatively different view of subject matter' (p. 6) and therefore qualify as threshold concepts, defined by Meyer and Land (2006a) as 'akin to a portal, opening up a new and previously inaccessible way of thinking about something' (p. 3)?

The most likely criterion of a threshold concept that unpresented cheques, deposits and bank charges appear to meet is that of troublesome knowledge – 'knowledge troubled by partial and brittle understandings...' (Perkins, 2006, p. 37). He identifies five possible categories of troublesome knowledge, namely, ritual, inert, conceptually difficult, foreign and tacit knowledge. It can be argued that unpresented cheques and deposits represent conceptually difficult knowledge as they comprise money received or paid by a business that needs to be recorded in two different locations, that is, both inside the business (its cash book) and outside the business (on the bank statement). The business has no control over the latter. Similarly, bank charges need to be recorded in both locations. It could, however, be argued to the contrary that knowledge of the definitions and meanings of unpresented cheques, unpresented deposits and bank charges is not conceptually difficult, but rather that it is the process of how to account for these that qualifies them as troublesome knowledge.

A knowledge and understanding of unpresented cheques and deposits is not likely to be *transformative*, as it is not likely '...to occasion a significant shift in the perception of a subject....' (Meyer and Land, 2006a, p. 7). This knowledge is also not likely to be *irreversible*, that is '....unlikely to be forgotten, or will be unlearned only by considerable effort' (Meyer and Land, 2006a, p. 7). This is because a knowledge of unpresented cheques and deposits, without knowing how to treat them, could prove not to be very durable and could result in some confusion. This is shown in interview 12, when the student obtains the right answer, but uses the wrong terminology.

This knowledge is also not likely to be integrative as, in itself, it is not likely that the knowledge '...exposes the previously hidden interrelatedness of something' (Meyer and Land, 2006a, p. 7). Rather, as stated previously, it is the skill to use the unpresented items that results in the correct integration of items in a bank reconciliation statement.

A further criterion for an item to be classified as a threshold concept is that it may, but need not necessarily be, *bounded*. According to Meyer and Land (2006a), this means that '...any conceptual space will have terminal frontiers, bordering with thresholds into new conceptual areas' (p. 8). The knowledge of unpresented cheques and deposits could be argued to be bounded, as it is limited to a finite area of Introductory Accounting and does not relate to other topics within the discipline. It does not, however, either permit or prevent the ability to progress to mastery of other areas of the discipline and for this reason its boundedness is not significant.

The preceding discussion suggests that students' *Problems with definitions and concepts* are not likely to be considered threshold concepts according to Meyer and Land's (2006a) criteria. This is primarily due to the lack of convincing arguments in favour of knowledge of certain bank reconciliation-related concepts being sufficiently transformative or integrative in their impact on student learning. These definitions and concepts could be rote learned, but this in itself should not diminish the importance of learning the definitions and concepts as, according to Meyer (2000), Lucas (2002) and Lucas and Meyer (2003), a surface learning approach, such as memorisation, can be implemented as an initial step towards gaining and progressing towards deeper understanding.

Cognitive Difficulties – or Threshold Concepts?

As illustrated in Table 1, a wide range of cognitive difficulties were identified from the protocol analyses of the talk-aloud interviews. These were evident in all of the phases of the mental act (Feuerstein et al., 1980), and several of the difficulties recurred frequently, such as *lack of inferential-hypothetical reasoning.* The discussion which follows focuses on three of the cognitive difficulties, namely, *lack of inferential-hypothetical reasoning, narrowness of the mental field and poor visualisation of relationships.* These three difficulties are very similar, illustrating

Feuerstein et al.'s (1980) view that their list of deficient functions is neither definitive nor exhaustive and that overlaps exist between the functions. The three cognitive difficulties can all be placed within the general description of poor perception and manipulation of relationships; inferential-hypothetical reasoning relates to cause and effect relationships, narrowness of the mental field relates to an inability to think broadly enough about the impact of an accounting transaction or event and poor visualization relates to an inability to see how one action relates to another – for example, the mirror image that the bank statement and cash book have with each other.

Lack of Inferential-hypothetical Reasoning

Several students had difficulty with the preparation of a bank reconciliation statement, especially with regard to the reasoning involved in deciding whether to add or subtract amounts to or from the bank statement balance respectively.

A good example of this deficient cognitive operation is provided in the analysis of interview 1. When answering the question, the student relies on a mechanical technique which involves the insertion of amounts into either a debit or credit column and, by the process of adding or subtracting, the derivation of a balance. Such a technique is not, in itself, incorrect. The student, however, is uncertain whether the derived balance is favourable or unfavourable, thereby indicating his reliance on the purely mechanical insertion of amounts into columns, without a concomitant understanding of the effects and consequences of these entries on the relationship which he is considering. After some confusion, he settles for a favourable cash book balance, which is correct. When asked, however, to explain his decision in more detail, he displays an ability to reason in terms of , '….if this happened in the bank statement, then that happened, or will happen, in the cash book'. This brings the student to the opposite of his previous answer, with his concluding comment being, 'No, I am not really sure of myself here' (Weil 1989, B8).

Interview 9 provides further evidence of the use of a purely mechanical technique by a student. When explaining how unpresented cheques should be treated in the bank reconciliation statement (Part B(ii)), the student uses debits and credits to obtain the correct answer. When asked, however, to explain the reason for debiting outstanding cheques, he become confused and is unable to do so. He displays an inability to reason in terms of causes and effects, i.e. how cheques made out will affect initially the cash book and subsequently the bank statement and accordingly why unpresented cheques should be debited, as opposed to credited, in the bank reconciliation.

The student demonstrates similar difficulty when answering Part C of the question. By using the same mechanical technique, he correctly obtains a cash book balance of R55[3], but incorrectly regards this as an unfavourable, instead of a favourable balance. Rather than reasoning in terms of 'cause and effect', the student relies on mechanical technique which, in this case, produces an incorrect answer.

A different illustration of a weakness in inferential-hypothetical reasoning is found in interview 14. This student had previously defined the term 'unpresented deposits' incorrectly. Consequently, when preparing his bank reconciliation statement, he shows these deposits as outstanding in the cash book, instead of the bank statement.

That is not his only error, however. Assuming, as he does, that the deposits are not yet in the bank statement, this would mean that the balance in the cash book *before* entering the deposits should be R875 (unfavourable), rather than the R55 (favourable) determined by him. Because of his weakness in reasoning in terms of 'before and after', he has incorrectly deducted the unpresented deposits of R465 from the (unfavourable) balance of R410 (to obtain R55), instead of adding them (to obtain an unfavourable balance of R875).

Do the difficulties described previously fit the definition of a threshold concept? Although understanding the impact of unpresented cheques and deposits on the cash book and bank statement clearly fits Perkins' (2006) description of troublesome knowledge – especially – conceptually difficult knowledge, it is more likely to be the process of visualizing and comparing the relative impacts of the unpresented items that presents a barrier to students' effective learning. A bank reconciliation statement *cannot* be completed successfully unless a student can visualize the impact of unpresented cheques and deposits on the cash book and bank statement. This skill can, therefore, be argued to be *transformative*, in that once mastered, it may 'occasion a significant shift in the perception of a subject' (Meyer and Land, 2006a, p. 7), by permitting the completion of a bank reconciliation statement with confidence.

It is also likely that once a student understands the cause and effect that cheques and deposits have on the bank statement and cash book and can make the necessary entries, that this ability will be *irreversible*, as it is not based primarily on memory, but rather on inferential-hypothetical reasoning. It can be argued similarly that this skill is *integrative*, in that it exposes the 'interrelatedness' (Meyer and Land, 2006a, p. 7) between the bank statement and cash book.

Poor Visualization of Relationships

Evidence of poor visualization is provided in interview 10, when the student draws up a T-account[4] for *Bank*, showing a credit balance of R410. This amount is correct, but only *before* the unpresented deposits are credited by the bank. Although not yet in the latter, this deposit will already have been entered in the cash receipts journal and posted to the bank account, thereby giving a debit balance of R55[5]. The student is confusing what has been entered by the business in its cash book with what has been entered by the bank on its bank statement, not clearly understanding the impact that the unpresented deposits have on both balances.

Further evidence of poor visualization is found when the student completes the bank reconciliation statement. He obtains an adjusted cash book balance of R55 (credit), whereas had he considered the consequence of depositing cheques in the bank and not simply adhered to a mechanical technique when doing the statement, he would have realized that the balance should have been favourable.

Narrowness of the Mental Field

Feuerstein et al. (1980) define this deficient cognitive operation as '…a narrow mental field which limits drastically the number of units of information that can be processed and manipulated simultaneously.' (1980, p. 93). An example of this is found in interview 5, when the student decides to account for the unpresented cheques by increasing the cash book balance by the amount of the cheques, effectively nullifying the payments previously entered as cheques. This will reconcile the cash book with the bank statement, but is conceptually incorrect, as the cheques have not been cancelled and should not be written back to the cash book. They have simply not yet been presented to the bank – a timing issue, which will presumably be resolved in the next accounting period, when the recipient of the cheques presents them for depositing to its bank.

Had the student not limited his thinking solely to making the cash book and bank statements agree, he may have considered what would happen when the cheques were subsequently presented for payment to the bank. There will again be non-agreement between the balances; the bank balance will have been reduced by the recording of the previously unpresented cheques, but not the cash book balance, as the original entry of the cheques when made out will have been neutralized. To correct this, will require the entry of further cheques in the cash book; this is clearly incorrect, as no additional cheques have been made out.

The student could have avoided this error by thinking ahead to the future consequences of his decision. This would have left him with no possibility other than showing the unpresented cheques (correctly) as a reconciling item in the reconciliation statement. The preceding examples of poor visualization of relationships and narrowness of the mental field appear, like lack of inferential-hypothetical reasoning, to meet Meyer and Land's (2006a) criteria for classification as threshold concepts.

THRESHOLD CONCEPTIONS

The preceding deficient cognitive operations all have an impact on the effective usage of data. Given, however, that these cognitive operations relate to thinking skills, rather than to concepts, it raises the question of whether these are not threshold *conceptions*, rather than *concepts*. Lucas and Mladenovic (2006) describe threshold conceptions as 'comprising an *organising structure* or *framework* which provides the explanatory rationale for accounting techniques' (pp. 153–154). It could be argued that the cognitive operations necessary to use data effectively in accounting courses comprise such an *organising structure* and therefore constitute threshold *conceptions*, rather than threshold *concepts*. This argument concurs with what Perkins (2006) describes as 'epistemes' – '….a system of ideas or way of understanding that allows us to establish knowledge. … the importance of students understanding the structure of the disciplines they are studying. … epistemes are manners of justifying, explaining, solving problems, conducting enquiries, and designing and validating various kinds of products or outcomes.' (p. 42).

Furthermore, the cognitive operations identified in this chapter as being part of an organising structure for studying Introductory Accounting could be argued to represent an ontological shift in how the study of accounting is viewed. A focus on the thought processes underlying a topic area, such as bank reconciliations, rather than on the content itself, may be a spark to ignite a major shift in how student's perceive – and ultimately study – the discipline of accounting.

CONCLUSION

By using threshold concept theory to conduct a threshold concept analysis, this chapter has attempted to inform the question posed by Lucas and Mladenovic (2007), namely, whether or not threshold concepts will develop into its own distinctive theoretical framework. Lucas and Mladenovic (2007) consider threshold concepts to be a 'fruitful emerging theoretical framework for a review of educational research and practice' (p. 246). In encouraging its theoretical development, they recommend that threshold concepts draws on other fields of research, for example, transformative learning (Mezirow, 1991) and makes connections with other existing works in order to develop 'its own distinctive theoretical framework' (Lucas and Mladenovic, 2007, p. 245). One such existing research area is cognitive psychology, within which the Feuerstein et al. (1980) deficient cognitive operations' paradigm fits. This chapter, by analysing and evaluating the findings of a study (Weil, 1989) conducted in terms of the Feuerstein et al. (1980) paradigm, suggests that cognitive psychology and threshold concept theory may well be compatible in that cognitive operations, although not necessarily concepts in a traditional sense, may well possess most of the attributes of Meyer and Land's (2006a) threshold concepts. This confirms and adds to the work done by the Lucas and Mladenovic (2006) when utilizing Biggs and Collis' (1982) Structure of Observed Learning Outcomes (SOLO) categories of cognitive effort and conceptual complexity within a threshold concept context. There may also be a strong case for arguing that cognitive operations fit Lucas and Mladenovic's (2006) description of threshold conceptions.

The chapter has restricted its scope to an examination of the requisite learning structure for bank reconciliations – a single, traditionally difficult topic in Introductory Accounting. Future researchers might wish to consider and assess whether it is possible to reconfigure an entire Introductory Accounting course into requisite thinking skills framed within an appropriate organising structure. Such a significant shift would bring threshold concept theory firmly within the realm of ontological change for accounting students.

NOTES

[1] In South Africa prior to 1994, government legislation classified the population of the country into four groups: White, Black, Coloured and Asians. These designations have been used in this sense in this chapter.

[2] South African Rands.

[3] R55 is the difference between the debit balance on the bank statement of R410 and the unpresented cheques of R465 in Part C of the question.

[4] A T-account is the name given to a simplified general ledger account, which contains a debit and a credit side. Its name derives from its appearance; it has a horizontal line at the top, with a vertical line running downwards from the middle of the horizontal line, thus resembling a T.

[5] Obtained by deducting the unpresented deposits of R465 from the debit bank statement balance of R410.

REFERENCES

Biggs, J., & Collis, K. (1982). *Evaluating the quality of learning: Thr SOLO taxonomy (Structure of the Observed Learning Outcome)*. New York: Academic Press.

Chi, M. T. H., Bassok, M., Lewis, M. W., Reimann, P., & Glaser, R. (1989). Self-explanations: How students study and use examples in learning to solve problems. *Cognitive Science, 13*, 145–182.

Chi, M. T. H., de Leeuw, N., Chiu, M. H., & LaVancher, C. (1994). Eliciting self-explanations improves understanding. *Cognitive Science, 18*, 439–477.

Cousin, G. (2007, April). *Exploring threshold concepts for linking teaching and research*. Paper presented to the International Colloquium: International Policies and Practices for Academic Enquiry, Winchester. Retrieved March 5, 2009, from http://portal-live.solent.ac.uk/university/rtconference/2007/resources/glynis_cousins.pdf

Davies, P. (2003, August 26–30). *Threshold concepts: how can we recognise them?* Paper presented at the European Association for Research into Learning and Instruction (EARLI) Conference, Padua.

Ericsson, K. A., & Simon, H. A. (1985). *Verbal Reports as data*. Massachesetts Institute of Technology Press.

Financial Mail. (1981, April). *Accountancy – too many failures*. pp. 43–44.

Feuerstein, R., Rand, Y., Hoffman, M., & Miller, R. (1980). *Instrumental enrichment*. University Park Press.

Konold, C. E., & Well, A. D. (1981). *Analysis and reporting of interview data*. Working paper, University of Massachusetts.

Lucas, U. (2000). Worlds apart: Students' experiences of learning introductory accounting. *Critical Perspectives on Accounting, 11*(4), 479–504.

Lucas, U. (2002). Uncertainties and contradictions: Lecturers' conceptions of teaching introductory accounting. *British Accounting Review, 34*(3), 183–204.

Lucas, U., & Meyer, J. H. F. (2003). *Understanding students' conceptions of learning and subject in 'introductory' courses: The case of introductory accounting*. Study presented at the Symposium Meta learning in higher education: taking account of the student perceptive, Padova, August: European Association for Research on Learning and Instruction, 10th Biennial Conference.

Lucas, U., & Mladenovic, R. (2006). Developing new 'World Views': Threshold concepts in introductory accounting. In J. H. F. Meyer & R. Land (Eds.), *Overcoming barriers to student understanding: Threshold concepts and troublesome knowledge* (pp. 148–159). Oxford, UK: Routledge.

Lucas, U., & Mladenovic, R. (2007). The potential of threshold concepts: An emerging framework for educational research and practice. *London Review of Education, 5*(3), 237–248.

Mehl, M. C. (1984). *Using the cognitive difficulties of disadvantaged students to improve university teaching*. Maryland: Tenth International Conference on Improving University Teaching.

Mehl, M. C., & Weil, S. H. (1988). Accounting education in a disadvantaged socio-economic environment: A South African case study. In *The Proceedings of the Sixth International Conference on Accounting Education* (pp. 846–855). Greenwood Press and Yushodo Co.

Meyer, J. H. F. (2000). The modelling of 'dissonant' study orchestration in higher education. *European Journal of Psychology of Education, 15*(1), 5–18.

Meyer, J. H. F., & Land, R. (2003). Threshold concepts and troublesome knowledge: Linkages to ways of thinking and practicing within the disciplines. In C. Rust (Ed.), *Improving student learning theory and practice – 10 Years On* (pp. 412–424). Oxford, UK: OCSLD.

Meyer, J. H. F., & R. Land (2006a). Threshold concepts and troublesome knowledge: An introduction. In J. H. F. Meyer & R. Land (Eds.), *Overcoming barriers to student understanding: Threshold concepts and troublesome knowledge* (pp. 3–18). Oxford, UK: Routledge.

Meyer, J. H. F., & Land, R. (2006b). Threshold concepts and troublesome knowledge: Issues of liminality. In J. H. F. Meyer & R. Land (Eds.), *Overcoming barriers to student understanding: Threshold concepts and troublesome knowledge* (pp. 19–32). Oxford, UK: Routledge.

Mezirow, J. (1991). *Transformative dimensions of adult learning.* San Francisco: Jossey-Bass.

Mladenovic, R. (2000). An investigation into ways of challenging introductory accounting students' negative perceptions of accounting. *Accounting Education: An International Journal, 9,* 135–154.

Nickerson, R. S., Perkins, D. N., & Smith, E. E. (1985). *The teaching of thinking.* Lawrrence Erlbaum Associates.

Perkins, D. N. (2006). Constructivism and troublesome knowledge. In J. H. F. Meyer & R. Land (Eds.), *Overcoming barriers to student understanding: Threshold concepts and troublesome knowledge* (pp. 33–47). Oxford, UK: Routledge.

Sharma, D. S. (1997). Accounting students' learning conceptions, approaches to learning and the influence of the learning-teaching context on approaches to learning. *Accounting Education: An International Journal, 6*(2), 125–146.

Weil, S. H. (1989). *Addressing the problems of cognition in a first year accounting course at the University of the Western Cape.* Unpublished Ph. D. thesis, University of the Western Cape, Cape Town.

Sidney Weil and Nicholas McGuigan
Centre of Accounting Education and Research
Lincoln University

JANE OSMOND AND ANDREW TURNER

21. THE THRESHOLD CONCEPT JOURNEY IN DESIGN:

From Identity to Application

INTRODUCTION

This chapter builds upon previous research (Osmond and Turner 2008) outlined in Land and Meyer's *Threshold Concepts within the Disciplines* published in 2008. Specifically, it outlines the use of threshold concepts as a research framework within the transport and product design course at Coventry University, and then considers the journey from seeking to identify a threshold concept to a consideration of its potential impact on teaching and learning.

BACKGROUND

The research began in 2005 within the Centre of Excellence for Product and Automotive Design (CEPAD), established from a successful bid to the Higher Education Funding Council for England (HEFCE), as part of the CETL initiative. Pedagogical research has been a key activity within CEPAD with three inter-related strands of enquiry: identifying threshold concepts in design, examining the development of spatial awareness and investigating the internationalisation of the design curriculum. This chapter focuses on the research relating to the identification of threshold concepts in design.

As previously reported by Osmond and Turner (2007), at the outset of the research it was soon evident that in relation to pedagogical theory, the Transport and Product Design discipline was relatively untheorised, and approaches to teaching used by the Transport and Product Design staff were underpinned by a 'tacit underlying agenda of things that students need to have' (ibid). A similar observation by Buchanan in relation to design research is that within the design community there has been relatively little consideration of the nature of design research and its value, and questions about whether there is 'design knowledge that merits serious attention.' (1999: 3). This is echoed by Dorst (2008), who argues that most research into design has focused on the *process* of design at the expense of the development of the designer, and Rogers: 'In this respect, design research is a relatively young discipline and does not possess a well established knowledge base when we compare it to the likes of the sciences, humanities and other more established scholarly disciplines [4].

J. H. F. Meyer, R. Land and C. Baillie (eds.), Threshold Concepts and Transformational Learning, 347–363.
© 2010 Sense Publishers. All rights reserved.

Further, a pilot study using an existing research methodology (ELTQ 2002) based on phenomenographic research was found to have little relevance to this context. The pilot used the Experiences of Teaching and Learning Questionnaire (ELTQ 2002), developed from the ESRC-TLRP project "Enhancing Teaching-Learning Environments in Undergraduate Courses", but notions of deep and surface learning were found not to be particularly applicable to the course, with the questionnaire itself found to be both too atomistic and generic a tool. Similarly, the notions and characteristics of deep and surface learning had little resonance with staff and students in relation to the nature of learning or student engagement, perhaps reflecting the increasing debate around the notion of deep/surface learning exemplified by Beattie et al (1997) and Haggis (2003).

The research therefore focused on the notion of threshold concepts (Meyer and Land), which were introduced to characterise the idea that in certain disciplines there are concepts that:

> ...represent a transformed way of understanding or interpreting, or viewing something without which the learner cannot progress. (2003)

Since the initial definition, the notion of threshold concepts has been further developed (Meyer and Land, 2005) and threshold concepts have been identified across disciplines as diverse as health, accounting, languages, communication studies and online spaces (Clouder, 2005; Lucas and Mladenovic, 2006; Orsini-Jones 2008, Cousin, 2006, Savin-Baden, 2008). The applicability and relevance of the notion of threshold concepts across disciplines is also reflected in an increasing body of literature and events focusing on threshold concepts both generally and within disciplines.

Within this context, the threshold concept framework was applied as a lens to research the Transport and Product Design Course in order to identify key concepts that students need to acquire in their development as designers and enable them to enter both national and international transport and product design industries. The concept provided a very useful starting point for opening up a research dialogue with both students and staff of the courses. Staff in particular engaged enthusiastically with the pedagogical research team in both interviews and whole-staff meetings and found the thresholds approach accessible in terms of a theoretical concept and the language (Osmond et al., 2007, 2007a). From the perspective of the pedagogical research team, threshold concepts provided a 'way in' to conducting pedagogical research with staff who may have had little or no engagement or knowledge of existing pedagogical research or theory.

Initially, to help identify potential threshold concepts in this area, and bearing in mind that staff saw possessing and developing spatial awareness as a crucial aspect of the student journey, a research question was posed: 'Is spatial awareness a threshold concept for the Transport and Product Design course?'. A concomitant research aim was to develop a discipline specific tool to measure the student journey in terms of spatial awareness from entry to the end of the first year.

Interviews with staff were carried out using the above research question as a baseline and a key finding was that there was no common definition of the meaning of spatial awareness as it related to the Transport and Product Design course. Staff responses ranged from 'all round awareness' to 'design sensitivity'. In addition, student responses were gathered through a mixture of qualitative interviews and questionnaires and these responses were categorised as 'having no knowledge', 'little knowledge' and 'guessing' (see Table 1 below).

Table 1. Staff and student perceptions of the term 'spatial awareness' (Osmond et al. 2007)

Category	Indicative response: staff
All around awareness	I don't think there is any area of conscious thought about anything that the design business doesn't touch on in a way that few others do: it is this business of this incredible all-round awareness.
	Holistic approach: cloud of information with polarised areas.
Co-ordination	Hand/eye/brain co-ordination.
Design sensitivity	Sensitivity: being able to 'see' design; some see it as a picture, others see it as presenting and manipulating information.
	Seeing things as a whole, but having an instinct to knowing which bit to highlight to achieve certain purposes.
Space	Displacement of space.
	'Relationship between form and spaces.'
'Intuitive/6th sense.'	Intuitive/6th sense.
Looking at an object from the outside	I think it really has to be looking at an object.
	Awareness of an object at a distance.
Mental rotation	2D to 3D translation.
	Looking at an object at a distance, but able to perceive it in the round in detail.
Positioning system	Spatial positioning system working on several planes.
	Is about navigation and urban environments.
Time	Relates to time especially when orienting through large spaces.
Visualisation	Somebody being able to sit in a chair and visualise what the space around them is and look at that on drawings and have a concept of what that means.
	Understand what that means in terms of space around a product, car, phone...
Volume	Relates to the ability to transform volume.
Category	Indicative response: students
No knowledge	I can't say I do. I would like to guess but I might be wrong.
	Never heard of it before.
Some knowledge	No, I have heard the term but I am not aware of it.
	I've heard of it before…
	Like distance from things and if something will fit into a certain space or if it doesn't?
	In what sense – when you walk into a room and feel a lot of space?

However, although no common definition of spatial awareness was reached, a number of possible threshold concepts did emerge from the data, some of which were used to inform the development of a pilot spatial awareness measurement tool (©TPD Test) which was implemented with 114 first-year students alongside an existing spatial awareness test (PVRT[1]), the latter specifically designed as the basis for evaluating courses developed to enhance students' spatial skills. (Figure1)

Analysis of the PVRT test results were undertaken and the mean score was comparable to previously published scores for this test carried out by Purdue University; in addition the TPD Test results correlated with the PVRT results indicating that the tests were assessing similar aspects of spatial awareness[2]. The results were then compared with students' end of year assessment results, with a specific comparison undertaken with a 2D and 3D representational module, but no correlation was found. In other words, scoring well or not so well in both tests did not correlate with how the students performed in their assessment results, and therefore whether they passed their first year of study.

Due to the lack of common definition of spatial awareness amongst staff and students and the lack of correlation between the tests and end of year assessment results, the research team concluded that spatial awareness, as represented in the tests, was not a threshold concept in the first year of study. This lead to a reconsideration of the meanings inherent in the term 'spatial awareness' and how

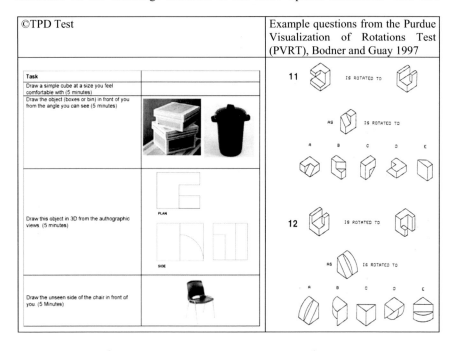

Figure 1. ©TPD Test (Osmond 2007) and existing spatial awareness test.

relevant it was to the Transport and Product Design course. Current work focusing on the term 'visual creativity' is currently under investigation. Meanwhile, whilst spatial awareness was not seen as a threshold concept, a number of possible threshold concepts did emerge, with the notion of 'confidence to challenge' tentatively identified as a threshold concept within the first year of the course. (see Osmond et al. 2007a)

DEFINING THE THRESHOLD CONCEPT

As described above, the research tentatively identified 'confidence to challenge' as a first year threshold concept, defined by an Industrial Design tutor as:

> the ability to inculcate design conventions and expand upon them using information from a variety of sources and experiences.

This 'confidence to challenge' allows students to tackle what Buchanan (1992) calls 'wicked problems', which

> ...have incomplete, contradictory, and changing requirements; and solutions to them are often difficult to recognize as such because of complex interdependencies.'

Without this confidence students can remain in a liminal state, constantly 'surfacing around' in search of a solution, and this seemed to present even more difficulties to those international students who are used to a more prescribed style of teaching and curriculum:

> I think during the very beginning I really struggled to really know what I should do in my projects – you really spend a lot of time to think about it but the result is not really that good as you expected because you keep surfacing around, you can't really make decisions about doing ... that's one of the most negative feelings because you don't know what to do sometimes – I mean I understand you do projects it is not really satisfying teachers, you learn during the process, but still you want to know what they really want. (first year international student)

A search of the design literature reveals that the 'surfacing around' described by the student quote above, chimes with Tovey's (1984) notion of an 'incubation period' that designers tend to experience:

> It is possible that the incubation periods, that time of apparent inactivity during which the designer's brain furiously grapples with the problem, is simply the period during which the two halves of the brain are out of touch or unable to agree. But contrast the moment when they do suddenly come into alignment would be the classic 'eureka' point.' (226)

This is also described by Cross as the attention of the designer oscillating between the problem and the solution, epitomised by this quote from Archer (1979):

> The design activity is commutative, the designer's attention oscillating between the emerging requirement ideas and the developing provision ideas, as he

illuminates obscurity on both sides and reduces misfit between them.' (quoted in Cross 1992: 5)

Whereas Dorst likens this uncertainty to 'tightrope walking' in that designers can work on a design for indefinable lengths of time, not knowing whether the design will be successful or reach a 'satisfying conclusion.' (2003: 97).

This incubation period can also be likened to Wallace's concept of a 'bubble' (Figure 2), which he describes as:

> Progress through many simultaneous tasks involves solving hundreds of individual problems...To solve a particular design task, the complete set of problem bubbles associated with the task must be solved; but many, many bubbles not directly related to the task will be entered between starting and finishing the task...' (1992: 81)

Wallace therefore marks out the terrain a designer routinely enters when first approaching a design, which one member of staff described as 'the explosion in the head which actually makes them better designers', and is a sentiment echoed by Cross when he states that a good designer '...is someone who has no limitations in having odd and strange ideas in that early stage of the concept phase.' (IBID:13)

Further, Dorst and Lawson's (2008) 'Levels of Design Expertise' model (based on a model originally developed by Drefus) and outlines six levels of expertise in relation to a designer's development. A fledgling designer will begin in the 'naive'

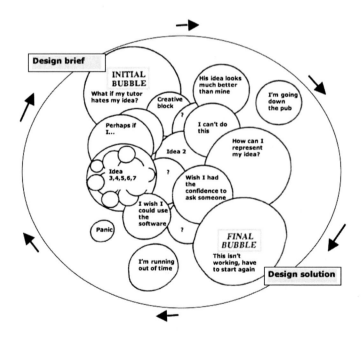

Figure 2. Stuck in the Bubble (adapted from Wallace 1992).

category, where the student has not yet realised that 'design is a series of activities'. The student then moves to the 'novice' category where rule-based design is the norm. The next stage is to 'advanced beginner' which involves situation-based design, followed by the 'competent' design stage where the focus is on strategy-based design. The student then moves into the expert category where pattern based design is used, and finally to the 'visionary' category where designers incorporate all the previous categories and strive 'to extend the domain in which they work...new ways things could be, defines the issues, opens new worlds and creates new domains.' (2008: 9). Therefore, it appears that the students can be characterised as being as the 'naïve' stage, where they do not yet realise that 'design is a series of activities' and the surfacing around and/or incubation period experience is perhaps the initial stage on the journey to becoming a 'visionary' designer.

The period of uncertainty or being 'stuck in the bubble' when looking for solutions and considering alternatives for solutions has also been identified as an important part of the process of the 'creative thinking' process. Although the terms and context vary, the principle and importance of a period of uncertainty is well recognised. For example, Kleinman talks about 'Creativity-as-process':

> Creativity-as-process is conceptualised [and] conceived as leading to implicit or intangible outcomes and...as not linked to any outcome. While the latter may appear illogical, in that all processes must lead to some form of outcome, and seems perhaps counter-intuitive, it recognises that creativity sometimes requires an acceptance of a lack of structure and direction, e.g. 'playing for the sake of playing'. (2008)

DeBono (1995) in describing his six 'thinking hats' system refers to the importance of creating time and space for creative thinking. The coloured hats are used as a tool to allow time and space for creativity, with the different coloured hats denoting a particular type of thinking. There is no set order to 'wearing' the hats but ideas such as thinking for 'ideas and proposals' and 'evaluating the alternatives' clearly resonate with the ideas of 'surfacing around' for solutions identified in this research. In addition, DeBono identifies 'provocations' to achieve 'movement' to come up with new solutions, defining movement as a mental operation requiring 'confidence and practice'. Amabile (1983 *in* Vidal 2009) in defining the creative person describes how 'creative thinking skills determine how flexibly and imaginatively people approach problems and tasks. It demands courage to be creative because you will be changing the status quo', and Baille (2003) focuses on fostering students' creative thinking skills in particular through a series of case studies entitled *The Travelling Case*. Other publications that identify the importance of creativity in problem solving include Vidal (2009); Kotzé & Purgathofer (2007) and Dekker (1995).

It is likely then that some first year students, when faced with a design brief for the first time, can get 'stuck' in Wallace's bubble, perhaps lacking 'the ability to entertain ambiguity and complexity' (Wylant 2008), and subsequently may panic as they search for solutions. In practice then, they may be afraid of admitting that they don't understand the brief or can't get past a creative block and constantly enter and re-enter the bubble as they struggle for inspiration, and, at this stage, lack the 'confidence to challenge'.

INVESTIGATING THE THRESHOLD CONCEPT

The notion of 'confidence to challenge' as a threshold concept was explored further during the third year of this research through a whole-staff meeting and one-to-one interviews with five third year students (including one international student) who were originally interviewed as first year students.

The aim was to establish evidence of progression through the threshold concept, perhaps identifying critical points (such as key experiences and assessments) which enabled this and to this end each student was presented with a picture of a piece of assessed first year work and asked to describe how they would approach such a brief from their 3rd year perspective. Two students were quite taken aback to be presented with a piece of work that they hadn't seen for over two years:

> Hmm, 40% didn't do very well, I don't think I read the brief properly – I think that was what – my drawing skills don't look fantastic either.

> I look at my first year work now and I think I shouldn't really be here. Yeah, at the time I knew for example some of the things could have been better, but compared to what I can do it is like I am looking at myself 10 years ago thinking what were you doing – quite shocking.

They all recognised that there was a real difference in how they would approach the same brief and talked about how they felt they had progressed quite significantly since their first year, typified by this comment from one of the students:

> I can approach things in a more homogenous way...a holistic approach now. I can actually look at things and think well it looks good – works well. First year I felt like I approached things from separate angles and hoped that they would collide in the middle and I would have something that looked good and worked well, but now I find that I can merge things together while I am doing it, it is more controlled.

Interestingly, three students felt that their actual thought process had not changed since the first year, rather, that they had been given the tools to underpin and express the process in improved designs:

> ...it is kind of an emotional/emotive thing that goes on in your head - as you progress along the year, you do learn new skills and new ways of handling/tackling a project or handling different stages, but in the thought processes – I would say that the actual rigid structure of thinking in the way to tackle the project hasn't changed that much...you just improve on what you have got, rather than a total overhaul of your thinking processes

> I still think my thought processes are quite similar to the way I used to think compared to the way I used to think in the first year or second year

I think there is a natural thought process that you actually do compose as the project goes along

However, the students did confirm that the sense of being stuck in the bubble when faced with a new brief was still present in their third year:

It has happened to all of us at one point or another, when you have had that soul crushing moment when you think I can't do it or something has gone wrong and you haven't got time.

Oh yes there are still some briefs that you do have to rack your brain over and think what is going on here

This difference between the first and third year appeared to be that the students had inculcated and used coping strategies:

If [it] happens in the 1st year I don't think you would be equipped to deal with it, but in the 2nd and 3rd you have learnt the skills to get round that problem.

I have actually found that I am quite good at pressing the reset button and getting everything back together.

I think actually understanding of the briefs you really need to know what you are talking about and be able to understand it right from the beginning and make sure your understanding of it is the right one – because if you think you completely understand and it comes to the end of the assessment, and yeah but I understood the brief, they are like no you didn't understand it in the correct way so you have to make sure you understand right from the very beginning– I think that is definitely something that I need to make sure is happening,

It seems then that by their third year of study, the students were still getting stuck in the bubble, but had developed strategies to deal with it by accepting that this is part of the design process:

Pressure – you are up against the wire and you have got a few hours left and you think to yourself...what am I going to do? It is that pressure that forces you to condense your skills into something useful – I feel that's when I have learnt most – when I have been up against the wire.

The result is an increased confidence in not only drawing on different strategies to cope, but also translates to presenting and defending their actual design work. All the students mentioned that the work they carried out as part of a group in their third year, aided by an assignment that required them to present designs to companies who agreed to pose as 'clients', boosted their confidence:

Yes, I was able to stand in front of the editor of [...] today and wing the presentation when the video wasn't working and he really liked it. I felt that I can do that a lot more effectively now, you have the practice of defending everything you have done.

To explain why you have done something and why you think it is good I feel that I have got a lot more confidence

I think [my confidence] has definitely improved – I am still not 100%...the group work we were doing a lot of in the studio in front of everyone else – I had to be confident with my work and I was proud of it in the end, I would be drawing something and this doesn't look quite right and someone else would tell me if there was something wrong with it that they could see or they would say it was really good.

It appears then that during the first three years of the course, the students undergo a series of transitional moments that enhance their ability to progress through the bubble when faced with a design brief, which is underpinned by the development of an inquisitive attitude/hunger for knowledge; a 'playfulness' that facilitates the stretching of boundaries; a lateral and logical approach to tackling problems and an ability to evolve, change and refine ideas. Further, tutors feel that releasing students' creativity comes to the fore during the process of design; '...through problem solving, direct modelling, sketch modelling...experiencing it where it really takes place.' (Osmond and Bull 2007). Previous research (Osmond et al., 2007) observed that this facilitation of creativity is underpinned by the provision of a studio environment that favours a teaching approach akin to the atelier principal of teaching, defined by Craddick and O'Reilly (2002) as involving a group of students...working with one or two tutors...through a year-long cycle of design.' facilitated by a staff who cultivate a 'respect for the creative mind' (Design Tutor). In this, the teaching method resembles the apprenticeship model, in which effective teaching, according to Pratt is

...a process of socializing students into new behavioural norms and professional ways of working. Effective teachers are highly skilled practitioners of what they teach. Whether they are in classrooms or in clinical settings, effective teachers are recognized for their professional knowledge and expertise. (2005)

TRANSITION POINTS

For the first year students, one member of staff talked about how the result of the first assessment was an important transitional moment, almost like a reassurance that the students 'had the right' to be on the course:

...something about having gone through the process and being reassured...[they feel] am I still here? Can I stay? Now can I actually call myself a designer?

With second year students a seminal moment occurs when the students use clay for the first time. This experience brings a number of concepts together, in particular, space – physically in terms of the actual studio environment, and conceptually, in terms of the brief which requires them to produce a 'clay head' based on their imagination (Figure 3), and an awareness of each other as a.group:

Somewhere towards the end of the 5-week clay head part – their own studio, freedom they are given – and their understanding all of a sudden of who they are in the group and working together in a sustained way, and achieving.

Figure 3. Clay heads project.

Just after the experience with the clay heads, the staff mentioned an increase in confidence in terms of students approaching them:

> Another gateway is just after the clays, because I tend never to see any students come to tutorials until they are in year 2 and then we do the empowering 'yes you can go and do this'.

> Being mature enough to turn up and talk to us...We are perhaps changing their view from us being teachers to just people, to facilitators

A transition for third year students was mentioned in reference to being exposed to the 'world of work' either through a company placement or an in-house design placement:

> Going out on a real placement or a placement alternative here, where you do need to get up for work and behave in a professional way – when they finish that, there is definite change from then on.

Another change noticed by staff is how the students use technology differently during their third year:

> [in their second year, the students] get locked behind what is technically feasible, whereas we want the technology to enable their design rather than solve all the technology first – 2nd years seem to get locked behind that, whereas the third years don't.

Other transitional moments discussed by staff as spanning the students' journey through the course were group work and empathy. For the former, the key moment was when individual students realised that they had concede that their design was perhaps not the design that should be pursued:

> One of the big ones is working in groups – if their personal piece of work isn't the bit that gets chosen – a big one is to recognise is 'that idea is better than mine and I have to stop making that one work, and try and make this one work'.

For the latter – empathy – this relates to students having to expand their awareness to include the needs of other people, a particularly important transition for a designer:

> ...because what the students have to be able to do as a designer is not think like themselves, not got to design for themselves – and I think that is one of the most difficult – it is actually taking them out of themselves, and making them think like a 60 year old or like a child. I think that is one of the important breakthrough moments, when they stop doing that, when they stop thinking like a petrol–head. When they can think like an old lady trying get a bag onto a bus I think that is the breakthrough moment when they can achieve interesting design because it is that ability to think outside [of themselves]

The pedagogical design of the transport and product design course appears to be key in providing opportunities and experiences for key transitions in the student identity to occur and for the development of key design competencies. By the third year of study students are able to use learned competencies to negotiate the bubble – for example, knowing where to look for inspiration, tolerating a creative block until inspiration strikes, possessing relevant technological competencies, knowing how to use clay and not being afraid to approach peers and teachers for help. This progression is evidenced by the students' increased confidence in their own ideas and proposals, an example of which was discussed earlier when a third year brief involved the students presenting their ideas and proposals to real clients.

THE THRESHOLD CONCEPT

The key aspect identified in this research is the need for students to accept as an important and necessary part of design process, that period of uncertainty when they are searching and trying out different solutions or 'surfacing around'. We are therefore arguing that toleration of being stuck in the bubble – or Meyer and Land's liminal space – leads to the 'confidence to challenge', defined as inculcating design conventions and expanding upon them using information from a variety of sources and experiences. In other words, although the 'confidence to challenge' was originally identified as the threshold concept within this context, it is the *process*– the toleration of uncertainty – that brings about the transformation in the student, and this achievement of tolerance is linked to an increasing confidence in their own capability and identity as a designer to identify and propose design solutions. Using Meyer and Land's characteristics of threshold concepts, achieving toleration of being stuck in the bubble is *transformative* in that the students accept that this is what a designer 'does' and thus they begin their journey to the designer identity. It is *irreversible* in that they would find it very difficult to 'un-think' themselves from a design identity. It is *integrative* in that that they realise that everything they know, learn and experience is a legitimate source of inspiration (for example accepting that those moments when they dance around the bubble thinking about subjects that are not directly related to their task may turn out to be the most important part of the process). And, most of all it is *troublesome* in that the students will constantly experience and re-experience the 'surfacing around' as they hunt for a solution, even when they attain the status of professional designer.

In other words, when students accept that part of the creative process is being stuck in the bubble – or they accept *the toleration of uncertainty* – while they search for inspiration, then they have achieved the confidence to play with both conventional ideas and challenge these with new thoughts, or perhaps develop the capability for what Perkins (2000) describes as 'breakthrough thinking' which leads to the 'kind of creativity that involves thinking outside the box.', or even 'thinking in a very different box.' (Wylant 2008).

IMPLICATIONS FOR TEACHING AND LEARNING

According to Davies and Mangan (2007) it is not enough to identify a threshold concept – for this activity to be useful, consideration of how this can affect the design of teaching and learning must be the next step. A characteristic of the assessments and activities associated with the transitional moments where students appear to progress through the threshold concept, appear to be problem-based, experiential, related to work and 'real-world' design activities and often involve group work; in other words there is a focus on 'doing as learning'. This reflects the growing interest evident in the literature in curriculum design incorporating work-related learning, the use of serious games and simulations using immersive virtual worlds (e.g. Savin-Baden and Wilkie, 2006, Gauntlett, 2007).

In contrast, development of the toleration of uncertainty seems to be implicit – almost an underlying agenda – in the teaching and learning process and to help first year students, in particular international students, perhaps explicitly surfacing this may enable them to develop suitable coping strategies during their first year on the course. In other words, by legitimising the 'stuck in the bubble moment', it is possible that students may feel more comfortable in this moment at an earlier stage.

However, surfacing the underlying agenda in a creative discipline such as this one could be problematic and surfacing 'the stuck in the bubble' moment may not enhance students' creative abilities. The course as it stands is very successful, and some members of staff would argue this is precisely because of the freedom the students are given to experiment and 'play' during the design process and that 'the stuck in the bubble' moment, if described and explicitly surfaced, may hinder their progress, or as a member of staff comments:

> Can't write it in a document. Sometimes to write things down kills them – you finally isolate it and nail it down and write it down it looks trite and stupid – it's not worth the paper it is written on – you can say it in the heartfelt way – it's meaningful – probably works as a quote – but it wouldn't work in text...'

Dorst echoes this when he talks about how existing models of the 'design process' exclude everything else that is happening when designers are in design mode and that 'it takes only an afternoon to explain one of the design process models to a group of design students. But knowing that model doesn't make these students designers at all...' (2008: 5)

Conversely, Perkins argues that by not surfacing the underlying agenda, or what he calls the episteme:

...many students never get the hang of it, or only slowly, because the epistemes receive little direct attention. For [students], surfacing the game through analytic discussion and deliberative practice could make a big difference. (2006: 43)

Wallace concurs when he states that design thinking is improved 'through being consciously aware of the design process' (1992: 75) whilst at the same time 'hovering' above the bubbles.

Perhaps a way forward may well be to focus on the concept of negotiating the bubble as a way to assess gaps in student knowledge. If, in the first year, students were encouraged to articulate the reasons as to why they are stuck in the bubble – for example, 'I would like to produce a rotational 3D model on screen so I can play with it, but I don't know how to use the Alias software'; I can't seem to make this clay model work'; 'I am afraid of admitting that I don't understand the brief'; 'my mind is blank at the moment and I don't know how to get past it', then this feedback could facilitate appropriate interventions and support as well as legitimising their feelings of being unable to make a conceptual leap at this point in the course.

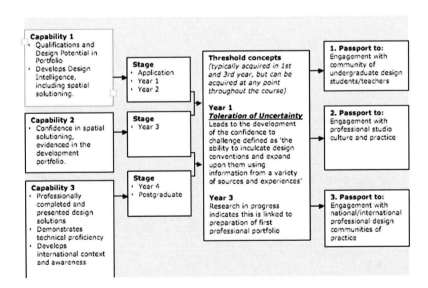

Figure 4. Representation model of threshold concepts in Transport and Product Design (work in progress).

At this point in the research, having identified a first year threshold concept, the intention is to explore the notion of introducing teaching and learning interventions along the lines of the discussion above. Further, research in progress indicates another threshold concept during the third year of the course which is linked to engagement with professional practice and the preparations of early professional portfolios. Finally, work is currently taking place on the development of a representational model of the research outcomes (see Figure 4 for early model development) which has the potential to be of use within the design disciplines and similar both within and outside Coventry University.

CONCLUSION

This paper has charted the identification of a threshold concept – the toleration of uncertainty. The research has also clearly identified nature and importance of the design of learning, teaching and assessment activities in facilitating the development of the identity of a designer- and has discussed some possible implications for teaching and learning for the transport and product design at Coventry University.

The researchers found that using threshold concepts enabled a useful and constructive dialogue with both staff and students within a relatively untheorised discipline. Although the research found that spatial awareness, considered as being at the heart of the course by staff was not a threshold concept but a design capability, it did allow the 'confidence to challenge' to emerge as a possible contender.

A search of design literature allowed the linking of the threshold concept to the work of Tovey's incubation period, Cross's oscillation between problem and solution, Dorst's tightrope walking, strategic thinking and visionary designer category; and, of particular interest, Wallace's idea of representing design tasks as a set of 'problem bubbles'. Links were also found in the creativity literature, particularly in the work of Kleiman, De-Bono, Baillie and Amabile.

We have argued that it is only when students have mastered toleration of a period of uncertainty that they gain the 'confidence to challenge' and are ready or able to tackle design briefs that typically contain 'wicked problems'. Further investigation of the 'confidence to challenge' with third year students showed that between entry and the third year of study they have developed a tolerance of being in a period of uncertainty due to inculcating skills, capabilities and coping strategies delivered via an apprentice-like immersive method of teaching underpinned by an atelier, or studio-based, environment. Staff also identified particular moments during the course that moved the students on, including first year assessments, the use of clay in the second year, exposure to the professional community of practice during the third year, coupled with the ability to work in groups and the development of empathy.

As such, the threshold concept has been identified as *the toleration of uncertainty* which precedes the development of the 'confidence to challenge' and it adheres to Meyer and Land's threshold concept characteristics in terms of being transformative, irreversible, integrative and, most of all, troublesome.

Implications for teaching and learning of the identification of the threshold concept are still a focus for research, but may include the introduction of teaching and learning interventions such as a first year module that surfaces the process to allow the identification of 'gaps' in the students' knowledge. Finally, the development of a model of the process is planned, as is further investigation into possible a third year threshold concept linked to students' exposure and engagement with the profession design community of practice.

REFERENCES

Baillie, C. (Ed.). (2003). *The travelling CASE: Fostering creative thinking in higher education*. UK Centre for Materials Education. Learning and Teaching Support Network.

Bodner, G. M., & Guay, R. B. (1997). The purdue visualization of rotations test. *The Chemical Educator, 2*, 1–17.

Buchanan, R. (1999). Design research and the new learning. In *Design Issues* (Vol. 4, Issue 4). Autumn 2001.

Buchanan, R. (1992). Wicked problems in design thinking. In *Design Issues* (Vol. 8, Issue 2). Spring.

Beattie, V., Collins, W., & McInnes, W. (1997). Deep and surface learning: A simple or simplistic dichotomy? *Accounting Education, 6*(1), 1–12.

Clouder, L. (2005). Caring as a 'threshold concept. Transforming students in higher education into health (care) professionals. *Teaching in Higher Education, 10*, 505–517.

Craddick, M., & O'reilly, D. (2002). Structures for facilitating play and creativity in learning: A psychoanalytical perspective. In J. Wisdom (Ed.), *Academic and educational development: research, evaluation and changing practice in higher education*. London: Kogan Page.

Cross, N. (1992). Research in design thinking. In C. N. Dorst & K. Roozenbury (Eds.), *Research in design thinking*. Delft University Press.

Cousin, G. (2006). Threshold concepts, troublesome knowledge and emotional capital: an exploration into learning about others. In J. H. F. Meyer & R. Land (Eds.), *Overcoming barriers to student understanding: Threshold concepts and troublesome knowledge* (pp. 134–147). London and New York: Routledge.

DeBono, E. (1995). Exploring patterns of thought: Serious Creativity. *Journal for Quality and Participation, 18*(5), 12–18.

Davies, P., & Mangan, J. (2007). Embedding threshold concepts: From theory to pedagogical principles to learning activities. In R. Land & J. H. F. Meyer (Eds.), *Threshold concepts within the disciplines*. Rotterdam, The Netherlands: Sense Publishers.

Dekker, D. L. (1995). Engineering design processes, problem solving and creativity. In *Proceedings in Frontiers in Education Conference 1995, Atlanta, GA, USA*.

Dorst, K. (2008, January). Design research: a revolution-waiting-to-happen. In *Design Studies* (Vol. 29, Issue 1, pp. 4–11). Elsevier.

Dorst, K. (2003). *Understanding design 150 reflections on being a designer*. BIS. Amsterdam.

ETLQ. (2002). *ETL Project, Universities of Edinburgh, Durham and Coventry*. Retrieved from http://www.tla.ed.ac.uk/etl/project.html

Gauntlett, D. (2007). *Creative explorations: New approaches to identities and audiences*. Routledge.

Haggis, T. (2003). Constructing images of ourselves? A critical investigation into 'Approaches to learning' research in higher education. *British Educational Research Journal, 29*(1), 89–104.

Kleiman, P. (2008). Towards transformation: Conceptions of creativity in higher education. *Innovations in Education and Teaching International, 45*(3), 209–217.

Kotzé, P., & Purgathofer, P. (2007). A framework for design Exercises – From creativity to real world use. In *HCI Educators 2007 – Creativity3: Experiencing to educate and design. 2007* (pp. 59–68). Aveiro, Portugal: GPCG.

Land, R., Meyer, J. H. F., & Smith, J. (Eds.). (2008). *Threshold concepts within the disciplines.* Rotterdam, The Netherlands: Sense Publishers.

Lucas, U., & Mladenovic, R. (2006). Dissolving the boundary between research and teaching: Exploring threshold concepts within introductory accounting. In *Beyond boundaries: New horizons for research into higher education.* SRHE: Brighton.

Meyer, J. H. F., & Land, R. (2005). Threshold concepts and troublesome knowledge (2): Epistemological considerations and a conceptual framework for teaching and learning. *Higher Education, 49*(3), 373–388.

Meyer, J. H. F., & Land, R. (2003). Threshold concepts and troublesome knowledge: Linkages to ways of thinking and practising within the disciplines. In C. Rust (Ed.), *Improving student learning. Improving student learning theory and practice — 10 years on* (pp. 412–424). Oxford, UK: OCSLD.

Orsini-Jones, M., & Jones, D. (2008, June). Troublesome language knowledge 2: Identifying 'threshold concepts' for students on a linguistics-based English degree course. In *From theory to practice conference.* Ontario.

Osmond, J., & Bull, K. (2007). Can creativity be taught: Creativity in Transport and Product Design. *ELIA Teachers' Academy.* Brighton. Retrieved from http://www.elia-artschools.org/activities/programme_ta.xml (strand A2)

Osmond, J., Turner, A., & Land, R. (2008). Threshold concepts and spatial awareness in automotive design. In R. Land & J. H. F. Meyer (Eds.), *Threshold concepts within the disciplines.* Rotterdam, The Netherlands: Sense Publishers.

Osmond, J., & Turner, A. (2007a, September). Measuring the creative baseline in transport design education. *Improving Student Learning Conference.* Dublin.

Perkins, D. (2006). Constructivism and troublesome knowledge. In J. H. F. Meyer & R. Land (Eds.), *Overcoming barriers to student understanding: Threshold concepts and troublesome knowledge* (pp. 33–47). London and New York: Routledge.

Perkins, D. (2000). *The Eureka Affect: The Art and Logic of Breakthrough Thinking.* New York and London: W.W. Norton & Co.

Pratt, D. (2005). *Five perspectives on teaching in adult and higher education.* Malabar, Florida: Krieger Publishing.

Savin-Baden, M. (2008, June). *After the death of privacy: Liminal states and spatial identities.* Threshold Concepts: From Theory to Practice Conference. Queen's University, Kingston, Ontario.

Savin-Baden, M., & Wilkie, K. (Eds.). (2006). *Problem-based learning online.* Maidenhead: Open University Press/SRHE

Tovey, M. (1984, October). Designing with both halves of the brain. In *Design Studies* (Vol. 5, Issue 4, pp. 219–228). Elsevier.

Vidal, R. V. V. (2009). Creativity for problem solvers. *AI and Society, 23,* 409–432.

Wallace, K. (1992). Some observations on design thinking. In N. Cross, K. Dorst, Roozenbury (Eds.), *Research in design thinking.* Delft University Press.

Wylant, B. (2008, Spring). Design thinking and the experience of innovation. In *Design studies* (Vol. 24, Issue 2, pp. 3–14). Elsevier.

Jane Osmond and Andrew Turner
Coventry University
Coventry
England UK

MING FAI PANG AND JAN H.F. MEYER

22. MODES OF VARIATION IN PUPILS' APPREHENSION OF A THRESHOLD CONCEPT IN ECONOMICS

INTRODUCTION

Recent work on developing pupils' acquisition of threshold concepts has brought into focus the importance of transformative learning in particular critical content elements within a discipline, as opposed to learning in general in a disciplinary context: 'Student learning engagement' is a broad term, and the variation within it can be generally formalised in terms of empirical (or conceptual) 'models' of differing multivariate complexity....[however] generic models [of learning] are only useful, and indeed 'actionable', up to a rapidly reached point at which they become inadequate proxies for the dynamics of student learning within discipline-specific courses. It is here, at this interface of reached uselessness, that the existence of threshold concepts provides immediate and compelling signposting for avenues along which to solicit variation in student learning and understanding (and misunderstanding) in a far more critical sense. The responsiveness to variation is no longer in the general sense (how are you going about learning?), or even the discipline sense (how are you going about learning subject x?), but is now operating at a critical micro-perspective level within the epistemology of the discipline itself and its discourse (Meyer and Land, 2005 pp. 380–381).

In further developing a theoretical framework for threshold concepts Meyer, Land and Davies (2008) distinguish between four modes of variation in the acquisition of a threshold concept. The first of these modes captures the extent of the learner's awareness and understanding of an underlying game or episteme – a 'way of knowing' – which may be a crucial determinant of progression (epistemological or ontological) within a conceptual domain. Such tacit understanding might develop in the absence of any formalised knowledge of the concept itself; it might, *for the learner*, represent a 'normal way of thinking'. Variation in such thinking constitutes a mode of subliminal variation. The second mode, that of preliminal variation, captures variation in how a threshold concept initially 'comes into view', that is, how it is initially perceived or apprehended, and with what mindset it may therefore be approached or withdrawn from. These two modes of variation provide a focus for the work reported here.

CONCEPTUAL FRAMEWORK AND CONTEXT

A first concern is the identification of a suitable candidate threshold concept – that of *opportunity cost* – that can plausibly serve as a basis for eliciting variation

*J. H. F. Meyer, R. Land and C. Baillie (eds.), Threshold Concepts and
Transformational Learning, 365–381.*

across the two modes of variation. Davies and Mangan (2008, p. 39), building on the findings of a completed research project on 'Embedding threshold concepts in first-year economics' specifically identify (the acquisition of) the discipline threshold concept of 'opportunity cost' as one that goes beyond facilitating a transformed 'understanding of everyday experience through integration of personal experience with ideas from [the] discipline' to the 'understanding of other subject discipline ideas (including other threshold concepts) integrated and transformed through acquisition of theoretical perspective'. Indeed, in terms of finer grain, the concept of *choice* itself, and the value placed on the next best but rejected alternative when making choices (the definition of 'opportunity cost') represents a fundamental element of economic discourse and analysis. The importance of the concept of opportunity cost cannot be overstated, and the pedagogical challenge lies in the fact that many pupils of economics fail to understand it. As Frank (1998, p. 14) puts it: '…the opportunity cost concept, so utterly central to our understanding of what it means *to think like an economist*, is but one among hundreds of other concepts that go by in a blur (emphasis added).

Reimann and Jackson (2006) provide a some justification for the suitability of 'opportunity cost' in the context of the present study in that they have demonstrated that this concept can be 'brought into view' for first-year pupils of microeconomics in the form of hypothetical scenarios within which pupils position themselves and externalise relevant aspects of reasoning and explanation. The conjecture here is that such *proxies* can be found that in effect bring a threshold concept 'into view' (within the preliminary and subliminal modes of variation) for pupils (school pupils in this case) *without* any formalised prior knowledge of economics or economic language. This conjecture addresses directly the important question raised by Meyer and Land (2009) (Chapter 4) in relation to the dynamics of assessing pupils' understandings of threshold concepts in situations where, in particular, an apprehension of what a threshold concepts represents in transformative terms lies *beyond* the ontological horizon of the student.

The present study is contextualised within a strategic framework: The New Senior Secondary (NSS) Curriculum – Proposed Economics Subject Framework for Secondary 4–6 pupils in Hong Kong. The aims are to develop pupils' interest in exploring human behaviour and social issues through an economic perspective, and to have a deeper understanding of the world in which they live through mastery of basic economic knowledge. Pupils are expected to develop a good mastery of the fundamental economic themes such as 'economic decisions involving choices among alternatives' and the 'concept of cost in Economics'.

RESEARCH PLAN AND METHODOLOGY

The research question is located in the two modes of variation that precede the acquisition of the concept of 'opportunity cost' and sets out to determine the dimensionality of sub- and pre-liminal variation in secondary school pupils' initial apprehension, via a range of proxies, of the threshold concept of 'opportunity cost'.

Subjects were forty Secondary 3 pupils in Hong Kong who had not taken economics as a school subject prior to the commencement of the present study. These pupils, of both genders, were at schools of different bands/levels in terms of academic attainment and in different physical locations in Hong Kong.

A semi-structured interview method was used for data collection. Pupils were invited to attend an individual interview, conducted in Cantonese, during which they were asked to respond to questions related to a number of scenarios in which the concepts of 'choice' and 'opportunity cost' were implicitly embedded. The intention was to firstly explore their experiences of making choices in a personal context, and in terms of relating to the economic contexts implicitly represented by the scenarios, and specifically so to reveal variation in any tacit understandings that might link choice-making to a sacrifice of alternatives. All the interviews were recorded and translated verbatim into English. These transcripts were the units of an analysis that sought to categorise similarities, differences and complementarities at the collective level.

FINDINGS

In order to determine the dimensionality of sub- and pre-liminal variation in secondary school pupils' initial apprehension of the threshold concept of 'opportunity cost', there is a self evident emphasis in exploring pupils' understanding of the concept of 'opportunity cost' before the concept is taught. Towards this end four scenarios were trialled, three of which (Scenarios 1, 3 and 4) worked very well as proxies for revealing variation in pupils' understanding of 'opportunity cost'. Results based on these scenarios are now presented.

Scenario (1)

Ben woke up at eleven and he planned to study for his exam in the afternoon. At noon, the phone rang. His girlfriend asked him to go to a movie. He decided to spend 4 hours in the afternoon with her.

a. What choice did Ben make? Why did Ben have to make choice? What was the cost for Ben to go to see the movie?

b. If the movie was boring, would it have increases his cost of going to the movie? Why or why not?

These questions, in two parts, worked well in soliciting pupils' prior experience of the notions of 'choice' and 'opportunity cost'. Based on answers to the questions in the first part, pupils exhibited in varying degrees an intuitive economic understanding of the notion of 'choice' insofar as they could identify the scarce resource (time), consider the notion of 'choice' with a focus on sacrifice *and* identify the opportunity cost of choosing the option of going to the movie with the girlfriend as the foregone option of using the limited time to study for the examination.

However, although quite a number of pupils understood that the time for studying would be sacrificed if the option of going to movie was chosen, some of them focused on the monetary cost of the option chosen rather than the opportunity cost involved. This can be demonstrated by the following interview excerpt of Pupil S1, School C:

R   What is the cost if he chose to go to a movie?

S   What is the cost if he chose to go to a movie…let me think about it……his cost is to… watching movie…watching movie he might have to pay for the movie ticket…the fare of the public transport.

R   What did he give up if he chose to go to a movie?

S   He gave up the opportunity to study if he chose to go to a movie. It wasted his time to study and probably made his exam results worse. It would make his study lagging behind. This effect is more long-lasting.

R   Would it increase his cost of going to the movie if the movie was boring?

S   Yes, it would increase his cost of going to the movie. Probably because he knew that the movie was boring….but he had to make his girlfriend happy, he would probably buy some snacks or drinks for watching the movie. So, he might have to spend extra money to buy snacks and drinks. So, it would increase the cost.

Overall, many pupils managed to demonstrate a basic level of economic understanding of opportunity cost, as shown by the following answer of Pupil S7, School D

R   Ben woke up at eleven and he planned to study for his exam in the afternoon. However, at noon, his girlfriend asked him to go to a movie. He decided to take her to a movie and spent four hours in the afternoon with her. I would like to ask, what options were open to Ben when he made his decision?

S   Study or go to watch movie with his girlfriend.

R   What did Ben choose finally?

S   Watch movie with his girlfriend

R   Why did he have to make such a choice?

S   Because he thought that study can be done at any time but not for being together with his girlfriend. Perhaps the girlfriend would be angry with him and as a result they would not watch movie.

R   Why was it necessary for him to make a choice? Why couldn't he avoid making a choice?

S   He could not avoid making a choice. They both happened in the same afternoon. He did not have enough time to do both of them.

R   What is the cost for him to go to the movie?

S   Give up…give up the opportunity to study.

For some pupils there was an increasing level of reasoning of 'opportunity cost' in the first part questions. Three levels of analysis were identified: (a) They attended to the scarcity of time – the 4 hours; this could have been used for going out with the girlfriend or for studying. (b) They considered the consequence of the choice made – choosing to go out with the girlfriend and thus not to study would probably mean a lower performance in the examination and a lower grade that could be considered as part of the cost (of the choice). (c) They extended their analysis to consider the consequence in the future. Following the same line of reasoning, not doing well in the exam would also affect the overall academic performance results and would thus probably adversely affect future studies and future career prospects.

R OK What is the cost for him to go to the movie?
S What is the cost for him to go to the movie? Other than paying for the movie, he also gave up the time to study, and consequently he might get poorer exam result. This is the cost. (Pupil S4, School D)

The questions in the second part required a considered decision as to whether the cost of going to the movie would increase (or not) if the movie was found afterwards to have been boring. In economics, 'opportunity cost' is the (value of) the highest-valued option forgone. The opportunity cost of choosing an option will change only when there is a *change* in the (value of) the highest-valued option forgone. In this case, although the value of going to see the movie with the girlfriend dropped because the movie was found boring, the opportunity cost of doing so did not change, as the value of the best option foregone; that is, study for the examination, did not change. (A more advanced answer may involve the notion of 'sunk cost' but this is not elaborated on here).

This way of understanding can be exemplified by the following student answer (Pupil S1, School E):

R What was the cost of choosing to watch the movie?
S He would use up his time
R Use up his time. What is the significance of the time to him?
S He planned to study for the examination in the afternoon, but he took this time to go to movie with his girlfriend, which was the cost.
R Would the cost of going to the movie increase if it was boring?
S I don't think so because he had spent this time in watching the movie. The fact that the movie was boring was his feeling after the movie, or he thought about it afterwards. I think it has nothing to do with these four hours, no matter the movie was good or not.

In answering the questions related to scenario one, a number of pupils exhibited a *shift* in their understanding of 'opportunity cost'. Quite a number of them exhibited a correct way of understanding the notion of 'opportunity cost' in the first part questions, but still expressed that the opportunity cost of going to the movie would decrease or increase because the movie was boring and therefore wasted time and/or money. An example is shown below.

R Ben woke up at eleven and he planned to study for his exam in the afternoon. At noon, his girlfriend asked him to go to a movie. He decided to take her to a movie and spent four hours in the afternoon with her. I would like to ask, what options were open to Ben when he made his decision?

S   Study or play with his girlfriend.
R   What did he choose finally?
S   Choose to be with his girlfriend.
R   Why did he have to make a choice?
S   Why did he have to make a choice…because of the time clash
R   What is the cost if he chose to go to a movie?
S   Study…cannot study
R   Cannot study. Would it increase his cost of going to the movie if the movie was boring?
S   Of course. He would waste money, waste time and money. (Pupil S5, School C)

In contrast some other pupils argued that the cost of watching the movie did not change because what they were concerned and cared about, and focussed on, was the (option) to go out with the girlfriend. These pupils argued that the issue of whether the movie was boring or not was irrelevant because it did not affect the value of the option chosen. It seemed that their answers were correct but their way of reasoning was absolutely wrong. The fact that the opportunity cost did not change was not because the value of the option *chosen* did not change; rather it was because the value of the highest-valued option *forgone* did not change. The following excerpt manifests this seemingly clever answer:

R   Would the cost of going to the movie that we just talk about increase if it was boring?
S   The movie was boring…I think it would not increase the cost of his choice because he would not know whether the movie was boring until he had watched it. He actually was choosing between examination results and his girlfriend, which was not directly related to the movie itself. It means that his focus was on his girlfriend…the relationship with his girlfriend rather than the movie. (Pupil S7, School B)

These pupils correctly identified the opportunity cost of having the chosen option is the highest-value option *forgone* in the first part questions. However, in the second part, all of them focused on the chosen option itself, to be more exact, the value of the chosen option (the value of going to the movie) and treated it as the 'opportunity cost' of having the chosen option. Obviously, they mixed it up with the *opportunity cost of the option chosen*; that is the value of the best option rejected (the value of the studying).

Scenario (2)

Peter plans to attend a Spanish course. He attends 10 hours of classes every month and the course fee is $1000 per month. His time can also be used to earn $100 per hour as a part-time helper for his professor.

a. What choice does Peter need to make? Why did Peter have to make choice?

b. What is Peter's cost of attending the Spanish course in a month?

This scenario did not work very well in revealing pupils' understanding of 'opportunity cost'. One possible reason is that questions based on it require answers involving some mental arithmetic. Many of the Secondary three pupils got confused in the calculating process and did not come up with clear answers because of their weak foundation in doing mental arithmetic. Another possible reason is that this case involves both the explicit and implicit cost of choosing an option, which may be too complicated and difficult for a Secondary 3 student to grapple with.

Scenario (3)

Carol is an accountant and is also very good at doing housework. However, she employs a maid to do the housework for her.

a. Why does Carol employ a maid instead of being a full-time housewife?

b. In terms of cost, explain why accountants in Hong Kong seldom change their occupation.

A number of pupils were able to demonstrate quite a good understanding of the concept of 'opportunity cost' in this context. They could explain the two cases in terms of 'opportunity cost' by arguing firstly that the opportunity cost of being a full-time housewife (the high income of being an accountant forgone) is much greater than the salary that would be paid to get a maid and, secondly, that the reason why accountants in Hong Kong seldom change their occupation is due to the high opportunity cost involved in doing so (the high income of accountant forgone). This success may be attributable to the fact that the scarce resource in question is time, something the pupils could make sense of. The following student answer clearly illustrates this way of understanding.

R   OK. Let's move on to the third scenario. Carol is an accountant and is also very good at doing housework. However, she employs a maid to do the housework for her. I want to ask why Carol employs a maid instead of being a full-time housewife.

S   Because she does not have enough time.

R   Can you explain, in terms of cost, why accountants in Hong Kong seldom change their occupation?

S   Cost ... explain in terms of cost.

R   Yes.

S   Accountants can earn a lot of money without bearing a high cost. And being an accountant is not a hard job.

R   You mean there is a low cost of being an accountant.

S   Yes.

R   Then I want to ask, what is the cost for Carol to employ a maid?

S   The cost is that she has to pay for the maid.

R   Given that she is an accountant, what is the cost if she becomes a full-time housewife?

S   Cannot earn the salary of accountant.

R If comparing these two costs, can you tell me why Carol finally decides to work as an accountant rather than a housewife?

S Because if an accountant can get a higher return with a lower cost, it means that she can have more monetary returns after all.

R Is the cost higher for her to employ a maid or to be a full-time housewife?

S To be a full-time housewife.

R Why?

S Because the amount of money she can earn as an accountant is larger than that she pays for a maid.

R If you follow this line of reasoning, can you explain why Carol finally decides to work as an accountant rather than a housewife?

S Because she can make more money by working as an accountant. (Pupil S2, School C):

Also, all interviewees are Secondary three pupils who do not have any working experience at all. Since this question is set in the context of some authentic local experience that pupils may have in their daily lives, some of the pupils tended to appeal to their common sense and everyday conversations about how accountant earn their living when they attempted to put forward their reasoning within the scenario. (For example, since accountants are professionals and work very hard to get the qualification, they seldom change their occupations). Some pupils even argued that the cost for Carol to be a full-time housewife is more than the salary of an accountant which is to be forgone, in that the cost includes the hard-earned accounting qualification and their precious working experience. This reasoning obviously goes beyond what the questions where intended to reveal, as shown below.

R What is the cost if she employs a maid?

S It is the wage of the maid.

R What is the cost to her of being a full-time housewife?

S She will lose the salary of being an accountant and the opportunities of promotion and further study.

R Regarding these two costs, which one is higher?

S I think there is a higher cost for losing the salary of an accountant and the opportunities of being promoted

R Can you explain, in terms of cost, why accountants in Hong Kong seldom change their occupation?

S Because accountant is a well-paid occupation and accountants have to spend a lot of time in studying before having a certain level of achievement. They may have nothing left if they suddenly change occupation.

R Can you see if there is any relationship with cost?

S You will...you will lose all the achievements obtained and the experiences established before.

R Is it a cost?

S The efforts and time you paid to gain the achievements and experiences are the costs. (Pupil S8, School C)

Scenario (4)

Eric runs a grocery store in the downtown. He operates it from 7 a.m. to 11 p.m. daily in premises which he owns. His son gives up his job in an insurance company in order to help in the business.

a. What is the cost to the son when he chooses to work in the grocery store?

b. What is the cost of using the store premises? Will there be any change in the cost of using the store premises if Eric extends the closing time till midnight?

This was the most difficult scenario among the four, as pupils were unfamiliar with the scarce resource; namely, the premises in part (b), which is a resource beyond their own life experience. Also, pupils could not identify the options available, as they did not understand the notion of 'using' the store premises. Some of them misinterpreted it as a choice of 'buying' premises.

Quite a number of pupils managed to do well in part (a), successfully identifying the cost to the son when he chooses to work in the grocery store, i.e. the income or benefits of working in the insurance company forgone. However, when pupils handled part (b), most of the pupils confused the accounting cost or operation cost with the opportunity cost. For instance, they claimed that the cost of using the premises would increase when extending the closing time of the shop till midnight because of additional electricity costs, labour wages, and other expenses, that would be incurred. However, the opportunity cost should be equal to zero if there is no alternative use of using the premises till midnight, which has nothing to do with the operation cost. Pupils tended to confuse the monetary cost of getting the option chosen with the value of the best option rejected. The following exemplifies this commonly-found way of understanding.

R Good. We move on to the last scenario. Eric runs a grocery store in the downtown. He operates it from 7 am to 11 pm in the premises which he owns. His son gives up his job in an insurance company in order to help in the business. I want to ask, what is the cost to the son when he chooses to work in the grocery store?

S His cost is the job in the insurance company that he has to give up.
.....

R If this is a cost, will there be any change in the cost of using the store premises if Eric extends his closing time till midnight?

S It will. Because the lighting and electricity, electricity charges, wages and so on, i.e. the operating costs, would get higher. (Pupil S6, School C)

But for a small number of pupils this scenario worked well. They could identify the options available for 'using' the premises; that is, either use by the owner of the store or renting it out to other potential clients. They further reasoned that if the store could not be rented out to earn income over the time between the original closing time and midnight, there will not be any extra income forgone and thus the opportunity cost would not change. Clearly, these few pupils were advanced in their reasoning, and demonstrated a solid intuitive understanding of the notion of 'opportunity cost'. This demonstration is quite remarkable given that they have not received any formal teaching the threshold concept involved and also that scenario is relatively complicated to understand and alien to their own life experience. The following is an example.

R   The premises are owned by him. If he runs the business making use of the premises which he owns, what costs are involved?

S   The cost is the rent you can get from leasing it out.

R   So this is the cost. Then I want to ask, will there be any change in the cost of using the store premises if he extends his closing time till midnight?

S   No.

R   Why?

S   Actually, if he leases out the shop to others, it won't increase the rent, no matter how long he himself extends the opening hours of his grocery store or even operating for 24 hours. (Pupil S8, School B)

SOME INTERIM OBSERVATIONS ON CONCEPTIONS OF 'CHOICE'

What arises repeatedly in the transcripts, as offered spontaneously by a majority of pupils, is that choice (as a *selection* between two or more alternatives) is exercised in terms of personal preference 'Whether I like it or not' or perceived benefit to self or others. In fact practically all the pupils talked about choice being exercised in the latter terms. There is a sense in the transcripts that choice is about the ranking of the order of preference and optimal allocation of benefit. And, as an aside, it can be noted that when this process also involves allocation relative to cost, we have the essence of the Economic concept of *rational choice*.

To be rational in choice making, one will choose the option which carries the maximum value or benefit or one which minimises the (opportunity) cost involved, and the outcome will be the same. For instance, assume that one has $5000 and may spend it on either one of the following three options: option (1) buying a leather bag; option (2) joining a travel tour to Japan; and option (3) paying tuition fee for piano class. Suppose option 1 (buying a leather bag) is the most preferred option which carries the highest value and thus has the maximum benefit to the decision-maker, option 2 is the second best and option 3 is the least preferred. If one adheres to the principle of getting an option with the maximum benefit, one will opt for Option 1. Similarly, if one follows the principle of minimising the opportunity cost involved, one will still choose Option 1 because its opportunity cost, the value or benefit of the highest-valued option forgone (i.e. Option 2), is the lowest. (Note: if one chooses Options 2 or 3 instead, the opportunity cost involved will be the value or benefit of Option 1 which is higher).

People who have developed an economic way of thinking are able, in their reasoning, to consider both the benefits and costs involved in reaching a rational decision; they focus on both the option chosen as well as the highest-valued option forgone at the same time. However, most of the pupils interviewed seem only to have some innate grasp of the allocation of preference or benefit part, and they thus focus only on the option chosen, taking for granted or ignoring the sacrifice or cost involved in choice making. Even though some pupils may have a sense of cost, what they focus on is the monetary cost involved in getting the chosen option, rather than the opportunity cost of getting the chosen option.

SUMMARY AND CONCLUDING DISCUSSION

At one extreme, some pupils were found to have no clues of what was being asked about the notion of 'choice' and 'opportunity cost'. They were unable to give coherent answers to the questions or demonstrate a way of reasoning.

R   What goes through your mind when you make choice between alternative options?

S   I have no idea.

R   No idea?

S   No idea.

R   If you are asked to choose between alternative options...

S   ....(silent) (Pupil S4, School C)

R   What is the cost to her as an accountant? I mean she is an accountant and is also good at housework, and she employs a maid to do the housework. What costs are involved here?

S   She has to train the maid to do housework but she has to work too, so it takes her more energy to train the maid.

R   I want to ask what the costs are if she employs a maid.

S   Have to pay for the maid and accommodation.

R   What are the costs involved if she doesn't work as an accountant but to be a housewife?

S   She will have no salary, her salary. And she may feel bored if staying at home to do the housework.

R   You have provided good answer for the two costs. But can you explain why Carol employs a maid to do housework if you consider the two costs?

S   Because she loves her job as an accountant. She may think that her home is in a terrible mess and she doesn't have time to do the housework. That's why she employs a maid to do it for her. (Pupil S5, School D)

At another extreme, based on some partial evidence, a small number of pupils may have reached the *preliminal stage* already, although they may not have formally learnt the concept of 'opportunity cost'. Judging from their answers, these pupils are clearly conscious of an embedded, consistent way of rationalising the phenomenon, although without the language to formalise it. They have developed an implicit way of using the concept of 'opportunity cost' to make sense of the world through the scenarios and they seemed to be 'thinking like an economist' without being aware of it. They implicitly have something 'in view' (the concept of 'choice' and 'opportunity cost') but cannot put a label on it because they do not have the technical language to express it. For instance, one student said "Let me explain to you..."

R   If there is somebody younger than you asked you to explain to them what the meaning of 'choice' is, what would you tell them?

S   It is you choose… what is the meaning of "choice'? It is that you are given two things for you to do at the same time, and you have to give up the other one in order to get this one. This is a choice.

......

R   Have you thought about what factors would be considered when you make a choice?

S   For making a choice you should pick the best one. But it means that you have to see if there are any alternatives and compare all the options to identify which one is the best. And when you choose this one, you have to consider the loss as a result of what you give up. (Pupil S3, School E)

Scenario 3

R   Let's move on to the third scenario. Carol is an accountant and is also very good at doing housework. However, she employs a maid to do the housework for her. I want to ask, why does Carol employ a maid instead of being a full-time housewife?

S   First of all, she is a professional, an accountant. Clearly her time is worth more than that of maid. Perhaps she earns $40,000, $50,000 or more each month, but it is only $3000 for a maid. So, although she is good at housework, considering the cost, it is better for Carol to have one or, if you are smart enough, two maids instead of doing it by herself

R   Can you explain, in terms of cost, why accountants in Hong Kong seldom change their occupation?

S   Accountants in Hong Kong seldom change their occupation …

R   Try to explain in terms of cost.

S   Specifically for accountants?

R   Not specifically for accountants. It can be any kind of professionals.

S   Actually for every occupation you have to get adapted to a new environment if you change to a new occupation. You will waste some time and you…

R   Or maybe we look at Carol's case. What cost is involved if she employs a maid?

S   It will involve the $3000 salary for employing a maid.

R   What is the cost involved if she becomes a full-time housewife rather than employing a maid?

S   It is the monthly salary of being an accountant.

R   So why does she finally choose to be an accountant rather than being a housewife?

S   It's because if she can have a maid to take up the housework for her and the salary of the maid is lower than her salary, then she can get the housework done as well as having more money at the same time.

Scenario 4

R   We move on to the last scenario. Eric runs a grocery store in the downtown. He operates it from 7 am to 11 pm in the premises which he owns. His son gives up his job in an insurance company in order to help in the business. I want to ask, what is the cost to the son when he chooses to work in the grocery store?

S   It is the promotion opportunity of his job in the insurance company or his prospect. Since there is dim prospect if you work in grocery store. At most, you will become the boss, or you are working there to make your father happy. But you have to give up the job in the insurance company. It means that you would spend a long time, your whole life in the grocery store. If you work in the insurance company, provided that you are an ordinary fellow working there, the cost he gives up is not only the current salary, but also the salary after he gets promoted in the future.

R   Since the premise belongs to Eric himself, what is the cost if he uses the premise?

S   Obviously, it could be leased out to others. If it is leased out to others, he can get back rentals for the premise. If he runs the grocery store in his premise, he will give up the time for working in the insurance company. It means that his cost would include the rentals plus his salary.

R   If what you said is a cost, I want to ask, will there be any increase in the cost of using the store premises if he extends his closing time till midnight?

S   For sure, the cost of using the premise will not increase at all because people pay a fixed amount of rentals every month. If he runs the grocery store, he still receives such an amount of rentals; that means the value of rentals is still the same. (Pupil S3, School E)

In fact, most of the pupils were found between these two extremes. When these pupils (e.g. Pupil S2, School E) were asked to talk through the four scenarios, the way of rationalisation or the conception exhibited was naïve for one particular situation (such as in Scenario 4) but not in the sense of a 'misconception'. However, in another scenario (such as Scenario 2) the conception manifested was quite sophisticated. Pupils generally seemed unable to adapt from one scenario to another, thereby displaying a shift in their understanding of 'opportunity cost'.

Scenario 2

R   Ok, let's go to the second scenario. Peter plans to attend a Spanish course. He would have to attend 10 hours of classes every month and the course fee is $1000 per month. However, he can also use this time to work for his professor to earn a return of $100 per hour. I want to ask, what choice should Peter have to make now?

S   If he wants to attend the Spanish course, he has to pay $1000. If he wants to help his professor, he can earn $100 per hour

R   Why does he have to make a choice?

S   Because he has to spend 10 hours to attend the Spanish course per month and also $1000. If he helps the professor, he can earn $100 using this time

R   Why does he have to choose?

S   Because that 10 hours may make him…that is, if he spends 10 hours on the Spanish course then he couldn't have time to help the professor

R   And I want to ask you, what is the cost for Peter to attend the Spanish course in one month?

S   His $1000 course fee per month and the income from working for the professor is the cost.

R   Why is the income from working for the professor also a kind of cost?

S   If he helps the professor, then he could get that er…the return per hour. But if he chooses to study the Spanish course, he would lose not only $1000, but also the income from the professor

Scenario 4

R   For Eric, the grocery store the premise belongs to him, then what costs would be involved if he uses the premise for himself ?

S   He has to manage it by himself. That means he has to do cleansing, pays electricity and water charges if the premise is used by him

R   If the premise is used by him, what would he give up?

S   As he has to work for a long time, he wouldn't be able to be with his family.

R   Are there any others? If the premise belongs to him and it is used by him, what would be given up?

S   Give up…maybe he can't go out in the evening, as he has to take care of the grocery

R   Is there any other usage for the premise if it is not used by him?

S   He can rent it to other people or employ someone to help him

R   Will the cost of using the store premise increase if Eric extends his closing time till midnight?

S   Yes

R   Why?

S   The water and electricity charges would increase. Perhaps not many people would go out in the midnight, so it would have not much business to do. Also, the time he spends with his family would decrease (Pupil S2, School E)

Moreover, some pupils frequently *changed their minds* when they talked through the same scenario, demonstrating their changing way of understanding the notion of 'cost'. There appeared to be genuine oscillation taking place possibly indicating that these pupils may be situated somewhere between the sub- and pre-liminal modes of variation. This is quite evident in the following interview excerpt, as the pupil seemed to have been able to identify the value of the option of using the premise forgone in the first part of his answer but he then shifted to the layman's conception of cost in terms of time spent in the second part.

R   As the premise belongs to Eric, what costs are involved if he uses the premise?

S   The cost of using the premise is…actually he could use the premise for other different activities. That means the premise is not necessarily used as a grocery store. Grocery store only sells groceries, and money earned from a grocery store wouldn't be so much… But if the premise is used…you know it is a premise, he could have many different activities in the premise. For example, he may build his home in the premise or alternatively he could do different businesses in it. That means he could use the premise to do more than just a grocery store.

R   The last question is, will the cost of using the store premise increase if he extends his closing time till midnight?

S   Yes. If he extends the closing time, then he would spend more, that is, the time he uses would be more. The opening time of the grocery store is longer…if the closing time is extended till midnight, his rest time would decrease. This would harm his body. So, the cost would be rather high

R   Just now, you mentioned that the cost of using premise is to use it in other ways. If he extends the business hours, would this cost increase?

S   Business hours…I don't think so. Because the extension of business hours has nothing to do with the business. It is a premise; it could be used for doing different businesses. Different companies could choose doing different businesses… I mean, the different operation hours could be controlled by oneself (Pupil S8, School E)

The findings of the proposed research have particular educational significance insofar as they can inform pedagogical practice. It is well established that threshold concepts in general, and 'opportunity cost' in particular, may represent barriers to student understanding. There is furthermore emerging evidence that, for some pupils, the acquisition of 'opportunity cost' may be impeded by what would otherwise be considered to be good teaching practice. But the variation present in such impediment is not known, and it is here that the proposed research seeks to make a contribution to pedagogical practice.

In this study, pupils were found to exhibit different tacit understandings of the notion of 'choice' and 'opportunity cost'. Some students developed an intuitive and quite a sophisticated, economic way of reasoning in relation to the scenarios in terms of 'opportunity cost'. Some oscillated between an economic way of understanding and a lay person's way of understanding, both within and across the scenarios. And some had no economic sense of opportunity cost at all. Evidently, some of the pupils had unconsciously entered the preliminal mode in the absence of formal instruction and technical language whereas others appeared still to be in the subliminal mode. In short, there is variation in their 'normal way of thinking', that reveals what is interpreted here as both subliminal and preliminal modes of variation.

To help students pass through the preliminal and subliminal modes and acquire, threshold concepts ('opportunity cost' in this case), a 'transformative pedagogy' is proposed that targets the *transformation of* pupils' ways of thinking and reasoning. In order to achieve this transformation it is necessary to first ascertain pupils' original, intuitive and normal 'ways of knowing'. Teachers need to understand (the variation in) *how* pupils initially perceive, apprehend, conceptualise or experience the threshold concept in the absence of any formalised knowledge of the concept itself. This knowledge will, in turn, inform an understanding of where *and why* pupils may find themselves in 'stuck places' on their learning trajectory.

It is furthermore important for teachers to identify pupils' subliminal and preliminal variation in relation to the threshold concept(s) *in question* by, for instance, inviting pupils to respond to some well thought through questions or scenarios of the form discussed here. In this way, the *critical features* of pupils' initial different ways of apprehending phenomena that act as proxies for threshold concepts can be identified. It seems reasonable to argue that a knowledge of the variation in these critical features can inform the design of early learning experiences in students learning trajectories involving both cognitive and ontological shifts.

Pang (2003) has argued that learning can be seen as the capacity to discern and focus on the critical aspects of a concept or practice. Identifying threshold concepts and their critical features as an 'object of learning' invites a pedagogy based on *variation theory* after, for example, the work of Marton and Booth (1997), Marton and Tsui (2004) and Marton and Pang (2006). Variation theory posits that pupils' variation in the understanding of a disciplinary concept or practice, or alternative conceptions of the concept, hinges on those critical features of the concept or practice that pupils are able to *discern and focus on simultaneously*. To help pupils develop a particular professional or disciplinary way of thinking and practising, it is thus important to focus their attention on the critical features of the threshold concepts in question. Delineating these critical features is thus an important consideration for future threshold concepts research. It is furthermore important to further develop domain-specific generic capabilities by designing curriculum and pedagogy embedded within corresponding patterns of variation and invariance that are *specific* to the threshold concepts identified as well as to the cohort of pupils in question. Foundation work by, for example, Pang and Marton (2003, 2005), and Marton and Pang (2006), grounded in the variation theory framework, and aimed at improving pupils' grasp of disciplinary concepts, offers much to build on in terms of threshold concepts.

ACKNOWLEDGEMENTS

This research was made possible by grants from the University of Hong Kong.

REFERENCES

Davies, P., & Mangan, J. (2008). Embedding threshold concepts: From theory to pedagogical principles to learning activities. In R. Land, J. H. F. Meyer, & J. Smith (Eds.), *Threshold concepts within the disciplines* (pp. 37–50). Rotterdam, The Netherlands and Taipei, Taiwan: Sense publishers.

Frank, R. H. (1998). Some thoughts on the micro principles course. In W. B. Walstad & P. Saunders (Eds.), *Teaching undergraduate economics: A handbook for instructors* (pp. 13–20, chap. 2). Boston: Irwin/McGraw-Hill.

Meyer, J. H. F., & Land, R. (2005). Threshold concepts and troublesome knowledge (2): Epistemological considerations and a conceptual framework for teaching and learning. *Higher Education, 49*(3), 373–388.

Meyer, J. H. F., Land, R., & Davies, P. (2008). Threshold concepts and troublesome knowledge (4): Issues of variation and variability. In R. Land, J. H. F. Meyer, & J. Smith (Eds.), *Threshold concepts within the disciplines* (pp. 59–74). Rotterdam, The Netherlands and Taipei, Taiwan: Sense publishers.

Marton, F., & Booth, S. (1997) *Learning and awareness*. Mahwah, NJ: Lawrence Erlbaum.

Marton, F., & Pang, M. F. (2006). On some necessary conditions for learning. *The Journal of Learning Sciences*, *15*(2), 193–220.

Marton, F., & Tsui, A. B. M. with Chik, P. M., Ko, P. Y., Lo, M. L., Mok, I. A. C., Ng, F. P., Pang, M. F., Pong, W. Y., Runesson, U. (2004). *Classroom discourse and the space of learning*. NJ: Lawrence Erlbaum.

Pang, M. F. (2003). Two faces of variation – On continuity in the phenomenographic movement. *Scandinavian Journal of Educational Research*, *47*(2), 145–156.

Pang, M. F., & Marton, F. (2003). Beyond "lesson study" – Comparing two ways of facilitating the grasp of economic concepts. *Instructional Science*, *31*(3), 175–194.

Pang, M. F., & Marton, F. (2005). Learning theory as teaching resource: Another example of radical enhancement of students' understanding of economic aspects of the world around them. *Instructional Science*, *33*(2), 159–191.

Reimann, N., & Jackson, I. (2006). Threshold concepts in economics. In J. H. F. Meyer & R Land (Eds.), *Overcoming barriers to student understanding. Threshold concepts and troublesome knowledge* (pp. 15–133). London and New York: Routledge.

Ming Fai Pang
The University of Hong Kong
Hong Kong SAR
China

Jan H.F. Meyer
University of Durham
United Kingdom

DAGMAR KUTSAR AND ANITA KÄRNER

23. EXPLORATION OF SOCIETAL TRANSITIONS IN ESTONIA FROM THE THRESHOLD CONCEPTS PERSPECTIVE OF TEACHING AND LEARNING

INTRODUCTION

Threshold concepts perspective developed by Meyer and Land (2003, 2005) and applied first to teaching and learning in economics by Davies (2006) and Reimann and Jackson (2006) was broadened to include various disciplinary contexts and pedagogic directions (see: Land et al., 2008). This new conceptual framework integrates several theoretical perspectives combining learning theories with social constructivism and it draws several models from anthropology. Being in some way eclectic, the threshold concepts perspective is rich with those 'aha!' moments when ideas you have tried to clarify to yourself suddenly click in your mind and you wonder how they could have looked so different. Something similar happened to us, the authors of the current article, when after getting closer to the ideas within the threshold concepts perspective we felt an increasing curiosity to explore its reliability on a topic, of which we had a clear understanding.

We, the authors, formed an interdisciplinary team and started our joint cognitive journey. Dagmar Kutsar was educated in clinical psychology and now teaches subjects at the crossroads of psychology, sociology, social work and social policy brought to the common 'hold-all' of know-how her expertise and a broad knowledge collected from family, childhood and welfare studies. Anita Kärner is a specialist in educational sciences, who brought to the 'hold-all' her knowledge gained from studies on the issues of learning and teaching in higher education and more specifically, aspects of doctoral training.

The aims of the current paper are twofold. First, to broaden the explanatory potential of the threshold concepts perspective of teaching and learning to examine societal transition processes in society; secondly, to develop a cognitive learning exercise from the experiences of students seeking new explanations, visions, and meanings of "the known". This is an attempt to look at society as a learning and teaching environment during an extremely intensive period of societal changes, when one socio-economic and political system collapses and is exchanged for another. The transitions are meaningful events, accompanied by uncertainties, learning the new and changing identities and structures. During the transitional period, society is overwhelmed by a liminal space – no longer what it was and not yet what it will be. The liminal space is shared by the actors of transition, the institutions, groups and individuals all filled with a mixture of new and old cognitions, emotions, myths and behavioural patterns.

J. H. F. Meyer, R. Land and C. Baillie (eds.), Threshold Concepts and
Transformational Learning, 383–397.
© 2010 Sense Publishers. All rights reserved.

In summary, the aims of our academic curiosity are to deconstruct society at a time of rapid societal transition and refresh our academic understanding in the field of transitional studies with the help of the threshold concepts perspective. We have taken academic texts as descriptive data, and combined them with our personal reflections as participants in the transitional processes. We will deconstruct the meanings and understandings of societal transitions by integrating the *etic* and *emic* approaches of social constructivism. Our cognitive trip opens us up akin to a portal and a new way of thinking about the chosen subject and directs us towards revisions of teaching the subject as an outcome. We are going to integrate the threshold concepts perspective, with references, into our analysis when we introduce and explore a subtopic. The society we are going to focus is post-communist Estonia.

GENERAL FRAMEWORK OF SOCIETAL TRANSITIONS IN EASTERN AND CENTRAL EUROPE LATE 1980S – EARLY 1990S

Since the Second World War, the Eastern and Central European countries have undergone different social, economic and political experiences compared to Western Europe. Their development was directed by a totalitarian system, which diverted them from their own developmental tracks. The collapse of the totalitarian system provided the opportunity for societal transitions towards the free-market democracies of Western Europe.

Societal transitions in the late 1980s and early 1990s were characterised by changes from totalitarian to democratic societies and from planned to free-market economies. These were high-speed processes that involved the whole population, requiring them to coping intensively with rapid changes in all spheres of their private and social lives, which led to new knowledge, skills and identities. The phenomenon of *social stress* (distress as well as eustress) became observable at times when people felt their lives to be directly influenced by the events at the societal level. The process of rapid transitions in a society created an extra burden of tensions which needed to be coped with and adapted to (Kutsar, 1995). These social learning processes were not only extensive but also intensive, which according to Gibbs (1992) helped to understand reality and enabled individuals to perceive the world differently. For real learning to occur changes are needed – in what we know and understand, or in what we do. Gibbs argues this new knowledge is, as a result of what is learned, personally meaningful.

Davis (2006) says an act of learning is an act of identity formation. Learning in rapid societal changes does not have a clear curriculum and all those involved are students. Meeting uncertainties and the "unknown" leads to new perceptions and ('troublesome') knowledge. The following exercise will look at actors of the societal transitions and their state of liminality (the term is drawn from Turner, 1969) of the concept mastery, the conflicts of "old" and "new" (concepts); "wrong" and "right" (common sense) and coping strategies (social myths, illusions, social polarisations) with meeting uncertainties and overcoming the threshold (see also: Kutsar, 1997; Kutsar et al., 1998; Lauristin & Vihalemm, 1997).

Examining rapid societal transitions in a particular country from the threshold concepts perspective, feels like putting the social learning process under a magnifying-glass. Estonia is a small country with a population of 1,371,835 (Statistical Office..., 2000), which is situated on the eastern shore of the Baltic Sea. From the early 13th century to the early 20th century Estonia was ruled by a succession of Danes, Germans, Poles, Swedes and Russians. Estonia, the modern nation-state, declared independence in 1918. Estonia was invaded and occupied by the Soviet Union in 1940 and 1944, and remained under the alien power of the Soviet Union until 1991 when independent statehood was regained.

In the late 1980s, Mikhail Gorbachev introduced into the Soviet Union the policies of *glasnost* (openness) and *perestroika* (restructuring). These policies promoted public discussion about current and historical problems in the Soviet Union and encouraged the Estonians to re-establish independence and to obtain freedom from Soviet rule. In March 1991, a referendum supported an independent Estonia and on August 20, 1991, Estonian independence was proclaimed. On September 6, 1991, the Soviet Union accepted Estonia's independence (about this historical period read more: Estonian Institute, 2002). On the 1st of May 2004 Estonia joined the European Union among a group of ten post-communist countries of the Eastern and Central Europe.

Our current cognitive exercise will make insights into the social and psychological processes that led to the restoration of independence, starting with national awakening of Estonians in the late 1980s and followed by the peaceful revolution (called The Singing Revolution). Historically this was the most meaningful time for people of leaving *the old* and meeting *the new*. The whole population in Estonia went into the state of liminality – (*no-longer-not-yet-status* coined by Turner, 1969) and the majority emerged from it in the mid-1990s when the new socio-political and economic order and new social structures were established.

THE ACTORS OF SOCIETAL TRANSTIONS

The Communitas

Two key problematic aspects of societal transition emerged during the second national awakening of The Singing Revolution, 1987–1989, national identity and ethnic survival. Emerging hopes about national independence were realised in rapid civic initiatives. This was the time when the *Communitas* was formed. Turner defines *Communitas* as a group experience in which a sense of a common goal and collective emotional bond may transcend individual social status, creating a feeling of shared equality (Turner 1969, cited in Letkemann, 2002). This is a feeling of autonomy and collective goals producing an intense bond of "togetherness".

Togetherness was expressed in enormous mass actions and shared feelings of belonging. On 14 May 1988, the first expression of national feeling occurred during the Tartu Pop Music Festival. "Five patriotic songs", based on poems and songs originating from the first national awakening in the late 1890s were performed for the first time during the Soviet occupation. People linked their hands together and through the ritual of expressing a common will and fervent emotions, national bonding began. On 11 September 1988, a massive song festival "Song of Estonia" was held at the Tallinn Song Festival Arena. Almost 300,000 people, more than a quarter of all Estonians, came together to sing songs and hymns, which reflected their ethnic pride and desire for independence. Some of the older, traditional songs had been strictly forbidden during the years of Soviet occupation. Throughout the day-long festival, political leaders gave emotional speeches about the desire for independence alongside the popular and charismatic leaders of the *Communitas*. This was the first time political leaders in Estonia were openly insistent about the restoration of independence. They empowered the feelings of togetherness.

Another remarkable mass event where the *Communitas* was evident was The Baltic Chain a peaceful protest held on the 23 August 1989. This date was the 50th anniversary of the 1939 Molotov-Ribbentrop pact between Germany and the USSR, which apportioned the Baltic countries into the Soviet sphere of interest and formed the basis of the subsequent Soviet occupations of 1940 and 1944. The *Communitas* of Estonia, Latvia and Lithuania joined together in a human chain, hand–in-hand, from Tallinn, through Riga to Vilnius as a symbol of the shared destiny of the Baltic countries and the expression of the common goals of regaining their independent statehood. Approximately 2,000,000 people joined their hands over the 600 kilometre route to show that the Baltic people had united and shared their visions of the future. During this ritual, a mantra *"Estonia/Latvia/Lithuania belongs to us"* was echoed from person to person the length of the entire human chain. This event created hope for new opportunities for gaining independence and finding greater international support for their aspirations.

Togetherness was not always accompanied by positive emotions. In the situation of rapid societal change, individuals are often unable to adapt as rapidly as changes occur. For that reason, rapid change, even positive in essence, brings emotional tensions and fears of loss of cognitive control over the situation, which results in feelings of powerlessness, dissatisfaction and alienation. Well-being acknowledges the *possibilities* as well as *limitations* for action. In general, the process of societal transitions in Estonia was tense for everybody involved in the manner of decreasing their perceived quality of life, i.e. well-being. The results of the survey "Social Stress in Estonia" (1993) revealed that over a third of the respondents expressed high levels of social distress (negative emotions like anxiety, discomfort, different kinds of fears, etc); these respondents were mostly male, non-Estonians, and from the older generations (Kutsar, 1995).

A collective experience results from a crisis in the social process – as Turner discovered in primitive tribal societies (Turner 1969 cited in Deflem, 1991 and Letkemann, 2002). The Estonian *Communitas* collective experience was performed as a social ritual and functioned by disconnecting people from the old social structures and social status and bonding them together on new grounds to meet the unknown but strongly wished for future. The *Communitas*, using Turner's (1969) approach, expressed the readiness for creation of the 'anti'-structure in Estonian society. Springing forth from the ruins of the collapsing totalitarian system and fed by opposition towards it, the *Communitas* was destructive towards the old system and its power structures. This destructive societal participation was supported by national trust in the actions of the new popular, charismatic leaders and the new political elite.

The most essential result of this initial period of transformation was the formation of new social structures in the forms of informal organisations (popular front, heritage society, green movement, creative unions, the Congress of Estonia, etc.) and new initiatives to disconnect the Estonian economy from the USSR (the Estonian *IME-programme* for economic autonomy was signed in 1987). The new structures operated as pressures for restoration of democratic relations and independent statehood. As a result of public pressure the Supreme Soviet passed a sovereignty declaration on 16 November 1988, which acknowledged the supremacy of Estonian laws and declared all resources in Estonia to be Estonian property. In 1989–1990 the first attempts for restoration of the civic society were made: a free press started to develop, a multiparty political system emerged, society became more open, free elections were successfully carried out. Many people became enthusiastic in starting with individual entrepreneurship (initially as a 'cottage industry'– individually producing illegal income until this was legalised as individual work).

Who in a social context formed the Communitas? In general, these were people who had disconnected from their social status and position in Soviet society and converged on ethnic grounds (Estonians). By intensively seeking their own identity, they disconnected themselves from being Soviet and opposed everything that was related to Soviet society or was labelled as 'old'. They were looked back at the long history of conflicts with different nations and life under alien powers (e.g., Denmark, Poland, Germany, Sweden and Russia, which Estonia had experienced. Their ethnic identity of being Estonians was bolstered by these insights into the nation's historical past. The right of owning this land forever was strongly acknowledged and a politically independent existence (new social structure) was perceived as a highly deserved reality-to-be.

The *Communitas* was led by popular, charismatic leaders who sprang from several origins. First, the new political elite grew from the union of creative intellectuals – writers, artists, actors, etc., and academic people with high social and political sense. This group of leaders was supplemented by Estonians who had lived in exile and now repatriated as experts or teachers with "valid" social and political experiences acquired in the West. They were joined by the victims of the repressions of Soviet power (e.g. sentenced to prison on the political grounds). These former dissidents became actively seen and heard. The leaders also involved a mix of the politically well-oriented younger generations and the older generation who had held political power in the Soviet system but were collaborating with the new alternative political elite.

Constructive participation in the new political elite was strongly supported by the majority of the population. This was due to the *'valid social-political experience'*, which had been and still was reflected in the oppositional attitudes towards the Soviet system, as well as in their active participation in the mass movements of national liberation (the *Communitas*). Interestingly, young people who had had a '*missing experience*', no participatory experience in the Soviet system, were popularly viewed to have more worth in facing the challenges inherent in rebuilding the nation than those, like the nomenklatura, whose experience was deemed an '*invalid experience*'. As a result, many young people, and former dissidents, as well as representatives of the creative intelligentsia and a few repatriated Estonian refugees acquired Ministerial positions in the first democratically elected Parliament (still called the Supreme Soviet at that time) or became national experts or counsellors. Mr Mart Laar, for example, became the first Prime Minister of independent Estonia at the age of 32 years. The appreciation of a '*missing experience*' continued until people acquired a new '*valid experience*' that was expected to favour the development of the country.

"The Others"

Although the *Communitas* involved the majority of the population, there was a sizable part, '*The Others*' which was not involved by their own choice (self-exclusion) because they did not share the aims, goals and values of the *Communitas*. During the national awakening and the following the peaceful 'Singing' revolution, non-Estonians who had migrated from different parts of the Soviet Union found themselves in a troubled situation feeling both alien and excluded from the development of Estonia. Besides regular societal changes that were too rapid, they faced additional changes, mostly connected with their own identity.

The non-Estonian population (mainly Russian-speaking) needed more time for self re-identification and for re-positioning in the transition from being accepted as the dominant ethnic group and the speakers of the former state language (Russian) to being labelled as the ethnic minority with either weak or zero command of the state language (Estonian).

The problems of ethnic relations emerged in several of the former Soviet Union countries in Central and Eastern Europe. The complicated ethnic relations within the borders of a single country became serious barriers to national development in times of the intensive nation-building. In Estonia the ethnic minorities (of whom approximately 90% were ethnic Russians and Russian-speaking Slavs – Ukrainians and Byelorussians) comprised one third of the total population.

Another group which chose to stay out of the *Communitas* was the Soviet *nomenklatura* (of both Estonian as well as non-Estonian origin) whose '*invalid experience*' was popularly deemed to be of no value to the development of Estonia.

The actions taken by *The Others* were aimed at actively keeping the old social structures (the Communist Party in particular) and the old identities. They perceived the actions of the *Communitas* as dangerous to the existing system. *Interrinne*, the Interfront movement was organised by the Soviet military-industrial complex with the aim of spreading social tensions to keep the old structures in place.. The majority of *Interrinne*'s members were ethnic Russians.

"The Teachers"

The developmental path from a totalitarian system with a command economy towards a civil society with advanced free-market economies was original in global history. The Central and Eastern European countries, including Estonia, by standing at the crossroads of choices needed wise advisers and experts with 'know-how', both internally as well as externally. Estonia did not aspire to copy foreign practices but sought its own paths that put the competence of the foreign experts to the test. The only 'teacher' organisations with a clear curriculum were the supra-national agencies (the World Bank, the International Monetary Fund and others), which appeared after independence was restored in 1991.

THE LIMINALITY OF SOCIETAL TRANSITIONS AS A LEARNING PROCESS

During Estonia's societal transitions the entire population was overwhelmed with the learning process where common sense, meeting uncertainties and the "unknown" led to new perceptions, ('troublesome') knowledge and identities. The transition processes, proceeding from the thresholds concept perspective, were liminal and went through three phases, as referred to by Turner (1969). Preliminal occurred with the national awakening, when individuals, disconnected from Soviet social status and position, converged on ethnic grounds. Liminal occurred with confronting social memories, experiences and attitudes using common sense and newly acquired perceptions (being between the *known* and the *unknown*). Postliminal occurred with new understandings, identities and disillusions as well as social polarisations of the 'winners' and 'losers' of the transitions.

The liminal state was launched when rapid societal changes started and problems were experienced in understanding and re-constructing them. For the *Communitas* this meant the orientation towards the desired future and negating the 'old', whereas for "*The Others*" this meant resisting the 'new' as the alien challenge and keeping the 'old'.

Confrontation of the "Old" and the "New"

The state of liminality meant confrontation of the old and the new terms, principles and situations. People disconnected from the former experiences of the Soviet way of life and re-evaluated them as "*invalid* " (Kutsar et al., 1998). By denying the 'old' they filled new life situations, which reflected the societal changes, with highly positive meanings until personal experiences with the issues occurred. For example, unemployment was perceived as a 'good' term because it was supposed to create competition and to force higher work standards. However, the moment a person, family member or close friend lost their job as an outcome of the structural changes within the country, the positive meanings became profoundly negative. This was also true for the overarching concept of the free market economy (Järve, 1995), which was supposed to be positive because it provided numerous possibilities for a better life, until one faced the problems inherent in the labour market of a free-market economy.

In a country in the process of transforming from a totalitarian system, the meanings of an individual's previous position and status were also re-evaluated. For example, a person who had been doing well in former Soviet period might not be preferred because their previous experience was evaluated as '*invalid*'. Denial of the old social and political order as *wrong* cognitively excluded habitual coping strategies and put an individual in a situation of higher uncertainty and in a process of learning new life strategies.

Social Myth as a Coping Strategy

During the state of liminality, several social myths (irrational beliefs) emerged to help in coping with the *unknown*. They were cognitive constructions with high affective and directive (behavioural) components. Nobody could read or see the social myths anywhere but everybody knew and felt how they guided the people's behaviour. As a coping strategy, they helped to survive during the most severe and unknown situations. The myths were formulated in a form of conditional sentences, also indicating to the date of their completion. Some examples, "w*e are ready even to starve until independence will be real*", or: "*when the Soviet Army will leave the country, everybody will start feeling safe*", or: "*when we shall have our own currency our country will flourish*" (Kutsar, 1995).

As social myths, there were also several imaginary images spread among society about Western way of life as affluent and most desirable. Once the free market economy became real, people started to compete for places in the labour market, and the socio-economic re-constructions were accompanied by decreasing levels of wellbeing of the population.

The therapeutic function of a myth was to help in coping with unfavourable life situations until the completion date. They were myths because after their irrational content of the truths became evident, they disintegrated. However, in the state of liminality, people created new social myths to substitute the disintegrated ones, as means to maintain control over rapidly changing social situations (Kutsar, 1995). The obtained knowledge after the disintegration of a social myth comprised a new understanding and relation to oneself and the others, which Meyer and Land (2005) referred to as repositioning and transformed thought. It also paved the way towards new skills and experiences. Sometimes this new worldview led to 'troublesome' knowledge and disillusionment; for example after the Soviet Army left the country, people continued feeling unsafe and the monetary reform in 1992 led to social inequalities and exclusion. Social myths can be interpreted as threshold myths (Atherton et al., 2008), the functional value of which exceeds their value of being true. They are ideological beliefs with strong affective and political elements, which according to Atherton et al., (2008) serve as threshold concepts.

Social myths of people of older age were positive in their context and more concrete because the myths proceeded from their own experience in the past. On the other hand, the disintegration of a social myth was more painful for an older person because there was not so much time left for waiting for an improvement of the situation (Kutsar, 1995).

In the instance of the non-Estonian population, there was a lack of authentic information. This was because many of them could not speak and understand the Estonian language; and living in the homogeneous Russian-speaking regions, they received information that was filtered by misunderstandings spread through gossips and politically elaborated materials. Nevertheless, there is acceptance of the negative context of turning non-Estonians social expectations into social myths, which supported the role of outsiders and so enabling the alienation from society processes. These alienation processes in turn bolstered the feelings of togetherness among *"The Others"*. The social myths of many non-Estonians decreased their cognitive control over new life situations and increased the levels of social distress. It was the time of re-construction of the national state of Estonians which easily created an extra burden of tensions to the non-Estonian population leaving them in the positions of outsiders.

The total learning process during societal transitions, referring to Meyer et al. (2006), and (Cousin, 2006), involve the occupation of a liminal space during the process of threshold mastery. In the case of the rapid societal transitions in Estonia, nobody was unaffected, however the learning processes created both 'convenient' as well as 'troublesome' knowledge accompanied by anxieties and stress. The 'convenient' knowledge was easily acceptable because of its shared intellectual and emotional meanings of the *Communitas* and its charismatic leaders. The 'troublesome' knowledge stayed far from common sense for several reasons: new perceptions developed too early or were misunderstood by the learners or were imported from outside and were thus alien or were simply related to the decreasing wellbeing of the individuals concerned.

Perception of New Social Adequacy and Personal Challenge

Looking for new self-identity, people evaluated their own new perspectives by confronting their individual characteristics and social demand (Kutsar et al., 1998). As a result, a new understanding of one's social adequacy was formed. The level of social adequacy was highly dependent on how much an individual was able to meet new social demands.

For example, starting private business did not have age, gender or family status restrictions. Indeed this action was more dependent on the individual's ability to understand the new principles of property and work organizations; their psychological readiness to take risks and responsibilities, and to look for new technologies and find new trajectories in the market. Those not overcoming these thresholds found themselves rejected and excluded from society and its development.

Loss of social participation favoured the loss of personal identity and the development of alienation (Kutsar, 1997). In the transition from a totalitarian society, alienation was a problem of over-choice rather than under-choice. Everyone had to make a choice between different social groups, political parties, even nationalities and countries, in order to create a new personal identity in a new social, economic and political situation. At the time of societal transitions, the old meaning of social participation was also replaced with new one.

Social Polarisations

Estonian society became polarised by several dimension – gender, age, ethnic origin, success in coping with societal changes, etc. An interesting example was the polarisation by gender (Kutsar et al., 1998). The unisex 'comrades of Soviet society' with ideological equalisations in the labour market polarised into men and women through looking for their own gender identities. This process, supported by the slogan "Back Home!" during the Singing Revolution, was regressive because it went back to the traditional gender roles. Men became more ready to take responsibilities over family welfare while women became more enthusiastic than ever to form a family, to have several children and stay at home to care for their children (Narusk & Hansson, 1999). Due to the economic re-construction of the country and the overall decrease of welfare, men experienced high distress at the loss of a job and not for failing to meet the changed standards of their gender, while women continued in the labour market to make ends meet.

In the late 1990s, the "winners" and "losers" of the transitions became evident (see: Narusk & Hansson, 1999; Lauristin & Vihalemm, 1997; Titma et al., 1998). The "winners" were most often people in their thirties, called the winners' generation, educated and successfully repositioned in the labour market.

Age performed as a social-cognitive factor in Estonia, determining the levels of overcoming the threshold through socially driven higher positive challenges and the preference of the younger generations. This was connected with their rapid socialization process, their flexibility in changing habitual ways of life, re-orienting to new jobs, meeting new demands, and last but not least, with their incorrupt and unspoiled social experience. The younger generations were less overwhelmed with stress. They had clearer future orientations than older people who revealed more nostalgic attitudes towards past achievements and hard work. Older people also felt that they had less control over the new circumstances and more often than young people they perceived themselves as having few opportunities to better themselves.

The "losers" were the people who had been unable to re-construct their life philosophies. They mostly had lower educational levels and came from older age groups and were those for whom the welfare decrease had the most impact (the long-term unemployed, socially excluded and the poor).

SOURCES OF 'TROUBLESOME' KNOWLEDGE

Learned Helplessness – the Legacy of the "Old"

The Soviet socialist state took responsibility for giving work, free education, medical services, and low priced public transport. Family policy was oriented to support a working woman and, therefore, the state provided a well-organized set of preschool institutions for children. Housing costs were partly paid by the state and expenditure on rent was low for a family-budget. The state, through work agencies, or trade unions, took care of anyone who had good work records, and established opportunities for staying in holiday homes and Soviet type sanatoriums. The state solved the lack of consumer goods by providing these through the workplaces.

Deacon (1992) called this type of social security system 'party-state/workplace paternalism'. Allocation according to work record rather than necessity led to failing to meet the needs of those falling outside the insured categories of risk. Deacon (1992: 7) concludes: "Welfare recipients were objects of provision and never active subjects in defining needs and running services that met needs".

A policy of full employment in the Soviet system made people unconcerned about the quality of work, since they never feared losing their job. Increasing unemployment during the societal re-constructions produced a real shock for those experiencing it. The life philosophy of the planned economy and the paternalistic care of the state had produced '*learned helplessness*' and an absence of any '*self-help mentality*'. There were people who, after the loss of work or permanent income, unexpectedly found themselves among the group which, at least temporarily, needed social welfare services.

The 'old life' philosophy intervened into the process of re-construction of a societal change. Lacking any self-help mentality suppressed one's own activity and entre-preneurship and left an individual passively waiting for the '*paternalistic*' help, which society had given earlier. Becoming aware that there was no help any more, made people overwhelmed with discontent and confusion (see: Kutsar et al., 1998).

Changed Societal Demand

Societal demand in the post-communist country was aimed at fostering new purposeful developments of the country and social preference was given to those people who were presumably able to meet the new demands. Concomitant with the process of change in societal demand social myths intervened in the process by placing social groups in opposition to one another. These groups were essentially the 'winners and losers' of the transition process, the younger *versus* the older generations, men *versus* women, the representatives of the new ethnic majority *versus* the new ethnic minority, people acquiring a new valid experience *versus* those who had an '*invalid experience*' (Kutsar et al., 1998).

As the goal was on reaching a *normally functioning society* in the quickest possible way, the development of the post-communist Estonia favoured young men of the new ethnic majority. Even when married, they had more opportunities for professional growth and self-realization compared to married women with dependent children.

The re-construction of the national state created an extra burden of tensions for the non-Estonian population who for a number of reasons were left in the position of outsiders. Their deficiency in speaking and understanding the state language (Estonian) left them without authentic information and, at the same time, decreased cognitive control over the new life situations and so decreased their levels of well-being. Furthermore, many non-Estonians found themselves in the situation of social vacuum. In many cases, all of their friends and relatives had been repatriated, and visa constraints and restrictions made for complications in visiting and keeping in close contact with their friends and relatives.

Social Justice and Unpopular Political Decisions

Deacon (1992) has pointed out that it is not an easy task to create democracy and a civil society while retaining an acceptable concept of social justice. People find it undeserved to be unemployed or to experience severe problems in coping the economic and psychological aspects of everyday life.

On the other hand Lamentowicz (1993: 215) in discussing 'arrogant elites', points out that both domestic and international pressures push new elites into shock therapy based on the assumption that a rapid transition to a market economy is preferred to a slower transition. Over-politicized and over-ambitious liberal reformers tend to alienate themselves from the main-stream of public opinion by the top-down design of guided change, by their open hostility to trade unions and workers' self-management, and, last but not least, by their insistence on special powers to legislate the executive branch of the government.

The data from the Social Cognition Test (1994)[1] supported the ideas of Lamentowicz and revealed that the most relevant values perceived by the leaders in Estonia were power, decent standard of living, wealth, career, personal profit, control and influence over the people. The international research project Social Justice and Political Change (1990/91)[2] also reported the public dissatisfaction with the methods applied by governments, which are in ignorance of public interests. The majority (80.6%) of respondents in Estonia agreed with the statement that public officials do not care what ordinary people think. The social and political reconstruction of Estonia required numerous unpopular decisions from the policy makers.

The expectation, which was born in the light of events in 1988, that after the collapse of communism, the just (i.e. democratically elected) Parliament and competent Government in Estonia would attain power was shattered in 1993. People became dissatisfied with the rapidly diminishing standard of living and perceived the system and state representation as alien, "not mine", a source of threat rather than a guarantee of rules which could be used to defend their rights. The survey "Living Conditions in Estonia" (1994)[3] revealed the respondents' high suspicions of the power structures. For example, 52% of the respondents stated that the public authorities concealed important information; 41% suspected that public officials took bribes; 60% agreed that it was difficult to understand politics, and only 40% were really interested in politics (Kutsar et al., 1998).

However, in the late 1990s Estonia was regarded as one of the most successful East and Central European countries coming out of the collapsed totalitarian regimen.

CONCLUSION

This article was written at the time Estonia celebrated the 20th anniversary of the (second) national awakening and the Singing Revolution. About 70,000 people gathered at the Tallinn Song Festival Arena from all over Estonia on the 19 August 2008 to sing old and new patriotic songs. This six hours celebration was to commemorate the *Communitas*, as well as to introduce its feelings of togetherness to the new younger generations. The event revived the *Communitas*, the feeling of togetherness was present again with its liminality – being *here and now*, between the past and the future, in the *no-longer-not-yet* status. The same day, the Estonian discus thrower Gerd Kanter won a gold medal at the Olympic Games in Beijing, which supplemented the arousing eustress, but anxiety was also present at the ongoing conflict between Russia and Georgia.

Transition from the totalitarian society with a planned economy to a civil society with a free market economy has been rapid and provided new challenges, as well as the risks in coping with the economic and psychological aspects of life for individuals and households in Estonia. New knowledge obtained, in terms of Meyer and Land (2005), was transformative, irreversible and integrative. The transition occasioned a significant shift in the worldviews of the whole nation and led to new identities. Even if troublesome, this knowledge is unlikely to be forgotten and exposes the hidden interrelatedness of the past and the future.

The threshold perspective led us, the authors of this article, on a cognitive journey back into the past, recalling the events that had happened 20 years ago, in which we have our participative cognitions. We are not the same people any more. Reading the texts written on societal transitions in Estonia years ago and trying to re-analyse the processes from the threshold concepts perspective placed us in a learning process, which provided us with many new insights. On this journey, we experienced a state of liminality of being between different times, experiences, knowledge and identities.

The reader may well ask: *"So what? How this is related to teaching and learning in higher education, the main focus of the current book?"* First of all, this journey gave us new insights into how this subject would be better taught. Secondly, but no less important is the personal experience of looking at things differently, exploring new meanings and understandings and becoming surprised because the threshold concepts perspective, while it having been developed for teaching and learning in higher education, has a great potential for understanding social learning processes. Now we are ready to collect our 'hold-all' again and start new journeys with our students. We believe that every class we teach is a cognitive journey with its liminal space shared by actors meeting thresholds when they open up to akin to a portal to a new way of thinking and identity formation.

NOTES

[1] "Social Cognition Test" elaborated by a research team led by Olev Must, Phd, at the University of Tartu in 1994, was aimed to study people's perceptions of the rapidly changing Estonian society. The Test was based on pictogram-method developed by Evans, Kelly and Kolosi (see: Evans, M.D.R, Jonathan Kelly & Tamas Kolosi (1992) Images of Class: Public perceptions in Hungary and Australia. *American Sociological Review,* 57. 461–482).

[2] I.S.J.P International Social Justice and Political Change (1990/91) See at: http://www.butler.edu/ISJP/intro.html.

[3] "Living Conditions in Estonia" (1994) See at: http://www.fafo.no/norbalt/index.htm.

KUTSAR AND KÄRNER

REFERENCES

Atherton, J., Hadfield, P., & Meyers, R. (2008). *Threshold Concepts in the Wild*. Expanded version of a paper presented at Threshold Concepts: From Theory to Practice conference, Queen's University, Kingston Ontario 18–20 June 2008. Retrieved January 30, 2009, from http://www.bedspce.org.uk/ Threshold_Concepts_in_the_Wild.pdf

Cousin, G. (2006). An introduction to threshold concepts. *Planet*, (17).

Davies, P. (2006). Threshold concepts. How can we recognise them? In J. H. F. Meyer & R. Land (Eds.), *Overcoming barriers to student understanding. Threshold concepts and troublesome knowledge* (pp. 70–84). London and New York: Routledge.

Deacon, B. (1992). East European welfare: Past, present, future in comparative context. In B. Deacon, M. Castle-Kanerova, N. Manning, F. Millard, E. Orosz, J. Szalai, & A. Vidinova (Eds.), *The New Eastern Europe: Past, present and future for social policy* (pp. 1–31). London: Sage Publications.

Deflem, M. (1991). Ritual, Anti-Structure, and Religion: A Discussion of Victor Turner's Processual Symbolic Analysis. *Journal for the Scientific Study of Religion*, 30(1), 1–25.

Estonian Institute. (2002). *The restoration of Estonian independence*. Retrieved August 21, 2008, from http://www.einst.ee/factsheets/factsheets_uus_kuju/the_restoration_of_estonian_independence.htm

Gibbs, G. (1992). *Improving the quality of student learning*. Bristol: Technical and Educational Services.

Järve, P. (1995). Transition to democracy. *Nationalities Papers*, 23(1), 19–27.

Kutsar, D. (1997). *Multiple welfare losses and risk of social exclusion in the Baltic States during societal transition. – The Baltic Countries revisited: Living conditions and comparative challenges.* The NORBALT Living Conditions Project. Aadne Aasland, Knud Knudsen, Dagmar Kutsar, Ilze Trapenciere. Oslo: Fafo Report 230: 79–104.

Kutsar, D. (1995). Social change and stress in Estonia. *Scandinavia Journal of Social Welfare*, 4, 94–107.

Kutsar, D., Trumm, A., & Oja, U. (1998). New democracy: Boundaries and resources for development. In S. MacPherson (Ed.), *Social development and societies in transition* (pp. 248–264). Hoi-Kwok Wong. Aldershot, Brookfies, Singapore, Sydney: Ashgate.

Land, R., Meyer, J. H. F., & Smith, J. (Eds.). (2008). *Threshold concepts within the disciplines. Educational futures: Rethinking theory and practice* (Vol. 16). Rotterdam, The Netherlands: Sense publishers.

Lamentowicz, W. (1993). Prospects for civil society in Eastern Europe. In W. Weidenfeld & J. Janning (Eds.), *Europe in global change* (pp. 209–221). Gütersloh: Bertelsmann.

Lauristin, M., Vihalemm, P., Rosengren, K. E., & Weibull, L., (Eds.). (1997). *Return to the western world. Cultural and political perspectives on the estonian Post-communist transition*. Tartu: Tartu University Press.

Letkemann, P. G. (2002). The office workplace: Communitas and hierarchical social structures. *Anthropologica*, XLIV(2), 257–270.

Meyer, J. H. F., & Land, R. (2003). Threshold concepts and troublesome knowledge (I): Linkages to ways of thinking and practising. In C. Rust (Ed.), *Improving student learning – ten years on*. Oxford, UK: OCSLD.

Meyer, J. H. F., & Land, R. (2005). Threshold concepts and troublesome knowledge (2): Epistemological considerations and a conceptual framework for teaching and learning. *Higher Education*, 49, 373–388.

Meyer, J. H. F., Land, R., & Davies, P. (2006). Implications of threshold concepts for course design and evaluation. In J. H. F. Meyer & R. Land (Eds.), *Overcoming barriers to student understanding: Threshold concepts and troublesome knowledge*. London and New York: Routledge.

Narusk, A., & Hansson, L. (1999). *Estonian families in the 1990s: Winners and losers*. Tallinn: Estonian Academy Publishers.

Reimann, N., & Jackson, I. (2006). Threshold concepts in Economics: a case study. In J. H. F. Meyer & R. Land (Eds.), *Overcoming barriers to student understanding. Threshold concepts and troublesome knowledge* (pp. 115–133). London and New York: Routledge.

Statistical Office of Estonia. (2000). *Population and housing census, part VI: Household*. (Tallinn: SOE, 2002).

Titma, M., Tuma, N. B., & Silver, B. D. (1998). Winners and losers in the postcommunist transition: New evidence from Estonia. *Post-Soviet Affairs*, *14*(2), 114–136.

Turner, V. (1969). *The ritual process: Structure and Anti-structure*. London: Routledge & Kegan Paul.

Dagmar Kutsar
Institute of Sociology and Social Policy
University of Tartu
Estonia

Anita Kärner
Centre for Educational Research and Curriculum Development
Faculty of Education
University of Tartu
Estonia

MARGARET KILEY AND GINA WISKER

24. LEARNING TO BE A RESEARCHER:

The Concepts and Crossings

ABSTRACT

This chapter has as its main focus the research we have carried out with supervisors regarding their identification of candidates' "learning leaps" or conceptual threshold crossing, with reference to the threshold concepts that have been identified as part of the process of learning to be a researcher. Experienced supervisors across a range of discipline areas and a number of different countries were surveyed or interviewed with the aim of identifying supervisors' views on: conceptual challenges that candidates encountered when learning to be a researcher, how supervisors recognised that a candidate had successfully met those challenges, and how they might have assisted the candidate in that process.

As an outcome of the study we suggest that with the development of research supervisors' ability to appreciate the concepts involved, to identify moments of research learning, and to have access to a range of strategies, they might be more able to assist candidates when they struggle in their engagement with these concepts and threshold crossing.

INTRODUCTION

Most research focusing on threshold concepts has considered the learning of undergraduate students and definitions of subject-related threshold concepts with examples of strategies and practices, which aim to encourage students to make the crossing through a liminal space to the position of understanding and using the concepts in their work (Cook-Sather, 2006; Deegan & Hill, 1991; J. Meyer & Land, 2006; Turner, 1979; Wisker, Robinson, & Kiley, 2008). This crossing of the threshold, a process which in this paper we call *crossing conceptual thresholds*, can alter the learner's approaches to, and perceptions of learning in the subject and often of learning itself. This change, it can be argued, means that the learner has not only revealed a more complex landscape of knowledge, but can understand, manipulate, and create knowledge, a type of learning defined by Flavell (1979) as meta-learning. Such a developmental change can be troublesome, causing disruption in the learning practices of the doctoral student and so affect both ontology, their identity, and epistemology, their construction of and contribution to knowledge.

J. H. F. Meyer, R. Land and C. Baillie (eds.), Threshold Concepts and
Transformational Learning, 399–414.
© *2010 Sense Publishers. All rights reserved.*

The theory and use of threshold concepts in student learning has developed dramatically over the past few years, for example, with conferences in Scotland, 2006 and Canada 2008; books, Land, Meyer & Smith, 2008; Meyer & Land, 2006; funding for research projects such as the UK National Teaching Fellowships Scheme Project on Doctoral Learning Journeys (2007–2010) based at the Universities of Brighton and Anglia Ruskin, the Australian Learning and Teaching Council project at the Australian National University, and numerous conference and journal papers. We have paralleled this work with research into threshold concepts in research education, and with research into the crossing of conceptual thresholds, those learning moments at which doctoral students begin to view the construction of knowledge and to work at a more complex, conceptual, critical and creative level.

Our research into threshold concepts in research education began with the Reflections on Learning Inventory (ROLI) (Meyer & Boulton-Lewis, 1997) which aimed to identify student learning approaches, motivation, and their meta-cognition, that is when they knew they were learning and what they thought learning was for them (Flavell, 1979; Wisker, Robinson, Trafford, Lilly, & Warnes, 2004). The ROLI was used in a study in the UK with a large international, cohort-based PhD programme spanning 1998–2008. It was administered at the start and end of the candidate's doctoral learning journey. Used in conjunction with interviews, focus groups, supervisory dialogues and set group dialogue events. The action research accompanied a five stage research development programme. It focused on postgraduate student learning and moved through the identification of various moments when students can be seen, or not, to develop their approaches to, and perceptions of, the learning necessary at doctoral level. Initially, much of this research focused on the identification of questions or problems at doctoral level for example, methodology and the development of the literature review. Dialogues between candidate and supervisor have identified where students find their own voice and are able to explain and argue their contribution. Recently, the research has focused on candidates working at conceptual levels in their research, for example conceptual levels of enquiry, research, design, data management, interpretation of findings and conclusions. These findings related to candidates' conceptual level of learning that has been referred to as 'doctorateness' (Trafford, 2003).

A further related stage in the emerging work on research learning was the development of the Students' Conceptions of Research inventory (SCoRi) which aimed to identify what it was that students understood 'research' to be, leading further to conceptions of research held by academics, particularly research supervisors Kiley & Mullins, 2001, 2002, 2003, 2005, Meyer, Shanahan & Laugksch, 2001).

Additionally, research on the examination of the doctoral dissertation and viva/oral suggested not only that work that was deemed to have achieved the level of the doctorate had made a contribution to knowledge, but also that candidates were able to present their work conceptually and to theorise and abstract their findings in ways which allowed them to have broader application (Bourke, Hattie, & Anderson, 2004; Hartley & Wisker, 2004; Holbrook, Bourke,

Farley, & Carmichael, 2001; Isaac, Quinlan, & Walker, 1992; Johnston, 1997; Kiley & Mullins, 2004, 2006; Mullins & Kiley, 2002; Tinkler & Jackson, 2004; Winter, Griffiths, & Green, 2000).

The combination of these aspects of our work with the theory of threshold concepts became a turning point in our own research. Student meta-cognition, conceptual level thinking and developing facility and ability to articulate their research learning were seen as crucial in the development of postgraduates' doctoral learning journeys through to the crossing of conceptual thresholds and the achievement of their doctorate. We argue that conceptual thresholds are the stages or critical points in students' research journey where they move into work at a conceptual, critical and creative level. Such moments include, for example, the identification of a research question from a topic, and engagement in dialogue with the literature, placing their own work and findings in their own voice in this dialogue. This work led to the first paper on research candidates' threshold concepts at the Quality in Postgraduate Research conference in 2006 (Wisker, Kiley, & Aiston, 2006) and further papers on conceptual thresholds in literature and art, and in education (Wisker, Robinson, & Kiley, 2008) and on supervisory recognition of this conceptual threshold crossing (Kiley & Wisker, 2008).

The research has advanced with four main aims:

1. The identification of concepts in research learning that might be argued to be threshold concepts
2. The identification by research supervisors of the moments of development or crossing of the conceptual threshold associated with having understood one of these concepts, often referred to in this paper as the "learning leap"
3. The ways in which research supervisors might be able to assist candidates in understanding these concepts and cross conceptual thresholds or making the learning leap, and
4. The identification by research candidates of the moments of understanding or learning leap that is their own meta-cognitive understanding of learning.

This chapter has as its main focus the second and third of the above aims. However, we begin with an overview of the Threshold Concepts that have been already identified in research education (Kiley, in press, Kiley & Wisker, submitted for publication). Following this we present the study that identified how supervisors recognised the crossing of these thresholds.

In our earlier work, we suggested that there were six initial threshold concepts emerging from the data. The first was the concept of *argument* or thesis, a concept which the research on doctoral examination frequently cites either because of its presence, or lack of it, in the dissertation (Bourke, Hattie, & Anderson, 2004; Kiley & Mullins, 2004, 2006; Lovitts, 2007; Mullins & Kiley, 2002). The second threshold concept identified was the concept of *theory* either underpinning research or being an outcome of research. A research students' understanding of the role and use of theory was a critical issue raised in the earlier work. A third concept identified in the research was that of *framework* as a means of locating or bounding the research.

The other three possible threshold concepts suggested by the earlier research include the concepts of knowledge creation, of analysis, and of research paradigm. The concept of originality and *knowledge creation* was one reported to challenge students. The idea that in undertaking original research one is contributing something new to our knowledge and understanding is a substantial leap for many. In the earlier research it was not uncommon for supervisors to report that some candidates had difficulty appreciating the concept of *analysis.* Again the research on examination (Kiley, 2004; Kiley & Mullins, 2004; Lovitts, 2007; Mullins & Kiley 2002, and (Lovitts, 2007; Winter, Griffiths, & Green, 2000) suggests that examiners frequently comment negatively on lack of analysis or analysis that might be termed "haphazard" or "undisciplined". The sixth threshold concept to be identified to date is the concept of *paradigm* that is the epistemological framing of one's approach to research.

Having outlined our previous work on identifying threshold concepts we now move to the more recent study which examined how supervisors recognised when students had grasped one of those concepts and crossed the threshold.

AIMS OF STUDY

Work being discussed and reported in this chapter comes from an early invest-tigation into the awareness and articulation by research supervisors, who are engaged in encouraging students to cross conceptual thresholds and gain threshold concepts at doctoral level. This specific contribution focuses on ways in which they intervene in working with their postgraduate students' learning that is how they "nudge" students across conceptual thresholds.

Hence, the specific aims of this particular part of the study were to identify:

1. How research supervisors recognise the acquisition of the threshold concepts
2. Where and how they recognise evidence they are crossing, and
3. How they "nudge" candidates in the crossing of this threshold.

For us as supervisors in an educational development context we might ask what it is we do or could do to help students engage at this conceptual level to gain the threshold concepts and get through the conceptual thresholds.

METHOD

We have used face-to-face interviewing of individuals and small groups (n = 40) (see Table 1) and written surveys (n = 26) (see Table 2) with experienced supervisors across a range of disciplines to identify if they are aware of such conceptual threshold crossing and the gaining of threshold concepts. We were seeking to find how this "crossing" might appear and take shape in terms of "articulation" i.e. in the written and spoken work of their students. In addition we wanted to know what they felt was their contribution to "nudging" students through the various thres-holds. Early work has suggested that supervisors identify key issues in what can be termed doctoral work that is: conceptual, critical and creative (enough) to be accepted as doctoral work.

Responses were coded by discipline e.g. SS for Social Science, and each respondent identified numerically e.g. SS10. Where terms exist in the transcripts that might identify the respondent they have been removed and replaced with … which has also been used when parts of the quotes are not specifically relevant. False starts and "words" such as um and err have been removed to aid in reading.

Table 1. Interviewees by discipline cluster and country

Discipline cluster	Australia	UK	Jamaica	Trinidad	Canada	Total
Engineering & IT	2			1		3
Humanities	4	2		2		8
Science & Health Science	9	2		1		12
Social Science	11	2	3		1	17
Total	**26**	**6**	**3**	**4**	**1**	**40**

Twenty-six experienced doctoral supervisors across eleven universities, in five countries were invited to complete a short survey. As Table 2 demonstrates the supervisors represented the same four main areas as in the interviews. In the survey, respondents were asked to identify the main learning challenges that they considered their research candidates experienced and the strategies that they as supervisors had adopted to assist learners overcome these challenges.

Table 2. Survey respondents by discipline cluster and country

Discipline cluster	Australia	UK	New Zealand	Malaysia	Israel	Total
Engineering & IT			1			1
Humanities		1	3	1		5
Science and Health Science			6	1		7
Social Science	3	1	6	2	1	13
Total	**3**	**2**	**16**	**4**	**1**	**26**

Hence, we have a total of 66 sources of data to assist us in answering our questions.

FINDINGS

The analysis of the transcripts suggested that there are a number of moments when candidates demonstrate that they have made a "learning leap" and are operating at a conceptual, critical and creative enough level for a doctorate. These moments are presented below followed in each case with examples of how supervisors in the study report that they have been able to nudge candidates to work at the appropriate level.

However, it is important to note that several supervisors indicated that some of their students have clearly reached the level of conceptual threshold crossing prior to their commencement of the doctorate. This is particularly true of some Masters students, or in the Australian context, First Class Honours graduates. Also, in the North American system, where course work and examinations, and often a *viva*, precede the development of the dissertation. In these cases it is anticipated that many candidates would have reached these levels of conceptual thinking in their pre-dissertation learning experiences, for example:

> Some students seem to be like that [thinking conceptually] from the beginning almost even in their proposals. I have a couple of really good Masters students, none of them are moving along very well but what they are capable of, and in terms of what they write, I am very impressed. So often these are people who are adults, they have problems, they have families, a couple of them have had crises.

> Interviewer: And that stops them from working at anything other than university level?

> It stops them from working at all, once they have finished their coursework, and they have gone off to deal with their family issues. (SS25)

Some students, conversely, never reach this conceptual, critical and creative level of threshold crossing in their work and some cannot even glimpse the portal let alone get through it. Supervisors have indicated that at this point they feel it is wise to ask whether such students could develop to achieve this level and whether they could or should receive a PhD. Many universities are now introducing probationary enrolments and assessed proposal seminars in the first year of candidature as a means of identifying those candidates for whom a research degree might not be the most appropriate award.

Having addressed the issue for whether the candidate should/could continue, it might be here that the question of the 'good enough PhD' is raised. This is particularly the case with good 'journeyman' work where the PhD is solid but not earth shatteringly new or conceptualised. Many examiners of doctoral dissertations report that a substantial number of dissertations they receive could be classified as 'passable' in that they are 'good enough' without being exciting, ground breaking, and 'short, simple, elegant, surprising, beautiful, and out of the ordinary' (Lovitts, 2007, p. 203).

Hence, we are at pains to make it clear that we are aware that we are not dealing here with a cohort of learners who are starting from the same learning point and moving through a staged development. Rather we are considering learners who come with diverse experiences, capabilities and motivations, all within an overlay of disciplinary and inter-disciplinary variation.

"Nudging," i.e. the constructive intervention of the supervisor to aid the student's conceptualised work, takes place through staged interventions during the development of the supervisory relationship. The interventions are aimed at working with candidates in terms of their own development of the research and the writing and preparation of the dissertation. These interventions occur at many stages of candidature, with some of the more specific and critical being:

> The development of research questions.

The movement from other-directed reading to self-directed and 'owned' reading of the literature leading to the development of a sound literary review.

Working with data at different conceptual levels, analysing, interpreting and defining findings which make a contribution to understanding as well as factual knowledge.

Developing an argument or thesis which can be sustained and supported.

Producing the abstract and the conceptual conclusions.

All of the above are seen as key moments for making "learning leaps" and articulating at a conceptual level and we address each one in more detail below. However, as one very experienced supervisor suggested, these breakthroughs might not always be evident in the outcome:

> In terms of conceptual breakthroughs, the students I've supervised I think would have made conceptual breakthroughs that wouldn't be evident necessarily to an independent examiner. But as a supervisor you see it all the time. They're making a series of conceptual breakthroughs themselves as a learner. Whether they're a contribution to the field in the end or whether other people are able to see what's been accomplished hopefully yes, but not always. Sometimes I think people in the end produce a more modest piece of work. (SS18)

The Development of Research Questions

A commonly reported 'identification' of having crossed a threshold was when a candidate was able to define a research question from a broad topic, and then ask questions of the field, their data and themselves.

Supervisors comment on the quality and cognitive level of the students' discussion with them as providing evidence of not just ownership of, and contribution to the field but a deep level of understanding and engagement with the discipline and the doctoral level of work:

> One of the things that you get an idea that the students have actually crossed that threshold is when they start to ask you higher level questions. And all of a sudden they are not asking any more if this is red or if this is blue but all of a sudden their level of questioning is on a whole different plane and its very exciting. (Hum02)

A Social Sciences supervisor talked about the mature-age candidates with whom she mainly works. She suggested that they have had many years of professional practice and generally find it difficult to ask questions of the literature and work at a theoretical or conceptual level as they are keen to find an answer to a specific practice question, which they come with when starting the research process. She then went on to talk about one student who had just started and who was different from the other mature-age, practice-oriented candidates she had supervised:

> One extreme example then in terms of conceptual breakthroughs, this is in just the last week. I had another student who even though he's a very experienced educator and worked for many years in three different school sectors and now working in policy, but he's a theory junky. I'm never going to stop this guy he's never going to get down to the project. The other co-supervisor was away so I put a bit of pressure to see what happened if we push it a little bit to try and get to the proposal. Here we have a colloquium process that they need to do within the first twelve months. (SS18)

The supervisor decided to use the proposal colloquium as an opportunity for the candidate to engage with 'a few very well read people who were also of a theoretical bent to really push him a little bit' (SS18).

Similarly, in Engineering.

> I can't say…that there is a specific time when it happens, I believe in my case it happens gradually over a period. Of course there are those students who quickly grasp what is required of them and get on with their thesis. There are some however, I have one who is taking time to bring it together and it is a gradual thing over time, one thing will happen, the methodology that they will use as an engagement, a discussion.

> Interviewer: A dialogue

> Very much of that and I would ask engaging questions to try to remove from them, establish, determine in my own mind whether they know what is taking place.

> As a supervisor I would see, what I would do I make suggestions to them often I would give them an example of a system that would do something similar, for them to start them off, rather than them searching the literature, I would give them a sample of something and encourage them to come back and let us discuss these techniques and eventually I expect them to come up with what I call a conceptual solution to the problem which is just what you have to do to get the data across…So I don't think it happens in a discrete manner, it's more gradual, at least in my experience. (Eng04)

The Movement from Other-Directed Reading to Self-Directed and "Owned" Reading

Supervisors report that they are aware of research candidates working in a different way when the candidate sees her/himself as part of the research environment:

> Undergraduate students talk about 'they' as the researchers but a research candidate identifies a relationship between their own work and the ideas of others and how these ideas advance theory. They are looking to be specific about the authoring of the literature and then advancing the development of research. (Sci10)

Similarly in the Humanities:

> Some of them really struggle to understand how to make choices in the literature review. How to produce a literature review which isn't almost a general history of the discipline but is actually focussed down to their particular part of the research. I think that for some students they really struggle with that and they can never figure out why that particular piece of literature is relevant and why it is important and how to summarise it so that people can understand why it links to what they're doing. (Hum07)

Another supervisor (Sci12) is aware of the student's ownership of and contribution to the field when they:

> Have finally understood where their work fits into the context of the entire field so that they know where they sit and they know…They know what forces can reinforce, or shift, or move their thesis basically so when they can identify other people's work.

> They know what they are looking for and they know what is relevant. Before that you have to keep saying you should look at this piece, have a look at this, have a look at this, see if you find anything on that. There comes a time when they are coming to you and telling you this is really important.

A Humanities supervisor reported that to help candidates to "own" the literature and place themselves with it 'I've tried a range of strategies: brainstorming with the student around a particular issue to get ideas going and build confidence, focussing particularly on what the student knows rather than what critics have said.' (Hum05)

Working with Data at Different Conceptual Levels: Interpreting Findings and Presenting Arguments

This stage is where students are analysing, interpreting and defining findings which make a contribution to understanding as well as to factual knowledge. They then can contribute to understanding and conceptual levels of debate in their presentation of the dissertation or a *viva*.

The following extract is taken from an online supervisory discussion about recognising conceptual threshold crossing and considering ways of enabling candidates in their crossing.

> Message no. 65: [Branch from no. 40] posted by (hedgehog2) [candidate] on Wed Feb 19, 2003 09: 57

> "Framework'"', "architecture", "underpinning", "scaffolding"—the discussion has focused on building metaphors which seem OK for hard scientific/ engineering models of research but are hardly appropriate for softer approaches. I'd want to encourage students to look at different and more flexible ways of characterizing their research. For example, a stance or perspective I favour may be termed pragmatic or pragmatist which admits that the concepts or

principles we use are far from exact and indeed may be termed fuzzy. Concepts like freedom, democracy, equality, growth, variety—all key terms in the pragmatist's lexicon—are fuzzy and essentially contested but should we run a mile from them if they are relevant to what we are studying? The scientist's answer is of course to define them so narrowly that they can be chopped up and measured thereby turning them into some sort of impoverished version of the messy original. I think we inhabit a fuzzy old world and we do it and ourselves a disservice by pretending otherwise. I don't think we are in the building trade.

Response: Message no. 66: posted by Supervisor Team on Fri Feb 20, 2003 14: 45

Yes indeed—many of us prefer more organic metaphors and language. X talks of completing the thesis like threading beads, and I use metaphors of weaving indicating the setting up of theories and theories/theorists and how these threads interweave throughout the whole until they are apparent in the finished thesis and can be seen to underpin it and can be discussed in the viva.

This supervisor encourages novice researchers to work with the meaning of those words, not just adopting popular technical terms, but instead using them as terms which are questioned, understood and put to work in the research and the dissertation.

Some of the early work of nudging takes place in the problematising of terms and the development of meaning, so that candidates can take ownership of the discourse and ideas which they then articulate in their research.

I think conceptual insights also come through sitting down and having free serious discussions with them…So what do you think about it?…What do you mean by this?

I'll give you one example…what I do is I take them etymologically through their title as a conceptual entity. I always say it's going to change, at the change…and you are getting closer and closer to what you are dealing with, the title of your thesis. (SS22)

Another supervisor comments on a constructive dialogue involving the appropriate use of the subject and doctoral level discourse:

Usually their first drafts are hardly ever very good. They just don't know where to start. But you can help them a lot by a couple of helpful things like what does this concept mean? And they will often write to the wrong audience…If they start using very technical terms, like "hybridity", they will lose people that read it, so you have to help them with that. (SS25)

In terms of "helping students through conceptual thresholds". In my experience the student has identified a blockage, the nature of the blockage has been discovered through supervisory dialogue and the conceptual threshold has been crossed when a deeper and usually more conceptual understanding has been reached. These have been moments of "insight" and connected to being able to identify the particular threshold concept that has enabled the making of new connections from what was previously a "collection" thus removing the "blockage". (Hum09)

And another supervisor…

In discussion with students about their theses there's moments which I can visualise a kind of matrix of interlocking ideas and images which represent the unique contribution of their work and the step up they're making. This emerges out of a grey, blank, left space – and then if I can articulate it, they have to work to understand those nudges through questioning e.g. Can you see it? What does it mean? How do these things connect to you?

When you realise it, you can steer the discussion to enable the student to clarify, arrange, challenge, destruct and reconstruct and create a way to move forward as mini thresholds. (Hum10)

These supervisors suggest that is it necessary to recognise blockages in their own learning, as well as that of the student in order to 'nudge' candidates into more conceptual work in ways which are acceptable to, and can be owned and actioned by, the student.

Writing is an important step – and the learning of both supervisor and student need to be matched, as one of the authors has suggested is necessary in a good supervisory dialogue (Wisker, 2005). Hence:

When they are writing that's when I work really hard with the students. They send me each chapter sometimes several chapters. It's me that goes through the threshold…I also run a study group which is very important for my students, about once a month, call it a thesis support group, they turns up if they can, sometimes one person is under spot light and talks about what stage they are up to, sometimes it is an open session where everyone talks, or sometimes I'll focus on a particular thing, like how to publish, when someone comes up to their oral exam, we do a practice. (SS25)

Developing a Sustained and Supported Argument or Thesis

The concept of argument is one which many supervisors mentioned was difficult for some of their research candidates to understand and develop. Some are stuck in the journeyman, busy work of data collection and even analysis, rather than the interpretation. For example:

It doesn't matter how much fieldwork you do, it will never be a PhD. It's the next stage, taking that information and utilizing it to produce a coherent, sustained argument which makes it a PhD and that I think is where there is a problem. (Hum07)

A supervisor from Engineering agrees that candidates often find it difficult to mount an argument supported by evidence:

> With the students who seem to struggle to get 'it', often the 'it' is the notion of what a thesis is, that is, a claim and defence. It is more than just a body of work. In the experimental sciences and engineering it's a whole kind of building evidence to find out if a hypothesis will be proven or not. (Eng02)

An experienced supervisor in the Social Sciences appreciates when candidates have made the breakthrough and can tell that it happened. This is an indication of meta-learning:

> When they begin to surprise me with their discussions and their ideas. When they are discussing something and they see something that I don't expect them to have [and] during the discussion. They managed to surprise me in the arguments they are making or the direction that they are taking. Also when they begin to be the ones who retrieve relevant articles and present them to me.

> They know what they are looking for and they know what is relevant. Before that you had to keep saying 'You should look at this piece, have a look at this, have a look at this, see if you find anything on that'. There comes a time when they are coming to you and telling you 'This is really important'. (SS23)

Assisting candidates to develop a position and argument has clearly been an issue for many supervisors, including those who are now successfully at the professorial level: 'My supervisor said to me, and I say to my students, "The day that you come into my office and sustain an argument with me about your research is the day I know you are close to submitting"' (Pers. Com. Professor T. Smith, The Australian National University, July 2008). This comment was made to a group of new doctoral candidates by a supervisor in Finance who has supervised, to completion, over 40 doctoral candidates.

Challenging candidates to be able to argue their position might not actually assist the candidate in being able to understand the concept of argument and the skill of being able to develop and sustain one. One supervisor suggested that she has found it helpful:

> Playing 'Devil's Advocate'. It's delicate because picking holes in their work can hurt confidence, so instead I take the perspective that we need to think of opposing arguments for the purpose of handling them (as opposed to suggesting that their arguments might mean that the student's thesis is not supportable, although conceivably it could come to that)' (Hum03)

> I think the skill of helping somebody through this thought process in terms of research came from my own PhD. I mean, it has to, because I think that I had such a struggle and because I had such a struggle, I knew where I was coming up against brick walls and where I could have done with understanding the process better as I went along. And so I think that it was out of my own sort

of conflicts that, that I recognised those in other people's. It is being able to see that problem and then just sort of say, 'Well, what do you think?' You know, 'which way do you think that you are going to go? (SS26)

These comments indicate a sense that the blockage and the gradual development in learning are perceived as troublesome in the first instance. For several supervisors in the study to date, students have been seen to indicate their threshold crossing achievement in writing the conclusions only when students stand back, view the whole, define what they have understood and contributed to meaning, and then return to their writing and make it explicit, articulate it:

> It is always very nice when it happens…when I think it happens a lot is when there is a bit of a break in conclusion, when a conclusion is written, a conclusion is a summary of factors that occurred and you conclude…without understanding that your conclusion actually draws out and creates that pivotal point around which your thesis really contributes scholarship and knowledge. If you can get them to put down the thesis for a month, literally put it down, don't even look at it and then go back, and start as if they were somebody reading it afresh, as they go through read every chapter, think about the insides…and start listing, making the links. (SS22)

Here the supervisor is nudging the student to look for the insights rather than merely to rewrite. She is inviting the candidate to step back from the text itself to see what it means, what the overall structure and emerging meanings are, and how the ideas work at a conceptual level throughout.

SUMMARY

Research conducted so far with experienced supervisors across a range of subject areas and from different countries throughout the world suggests that they are aware both of the kind and quality of student work when they have crossed conceptual thresholds and achieved conceptualized levels of learning and articulation at a doctorate level. Such work appears when these novice researchers:

Develop a research question from a topic ensuring a feasible and conceptual-level question.

Develop an appropriate design and research processes for their work.

Focus on conceptual framework, methodology and methods

Enter the dialogue with experts in terms of their selection and engagement with their reading in the literature review/theoretical perspectives chapter and then throughout the thesis.

Put forward an argument supported by evidence.

Produce an abstract and a conclusions chapter which deal with concepts, not merely facts.

The responses also indicate that supervisors are equally aware of ways in which specific elements in their supervision practices with students can lead to developments in the level of the students' work which we define as conceptual threshold crossing. Supervisors comment on moments of what can be called "nudging" of students' work towards the achievement of a high conceptual level including the following activities:

Encouraging engagement with the research question.

Offering and prompting opportunities for engagement with the literature in relation to themes, issues and then in a dialogue with the candidate's own work.

Oral prompting of conceptual work in groups, supervisory meetings, and individually.

Encouraging conceptual and critical work with prompt feedback.

Pointing out contradictions and tensions.

Encouraging careful data analysis, developing themes, engaging with theories.

Encouraging early writing and much editing-sharing and reflection.

Using the language of 'doctorateness' e.g. conceptual framework, and the ideas, the research and theories of learning e.g. meta-cognition.

Offering opportunities to articulate ideas and achievements in mock vivas and other oral presentations.

DISCUSSION AND CONCLUSION

Theories of threshold concepts and conceptual threshold crossing indicate that students who have crossed conceptual thresholds can be seen to have developed in the ways in which they see themselves (ontology) and the world, and the ways they perceive, construct and express knowledge and meaning (epistemology). This early research with supervisors from a range of discipline areas and a number of different countries indicates both that they are aware of such changes in the conceptual levels of operation of research students and that they are equally aware of some of the ways in which their interventions with students can nudge, support and contribute to the candidate working at more conceptualised, critical and creative levels. Students are perceived to be changing their ways of working, their contribution to meaning, and also changing in terms of behaviour, particularly their ways of going about their learning. Identity is then an important factor noted by supervisors in terms of the changing ways students engage with, conduct and articulate their research.

We argue that when a candidate's behaviour changes it suggests that they have crossed a particular conceptual threshold and that this indicates a shift, a change, in the learner's appreciation and understanding of her/himself as well as what has been learned. These shifts or learning leaps might well be perceived by the student and or supervisor as troublesome, challenging, certainly in the first instance, but generally leading to new insights and levels of work.

Two of the four aims of our current research have produced compelling results which is hoped to encourage support for the work of research supervisors in their supportive engagement with student work at conceptual, critical and creative levels, such as are appropriate for a doctorate.

REFERENCES

Bourke, S., Hattie, J., & Anderson, L. (2004). Predicting examiner recommendations on PhD theses. *International Journal of Educational Research, 27*(4), 178–194.

Cook-Sather, A. (2006). Newly betwixt and between: Revising liminality in the context of a teacher preparation program. *Anthropology and Education Quarterly, 37*(2), 110–127.

Deegan, M. J., & Hill, M. (1991). Doctoral dissertations as liminal journeys of the self: Betwixt and between in graduate sociology programs. *Teaching Sociology, 19*, 322–332.

Flavell, J. (1979). Metacognition and cognitive monitoring: A new area of cognitive-developmental inquiry. *American Psychologist, 34*(10), 906–911.

Hartley, P., & Wisker, G. (2004, December 14–16). *Using the Interviewer software to simulate the postgraduate viva.* Paper presented at the 'Whose Higher Education? Public and Private Values and the Knowledge Economy' University of Bristol.

Holbrook, A., Bourke, S., Farley, P., & Carmichael, K. (2001, February). *Analysing PhD examination reports and the links between PhD candidate history and examination outcomes: Methodology.* Paper presented at the HERDSA Conference, Newcastle.

Isaac, P., Quinlan, S., & Walker, M. (1992). Faculty perceptions of the doctoral dissertation. *Journal of Higher Education, 63*(3), 241–268.

Johnston, S. (1997). Examining the examiners: An analysis of examiners' reports on doctoral theses. *Studies in Higher Education, 22*(3), 333–346.

Kiley, M., & Mullins, G. (2001). *Supervisors' and students' conceptions of research: A comparison.* Paper presented at the Paper presented at 'Bridging instruction to learning' 9th European conference of the European Association for Research on Learning and Instruction, Fribourg, Switzerland.

Kiley, M., & Mullins, G. (2002). Supervisors' and students' conceptions of research. In M. Kiley & G. Mullins (Eds.), *Quality in postgraduate research: Integrating perspectives* (p. 178). Adelaide, Australia: CELTS, University of Canberra.

Kiley, M., & Mullins, G. (2003, August 26–30). *Why conceptions of research might be significant in postgraduate education.* Paper presented at the Paper presented at the 10th European Association of Research in Learning and Instruction, 'Improving learning: Fostering the will to learn', Padova, Italy.

Kiley, M., & Mullins, G. (2004). Examining the examiners: How inexperienced examiners approach the assessment of research theses. *International Journal of Educational Research, 41*(2), 121–135.

Kiley, M., & Mullins, G. (2005). Supervisors' conceptions of research: What are they? *Scandinavian Journal of Educational Research, 49*(3), 245–262.

Kiley, M., & Mullins, G. (2006). Opening the black box: How examiners assess your thesis. In C. Denholm & T. Evans (Eds.), *Doctorates downunder: Keys to successful doctoral study in Australia and New Zealand* (pp. 200–207). Melbourne: ACER.

Kiley, M., & Wisker, G. (2008, June). *"Now you see it, now you don't": Identifying and supporting the achievement of doctoral work which embraces threshold concepts and crosses conceptual thresholds.* Paper presented at the Threshold concepts: From theory to practice, Queen's University, Kingston Ontario Canada.

Lovitts, B. (2007). *Making the implicit explicit: Creating performance expectations for the dissertation.* Sterling, VA: Stylus.

Meyer, J., & Boulton-Lewis, G. (1997). Variation in students' conceptions of learning: An exploration of cultural and discipline effects. *Research and Development in Higher Education, 20*, 481–487.

Meyer, J., & Land, R. (Eds.). (2006). *Overcoming barriers to student understanding: Threshold concepts and troublesome knowledge.* Abingdon: Routledge.

413

Meyer, J., Shanahan, M., & Laugksch, R. (2001, Aug 28–Sept 1). *A quantitative analysis of students' conceptions of 'research'*. Paper presented at the Paper presented at 'Bridging instruction to learning' 9th conference of the European Association for Research on Learning and Instruction, Fribourg, Switzerland.

Mullins, G., & Kiley, M. (2002). 'It's a PhD, not a Nobel Prize': How experienced examiners assess research theses. *Studies in Higher Education, 27*(4), 369–386.

Tinkler, P., & Jackson, C. (2004). *The Doctoral Examination Process: A handbook for students, examiners and supervisors*. Buckingham: SRHE and Open University Press.

Trafford, V. (2003). Questions in doctoral vivas: Views from the inside. *Quality Assurance in Education, 11*(2), 114–122.

Turner, V. (1979). Betwixt and between: The liminal period in rites de passage. In W. Less & E. Vogt (Eds.), *Reader in comparative religion*. New York: Harper and Row.

Winter, R., Griffiths, M., & Green, K. (2000). The 'academic' qualities of practice: What are the criteria for a practice-based PhD? *Studies in Higher Education, 25*(1), 25–37.

Wisker, G. (2005). *The good supervisor: Supervising postgraduate and undergraduate research for doctoral theses and dissertations*. Basingstoke: Palgrave Macmillan.

Wisker, G., Kiley, M., & Aiston, S. (2006). Making the learning leap: Research students crossing conceptual thresholds. In M. Kiley & G. Mullins (Eds.), *Quality in postgraduate research: Knowledge creation in testing times* (pp. 195–201). Canberra, ACT: CEDAM, The Australian National University.

Wisker, G., Robinson, G., & Kiley, M. (2008). Crossing liminal spaces: Encouraging postgraduate students to cross conceptual thresholds and achieve threshold concepts in their research. In M. Kiley & G. Mullins (Eds.), *Quality in postgraduate research: Research education in the new global environment – Part 2: Conference Proceedings*. Canberra, ACT: CEDAM, ANU.

Wisker, G., Robinson, G., Trafford, V., Lilly, J., & Warnes, M. (2004). *Achieving a Doctorate: Meta-learning and research development programmes supporting success for international distance students*. Paper presented at the Quality in Postgraduate Research: Re-imaging research education, Adelaide, Australia.

Margaret Kiley
Centre for Educational Development and Academic Methods
Australian National University

Gina Wisker
Brighton University
United Kingdom

LIST OF CONTRIBUTORS

Caroline Baillie has recently been appointed Chair of Engineering Education at UWA Perth, before which she was Chair of Engineering Education, Research and Development at Queens University in Canada where she hosted the June 2008 Threshold concepts conference. Her role is to enhance the learning experience of engineering students across the Faculty whilst maintaining her research and teaching interests in materials science and engineering. She has over 160 publications, papers and books in materials science and education. Her most recent books include a Morgan and Claypool 2009 publication *Engineering and Society: working towards social justice* (with Catalano) and *Natural Fibre Composites: Turning Waste into Useful Materials* (with Thamae, VDM publishers).

Jonas Boustedt has a University Diploma in Electronics and Computer Engineering from University of Gävle, a Master of Education in Mathematics and Computer Science from Uppsala University, a Master of Science in Computer Science from Uppsala University, and a Licentiate of Philosophy in Computer Science with specialization in Computer Science Education from Uppsala University. He holds a tenure position as lecturer at the Computer Science Department at University of Gävle (Sweden) and is currently working on the second part of his Ph.D. He started his working career as a developer of embedded systems for tele and radio communications in the rescue industry.

Lyndon Cabot is Senior Lecturer in Prosthodontics, Director of Admissions and Deputy Director of Education (Undergraduate Programmes) at King's College London Dental Institute. His research interests involve modelling professional expertise and the development of clinical pedagogy and his recent published work has been within these areas. Lyndon's work as Admissions Director at the Dental Institute has led to his recent appointment as Chair of the Test Development Group of UKCAT, the aptitude test used by the majority of United Kingdom medical and dental schools. He is also a Fellow of the Higher Education Academy.

Kim Cheek is an Assistant Professor of Education at Valley Forge Christian College where she teaches science and mathematics courses for future elementary school teachers. Prior to teaching at the university level, Kim taught for 11 years in several elementary and middle schools. Her current research is focused on how students understand concepts in geoscience, especially geologic time.

Monica Cowart is Associate Professor and Chairperson of the Philosophy Department at Merrimack College in North Andover, Massachusetts. Her research interests in philosophy of psychology include embodied cognition, mindfulness-based therapeutic interventions, gendered conceptions of post-traumatic stress disorder and scaffolded learning environments. For over ten years, she has used experiential learning techniques to enhance her student's understanding of philosophical concepts. This research has been supported by three grants and has resulted in a number of presentations and publications that explore the link between experiential learning and recent developments in cognitive science. In addition, she has been recognized by two universities for her exceptional teaching.

Peter Davies is Professor of Education Policy and Director of the Institute for Educational Policy Research (IEPR) at Staffordshire University, Stoke on Trent, UK. His current research focuses on participation and engagement in learning, particularly within the context of higher education. He is co-editor of the International Review of Economics Education.

Anna Eckerdal has an M.Sc. in Scientific Subjects Education including Mathematics and Physics, and a Ph.D. in Computer Science with a specialization in Computer Science Education from Uppsala University. She taught high school mathematics, physics and programming for many years, and since 1999 has taught in the Department of Information Technology at Uppsala University where she holds a tenured position as lecturer. Her current primary research interests lie in how students learn object-oriented programming. From this research she has published a number of empirical-computer-science-education papers.

Mick Flanagan is a Senior Research Associate in the Department of Computer Science and a Teaching Fellow in the Department of Electronic and Electrical Engineering, University College London (UCL). His research is centred on undergraduate engineering education and the development of technology enhanced learning for industrial continuing professional development. He maintains a website that provides a comprehensive reference list of current work on the Threshold Concept (http://www.ee.ucl.ac.uk/~mflanaga/thresholds.html).

Gigi Foster received her PhD in economics from the University of Maryland. She spent six years with the University of South Australia, and is now a Senior Lecturer at the University of New South Wales School of Economics. Her research interests are in applied micro-economics and include specific topics in education economics, human social selection patterns, the influence of the social environment on economic outcomes, and behavioral economics. She is currently working on two Australian government-funded projects, one of which is a longitudinal study of Australian undergraduate educational outcomes. Gigi's research has also been supported by the University of South Australia, the University of Maryland, and the Spencer Foundation, and has been published in leading international and interdisciplinary journals.

Simon Gray is an Associate Professor in the Department of Mathematics and Computer Science at The College of Wooster in Ohio USA. He is currently serving as a program officer for the Great Lakes Colleges Association where his role is to promote faculty development in a liberal arts environment. He is the author of *Abstract Data Types and Object-Oriented Programming with Java* (2007, Addison-Wesley). His research interests lie in student learning, pedagogy, and assessment.

David Hay is currently Senior Lecturer in Higher Education at King's College London. His research and teaching concern the trajectories of student learning in a variety of disciplines and he is particularly interested in the ways that students learn to read their disciplines. Much of his previous work concerns the use of concept mapping for the visualisation of change in learners' knowledge structures. Now his work focuses rather more on the dialogic interactions of higher education and the role of insight in particular. Learning from the personal perspective has therefore come to feature most prominently in his recent research and he is particularly interested in the notion of ideas made personal – a concept that includes the relations of interpretation as the student learns to understand ideas embodied in their disciplinary texts.

Chris Hughes is an Associate Professor in the Medical Education and Student Office and the School of Public Health and Community Medicine at UNSW. He has a multidisciplinary background in the sciences and the humanities, and a doctorate in adult education. He has over 30 years f experience in curriculum and teaching development. For the last nine years Chris has been working on the undergraduate Medicine Program at UNSW, focusing on the program and course structures, assessment, and information technology systems. Chris convenes the first phase of this program and tutors in medical ethics. His research focuses on medical education, particularly on assessment systems and the use of student generated resources.

Jens Kabo is a doctoral candidate in the Department of Chemical Engineering, Queens University, Kingston, Ontario conducting research in the area of engineering education with an aim to graduate in 2010. His research interest is engineering and social justice with a focus on student learning in courses that highlights the social context surrounding engineering and introduces alternative views of the profession. Jens has studied student learning at Queen's and at three universities in the United States. Prior to Queen's Jens acquired a MSc in Engineering Physics from Chalmers University of Technology, Gothenburg, Sweden focusing on Technical Communication. The title of his thesis was 'What is technology? A qualitative study of engineering physics students' conceptions of technology'.

Anita Kärner is the Head of the Centre for Educational Research and Curriculum Development at the Faculty of Education, University of Tartu in Estonia. Her main fields of interest are the organisation of doctoral education, comparative studies of the systems of doctoral education, practices of doctoral supervision and supervision pedagogy. She is a member of the Expert Committee of the National Curriculum and of the Committee of the National Educational Research and Teacher Education Developing Program ('Eduko').

Margaret Kiley researches in the area of research education with particular topics including: The examination of theses; Students' and supervisors' conceptions of research; Students' and supervisors' expectations of the research experience; and Threshold concepts in research. She has been a member of the organising committee for the international *Quality in Postgraduate Research* biennial conferences held in Adelaide, South Australia, since their inception in 1994. She has been co-editor of the proceedings, and initiated and manages the QPR web site http://qpr.edu.au which houses copies of all papers presented at the conferences. Margaret has worked, to date, in four Australian universities, and is currently at the Australian National University where she works extensively with staff involved in supervising research students.

Ian Kinchin is Senior Lecturer in Higher Education and Assistant Director (programmes) within King's Learning Institute (KLI) at King's College London. He is course leader for the MA in Clinical Pedagogy and spends much of his time making direct observations of university teaching to support new academics in the development of their teaching role. His research interests have stemmed from the application of concept mapping to higher education contexts and have focussed on the development of clinical (particularly dental) pedagogy in recent years. Ian has published within the fields of zoology, science education and university pedagogy. He is the author of *The Biology of Tardigrades* (Portland Press 1994) and is a Fellow of the Institute of Biology.

Michelle Kofod is presently the Manager of the Education Development Unit at the Australian School of Business, University of New South Wales (UNSW). Prior to this Michelle worked in the Faculty of Science UNSW, where she has been involved in working with education technology, mapping graduate attributes, e-portfolios, peer mentoring and tutor training. Michelle was awarded an ITET Fellowship and an Australian Teaching and Learning Council (previously Carrick Institute) Citation for her contribution to student learning and holds a Graduate Certificate in University Learning and Teaching. In 2007–2008 she was the Australasian Co-VP for the International Society for the Scholarship of Teaching and Learning (ISSOTL).

Dagmar Kutsar is an Associate Professor of Social Policy of the Institute of Sociology and Social Policy at the University of Tartu in Estonia. She has broad experience of teaching and supervising students and is interested in cognitive aspects of teaching and learning. Basically trained as a psychologist, her research interests include family and childhood studies linked to social problems – poverty and social exclusion. Getting familiar with *threshold concepts* inspired her to reconstruct the societal transition processes from national awakening to establishment of an independent statehood as a social learning process, by applying this theoretical framework.

Ray Land is Professor of Higher Education and Head of the Centre for Academic Practice and Learning Enhancement (CAPLE) at the University of Strathclyde, Glasgow. His research interests include educational development, threshold concepts, research-teaching linkages, and theoretical aspects of digital learning. He is the author of *Educational Development: Discourse, Identity and Practice* (Open University Press 2004) and co-editor of *Education in Cyberspace* (RoutledgeFalmer, 2005), *Overcoming Barriers to Student Learning: Threshold Concepts and Trouble-some Knowledge* (Routledge 2006), *Threshold Concepts within the Disciplines* (Sense Publishers 2008) and *Research-Teaching Linkages: Enhancing Graduate Attributes* (QAA 2008).

Gregory Light is the director of the Searle Center for Teaching Excellence and an associate professory in the school of education and social policy at Northwestern University. Prior to Coming to Northwestern, he was on the faculty of the Institute of Education, University of London in the U.K. where he was deputy head and then interim head of the department of Life Long Learning. He has taught post-graduate courses in higher and professional education and consulted across the higher and professional education sector in North America, Europe and Asia. His research and scholarship focuses on the theory and practice of learning and teaching in higher and professional education. His research and his many publications are focused on student learning and the professional development of teaching in higher education. He is author (with Roy Cox and Susanna Calkins) of the book *Learning and Teaching in Higher Education: The Reflective Professional,* (2009).

Louise Lutze-Mann is a senior lecturer in the School of Biotechnology and Biomolecular Sciences and the Academic Coordinator of Learning and Teaching Enhancement for the Faculty of Science at the University of NSW. She has been involved in curriculum development within the School, focusing on the rationa-lization of courses, the introduction of technology and the embedding of graduate attributes. Louise spent 2002–03 working on the development of the curriculum, policy and procedures for a new university for the California State University System and was Chair of the Academic Senate. Apart from threshold concepts, her research interests are the development of novel cancer chemotherapeutics and the engagement of students in learning.

Jean Mangan is a Professor of Education Economics in the Institute for Education Policy Research at University of Staffordshire in the United Kingdom. With Peter Davies and others she has extended the *threshold concepts* framework and in particular the application to economics. She was the project manager of *Embedding Threshold Concepts,* a four-year Fund for the Development of Teaching and Learning project involving four universities, under the auspices of the Higher Education Academy. In addition, she has published articles on the economics of education, including aspects such as the effect of resourcing and government initiatives on examination performance, and the effect of changes in the funding of university students on university choice.

Robert McCartney earned his B.S. and M.S. degrees in Natural Resources from the University of Michigan. After a number of years working in a photobiology lab at the Smithsonian Institution, he returned to school at Brown University, where he earned his Sc.M. and Ph.D. degrees in Computer Science. He has published papers in artificial intelligence (planning, robotics, and diagrammatic reasoning) and computer science education. He is currently a faculty member of the Computer Science and Engineering Department at the University of Connecticut, and co-editor-in-chief of the ACM Journal on Educational Resources in Computing.

Nicholas McGuigan lectures in accounting within the Centre of Accounting Education and Research, Lincoln University, New Zealand. He is directly involved in applied research focussing on the enhancement of educational and training programmes for New Zealand accountants. His research interests include threshold concepts and conceptualisations within an accounting curriculum, development of generic learning skills in accounting graduates, student perceptions and learning approaches towards accounting, mobile learning technology and innovative teaching practice. He has also published in the field of sustainable development and disclosures of financial institutions with particular emphasis on socially responsible lending practice of banking institutions and environmental management system implementation.

Jerry Mead is Associate Professor of Computer Science at Bucknell University in Pennsylvania, USA. He is co-author (with Anil Shende) of two books, *Persuasive Programming* and *A Guide to Persuasive Programming in Java* (both with Franklin, Beedle & Associates). His research in computer science education has focused on the development of project-based courseware, on constructivist pedagogy, and threshold concepts.

Jan Meyer is a Professor of Education and the Director of the Centre for Learning, Teaching, and Research in Higher Education at the University of Durham in the United Kingdom. Much of his research career has been devoted to exploring mechanisms for developing metalearning capacity in students, to the modelling of individual differences in student learning, and to the construction of discipline centred models of student learning. He has more recently developed with Ray Land and others the conceptual framework of *threshold concepts* – a framework that provides a new lens through which to focus on critical aspects of variation in student learning and the acquisition or not of disciplinary-specific ways of thinking, reasoning and explanation.

Jan Erik Moström has an M.Sc. in Computer Science from Luleå Technical University, Sweden and a Technical Licentiate from Umeå University, Sweden. He currently holds a tenure position as lecturer at the Department of Computing Science at Umeå University and has extensive experience in teaching a wide range of computer science related subjects, ranging from software development and operating systems to human computer interaction to computer architecture. He has also been teaching software courses for several companies. He has published a number of computer science education articles.

Marina Orsini-Jones is Principal Lecturer in the Department of English and Languages at Coventry University (UK) and has carried out research on the integration of e-learning into the languages curriculum to support the crossing of threshold concepts since 2003. She has published work on the impact that the use of education technology can have on the undergraduate students' learning experience and is particularly interested in developing constructivist tasks that can enhance the development of students' critical digital multiliteracies and cybergenre awareness. Marina is currently investigating more generic troublesome knowledge relating to academic literacies and collecting data on the epistemological and ontological issues students face when engaging in research for their dissertation. Curricular action research is Marina's methodology of choice.

Jane Osmond is Senior Research Assistant for the Centre of Excellence for Product and Automotive Design (CEPAD) at Coventry University, England. Her current research includes tracking student development of spatial awareness; identifying threshold concepts in design and enabling internationalisation of the design curriculum. Previously, Jane worked on research projects such as *Improving Retention, Supporting Students*, *Mapping good practice in equality and diversity* and *Meeting the Challenge – Managing Equality and Diversity in HE*. Selected publications include Osmond, J. *et al* (2008) 'Measuring the creative baseline in transport design education.' In Rust., C. (ed) *Improving Student Learning – For What?* OCSLD. Oxford, and Osmond, J. *et al* (2007) 'Threshold Concepts and Spatial Awareness in Automotive Design.' In Land, R., and Meyer, JHF. (eds) *Threshold Concepts within the Disciplines.* Sense Publishers. Rotterdam.

Ming Fai Pang is an Associate Professor at the Faculty of Education, the University of Hong Kong. His research interests include learning and instruction at various levels (i.e. early childhood/primary/secondary/higher education), economics education and teacher education. In particular, he specializes in the use of phenolmenography, variation theory and learning study to improve learning and teaching. The focus of his recent research projects lies on the development of domain-specific generic capabilities and discipline-specific ways of thinking and reasoning, such as financial and economic literacy. He was the co-ordinator of the Special Interest Group "Phenomenography and Variation Theory" of the European Association for Research on Learning and Instruction (EARLI) in 2003–07.

Eun-Jung Park is a Research Associate of the Searle Center for Teaching Excellence at Northwestern University (USA) and works for the NCLT (the National Center for Learning and Teaching in Nanoscale Science and Engineering) program. Her research interests include students' learning, threshold concepts, mental models, learning progression, teacher preparation, and currently, she is working on a project that investigates students' understanding of some key nano-concepts and conceptual change for learning the concepts.

David Perkins is a Senior Professor of Education at the Harvard Graduate School of Education. He is a founding member of the well-known research and development group Harvard Project Zero, co-directed it for almost 30 years, and now serves as senior co-director. He has conducted long-term programs of research and development in the areas of creativity and reasoning in the sciences and arts, learning for understanding, organizational development, and online learning. He is the author of *Archimedes' Bathtub, Smart Schools, Outsmarting IQ, Knowledge as Design,* and several other books, as well as many articles. He has helped develop instructional programs and approaches for teaching for thinking and understanding, including initiatives in South Africa, Sweden, Australia, Israel, and Latin America.

Rosanne Quinnell is a senior lecturer in the School of Biological Sciences at the University of Sydney (Australia). For the past 2 years she has been the Learning and Teaching Fellow in the Faculty of Science at the University of New South Wales (Sydney, Australia). Rosanne's research interests in higher education include: exploring academic numeracy as a threshold concept for students of biology, medicine, and more recently physics; information and communications technologies, particularly Web 2.0, for learning and teaching science; and, 'learner profiling' where cohorts of undergraduate tertiary biology students, with shared approaches to learning and conceptions of biology, can be grouped using hierarchical cluster analysis. Here she is working to determine which 'learner profile' is most resistant to change.

Aidan Ricketts is a legal educator and educational designer, holding post graduate qualifications in both law and education. He currently teaches constitutional law and environmental law at the University of the South Pacific in Vanuatu, and has previously taught in universities in Australia. Aidan has specialised in curriculum reform processes in law schools to encourage deep and critical learning and in the development of converged models of flexible delivery. Currently his teaching in law is conveyed to students located in twelve different Pacific island nations by means of online, print and other forms of educational delivery. Aidan's research interests centre around a deep commitment to participatory democracy and have included publications in the disciplines of law, education and social history. Aidan is currently working on a new book on community based activism and advocacy, a field in which he has also previously designed university based and community based courses.

Pauline Ross is an Associate Professor and Assistant Associate Dean Academic at the University of Western Sydney, Australia, working to enhance the student learning experience. She conducts and coordinates research in both biology and science education, specifically biology. She has received numerous awards for their work, including the AAUT/ALTC 2009 Teaching Excellence Award in Biology and related fields, a 2008 ALTC citation for an Outstanding Contribution to student Learning, recognising her contribution to curriculum development and the University of Western Sydney Vice Chancellor's Excellence in Teaching award 2007. She has identified and synthesise a new understanding of threshold concepts in the sciences and biology emerging from an ALTC funded project on

"Identifying Threshold Concepts in Biology", jointly conducted with the University of Sydney and the University of New South Wales. She is well known for her inquiry approaches, particularly those which infuse research in teaching, having several examples showcased on the Teaching Research Nexus (http://trnexus. edu.au/index.php?page=year-level-groups) and BioAssess (http://www.bioassess. edu.au/bioassess/go)

Kate Sanders has an A.B. in classics from Brown University, a J.D. from Harvard Law School, and Sc.M. and Ph.D. degrees in computer science from Brown University, with a dissertation on artificial intelligence and law. She is a Professor in the Mathematics and Computer Science Department at Rhode Island College, in Providence, Rhode Island (USA). In addition to her work in artificial intelligence, she has published numerous empirical computer-science-education papers and an introductory programming textbook, Object-Oriented Programming in Java: a graphical approach (with A. van Dam).

Leslie Schwartzman received her doctorate in computer science from the University of Illinois, Chicago, in 2001. Prior to that, she worked at Bell Laboratories for six years. Her primary research interests are related to software quality (which she regards as an ethical issue), and learning (for which she also draws on her Feldenkrais training and practice). The software quality concerns are organized around considerations of what constitutes good quality in software, and what practices and procedures lead to its development. As a teacher and as a student, she regards learning as a high form of self-use, and is drawn to questions of how best to support and facilitate it. Dr. Schwartzman is currently affiliated with the University of Illinois, Springfield.

Martin Shanahan is Associate Professor in Economics, and Dean of Research, at the University of South Australia. An economic historian by training, he has written extensively in the field of economic education. He is a co-winner of an Australian Carrick Award citation for making an outstanding contribution to student learning in the scholarship of building metalearning capacity in first-year students. Together with Jan H.F. Meyer and others, he has researched the measurement of students' learning and meta-learning, post-graduate students' conceptions of research and investigating threshold concepts in Economics.

Leah Shopkow is an associate professor of history at Indiana University, Bloomington. Her disciplinary research is in medieval historiography; she is currently doing a critical edition and translation of the 'Chronicle of Andres.' Her interest in history learning grew out of her scholarly interest in how people understand and write history. As a member of the History Learning Project at Indiana University with Arlene Díaz, David Pace, and Joan Middendorf, she has co-authored "The History Learning Project: A Department 'Decodes' its Students" in the Journal of American History, which has won the McGraw Hill-Magna Publications Scholarly Work on Teaching and Learning Award, as well as other collaborative pieces with them and with Vicky Gunn of University of Glasgow.

Charlotte Taylor is a senior lecturer in biology and Director of Learning and Teaching in the Faculty of Science at the University of Sydney. She has 20 years experience in the course design, staff training, assessment and online learning associated with cohorts of 1000–1500 students. Her research integrates projects on science education and biology to investigate quality learning in formal and public education in the context of urban ecology. Outcomes of these activities include numerous publications, development of educational resources such as the BioAssess website, a university excellence award for enhancing the first year experience, and a national Eureka Prize for Environmental Sustainability Education. Her initial work on defining biological threshold concepts laid the basis for the collaborative ALTC project 'Using threshold concepts to generate new ways of teaching biology'.

Philip Taylor carries out research which focuses on the challenges associated with the widespread integration and control of distributed generation in electrical distribution networks. He received an Engineering Doctorate relating to intelligent demand side management techniques from the University of Manchester Institute of Science and Technology. He has significant industrial experience as an electrical engineer including a period working in the transmission and distribution projects team at GEC Alsthom. His most recent position was Research and Development Director at Senergy Econnect. He is a Professor and the Deputy Director of the Durham Energy Institute and the Director of the Multi-disciplinary Centre for Doctoral Training in Energy. He is also a member of the CIGRE working group C6.11, 'Development and Operation of Active Distribution Networks'.

Lynda Thomas has a B.Sc. and an M.Sc. in Mathematics from McMaster University, and an M.Sc. in Computing from Southern Illinois University. As a mathematician, she specialised in Geometry, which led her to complete a Ph.D. in notations to support object-oriented design at the University of Wales, Aberystwyth, where she is now a Senior Teaching fellow in Computer Science. She has worked in industry and taught in both the United States and the United Kingdom and her research interests have evolved into the area of computer science education and introductory programming.

Rachel Thompson is a lecturer in the undergraduate medical program at the University of New South Wales (Australia). She convenes the Quality of Medical Practice element (QMP) and the 1st/2nd year Health Maintenance courses (adult medical science and clinical medicine). QMP is taught through all six years of the program, encompassing evidence-based medicine, medical statistics, and the quality and safety of medicine. In mid 2007 Rachel was appointed Fellow in Learning and Teaching for the Faculty of Medicine. This position involves a wider role in promoting, organising and supporting learning and teaching within the faculty. It was through the Fellow appointments at UNSW that Rosanne Quinnell and Rachel discovered their shared perspective of academic numeracy as a threshold concept for students of biology and medicine.

Julie Timmermans is a Ph.D. candidate in Educational Psychology at McGill University with special interests in instructional psychology, higher education, and educational development. While she has many academic passions, a primary focus of her dissertation is investigating threshold concepts in educational development. Julie has taught courses at both the undergraduate and graduate levels and through her work at Teaching and Learning Services at McGill has coordinated and facilitated workshops for graduate students and professors. Much of the inspiration for her work comes during intensive writing sessions over good books and coffee at the local café.

Andrew Turner is Programme Manager for Teaching and Learning in Organisational Learning and Development at Coventry University where he leads the Postgraduate programmes in Higher Education Professional Practice. He was formerly in the Centre for the Study of Higher Education (CSHE) at Coventry University where he led the iPED Pedagogical Research Network and the team of Teaching Development Fellows. In addition, he is Research Fellow for the Centre of Excellence for Transport and Product Design. Andrew has a background as an environmental biologist and made the move to education research and development around 4 years ago although he still maintains an interest in science communication and education. His main research interests are in the student experience of Higher Education and the scholarship of educational development.

Vicky Tzioumis is a Project Officer at the University of Sydney, working on an educational research project into the definition of a Threshold Concept in Biology. She has a Ph.D. in marine ecology (University of Sydney) and a broad knowledge of the natural sciences. She has extensive experience in editing scientific papers and reports for publication in International Journals. She has managed interdisciplinary projects involving the scientific community within NSW Universities and Australian State and Federal Government Departments.

Sidney Weil is an Associate Professor in accounting at Lincoln University, New Zealand. Formerly from South Africa, he developed an interest in accounting education at the University of the Western Cape, completing his Ph. D. by investigating the learning difficulties of first year accounting students. He developed this research interest further as the Director of the Associate in Management (AIM) programme – an intensive management development programme designed to empower formerly disadvantaged South Africans to move into and through middle management – at the Graduate School of Business of the University of Cape Town. The author of several books and numerous journal articles, his primary research interest in recent years has been in the perceived benefits of the use of case studies by accounting students.

Noel Whitaker is a senior lecturer in cell and cancer biology in the School of Biotechnology and Biomolecular Sciences and is Associate Dean (Undergraduate Programs) in the Faculty of Science, UNSW. He has received Education prizes (including an ALTC citation and Faculty Teaching award) and educational fellowships. He has established a number of intra and inter University Science Education Networks. He has carried out a number of initiatives including University curriculum development and curriculum mapping for the Faculties of Science and Medicine. His research interests are viruses causing cancer and teaching students to think like scientists.

Gina Wisker is the Head of the Centre for Learning and Teaching at the University of Brighton UK and professor of higher education and contemporary literature. She also teaches English and supervises postgraduates. Gina has researched extensively into postgraduate student learning and supervisory practices and is author of *The Postgraduate Research Handbook* (2nd edn. 2008) *The Good Supervisor* (2005) *Teaching One to One* (ed. 2008) as well as a number of essays, chapters and conference papers on conceptual threshold crossing and threshold concepts in research education. Gina is co chair of the Heads of Educational Development Group (HEDG), co-editor of the SEDA journal Innovations in Education and Teaching International (IETI) and on the board of a number of other journals in education and literature.

Carol Zander has an A.B. in Mathematics from San Diego State University and an M.S. in Mathematics from the University of Colorado. After a short hiatus working at IBM, she received an M.S. and Ph.D. in Computer Science from Colorado State University, with a dissertation in Distributed Artificial Intelligence. She has taught at the University of Maine, Colorado State University, Seattle University, and is currently on the faculty at the University of Washington, Bothell. Her current primary research interests lie in computer science education, in particular object-oriented design and issues relating to software development in general.

INDEX

Note: Page numbers in italics refer to illustrations, e.g. *85*. References to tables and notes are shown as, for example, 171t or 199n1.

Printed by BoD™in Norderstedt, Germany

9 789460 912054